The Battle for the Fourteenth Colony

Mark R. Anderson

THE BATTLE FOR THE
FOURTEENTH COLONY

America's War of Liberation in Canada, 1774–1776

University Press of New England
Hanover and London

University Press of New England
www.upne.com
© 2013 University Press of New England
All rights reserved
Manufactured in the United States of America
Designed by Mindy Basinger Hill
Typeset in Adobe Caslon Pro

University Press of New England is a member of the
Green Press Initiative. The paper used in this book meets
their minimum requirement for recycled paper.

Front matter images: detail of *An East View of Montreal, in Canada,*
by Pierre-Charles Canot (full view and credit, p. 156); details of
View of Fort St-Jean from East Side of Richelieu (p. 105); detail
of *French Fort at Chambly* (p. 131).

Library of Congress Cataloging-in-Publication Data

Anderson, Mark R.
The battle for the fourteenth colony: America's war of liberation in
Canada, 1774–1776 / Mark R. Anderson.
        pages   cm
Includes bibliographical references and index.
ISBN 978-1-61168-497-1 (cloth: alk. paper)—
ISBN 978-1-61168-498-8 (ebook)
1. Canadian Invasion, 1775–1776.
2. Québec (Québec)—History—Siege, 1775–1776.
3. United States—History—Revolution, 1775–1783—Campaigns.
I. Title.
E231.A64 2013
971.02'4—dc23   2013018801

5   4   3   2   1

For Pam

CONTENTS

MAPS

PREFACE

This book originated in 2006, while I was serving as a military planner, co-ordinating support for the United States' endeavors to liberate and spread democracy to foreign peoples in Afghanistan and Iraq. During that duty, I reflected on my studies in Professor Hal Shelton's American Military University graduate course on Canada in the American Revolution and recognized an apparent connection between these twenty-first-century military campaigns and the 1775 Revolutionary War invasion of Quebec. In both cases, it seemed that American liberators sought to bring their own concepts of freedom to a foreign culture: to a people with a starkly contrasting worldview and to a society inextricably welded to a seemingly antagonistic religion and lacking a tradition of popular rule. The parallels inspired me to dig deeper, to see how the 1775 episode compared and contrasted with its more recent counterparts.

Research proved that these "liberating" invasions shared many common elements beyond the ideological component: limited sociocultural understanding and errant intelligence, military-heavy intervention, and the inherent challenges of fostering or imposing a radically new form of government on an alien population. Even more important, it cast new light on the complexity of Canada in the critical years from 1774 to 1776, which defies the simple solutions generally applied to address the Quebec invasion's failure. Finding such a rich Revolutionary War story to tell, I elected to write a book focusing on the Canadian expedition itself and allowing readers to evaluate the modern similarities and contrasts on their own, rather than delving into the details of the twenty-first-century American wars and explicitly comparing them to the Canadian campaign.

ACKNOWLEDGMENTS

I owe many thanks for the wide-ranging assistance offered in the five-year course of research generating this book. The kind staffs at the New-York Historical Society, the Library and Archives Canada, and the Bibliotheque et Archives Nationale de Québec were tremendously helpful as I launched my first research efforts and pored through their exquisite and wonderfully accessible collections. Maurice Klapwald and the New York Public Library research staff were especially efficient in answering long-distance inquiries in the search for critical resources. Gilles Lafontaine at the Ville de Montréal Archives Section always was incredibly responsive to my repeated requests for assistance. The librarians at East Carolina University, Seymour Johnson Air Force Base, and Pikes Peak Library District all provided consistent support as well, with their dogged pursuit of hard-to-find interlibrary loans. I also have to thank the many unheralded archival pioneers who expanded the wealth of electronic resources: scanning, applying metadata, and cataloging numerous digitized collections, and as a result, contributing significantly to this book's research foundations.

Most important, I would not have been able to undertake this project without my family's understanding and support. Pam, Kira, and Karl willingly sacrificed innumerable hours of "quality time" as I made trips to libraries, took notes, organized ideas, and wrote. Pam and my great friend Dave Eblen unhesitatingly volunteered to provide the vital first proofread, significantly refining and clarifying the book. Adam Derenne provided great insight from his exquisitely detailed knowledge of the 1775 Richelieu Valley campaign. Douglas Cubbison and Michael Gabriel graciously offered sage advice and professional guidance to dramatically improve my manuscript. Editor Richard Pult played an essential and much appreciated role in patiently shepherding me through the process of translating my manuscript into a publishable work.

Returning this project to its deepest roots, I have to thank two early mentors: childhood neighbor George Klopp, who fed my young appetite for military history, and Purdue's Professor Charles Ingrao, who provided me with the essential skills to practice the historian's craft. Finally, I have to thank my parents, who selflessly supported my interests from a young age, regularly taking me to local libraries and countless historic sites across North America. The book would be a pale shadow of its current form without the generous contributions of all of these people.

The Battle for the Fourteenth Colony

INTRODUCTION

The Canada expedition is one of those measures which the enemies
of American peace having first rendered necessary, will now strive
to misconstrue into hostility and offence. | *William Smith, "Oration
in Memory of General Richard Montgomery" (1776)*

The American Revolution's Quebec Campaign of 1775–1776 has generally remained a footnote in the histories of both the United States and Canada. In
large part, this has been because it has not fit comfortably in either country's
national narrative. The episode's results were unspectacular for both sides, leaving a chastened United States and a fractured, tenuously held British Canada.
When remembered in American history, the campaign has been painted largely
as a defensive measure to shore up the colonies' weak northern flank, with the
only notable highlights being Benedict Arnold's epic Kennebec march and
Richard Montgomery's tragically dramatic attack on Quebec's capital. For
modern Canadians, the conflict does not square well with national historical
themes: in 1775, most of the country ignored or defied Royal authority, and
only the stalwart defense of Québec City prevented a sweeping Continental
(and rebel Canadian) military victory. North of the border, it has been easier
to portray the conflict as a prelude to the nation-defining struggle in the War
of 1812, in which grasping Americans were whetting their appetite for Manifest Destiny. However, two important, and previously underexplored, themes
to the northern struggle of 1775–1776 *do* fit the national history and character
of both nations.

For the soon-to-be United States, it was their first war of liberation, an
effort to bring liberty to an "oppressed" people who presumably yearned for
freedom.[1] The historical record shows that the driving motivations underlying
the Continental invasion were focused more on ideological expansion, rather
than on territorial acquisition. Thus, the Canadian campaign is the leading
edge of a two-centuries' long thread of American wars of liberation: one with
prominent knots in the Spanish-American War, several twentieth-century
interventions, and the more recent wars in Afghanistan, Iraq, and Libya, but

which is also an important part of the "cloth" in both World Wars, Korea, Vietnam, and even the American Civil War.[2]

Few Americans remember that between Bunker Hill and the Declaration of Independence, the Revolution's most active military campaigning took place in Canada. Generally, American Revolutionary War historiography has marginalized the campaign, rarely addressing its political background, strategic objectives, or sources of failure. The few works that have attempted to identify why Quebec did not end up joining the Continental confederation have tended to reiterate basic military and financial causes—similar to those identified by Congress in 1776—or have focused on allegedly insurmountable ethnic and religious barriers between the old British North American colonies and their northern neighbors. The true origins of the Continental defeat in Canada actually have more widespread political roots, sharing much in common with later American "wars of liberation."

In Canada, the character and sources of the early Revolutionary struggle in Quebec inevitably have been miscast as well. Canadian historiography has generally ignored the anti-administration uprisings in the summer of 1775, or mistakenly linked them directly with American intervention. The historical record, however, shows that there was a real, local Canadian protest and rebellion against developments in the provincial government, well before Continental forces arrived in the province. Elements of this local Canadian opposition connected with the continent-wide patriot movement, sharing a similar spirit of resistance to recent government "innovations," even if their specific grievances may have differed. This ultimately encouraged American intervention and generated varying levels of cooperation with the invaders. Where other popular armed antigovernment demonstrations have been fairly acknowledged and incorporated into Canada's national narrative—the 1837–38 Patriot Revolt being the most obvious parallel—the 1775 agrarian resistance and urban agitation have largely been dismissed and delegitimized as products of American influence, ignoring their strong grassroots origins, which reflected valid Canadian concerns about the nature and application of their provincial government. It is hoped that this book's reassessment of Quebec politics will spark additional research into this volatile period in Canadian history.

It is important to note that from 1774 to 1775, both the United States and Canada were prenational; the former officially framed its conceptual identity in July 1776, and the latter developed national self-awareness in a process spanning many subsequent decades. The vast majority of North Americans in this era, especially in the Anglo-colonial community, identified themselves by local or imperial affiliations rather than Canadian or American labels; yet much of the historiography has attempted to impose a hindsight perspective on their "nationality" at the beginning of the Revolution. Through this anachronistic filter, the "national" identities of Quebec Province's rebels and loyalists have been categorized based on the war's outcome, rather than on their position at its beginning.

While American historiographical trends have slowly recognized the "Americanness" of Tory "friends of the King" in the colonies and nascent United States, Canada's 1775 patriot Whigs have yet to receive comparable recognition for their "Canadianness." Instead they are often portrayed as nomadic Americans passing through Canada, or deluded, ignorant, or even fickle miscreants—denying those individuals their valid contemporary political motivations as earnest inhabitants of the Province of Quebec. In Canada's first post-Conquest decade, such men as Thomas Walker and Christophe Pélissier played roles comparable to many of that country's historically recognized national figures; but much like the American Tories, these opposition leaders' political views put them on the losing side of the Revolution. Just as thousands of American loyalists chose to become Canadian when their opponents gained political control from New England to Georgia, the Canadian "patriots" who fled to the United States during the American Revolution were not inherently "American," but felt compelled to become so, based on politically intolerable conditions in their Quebec homeland.

This book focuses on these two overarching, interwoven themes: America's ideologically focused Canadian "intervention," and Quebec's own parallel unrest in 1775 and 1776. While this work is painted on the canvas of a military campaign, it tells an even more important political, social, and diplomatic story, expanding the understanding of historically relevant developments for both Canadians and Americans, and breaking from traditionally marginalized characterizations of the early American Revolution's Quebec episode.

NOTES ON TERMINOLOGY, LANGUAGE, AND PRESENTATION

One of the most difficult challenges in telling this story, without imposing anachronistic biases, is determining the terminology and labels. Generally, I have tried to use historically appropriate terms. I do not intend to pass judgment through expressions such as "American liberty" or "oppressive British

Ministerial tyranny"; the goal instead is to characterize the struggle in its participants' terms. Accordingly, I refer to the "Americans" and their Canadian anti-administration counterparts as patriots, Whigs, "friends of liberty," or rebels; and I describe their opponents as Tories, loyalists, royalists, or "friends of government." Since the United States did not yet exist for most of this story and all participants were initially still "British," I label the King's government as "Ministerial," Crown, or Royal; the opposition is broadly "Continental," embodied in "patriot" provincial governments, the Continental Congress, or the confederation of the United Colonies. Surprisingly few people in the thirteen colonies identified themselves foremost as "Americans" until 1776, so the use of that national appellation is restricted to situations in which it was used by participants or it provides a specific differentiation. By contemporary *Canadien* convention, everyone from the United Colonies was labeled *Bastonnais* (Bostonian), roughly equivalent to "Continental"; while British North Americans were more specific, using "Yankees" when referring to New Englanders and calling New Yorkers simply "Yorkers."

Canadian ethnonational differentiation presents more challenges. Given the province's previously discussed prenational character, I have opted to use "Canadian" as a colonial and geographically focused label to apply to everyone electively living in Quebec Province. Contemporary sources differentiated the two major ethnic elements as "English" or "French," and generally used "Canadian" only for Franco-Catholic inhabitants. I have employed other labels to avoid biases and judgments on anyone's "Canadianness," preferring Anglo-Canadians or "Old Subjects" (a term explained in the text) and French-Canadians, *Canadiens*, or New Subjects. When employing participants' terminology, I use quotation marks with the labels "English" or "French" to distinguish those groups from Europeans of those nationalities and I identify those Canadians actually born in France as "French-born."

I have elected to describe Native Americans and Canadian First Nations with period terminology—generally as "Indians," with appropriate recognition of the village or tribal affiliation, again with eighteenth-century nomenclature. The Iroquois/Haudenosaunee and Canada Indians, especially the Caughnawagas/Kahnawakes, played critical roles in the American Revolution, managing a cautious, rational political effort to protect their own interests in the internecine British conflict. Theirs is an interesting story in its own right, but in an effort to keep this work manageable, I have limited them to a supporting role in the narrative.

Regarding French words in the text, I have elected to minimize italicization. Frequently used words such as *habitants* (Canadian tenant-farmers) and *seigneurs* (their landlords) will remain unitalicized throughout the rest of the work. Other less frequently used words such as *curé* and *corvée* will follow convention, and *Canadien* will remain italicized to help the reader easily differentiate it from "Canadian." The names of Canadian individuals offer their own challenges. Many Canadians used traditional family nicknames. In the first reference to such individuals, I will provide their proper name, followed by the contemporary French term *dit* (called) and their family nickname, which will subsequently be used; that is, Jean Ménard *dit* Brindamour will be simply Brindamour after the first reference. I have also reverted to the old French convention of hyphenating proper names (for example, St-Thomas-de-Montmagny and Hertel-de-Rouville) and ranks (militia-captain) to minimize confusion with multiple names and to differentiate those with similar names.

Except in quotations, place names will be historical, with preference given to the form in the native language; therefore, Quebec parishes, towns, and so on will be French, with the Anglicized or other modern equivalent identified in parentheses. British administrative divisions, such as the Montreal, Three Rivers, and Quebec Districts, as well as the Province of Quebec, will be in the English form.

Perhaps the most challenging standard for many readers will be geographic. Generally I have provided relative descriptions in accordance with contemporary references to waterways, in which "up" (upstream, upriver, and upper) and "down" are relative to the flow. For north-centric thinkers, this may require some processing, as "up" is almost inevitably to the south; that is, a boat traveling up Lake Champlain would arrive at Crown Point on the south end, and lower Quebec District is the northeastern-most section of the province, closest to the Atlantic. I have adopted this convention both to reflect historical terminology and to emphasize the criticality of water transport.

Regarding quotations, I have minimized the use of the distracting term "[*sic*]"; if the meaning of a misspelled or misconjugated word still seems clear, I have left it unmarked, and where spelling can be corrected easily, I have substituted the correction in brackets (i.e., Ticonderog[a]). I have also kept the characteristically erratic eighteenth-century capitalization in quotations. There is one significant exception to these rules: I have standardized both the spelling and the punctuation in the introductory epigraphs for the chapters.

Chapter 1

THE ONLY LINK WANTING

The First Continental Congress Invites Canada

Your Province Is the Only Link Wanting to Complete the Bright
and Strong Chain of Union. | *Continental Congress, "Address to the Inhabitants
of the Province of Quebec," 26 October 1774*

On 26 October 1774, the fifty-two distinguished delegates of the first Continental Congress prepared to conclude their session; it was an unprecedented
attempt to resolve the escalating political crisis in British North America
while defending colonial rights. Before the representatives departed from
Carpenters' Hall that day, they approved one final message: the "Address to
the Inhabitants of the Province of Quebec." This letter served as the initial
step in what would develop into a twenty-month campaign to bring Quebec
into a confederation with its southern neighbors—an effort to help the Canadians free themselves from an "oppressive government."

Quebec Province would seem to be an odd field in which to expand the
patriot cause. British colonists had been engaged in near-continuous conflict
with Canada for generations, as part of the Atlantic struggle of empires that
had ended only fourteen years earlier in the decisive conquest of New France.
As a result, the British Empire formally incorporated the conquered colony
only in 1763, when it was renamed the "Province of Quebec."

Quebec was decidedly different from the empire's other North American
colonies. In contrast to the dominant Anglo-Protestant culture of their neighbors to the south, the vast majority of the Canadian populace was francophone,
ethnically French and homogenously Catholic. For more than a century, these
particular characteristics had defined "the enemy" to Englishmen on both
sides of the Atlantic. Despite these differences, Congress believed it had good
reason to invite the Canadians to join its cause.

This revolutionary new Canadian venture was born in the rational, diplomatic era of the first Continental Congress. Political developments earlier that year had forced the convening of an intercolonial body that would not focus simply on a single issue, like its predecessors, but would serve to unite liberty-loving North Americans as a bulwark of freedom to address the "series of oppressions" emanating from Parliament, perceived as "a deliberate and systematical plan of reducing" the colonists to political slavery.[1]

The British North American colonies and Parliament had drifted apart in the decade following the conclusion of the French and Indian War. The core of their conflict rested on diverging interpretations of the unwritten, tradition-based English constitution. Starting with the Stamp Act of 1765, many colonists believed the next ten years of Parliamentary acts represented constitutional innovations — a fundamental change in the relationship between the colonies and the motherland. As the London government seemed increasingly distant from the colonies and the train of perceived abuses continued, more and more American subjects saw the Ministry as an enemy of freedom. Many even believed there was some conspiracy among the King's ministers to enslave the colonists politically by progressively denying their English rights. Those Americans resisting the government's tyrannical policies identified themselves as patriots, because they felt they were defending traditional British liberty.

Almost every action and reaction on either side of the Atlantic only served to reinforce and harden opposing sentiments, driving the parties farther apart. The situation escalated dramatically in December 1773. In the Boston Tea Party, patriot Sons of Liberty protested the latest tax policy by blatantly destroying commercial property. This act brought the British government to the point at which it felt obligated to take drastic and decisive action to rein in the radical vandals of Massachusetts.

In the first months of 1774, Parliament implemented a new series of punitive laws, dubbed the "Intolerable Acts" in the colonies. These measures completely changed the character of the British imperial crisis. The London government was intent on vigorously enforcing order in North America. However, colonial patriots saw Ministerial conspiracy theories becoming fact: with the Intolerable Acts, arbitrary rule had become a reality in Massachusetts — a new government was imposed, trade was blocked, and rights were suppressed. These acts served as a harbinger of what could happen to the other colonies. Upon receiving first word of the Intolerable Acts in May 1774, patriot Americans raised an alarm from Georgia to New England. Within weeks, colonial Committees of Correspondence and radical Sons of Liberty cells responded, developing a plan for a collective response: a "Congress from the different Colonies has been proposed, as the most effectual step to give at once Consistency and Weight, to such Measures, as shall be adopted & pursued to counteract the cruel designs of our Enemies."[2]

In September 1774, delegates from twelve British North American colonies gathered in Philadelphia for the first Continental Congress. Loyalist elements prevented the election of delegates from Georgia, which would eventually become the thirteenth colony, and New York faced a similar challenge to participation. Its conservative government stifled the patriot movement and ensured that delegates would not be authorized at a provincial level, yet persistent New York City patriots elected local delegates, followed by a handful of counties that endorsed representatives for the first Congress. Quebec, of course, was unrepresented as well; the province had not participated in the swelling intercolonial patriot correspondence leading to the Congress.

The Philadelphia Congress was an extralegal, ad hoc forum for intercolonial political cooperation. As gathered, the assembly was legally impotent and had no constitutional foundation in the British Empire. Its only power came from the limited authority that the colonies granted their delegates. Any action Congress proposed was utterly dependent on implementation by individual colonies. Many delegates from radical colonies, especially Massachusetts and Virginia, came to Philadelphia to spark decisive continent-wide action; representatives of more conservative colonies aimed to temper the tenor of the assembly, ensuring that it did not go too far. At this early date, independence and armed conflict were horrifying prospects, which almost every delegate ardently sought to avoid by any means.

The first Continental Congress began slowly, immersing itself in legalistic detail—days of serious committee work focused on defining "continental" colonial rights. Finally, on 17 September, a powerful set of political resolves reached Congress from Boston's Suffolk County, jolting the assembly to take new steps. The Suffolk Resolves began by confirming loyalty to the King and then enumerating grievances with Parliament and its acts, a format that would be adopted in most of the messages from this Congress. Suffolk County also called for action. Among nineteen measures, their resolves advocated the cessation of imperial trade, denied imperial authority in the Coercive Acts, obliged able-bodied citizens to "acquaint themselves with the art of war"—albeit with a caveat for defensive intent, encouraged the formation of a Massachusetts provincial congress called by the people, and recommended "due respect and submission" to any measures that might be offered by the Continental Congress.[3]

The heretofore silent Congress promptly moved both to formally support the Suffolk Resolves and to publicize all of its own resolutions. The time had come to inform the people and prepare for action. Within a week, Congress narrowed its focus to two principal approaches: a plan for economic coercion, to be known as the "Association," and an information campaign of addresses, memorials, and petitions to share the confederated colonies' message, explaining the origins and nature of their political opposition to the Ministry.

Economic measures had been the tool of choice for previous colonial patriot protest. Since the Stamp Act, the colonies had implemented a number of embargoes and trade restrictions to express dissent with Parliamentary acts. In 1774, a united colonial agreement to prohibit trade with Great Britain and its other colonies seemed appropriate as a logical next response to increased Ministerial oppression. Only five days after receiving the Suffolk Resolves, Congress began to shape its plan for a new economic protest.

The delegates collectively established dates for the nonimportation and nonconsumption of British and Irish products, and for ceasing to export American goods to Great Britain, Ireland, and the West-Indies: 1 December 1774 and 1 September 1775, respectively. To ensure the effective implementation of the plan, Congress appointed a committee of six, including Virginia's Richard Henry Lee, to flesh out the plan's details.

Lee was one of the main engines for early congressional action, continually pressing for immediate, concerted measures, rather than patiently awaiting London's responses. Along with Samuel Adams, the energetic and persuasive Lee is credited with sparking the colonial Committee of Correspondence movement that truly brought the colonial cause together in 1774. Now, he would draft a solid blueprint for colonial action known as the "Continental Association."

The final Association plan was approved on 18 October. Lee anchored the project in the American patriot movement's roots: local committees. Every county, city, and town would elect committees to "observe the conduct" of their fellow citizens; provincial committees would manage and coordinate colony-wide participation. Through the Association, the extralegal Congress gave "authority" to quasi-official, popularly elected local bodies. Although these committees initially were founded to enforce Congress's economic policies, they would become an immediate means of sustaining patriot activity and fostering the cause of liberty after the first Continental Congress dissolved. These were the first "cells" of revolutionary government in each colony, "engines of mobilization" that "vertically integrated organized resistance" to the Ministry, which would become the "framework for sustaining and strengthening the insurgency."[4]

Concurrent with the development of the Association plan, the delegates in Philadelphia launched the second element of their agenda: a public diplomacy program to inform the British world about the colonial patriot cause. In October 1774, Congress generated five separate appeals: to the King, to the people of Great Britain, to the people of the twelve colonies with delegates in Philadelphia, to the unrepresented British North American colonies, and to the inhabitants of Quebec.

The first of these was the "Petition to the King," which was approved on 26 October. It was a plea describing colonial grievances, justifying the colonies' protests, and respectfully requesting royal support to resolve the crisis. At this point, the King was still considered an outside party in the conflict between Parliament and the colonies. While the Petition to the King was being refined, Congress developed public messages for the two principal parties involved: a "Memorial to the Inhabitants of the Colonies" of British North America—those represented in Congress, and an "Address to the People of Great Britain." Through these appeals, the delegates sought to unite efforts at home and garner additional support from like-minded patriots in the British Isles. Congress approved both of these documents on 21 October.

With the session winding down, Congress created a final pair of messages, expanding the appeals to fellow colonists who were unrepresented in Philadelphia: one for the nonattending "old" British North American colonies—Georgia, Nova Scotia, St. John's (Prince Edward Island), and East and West Florida, and the other for the Province of Quebec. A single committee, consisting of Richard Henry Lee, Massachusetts's Thomas Cushing, and Pennsylvania's John Dickinson, prepared both messages.

The drafting committee benefited from the powerful combination of Lee's energy and Dickinson's genius. John Dickinson, "the Penman of the Revolution," was the most respected and widely recognized patriot thinker of the time, and he came to Congress with a reputation as a skilled political writer. He rose to prominence in 1767 after composing his famous "Letters from a Farmer in Pennsylvania." A response to the Townshend Acts, these rhetorical letters captured and clarified the conservative patriot perspective and resonated across the British Atlantic community.

Dickinson had been a latecomer to the Congress. Because of Pennsylvania's provincial policies, Dickinson was not qualified as a delegate until mid-October; yet once he arrived, he was immediately employed in refining the Petition to the King. As Congress was winding down, he also composed the "Letter to St. John's, &c.," a concise cover message to be provided to the five colonies with copies of Congress's resolves. The letter was produced and approved in one day, a simple appeal to an audience sharing a common Anglo-Protestant heritage. Yet the recipient colonies were relatively insignificant, sparsely populated and more dependent on the motherland than the twelve colonies in Congress. The letter clearly offered those five colonies the opportunity to join the confederated colonies in action—principally through the Association—"with all the earnestness that a well directed zeal for American liberty can prompt." However, the letter did not include an explicit invitation for any of these colonies to join the second Congress, planned for May 1775.[5]

Finally, Dickinson, Lee, and Cushing focused on the Quebec letter. They had good justification for addressing that province singly. Not only was Canada the newest addition to Britain's North American empire, but it was also the most populous continental colony still unrepresented in Philadelphia. Most important, the Congress had fundamental concerns with Quebec that were not a factor elsewhere on the continent.

By nature and history, Quebec Province still posed a physical threat to the neighboring colonies. For generations, British North Americans remembered invading Catholic French-Canadian armies and frontier raiders descending to attack them from the north. Even though Quebec was now part of the British Empire, they still feared that the Ministry would arm the Canadians to intimidate and subdue the restive patriot colonies. As recently as the 1774 Quebec Bill debates, one of the lords had been quoted as saying "he saw no reason why the loyal inhabitants of Canada should not co-operate with the rest of the empire in subduing" upstart colonists "and bringing them to a right sense of their duty." If Canadians were brought into the Continental confederation, they would no longer be potential tools of the Ministry.[6]

A second motivation to address Canada separately was the new Quebec

Act, which affected both its namesake province and the rest of North America. Approved in 1774, this Parliamentary measure was considered to be the last of the Intolerable Acts, part and parcel of the other punitive measures aimed at the rebellious colonies. Unlike the other acts, though, the Quebec Act was not a reaction to Boston's unrest, but instead answered a long-recognized need: Quebec had lacked a properly defined government since its incorporation into the British Empire. Parliament's solution, however, was unacceptable to many both inside Canada and out, and the timing was inopportune, to say the least, following coincidentally on the heels of the other Intolerable Acts.

The Quebec Act contained many controversial aspects: protections for the Catholic Church, expansion of provincial borders, and reintroduction of French civil law, to name a few. For many of the recent English-speaking settlers in Canada, however, the most disturbing element was that under the Quebec Act the government would not have a general assembly; it would be ruled by the governor and his council. This seemed to be a direct contradiction of the Royal Proclamation of 1763, issued after Canada's official cession to Great Britain, which explicitly promised an assembly as soon as circumstances permitted. The patriots considered these Anglo-Protestant Canadians, denied the English constitutional government they had been guaranteed, to be immediate victims of Ministerial oppression, on a par with Massachusetts. Many felt this was a foretaste of the tyrannical British government's plan for the entire continent. Pennsylvania Lieutenant-Governor John Penn observed that the patriot radicals "persuade themselves there is a formed design to enslave America, and though the Act for regulating the government of Canada does not immediately affect the other provinces it is nevertheless held up as an irrefragable argument of that intention."[7]

Looking beyond British colonial fears, there was a strong positive motivation for inviting Quebec into the Continental confederation. If Canada were to join the Congress, it would demonstrate continent-wide resolve in opposition to the Ministry's program. Canadian participation in the Association would amplify the effects of the colonies' economic protest, as well.

When Congress decided to address the Canadians on 21 October, it was not the first time that patriot organizers recognized the need to communicate with Quebec. Seventeen days earlier at a dinner party, John Adams reported that half-pay British officer and Whig radical Charles Lee had shown him a proposed address to Canada. No copy of this draft has been found, and there is no evidence to indicate whether it was used in any way to develop subsequent messages. Regardless of its content, this draft is significant because it demonstrates an early intent to involve Canada in the growing patriot community.[8]

Less than two weeks after Charles Lee's draft circulated, the first confirmed Quebec-focused patriot message was broadcast by a newspaper, rather than by Congressional action. A patriot group calling itself "The Sons of New-England" sent a short address to the Canadians in the 19 October *Essex Journal*. These "Sons" declared their "aim to establish a pure system of civil and religious liberty through all America," in which their northern neighbors "should in all respects be as perfectly free as ourselves."[9]

The letter told "brethren" Canadians they were "entitled to all the liberties and privileges of English men, and free Americans." The Yankee authors succinctly explained their opposition to the Quebec Act; the only reason New England patriots condemned the Canadian government plan was that it laid "a foundation" for continent-wide political slavery. Offering an alternative, "The Sons" called on their northern neighbors to join them in establishing "free" government across North America. Catholicism was not an obstacle to cooperation; the letter reassured the Canadians that Yankee patriots recognized the principle of religious freedom. "The Sons" concluded with an appeal for Canadian support: "We trust your generous bosoms are animated with the most free and noble sentiments and that you will, with us, resolve to exert all your powers and risk every thing for the defence of AMERICAN LIBERTY."[10]

When these New Englanders asked Quebec to support the cause of liberty in the fall of 1774, they were not referring to armed conflict; the common aim was participation in the next Congress and compliance with the impending Association. The Canadians might decline to participate in the Continental Congress, but the economic protest would affect them whether they chose to support it or not. In the Association's enforcement provisions, Congress proclaimed, "[W]e will have no trade, commerce, dealings or intercourse whatsoever, with any colony or province, in North-America, which shall not accede to, or . . . [does] violate this association, but will hold them as unworthy of the rights of freemen, and as inimical to the liberties of their country." Even at this early stage of the growing conflict, Canada was being called on to choose sides.[11]

There is no clear indication that the "Sons of New-England" message was received or disseminated in Quebec. Probably not many, if any, Canadians subscribed to Massachusetts's *Essex Journal,* yet "The Sons" could depend on the British Atlantic merchant network to spread the word and eventually deliver it to the north. Even if the only Canadian newspaper, the conservative *Quebec Gazette,* was unlikely to reprint the piece, the patriot Yankee authors could expect the message to be transmitted from person to person and reach sympathetic Canadian audiences.

An even earlier correspondence between Continental patriots and Canada appears to have existed, the source of which is a mystery. The 25 October *Nova Scotia Gazette* reported that "the principal merchants" of Québec City had received "a Letter from the General Congress; inviting them to subscribe to the Measures adopted by the southern Colonies." It would have been physically impossible for the newspaper form of the "Sons of New-England" message to have traveled to Québec City, and then for the news of its receipt to reach Halifax, all in less than one week. That leaves two possibilities: that the "Sons of New-England" message was delivered earlier, in a different format, and that the *Essex Journal* was merely reprinting an earlier iteration of that address; or that there may have been a completely different message that has been lost to history.[12]

Dickinson, Richard Henry Lee, and Cushing did not receive their task to compose the official Congressional address to Quebec until two days after the "Sons of New-England" message was published. "The Penman" Dickinson drafted the formal letter over a single weekend, which after some revision, was finally approved on 26 October, the last day of the Congress.

In composing this letter, Dickinson faced the challenge of addressing an essentially foreign audience, "educated under another form of government" and "artfully kept from discovering the unspeakable worth" of British civilian government despite their ten years' experience in the empire. There was little common ground to build on. In addition, Dickinson lacked any firsthand experience with Quebec and did not even have any realistic assessments of Canadian political views and interests on which to form his appeals. Given these hurdles, it is not surprising that Canada was given an eighteen-page address, while Congress sent the other British North American colonies only two long sentences in their equivalent appeal.

As the anonymous author of the "Sons of New-England" address had done, Dickinson tackled the long history of conflict between the Canadians and the other colonies head-on. The Congressional address proclaimed that the "old" colonies had "rejoiced in the truly valuable addition" of Canada to the empire, both for the Canadians' and their own benefit. Since the Conquest, "brave enemies" had become "hearty friends."[13]

Dickinson also dealt with the issue of religion, the other serious obstacle to union between the Protestant confederated colonies and Catholic Canada. Congress offered the Swiss federations—"composed of Roman Catholic and Protestant States, living in the utmost concord and peace with one another" and cooperating to "defy and defeat every tyrant" that dared attack them—as a model for the sort of religious harmony they expected in their loose North American union. Dickinson also tried to make light of the religious freedom offered by the Quebec Act. In a weak and specious argument, he maintained that "Liberty of conscience" was God-granted; the British government did not need to legislate it.[14]

The bulk of Dickinson's message to the people of Quebec—with their warring past behind them and their religious differences reconciled—employed a different approach from other Congressional messages. In an attempt to span the gap between their political traditions, Dickinson aimed to use this address as a primer on the characteristics and benefits of English government—a political education for Quebec. By arming Canadians with an adequate understanding of the British political system, Congress could prepare them to join the other colonists as liberty-loving patriot citizens.

Canadian historian Pierre Monette dubbed this address an "American catechization," which gave the Canadians their "first political lexicon and taught them their first lesson in constitutional law." Dickinson informed the Canadians of five essential rights, vital for liberty, but now being threatened by the Quebec Act. The "grand right" was government representation as a means to protect property. The other specified rights were: trial by jury, habeas corpus, land holding, and freedom of the press. The letter explained, "These are the rights, without which a people cannot be free and happy . . . These are the rights a profligate Ministry are now striving, by force of arms, to ravish from us."[15]

Perhaps the most interesting approach taken by Dickinson, given the message's predominantly uneducated Canadian audience, was his heavy reliance on Enlightenment philosophy, including citations from and allusions to "the immortal Montesquieu's" *Spirit of Laws* and Cesare Beccaria's *Of Crimes and Punishments.* Such references were beyond the grasp of most Canadians. This Enlightenment touch was more a reflection of the delegates in Congress than of the Address's intended audience. As Thomas Paine's *Common Sense* would later prove, even among the generally literate British colonists, a mass audience could be influenced with tremendously more effect through Biblical and natural references, rather than via Enlightenment ideology and legalistic arguments.[16]

Congress reinforced the appeal of their political "catechization" with a gentle reminder of Canada's security—a thinly veiled threat. The Address warned, "You are a small people, compared to those who with open arms invite you into a fellowship. A moment's reflection should convince you which will be most for your interest and happiness, to have all the rest of North-America your unalterable friends, or your inveterate enemies."

After persuading the Canadians of the benefits of British liberty, and the dangers of opposing it, Congress ended the letter by explaining its goal: "unity" with Quebec. Canada was "the only link wanting, to compleat the bright and strong chain of union" in North America. The ultimate goal of the newly offered confederation was "the perfect security of the natural and civil rights of all the constituent members . . . and the preservation of a happy and lasting connection with Great Britain." Once united with their neighbors, Congress promised the Canadians, "That we should consider the violation of your rights . . . as a violation of our own." Quebec would not suffer based on the "small influence" of a "single province," but could rely instead "on the consolidated powers of North-America."[17]

Dickinson also suggested that Quebec adopt the same political pattern already used by the colonies in Congress. The Canadians should "meet together in your several towns and districts, and elect Deputies"; in turn, these local representatives could meet in a provincial congress and select delegates to represent the province at the second Continental Congress in May 1775. This was the critical point of the address—the ultimate aim—to provide a unique opportunity for the Canadians to join the confederated colonies.[18]

Chapter 2

NEW SUBJECTS TO THE KING

Canadians and the Province of Quebec

The Inhabitants & Chiefly the Peasantry seem very happy in the Change of their Masters. | *Colonel Ralph Burton, "Report of the State of the Government of Three Rivers [Quebec]" (1765)*

In addressing its letter to the "Inhabitants" of Quebec, the first Continental Congress was communicating with several audiences in that province. Not only were there French-Canadians and Anglo-Protestants who had settled there from elsewhere in the British Empire, but within those two broad categories, markedly different class divisions existed as well.

At the time of the Revolution, there were an estimated 110,000 Canadians; in comparison, there were almost two hundred thousand people in relatively small Connecticut. In Quebec, French-Canadians were still the vast majority. They were called "New Subjects," having been added to the King's realm only in 1763. Until that time, the *Canadiens* had been enemies and rivals of the other North American colonies for generations: in war, the fur trade, and territorial expansion. In fact, the fourth and decisive North American colonial war, the French and Indian War, or Seven Years' War, began as a conflict over the Ohio Valley and spread to global proportions. After a stout initial five-year defense, New France was eventually overwhelmed as the British focused their strategic efforts on North America and gained the initiative. In the summer of 1759, a British force, with colonial auxiliaries, attacked Québec City and forced the capital to surrender in September. Montréal capitulated the following year, completing the British military conquest. The province remained under military occupation until formally transferred to Great Britain by the Treaty of Paris.[1]

The few "British" Old Subjects in post-Conquest Quebec were demographically inconsequential; by 1774 they numbered only in the low thousands and were heavily concentrated in Québec City and Montréal. Many of these Anglo-Canadians had been enticed to the province by economic opportunity; there were new markets to bring into the British Empire, and the Royal Proclamation of 1763 seemed to offer assurances that they would soon have an "English" form of government in Canada as well. They entered Quebec expecting to have disproportionate economic and political influence, and they did, but there were still ninety-nine *Canadiens* for every Old Subject in the province.

While the other British colonies had developed along the Atlantic coast and spread west, the Canadians were settled chiefly on a narrow two-hundred-mile ribbon of civilization along the province's dominant geographic feature, the St. Lawrence River, flowing northeast to the Atlantic. Two smaller strips of the population strayed south from the mainstream along two tributaries, the Richelieu River, east of Montréal, and the Chaudière River, south of Québec City. Virtually the entire settled population lived within two miles of these waterways.

Canada's first novelist, Frances Brooke, noted how, "The road from Quebec to Montreal is almost a continued street . . . so extended along the banks of the river St. Lawrence as to leave scarce a space without houses in view." This settlement pattern was known as a *côte*, where farms sat side by side on narrow strips of property, roughly perpendicular to the rivers. At the southwest end of settled Canada, Montréal served as the province's market gate, opening to the wilderness and the up-country fur trade. On the opposite end, the fortified capital Québec City not only acted as a defensive gate protecting the province from seaborne threats, but also provided Canada's primary connection to the Atlantic World. These two major cities each had roughly 10,000 inhabitants, putting them on a par with the lower colonies' smaller cities, such as Albany or Hartford. The third Canadian city, Trois-Rivières (Three Rivers), sat geographically midway between the other two. It was a glorified village, with an urban population closer to one thousand. Outside the cities, there were fewer than a dozen small villages of only a couple hundred residents, breaking the otherwise evenly spread population of the riverbank *côtes*.[2]

JEAN-BAPTISTE — THE HABITANT

Canada's primary population consisted of tenant farmers known as habitants, a people personified by the soubriquet of "Jean-Baptiste."[3] The habitants were tied to their land, living a peasant lifestyle for which they seemed well

Habitant, by Millicent Mary Chaplin.
Library and Archives Canada, Acc. No. 1956-62-124.

adapted. A contemporary Canadian observed, "I believe, without exaggeration, that throughout the whole Canadian population, no instance can be found of a family unprovided with the complete and comfortable means of subsistence." Foreign observers considered the typical Jean-Baptiste to be tall, robust, strong, and healthy in comparison with contemporary European counterparts. Jean-Baptiste's wife played a critical role in running the household and raising a large family of perhaps eight or ten children. Considered the brains of the family, female *Canadiennes* typically had little education; their men had virtually none, prompting writer Frances Brooke to observe, "all the little knowledge of Canada is confined to the [female] sex."[4]

Rural New France had been organized into land grants known as seigneuries, a practice sustained under British rule. This system contrasted with that of most "old" British American colonies, where land was a free-held form of personal property, but it was similar to New York's manorial grants. At the time of the Conquest, Canada was divided into roughly 250 seigneuries. Although these land allotments were "owned" by a lord, called the seigneur, Jean-Baptiste and his heirs held rights to their individual land cession for as long as they met their tenant obligations.[5]

Jean-Baptiste lived on a parcel of perhaps 300 arpents (about 250 acres) with two or three thousand feet of river frontage. Jean-Baptiste's property included a small, sparsely furnished house near the river, surrounded by a few farm outbuildings. In his arable fields, "every bit of wood is cut down, so that there are neither hedges nor trees left, but only fields of corn or grass separated from each other by palings of dead wood, and behind this half-cultivated country [were] the natural wild woods."[6]

Jean-Baptiste's life was ruled by the climate and the seasons. From the spring thaw, around May Day, to the September harvest, he was tied to his fields. Wheat was his mainstay crop, but he might also grow oats, barley, rye, or peas. The climate permitted only one planting a year, surplus labor was rare, and the soil was fertile, so Jean-Baptiste scraped by without intensive farming methods.[7]

Following the harvest, Jean-Baptiste slaughtered a winter's worth of livestock and prepared for the long freeze. He had to carry out a slew of down-season subsistence tasks: threshing wheat, cutting and carrying fire- and fence-wood, and hunting. The women would "card and spin their wool, weave their cloth, knit their stockings, and make the mo[c]casins, or shoes."[8]

The last major step in this annual agricultural cycle occurred early in the calendar year, before the thaw rendered roads and rivers unfit for transporting heavy loads. Jean-Baptiste delivered grain he owed as back rent to his seigneur, as a tithe to his priest, or as a debt payment to creditors, and might sell any surplus to merchants. Then, once the snow cleared in late April or May, it was time to begin the next crop cycle.[9]

Jean-Baptiste's world was relatively remote. He might see nearby relatives and immediate neighbors on a daily basis, but was unlikely to see anyone else until Sunday, which offered a chance to meet with the entire parish gathered for Mass. Other contacts occurred episodically—Jean-Baptiste would typically see his seigneur once or twice a year on official business, and occasionally meet with merchants or village artisans. Jean-Baptiste's connection to the outside world was weak, and he was not particularly well informed about anything beyond the concerns of his immediate parish.

JEAN-MARIE VERREAU — THE PARISH PRIEST

"In the centre of each Parish are to be found a church and a parsonage," and the parish priest, or *curé*, anchored his community. The Canadian Church used a parish system to distribute the limited number of priests and establish physical boundaries for each *curé's* flock within the seemingly endless *côte* stretch of population. Parish boundaries often matched seigneurial limits, but a seigneury might include multiple parishes, or vice-versa.[10]

Jean-Marie Verreau was the parish priest for Ste-Marie-de-Beauce on the Chaudière River, and had served this community of about eight hundred habitants for eight years. He was in his mid-thirties, had been born in the local area, and had attended seminary in Québec City—fairly typical for priests across the province—although there were still many who were French-born and educated.[11]

Verreau led all formal church functions for his parish, performing Mass, providing the sacraments, and giving counsel. In some parishes, the *curé* also offered basic elementary education to the few children who could be spared from household chores. Although *Curé* Verreau's power was theoretically limited to religious matters, his dominant position at the hub of habitant public life combined with his literacy gave him additional influence on many aspects of community life. Even the parish's sole community meeting space, the *salle des habitants*, was part of his presbytery home.[12]

Since Ste-Marie parish was in the Quebec District, *Curé* Verreau received official Church guidance directly from Bishop Jean-Olivier Briand. Verreau's counterparts in the Three Rivers and Montreal Districts communicated through vicars-general — regional deputies to the bishop. Verreau's parishioners held a limited voice in their local church operations too. Annually, a parish assembly elected peers as vestry board churchwardens, who handled church property and finances with the *curé's* guidance.

Since the British arrival in 1759, the Canadian Church had faced tremendous challenges. During the war, the British destroyed one in five churches and 15 percent of the presbyteries. Financially, the pre-Conquest Church was heavily subsidized by France; now, under British rule, the Church relied solely on tithes, parish assessments, and donations to cover expenses. As an additional strain, 10 percent of the priests, especially the French-born, left Quebec after the Treaty of Paris. Despite all these setbacks, the Canadian Church had recovered effectively a decade later, having rebuilt churches, replaced and redistributed priests, and even added twenty-five new parishes. Yet a few priests still served multiple parishes; *Curé* Verreau happened to be one of those, also tending the neighboring St-Joseph-de-Beauce parish.[13]

PIERRE BOUCHARD — THE MILITIA-CAPTAIN

In the secular realm, the militia-captain was the primary local authority figure. Prominent habitant Pierre Bouchard filled this role for the south bank parish of St-Vallier, downriver from Québec City. The third child of a fourth-generation Canadian family, he was in his mid-forties when the governor appointed him parish captain in the newly reinstated 1775 militia. A successful farmer, at the age of twenty-two Bouchard had married a widow, and he had prospered enough in the 1760s to purchase rights to a few neighboring plots of land — indicative of his remarkable drive.[14]

Within the parish, militia-captains and bailiffs were the manifestation of government authority, parish-nominated and appointed by the governor. Primarily selected for community rapport and leadership, these officials were also expected to be functionally literate in order to perform their duties. Under New France and in the immediate post-Conquest regime, the militia-captain's role was preeminent, until Governor Murray disbanded the entire militia system in 1765. A decade later, in the overture to the Revolutionary crisis, Governor Carleton restored the captaincy. As militia-captain, Pierre Bouch-

A View of the Château-Richer, Cape Torment, and Lower End of the Isle of Orleans, near Quebec, by Thomas Davies (1787). This is an example of a north-shore St. Lawrence *côte* settlement. National Gallery of Canada No. 6275.

ard had myriad duties in St-Vallier: publishing and enforcing government orders, delivering messages, enforcing police laws, and ensuring that roads and bridges were in proper repair. If the militia were called to arms, Pierre Bouchard commanded a company of 120 parish men, assisted by a lieutenant and four sergeants. Symbolic of his community authority, while holding office Bouchard was given a front pew in the parish church.[15]

During the decade when the militia was disbanded, government bailiffs had adopted the militia-captain's administrative and law-enforcement roles, in addition to their traditional legal duties of managing the local court justice process. By coincidence, in 1765 Pierre Bouchard had been the first St-Vallier bailiff to serve with those newly expanded powers, just as in 1775 he would be the first militia-captain under the Quebec Act government. When the militia-captain office was returned with full powers, the bailiffs' duties returned to the bounds of the legal realm.[16]

LOUIS-JOSEPH GODEFROY-DE-TONNANCOUR —
THE SEIGNEUR

Theoretically, the most powerful local figure was the seigneur. As an example, by 1774, Louis-Joseph Tonnancour's family had controlled the north bank Seigneury of Pointe-du-Lac, southwest of Trois-Rivières, for 140 years — and it was just one of several local landholdings belonging to the sixty-two-year-old. Tonnancour's family had played a major role in New France's history, and Louis-Joseph did his part, having served as the French king's storekeeper and as attorney for Trois-Rivières. Following the Conquest, however, he quickly attached himself to the British regime. In 1776, a Brunswick officer provided a snapshot of the ever-powerful Louis-Joseph as " . . . one of the wealthiest persons in all Canada. He is a large contractor, merchant, corn- and cattle-dealer . . . has numerous outlying country-houses; likes to loan money on houses and farms; and, in short, is universally known as the 'Pope of Canada.'"[17]

While Tonnancour had considerable regional power, his direct personal influence on Pointe-du-Lac's residents was relatively minor. As long as habitants met their obligations, Tonnancour did not interfere with their day-to-day lives; their most significant tenant responsibility was the annual rent payment, paid at the seigneurial manor house, typically around the November Feast of St. Martin. Rent was not particularly onerous for the habitant, and was of such limited value to most seigneurs that it might be considered symbolic. The other major privilege Tonnancour and his peers shared was the mill banality; this gave the seigneur first right to operate a mill and thus receive a percentage of the residents' milled grain. Louis-Joseph had taken advantage of this privilege — in fact, the mill still stands today.[18] Less commonly, seigneurs held minor fish, wood, or pasture rights and might be owed a few days of habitant *corvée* duty (compulsory labor). Another quaint traditional habitant duty took place on May Day, when the habitants visited their landlord's manor to raise a Maypole in his honor. Like militia-captains and bailiffs, the seigneurs had prestigious front pews reserved in the parish churches, plus designated burial plots.[19]

To maintain their positions, Louis-Joseph and his peers had their own responsibilities. First, they had to grant any unsettled land to available tenants. They also had a duty to keep a manor house on the seigneury, but did not need to live there. The manor was typically modest; few were larger than habitants' houses, but were undoubtedly better furnished and constructed. During war, Tonnancour and his fellow seigneurs could expect military commands, but not necessarily to lead their own habitants.

Like the two-thirds of his peers who were wealthy enough to support an urban home, Tonnancour lived in a city, in his case, Trois-Rivières. From there, Louis-Joseph generally acted as an absentee landlord, visiting seigneuries only as needed to meet obligations or resolve issues. The city provided him with a much greater opportunity to enjoy his economic and social position and keep involved in provincial politics.[20]

Tonnancour had noble heritage, but many of his peers did not. In one inventory, only twenty-two post-Conquest seigneurs were connected to hereditary noble families. Another few had received French nonhereditary titles as *chevaliers de Saint Louis* from their old king—an award for exceptional achievement. Now, Louis-Joseph and the remaining *Canadien* seigneurs cultivated a new set of political allies and social cohorts in Quebec. British government officials and senior military officers found that their common social status and education helped cement an affinity with the seigneurs, despite linguistic and ethnic differences. During the first dozen years of British rule, a considerable number of intermarriages took place between the ruling British and French-Canadian elite. In addition, as many as thirty Old Subjects joined the seigneurial ranks by purchasing rights, primarily from those "French" who abandoned Canada under British rule.[21]

SAMUEL JACOBS — RURAL MERCHANT

The British elite were definitely not the only newcomers in Quebec. A significant number of new Canadians were businessmen such as Samuel Jacobs, a European Jew who came as a British Army purveyor immediately following the Conquest. In 1763, he settled in St-Denis, on the lower Richelieu River. Rural merchants such as Jacobs had a powerful role in Jean-Baptiste's world, serving as the habitant's only regular connection with the Atlantic economy.[22]

The primary habitant commodity was wheat. By the 1770s, the Richelieu River valley achieved particular attention as a "breadbasket," feeding both provincial and Atlantic markets. Samuel Jacobs and his rural merchant cohorts functioned as middlemen, offering habitants those goods they could not make—fabric and blankets, tools and utensils, wine and liquor—in exchange for grain. In turn, Jacobs would sell wheat and buy goods from city whole-salers or traveling merchants, one of whom included a young Connecticut businessman named Benedict Arnold.[23]

Almost all habitants needed credit to cover purchases from one harvest to the next. Often, though, the peasant farmers did not produce enough wheat to cover their own needs, seigneurial dues, and church tithes, and ended up in arrears with the merchant. This was an accepted business fact, but with rival merchants contending for the high-demand grain, traders were inclined to be lenient; many habitants stayed indebted to them for years.

Jacobs and his competitors were a crucial link between Canada's parishes and the starkly different social environment of Montréal, Québec City, and Trois-Rivières. These cities were a sphere of merchants and officials, with connections throughout the Atlantic world. Just as the habitants formed the bulk of the rural populace, urban residents were primarily laborers, sailors, and artisans; but the cities were also home to the province's movers and shakers.

GEORGE ALLSOPP AND PIERRE GUY — URBAN MERCHANTS

English-born George Allsopp was one of 110 Old Subject merchants in Québec City at the end of the 1760s; Montréal had only forty-five. Allsopp's peers formed the Canadian demographic group with the closest links to the delegates assembled at Philadelphia in 1774; they spoke the same language, shared common traditions, and relied on similar communication networks. Allsopp, like two out of three Old Subject merchants, had relocated from the British Isles; but more than 10 percent of the Anglo transplants had their origins in the old British North American colonies.[24]

Allsopp, like many merchants, got his start in Quebec supporting the military. In 1761, two years after his arrival, he settled in Montréal at age twenty-eight. He began his Canadian mercantile career representing a large British firm, a pioneer in connecting imperial trade networks to the province. Most Old Subject merchants arrived with an inclination to rapidly exploit new market developments and establish business relationships of opportunity, and Allsopp did exactly that. He moved to Québec City and progressively diversified into every major Canadian trade, working with numerous com-panies and even purchasing his own seigneuries.

Pierre Guy was one of Allsopp's *Canadien* counterparts. Guy was born into a Montréal merchant family, wealthy enough that he could complete his education in France. Fresh from school, he returned to New France to fight as a militia officer in its last war. After the Conquest, even though almost half of the large-scale New French merchants chose to abandon Canada, the Guy family remained in North America. To support his family's business in the new conditions of British rule, Pierre traveled to London, established Atlantic trade connections to the new metropolis, and returned home to Montréal in 1763.[25]

Guy and his New Subject merchant compatriots benefited from established relationships in Quebec, along with a well-developed understanding of the traditional fur trade and its supporting economies. Now they were challenged by British business and government practices that prioritized imperially focused entrepreneurship and diversification over traditional *Canadien* local business relationships. By the 1770s, however, Guy proved that he could adapt successfully to the new market environment, expanding his business with English trading firms and integrating into the British imperial economy.[26]

If the Continental Congress hoped to spread its message to these diverse Canadians, it would have to rely on Quebec's own communication networks. When the Congressional delegates approved their October 1774 Address, they did not dwell on the means needed to distribute their letter's content, but trusted that such an important message surely would find its way throughout Canada. It would not be as simple as publishing it in a newspaper, which had proved to be effective in the twelve confederated colonies; in contrast, Quebec's print media were limited, and roughly 90 percent of *Canadiens* were illiterate. The province was still tremendously reliant on word of mouth.

In the countryside, news tended to flow from the parish church and commercial interaction. The priest had a key role in keeping the parish informed and in shaping public opinion. For example, he shared official church messages, such as Episcopal mandates; and his sermons might address current issues. The parish priest received the *Quebec Gazette* to obtain official news, but it also offered him a window on Canadian and world events. Government proclamations were posted at the church door, but the vast majority of habitants relied on militia-captains to "publish" them by reading the notices aloud, being unable to decipher the printed messages on their own.[27]

In his intermittent and seasonal commercial interaction at the local store,

Jean-Baptiste might converse with the merchant and habitants from nearby parishes; literate associates also might explain posted notices to him there. More aggressive merchants, such as peddlers, horse-, or wheat-traders, might visit Jean-Baptiste at home; their conversations certainly included more than just business. Successful merchants had a closer link to world events, relying on accurate news to make good trade decisions. Skilled businessmen had extensive correspondence networks, and if any rural layperson subscribed to a newspaper, it was probably a trader.

The situation in the cities was starkly different. Information was exchanged casually on an almost constant basis. Official news sources, such as the Church or "published" government proclamations, were still valuable in the city, yet they were less influential for a citizen of Québec City, Trois-Rivières, or Montréal than in the parishes. Daily business communication dominated the urban information exchange.

News spread primarily from the city waterfront. Each arriving ship carried letters, newspapers, and word-of-mouth information from previous ports of call. In the fall of 1774, almost half of the inbound traffic came from the British Atlantic seaboard colonies, especially New England. This was an efficient, but seasonal means of obtaining information; ships could travel up the St. Lawrence only from May to November, leaving the province isolated and short on winter news. Fortunately, an efficient postal system ran year-round, bringing communication from other colonies. By the summer of 1774, twice-weekly service ran between Montréal and New York. A post-house network on the north-shore "King's Way" road connected the Canadian cities; it took only three days for a letter from the capital to reach Montréal.[28]

Once information arrived in Canada's cities, the primary public forums for mass communication were taverns, inns, and coffeehouses. Both Old and New Subjects met in these establishments for business, relaxation, entertainment, and political action. Public houses were not merely forums for oral communication, but offered print media collections too. Typically newspaper copies were available for customers' perusal, and an evening's activities might include the public reading of interesting articles or current handbills, expanding the "print" audience to the urban illiterate. Even in the cities, slightly more than half of the francophone New Subject population could not read; yet almost every Old Subject Canadian was literate.[29]

There was only one newspaper printed in Canada, the *Quebec Gazette/La Gazette de Québec*. Partners William Brown and Thomas Gilmore founded the paper when they brought a printing press from Philadelphia—Canada's first. Brown and Gilmore published the premier issue of the *Gazette* on 21 June 1764. However, their company relied on the government to bring them a profit; more than two-thirds of their production was "job printing" of official messages and administrative forms. They also produced business and advertising products, and occasionally published books.[30]

The *Gazette* had only a few hundred subscribers, but a typical copy traveled through several sets of hands. In terms of format, the paper was fairly standard for the day, except that it was bilingual. Most items were printed in English and French, typically on parallel columns of the same page. Like other colonial publishers, Brown and Gilmore borrowed external news from other papers, and typically less than a half column was used for locally generated news, excluding official announcements and advertising.

The inaugural issue of the *Gazette* touted its "Accuracy, Freedom, and Impartiality," and in its early years the paper occasionally addressed controversial topics. Yet overall, it was quite conservative—Brown and Gilmore depended on government business, after all. By 1770, the government muzzled potentially divisive material, approving all of the *Gazette*'s content before printing. Gilmore died in 1773, leaving Brown in charge of the business on the eve of the Revolutionary crisis. As imperial tensions increased, Brown often took the easy option of simply publishing contentious acts and proclamations in their entirety, leaving readers to independently interpret the greater meaning of measures such as the Intolerable Acts. In 1774, the *Gazette* occasionally referenced the establishment and conduct of the Continental Congress, but only in a matter-of-fact form. When compared to the *Nova Scotia Gazette*, a paper operating in a similar political environment, the *Quebec Gazette* still seems cautious and implicitly progovernment.[31]

Beyond the *Gazette*, a number of other newspapers reached Quebec through various means. Some even offered direct subscription; in 1772, the London Post-Office advertised subscriptions for various English papers, to be delivered to Canada with each mail-packet boat. A year later, James Rivington's *New-York Gazetteer . . . and Quebec Weekly Advertiser* boldly included the province in its full title, and promised that "The Subscribers in Quebec, Montreal, and Three-Rivers, may depend on the Papers being constantly dispatched by the Post." These external papers offered analysis and viewpoints that differed from the generic coverage provided by the *Quebec Gazette*, but they were less accessible outside of Québec City and Montréal.[32]

In these conditions, the Continental Congress faced the daunting task of simply getting information to Quebec and distributing it around the province to the diverse groups represented by *Curé* Verreau, Pierre Bouchard, Seigneur Tonnancour, and merchants Jacobs, Allsopp, and Guy—and especially to the remote and illiterate habitants characterized by Jean-Baptiste. Effectively persuading these Canadians, of such different backgrounds and classes, to adopt a common patriot cause might seem impossible. Yet that was exactly what those represented in Philadelphia hoped to achieve at the end of 1774.

Chapter 3

FUEL FOR REBELLION

The British Party and the Quebec Act of 1774

The King trusts that when the Provisions of [the Quebec Act] have taken place . . . prejudices which popular Clamour has excited will cease, and that His Majesty's Subjects of every description will see and be convinced of the Equity and good Policy of the Bill. | *Secretary of State Dartmouth to Governor Guy Carleton, London, 10 December 1774*

Quebec's New French heritage had an undeniable influence on *Canadien* views and sentiments; their basic societal structure and many core values were clear products of that earlier era. Yet by the time Congress wrote its first address to Quebec, almost an entire generation had lived with a British presence in the colony. From the 1759 arrival of Royal Navy warships on the St. Lawrence, to the British government's Quebec Act, milestone events and sociopolitical undercurrents played a critical role in shaping the choices Canadian habitants, merchants, seigneurs, and clergy would make when the continent erupted in the 1774 Revolutionary crisis.

Beyond the change of kings dictated by its outcome, the French and Indian War left indelible marks on the Canadian psyche and ushered in meaningful changes to the colony's demographic landscape. When General James Wolfe brought his British force to the St. Lawrence in 1759, he began with a bombardment of heavily fortified Québec City. The British who occupied the city that fall found it "in a most ruinous condition." Many buildings had been burned and most damaged by "shot or shell . . . scarcely ha[bit]able without some repairing."[1]

While raining fire on the capital, Wolfe also unleashed a campaign of destruction across rural Canada. The general gave the habitants two options. He preferred that the people would "take no part in the great contest between the two crowns." If they took up arms, however, there would be "most fatal consequences; their habitations destroyed, their sacred temples exposed to an exasperated soldiery, their harvest utterly ruined." In a military policy applied for more than a year, the British laid waste to swathes of the Canadian countryside; whenever Canadian militia dared to resist, parishes were ravaged in retribution.[2]

Prior to Wolfe's operations, British Nova Scotia served as another example of British ruthless wartime policy. Unsure of Acadian loyalty at the war's outset, the government ordered the removal of the colony's entire ethnically French population. Exiles were relocated within the empire, many to New England. Three years after the war ended, Quebec Governor James Murray offered these displaced Acadians access to Canadian land, the only requirement being an oath of allegiance to the Crown. Over the next four years, an estimated 8,000 Acadians arrived in Quebec, increasing the province's population by more than 5 percent. Many Acadian-Canadians concentrated in the sparsely populated sections between Montreal District's south bank and the Richelieu River, including a region eventually called L'Acadie.[3]

Another wartime legacy would have tremendous influence on the American Revolution in Quebec, but this one originated in France. With its mercantilist cash flow perpetually biased toward the metropolis, New France never succeeded in obtaining sufficient specie (coin currency) to meet its internal financial needs. Instead, the colony relied on various forms of paper money or "bills of exchange." With the escalation of the French and Indian War, the situation in Canada only grew worse; the administration profligately issued more bills and *ordonnances*, which rapidly depreciated in market value by 60 to 70 percent. Although theoretically the paper could be redeemed for specie payment, grossly indebted France implemented serial policies to slow and eventually freeze such payment. The French government owed Canadians over 40 million *livres* at the time of the Conquest. While the British government tried to arrange for French repayment after the war, between merchant speculation, negotiated devaluation, and eventual default, "this huge mass of credit had become as worthless as the paper on which it was written." Having endured such a tremendous collective financial loss through this experience, *Canadiens* dreaded paper money of any sort.[4]

When allegiances were tested by the Revolution from 1774 to 1776, individual *Canadien* and Acadian-Canadian responses varied widely. Although there are no substantive written records to evaluate or quantify related habitant attitudes, the French and Indian War experiences must have weighed heavily

in many of their decisions. Presumably some habitants were driven to vengeance for hostile British acts; while others were intimidated or neutralized
by the lessons of their recent past, both military and economic.

As an additional factor, the Canadian situation had drastically improved
following the 1760 Conquest. British leaders offered liberal terms at the
capitulations of Québec City and Montréal, including "free exercise" of the
Catholic faith. As long as the people laid down their arms, they could expect
magnanimous treatment.[5]

Hand-in-hand with these reassurances, the Church did its part to promote
Canadian cooperation with the occupiers, even as the war was still being
fought. Bishop Henri-Marie Dubreil-de-Pontbriand issued a circular letter
insisting that his flock remain respectful and obedient to their new rulers—a
propitious step for future Church-state relationships. However, Pontbriand's
death in June of 1760 created a new provincial religious crisis that carried over
into the post-Conquest era.[6]

The Canadian Catholic Church could not function long without a bishop,
but the Protestant British proved hesitant to allow one. The Canadian clergy
took the initiative, nominating Montréal's Vicar-General Étienne Montgolfier, a French-born Sulpician superior who had lived in Canada for only
about a decade. This move was ill received in London; the British countered
by recommending that the Quebec vicar-general, French-born Jean-Olivier
Briand, lead the diocese instead; among his qualifications, Briand had served
in Canada twice as long as Montgolfier. After considerable behind-the-scenes
wrangling in London, Rome, and Paris, on 16 March 1766, the new fifty-one-
year-old bishop was consecrated quietly in France. Briand immediately and
steadfastly sustained his predecessor's policies in support of the new British
rulers, relying on St. Paul's guidance in Romans 13:1, " . . . the powers that be
are ordained of God."[7]

For a year after the Conquest, Canada was governed by a military regime,
under Brigadier-General James Murray's overall command. British policies
were accommodating to the *Canadiens* and encouraged a return to normal
productive life. The regime helped Canadians adapt to their new government
by promulgating official acts in French and relying on traditional militia-captains and bailiffs for local control. Citizens even received decent compensation
when forced to quarter troops in their homes.

In August 1764, the Province of Quebec received its first civil government, defined only in the broadest terms. General Murray became the first

governor and executed provincial rule along with his council, consisting of three appointed officials and eight members selected from the colony's "most considerable" residents. French-Canadians were effectively disqualified from council service due to the British "Test Act," which required the renunciation of Catholicism in order to serve in office anywhere in the empire. Military officers and administrators, sympathetic to the *Canadiens,* recognized the injustice that such laws created specifically in Quebec. Crown officials, joined by the seigneurs and Church leaders, formed a lobby known as the "French Party," which promoted French-Canadian interests. The governor stood at the head of this bloc.[8]

An opposing set of Canadian interests, concentrated in the small Anglo-merchant community, viewed Murray's liberal regime as excessively pro-"French" and counter to the Quebec government clauses in the Royal Proclamation of 1763. Collectively, these politically active Old Subjects formed the "British Party" to counter the governor's policies. Murray viewed these opponents as self-interested, profit-seeking Yankees and Yorkers — "Licentious Fanaticks" who would only be satisfied by "the expulsion of the Canadians" from their own province. By October 1764, the party conflict intensified and personal animosities exploded, leading Governor Murray to observe: "At Montreal the [British Party] Civilians & the [French Party] Military are Inveterate Enemies." The most notable result of these tensions occurred two months later — the Thomas Walker Affair.[9]

Walker was an enterprising English-born merchant who moved to Canada to profit from the fur trade, after a decade of doing business in Boston. Like many Old Subject newcomers, he became a justice of the peace shortly after arriving in Montréal — a reality driven by the Test Act's candidate restrictions. Through his legal decisions — particularly related to billeting soldiers in the city, which he viewed as unconstitutional — and other political outbursts, Thomas Walker highlighted himself as one of the most radical of the British Party troublemakers. Army officers were seriously offended by the "Oppressive Proceedings of the new Magistrates" epitomized by Walker. On the dark winter night of 6 December 1764, an unidentified band of his enemies, almost assuredly soldiers, made a "daring Assault" at the outspoken merchant-judge's Montréal home. The vengeful party attacked Walker, leaving him "cruelly maimed" by severing part of his ear.[10]

The search for conclusive evidence in the case proved fruitless, and Walker wrangled with the administration for years in a vain pursuit of justice. The controversy burned so hot that Governor Murray rotated the implicated Twenty-eighth Regiment out of Montréal. Having failed to obtain redress from the government, Walker burned with spite for the proadministration French Party, a venomous hatred that would have tremendous future implications. The governor's handling of the "Affair," added to the British Party's numerous complaints against his pro-"French" policies, contributed to Murray's recall the following year.[11]

While the British Party was busy opposing the governor, the New Subjects in the French Party worked to defend their own interests. During Murray's tenure, the *Canadien* elite regularly petitioned London on diverse topics. By 1765, a group of seigneurs received the governor's permission to hold their own informal political convention. The situation prompted protests and alarm from "British" Montrealers, especially when French Party leader Judge Adam Mabane barred them from observing a preliminary *Canadien* gathering held in their city. The subsequent Québec City "French" assembly was anticlimactic, but delivered a formal statement of elite *Canadien* concerns: fur-trade concessions, religious equality, and the need for a bishop—as Briand had not yet been consecrated.[12]

For the most part, the habitants remained uninvolved in provincial politics, leaving the debates to their traditional *superieurs*. During this period only one event really caught the habitants' attention. At the height of the 1763–64 Amerindian uprising, known as Pontiac's War, Murray sought to recruit a new Canadian regiment, primarily to convince "rebellious" Indians that they could not expect any assistance from the French. Murray's proclamation of 6 March 1764 called for militia-captains to recruit volunteers, a radical change from New France's traditions in which call-ups were handled through a parish quota system, with limited personal choice in participation.[13]

Many parishes showed an early disinclination to enlist, and Murray resorted to threats: if acceptable numbers of recruits were not reached, troops would be drafted and the resisters disarmed. Some habitant opposition originated in rumors alleging that the government intended to send volunteers "to serve in distant possessions of the British Empire," or that enlistees would be soldiers for life. The conditions for service seemed to hint at a grand nefarious purpose; voluntary enlistment, good pay, and a mandatory oath of loyalty all seemed suspiciously unusual to the habitants.

Despite the cautious, half-hearted response, the Canadian regiment eventually was fielded with proportional representation from all three districts.

Several seigneurs formed the unit's officer corps.[14] However, the regiment's primary achievements were mobilization and movement to Niagara. The unit was rapidly disbanded when Indian tensions subsequently cooled.[15]

The other major colonial crisis during Murray's regime passed relatively uneventfully in Quebec. While the Stamp Act caused great unrest in the lower thirteen colonies, Canadians of all stripes generally accepted the tax without meaningful opposition, particularly as Canada's tax and government situations were so different from those in the agitated "old" colonies. The Old Subject community debated the issue, resulting in "great disputes and very high words in the coffee house," but failed to produce a common political stand.[16]

=====

In the fall of 1766, a new government leader arrived in the capital, the stiff and distant forty-one-year-old Lieutenant-Governor Guy Carleton. After Murray's recall, Carleton would serve as acting governor for the next two years before receiving full gubernatorial authority. The province's new executive was another soldier-statesman, an Irish-born British officer who had served in both the War of Austrian Succession and the Seven Years' War/French and Indian War. During the latter conflict, none other than King George II initially stifled Carleton's military advancement. The monarch was displeased with Carleton, apparently over indiscreet comments the young officer made regarding troops from George's other kingdom, continental Hanover. Carleton was permitted to join the 1759 Quebec expedition only after his close friend Brigadier-General James Wolfe persistently pressed the King on the matter. During the campaign, Wolfe added to Carleton's assigned quartermaster-general duties, employing him as chief engineer and giving him command of the elite corps of detached grenadiers. Carleton was wounded leading these troops during Wolfe's fatal battle on the Plains of Abraham outside Québec City. Following the Conquest, Carleton received additional praise while serving as a brigadier-general in the 1761 French Belle-Isle operation and in the 1762 Havana campaign.[17]

A military leader rather than politician by trade, Carleton's 1766 lieutenant-governorship could also be attributed indirectly to the now-deceased James Wolfe's influence. In the early 1750s, between wars, Wolfe had recommended Carleton to escort the young Charles Lennox, Duke of Richmond,

Guy Carleton (detail). Library of Congress Prints and Photographs Division.

on a tour of fortified European cities. The two travelers developed a strong, enduring relationship, which subsequently benefited Carleton as Richmond's influence grew. As biographer Paul David Nelson recorded, "The Duke of Richmond . . . persuaded his friends in the cabinet that Carleton should be sent to Quebec as lieutenant governor to replace Murray in his absence. Despite the fact that Carleton had no experience in civil administration, neither [Prime Minister Charles Watson-Wentworth, Marquis of] Rockingham nor King George III had any objections to his appointment." It was this path of patronage that brought Guy Carleton back to Quebec.[18]

Reaching his new post, Lieutenant-Governor Carleton served as a calming influence, tempering British Party opposition while continuing government advocacy of elite *Canadien* interests. Early in his term, Carleton expressed his core belief that "the Common People are greatly to be influenced by their Seigniors." Heavy reliance on the "French" upper class would be the cornerstone of his governing philosophy through the Revolutionary crisis.[19]

The Catholic role in government still remained a key long-term political issue. The London government, however, was particularly unstable in the late 1760s, and the resolution of Quebec's core provincial government issues never quite warranted Parliamentary action. However, the Anglo-Canadian opposition persisted in pleading for a general assembly.[20]

The British Party, which relaxed temporarily following Murray's recall, rallied for a renewed political push in 1767. Led by Northern Irish–born Québec City entrepreneur John McCord, the Anglo-merchants met in coffee houses[21] and taverns to shape their way ahead. They continued to anchor their political position on the Royal Proclamation of 1763, maintaining that they "never would have set foot" in Quebec if there had been any doubt that English-style government would be established. In 1770 the King received a petition from more than thirty British Party leaders, asking His Majesty to issue a mandate for a Quebec general assembly. Carleton frowned on the British Party's tactics. He mocked the upstarts' common origins, and was surprised that the Old Subjects could not see that "tumultuous meetings" would result in anarchy—"the lowest dregs of the people . . . would of course become the lawgivers of the country."[22]

Carleton led the provincial struggle into its next phase, traveling to London in August 1770 to help draft a permanent plan for Canadian government; Lieutenant-Governor Hector Cramahé was left in charge. That same summer, fifty-nine French Party *Canadiens* wrote their own contrasting petition to the Crown, respectfully requesting a return to French law and customs in the province, which added more ammunition for Carleton's case.[23]

With the governor away, the province simmered. The next major volley of petitions originated in late 1773, as John McCord launched a final push to counter Carleton's influence in London. On 30 October, more than forty British Party members met in a Québec City tavern and overwhelmingly elected to send another petition for a House of Assembly.

The British Party's leadership committee sought to adopt a new tactic to break the ethnic divisions in the provincial political struggle. They invited fifteen substantial "French" merchants to join in the petition, even though the Test Act prevented full *Canadien* political participation, believing they had common class and economic interests. After a couple days' delay for consultation, the New Subject invitees made it clear there would be no French-Canadian support for the British Party petition; in the end, the only French names affixed to the petition came from a handful of Protestant Huguenots.[24]

When Lieutenant-Governor Cramahé received the British Party's petition in early December 1773, he politely replied that the subject was too important for him to address. The British Party responded by directly petitioning the King once more, with no substantial difference between this petition and its 1770 predecessor. However, the documents were not completed until Montrealers affixed their signatures on 15 January 1774.[25]

In the meantime, the French Party reacted. Sixty-five "divers[e] Roman-Catholic Inhabitants," primarily from Montréal, preempted their Anglo rivals, generating a December petition from "the Roman Catholic Inhabitants of Quebec." Their overarching request was for "a settlement of the Laws" to eliminate the "confusion which, at present, overspreads the Province." Their recommended approach shared many key points with Carleton's plans, hinting at some degree of collaboration. They also countered the British Party's principal arguments for a general assembly, arguing that the province was "not, as yet, in a condition to defray the expenses of its own Civil Government, and, consequently, not in a condition to admit of a General Assembly"—a reverse colonial position of "no representation, without taxation."[26]

As both Canadian parties had staked out their positions, it was up to Parliament to find a solution. Following a few weeks' debate in both houses, including testimony by Carleton and a handful of Canadian experts, Parliament approved the Quebec Act on 17 June 1774, to be implemented on 1 May of the following year. When the King provided his assent to the Act, he noted it was "founded on the clearest Principles of Justice and Humanity," and hoped it would "have the best Effects in quieting the Minds, and promoting the happiness" of his Canadian subjects. He may have been correct in the first sentiment, but events in the next year and a half would prove him wrong on the second.[27]

The Act handed the French Party a decisive victory. The law's key elements were "Free Exercise of the Religion of the Church of Rome"; tremendously expanded provincial boundaries, to include the northern Ohio Valley and the Great Lakes; and a restructured provincial government. Canada would be governed by a hybrid of French civil law and English criminal law, and the Governor's Council was expanded to a maximum of twenty-three members. Most important, the "Test Act" was replaced by an alternate oath, acceptable to Catholics, so *Canadiens* could serve on the council. Much to the British Party's chagrin, the Act specified that it was "at present inexpedient to call an Assembly."

Canada did not see the Act's full English text until its publication in the 8 September *Quebec Gazette*. A French version was not provided for another two months because of the "precision necessary in the translation." In New

England, however, the Act had been printed by the end of August; dissemination of the controversial Act's details certainly helped draw patriot attention to Canada, just as the first Continental Congress began its session.[28]

The Quebec Act's greatest advocate, Governor Carleton, returned to the provincial capital on the heels of the measure's initial Canadian publication. He arrived on 17 September, the same day Congress received the Suffolk Resolves and six days before his fiftieth birthday. He was accompanied by his wife of just two years, Lady Maria Carleton, who had been educated in Versailles and was fluent in French. The capital provided an incredibly warm welcome to them, with a reception committee, military honors, and the celebratory illumination of Quebec's Upper Town. Within a week the clergy and "the inhabitants" presented the governor with flattering addresses recognizing his contribution to the latest measures, prompting Carleton to inform Secretary of State Dartmouth that "All Ranks of People" were vying with each other "in testifying their Gratitude and Respect" over the new form of government.[29]

The clergy had a lot to celebrate. The Act essentially restored Catholicism as the colony's established religion. The seigneurs were excited because their place in provincial leadership could be formalized by Council participation. However, there is a dearth of firsthand evidence regarding the habitants' immediate response, if any, to the Quebec Act. The new form of government certainly did not offer them any immediate, tangible benefits. By fortifying the seigneurs' and priests' positions and privileges, the Act could be seen as an infringement of the "liberties" Jean-Baptiste had realized under British rule—an injury that might give the British Party an opportunity to politicize the heretofore silent peasantry.

The British Party's response was unsurprising. First and foremost, they were shocked to find the promises of the Royal Proclamation of 1763 abandoned and their perceived English constitutional rights ignored; they were to be denied an assembly indefinitely and would be yoked by "foreign" French civil law. What was previously perceived as the Canadian governors' personal biases toward the French Party had now been made a legal fact. With their political platform having received such a decisive defeat in London, some Anglo-Canadians talked of leaving the province, while others committed themselves to redoubling their political efforts. The time had come when they might need to seek a new set of allies. As Old Subject extremists argued that they had "no Security for our Property nor Religion" with the new government, the recent agitation of other North American colonists seemed to provide an excellent opportunity for cooperation in a common fight against Ministerial impositions.[30]

═══════

In the fall of 1774, the Quebec Act was reprinted and debated along the British-American seaboard at a remarkable pace, whipping patriot colonists to new heights of anger at the Ministry. Newspaper editors eagerly published antigovernment opinion pieces maligning the Act, including reprints of many highly critical examples from London. When issuing political resolves, communities, assemblies, and the Continental Congress now included the Quebec Act in their grievances with the Ministry. While the Anglo-Americans had many reasons to dislike the Act, the opposition focused on three core issues: "The establishment of the Roman [Catholic religion], "The institution of an arbitrary government," and "The extension of the Colony by excessive limits."[31]

Especially in zealously Protestant New England, the newly recognized status of the Canadian Catholic Church caused great alarm. Some patriot leaders, immersed in Enlightenment philosophy, held more tolerant views; yet most British North American colonists still clung to vitriolic anti-Catholic English tradition. The last 150 years of English and colonial experience inculcated such beliefs; in the episodic string of wars against France and Spain, Catholics had caused the "massacre and destruction of so many thousands of protestants." British America's strong ideological ties to the seventeenth century's Glorious Revolution, in which the Stuart kings had tried to implement their "corrupt system of tyranny and oppression" in England, also led many patriots to suspect "Catholic tyranny" behind any plot against liberty.[32]

Fearmongering rumors played upon such apprehensions. An October 1774 propaganda anecdote maintained that "A Gentleman lately arrived from Quebec" reported that the province's Protestants "were obliged to exercise their Religion in secret for fear of the Roman Catholics." The religious component of the Quebec Act was a clear challenge to core British colonial values; it was interpreted as a sign of Parliament's corruption, an imposition on Canada's Protestants, an indication of impending danger for the other North American colonies, and a violation of the King's coronation oath. Even the most progressive delegates in Philadelphia were unable to recognize the Quebec Act

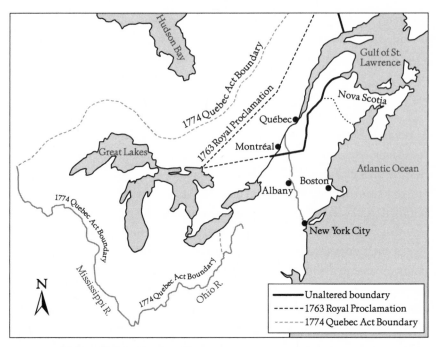

MAP 1: Quebec Province, 1763 and 1774.

as a fair, enlightened attempt by London to address the extreme challenge of grafting the large Canadian Catholic population to the otherwise vehemently Protestant British Empire in a just and enduring manner.[33]

The second vein of North American opposition to the Quebec Act came from the same political concerns expressed in Congress's "Address to the Inhabitants of the Province of Quebec": that a tyrannical government was being imposed on the Canadians, even though they had been "conquered into liberty" as New Subjects of the empire. The Act was decried as the "only statute which has been passed these two hundred years to establish Popery and arbitrary power in the British dominions," bringing provincial rule under executive prerogative and French law, rather than the traditional English constitutional forms promised by the Royal Proclamation of 1763. In patriot eyes, the Ministry's plan for Canadian government was "founded on injustice and violation, contempt of law and customs of the realm"; paired with the impact of the other Intolerable Acts on Massachusetts, the Quebec Act seemed to forebode despotism for all North American colonial governments, warranting immediate, active opposition.[34]

Many British North Americans also feared that Quebec was part of a "well concerted scheme" to check the other colonies and "to keep them in awe." It was easy to believe that the Ministry could persuade the Canadians—perpetual foes of British North America—to fight colonial patriots. Such fears were supported by early reports that London had sent orders to Canada, "to arm the Militia of that Country with all convenient Speed . . . to have a Body of Forces in Readiness" to suppress the "malcontents" in the lower colonies.[35]

As a third major cause of opposition, the Quebec Act's boundary provisions directly attacked economic interests as well, particularly those of land speculators and fur traders. Many prominent British North Americans, especially from the middle colonies, had long planned to develop the Ohio Valley land.[36] The new Act seemed to transfer the entire northern valley arbitrarily into Quebec Province (see Map 1), destroying Anglo-Protestant land development opportunity in the West. It seemed a cruel irony that Anglo-American claims on the contested region had been confirmed by the outcome of the French and Indian War, only to have the valley barred from settlement by the Royal Proclamation of 1763, then be restored to the conquered Canadians. The oddly worded caveat that the Act would not "make void . . . vary or alter" any other colony's territorial rights did nothing to comfort western investors who saw their economic prospects being stolen by a grasping Ministry.

Similarly, the drastic provincial boundary shifts seemed to remove any theoretical benefit the Anglo-colonial fur traders may have gained from the Conquest. The concurrent Quebec Revenue Act of 1774 gave an additional decisive market advantage to the Canadians. That measure not only taxed North American rum at a higher rate than that from competing markets, but also required all rum entering the newly expanded territory of Quebec—now encompassing all the prime trading ground—to clear a Quebec provincial customs house. From Albany, this meant a detour of more than a hundred miles from normal trade routes to St-Jean, which would naturally redirect much of the business to Montréal. With little exaggeration, the New York Assembly protested that the two acts had "in a great measure destroyed" the province's Indian trade. The Quebec Act affected political, religious, and economic interests in the confederated British North American colonies—a clear cause for alarm.[37]

Only a few colonists dared to recognize the generous and progressive character of the Quebec Act. Staunch loyalist Bostonian Benjamin Hallowell offered a balanced analysis of the entire British colonial response to the Act.

He observed that if the "very good and salutary" bill had passed "at any other than the present time, [it] would have answered many valuable purposes." Yet, with its passage at a time when many expected to see another tyrannical imposition from London, the Quebec Act "had an amazing effect and . . . increased the clamour and opposition against the mother country." Despite the Act's most liberal intentions, to the conspiracy-fearing North American patriot eye, it showed all the classic characteristics of tyranny and seemed only to confirm the Ministry's villainous role.[38]

Chapter 4

AUTHORS AND AGITATORS

Patriot Correspondence and John Brown's Mission

The Canadians in general are greatly alarmed. | *A Gentleman in Montreal, 9 October 1774*

We have lately opened a Correspondence with Canada which I dare say will be attended with great and good effects. | *Samuel Adams to Arthur Lee, Boston, 4 March 1775*

In September and October 1774, coincidental developments in Canada and Philadelphia generated a slow convergence of two growing political crises: the struggle over Canada's form of government, and the Continental colonies' conflict with the Ministry. The Quebec Act helped draw both movements closer. By the end of that winter, increased Continental influence in Canada and changes in the provincial political landscape would significantly alter the character of Quebec's political struggle.

Unlike its North American neighbors, Quebec had not been part of the Committee of Correspondence movement leading to the first Continental Congress. Over the summer of 1774, patriots from Augusta to Portsmouth used this system to share news and refine a mutual understanding of events, developing a common cause even before Congress opened its first session. Patriot organizers had advocated, "Let Towns be connected together. You will then be a band of brothers, which no force can break, no enemy destroy." The first hint of any such Canadian correspondence came from a short 6 September letter, sent by Québec City merchant Jonas Clarke Minot to a friend in Massachusetts. Minot's message accompanied a wheat donation, collected by capital merchants, to be "distributed amongst the innocent and necessitous sufferers of the Town of Boston," who were vexed by London's closure of their port. After receiving the relief shipment and letter, the Bostonians responded on 10 October, expressing gratitude for the wheat and joy over the first public correspondence with the Town of Quebec. They hoped to continue a "brotherly" connection with their "friends in Canada."[1]

In the time between Minot's letter and the Boston response, the British Party had the opportunity to read all the painful details of Parliament's Quebec Act. They could not accept measures so contrary to British tradition and vowed to oppose the Act. Montréal's British Party reacted with particular vigor, taking the lead in the provincial struggle. Within a few weeks, they assembled a meeting of "all the English Inhabitants" in the city, launching their new fight for the Act's repeal. A committee of six, including Thomas Walker, Isaac Todd, John Blake, and James Price, was appointed to organize party activities. This was Price's entry into opposition leadership, a role that would expand significantly over the coming year. Originally a New Englander, Price had lived in Montréal since 1764, and had established an exceedingly profitable business partnership with politically like-minded William Haywood.[2]

The Montrealers made an early effort to share their sentiments throughout North America. On 9 October, "a Gentleman in Montreal" offered his views on the Quebec Act to a friend in New York. The anonymous author explicitly requested that his letter be published in the *New-York Journal*, making it an unofficial British Party report to the other colonies. The "Gentleman" conveyed his fellow citizens' "Abhorrence of the Quebec Act" and reported that the measure had caused great alarm. Except for "a few Tools and Dependents of the Governor," English-Canadians were "unanimous" in opposition to the Act and were determined to "struggle hard to obtain a repeal." The anonymous Montrealer claimed that *Canadien* merchants and habitants were "greatly dissatisfied" as well, but dared not complain for fear of angering their priests. Only "the French Noblesse and Gentry" were pleased with the Act; they expected to "lord it over the industrious Farmer and Trader, and live upon their Spoils, as they did before the Conquest."[3]

Two weeks later, on 24 October, British Party correspondents added to the "Gentleman's" views when they forwarded another letter, again intended for publication. Allegedly this message was a copy of instructions that "the Canadian Farmers" had given to the Montréal Committee. According to this document, rural *Canadiens* shared the British Party's alarm at the Quebec Act, and offered to support "any legal Steps" for its repeal. By sharing these reports, Quebec's Anglo-merchants were developing a foundation for future cooperation with patriots in the neighboring colonies.[4]

━━━━━

At the end of October, Walker, Price, and their fellow Montréal committeemen ventured downriver to consult with their Québec City counterparts. When they arrived, "an anonymous summons was posted in the coffee-house for all British subjects to meet at a particular tavern." In the ensuing meeting, the capital's British Party elected its own seven-member committee, including Zachary Macaulay and Jonathan Welles, individuals who had served on that city's 1773–74 petition committee. Several "town-meetings" followed in which the joint committees developed strategy, sent thanks to supporters in England, and composed new petitions to London.[5]

Carleton was aware of these events and tried to monitor opposition activities, but the "malcontents" took "uncommon pains to keep their whole proceedings" from his knowledge. The governor was concerned that there was a political "infection" being "imported daily" and fed by Old Subject Canadians who "imagined themselves . . . wiser than the Parliament of Great Britain"; yet Carleton took solace in the fact that his *Canadien* friends, seigneurs and clergy, seemed equally unsettled by the British Party's "meetings and nocturnal cabals." According to some of the governor's sources, the British Party had been coercing French-Canadians into signing anti–Quebec Act petitions, either "under the awe of menacing creditors" or from "ignorance." To conservative government supporters, the Canadian political opposition seemed to be entering a new phase in which the British Party advocates were employing "extreme" means to reach their goals.[6]

Despite the hints of radicalization, the formal product generated by the two weeks of joint committee meetings stayed within traditional form: petitions to the King and both Houses of Parliament. In the 12 November 1774 documents, the British Party members dropped their long-standing plea for an Assembly and focused their requests on the repeal of the Quebec Act, which had "deprived" them of traditional "franchises," denied them "the protection of the English Laws," and exposed them to the governor's "arbitrary" acts. Based simply on the number of signatures, 181, this appeal had considerably more support than previous petitions. The Old Subject subscribers included both future loyalists and rebels: English, Irish, Scots, Huguenots, Jews, and North American–born British, but there were still no *Canadiens* willing to add their names.[7]

Shortly after the joint committees completed their petitions, the first news-paper texts of Congress's "Address to the Canadians" arrived in Quebec. By the beginning of December, hundreds of English-language copies were circulating among antigovernment circles in the Canadian cities; however, Governor Carleton denied a British Party request to reprint it in the *Quebec Gazette*. In Canada, unlike the colonies to the south, there would be no newspaper campaign to help establish a "foundation of shared [patriot] experience" and "a collective commitment to the revolution."[8]

What was really needed to achieve the desired effect in Quebec, though, were French copies of the Address. Old Subject merchants did not need Congress's lessons on English liberty; the *Canadiens* did. Accordingly, when the Continental delegates approved their message, they simultaneously ordered "the translating, printing and publishing" of the Address in French, but this process took time. Two recent French immigrants were hired to complete the job in Philadelphia: Pierre du Simitière performed the translation, and Fleury Mesplet did the printing. Together, the duo generated a faithful version, with few Anglicisms in its politically technical language. It would be months, however, before this official French version reached Canada. In the meantime, sympathetic *Canadiens* made their own translation.[9]

In Montréal, and presumably Québec City, a few "manuscript copies of it [were] handed about among the French Bourgeois." Production was limited; without access to William Brown's sole Canadian printing press, each copy of the eighteen-page message was handwritten. The most interesting characteristic of this *Canadien* edition is its variation from the "purer" official du Simitière translation. In general, the Canadian translator's deviations tempered the original English rhetoric. Perhaps, in this unidentified individual's view, Congress made its case too vociferously, and he hoped his version might create more appeal.[10]

The French Party did not sit idly as the opposition campaigned against the Quebec Act. The *Quebec Gazette* printed various articles that supported the Act. After the British Party petitions and French translations of Congress's

Address circulated for a few weeks, the French Party launched a more overt counterattack, focused on New Subjects who seemed persuaded by the Anglo-merchants' arguments. On the day after Christmas 1774, a French address titled *Le Canadien Patriote* was shared at the entrance to Québec City's Upper Town market. [11]

Le Canadien Patriote (the Patriotic Canadian) was a pen name, but this particular letter is attributed to François-Joseph Cugnet. He had served in several posts under Governor Murray, but Carleton showered the Canadian with new offices, appointing him as French secretary to the governor and council, and as the province's official translator. Cugnet was an obvious and well-qualified advocate for the Quebec Act.[12]

The "Patriotic" Canadian tackled the British Party's arguments head-on, challenging his audience to "open your eyes" and see beyond the "artful representations" of political wolves in sheep's clothing. He mocked the opposition and its arguments — middling men, who had risen above the dirt only due to a "beneficial trade," now sought to become "masters" of the province. In *Le Canadien Patriote's* view, the Act's religious, legal, and boundary articles were everything that New Subjects might desire. Only ignorant fools should be deluded by the restive Old Subjects' appeals.[13]

Curiously, the *Quebec Gazette* never published this letter; however, *Le Canadien Patriote* was "circulated throughout the province." It was known publicly that Québec City Seminary students were employed to make the numerous manuscript copies necessary to achieve such an expansive reach without using the printing press.[14]

The British Party saw this new approach, French progovernment circular letters, as a tremendous challenge. Old Subject merchants lacked a comparable means to "communicate to the whole body of the Canadians," and they were unequipped to counter the "private and repeated suggestions of the priests," who unconditionally supported the government. Even if the British Party could have generated written copies of its own messages, "the Canadians in many places could not have read them" without the assistance of the clergy or militia-captains. This early experience with having been overmatched in the rural parishes forced the Anglo-merchant opposition to reassess its tactics. Rather than relying solely on print media, in the future they would have to achieve what they could "in the way of conversation." Before the spring thaw, these innovative businessmen would demonstrate their adaptability in delivering their message.[15]

The British Party still generated a written response to *Le Canadien Patriote*, simply titled "An Answer." Dated 8 February, this letter refuted the French Party's main arguments and added an appeal for readers to leave religious conflict in the past and enter a more enlightened and tolerant age. It is doubtful that "An Answer" was heavily circulated or translated; its small audience was probably concentrated in the coffeehouses and taverns, where bilingual merchants could debate its merits.[16]

The writer of "An Answer" added a notable comment at the end of his message, indicative of an emerging question within the British Party. If the disputes between the mother country and sister colonies proceeded to "extremities," the author believed the "English and Canadians" undoubtedly would show "attachment to the constitution and government of Great-Britain" and support the Crown rather than "rebellious" fellow North American colonists.[17]

There were other indications that many British Party supporters were hesitant to join the Continental colonies in pursuit of the revocation of the Quebec Act, and a rift between radical and conservative factions began to develop. In mid-January, a concerned Montrealer raised an important question with friends in the lower colonies, one that might be decisive in determining Canadian merchants' future affiliations. Referring to the trade-prohibiting Continental Association, the author wanted to know if the colonies intended to adhere to "the Resolve of the Congress . . . dropping connection with us, unless we come into their measures." If it appeared that economic ties between Quebec and its neighbors were to be severed, the writer shared that Canadians intended to "order shipping from England"; they were unwilling to sacrifice their fur and wheat trade for political ends.[18]

As the *Canadiens* became more politically engaged and copies of Congress's Canadian address spread, loyal French Party Catholics found another good reason to attack Congress — its hypocrisy. By late March 1775, Montréal sources reported an anecdotal case in which an unofficial translator publicly shared the content of both Congress's Canadian Address and its "Address to the People of Great-Britain." The hostile "picture of the Catholick Religion, and the Canadian manners" in the letter to Britain contrasted so sharply with the pleasant, conciliatory language of its Canadian equivalent that the audience was stunned, allegedly wailing, "Oh! The perfidious, double-faced Congress . . . whose Addresses, like their Resolves, are destructive of their own objects."[19]

In fact, Congress was duplicitous in these two messages. By creating four separate official addresses, the delegates created an opportunity to specifically craft their message for each major demographic audience, but failed to "de-conflict" their appeals. Some of the language in the "Address to the People of Great-Britain" was highly inflammatory to *Canadiens,* including an accusation that Catholicism had deluged Great Britain "in blood, and dispersed impiety, bigotry, persecution, murder and rebellion through every part of the world." For a British audience, this may have been a boilerplate reference to the turbulent seventeenth-century fight for liberty, but it was patently offensive to the very audience with whom Congress sought to achieve direct political union. Such inherently conflicting messages were a clear case where Congress was politically and procedurally immature, with much still to learn about public diplomacy. However, the actual effect of their hypocrisy on the *Canadien* audience was probably less dramatic than the March letter and other progovernment reports portrayed.[20]

Sometime around the end of January 1775, Thomas Walker finally received a few hundred official French copies of Congress's "Address to the Inhabitants." He did not hold onto them for long; "in less than fifteen days," they were "distributed from one extremity of the province to the other." Walker accomplished this by delivering the printed letters "into the hands of Mr. Cazeau" and several others.[21]

François Cazeau was a former French soldier who elected to remain in Canada after the last war. He quickly excelled as a fur trade merchant and soon bought property rights on the St. Lawrence shore, opposite Montréal. Considered one of the most "prominent citizens of the region," Cazeau seemed an unlikely friend of the British Party; yet generally speaking, French-born Canadians were more disposed toward political cooperation with their Old Subject neighbors. Cazeau became Walker's most prominent New Subject collaborator, zealously giving Congress's letter "a speedy and extensive circulation in Canada," even employing his fur trade agents for the task.[22]

Over the next few months, under Walker's direction, "Many English merchants ran through the rural districts on the pretext of purchasing wheat of the farmers." In reality, the roving "traders" were proselytizing in the parishes, reading Congress's letter and making their case against the Quebec Act. These skilled marketers deftly adapted their talking points to draw Jean-Baptiste's attention and raise emotional responses. They surely discussed ethereal themes such as "Oppression and Tyranny," but dwelt on the more tangible considerations such as taxes and tithes, exorbitant government salaries, and arbitrary law—all appropriately embellished to convince the farmers they were "on the brink of misfortune" if they did not support the cause. French Party spies reported that in the countryside the "disaffected Subjects who cooperated with the Congress" were succeeding to such a degree that government supporters "were obliged to remain silent." At the very time that some urban opponents of the Quebec Act began to temper their activity as they began having doubts about creeping toward rebellion, the British Party's radical wing found a new pool of supporters in the rural parishes.[23]

Yet as Canada simmered, it took surprisingly long for the other individual colonies to open their own correspondence with the province. Massachusetts led the way, but the effort developed at a painfully slow pace. In early October 1774, a recommendation was offered that the Provincial Congress should "depute an agent or agents from that body to go to Canada and there treat with the inhabitants," but it remained a low priority. It was not until 6 December that Massachusetts finally formed the Committee for Correspondence to Canada, charged with maintaining communication and gathering "very frequent intelligence." The high-powered but very busy committee members, Samuel Adams, Joseph Warren, Benjamin Church, and John Hancock, remained preoccupied and were distracted from the task for another two months.[24]

While Massachusetts dithered in Canadian correspondence, patriot committees wasted no time intercepting loyalist communications to the north. As early as November, Governor Carleton reported that, "all persons from Boston for Canada are searched for letters and strictly examined" to ensure they were not bearing messages. By February, Quebec postal authorities reported the curious lack of New York mail, and by the end of April, they confirmed that correspondence was "being taken from the Post Office at Hartsford." Letters from General Gage were "taken out and burnt," as were hundreds of copies of the allegedly loyalist *Rivington's Gazette*.[25]

In mid-February, the Massachusetts Provincial Congress finally delegated Canadian communication to the Boston Committee for Correspondence, which was to "open and establish an intimate correspondence and connection" with Quebec, "for and in behalf of" Massachusetts. In less than a week, on 21 February, the Bostonians sent their opening letter to "the Inhabitants of the Province of Quebec."[26]

The message identified common ground for cooperation, noting that the newly imposed governments in Quebec and Massachusetts were "of a kind nearly alike," distinctly un-British. The people in both provinces had been "deprived of the most valueable Securities of the British Constitution." Taking a positive view of Canada's recent activities, the Massachusetts correspondents noted that even if "the late Continental Congress" did not have "the Advantage of Delegates" from Quebec, the Bostonians were pleased that their "fellow Subjects in Canada, of French as well as English Extract" had petitioned against the Ministry's latest measures on their own. The committee hoped to see their northern neighbors "cheerfully adopting the resolutions of the late Continental Congress & joyning their own Delegates" in the second Continental Congress, adding "great Reputation & Weight to the Common Cause."[27]

Coincidentally, in early February the Montréal Committee had provided Boston with an update on their status. In a letter accompanying a cash donation to the closed port city, James Price and Alexander Hay expressed their doubts about the effectiveness of their political tactics. They noted that their situation prevented them from "effectually" cooperating with the Bostonians, as Montréal's *Canadiens* not only refused to join the cause, but had "adopted a conduct professedly to counteract" British Party efforts.[28]

A few days before the Boston letter was ordered, Samuel Adams had already conferred with John Brown, a young patriot from Massachusetts's western Berkshire County, on the best means of "establishing the Canadian correspondence." After the discussion, Brown offered to deliver the message himself, traveling all the way to Montréal. He maintained that not only could he ensure delivery this way, but he would also provide a "certain & Mutual Method of intelligence" between the two provinces "before the next session of Congress." On the same day the Boston letter to Canada was completed, the committee directed John Brown to execute the delivery mission, armed only with £20 and some letters of recommendation.[29]

Brown was energetic, charismatic, and well educated. A Yale graduate, he served as a king's attorney on the New York frontier before starting his own Pittsfield, Massachusetts, practice in 1773. His peers quickly recognized the quality of his character and influence, electing him as militia-captain and delegate to the Provincial Congress.[30]

John Brown expeditiously embarked on his voyage, but on reaching Albany, he found that thaws had rendered the ice unsafe on Lakes George and Champlain, and took the slower route along the shore. On his way north, he recruited two partners, Peleg Sunderland and Winthrop Hoyt, both from the volatile New Hampshire Grants region (Vermont). They were selected for their experience with Canada's settled "praying" Indians. Sunderland would visit St-François village, southwest of Trois-Rivières, and Hoyt would confer with the Caughnawagas, southwest of Montréal. Fighting "inconceivable hardships" along the flooded lakeshore, the trio ventured to St-Jean, near the provincial border, where they split up to execute their individual missions.[31]

On 28 March, Brown reached Montréal. He delivered the Boston letter to Thomas Walker and John Blake and was "very kindly received" by the city's British Party committee. A group of merchants subsequently assembled at the Coffee House, where the Bostonian letter was read aloud. Brown and Walker spoke for some time "in support of the letter," after which they made a motion to form a local Committee of Correspondence and elect delegates to the second Philadelphia Congress. The proposal was poorly received—presumably for its Continental Association-driven trade implications—and "the assembly broke up without anything being done that was proposed." From this meeting, Brown concluded there was "no prospect of Canada sending Delegates to the Continental Congress."[32]

The following day, after being rejoined by Sunderland and Hoyt, Brown dispatched an initial report to Boston. He lingered in the area for a few more days, staying at Laprairie, the westernmost of the two principal south bank ferry points opposite Montréal. On 1 April, he crossed back to the island for a meeting with merchants in Lachine, the fur trade *entrepôt* ten miles southwest of the city. Having consulted with Québec Committee representatives in Montréal, Brown elected not to venture far downriver to visit the capital; instead, he circulated among Montreal District parishes in the guise of a horse merchant, gathering habitant views.[33]

It seems Brown shared some of the British Party's exasperation with rural *Canadiens'* passive response to the fight for liberty. Unable to persuade them through positive interests, he threatened that if any Canadians dared to take up arms for the government, thirty thousand Bostonians would "immediately march into Canada and lay waste the whole Country." Brown may not have been alone in adopting this tactic. In his report to Boston, he shared that the

British Party's primary "weapons" to "thwart the constant endeavours" of the "friends of government" seemed to have been similarly *in terrorem*.[34]

John Brown's initial report was starkly realistic: Quebec would not be sending delegates to Philadelphia. While there might be some support in the British Party to join the second Congress, the Montrealers would not, because the merchant cadre simply could not support the confederated colonies' nonimportation agreement. If the Anglo-Canadians tried, they argued that their New Subject counterparts, who refused even to consider the Association, "would immediately monopolize the Indian trade." Brown shared a negative overall view of the "French"—they were "ignorant and bigoted" and under the sway of the Church in "their temporal as well as spiritual affairs." *Canadien* merchants and gentry were "a set of people who know no other way of procuring wealth and honour but, by becoming Court sycophants," and were thus incorrigible "friends of government."[35]

According to Brown, the good news was that Quebec posed no immediate threat to the colonies' northern frontier. Sunderland and Hoyt likewise reported on the Indians' "peaceable disposition." Brown's sources indicated that the province's British troops were being held in readiness for deployment to Boston; and thanks to the "industry and exertions" of the colonies' friends in Canada, the government was "not at present able to raise ten men" to defend the province, in lieu of the regular army. In general, the *Canadiens* "appeared to have no disposition unfriendly toward the Colonies, but chose rather to stand neuter."[36]

After Brown's departure, the Montréal Committee provided its own written response to the Boston Committee's overtures. The British Party pleaded impotence; they had "neither numbers nor wealth sufficient to do . . . any essential service" to the Continental cause. The Anglo-Canadians were forced to rely "upon the wisdom, vigour, and firmness of the General Continental Congress" for their protection. If they tried to align themselves with the other colonies in Philadelphia, "the [French-]Canadians would join the Government to frustrate" the attempt. Brown and the Montréal Committee had reached the same overall conclusions. The "bulk of the people, both English and Canadians" wished the confederated colonies well, but dared "not stir a finger to help." The "noblesse and gentry" had been bought off by the Quebec Act, not having the slightest notion "of liberty and law." Despite the committee's pleas of helplessness, they did drop a final hint that economics really was the core issue when they asked "whether English Delegates would be accepted . . . without entering into the General Association?" It seemed that if Congress were willing to bend its policies, the Anglo-Canadians might be able to justify expanded cooperation.[37]

Brown's visit also had an unintended effect, feeding internal British Party tensions. Irish-Canadian Isaac Todd, one of the Montréal Committee members, "refused having any thing to do with" further Boston correspondence. He was part of a growing faction that was displeased with the party's direction and also had made a major investment in the fur trade for the year. Opposition to the Quebec Act was one thing; cooperation with rebellious Massachusetts and commitment to the economically ruinous Continental Association were quite another.[38]

It was hard to predict where Quebec would go in the coming months. With John Brown's assistance, the Old Subject agitators had further stirred up the cities, where despite the British Party's cracks, "A great many of the English merchants publicly manifested their devoutedness in favor of the Bostonians and endeavored to excite the people and to create confusion." Montréal notary Simon Sanguinet noted how, encouraged by the Carleton administration's hesitancy to rein them in, "several English merchants of Montreal and Quebec" operated with "impunity" and blatantly maintained correspondence with radical Continental counterparts. Chief Justice William Hey observed that habitants had been seduced by the appeals from the British Party and its external partners; the peasants' "fear, joined with extreme ignorance . . . and . . . credulity" had been "overmatched by the subtility & assiduity of some Colony agents." Even as radical Montréal Committee members lamented that they could not join Congress, the province's stability seemed in doubt. The British Party's rural spring propaganda campaign, supported by Congress's Address and Brown's visit, had sown revolutionary fuel across the Montreal District countryside. It would take only a few sparks—from outside forces, or through wrong moves by the administration—to ignite a rebellion.[39]

Chapter 5

PREEMPTIVE STRIKES

Ticonderoga and Fort St-Jean

The Fort at Ticonderoga must be seized as soon as possible. |
John Brown to the Boston Committee of Correspondence, 29 March 1775

It might be said that the gates of Canada were thrown open. |
Lieutenant William Lindsay, "Narrative of the Invasion of Canada . . ."

The Quebec Act went into effect on 1 May 1775, despite British Party calls for repeal. That morning, as Montréal's citizens stirred and soldiers called their morning roll, a shocking sight was discovered in the Place d'Armes. Under the shadow of Notre-Dame Church, the life-size white marble bust of King George III had been vandalized, "blacking it's face, hanging a chaplet of potatoes about it's neck, with a wooden cross, and a label on which was wrote, *'Le Pape de Canada ou le Sot Anglois'* (The Pope of Canada or the Fool of England)." The garrison commander hastily sent two men to clean the bust, while word of the incident shot through town.[1]

In a short time, the vandalism sparked two frays, landing citizens in jail. When agitated French-Canadian elites took offense at the Old Subject citizens' cavalier response to the affair, heated conversations escalated to fisticuffs. In both cases, "merchants" were arrested while their well-heeled *Canadien* adversaries were permitted to go on their way. This blatant show of official prejudice led some citizens to observe that such arbitrary justice was the first application of the Quebec Act. In the end, no one was charged with assaulting the King's bust, despite rewards totaling thousands of pounds. However, anonymous Canadian radicals had set a new precedent for the "extreme" demonstration of their opposition to the government.[2]

Still fretting about Montréal's momentous act of vandalism, citizens received unbelievable news from New York five days later—"shocking Accounts of a Battle between the Bostonians and the King's Troops." On 19 April, regular troops had marched out from Boston to seize military stores from the rebels, a move prompted by new guidance from London intended to demonstrate "firmness and decision" in the current crisis. The soldiers encountered Lexington militiamen and fired shots that killed five militiamen. A daylong running engagement ensued, driving the regulars back into Boston with numerous casualties. Overnight, thousands of New England militiamen flocked to surround Boston, isolating His Majesty's troops there. In a single event, Great Britain's relationship with the confederated Continental colonies entered an entirely new, dangerous phase.[3]

The recent battles and ensuing Boston blockade forced colonial patriot leaders to address military issues they willfully had ignored in the past. With no sitting Continental Congress at the time, the individual provinces were left to address immediate defensive concerns, such as reports that Carleton was forming "an Army in Canada to join the King's regular Forces in fighting against and enslaving the other British Colonies." If this were true, the Lake Champlain corridor offered the most-direct route for any Ministerial attack from the north. This traditional line-of-communication featured a two-hundred-mile chain of waterways, connected by well-used portages—a straight line between New York's Hudson Valley and Quebec's Richelieu River (see Map 2). Fort Ticonderoga, along with the destroyed works of nearby Crown-Point, controlled the southern end of this critical thoroughfare, a powerful choke point. Almost simultaneously, two different colonies recognized the critical advantage that the prompt seizure of Ticonderoga would provide in securing the northern frontier.[4]

In Connecticut, Silas Deane and a small group of "leading gentlemen" acted first. On 27 April, they issued secret orders authorizing a handful of officers to recruit volunteers and capture Ticonderoga. Even though the objective was in New York, that province was still too weak and divided to act on its own, or even to be trusted with information about the scheme. The party passed through Pittsfield, Massachusetts, and "fell in company" with John Brown, just returned from Canada, who had visited Ticonderoga en route. Brown and associate James Easton raised forty local men and joined the mission. The leaders separated to recruit in New York's contested New Hampshire Grants, planning to regroup in Castleton (Vermont) on 8 May for a final council of war before launching their attack.[5]

Meanwhile, the patriot government of Massachusetts initiated its own ef-

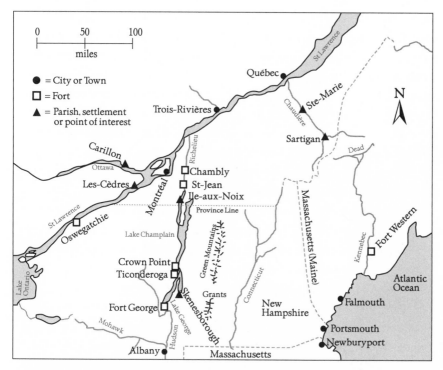

MAP 2: Lake and River Corridors.

fort, unaware of Connecticut's parallel activity. The Committee of Safety was prompted to act by the intelligence John Brown had sent from his Montréal trip as well as by a recent update of the fort's stores and defenses provided by an energetic and helpful Connecticut officer. This same gentleman volunteered to lead the expedition, and the Committee appointed him colonel. His orders were to recruit up to four hundred men, "reduce" Ticonderoga, and take possession of the artillery and stores there, as well as "the vessel . . . upon the Lake."[6]

This volunteer was Benedict Arnold, a bold, prosperous, thirty-four-year-old New Haven merchant, well-traveled in diverse American business endeavors, including repeated trips to Canada. At home, Arnold had cultivated enough respect to warrant command of an elite New Haven militia company, and already demonstrated a knack for keenly spotting opportunities and placing himself at the right place, at the right time. Arnold received his new Massachusetts command; but in the race for Ticonderoga, he faced the immediate disadvantage of a late start.[7]

Benedict Arnold. Library of Congress Prints
and Photographs Division.

Arnold rushed ahead to scout out his objective, leaving officers behind to gather recruits and join him later. In the New Hampshire Grants, he met the Connecticut expedition shortly after its final council of war, just as it was preparing to march on Ticonderoga. Almost two hundred "Green Mountain Boys" had joined, just as John Brown had predicted they would eagerly do, in his late-March letter from Montréal to Boston.[8]

The Green Mountain Boys were settlers in a disputed range (now Vermont), previously claimed by both New York and New Hampshire. In the 1770s, after London resolved the boundary issue in New York's favor, the frontiersmen resisted that province's attempts to impose authority, especially opposing powerful landholders' rival claims on their property. Under Ethan Allen's charismatic leadership, the "Boys" established their own local government and fought a successful insurgency to preserve it. The "robust, large framed," thirty-seven-year-old Allen used his "vehement and oratorical" style to steel his neighbors in their local cause, and adeptly intimidated and countered his opponents. Now, with the outbreak of violent resistance in Massachusetts, Allen and his associates recognized an opportunity to link their regional struggle with a larger ideological movement—a "continental" revolution that might erode their landed New York opponents' political foundations. As they prepared to seize Ticonderoga for this new cause, the "Boys" elected Ethan Allen as the operation's overall commander; Massachusetts's James Easton and "Green Mountain Boy" Seth Warner were his deputies.[9]

The leaders of the Connecticut and Massachusetts expeditions, Allen and Arnold, had much in common: they were strong-willed, enterprising, and fairly well educated. Now their competing ambitions brought them into conflict at a critical moment as they both "presumed to contend for the command" of the Ticonderoga mission. There are diverse partisan accounts of the Allen-Arnold showdown, but in the end, the two agreed to an ill-defined cocommand, each believing he was really in charge. However, Allen had hundreds of followers, while Arnold brought only one aide to the fight.[10]

In the early hours of 10 May, the Green Mountain Boys and west Massachusetts men surprised the few British guards at the sleepy outpost. With lightning action, they secured the fort "without bloodshed, or opposition," and the garrison commander surrendered his post to the rebels. A detachment under Seth Warner captured Crown-Point's ruins the next day, without a fight.[11]

The small Connecticut officer committee reinforced Allen's authority at Ticonderoga by giving him orders to command the fort. Meanwhile, Allen, Arnold, Warner, and Easton launched a barrage of letters to patriot colonial authorities. The expedition's officers

Colonel Ethan Allen (of Green Mountain Boys) (detail). Library and Archives Canada, Acc. No. 4312546.

shared news of Ticonderoga's capture, discussed plans, took credit for the success, and made accusations in the renewed Allen-Arnold spat.

As Ticonderoga's commander, Allen did not expect to keep his impetuous Green Mountain Boys at the fort for long; he encouraged Massachusetts and Connecticut to cooperate "in establishing a garrison in the reduced premises." Allen also appealed to the nearby Albany patriot committee for "Immediate Assistance . . . Both in men and Provision." Meanwhile, Arnold used his network of Canadian business associates to covertly deliver a letter informing Thomas Walker of the new conquest. The British Party leader was astounded to read Arnold's message dated from Ticonderoga: "I Breakfast here, & expect soon to see you & my friends at Montreal."[12]

Even before Ticonderoga fell, a detachment from the expedition had seized Skenesborough (now Whitehall, New York), a small community at the extreme south end of Lake Champlain, on 9 May. The patriots "Imprisoned" retired Major Andrew Skene, son of Skenesborough's landlord Governor Philip Skene, "and Seize'd a Schooner of his."[13] The detachment also intercepted intercolonial mail from Quebec within a few days, forwarding confiscated letters to New York authorities. The cooperative postmen shared intelligence that British regulars had armed a royal sloop at St-Jean, Quebec; the ship was only "waiting a Wind" before it headed to Ticonderoga.[14]

There was no time to waste. Arnold directed fifty of his late-arriving Massachusetts men to crew the Skenesborough schooner, renamed *Liberty*. They would sail north to St-Jean and seize the armed royal vessel. Whoever held the sloop at St-Jean controlled Lake Champlain; in Governor Carleton's hands, it could be used to counterattack and recover Ticonderoga, completely negating recent patriot gains.

St-Jean (St-John's) was the southern terminus of Canadian civilization on the Richelieu River, a decrepit military compound near a tiny settlement. The "fort," sitting on the west bank, consisted of a small barracks and the burnt-out shell of old French fortifications. Near the fort, the armed sloop was being fitted out in a rudimentary shipyard. For visitors, swampy and remote St-Jean's most memorable feature seemed to be its fearsome, smothering swarms of gnats and mosquitoes.[15]

On 15 May, Arnold impatiently led an advance party of thirty men toward

St-Jean by bateau,[16] while the *Liberty* finished its preparations for the mission. Before the rebel schooner rendezvoused with Arnold the next day, it stopped a southbound boat that happened to be carrying the Montréal mail, yielding another intelligence coup, "an exact list of all the regular troops in the northern department." Forwarded to Congress, this information proved critical in decision making for the rest of 1775.[17]

Nearing St-Jean, Arnold parted from the *Liberty* again, taking thirty-five men in two bateaux to seize the fort and royal sloop "by surprise at break of day." On the morning of 18 May, the rebels stealthily approached and made a short show of force, convincing the fourteen-man garrison to surrender. Arnold's Yankees "took the King's sloop, two fine brass field pieces, four boats," captured six sailors, and destroyed all other watercraft; then they made an efficient departure in anticipation of a British relief force coming from Montréal. A convenient northern gale sped Arnold's raiding party back to the *Liberty*.[18]

Later that day, about six miles out from St-Jean, Arnold's squadron met four boats carrying Ethan Allen and ninety men, intent on occupying Fort St-Jean. Arnold tried to dissuade Allen from proceeding, advising him that the scheme was "impracticable"—the sizeable Montréal garrison was too close and would easily drive him out. Allen scoffed at Arnold's warnings and pressed north. Arnold and his crew sailed back to Fort Ticonderoga, where he would order the *Liberty* and the King's sloop, renamed *Enterprise,* to "cruize on the lake, and defend our frontiers," asserting the rebels' newfound naval superiority.[19]

Meanwhile, retired British officer and upper Richelieu Valley seigneur Moses Hazen arrived in Montréal to inform the garrison commander, Lieutenant-Colonel Dudley Templer, of the surprise visitors he had encountered at St-Jean. After a short but friendly discussion with Arnold during the raid, Hazen had slipped away on the fifteen-mile Laprairie Road—a direct route between St-Jean and Montréal's southern ferry point. In the city, Templer immediately responded to Hazen's news by sending Major Charles Preston with a 140-man detachment to drive off any lingering rebels. Hazen could not confirm whether Arnold's men had stayed, and was completely unaware of Allen's approach. The city waited in suspense.[20]

Hearing of Hazen's intelligence from St-Jean, one of Montréal's British Party zealots, Joseph Bindon, joined Preston's troops in crossing the St. Lawrence. Bindon had his own mission, and while the regular troops marched on foot, he pressed ahead to St-Jean on horseback. In the meantime, Allen and his Green Mountain Boys landed at St-Jean and established ambush positions on the Laprairie Road. By nightfall, Allen reflected on his precarious situation and withdrew his men to the far bank of the Richelieu River, where they camped overnight. In the early morning hours of 19 May, Joseph Bindon reached St-Jean and warned the Green Mountain Boys that regulars were on the way. As Allen rallied his men, he handed Bindon a letter, composed the previous evening, and sent the helpful merchant back to the city.[21]

Allen's letter, addressed to merchants "friendly to the cause of Liberty at Montreal," assumed the tone of a triumphant liberator. He shared word that he was at St-Jean and that "the Colonies" now controlled the lakes, forts, and sloop. Expecting the letter's recipients to "be in the interest of the Colonies," he made a twofold request: to establish correspondence and send representatives to St-Jean, and to render "immediate assistance as to provisions, ammunition, and spirituous liquors." The Green Mountain Boys were willing to pay for the supplies; they need not be a donation. Allen emphasized that he came as a friend, with directions "not to contend with, or any way injure or molest the Canadians or Indians; but, on the other hand, treat them with the greatest friendship and kindness," a message he asked the English merchants to help disseminate. Allen must not yet have decided to withdraw when he gave Bindon such a letter; it would be irrelevant if the invading force retreated back to New York.[22]

Carrying the letter to Montréal, Bindon met Preston's eastbound troops on the Laprairie Road, very close to St-Jean. He "told the Major that a great many 'Bostonians' were waiting for him," presumably to slow down Preston's advance, giving Allen time to improve his defenses or withdraw. The two parted; Bindon proceeded to Montréal "at a full gallop" as Preston's men encountered the Green Mountain Boys "getting into the Battoes to return." The regulars wounded some of the "Free-booters" and took one prisoner. Allen and the rest of his men escaped, returning to Ticonderoga on 22 May.[23]

Upon arriving in Montréal, Bindon shared Allen's letter with British Party cohorts; some of them started promenading through the streets, deliberately causing an "alarm" and promoting the impression "that all the King's troops were killed" at St-Jean. Among the citizens a "terrifying panic . . . gripped everyone's mind"; some gathered their valuables and prepared to flee the city. Lieutenant-Colonel Templer intervened to restore order, posting troops around the city. Then he called a citizens' meeting; prominent city and suburb representatives attended, unanimously agreeing to defend Montréal. While the meeting was in progress, a letter arrived from Major Preston, relating recent events at St-Jean, including Bindon's treacherous delay of the column's advance and Allen's subsequent flight. The anxious citizens began to relax. The next morning, Templer convened another citizens' assembly, calling on Montrealers to form themselves into militia companies of thirty men each and elect their own officers. The colonel identified eight *Canadien* elites to establish the militia rolls.[24]

That afternoon, Preston's troops returned from St-Jean. After being dismissed, a group of soldiers launched their own vendetta against the malicious Bindon, presumably based on Preston's interpretation of his Laprairie Road encounter with the merchant, and perhaps further inflamed by hearing of the rebellious agitation following Bindon's return to Montréal. When they found the merchant, they started dragging him to the market pillory. Officers intervened, and instead of letting the troops administer their own justice, they took Bindon before a magistrate where he was accused of "willful recklessness" and forced to give bond.[25]

The drama in Montréal took an odd turn the following day, when a number of British Party "Grumbletonians" called their own town meeting at the Coffee House. Anti-administration agitators tried to spin Bindon's treatment — haranguing that "Honest men were no longer safe" and that any citizen might face similar vigilante justice. The "English" citizens lodged a complaint with Lieutenant-Colonel Templer, who undoubtedly was biting his tongue as he courteously reassured them that "he would have justice done."[26]

After he had warned Colonel Templer about Arnold's St-Jean raid, messenger Moses Hazen pressed on to Québec City to inform the governor of the developing situation. The forty-two-year-old Hazen was an inactive, half-pay army officer, with an inherent duty to serve the government in times like this. Originally born in Massachusetts, Hazen earned a great reputation as a ranger leader in the last war, fighting in the Louisbourg and Quebec Campaigns. He purchased a regular officer's commission in 1760, but retired with the postwar drawdown three years later. Settling in Quebec, Hazen served in minor offices and partnered in numerous business ventures, especially on the upper Richelieu River, purchasing sparsely populated seigneuries and farmlands around St-Jean. In 1770, he married a Montréal *Canadienne*. Despite some business distress early in the decade, Hazen was in a solid economic position by 1775 and also had the administration's trust.[27]

Hazen reached Québec City on Saturday, 20 May, and immediately informed Governor Carleton of both Ticonderoga's fall and Arnold's St-Jean raid. The governor assessed the situation and ordered army reinforcements to Montréal. By Monday evening, Carleton set out for that city himself.

═══════

The second Continental Congress convened on 10 May, ignorant of any operations against Ticonderoga or Canada; yet that assembly's deliberations immediately took on a very different character from the previous session. In addition to the Lexington operation, the Ministry had given clear indications that it had no wish to reconcile with the colonies. Royal governors were instructed to use their "utmost endeavours" to prevent the appointment of congressional delegates—the Philadelphia assembly being deemed an "unwarrantable proceeding." The ministry dispatched reinforcements to Boston and declared its "determination to inforce obedience to all the late laws." In London, the Petition to the King had been brought before the House of Commons where "a great majority" declined even to read it. Parliament could not deign to recognize any congressional authority as American representatives.[28]

On the third day of the Congress, there was one positive development. A Georgian appeared in the assembly and immediately was admitted as a delegate. He did not represent his entire colony, however, just one of Georgia's thirteen parishes, St. John's.[29] Frustrated by their province's failure to appoint delegates, radical St. John's Parish (home to many zealous Yankee settlers) elected to send its own. While not an immediate topic of discussion, the parish's "partial representation" model would eventually be adopted in the plans for Quebec, with the expectation that Montréal might be Canada's equivalent of St. John's, a foothold to help draw the entire colony into Congress.[30]

A few days later, on 18 May, Congress received its first news about Ticonderoga's capture, as John Brown personally delivered a report on "the disposition of the Canadians, the taking of Ticonderog[a] and the importance of that post." After considering the situation, the assembly generated a resolution addressing recent developments, somewhat distraught by what had happened without their foreknowledge. In Congress's interpretation of events, several northern colonists, with "indubitable evidence" of a Ministerial plan to launch a "cruel invasion" from Quebec and "impelled by a just regard for their own preservation," had taken Ticonderoga.[31]

Amazingly, Congress initially suggested Ticonderoga and Crown-Point be abandoned, offering that the captured military equipment should be removed from the forts and shipped to a more secure southern post on Lake George. The assembly advised New York to request "an additional body of forces" from neighboring colonies to guard the relocated artillery and stores. Even after Lexington and Concord, most delegates were not mentally prepared to conduct true "Continental" military operations, merely offering recommendations to individual colonies instead. There still was a heavy emphasis on economic measures, as well; just the day before, Congress unanimously resolved to cease exportations to all North American colonies outside the Association, including Quebec.[32]

In the midst of the clamor, a Canadian British Party "emissary to Congress" arrived. Montréal committeeman James Price had left his home city on 11 May, unaware that Ticonderoga had fallen, on a mission to visit Philadelphia, not as a delegate but as an ambassador. Upon his arrival he was examined before Congress. His message was probably similar to what he is known to have shared with Connecticut officials a couple of days earlier: "French officers" were now under the pay of the Quebec Act government, and one of those officers, St-Luc de La Corne, was trying to persuade northern Indian tribes "to take up arms against the New-England Colonies." Price assessed the situation among Canadians as well—"the plebeians, will not, but with the utmost reluctance, engage against the Colonists, but that the nobles are our bitter enemies"—which was not substantially different from other recent reports.[33]

Taking advantage of the Montrealer's presence, Congress also appointed John Jay, Samuel Adams, and Silas Deane (who had helped organize the Connecticut Ticonderoga expedition) "to prepare & bring in a letter to the people of Canada." The committee fast-tracked their draft, hoping Price could hand-carry the message when he left for Quebec in a few days. On 29 May, Congress approved the letter titled "To the oppressed Inhabitants of Canada."[34]

This second Congressional letter was more straightforward than its October predecessor. The core message still called for unity; Congress "perceived the fate of the protestant and catholic colonies to be strongly linked together . . . and therefore invited" their neighbors "to join with" Congress "in resolving to be free." Addressing current events, Congress justified patriot seizure of the forts and the "armed vessels on the lake"—actions that had been "dictated by the great law of self-preservation." The United Colonies declared that they would "pursue no measures whatever, but such as friendship and a regard for our mutual safety and interest may suggest." As might be expected, Congress also commiserated with the Canadians over the Quebec Act: "By the introduction of your present form of government, or rather present form of tyranny, you and your wives and your children are made slaves." Once again, Congress expressed hope that Canadians would unite to defend their "common liberty," while dreading the possibility that the Canadians would instead injure their southern neighbors and "reduce" the United Colonies to the "disagreeable necessity" of treating them as enemies.[35]

Much as it had done with its first letter, Congress ordered the immediate production of a French version with a thousand copies, and the French language translation was done by du Simitière and Mesplet in Philadelphia. This time, however, it was a rush job — the translation was more mechanical and prosaic than the first address; but James Price was able to take some of these hastily produced copies when he returned to Montréal.[36]

Concurrently, the New York Provincial Congress reacted to the St-Jean raids with astonishment, issuing a 25 May resolution, "earnestly" discouraging "any hostilities against the people" of Canada, and noting that such action would be "infamous, and highly inimical to all the American Colonies." The next day, the same Yorker body paralleled the Continental Congress by creating a letter to comfort and persuade the Canadians. Their end product was not too different from the one produced in Philadelphia, although there was an additional comment absolving New York of any role in Arnold's and Allen's Canadian forays. The message's ultimate hope was that "instead of consenting to become miserable slaves," the Canadians would "generously dare to participate" with their "fellow subjects in the sweets of that security which is the glorious lot of freedom." The letter was approved on 2 June; five hundred English and fifteen hundred well-translated French copies were ordered for distribution. When "dispersed throughout Canada," the letter was accompanied by a French translation of the 25 May Resolve.[37]

═══════

Back at Crown-Point on 23 May, Benedict Arnold received some distressing intelligence. The news was delivered by the sole member of Allen's St-Jean raiding party who had been captured by Preston's troops, but who had since escaped and made his way back to Crown-Point. The unnamed Green Mountain Boy reported that four hundred British regulars already assembled at St-Jean were "expected to be reinforced by more men," and were preparing to "cross the lake, and retake Crown Point and Ticonderoga." Without delay, Arnold forwarded this distressing information to patriot government authorities. Arnold was not sure whether to believe the "escaped prisoner report," but three days later he received "good Intelligence" that the regulars had actually withdrawn from St-Jean.[38]

The escaped Green Mountain Boy's report was based on that ex-prisoner's poor numerical assessment of Preston's 140 men, not uncommon in such high-stress situations. The British troops actually returned to Montréal on the same day the prisoner fled from their custody. In reality, there was no imminent challenge to the rebel hold on Ticonderoga; yet given the confederated colonies' limited information about Ministerial intentions in Quebec, this single threatening report took on a life of its own, with cascading consequences.

At this same time, Arnold had also been keeping up a correspondence with Thomas Walker in Montréal. He asked the patriot Montrealer to assist an embassy being sent to the Caughnawagas; a few days later he requested periodic updates on the number of troops in the city, and if Canadians or Indians had joined them in arms. Arnold also explicitly informed Walker that the "escaped prisoner report" had been found to be erroneous; it is interesting that while he sent a comparable update to Massachusetts, he does not appear to have sent one to leaders in Connecticut, New York, or Philadelphia. Instead, many in the United Colonies continued to anticipate a Ministerial counterattack for the next few weeks.[39]

In the last weeks of May, the northern colonies began to reach a consensus on handling Ticonderoga. Having weighed the advantages of holding the forts, and with the looming threat described in the as-yet-uncontradicted "escaped prisoner report," Connecticut, Massachusetts, and New York began to cobble together initial plans for cooperative northern defenses and asked Congress to reconsider its recommendation to abandon the forts. The Albany Committee prepared to send two hundred men as an expeditious reinforcement for the Green Mountain Boys. Connecticut sent an entire regiment to defend the forts. Both colonies were cautious though, ordering the troops "to exercise the greatest vigilance that no incursions be made into the Province of Quebeck, to disturb the inhabitants there." Now that control of the lakes had been temporarily secured, they did not want any repeats of Allen's rash St-Jean raid.[40]

The Continental Congress finally caught up with the rapidly changing situation on 31 May. That was the day the "escaped prisoner report" reached Philadelphia, prompting delegates to rescind their position on Ticonderoga. Now Congress belatedly asked Connecticut to forward a thousand troops to Ticonderoga and Crown-Point, and requested New York support with supplies and bateaux—measures already under way. The goal was to keep Ticonderoga and adjacent posts free from "all sudden attempts of the Enemies of America." Like New York, Congress felt compelled to reassure the Canadians about these moves. A 1 June resolution declared, "Congress has nothing more in view than the defence of these colonies," and "no expedition or incursion ought to be undertaken or made, by any colony, or body of colonists, against or into Canada." The resolve was ordered to be "translated into the french Language and transmitted, with the letter to the inhabitants of Canada."[41]

As defensive measures, the capture of Ticonderoga and Arnold's follow-on raid into Canada were important for the northern colonies' security. Massachusetts and Connecticut felt amply justified in launching expeditions into impotent New York without that province's consent—and the St-Jean operation had a comparable rationale. It would have been imprudent to let political boundaries, and a neighbor's feeble condition, keep patriots from securing the northern frontier against a plausible Ministerial threat.

The actions on the lakes would quickly generate additional effects. As events in the summer of 1775 would prove, the patriots "had broken down the fences which guarded the entrance" to Quebec. The St-Jean raids also led Carleton to implement a very different near-term reaction—the Canadian administration identified a new, direct external threat and responded with measures that would have tremendous consequences, almost all of them unintended.[42]

Chapter 6

THAT DAMNED ABSURD
WORD "LIBERTY"

Quebec's Own Rebellion

The Quebeck Bill is of no use; on the contrary, the Canadians talk
of that damned absurd word liberty. | *Thomas Gamble to Major Shirref,*
Quebec, 6 September 1775

These attempts of the seigniors have so disgusted the peasants of the
seigniories . . . that they have broke out into acts of open violence to resist
them. | *A Gentleman of Quebeck, of Exceeding Good Sense, 1775*

In Montréal, the atmosphere relaxed somewhat by the end of May, as the
chaos of the St-Jean raids slipped into the near past; but there were still tensions among the populace. Garrison commander Lieutenant-Colonel Templer sent his eight French-Canadian elite appointees[1] through the city and
suburbs to enroll citizens for the militia, anticipating future threats. Many
citizens demonstrated displeasure over the mission of these militia officials,
especially in the west suburb of St-Laurent, where women even threatened
to stone them. Overall the party had meager success; Governor Carleton
reported, "though the gentlemen testified great zeal, neither their entreaties
or their example could prevail upon the people." Working-class *Canadiens*
demonstrated their clear unwillingness to take up arms for the government.[2]

The most recent crises only served to encourage British Party radicals who
continued to preach politics to habitants and laborers. "These Parochial orators
held forth, that the liberty" the *Canadiens* "had enjoy'd for fifteen years was
to be taken from them." The seigneurs, "tools of the Governor," would keep
them enslaved; they would be taxed to pay "exorbitant" salaries for administration lackeys, and common people would be enlisted and sent from home

"to enslave their brethren of the lower Provinces." Government supporters noted that the speeches of "these ill-intentioned old subjects" were generally well received. As summer approached, all Quebec was aflutter.[3]

———

Quite early, the Canadian Church hierarchy committed itself to reinforcing government authority. On 22 May, just as Governor Carleton left Québec City for Montréal, Bishop Jean-Olivier Briand issued two mandates (*mandements*) to his flock. The first was expected; it officially announced the bishop's third diocesan tour and addressed specific Church issues. In many parishes, habitants had been showing "disobedience . . . outrages . . . disdainful insults" to their priests, and Briand reminded them, "The Church has lost none of its authority." While hoping that "the way of kindness" would win parishioners' hearts, he cautioned that the Church still held its ultimate "weapon"— interdict or excommunication.[4]

The second mandate was far less routine; titled "On the American Invasion of Canada," it dealt specifically with the current political crises. Having been a ceaseless British government advocate since the French capitulation of the last war, Briand ensured that his flock understood that his position remained unchanged. Beyond scriptural direction that "every soul be subject unto the higher powers" and that "Whosoever resisteth the power, resisteth the ordinance of God to obey civil authority"— as well as the Quebec Act's reassurances of religious freedom — the bishop had more mundane reasons to throw his weight behind Carleton. Bishop Briand was a respected confidant of the governor, and also received a £200 annual stipend from England.[5]

When Carleton asked Briand to issue Church guidance on the recent rebel "invasion," Briand initially planned to produce a circular letter. The governor requested a mandate instead, a form implying greater episcopal emphasis. The resulting mandate opened by maligning the rebels, who had "just burst into this Province, less in hope of being able to sustain their attack than with a view to dragging you into their revolt." The bishop expected *Canadiens* to support the Crown, not only out of gratitude for the "outstanding kindness and mildness" their sovereign had shown, but also because their post-Conquest "oaths and religion" imposed an "indispensable obligation to defend" their country and king. When British Party zealots warned that habitants

Portrait of Bishop Jean-Olivier Briand. Archives of
the City of Montreal, BM1, No. P0245-2.

were just being enlisted to be sent to distant lands, Briand explained that
their only obligation was "to strike a blow to repel the enemy and halt the
invasion," defending their own colony and property. Recognizing the role of
proselytizing radicals in the recent Canadian unrest, Briand warned his "Dear
Canadians" to close their ears, and not listen to the "seditious people" who
were trying to extinguish *Canadiens'* sense of "submission to . . . legitimate
superiors." The mandate left no doubt that the Church stood side-by-side
with Carleton's government.[6]

While the Montreal District was agitated by John Brown's visit and the
St-Jean raids, Quebec District's Beauce region, in the Chaudière valley (see

Maps 2 and 5), experienced its own taste of *Bastonnais*[7] visitors in May, more than one hundred miles to the east. Governor Carleton reacted to reports that "delegates from Boston" were approaching Quebec via little-used wilderness trails connected to the Chaudière, ordering seigneur Gabriel-Elzéar Taschereau to reintroduce the militia in that valley. In the area's largest parish, Ste-Marie-de-Beauce, only thirty river-miles from the capital, Taschereau appointed Militia-Captain Étienne Parent to enroll fellow parishioners. The *Beaucerons* (residents of the Chaudière Valley's Beauce region) cooperated, although there were some "impertinent" rumblings among the habitants.[8]

In neighboring St-Joseph, parishioners initially assembled, but when Taschereau attempted to address them, they "dispersed, refusing to hear him." Jean-Marie Verreau, parish priest of both Ste-Marie and St-Joseph, "used all of his influence to have them comply and was insulted several times." Taschereau prudently walked away. When authorities later tried to send militia officer commissions through *Curé* Verreau, parishioners still refused service, despite explicit government orders. St-Joseph demonstrated bold defiance to Carleton's first plans for a new Canadian militia.[9]

Some *Bastonnais* visitors did come to the Chaudière that spring. The first confirmed Yankee "spies" were Jabez Matthews and a three-man scouting party, commissioned by the town of Falmouth (Portland, Maine) as "an embassy," to see if the Canadians were preparing to attack frontier settlements.[10] Shortly after entering Quebec Province around the end of May, the scouts met with a "rough reception" from some Indians and "French bailiffs." It is unclear if Matthews and his men were the anticipated "Boston" delegates that had prompted the governor's Beauce region mobilization just a few weeks earlier.[11]

With confirmed word of the "three spies'" arrival in the valley, the administration directed Ste-Marie's Militia-Captain Parent to capture them; a party of twenty-five regular soldiers was also dispatched to the upper Chaudière to block future infiltration attempts. By the time Parent received his orders, he was already well aware of the Massachusetts scouts, even knowing the exact house where they hid. Rather than arresting the Yankees, he sent a sympathetic neighbor wife to warn them before conducting a half-hearted pursuit, going "slowly for fear of catching them." The "Bostonians" escaped. Upon his return to Massachusetts on 30 June, Jabez Matthews credited "the good disposition of the French people, especially the women," for keeping his party from Canadian jail, and reported, "the French people are determined not to come out against us."[12]

—————

Governor Carleton arrived in Montréal on 26 May, looking to restore order and defend the province. Militarily, his assets were spread thin; in 1774, two regiments had been stripped from Quebec to reinforce Boston. Almost half the remaining troops were garrisoned hundreds of miles away in remote up-country posts. The largest available element consisted of 250 soldiers garrisoned in Montréal and nearby Lachine. Another 186 regulars had been rushed to Fort St-Jean, where they immediately set about improving fortifications; almost fifty men held Fort Chambly, a dozen miles north on the Richelieu. In the Quebec District, fewer than one hundred soldiers were split between the capital garrison and the new Chaudière border post. Carleton would be hard pressed to meet any substantial rebel invasion with his regular army force.[13]

Not only were rebels knocking at Canada's door, but the province's British American subjects continued to demonstrate boldly against the government and did little to hide their correspondence with the "Bostonians." Council member Judge Adam Mabane warned the governor, "the sooner the laws are put in force so much the better; procrastination only encourages the seditious and weakens Government." All these pressures seemed to warrant the establishment of a provincial military body. In fact, for many months Carleton and General Gage had corresponded about establishing a Canadian regiment to "form a Junction with the King's Forces" in the lower colonies. The governor still hoped the habitants might be "favourably disposed" to raising such a provincial battalion, but grew increasingly skeptical.[14]

Montréal's citizens had already shown their unwillingness to mobilize as a militia in May. Carleton felt the people's minds had been "poisoned by the same hypocrisy and lies practiced with so much success in the other provinces." Only the clergy and seigneurial families stood strong, but as the governor noted, they "both have lost much of their influence over the people." The only exception to Canadian apathy was a "small corps of volunteers" led by Montrealer Samuel Mackay, consisting of a "few of the gentry." But these men were all traditional officer material; they needed men to lead.[15]

The final straw prompting militia mobilization may have come on 7 June, when Carleton was told the rebels had returned and had "taken post near to St. Johns," allegedly in great numbers. Although the report quickly was proven to be highly exaggerated,[16] it served as a reminder of the real dangers facing Quebec. Two days later, Carleton acted, declaring martial law and reestablishing the militia, because of the "rebellion" in neighboring colonies and the recent "incursions . . . into this province." Martial law was necessary to defeat "so treasonable an invasion" and to bring traitors and their "abettors" to speedy justice, so that Quebec's "publick peace and tranquillity" could be restored.[17]

On the basis of advice from prominent citizens, Carleton rejected Lieutenant-Colonel Templer's mid-May scheme to have *Canadiens* elect their own officers, which may have been more popular. Instead, the governor formed the militia on the "old plan" to minimize confusion and speed mobilization; the governor would appoint the officers. In any case, Carleton was not overly confident of the habitants' response: "What I shall be able to make of them or of the savages [Indians] I cannot yet positively say but I am sure it is become highly necessary to try." If the effort proved successful, the governor still harbored hopes that he could establish a provincial regiment for external service. The next step, though, was appointment of senior militia officers.[18]

Carleton had already angered some *Canadiens* with his recent selections for new government posts. The Quebec Act's "French" council seats and judgeships came solely from a core of powerful landed families, ignoring prominent New Subject bourgeois. Many Canadians expressed their "great disgust" that the governor was "wantonly and profusely inventing places for creatures and sycophants." The most egregious example was Montreal District Conservator-of-the-Peace René-Ovide Hertel-de-Rouville. A foe of many Canadians, this unpleasant individual's appointment led even an elite peer to ask, "How could the government possibly have cast its eye upon the greatest scoundrel and the biggest rogue on earth?" By relying solely on "friends" to fill new offices, Carleton missed opportunities to broaden his support, instead fostering widespread resentment against his government.[19]

The preferential appointments continued with martial law. The top Montreal District militia leaders, Colonel Thomas Dufy-Desauniers, Lieutenant-Colonel Pierre-Paul Neveu-Sevestre, and Major St-Georges Dupré, were appointed from the same elite class. As loyalist Simon Sanguinet recorded, "These three gentlemen began by committing injustices in favoring their families and friends," even commissioning some who were blatantly unqualified for their new militia posts. Needless to say, this produced even more discontent.[20]

The Montréal region had critical elements for an outbreak of direct class conflict. Seigneurs had complained for years that the "middling and lower sort of people" were losing the "deference and respect" they had formerly shown "their superiors." Now that the government was calling all *Canadiens* to arms, many of these seigneurs also believed they had "a legal right to command the personal service of all the holders of land under them, whenever the Sovereign . . . calls upon them"; while most habitants maintained that, in accordance with the old militia system, "their seigniors had no right to command their military service." They "owed them nothing further" than rents and "other just dues." These simmering tensions, heated up by British Party orators, would boil over with the brash acts of a few obnoxious seigneurs.[21]   ✓

In the summer months of 1775, Quebec's internal conflicts metamorphosed into an entirely new form of antigovernment struggle. When Canadians heard about Carleton's martial law, many considered the measures an "injustice" and vowed to resist militia call-ups. The governor's "weak" justifications for imposing the "dreaded Martial Law" were just the start, as many observed that the rebels had come and gone and "did not in the least molest the Canadians." Many suspected that Carleton's actual purpose was to legally compel habitants "to take arms" for use outside the province. Quebec's "canting Enthusiasts," both Continental envoys and British Party men, helped promote these skeptical perceptions.[22]

Coincidentally, several messages from the rebel colonists arrived in the province shortly after the martial law proclamation. On 1 June, Ethan Allen and James Easton composed the first of these, a letter to "the French people of Canada," sent direct to Thomas Walker. While the letter was laced with appeals for peaceful cooperation, the authors primarily sought to prove that a patriot scout skirmish near Fort St-Jean, which did not result in any casualties, had been sparked by Mackay's *Canadien* volunteers. Although the authors asked Walker to translate and disseminate their address, there is no evidence he did; based on its content, which proved armed patriots continued to meddle inside Quebec's border, the letter offered little benefit to the radical British Party cause and probably went no farther than Walker's desk.[23]

In late June, James Price returned to Montréal bearing several more patriot addresses: the second Continental Congress letter, New York's equivalent letter, and a new message from that colony, completed as Price left for Montréal on 12 June. This last document, addressed to the province's "Gentlemen Merchants," encouraged communication between "brethren in the northern parts

Portrait of Étienne de Montgolfier.
Archives of the City of Montreal,
BMı, No. Pı5ı2.

of this Continent." Price shared these letters with British Party compatriots, who distributed them throughout the district. Observers noted how the "vast importation" of the "Address & Letters of the Congress & others had got among the Canadians" who found them "very agreeable." Radicals also left night messages: a "scrip of paper" was "dropped at the door of every habitant in the parishes almost opposite Montreal." This note, written in French, cryptically adopted Biblical terminology, "He is evil who does not choose the good path,"[24] and was signed "Boston." These various publications reportedly had the desired effect, as a loyalist assessed that "nine in ten" Canadiens were in the rebel interest.[25]

The Church offered its own counterpoint in Quebec's battle of ideas. The most important contribution at this time was a 13 June circular letter composed by Montréal Vicar-General Étienne Montgolfier, calling *curés* to inspire their flocks in support of the militia establishment. Bishop Briand subsequently ordered the letter's distribution across the entire province; parish priests were to read it after Mass and post it on the church door. Many parishioners did not appreciate Church advocacy of specific government policies. Agitated *Canadiens* throughout the province insisted that the bishop was acting against the nature of his office; by threatening Church punishment to help enforce government policies, Briand was "making a tool" of their religion. The bishop's £200 London salary sparked innumerable questions about conflict of interest as well.[26]

Both Church and government officials observed that habitants seemed to be turning into "grave and subtle politicians." With their own government seemingly forcing them into the revolutionary contest, "Jean-Baptistes" began asking themselves which side they should support. Their recent antigovernment "education," along with an inherently conservative "peasant's" inclination to resist change—such as reinstitution of militia duty—led many rural *Canadiens* to oppose martial law; some refused commissions, and many "refus'd to take arms as Militia men." There were also three principal cases where the people "rose up in Arms" when "friends of government" attempted to mobilize them.[27]

The three incidents, all apparently occurring in late June to mid-July, followed a similar pattern (see Map 3). Gentry-class leaders traveled to family seigneuries and haughtily demanded that the militia form under their command. The habitants resisted; the government representatives lost control, made threats, and were subsequently forced to depart—leaving behind a volatile population, which anticipated further escalation of the conflict.

In Terrebonne, north of Montréal, Louis de La Corne Jr., the twenty-six-year-old nephew of St-Luc de La Corne, was the instigator. In this incident at the end of June, the young La Corne's "high tone" led to blows before he "left in a rage to make his complaints" to Carleton. Anticipating La Corne's return with regular troops, hundreds of habitants from Terrebonne and neighboring parishes Lachenaie, Mascouche, and Repentigny armed themselves, "some with guns," others with clubs, pitchforks, or hoes, to stand their ground at the Lachenaie ferry landing, resolving "to die rather than submit to be commanded by their seignior." Instead of attempting to suppress the north-shore uprising with troops he could not spare, Governor Carleton wisely sent regular army Captain Henry Hamilton to defuse the situation. In the ensuing exchange, the habitants reiterated their position against serving under seigneurs: "If General Carleton requires our services, let him give us Englishmen to command us," or "some of their neighbours such as they would chose"; they dispersed peacefully, but did not form into the desired militia companies.[28]

Opposite Montréal, in south bank Longueuil, the seigneur's twenty-nine-year-old son, Étienne Fleury-Deschambault, made a similar attempt to assemble the militia in the first part of July. After Deschambault harangued and insulted the habitants, a scuffle ensued in which the young gentleman drew his sword; the habitants "surrounded him, and beat him severely," driving him away. In this case the seigneur, Joseph Fleury-Deschambault, returned to the scene the following day. He warned the parishioners that, if they did not apologize to his son, the governor would punish them severely. Becoming even more agitated, the habitants chased the seigneur off and prepared

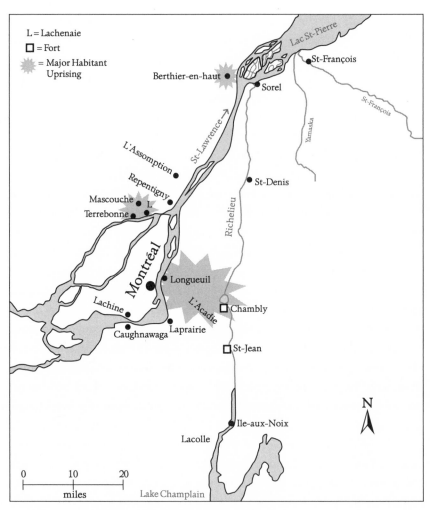

Map legend:
L = Lachenaie
□ = Fort
✦ = Major Habitant Uprising

Lac St-Pierre
St-François
Berthier-en-haut
Sorel
St-François
L'Assomption
St-Lawrence →
Repentigny
St-Denis
Mascouche
L
Terrebonne
Richelieu
Yamaska
Montréal
Longueuil
Lachine
L'Acadie
Chambly
Caughnawaga
Laprairie
St-Jean
N
Ile-aux-Noix
Lacolle
0 10 20
miles
Lake Champlain

MAP 3: Montreal District Rebellions, 1775.

to defend themselves. Reportedly three thousand[29] habitants gathered at Chambly and took up arms to face the anticipated arrival of regular troops. The habitants had weapons, but little ammunition, having bought what little was available from local merchants. Once again, a regular officer arrived to calm the situation, reassuring the *Canadiens* "that all would be well, if they would disperse, and retire, each to his home."[30]

The third incident occurred forty miles downstream from Terrebonne, in Berthier-en-haut. In this case, "English" seigneur James Cuthbert, one of the Quebec Act legislative councilors, called his "peasants" to the manor house.

The habitants refused and told Cuthbert that "if he had any thing to communicate, he might come to them," and they would be gathered at a nearby crossroads. When the seigneur arrived, the people informed him that if his goal were to enroll them in arms, "he had best retire to his own home and trouble them no more." Cuthbert departed without escalating the situation. Before dispersing to their homes, the habitants then took an oath against taking up arms; if any among them joined the government, his peers would "burn his house and his barn, and destroy his cattle"; if the government tried to compel them to serve, "they would repel force by force."[31]

In all three cases, the critical inflammatory issue was the seigneur's attempt to exert nontraditional authority as a militia leader; the habitants were not willing to concede additional power to the seigneur.[32] There were also myriad reports of less-blatant resistance elsewhere in the province. Militia-captains refused to acknowledge commissions, and four Quebec District "British" seigneurs failed in attempts to raise the militia on their lands. Throughout Canada, the habitants' first practical experience with the Quebec Act was the distinctly distasteful imposition of martial law. In "Jean-Baptiste's" eyes, martial law and the Quebec Act were one and the same.[33]

All these events show that Quebec had experienced its own small-scale rebellion in the summer of 1775, especially in Montreal District's fertile "corn countries." Publicly, Carleton refused to accept that he had just experienced a habitant revolt and that his seigneur friends had failed to form the militia to any effect. In a more honest moment, however, he reflected, "The difficulty I have found in proceeding so far convinces me, till their [habitants'] minds change, it will be unadvisable to attempt assembling any number of them," unless "absolutely necessary . . . for the immediate defence of the province and there is no other resource whatsoever."[34]

═══════

While government authority was becoming increasingly tenuous in the rural countryside, Governor Carleton and his supporters achieved a minor coup within the Old Subject population—the very same element that had initially provided the administration's staunchest foes. "Friends of government" worked to exploit the growing rift between British Party moderates and radicals. In Montréal, Chief Justice William Hey led conversations in the "English" community, convincing Old Subjects to reassess their loyalties. Many Montrealers came to the practical realization that it "would be extreamly prejudicial to their interests"—especially their business—if Continental patriots held sway in Canada. A good number of "Grumbletonians" decided they were "still friends to the Constitution," despite their fury at the Quebec Act, choosing to support the government rather than sticking with the doggedly radical faction that was embracing the neighboring rebels' cause. This conservative faction had been willing to agitate among the *Canadiens* for "a General application for a repeal of the act," but not to incite further "Rebellion."[35]

Québec City's merchants did similar soul searching and demonstrated support for government by forming an "English" militia; however, a core of patriot-minded Quebeckers led by Jonathan Welles hedged their commitment, trying to form an alternative "private company." Montréal formed an "English" militia company too; Isaac Todd characterized the shifting Old Subject loyalties, as the one-time "Malcontent" committeeman became the new company's lieutenant. Of course, "Thomas Walker, and one or two others" refused to join, persisting in "seditious" activities. In both cities, urban *Canadiens* seemed to be won over by the "English" merchants' change of heart; following their example, the New Subjects similarly "evinced great satisfaction in serving under" Carleton. By August, the governor had reasonable cause to believe the bourgeois, both Old and New Subjects, had returned to the administration's fold.[36]

There was another, concurrent effort to bring "British" Canadians into government service. Colonel Allan Maclean, a fifty-year-old Scots veteran of the French and Indian War, was raising a North American regiment of Royal Highland Emigrants. In the summer of 1775, eight officers recruited among Canada's sparse, but loyal, Scots community, primarily ex-Highlanders soldiers. Captains John Nairne and Malcolm Fraser, half-pay officers from the Seventy-eighth Regiment, were the two most prominent among them. Governor Murray had granted them seigneuries on Quebec's northern St-Lawrence west bank following the Conquest. A large group of Emigrants were recruited among the frontier Scots in New York's Mohawk Valley, as well. In return for service "during the present Troubles in America only," recruits were promised two hundred acres of land in the North American province of their choice.[37]

It took time to assemble a meaningful core for Maclean's regiment. In August, a Canadian patriot reported, "from Three Rivers to Chambly, he [Maclean] got not a single man," and he had very limited success in Montréal. Within a month, however, the Emigrants colonel reported that one hundred Scots-Canadians had joined, along with four hundred from New

SIR ALLAN MACLEAN, BART.

Colonel Allan Maclean. From John P. Maclean, *An Historical Account of the Settlements of Scotch Highlanders in America: Prior to the Peace of 1783* (Cleveland, OH: Helman-Taylor, 1900), p. 391. Courtesy of the Ohio Historical Society.

York, nominally giving him more than half of the regiment's 750 authorized men. Not all of the Mohawk Valley Highlander recruits were able to sneak into Canada, so an early September Continental report of "300 Beggarly Scotchmen" contributing to Quebec's loyalist defense was fairly accurate, at least in quantity. Colonel Maclean joined them in August, following a June meeting with General Gage in Boston and covert travels through New York. While Governor Carleton did not receive any regular army reinforcements during the tense summer of 1775, the Royal Highland Emigrants offered a critical source of military manpower for the province's defense.[38]

There was one other party that Carleton could call on to help defend the province: Canada's Indians. A handful of agents helped the governor work toward that aim in the summer of 1775: Major John Campbell was the official

Quebec Superintendent of Indian Affairs, and his father-in-law, St-Luc de La Corne, formerly a superintendent of New France, was also particularly active. New York Crown agents Daniel Claus and Guy Johnson also had a key role, after being compelled to leave their home colony because of their Ministerial loyalty. Carleton played a carefully balanced game. He wanted to ensure the Indians served as a deterrent to the rebellious colonies and did not join the rebels, yet he specifically did not want to unleash them as a means of terror on the frontiers. However, the New York agents were being encouraged by London officials to "induce" the Indians "to take up the hatchet against His Majesty's rebellious subjects," and fervently worked toward that goal.[39]

In late July, Guy Johnson brought sixteen hundred Indians to a "congress" in Montréal. Carleton and Johnson offered presents and secured promises of support from the leaders in attendance. While Johnson and the chiefs seemed intent on attacking neighboring rebel colonies, the governor discouraged those schemes. So that the Indians might "in the mean time be amused in the best manner that could be found," Carleton asked them to help guard the province by establishing "different camps on the Island of Montreal." He also asked that they "keep a party of 40 or 50 of their young Men at St. Johns [St-Jean] to have a Lookout" and monitor the rebels on Lake Champlain; the Indians agreed. The governor made it clear that he did not want them to cross the "Province Line" into New York or New England.[40]

Colonel Johnson rotated various Indian parties through St-Jean, trying to keep these auxiliaries "contented with their situation." Some St-Jean locals, however, worked to sabotage the effort: "Inhabitants . . . continued to sell liquor to the Indians and to strip them of their clothing." There seemed to be an ulterior motive behind this, as these same Canadians were "propagating . . . dangerous reports" among the Indians, and saying the habitants approved of rebel incursions into Quebec, "as it was for the interest of the Colony." Thus, the province's political agitators proved capable of influencing the Crown's Indian allies, even if not decisively.[41]

As Carleton's friends encouraged Canadians to reconfirm their loyalty, a new wave of progovernment messages appeared in the *Quebec Gazette.* In the 13 July issue, a French-only article emphasized the duplicitous discrepancies between Congress's Canadian letters and their British address. The anonymous author hoped that "some enlightened Canadians would, on this evidence, take pains to examine the three raids[42] they [the rebels] have recently made on this province," in considering whether their neighbors were indeed good friends of Quebec's Catholics.[43]

In July and August, the *Gazette* printed two additional anti-rebel letters. The first was another French-only piece, written by "Le Canadien Patriote,"[44] titled "A Canadian's Reply to a Foreigner." The second initially appeared in English, written by "An English Farmer" to "the People of Canada." Both letters argued against Canadian neutrality. To show the folly of passivity, "Le Canadien Patriote" and the "English Farmer" crafted a picture of a Yankee invasion: thousands of invaders would arrive as friends, initially seizing only royal property. Eventually they would need food from the Canadians, who would be paid in "Philadelphia" paper money, useless for Atlantic trade. Quebec would be "deprived of all intercourse with the mother country." Finally, their religion would be endangered, despite rebel professions to the contrary—"Bostonian fanaticism is world-renowned." The "English Farmer" even called on Canadians to take up arms to resist such an invasion, to "rescue the name of Canadian from being synonimous with those of Coward and Traytor." The letters made a good case, and would actually prove to be remarkably prophetic.[45]

Governor Carleton, meanwhile, was being criticized by some of his most zealous supporters for his failure to rein in the radical Canadian opposition's "seditious talk." Thomas Walker continued to spout patriot propaganda at will. When James Price returned to Montréal with all the rebel letters, the governor was "much enraged," yet only "interrogated" him. The governor arrested only a handful of low-level suspects—Continental "spies" and a patriot habitant messenger—and ordered the confiscation of external newspapers. Carleton seemed comfortable excluding outside influences, but hesitated to act against Canadian citizens of any substance, even when they openly preached in favor of a coming rebel invasion.[46]

———

At the end of August 1775, Quebec's Chief Justice William Hey composed a historically valuable letter detailing all of Canada's political developments over the summer. It was written toward the end of the first abbreviated Quebec Act Legislative Council session, which provided a forum for consolidating elite views from across the province, but was otherwise unproductive. While Hey's resultant assessment was biased toward upper-class "English" perspectives, it still provides tremendous insight into the state of Canada at the time. Hey believed the *Canadiens'* minds had been "all poisoned by emissaries from New England, and the damned rascals of merchants" in Québec City and Montréal, and "corrupted and persuaded by the circular letters" from the United Colonies. Despite Carleton's frustrations, the governor pitied the insubordinate habitants and did not condemn them, "because he knew that it was the city merchants that had seduced them" and "the lower class of British subjects" had taken "incredible pains to instruct the Canadians in what they called English liberty . . . they implanted a spirit of licentiousness in the minds of the new subjects."[47]

Hey also felt the governor had bet on the wrong horse to defend government interests in Quebec, noting "it may be truly said that Gen. Carleton had taken an ill measure of the influence of the seigneurs & Clergy over the lower order of people." The *Canadiens'* hostile reaction to seigneurial militia call-ups, and cynical responses to the bishop's instructions, showed that the old authorities did not have the power to force the habitants into unwavering obedience. The Quebec Act, "passed for the express purpose of gratifying the Canadians," had instead "become the first object of their discontent & dislike."[48]

By the end of the summer of 1775, the administration's apparent progress in fostering the Old Subject community's loyalty was offset by the habitants' *petite rébellion*. At best, Canadians were lukewarm Crown supporters; at worst, they were a powder keg waiting for Continental patriots to ignite into provincewide rebellion. By the end of August, the Quebec administration's only practical object was to keep rebel "Ruffians from invading" through winter, "& wait 'till better & more sober times" to properly implement the Quebec Act.[49]

TO ERECT THE GLORIOUS STANDARD OF AMERICAN LIBERTY IN CANADA

The Decision to Intervene

We are to leave this place, and set out on our march for St. John's, in order to erect the glorious standard of American liberty in Canada, the colony that now groans under British Tyranny! | *Extract of a letter from an Officer in the Continental Army, at Ticonderoga, 27 August 1775*

Even after Ethan Allen and the Connecticut expedition seized Ticonderoga for the patriot cause, the confederated colonies continued to have reason to worry in the north. Benedict Arnold's erroneous "escaped prisoner report" led decision makers to believe that Governor Carleton had hundreds of regular troops poised to recover the forts. Mail from Canada, intercepted on Lake Champlain, seemed to validate the northern threat, at least in intent if not details. One of these letters, which had fallen into the hands of the Albany Committee, reported that Carleton's new commission gave him "Power to raise a Canadian Regiment and send it where he pleases." In another letter, a regular soldier in Quebec shared that his regiment would probably "be sent very soon to serve against the rebellious New Englanders." Growing evidence supported fears that the Ministry could launch an attack on Lake Champlain at almost any moment.[1]

Another one of the intercepted letters appealed for the Continental colonies to act; the Canadian "English" were "in a deplorable situation, being deprived of all their Liberties and Priviledges . . . afraid to speak or Act relative to public affairs." Their only hope was for the other provinces to "succeed in their just Demands" and "then exert themselves to obtain a Redress for us."

This sort of news inspired aggressive patriot men of action to yearn for the opportunity to rescue their brethren in Quebec.[2]

Ethan Allen became a zealous advocate for a Canadian expedition in a series of letters sent to the Continental, New York, and Massachusetts Congresses, from 29 May to 9 June. He promoted an intervention to simultaneously liberate the Canadians and eliminate the Ministerial threat from the north; it would also "unite and confirm the Canadians and Indians" in the patriot cause. To skeptics who might argue that such an invasion would be offensive to Quebec's inhabitants, he offered that "Advancing an army into Canada" would be "agreeable to" patriot friends; and current intelligence showed that the "Canadians, all except the noblesse" appeared "at present to be very friendly."[3]

Since Governor Carleton had only about seven hundred British regular soldiers, Allen believed he could take Montréal with a patriot force of fifteen hundred men and some artillery. If augmented to a total of two or three thousand men led by "intrepid commanders," they could conquer the entire "ministerial party in Canada" and "vie with the re-enforcements that may be sent from England." Allen even laid out a twofold grand strategic benefit of this enterprise: "Such a diversion would weaken General Gage"—it was better to fight the enemy in Canada than in Massachusetts—and would block "the design of the Quebeck Bill," benefiting all of British North America.[4]

Allen's ally James Easton took up the same case with his own Massachusetts government, maintaining that "the Colonies must first help their friends in Canada" before the Canadians would be able to support the patriot cause. Easton's sources contributed to the intelligence picture also; in Montréal, St-Luc de La Corne had reportedly "been using his utmost influence to excite the Canadians and Indians to take part in the war against the united colonies." And at Fort St-Jean, "near two hundred regulars" had joined Mackay's "party of about fifty Canadians"—a fairly accurate assessment.[5]

Benedict Arnold was not to be left out, sending comparable letters to the Continental Congress and Connecticut Governor Jonathan Trumbull, arguing that Quebec should "be placed under a free Government" to secure the northern frontier "forever." Arnold added important flourishes of detail from Montréal sources—a merchant "friend," certainly Thomas Walker, and "Indian interpreter" Winthrop Hoyt. Arnold relayed their view that "great numbers of the Canadians have expected a visit from us for some time, and are very impatient of our delay," and these habitants were determined to join the cause whenever patriots appeared in Canada with substantial force. They even offered a prearranged plan in which the liberating army needed only to "show themselves off Montreal" for "friends" to open the city gates to welcome them.[6]

Arnold also offered the troop strength estimates necessary for such an endeavor, closely matching Allen's. He generously volunteered to "carry the plan into execution" and answer for its success. Arnold and Allen seemed postured to compete for the same command again. Yet while these dynamic officers were offering up visionary strategies and operational plans, colonial governments pondered and plotted their own courses for the early summer of 1775, grounded in the realities of their individual situations.[7]

Even though they were often referred to as the "United Colonies," in May and June 1775, the thirteen patriot provinces were in a very loose, poorly co-ordinated confederation. New York was still hobbled by split loyalties and moderate inclinations, and generally took a reactive approach. Although zealous in the cause, Massachusetts was preoccupied with the Boston blockade. Little New Hampshire simply lagged behind the other colonies; its every measure immediately seemed to be rendered obsolete by other colonies' more expeditious activities. All three of these provinces agreed on one thing, and it was not for a northern intervention; rather, it was the urgent necessity of reassuring the Canadians that the colonies held no malevolent intentions toward Quebec and did not want to invade.

Connecticut was the only northern colony in a position to exercise initiative on the Canadian frontier. It did not have Ministerial troops within its borders and was on the cutting edge of patriot activities. Of utmost importance, Connecticut, unlike its neighbors, kept its pre-Revolution government intact; its assembly and governor continued in their posts, smoothly transferring civil and military authority to the patriot cause. This was why Connecticut could lead the longer-term colonial military effort by embodying its provincial militia in May, on seven-month terms of enlistment. Yet even Connecticut was cautious about Canadian expeditions. Governor Jonathan Trumbull agreed that Arnold's proposals offered "great advantage," but he doubted they could be executed with the competing needs of the Boston blockade and coast defense. Trumbull told Arnold that if any such Quebec plan were undertaken, it would "be with great propriety first moved" by the Continental Congress.[8]

The colonies feared more than just the regular British troops in Quebec that summer; northern Indian activity seemed an imminent danger. Massachusetts and New Hampshire both sent envoys to the Canadian Indian villages to gather intelligence and promote amity. The single most influential Indian intelligence report, however, came from testimony given to the Albany Committee. Dirck Swart, a committee board member, had consulted with Udney Hay, a messenger direct from Montréal's "English" merchants. Most details were unsurprising; Carleton was trying to recruit the Canadians, and they were unwilling. Yet one item struck a chord: the merchants' urgent message was that Caughnawaga Indians "had taken up the hatchet." This was particularly alarming since regional Canadian tribes typically followed the Caughnawagas's lead. In reality, the Caughnawagas nominally had committed to Quebec's defense, but carefully continued to play the middle ground between Carleton and the United Colonies, retaining a degree of independent action. Yet to the patriot provinces, it appeared to be a credible warning of impending Indian attack; the Swart report would bear disproportionate weight, similar to Arnold's "escaped prisoner report," figuring prominently in a key Continental Congress decision in the following month.[9]

Connecticut Governor Trumbull's lukewarm mid-June response to Benedict Arnold's Canadian plans typified the patriot colonies' situation; having done what they could individually, they realized that larger efforts demanded intercolonial cooperation and Continental coordination. After Lexington and Concord, and with the Ministry's hostile attitude toward Congress, the confederation's needs took a more martial flavor. Ben Franklin characterized the new atmosphere in early June: with "hostilities being commenced by General Gage against America," a "Civil War" had begun."[10]

The patriot cause needed a Continental military establishment. On 14 June, Congress began by authorizing rifle companies and discussing "Rules and regulations" for "the American continental army." The next day, George Washington was unanimously elected general, commanding all Continental forces. On 19 June, four major-generals were added, including New Yorker Philip Schuyler, destined to command the separate northern "department."[11]

Major General Philip Schuyler (detail), painted by John Trumbull and engraved by Thomas Kelly. Library of Congress Prints and Photographs Division.

Schuyler was a wealthy Hudson Valley manorial landholder, "sincere, well-bred, & resolute." Forty-two-years-old, he had served with distinction in the French and Indian War, where he found his military calling as a superior logistician. Politically aligned with New York's Livingston party, Schuyler's patriot inclinations and "strong, fertile and cultivated mind" led to duty in the Provincial Assembly, Albany Committee of Correspondence, and second Continental Congress before adopting his new military role.[12]

In Philadelphia, on the day before his appointment as a Continental major-general, Schuyler was asked to take a private ride with Connecticut's Silas Deane.[13] Most likely, with Schuyler's generalship assumed and a New York command posting imminent, the two discussed plans "for another bold Stroke like the Ticonderoga affair." The exact nature of the scheme is unclear, but it may well have been an operation to secure St-Jean and Montréal for the patriot cause.[14]

A few days later, on 22 and 23 June, a flurry of notable events passed in Philadelphia: news arrived detailing the Battle of Bunker Hill outside Boston; Congress appointed eight brigadier-generals, including New York's Richard Montgomery (second in rank) and Connecticut's David Wooster (third in rank); and Congress started the Continental Army's war chest, authorizing Continental bills of credit worth up to two million Spanish-milled dollars.[15]

Ethan Allen and Seth Warner also visited Philadelphia at that time, encouraging Congress to bring the Green Mountain Boys into Continental service. Initially New York was asked to include the "Boys" in its provincial establishment, an odd request given the bad blood between the Green Mountain Boys and the Yorker government. When New York disregarded the request, Congress authorized General Schuyler to raise the "Boys" as a Continental regiment on 1 July. The army's Northern Department was slowly being assembled to defend the forts and also to provide a force that could move on Canada.[16]

Despite Congressional delegates' frequent conversations about the possibility of an "Expedition to Montreal" to liberate the "friendly" Canadians, when General Schuyler left Philadelphia on 23 June, he lacked specific orders for his new Northern Department. Two days later, when Schuyler parted from General Washington at New York City, the commander-in-chief provided written orders: Schuyler was to promptly man and repair the northern posts and to "Obtain the best information" possible regarding "the temper and disposition" of both the Canadians and Indians. This information could be used to "conciliate their good opinion" and "facilitate any future operation." That same day, Congress received a copy of Swart's Albany Committee testimony, relating Carleton's offensive intent and word of the Caughnawagas "taking up the hatchet."[17]

On 27 June, stirred to action by that report, Congress produced new orders for Schuyler. In addition to his defensive responsibilities, the Northern Department commander was to "exert his utmost power to destroy or take" any watercraft Governor Carleton prepared on Lake Champlain; the United Colonies wanted a preemptive strike to prevent any challenge to their Lake Champlain naval superiority. Yet there was an even more momentous article in the orders: if Schuyler found it "practicable, *and that it will not be disagreeable to the Canadians* [author's emphasis]," the general was authorized immediately to "take possession of St. Johns, Montreal, and any other parts of the country, and pursue any other measures in Canada" to promote Continental "peace and security."[18]

Schuyler had been given discretionary carte blanche to invade Quebec, a move that seemed contrary to Congress's earlier claims that they would act only for the "mutual safety" and "friendship" of the Canadians. In a letter accompanying the orders, the President of Congress specifically linked this change of heart to Swart's report, a pragmatic response to an apparent threat; yet the fact that Schuyler was expected to consider the Canadians' views in his decision pointed to the revolutionary nature of the invasion authorization—the fight was as at least as much about the Canadian people as it was about their territory and enemy forces.[19]

Initially, Schuyler had only one regiment to accomplish his missions in the north, Colonel Benjamin Hinman's Fourth Connecticut Regiment of about five hundred men. These seemingly ragtag, ununiformed soldiers had relieved the ad hoc Ticonderoga expeditionary force in mid-June. From the moment they arrived, these Yankees talked "as if it was fully determined they should soon march in to the Province of Quebec," well before Schuyler received orders even mentioning such an undertaking. While these few troops seemed ready to move on Canada, the department lacked sufficient manpower and supplies to conduct an invasion.[20]

Meanwhile, Congress finalized a "Declaration on Taking Arms" on 6 July, justifying its new martial posture, including references to the Quebec Act's dangerous "despotism" and "certain intelligence" that the Canadian governor was instigating his people to attack the United Colonies. Yet in the time between the issuance of Schuyler's orders and the declaration, it had already become apparent that Swart's northern intelligence sources may have rushed their conclusions. On 1 July, Richard Henry Lee shared more recent indications that had reached Philadelphia; only twenty Canadian "noblesse" joined the call to arms, and when Carleton asked the Indians "to take up the hatchet," they told him "it is buried too deep, they cannot find it." More frequent and accurate intelligence was clearly needed.[21]

Patriot authorities received another intelligence update from an unofficial source, direct from Canada: Connecticut-born James Dean. He was a Dartmouth College missionary supporting an Indian student program at Caughnawaga. When Dean returned to the lower colonies in the summer of 1775, he not only described the government's persistent approaches to bring the Caughnawagas onto a war footing, but also reported that British regulars were seriously exerting themselves to improve Fort St-Jean.[22]

In mid-July, the Continental Congress received reports from James Dean and an unidentified "gentleman from the province of Quebec." They all seemed to agree that neither the Indians nor the Canadians were an immediate threat. A report from Colonel Arnold shared similar content, but added that there were indications the British regulars were preparing to build a new ship at

St-Jean. Arnold also casually mentioned that he had left his command on the lakes, perhaps subtly hinting for a new posting.[23]

Arnold's departure from the northern posts resulted from Colonel Hinman's arrival as the new senior-ranking officer. Arnold resisted serving as a subordinate. A Massachusetts committee intervened to resolve the situation, and eventually Arnold was relieved or resigned; accounts differed. Arnold's men—soldiers and lake sailors—were initially unwilling to serve under Hinman; yet with the committee's persuasion, most of the ships' crews agreed to cooperate, and many soldiers transitioned to a new Massachusetts regiment commanded by one of Arnold's Ticonderoga-mission rivals, James Easton.[24]

———

Even before Schuyler arrived at Ticonderoga, the Northern Department entered a new phase of operations. In July and August, patriot scouts would make a handful of voyages "across the line" into Canada. Through these reconnaissance missions, Schuyler was kept apprised of the Canadians' shifting sentiments during that province's turbulent summer of habitant rebellion—invaluable intelligence to support the general's discretionary orders for invading Quebec.

The Liberty's Captain Jeremiah Halsey led the first mission, joined by Green Mountain Boy leader Remember Baker, a cousin of both Ethan Allen and Seth Warner. Baker was a bold, experienced woodsman and a French and Indian War veteran, a man who thrived on adventure. The overt purpose of the 13 July mission was to return an Indian student of the Dartmouth-associated Moor's Charity School to his Caughnawaga home along with two escorts; that party was immediately detained, however, when it crossed into Canada. Baker also intended to scout around St-Jean, but in an uncharacteristically cautious moment, did not venture near the fort. When Halsey and Baker returned to Crown-Point on 24 July, they brought back only secondhand information.[25]

While the Halsey-Baker scouting mission was under way, General Schuyler finally reached Ticonderoga on 18 July. The general was already predisposed to send an expedition to St-Jean, even though he did not believe "any great dependance" could be placed on recent Canadian intelligence. In his first report to Congress, he boldly stated, "This, then is the time to gain intelligence with certainty by going to St. John's with a respectable body, giving the Canadians to understand, when we arrive there, that we mean nothing more than to prevent the regular Troops from getting a naval strength, and inter-rupting the friendly intercourse that has subsisted between us and them."[26]

Schuyler's letter, however, would not be read in Philadelphia for six weeks; Congress had taken a summer recess from 1 August through 13 September, completely removing itself from any final decision regarding a Canadian intervention. However, Connecticut's Governor Trumbull prompted Schuyler for action, believing that Canadians needed relief to prevent Carleton from enlisting them through coercion. By 24 July, Trumbull wrote Schuyler, rhetorically pondering, "Is it not high time to proceed into, and even to hasten forward to secure the Government of Quebeck . . . in our interest and favour?" Yet even if Schuyler were inclined to move, his infant army was still desperately short of supplies, transportation, and troops.[27]

By late June, a surprising development occurred on the lower Richelieu River; in their opposition to the Quebec government, rural Canadians began to turn to the Continental cause. A leadership cell formed around Chambly. The group's origins are vague, but elements may have operated even before the "3000" habitants gathered around Chambly in that summer's Longueuil militia revolt. The leadership cadre consisted of about a dozen *Canadiens;* its principal "Head of Council" was Dominique Mondelet, a notary and surgeon from St-Marc. Only one of the organizers is known to have been an Old Subject: Chambly merchant James Livingston.[28]

Captain Joseph Ménard,[29] another Chambly patriot leader, dispatched *Canadien* Pierre Charlan to confer with Continental officers about the Richelieu situation in early July. Reaching Ticonderoga, Charlan reported that British regulars were trying to force the habitants to take up arms; Canadian resistance leaders wanted to know if the "Bostonians" "intended to come or not," so they could respond appropriately. Captain Ménard offered assurances that if the Continentals came into Quebec, the habitants were ready to offer "cattle, horses, carriages" as needed.[30]

When it was time for the Chambly messenger to return, he was attached to a new Continental reconnaissance team led by Major John Brown. On 24 July, this scouting party headed down Lake Champlain, "Compleatly in Disguise," with two goals in mind: to "discover the motions and intentions of the enemy" and "to engage the Canadians and Savages in the interest of the Colonies." After the party covertly infiltrated past Fort St-Jean, Charlan coordinated a conference between Brown and Captain Ménard at Chambly. Afterward, Ménard and Charlan departed to visit Thomas Walker, while friendly habitants helped secret Brown out of the province. During his departure, Brown had the opportunity to meet James Livingston on 3 August, which was the start of a tremendously important Continental-Canadian patriot relationship.[31]

Livingston was a longtime Quebec resident;[32] his family moved to the province from New York shortly after the Conquest. He spent his formative years in Montréal but moved to Chambly around 1770. He acquired a "landed estate" on the Richelieu and served as a wheat merchant, supplying British troops. Through that business, Livingston, who was perfectly fluent in French, established good relationships with many local habitants. With recent events in the province, he decided to commit himself to the nascent Canadian patriot cause, sacrificing his lucrative military contracts.[33]

As one of the Chambly patriot cell organizers, Livingston opened a correspondence with Ticonderoga, providing regular intelligence updates and reminding Schuyler, "The Canadians have waited with the utmost impatience your coming, and begin to despair of seeing you." Like Ménard, Livingston promised that *Canadiens* were ready to provide any supplies the liberating force might need. For his part, Livingston said he would "revive" Canadian patriot spirits by "sending circular letters to the Captains of the different Parishes of your coming soon to relieve them."[34]

Schuyler still had a voracious appetite for Canadian intelligence. Even before Brown returned, Remember Baker was dispatched on another scouting mission. On that early August mission, Baker made an important discovery at Fort St-Jean: two vessels were under construction, which he estimated would be ready in ten days.[35]

While traveling on Lake Champlain, Baker and his naval escorts detained two suspicious men, John Shatforth and John Duguid. They interrogated them back at Ticonderoga; among a wealth of mostly secondhand information, both said they had heard that "Indians were coming up the lakes to act against the Colonies when the Regulars were ready." Shatforth provided another valuable observation; he did not "suppose the Canadians would take it ill if the Colony troops were to pass the line" into Quebec. As these interviews concluded, new intelligence arrived from the north, especially reports of the Montreal District habitant rebellions in early summer.[36]

On 10 August, another messenger reached Ticonderoga from Chambly's increasingly active patriot cell. French-born *Canadien* Jean-Baptiste Féré came to "inquire whether the Army was coming down to Canada to relieve them or not, or whether the Canadians who are Friends to the Cause of Liberty are to remain unsuccoured by the [Continental] Army." Originally he had carried a letter from Livingston, but was forced to hide and abandon it in the woods near St-Jean when he feared he might be captured by an Indian patrol. He also reported that the "Friends of America" around Chambly could raise "about 1500 Men. . . . in 24 Hours & double that Number in 48 Hours," but cautioned that not all had arms. This was the first quantification of the Canadian patriot support to be expected if Continental forces were to venture across the line.[37]

=======

By the time he arrived at Ticonderoga in mid-July, General Schuyler had only Colonel Hinman's Connecticut and James Easton's Massachusetts Regiments available. At least half of those troops were needed to garrison Ticonderoga, Crown-Point, and Skenesborough. The general simply needed more men if he wanted to cross the lake into Canada. On 26 July, Congress had informed Schuyler that he could deploy two additional Connecticut regiments in the north—Wooster's and Waterbury's—but it would take time for them to move; and they needed provisions that Schuyler still lacked.

Another "new" regiment, the Continental Green Mountain Boys, was forming, but Schuyler had to help resolve an internal squabble in the unit first. When the people of the New Hampshire Grants elected the regiment's officers that summer, the "enterprizing & Heroic" Ethan Allen was completely slighted; Seth Warner was elected as regimental commander instead. Needless to say, Allen was livid and complained to Schuyler. After investigating the elections, the general supported Warner's appointment and the situation cooled off. Allen, however, was left without a command.[38]

New York troops were slowly mobilizing to help defend the northern frontier, but their Provincial Congress had not even authorized the formation of the first four regiments until 30 June, three days after General Schuyler received Congress's initial orders for the department. The First Regiment, formed by famous patriot Alexander McDougall in New York City, was designated to join Schuyler. On 8 August, its lead elements marched out of the city in their new blue uniforms, under the command of Lieutenant-Colonel Rudolphus Ritzema; radical "Liberty Boy" Captain John Lamb's independent artillery company followed a few weeks later. New York was starting to contribute, but Connecticut still bore the chief military burden of the Northern Army.[39]

=====

In mid-August, Schuyler's military strength was growing, and he certainly had ample intelligence to justify an attack on Quebec; yet he found himself with virtually no civilian guidance in making such a momentous decision. When the Continental Congress adjourned for its summer recess, President John Hancock told Schuyler to consult with New York's Provincial Congress; the Yorkers, however, notified the general they could not provide any instructions. The only input he actually received was a 10 August letter from Maryland delegate Samuel Chase,[40] who cautioned Schuyler that "a *sine qua non,* of Marching into Quebec, is the Friendship of the Canadians: without their Consent and Approbation, it is not [to] be undertaken."[41]

Further complicating his decision, Schuyler was severely distracted by a new set of responsibilities. He had been appointed senior commissioner to superintend Indian affairs in the Northern Department. With an important Indian treaty conference scheduled for 26 August in Albany, Schuyler departed from Ticonderoga, leaving fellow Yorker Brigadier-General Richard Montgomery in charge at the forts. Montgomery was a veteran British officer, familiar with both the New York and Canadian ends of Lake Champlain from his service in the 1759 and 1760 campaigns of the last war. He had adopted New York as his home less than three years earlier, but was quickly vaulted into important leadership roles in the Revolutionary Crisis, including New York's first Continental brigadier-generalship.[42]

Montgomery sent John Brown back to Canada one more time, on 19 August. He hoped to recover the Livingston letter that Jean-Baptiste Féré had abandoned near St-Jean, and he also gave the messenger a letter to deliver to Livingston. Brown dropped Féré off, along with "an Acadian," interpreter Winthrop Hoyt, and two soldiers. The soldiers escorted Féré to recover the letter, but abandoned the attempt when they were threatened again by Indian patrols. The Acadian, Hoyt, and Féré pressed on to Chambly to arrange further cooperation with Ticonderoga. Brown returned to Crown-Point on 24 August.[43]

While Brown was escorting Féré, Remember Baker set out on another

General Richard Montgomery (detail). Emmet Collection of Manuscripts, Etc., Relating to American History, *The Generals of the American Revolution,* Vol. 3: *Philip Schuyler,* Miriam and Ira D. Wallach Division of Art, Prints and Photographs, The New York Public Library, Astor, Lenox and Tilden Foundations.

scouting mission. On 22 August, across the province line near Lacolle, Baker and a five-man reconnaissance team met an Indian patrol from Fort St-Jean. Baker "wickedly snapped his firelock" at the Indians as they attempted to seize a boat he had left on the shore. The Indians immediately fired back, killing Baker. Both parties disengaged, leaving the corpse behind. The Indians returned to sever Baker's head, which they raised on a stake outside Fort St-Jean. This bit of savagery infuriated Continentals at the other end of the lake; they longed "bravely to revenge his death, or fall in the glorious attempt."[44]

Schuyler, busy with the Indian conference, was furious when he heard the news. Baker had defied "explicit and pointed orders" to avoid molesting either Canadians or Indians. The general hoped that "the intemperate heat and disobedience of Captain Baker" had not turned both friendly and neutral Canadians into enemies. Fortunately for the Continentals, average *Canadiens* did not seem bothered by the incident.[45]

On 27 August, Schuyler was informed about a dramatic new "Plan of an Expedition" for Canada. Washington was prepared to detach more than one thousand men from his camp at Cambridge, outside Boston, and march them to Quebec using an alternative route up the Kennebec River to the Chaudière (see Map 2). Washington did not want to launch this new mission until he confirmed that the Northern Army was actually moving on Canada; he emphasized, "Not a Moment's Time is to be lost," as the season was already getting late. Accordingly, the commander-in-chief requested that Schuyler send his "ultimate Resolution" on the Canadian invasion by express messenger. Schuyler replied that he intended to invade, seeing the "necessity of penetrating into Canada without delay." There is no indication, however, that Schuyler had previously committed to the attack; Washington's query may have been the pivotal input that convinced the Northern Army's commander that an advance on St-Jean was necessary.[46]

In any case, the decision was already being taken from his hands. In the last days of August, General Montgomery finally received compelling intelligence — something that demanded immediate action — and the brigadier determined that it was "absolutely necessary to move down the lake with the utmost dispatch." Montgomery felt he was "in a great Dilemma," making such a decision without consulting his commander, who was still in Albany, but if he were to err he would do so on the side of caution for the colonies' defense.[47]

The critical intelligence came from two key sources. A soldier named Peter Griffin returned to Crown-Point on 25 August, from a Canadian scouting expedition. He had joined Baker "as a Spy" a couple of days before the fatal Lacolle skirmish, and with the help of a Caughnawaga guide, had scouted within five hundred yards of Fort St-Jean. Griffin's most important observation was that two ships were being built: one definitely would be ready to sail soon; the other, somewhat obscured from view, seemed nearly complete. John Brown, who had been on the *Liberty* exchanging Livingston correspondence when it picked up Griffin, further prodded General Montgomery; if the army were not ready to march before the royal ships were completed, the United Colonies would "lose all . . . the Command of the Lake, which is tantamount."[48]

James Livingston's letters, delivered by Brown, completed Montgomery's intelligence picture. Through these updates, the general learned that the British regulars had "three Row-galleys . . . of about fifty Tons each," being brought from Chambly to St-Jean, which would "be fit for sailing" at the end of August. Livingston admitted that he was not sure if they intended to attack Ticonderoga, but had heard the boats' captains discuss the possibility. Hoyt and Féré delivered another Livingston letter a few days later, pleading for Schuyler to "hasten the troops under his command"; the Chambly patriots were ready for the Northern Army to "penetrate into Canada." Now a clear threat, as well as strong indications of Canadian support, called for preemptive action, clearly in the spirit of Congress's guidance for an invasion.[49]

"Being apprehensive that the enemy's armed vessels might get into the lake unless an immediate movement was made" into Canada, Montgomery "resolved to proceed with what force he could carry." The brigadier took several measures as he prepared to launch a mission up the lake. First, he ordered the preparation of two cannon and a log boom, to prevent British ships from gaining access to Lake Champlain "by taking post at the Isle aux Noix," a Canadian island on the upper Richelieu, thirteen miles south of St-Jean. Second, he ordered the schooner *Liberty* to the north end of the lake "to keep a watchfull look out for the enemy's vessels." The general also ordered troops to Crown-Point, for transportation up the lake. And finally, he sent John Brown back to Canada with a message for James Livingston: the troops were finally moving, and Montgomery requested "every Assistance" in the Chambly patriots' power.

After all the buildup, the final decision to invade Canada had been made by a second-tier Continental leader. With his superior officer prodded for action by Connecticut politicians Governor Trumbull and Silas Deane; supported by the zealous efforts of Allen, Arnold, and Brown; and most important, encouraged by the increasingly active Chambly patriot partisans, Brigadier-General Richard Montgomery launched the much-anticipated expedition into Quebec. With its grand ideological goals for the Canadians, the mission was ultimately triggered by the imminent readiness of the King's new ships, a matter of immediate defensive concern for the United Colonies.[50]

Chapter 8

THE CANADIANS
OPENED THE ROAD

Continentals and Partisans on the Richelieu River

The Canadians opened the Road and led them by the hand to the very gates of the Capital. | *John Bonfield to Robert Morris, 4 February 1776*

When the Continental Northern Army sailed down Lake Champlain at the end of August 1775, it was led by a man who had been an "American" for only three years, Brigadier-General Richard Montgomery. An Irish-born British officer, he had served with distinction at Louisbourg and in the Champlain-Richelieu corridor during the French and Indian War, rising to the rank of captain by the war's end. Frustrated when a less-deserving peer purchased a major's rank that Montgomery understood had been promised to him, he sold his captain's commission in 1772 and headed back to North America. Settling in New York, Montgomery soon married Janet Livingston and was embraced by the powerful Judge Robert Livingston family. This led Montgomery directly into patriot politics, including his May 1775 election to the Provincial Congress. Yet when the Continental Congress began appointing generals, he was still not well known; delegate Robert R. Livingston Jr. must have lobbied heavily for Montgomery's appointment as New York's first Continental brigadier, emphasizing his brother-in-law's vast military experience and patriot commitment.[1]

On 30 August, the "tall and handsome" Montgomery stood as a tower of authority guiding the Northern Army's chaotic Crown-Point embarkation. Almost twelve hundred men—chiefly from Waterbury's motley Fifth Connecticut Regiment and the blue-coated First New Yorkers—clambered into tightly packed ships and bateaux. The flotilla made slow progress down the lake, facing a "Barbarous North wind." General Schuyler caught up just before

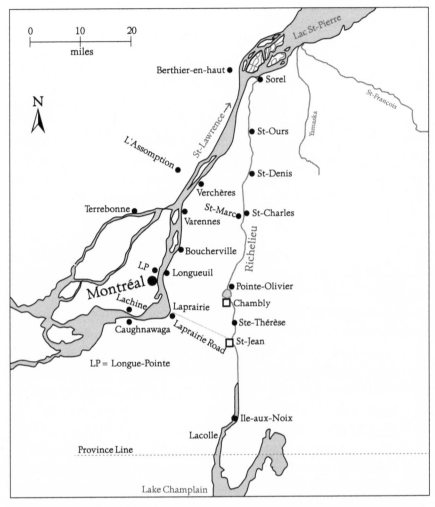

0   10   20
miles

N

Berthier-en-haut ●

● Sorel

Lac St-Pierre

St-François

St-Lawrence

L'Assomption ●

● St-Ours

● St-Denis

Verchères ●

Yamaska

Terrebonne ●

St-Marc ● ● St-Charles

Varennes

Richelieu

● Boucherville

LP ●
● Longueuil

Montréal ●

Lachine

Laprairie

● Pointe-Olivier

□ Chambly

Laprairie Road

● Ste-Thérèse

Caughnawaga

□ St-Jean

LP = Longue-Pointe

● Ile-aux-Noix

Lacolle

Province Line

Lake Champlain

MAP 4: Richelieu Valley Campaign, 1775.

it crossed the province line on 5 September. The expedition cruised ten more miles into Quebec and landed at Ile-aux-Noix (see Map 4).[2]

That low, marshy Richelieu River island formed a spearhead pointing into Canada, about a mile in length and five hundred yards wide. It was in a good position to block passage to the lake; any boat headed upriver would pass within three hundred yards. But it was an unpleasant remote post, home to thick swarms of biting insects, "much troubled with snakes &c.," and rank with stagnant air.[3]

A dozen miles north, at Fort St-Jean, about 450 British troops, Royal Highland Emigrants, and *Canadien* volunteers, augmented by Indian parties, stood between Schuyler's provincials and their patriot friends in Chambly and Montréal. Over the summer, Carleton's soldiers had built two earthen redoubts at the west bank fort, enclosing the barracks and a preexisting house. Ditches surrounded the works, and cannon dominated the river from mounts behind the grassy redoubt walls. The ramshackle old post had been transformed into a respectable frontier fortification. Beyond the fort's few-hundred-yard clearing, the land was "an impassable Quagmire," heavy with brush and timber. Adding to the available firepower, the recently completed, but not fully fitted schooner *Royal Savage* and a cannon-armed row galley sat immediately in front of the fort.[4]

General Schuyler knew Canadian support was the single most critical element for his success; using Clausewitzean terms, the Canadians were the operation's "center of gravity." John Brown had already been sent ahead to advise the Chambly partisans of their approach and to coordinate immediate assistance with provisions, boats, and auxiliaries. Reaching Ile-aux-Noix, the army fired three cannon blasts to signal its arrival to any Canadians within earshot. Once on the island, the general's next undertaking was to compose an address to the Canadian people. He hoped this "manifesto" would induce the *Canadiens* to join the patriot cause, or at least remain neutral, by conveying the United Colonies' intentions in the province.[5]

Schuyler's address explained that the Northern Army came to restore the entire Canadian population's "British rights," regardless of class or "religious sentiments," by expelling the Ministerial troops who served as tools of oppression. The general offered assurances that he would "cherish every Canadian, and every friend to the cause of liberty and sacredly guard their property." He described the United Colonies' recent entreaties to ensure Indian neutrality,

View of Fort St-Jean from East Side of Richelieu (1776). The numerous outbuildings were not present during the invasion. In 1775, the threatening ships were being completed in the river, close to the northern (right) redoubt. Emmet Collection of Manuscripts, Etc., Relating to American History, Miriam and Ira D. Wallach Division of Art, Prints and Photographs, The New York Public Library, Astor, Lenox and Tilden Foundations.

and apologized for the embarrassing Remember Baker incident. The address was purely informative, without explicit requests for Canadian support.[6]

Amidst the hubbub of unloading supplies and setting up camp, soldiers scrawled handbill copies of the address—there was no printing press. Swiss-born New York chaplain Jean-Pierre Tétard, Schuyler's interpreter, provided the indispensable French translation. The general called on a pair of veteran leaders—Major John Brown and volunteer officer Ethan Allen—to deliver copies of the address into *Canadien* hands. The duo was to infiltrate past Fort St-Jean, deliver the address to the Chambly patriot partisans, and open communications between the two camps.

Across Quebec, the Continental invasion instantly reframed the entire provincial political conflict. Conflicts between French and British Parties were passé. Now Canada, like its southern neighbors, was a scene of conflict between rebel, antigovernment "patriots," and government-supporting "loyalists" or Tories.

=====

Before embarking on a major mainland operation, General Schuyler sought tangible evidence of a friendly Canadian reception—something more than the Chambly partisans' promises. He sent a detachment toward St-Jean on 6 September, to test the waters of *Canadien* sentiment, encourage cooperation, and cautiously probe Fort St-Jean's defenses. Brigadier-General Montgomery led almost five hundred men, who disembarked about a mile-and-a-half south of the fort; General Schuyler joined them once the landings were complete. As the Continentals slogged through thick swampy woods, they encountered a party from the fort—almost a hundred Indians, a pair of *Canadien* volunteers, and a British captain. A short melee produced casualties of almost a score on each side. The Continentals held their own, but Montgomery observed there was "a good deal of confusion in the action; the Yorkers little acquainted with wood-fighting; the Connecticut men behaved well for the most part." The rebel army set up a couple of small earthworks and settled in for a night on the mainland. No habitants rushed to join the rebels, and Montgomery lamented the lack of clear indications regarding Canadian intentions.[7]

Only one "well dressed gentlemanly appearing" Canadian visited that evening. It was local seigneur Moses Hazen, the retired British officer who in May had rushed to notify Carleton of Arnold's St-Jean raid. Hazen offered a little intelligence on Fort St-Jean, as well as some advice. In his opinion, the Continentals would not be joined "by one Canadian"; the locals preferred "to be neuter." It was also "imprudent to attack" St-Jean. Instead Schuyler should withdraw to Ile-aux-Noix, send parties among the habitants, and open "an intercourse" with Montréal. It is hard to discern if Hazen's advice was an honest, yet skeptical assessment, or if it reflected a desire to protect his local interests from the ravages of war.[8]

General Schuyler called a council of war the following morning, 7 September, and opened the meeting by sharing the Canadian's information. All the field officers agreed that the army should reconsolidate at Ile-aux-Noix, take extra measures to bar enemy ships from the lake, seek "certain Intelligence touching the intentions of the Canadians," and await more reinforcements, especially artillery. Only then might they "send a strong detachment into the Country by land."[9]

As the Northern Army detachment returned to the island, James Livingston, Ethan Allen, and John Brown opened the real war for Quebec in the rural countryside of the mainland. During the night the Continentals spent south of Fort St-Jean, Allen and Brown parted from the main body, heading into the boggy wilderness to skirt around the fort and contact the Chambly patriots. They evaded vigilant Indian patrols and emerged on the banks of the Richelieu River the following day, 8 September. Friendly habitants escorted them to rendezvous with James Livingston. After a short conference, Allen, Brown, and Livingston considered traveling to the Continental camp, but there were rumors that Indian patrols expected them; and with word that the Continental landing party had withdrawn to the island, they adopted an alternate course of action. They sent a letter to Schuyler, declaring, "The Canadians are all Friends & a Spirit of Freedom seems to reign amongst them." They also established a patriot camp at Ste-Thérèse, between the two upper Richelieu River rapids, where they could organize valley partisan activities.[10]

This area south of Chambly was sparsely settled; the only road was a west-bank portage path. Yet from Ste-Thérèse, messengers and organizers could easily range into the lower, northern end of the valley, which was a continuous "string of villages" in the typical *côte* pattern, and visit the village of Chambly itself. That "beautiful small town" sat on the south end of the Richelieu River's mile-diameter Chambly Basin. A stone fort, east of the village, guarded the point where bubbling river rapids spilled into the basin. While the Canadian patriots generally felt free to move up and down the valley at will, Fort Chambly was one of two points the partisans still avoided—the other being the heavily patrolled St-Jean region.[11]

Allen and Brown delivered General Schuyler's "manifestos," and Livingston distributed them expeditiously to regional parish leaders. The two Continental officers also roamed through central Richelieu Valley communities with an armed escort "Night and Day," meeting with militia-captains and other "respectable Gentlemen" who came to meet the *Bastonnais* emissaries. Brown and Allen reassured Canadians that the Continental force had come to fight the Ministry's troops and had no issue with the habitants or their religion.[12]

Ethan Allen also opened communications with nearby Indians. Applying his personal mix of charisma and bluster, he persuaded the "praying Indians" to send a pair of representatives to join him when he returned to Ile-aux-Noix, so they could see the powerful Northern Army gathering at their doorstep. Allen liked to think he personally drew the Indians away from Carleton; the reality was that he happened to be a facilitator for their measured middle-ground strategy.[13]

Meanwhile, Livingston and his associates rallied *Canadiens* to gather provisions and help interdict Fort St-Jean's communications. Although they were surprised to hear the Continentals had landed and subsequently retreated, the Chambly patriots were still ready to raise "a considerable party" to join the "Bostonians" whenever they returned to the mainland. To some degree, habitant participation was facilitated by the timing of the invasion. Many farmers had an early harvest and were relatively free for a few weeks—a fortuitous opportunity to support the patriot cause as armed auxiliaries and provisioners, without meaningful impact on their own livelihood.[14]

Ministerial forces faced greater challenges in garnering significant Canadian support. Under Governor Carleton's direction, Brigadier-General Richard Prescott ordered seigneur Joseph Lemoyne-de-Longueuil to lead a corps of south bank militia to meet the rebels. Each parish, in a sixty-mile stretch from Châteauguay to the mouth of the Richelieu, was called to mobilize every tenth man, theoretically totaling about four hundred habitants. Moses Hazen received similar orders to organize Richelieu Valley parishes for the king. Prescott was optimistic, thinking the Canadian force would "enable us to repel all attempts." On the south bank, Longueuil found that militia-captains reported for duty; yet the men were allegedly "so corrupted" by patriot propaganda that they refused to march, despite incessant appeals from officers, priests, and seigneurs. There is no evidence that the waffling Hazen ever attempted to execute his orders.[15]

While parishes resisted mobilization, Montréal's citizens seemed fairly reliable. Following the rebels' arrival at Ile-aux-Noix, General Prescott twice assembled the city militia, drawing about three hundred men each time. In both cases he dismissed them when it was clear the city faced no immediate threat. A citizens' guard was established to man the gates, and several volunteer parties, composed exclusively of "young gentlemen" and prominent bourgeois, marched to augment Fort St-Jean's defenders.[16]

Governor Carleton assumed operational control of the province's defenses when he reached Montréal on 7 September. Prescott immediately presented him with substantial new evidence against the radical Thomas Walker—seditious correspondence between the merchant and the rebels. Letters had been found on Remember Baker's body and in the hands of Pierre Charlan; that Chambly patriot messenger had been arrested outside the city trying to reach Walker. The defiant Walker had taken refuge in his L'Assomption Parish country home, but his wife and servants were still harassed relentlessly by zealous loyalists and officials in Montréal. Martha Walker even met Carleton, trying to defuse the situation, but the patriot couple could not accept the governor's only offer: immediate relocation outside the province. Carleton still refrained from arresting known patriots, even after the Continental invasion, but on 16 September he issued a proclamation authorizing officials to examine suspicious "strangers" in town, who suddenly seemed more prevalent.[17]

The Continentals had hardly returned to Ile-aux-Noix when General Schuyler received letters from the Ste-Thérèse partisan camp on 9 September, prodding him to launch operations on the mainland. Livingston described the "Spirit of Freedom" reigning amongst the habitants and promised to raise "great numbers" of *Canadiens* to join the Northern Army, but only after the Continentals returned to shore from the island. He also specifically requested a detachment to "cut off the Necessary Communication between St. Johns & Lapriare [Laprairie], Chambly, &c."[18]

Schuyler decided "to go forward immediately" with another landing under Montgomery's direction. New York Lieutenant-Colonel Rudolphus Ritzema would lead a composite force of five hundred Yorkers and Connecticut Yankees to the east end of the Laprairie road, near the settlement of St-Jean. Once established, he would block the fort's communications and open direct correspondence with Livingston and Montréal. An additional three hundred troops would "cover their landing and bring back the boats." Ritzema was reminded to take all necessary measures to "cultivate the friendship of the Canadians."[19]

On the dark evening of 10 September, the troops landed about three miles south of Fort St-Jean. Ritzema had hardly commenced his night march in the swampy woods when the mission fell apart. Two parties of green troops ran into each other in the dark and panicked, convinced they had encountered the enemy. Montgomery rallied the skittish men and persuaded them to try again.

This time the advanced guard encountered a small party of loyalists, resulting in a short, sharp firefight. Many troops sprinted back to the landing site again, yet Ritzema led a small party to drive off the enemy Indians and *Canadien* volunteers. The general waited until morning before proceeding any further.[20]

At dawn, the senior officers held a council of war, initially electing to resume their mission; but before anyone marched, a Continental picketboat erroneously reported that the enemy's new sloop was approaching from St-Jean, sparking a short, terrified scramble for the landing boats. After officers regained control, Montgomery led another council of war and, with considerable frustration, agreed to withdraw to Ile-aux-Noix once again.[21]

General Montgomery, normally even tempered, was "Exceedingly chagrined and mortified" at his men's poor performance, especially since a few Canadian volunteers had witnessed the disgrace. Back on the island, Yorkers blamed Yankees, and vice-versa, fueling Northern Army internal tensions. However, the worst result was that the Canadian partisans were unsupported, still anticipating Continental aid to liberate the district.[22]

The local patriots were not passive bystanders, though. On 13 September, Ethan Allen and his habitant escorts sparked an opening engagement near Chambly, capturing five British artillerymen traveling on the Richelieu. Anticipating a counterattack from Fort Chambly, Livingston urgently sent reinforcements. Additional partisans reached the scene just before twenty regulars appeared in two bateaux. The rebel Canadians attacked the boats, killing or wounding a dozen; the rest of the King's troops escaped. Livingston was displeased with Allen's rash and "imprudent" action, believing the entire partisan operation was unnecessarily put at risk; yet *Canadien* patriots had successfully engaged regular soldiers in their first fight. Reports quickly spread across Quebec that 150 rebel habitants were roaming the Richelieu Valley.[23]

In reality, Livingston tallied three hundred supporters, and they had already established a second partisan post at Pointe-Olivier, the northeast corner of the Chambly Basin.[24] Yet Livingston complained that he was "almost harassed to Death" trying to keep his volunteers in good order; to avoid "losing ground" in his recruiting campaign, Livingston promised pay and purchased food to keep habitants in camp. A few trusted deputies gave vital assistance: Jean-François Hamtramck, an educated bilingual Chambly resident, served as a lieutenant and commissary, gathering provisions for both partisans and Continentals; St-Denis blacksmith Augustin Loiseau led various parties;

and Old Subject wheat trader Jeremiah Duggan stepped up as Livingston's right-hand man. Fluent in French and married to a *Canadienne*, Duggan had a strong rapport with the habitants and was credited with bringing in at least sixty men during the first weeks of September. After the Continentals failed to provide support, the partisans effectively stopped "Intercourse between St. John's and the Country" on their own. No one freely entered or exited the fort after veteran Canadian officer and legislative councilor François-Marie Picoté-de-Bellestre brought a final reinforcement of one hundred loyalist volunteers to Fort St-Jean at mid-month.[25]

On 14 September, Ethan Allen completed his first weeklong venture on the Richelieu, returning to Ile-aux-Noix with thirteen Canadian volunteers and a pair of Lorette Huron chiefs. He immediately updated General Schuyler on Canadian partisan activities. Twenty-one other *Canadiens* had also come to Ile-aux-Noix over the preceding week, some from as far away as the Quebec District. Based on these Canadians' encouragement and Allen's reports, the Continental generals ordered another attempt to support the partisans. On the fifteenth, Major John Brown landed with a combined force of about thirty Canadian volunteers and one hundred Continentals. Their mission was "to keep up the Spirits of the Canadians & to join the Army at St. Johns as soon as it shou'd arrive there."[26]

In the valley, Livingston and Duggan solicited habitant support by sending two circular letters to militia-captains on 16 and 18 September, invoking the authority of the "Bostonian" general. These letters, some of which even reached the Quebec District, announced the Continental Northern Army's arrival and called for aid: seeking flour, with a promise of payment, and requesting that militia officers lead habitants to join the "brave Canadians" fighting the Ministerial scourge on the Richelieu. If unable to send men, militia-captains could show goodwill by maintaining a "fraternal correspondence" with the partisans. Livingston and Duggan also built on the key points of Schuyler's manifesto; the "Bostonians" came only to make the *Canadiens* masters of their own property and to abolish taxes.[27]

In between the two patriot Canadian circular letters, another matter grabbed Livingston's attention. Governor Carleton was attempting to reclaim the lower Richelieu parishes from the rebellious partisans. On 15 September, some of the region's "principal Farmers" and militia officers informed the governor that St-Denis parishioners had been persuaded to return to the fold, and requested a pardon. Carleton wrote an amnesty proclamation and gave it to two loyalist volunteers, prominent Montréal merchant Jean Orillat and a man named Lévéille, for delivery to repentant parishes. The messengers reached St-Denis on 17 September and spent the night at *Curé* François Cherrier's rectory.[28]

When Livingston heard these men were coming to stir up habitant support for the government, he dispatched a party to seize the duo. At dawn on the eighteenth, a patriot force consisting of Pointe-Olivier, St-Denis and St-Charles habitants, and a Continental party led by Allen, appeared at Cherrier's presbytery. The *Canadiens* roughly demanded the surrender of Orillat and Lévéille, threatening to burn the house. During this showdown, a Continental accidentally shot the priest's maidservant dead — the only casualty of the affair — after which the loyalist messengers promptly yielded to the rebels' demands.[29]

Once again, the partisans had escalated the conflict: they had physically challenged a Catholic priest, and their companions had killed an innocent Canadian. When word of the affair reached Montréal, loyalists were shocked. They assumed Carleton would promptly send "a detachment to punish these rebels; but he did not do so." Instead, the ranks of opposition habitants grew unhindered. As events unfolded, Livingston reported, "We have nothing to fear here at present, but a few Seigneurs in the country, endeavouring to raise forces."[30]

While Livingston was dealing with Orillat and Lévéille in St-Denis, Major John Brown led his operation outside Fort St-Jean. His Continental-Canadian detachment deployed north of the fort to serve as a "corps of observation." Late in the night of 17 September, Brown's force ambushed a supply convoy approaching on the Laprairie road, capturing a number of heavily laden wagons and cattle. Coincidentally, Brown also encountered Moses Hazen that night, taking him prisoner, unsure of the Canadian seigneur's allegiances.[31]

Early in the morning, Fort St-Jean's commander, Major Charles Preston, was alerted to the convoy ambush and swiftly launched a two-hundred man counterattack. Brown's rebels "fir'd a few Shot and ran off into the wood," judging that they were outnumbered by the British regulars and loyalist *Canadien* volunteers. The British force was considering pursuit when it was alerted to a rebel approach from an unexpected direction.[32]

A few days earlier, immediately after Brown's force was landed, General Montgomery had also deployed to the mainland with four hundred Continentals, establishing positions south of the fort. Hearing Brown's skirmish, the general ordered New Hampshire Colonel Timothy Bedel to march a detachment toward the sound of the musket fire. It was Bedel's arrival that caught the British party off guard, forcing it back to shelter in the fort's redoubts. The fight cost the garrison two dead and one wounded. Rebel casualties totaled fourteen men, including three Canadians; the enigmatic Moses Hazen had also been "recaptured" by the British and taken into the fort.[33]

General Montgomery exploited his victory, strengthening Continental positions north and south of the fort and sending Brown toward Laprairie, on the banks of the St. Lawrence. At this time, the brigadier also discovered that he was the senior Continental officer in Canada. General Schuyler, bedridden by "a bilious fever and violent rheumatick pains," was evacuated to Ticonderoga. Schuyler retained his role as theater commander, responsible for strategy and logistics, while Montgomery became the operational field commander. Continental strength also began to grow, as Seth Warner's Green Mountain Boys, Bedel's New Hampshire Rangers, and additional Yorker infantry arrived in late September and early October. Most significant, New York artillery had joined the camp south of St-Jean on 19 September, bringing "great joy to the army."[34]

After the 18 September skirmish, Brown led his detachment along the Laprairie road's twelve "sunken, low & wet" wilderness miles, emerging at its west end to see a tremendous Laurentian vista framing the Island of Montréal. Brown's troops took in the sights of the village's whitewashed houses, "pretty" church steeple, and "old crazy windmill," before realizing they had arrived at a most fortuitous moment. *Canadien* loyalist volunteer Chevalier Joseph Boucher-de-Niverville had just crossed the river with ten cartloads of supplies for Fort St-Jean, escorted by Indians and militiamen. Completely surprised to find rebel soldiers so near Montréal, the veteran Niverville and his men fled to their boats. They rushed back to the island, abandoning the wagons and their cargo.[35]

The shock jolted Montréal: "Everyone in the city was in the greatest consternation." Citizens spied rebel troops marching on the far shore, slightly more than a mile across the river; these included Brown's detachment and fresh reinforcements led by Seth Warner. Government officials and military officers fueled panic by loading "papers and Baggage," as well as their families, onto ships—clear signs they intended to abandon the city. It was clear that the governor had lost control of not only the Richelieu Valley, but also the shore opposite Montréal.[36]

From his position south of Fort St-Jean, Montgomery dispatched Ethan Allen down the Richelieu again, with orders to "raise a Corps" of Canadians and "observe the disposition, designs and movement of the inhabitants of the country." Allen traveled down the valley "preaching politics" and reportedly raised 250 men in three days. One of his new *Canadien* lieutenants was Jean Ménard *dit* Brindamour,[37] who brought his own company of one hundred Canadians and helped purchase supplies for the Continentals.[38]

Allen marched his partisan corps up and down the lower Richelieu for three days. He initially planned to capture "slenderly Mann'd" ships stationed off Sorel on the St. Lawrence, loaded with government provisions and "warlike stores." Before executing that mission, he decided to return to St-Jean, having concluded the fort was the key to the province. Changing his mind once again, he headed north, reaching the mouth of the Richelieu and marching up the St. Lawrence's south bank to Longueuil, where he linked up with Major John Brown, who had arrived from the opposite direction. The Continentals now dominated the entire south shore region west from the mouth of the Richelieu.[39]

―――――

At the start of the Canadian campaign, General Washington had warned Schuyler that his men needed "strict Discipline" as "the most certain Means" of reaching their ultimate goal: the "Friendship of the Canadians." As the Northern Army established itself in Quebec, it complied remarkably well; the principal cases of plundering were targeted specifically against loyalists. Near St-Jean, Colonel Bedel had "thirty Bostonians and three Canadians" remove all the furniture and animals from Moses Hazen's manor—that seigneur's loyalist stance apparently having been confirmed when he was taken into the fort; troops maliciously vandalized his property as well. Livingston's Pointe-Olivier patriots likewise ransacked Fleury-Deschambault's Longueuil manor and "carried off every thing of value"; this was the same lord whose arrogance sparked that seigneury's summer rebellion. A few lesser incidents were also focused on the property of "friends of government." Considering the Continentals' many minor indiscretions while passing through New York, their restraint in Quebec seems a testament to the officers' enforcement of discipline and understanding of the need for good Canadian relations.[40]

Governor Carleton faced a different sort of discipline problem; habitants still would not form as a militia. Priests took a prominent role in addressing this issue, yet incorrigible parishioners defied both the governor and the Church, arguing that they would not fight colonial brethren and that they considered themselves permanently relieved from armed duty once the militia was disbanded in the 1760s. With his progovernment stance, Bishop Briand became a prominent target of habitant ire; *Canadiens* wondered why the bishop had become the "General of the country," using religion as a tool to promote martial affairs. A chorus of popular songs rang out through the countryside mocking the bishop: "his avarice, his love of power," and his government salary. The widespread intransigence drove Briand to authorize the extreme punishment mentioned in his May mandates—an interdict for parishioners who deliberately strayed from the proper path. Some reluctantly returned to their duty; others pressed deeper in defiance of Church and State.[41]

The only place the King's friends showed any real strength was at Fort St-Jean, where the garrison defiantly lobbed cannon shells at the Continentals. Yet by 24 September, Montgomery reported that he had lost only one soldier to such fire. However, disease took its toll; almost five hundred soldiers followed General Schuyler's path and were medically evacuated to New York that month. A few deserters slipped into the enemy's fort too, starting with some Yorkers; others would follow.[42]

While Major Preston welcomed those deserters, he dealt with a more puzzling case in handling Moses Hazen. After Hazen's 18 September "capture," Preston was unsure whether the retired officer was a friend or a traitor. On 23 September, the major finally ordered *Canadien* volunteer Claude Lorimier to slip through enemy lines, escorting Hazen to Montréal, where the governor could judge the seigneur's true loyalties. Upon reaching the city, Hazen failed to convince Carleton of his commitment to the Crown and was imprisoned indefinitely.[43]

Two days later, the Continentals established their first artillery batteries outside Fort St-Jean. With the wet ground and persistent rain, this simple siege construction taxed the inexperienced rebels' capabilities. Guns finally opened fire late on 25 September. Although the first shells did little physical damage, they directly affected some *Canadien* volunteers' will to fight. The next day, six loyalists deserted the fort. Livingston's partisans captured and interrogated some of these men, who reported that "St. John's cannot hold out long." By their report, morale was low and many Canadians were looking for an opportunity to desert.[44]

=====

Continentals under Warner, Brown, and Allen continued to rove opposite Montréal for a few days, but for such dynamic and ambitious leaders, it was painful to stay put, with the lightly defended city so tantalizingly close. On 23 September, Allen and Brown conferred and determined to make an attempt on Montréal, without consulting General Montgomery or James Livingston. Allen would cross from Longueuil and form his detachment north of Montréal; Brown would bring two hundred men from Laprairie, landing to the south; and Thomas Walker would deliver hundreds of north-shore patriot habitant supporters. Combined, they would make themselves "masters of Montreal." Allen and Brown parted to prepare their men and gather more *Canadiens*.[45]

On the night of 24 September, Allen covertly crossed to the Island of Montréal. Accompanied by Duggan and Loiseau, he visited the city's northeastern "Quebec" Suburb, meeting with several patriot friends and arranging details for the coup. Amazingly, not a single loyalist reported the nocturnal liaison to the authorities. As a result of the meeting, the colonel decided to bring his eighty partisans and Continentals across the St. Lawrence that night, in three bateaux. On the morning of 25 September, Allen's men gathered north of the city, ready for action.[46]

That same morning, two unidentified Continental officers[47] visited Thomas Walker in his north-shore country home. The three had closed discussions before calling L'Assomption Militia-Captain Jean-Baptiste Bruyères. They asked him to assemble the local militia the following day and join the Montréal operation. Bruyères cooperated, anticipating that his men would help secure the city, not fight for it. There was one significant problem with this plan, though: Allen was already on the island, poised to attack and expecting four hundred *Canadiens* to join him. The L'Assomption militia however, was not told to cross until the next day—a fatal timing error. While the problem may have been caused by an error in communication, there is also a realistic possibility that the reckless and bold Allen intentionally crossed a day early, believing he could enter Montréal unopposed, based on prior promises that

PLACE D'ARMES.
GOV. CARLETON REVIEWING HIS TROOPS BEFORE ATTACKING ETHEN ALLEN AT LONGUE POINTE, 1775.

Governor Carleton Reviewing Troops in Montréal, Before Longue-Pointe Place d'Armes en 1775, artist unknown, undated. Bibliothèque et Archives nationales du Québec, Centre d'archives de Montréal, Collection Édouard-Zotique Massicotte, No. P750, Album 4-63A-a.

the city gates would simply be opened to the liberators and that he could gather all the glory for himself.[48]

John Brown did not cross the St. Lawrence to join Allen on 25 September either. Although Brown never mentioned the coordination breakdown, it seems likely that he was operating on the same timetable as the officers at L'Assomption, expecting to cross a day later. Loyalists reported the presence of Allen's force at mid-morning, still at a distance from Montréal. City guards closed the gates, and hundreds of citizens rallied to defend Montréal. Compromised and isolated, Allen sent express messengers to Brown and Walker calling for "speedy assistance."[49]

Governor Carleton roused the citizens; with a real threat at the gates, they seemed ready to protect their own property. The governor villainized the rebels as "a pack of Banditti, coming to plunder the Town." Quebec Indian Superintendent Major John Campbell led thirty-four British soldiers and two hundred citizen volunteers, 60 percent of whom were *Canadiens,* to face the rebels.[50]

Allen was shocked to see that an armed force was emerging from the city, instead of a friendly welcoming committee. He withdrew to "an advantageous spot of ground" closer to Longue-Pointe, since only half his men had muskets. The two forces collided near some farm buildings, fighting for about fifteen minutes before most of Allen's men "scamper'd towards the woods," as they were about to be surrounded — although some accounts maintained that the *Canadiens* abandoned Allen "on the first fire." Given that many were unarmed, flight in the face of determined resistance would be a measure of prudence rather than cowardice. Thirty-five diehards fought on for a few more minutes before surrendering.[51]

On the loyalist side, one soldier was killed and three were wounded, one mortally. The loyalists marched Allen and his ragtag survivors back to Montréal as prisoners: seventeen "Yankees" and sixteen *Canadiens*, ten of them wounded — and two of whom died shortly thereafter. Five patriot Canadians were already dead on the field of battle. Ethan Allen was put on board the Royal Navy ship *Gaspée*, his legs in irons. Both Duggan and Loiseau were among the Canadians escaping to fight another day, and Walker still remained at large. Hearing of Allen's defeat the next morning, Walker sent the L'Assomption men home, just as they prepared to cross to the island.[52]

In the Battle of Longue-Pointe, Canadians fought each other in significant numbers, and both sides' commitment was notable. Although the opposing parties each claimed that the enemy had paid off its *Canadien* supporters, it is unlikely that simple pillagers or pay seekers would have fought such an engagement. Instead, it seems there were core Canadian ideological and security issues at stake, the sort that might lead men to march into combat.

The immediate patriot reaction was that this "Rash Attack" might have catastrophic consequences for habitant support. Allen received "much censure" from fellow officers for his failed, uncoordinated enterprise. Montgomery lamented the "imprudence & ambition which urged him to this affair Single-handed when he might have had a considerable reinforcement."[53]

In Montréal, the Battle of Longue-Pointe brought about a "sudden revolution in the spirit of the inhabitants," who demonstrated newfound respect for government authority. Carleton ordered a militia levy of fifteen men per company, and some of the island's southwest parishes complied almost immediately; seigneurs were notably uninvolved with the process this time. Loyalists began to hope Quebec was "out of danger"; yet, while many habitants "return'd to their Duty," the governor lacked confidence in their "good will" and was reluctant to employ them en masse. On 30 September, he sent a sixty-man detachment across the river to raid a weakly defended rebel supply depot at Longueuil. Wearing traditional pale hooded *capots* and red *tuques,* a mixed force of regulars and militia seized 550 pounds of provisions and ammunition before expeditiously returning to the island. The rebels avoided a fight. With such a meek follow-up by Carleton, as the first snowflakes fell at September's end it became clear that the impact of Allen's Longue-Pointe defeat was more moderate than initial loyalist hopes or patriot fears imagined.[54]

=====

Back in Philadelphia, the Continental Congress had remained completely uninvolved in the Canadian campaign from the time Schuyler received his initial June orders until reconvening on 13 September. A week into the new session, delegates finally read Schuyler's first reports of the Canadian invasion. After another week of discussion, they sent the general their "Approbation" of his measures, specifically in securing Ile-aux-Noix as a barrier keeping royal ships from the lake; they were still unaware that Continental troops had since encircled Fort St-Jean and roamed the St. Lawrence's south banks. Congress offered the Northern Army no immediate guidance, military or political.[55]

Major-General Schuyler, however, was already raising pointed questions about the Canadian campaign's future. In a 19 September letter to Congress, he queried, "What kind of conduct am I to pursue with the Canadians respecting civil matters?" Militarily he wanted to know what troops would remain in Canada, how they would be supplied, and under what terms they would be engaged—well aware that the enlistments of his current force expired in a few short months. Equally aware that "paper, of any kind" did not have "the least currency in Canada," Schuyler inquired about silver or gold specie. These were critical questions, but the United Colonies' political leaders were desperately far behind their army's advances, with little hope of regaining the initiative. They would not even receive these pressing questions for another twenty days.[56]

General Montgomery pestered Schuyler about Canadian political concerns, warning that it was "almost time to think of Politicks." To help handle affairs in country, Montgomery begged for "three enlightened members of the Congress as a council immediately," lest he "should make any *faux pas.*" Schuyler forwarded this request for political guidance, which he "most sincerely" supported, and begged "the explicit directions of Congress" regarding his subordinate's concerns.[57]

Outside of Montgomery's Canadian headquarters, the widespread expectation was that the Northern Army would cease field operations in November, perhaps giving all parties time to adapt to the new situation over the winter. Forward-thinking patriots wondered if winter quarters could be established in Canada, even if Montréal were not captured. Similarly, loyalists imagined, "The season of the year" would "in a short time, oblige the rebels to leave the Country." However, developments would prove that revolutionary warriors such as Richard Montgomery and James Livingston were ready to eschew traditional seasonal warfare.[58]

In its first month in Quebec, the Northern Army had floundered—conducting two failed landings and suffering Allen's defeat at Longue-Pointe—yet Canadian patriot partisans not only remained steadfast, but grew stronger. Somewhere between one-in-four and one-in-seven lower Richelieu habitants joined the fight for liberty in September.[59] Based on the initial *Canadien* response in the Richelieu Valley, it seemed the United Colonies were not overreaching in their expectations that the Canadians were ready to embrace the patriot cause, if only given the opportunity.

Chapter 9

THE TREACHERY AND

VILLAINY OF THE CANADIANS

Collaboration, Resistance, and Siege in the Montreal District

What Contributed most to the loss of the Country is the treachery and
Villainy of the Canadians. | *Colonel Allan Maclean, Royal Highland Emigrants,
to Viscount Barrington, 20 November 1775*

After Ethan Allen's Longue-Pointe defeat, archradical Thomas Walker's
days were numbered. Interrogated after the battle, rebel prisoners implicated
Walker in the affair, describing his promise to join them with hundreds of
men. The governor made a minimally confrontational attempt to detain him,
sending a British Army officer to L'Assomption, directing the patriot agita-
tor's immediate return to Montréal—a demand that Walker "peremptorily
rejected."[1]

In response, Governor Carleton issued an official order to arrest Thomas
Walker for high treason, on 4 October 1775. He dispatched twenty regular
soldiers under Royal Highland Emigrants Lieutenant John McDonnell to
capture the traitor. They were escorted by L'Assomption's militia-captain,
Jean-Baptiste Bruyères, who was redeeming himself after giving a self-
incriminating deposition, which detailed the L'Assomption militia's failed role
in Allen's attempt on Montréal.[2]

In the dark morning hours of 5 October, the governor's party approached
Walker's fine country manor house; given the radical's reputation, the soldiers
and militia had good reason to expect trouble. As men surrounded his house,
Walker opened fire. Ducking from window to window, he met the soldiers
with well-aimed musket shots, wounding a few, including the lieutenant.
After shooting at the house with no result, McDonnell called for the torch.
The Walkers surrendered as flames forced them out a second-floor window.

A large party quickly escorted the couple to Montréal, where Martha was released and Thomas was confined in the barracks prison. Governor Carleton had finally silenced Quebec's most rabid and persistent patriot.[3]

=====

By the beginning of October, Continental officers noted that Canadian partisans "seemed to grow cool and fearful, & some went off and left the Army." To revitalize local support, General Montgomery and James Livingston developed an innovative plan to involve Canadians actively in the siege. On 3 October, Livingston led about 250 partisans to raise and man a battery near Moses Hazen's home, on the Richelieu east shore. Not only would this work expose the fort's east side and ships to direct fire, but the loyalist garrison would also clearly see the Canadians fighting them, directly across the river.[4]

When the digging began, Livingston feared his men would "drop off by degrees," especially since they were receiving only minimal rations on the isolated east bank. The patriot habitants, however, shined in their first combat test. On 4 October, the second day of battery construction, Major Preston sent a party of British troops to drive them off, employing their row galley armed with swivel guns[5] and cannon. In an hour-long fight, one partisan was wounded as the rebel *Canadiens* "stood their ground well"; the loyalists withdrew. The Canadians also repelled two "feeble" attempts in subsequent days.[6]

With Livingston occupied by the siege, Colonel Timothy Bedel assumed new responsibilities, handling partisan auxiliaries from his post north of the fort. One of Bedel's lieutenants observed, "The French are as much engaged as our people in the camp." This scale of local support prompted the New Hampshire colonel to request additional guidance on distributing provisions and muskets to his partners. Montgomery responded that *Canadien* patriot "friends must certainly be supported" with victuals, but was more cautious on issuing firearms. The Northern Army was already locally purchasing guns to arm partisans; to ensure that no dishonest habitants swindled the Continentals by selling their weapons and then requesting replacements gratis, Montgomery directed Bedel to consult Livingston or his deputy Duggan before dispensing guns.[7]

Montgomery focused his main army's efforts on improving the Fort St-Jean siege, ordering a new western battery, constructed on a slight rise, that offered better lines of fire into both redoubts. Inside the fort, loyalist *Canadien*

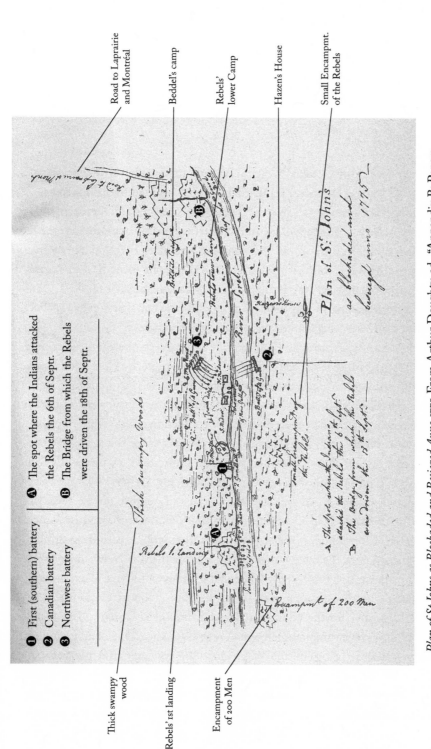

Legend (left):

① First (southern) battery
② Canadian battery
③ Northwest battery

Ⓐ The spot where the Indians attacked the Rebels the 6th of Septr.
Ⓑ The Bridge from which the Rebels were driven the 18th of Septr.

Road to Laprairie and Montréal

Beddel's camp

Rebels' lower Camp

Hazen's House

Small Encampmt. of the Rebels

Thick swampy wood

Rebels' 1st landing

Encampment of 200 Men

Plan of St Johns as Blockaded and Besieged Anno 1775. From Arthur Doughty, ed., "Appendix B: Papers Relating to the Surrender of St. Johns and Chambly," in *Report on the Works of the Public Archives for the Years 1914 and 1915* (Ottawa: L. Taché, 1916).

commitment wavered further. Some volunteers doubted their contribution to the defense and asked Major Preston's permission to leave the fort. The major reassured them of their value, yet on 5 October, three more volunteers "left quietly in the night."[8]

In the first week of October, General Montgomery discovered that one of Montréal's leading citizens, St-Luc de La Corne, wanted to open secret negotiations. La Corne, a rich sixty-four-year-old seigneur and merchant, had a reputation as a demonic "villain" in Continental circles, based on his role as an Indian officer in the last war, including the legendary Fort William Henry Massacre. This new "traitorous" overture was surprising given St-Luc's close administration ties: he was father-in-law to Indian Superintendent John Campbell and had personally joined Carleton in London, shaping the Quebec Act. But La Corne was a notorious conniver and schemer.[9]

Back in late September, as Continentals appeared on the south shore opposite Montréal and before the Battle of Longue-Pointe, La Corne and seven or eight prominent *Canadiens* asked Caughnawaga friends to carry a message to the rebel commander: the "nobility of Montreal city" were prepared to make peace with the rebels and "not interfere anymore," while begging forgiveness for past actions. It took almost two weeks for the message to be delivered, however. When the Caughnawagas presented La Corne's offer on 4 October, Continental officers were suspicious, but General Montgomery still offered to have an envoy meet La Corne at Laprairie on the seventh. John Brown would lead Continental negotiations, accompanied by James Livingston. Montgomery prepared detailed instructions, including diverse negotiating points, the most notable of which was that the New Subject elite should promise not to obstruct "the establishment of a free Government in Canada" and that citizens must be permitted to "choose Committees to depute Delegates for the Continental and a Provincial Congress," so Canada could join "that union which will . . . establish the rights of all Colonies on a firm basis"—a significant insight into the general's strategic goals in Quebec.[10]

This opportunity to co-opt the "French" elite "ended in Smoke." With growing government support in the aftermath of the Longue-Pointe victory, La Corne reconsidered his position and decided to hand Montgomery's written response to the governor. Carleton demonstrated his policy for rebel communications by destroying the correspondence unopened; the executioner was called to tread upon the letter before casting it into the fire with tongs. When Montgomery heard the result, he supposed the governor was "afraid of making a discovery which would have obliged him to treat St. Luke roughly."[11]

La Corne was not the only Canadian to rally to the Union Jack after Longue-Pointe. Sixty-seven Old Subject Montrealers published a resolution on 2 October, declaring their loyalty and explicit opposition to rebel "Invaders" and their Canadian accomplices. That same week, loyalist militia also began arriving from the south shore, including Sorel and St-Ours. The parish of Varennes, ten miles downstream from Montréal, was particularly dedicated; instead of bringing a quota, the entire three-hundred-man militia reported to the governor. Soon, more than twelve hundred habitants, six hundred city militia, and a few hundred Indians congregated in the city, anticipating Carleton's imminent orders to cross the river and cast out the rebels; instead, they sat.[12]

While several parishes near Montréal swiftly supported the governor's October militia mobilization, many refused to comply. Richelieu patriot partisans promoted resistance, advising regional parishes not to heed the call-up; by their account, the *Bastonnais* had proven their intent to liberate Quebec's habitants from oppression and not to harm them. Most parishes quietly failed to send militia to join the governor.[13]

Berthier-en-haut's habitants provided more blatant opposition. Initially, that parish had gathered its levy; but their seigneur, Legislative Councilor James Cuthbert, had arrived and arrogantly demanded that the entire parish, not just a quota, march to Montréal. Still angry with Cuthbert for his attempt to mobilize them the past summer, the entire parish defiantly refused service; instead of fifteen men, he would have none.[14]

Shortly thereafter, Governor Carleton's aide-de-camp Charles-Louis Tarieu-de-Lanaudière stumbled into trouble in Berthier as well. Lanaudière and Joseph-Marie de Tonnancour, son of the Trois-Rivières militia-colonel, gathered militia quotas from parishes in their family seigneuries — including Ste-Anne-de-la-Pérade, Yamachiche, Lac-Maskinongé, and Rivière-du-Loup — as well as Nicolet parish and Trois-Rivières city. This combined force of about one hundred militiamen marched to Montréal to receive weapons and join government service.[15]

When the lightly armed militia party approached Berthier on the King's Way, it was trapped in the woods by a band of parish habitants under Militia-Captain Hardoin Merlet. Tonnancour and Lanaudière were disarmed and detained; their militiamen fled when given the opportunity. The rebellious Berthier men threatened to deliver their prominent prisoners to the *Bastonnais,* until a priest intervened and convinced Merlet to release them — on the two conditions that Lanaudière would never return to Berthier for militia mobilization, and that he would obtain a governor's pardon for the parish.[16]

Elsewhere in Three Rivers District, prior to the Berthier event, south-shore Nicolet initially refused the militia levy as well. On 8 October, Militia-Colonel Louis-Joseph Godefroy-de-Tonnancour[17] sent his son Chevalier Charles-Antoine, along with notary Jean-Baptiste Badeaux, to encourage parishioners to meet their quota. Many habitants resisted the call to assemble, some telling messengers to "go to the devil." When a few gathered as an audience, the twenty-year-old nobleman courteously addressed them about responsibilities and obligations, and the consequences of rebellious behavior. Finally, ten men — of a fifteen-man quota — agreed to join the militia assembling at Trois-Rivières. The young Tonnancour coaxed Nicolet into a degree of cooperation, although these men soon returned home after Merlet's rebels blocked their march in the Berthier event.[18]

The parish was revisited by the King's officers within a week of Tonnancour's visit, however. Marching his Royal Highland Emigrants toward the Richelieu from Québec City, Colonel Allan Maclean heard of Nicolet's generally defiant spirit and decided to apply a martial solution to the problem. Crossing to the south shore, Maclean led a party of Emigrants and cooperative Trois-Rivières militiamen to arrest parish resistance leader Joseph Rouillard, but found only his wife at home. Suspecting Rouillard was hiding nearby, Maclean threatened to burn the house down; yet when it was apparent the wanted man would not be flushed out, the colonel extinguished the torch.

Meanwhile, habitants gathered on a Nicolet River island, armed to oppose Maclean's "fire and sword" demands. Hearing of this rebellious assembly, the bitter Scots colonel decided to challenge them all, leading the Emigrants toward the isle. Upon seeing the King's provincials approaching, the *Canadiens* dispersed into the woods, as if chased by the devil himself. Maclean's application of force was radically less effective than the younger Tonnancour's friendly speech, pushing Nicolet habitants firmly into the rebel camp, rather than gathering support.[19]

=======

Back in Montréal, restless loyalists were vexed by Carleton's inactivity. In particular, the dedicated Varennes militia begged for action, fearing rebels would burn their farms while they sat in the city. The governor, lacking confidence in the militia's commitment and resilience, persistently replied that it was "not yet time, but that they would soon cross."[20]

Without leave, a few rural militiamen departed from the city on account of boredom, anxiety for their homes, or needing to till their fields before snow covered the landscape. Although the governor seemed ambivalent about militia desertions, on 14 October he issued a proclamation requiring all militia officers to use nonmobilized parish men to tend the fields of those currently in arms. It removed the primary militia excuse for absconding, but the real impact was imperceptible.[21]

Finally, on 15 October, Carleton acquiesced to the pressure for action, sending a mission to south bank Verchères, roughly opposite L'Assomption. The target parish had failed to provide its militia quota, and the governor received intelligence that rebel partisans threatened its few staunch loyalists. Carleton would make a show of force, helping the habitants of Verchères to "return to their duty" and reassuring them that "they need not fear abuse" from a few wandering rebels.[22]

Carleton gave an experienced *Canadien* military man, Legislative Councilor Jean-Baptiste-Marie Bergères-de-Rigauville,[23] command of two hundred militiamen for the mission. The detachment cast off in eight bateaux on 15 October, but took three days to reach Verchères, only twenty miles away with the current. In passing downriver, they exchanged fire with Warner's Continentals at Longueuil. When Rigauville's task force reached Verchères, it was not welcomed; many habitants fled, fearing the King's men had come "to wage war against them." When Rigauville interviewed some locals, he was told the parishioners had no intention of taking up arms. The force might as well return to Montréal; if it did not, patriot parishioners would call the Continentals to drive the loyalist force out. Rigauville scoffed at the warnings, opting to spend the night in the parish.[24]

The loyalist commander took minimal security precautions, posting only a small guard before retiring for the evening. He had a "splendid" supper in a local home, allegedly going to bed drunk. With no real order, his men dispersed throughout the parish to find accommodations, some a mile away. Well before dawn on 18 October, three score of Warner's Continentals entered the parish, marching from Longueuil with local partisan guides. A single sentry raised the alarm, triggering a chaotic scramble; loyalist militiamen scurried for bateaux and rowed to a nearby Laurentian island for shelter. Rigauville stepped out to see what was happening, dressed only in pants, and was captured by the patriot raiders. He and one Verchères loyalist were taken to St-Jean as prisoners of war.[25]

In Montréal, the affair further discouraged loyalists and increased habitant militia disenchantment. Small groups immediately began to slip out of the city; ten rural *Canadiens* left the first day, with thirty or forty per day thereafter. There was a different effect in the Continental camp. General Schuyler considered the skirmish encouraging, a further indication of the Canadians' "friendly Disposition," of which he was still unsure.[26]

For the past few weeks, Northern Army soldiers had been making friends and becoming familiar with "alien" Canadian culture throughout the patriot-occupied triangle bounded by St-Jean, Laprairie, and Sorel. Despite the language barrier, it seemed that whenever Yankees and Yorkers were hosted in a habitant home, they were eagerly regaled with the best fare the family had to offer; many *Canadiens* proudly demonstrated their English vocabulary, which inevitably included a new word, *liberty*. In return, the Continentals generally regarded habitants as peers, in contrast to the characteristically arrogant British military treatment to which the Canadians were accustomed. This mutual respect certainly encouraged rebel tolerance of the radically different religious practices they observed in Quebec. Fervent Protestant Continentals marveled at the ubiquitous roadside crosses and the "follies their absurd religion calls upon them to attend" in Mass; yet there were very few, if any, overt insults to a religion the liberating invaders considered "superstitious" and fundamentally errant.[27]

Civility and religious respect were two legs of a critical triad of good Canadian-Continental relations. The third was respect for property; the *Bastonnais* were not looting or foraging. The one exception continued to be retributive pillaging against loyalists, as seen in Verchères loyalist François Maillot's "punishment" after Rigauville's defeat; Continentals occupied his home and stole his goods. Through such behavior, the patriots punished enemies, but gave friendly and neutral habitants little reason to fear for their own property.[28]

In addition, Northern Army officers were ordered to pay for everything they needed in the field, ensuring local support. General Montgomery was ill equipped to sustain this policy though, hard cash being "very scarce." Aware of the *Canadien* dread of paper money, the general prioritized payments; specie was to be spent only on provisions. Other "necessaries"—clothing, equipment or transportation—were purchased with credit or Continental bills. It was not yet a crisis, but General Schuyler already had warned Congress that "the want of specie will be fatal to us," even "should every thing else go well."[29]

By mid-October, Montgomery felt increasing pressure in his own camp. Impertinent Continentals were unhappy with the "present confined state of operations" and demanded "to know the reason of every maneuvre." The general was equally displeased with his "unstable" authority over the men; yet he continued to press Fort St-Jean. He brought more guns into the fight and added another battery on the east bank under New York Major Zedwitz, south of the Canadian emplacement.[30]

Resentment simmered as the days grew shorter and colder, the terms of enlistment rapidly wound down, and the siege showed no real progress. Yorkers and New Englanders chafed on each other. Officers squabbled. Montgomery tried to avoid "disgusting the New Englanders by any partiality to New Yorkers," while begging Schuyler for more Yorkers, as "they don't melt away so fast as their eastern Neighbours." Meanwhile, Yankees such as Colonel Samuel Mott held "no great opinion" of Montgomery's generalship. The general was also frustrated by the "shocking embezzlement" of goods captured from loyalist convoys, which simply disappeared, especially ammunition, provisions, and clothing, which were so precious to the army.[31]

On 13 October, Major Brown finally confronted General Montgomery about the Northern Army's "general dissatisfaction." Without some change, he loyally cautioned that the brigadier faced a mutiny in the next few days. The general called a council of war to address the myriad issues. Senior officers supported continuing the siege, yet Montgomery remained pessimistic, skeptical even of taking Fort St-Jean. Further complicating matters, the artillery was running short of powder and ammunition; however, James Livingston and the *Canadien* partisans proposed a new operation.[32]

Livingston had long eyed Fort Chambly. The isolated strongpoint was not a significant threat, but it seemed a tempting target for a patriot coup, a concept Livingston proposed to Montgomery in late September. Now, with a growing shortage of gunpowder and shells, the plan gained energy; the fort held significant quantities of "warlike stores" to meet pressing Continental needs. Montgomery agreed to support the fort's capture, but Livingston was preoccupied at the Canadian siege battery; John Brown and Jeremiah Duggan were delegated command of the Chambly mission. The duo refined the tactical plan while Livingston coordinated the delivery of two artillery pieces down the Chambly rapids, a mission further facilitated when the moored British schooner *Royal Savage* finally was "sunk up to her ports," on 16 October. Brown brought fifty Continentals, while Duggan led about three hundred *Canadien* patriots; in this operation, the Northern Army was auxiliary to the Canadians.[33]

Fort Chambly seemed impressive from the outside, "having the appearance of a castle." The stone walls were deceptive, intended only as a defense against Indian attacks; they could not withstand cannon fire, even from the relatively small Continental guns sent by Livingston. The fort was occupied by eighty-three British troops under Major Joseph Stopford, and also housed a disproportionate number of civilians, including many Fort St-Jean soldiers' families.[34]

The ensuing battle was short; Canadians and Continentals surrounded the fort and cannon began playing on the walls around 2 A.M. on 17 October. Shells soon "made a Breach into the thin Walls." Even though neither side had suffered a casualty, Major Stopford offered to capitulate the next day, unaware that the rebels were almost out of shot. Symbolically, Brown offered to have Livingston sign the capitulation; the recently arrived Canadian declined, "considering himself as a Volunteer," not an official officer. Partisans and Continentals occupied the fort on 19 October and immediately forwarded gunpowder to Montgomery. The *Canadiens* were authorized to take all the fort's muskets.[35]

In addition to providing much-needed gunpowder, Fort Chambly's conquest fired up Continental morale. Now Montgomery ventured that "unless some unlucky accident befalls us we shall accomplish our Business here." On 21 October, the general sent a flag of truce, requesting unhindered passage for vessels carrying Fort Chambly families and prisoners' baggage upriver to Lake Champlain, and conveniently advertising the recent victory. Preston agreed to the transit; and within two hours, a parade of bateaux passed, reminding Fort St-Jean's defenders that they were the last loyalists on the south shore, and for some, that their families were in rebel hands.[36]

French Fort at Chambly (detail). Library and Archives Canada, Acc. No. R9266-55, Peter Winkworth Collection of Canadiana.

Somewhat surprisingly, Fort Chambly's capture sparked a spat in the Canadian partisan camp. Livingston arrived at the fort at the time of surrender and was surprised to see patriot *Canadiens* rifling through the prisoners' baggage, unaware that Duggan had condoned it. In the process, he found that Brown and Montgomery had corresponded about the division of spoils, excluding him from the conversation. After a month and a half of constantly draining, dynamic operations, Livingston had a momentary breakdown; he was convinced that Duggan was jealously conspiring against him and that his Continental friends had turned on him. He threatened to retire. Fortunately for the Canadian patriots, the episode quickly passed, and the men reconciled. Coincidentally, when word of Fort Chambly's fall reached the United Colonies, Brown's role was widely advertised, but Rhode Island's Congressional delegation was astute enough to comment that the report did not "do justice to Maj[o]r Livingston and 300 Canadians."[37]

Fort Chambly's fall also seemed to assure Fort St-Jean's surrender. On 27 October, Montgomery ordered a new battery north of the fort, in part to prevent a frequently rumored garrison breakout. Just as had been done for Chambly, some "trusty Canadians" took two cannon downriver past the fort at night. Once the battery was established, Montgomery planned to move almost the entire army there; troops south of the fort were increasingly irrelevant.[38]

With detachments spread down the Richelieu, at Longueuil and Laprairie, and most recently at the Caughnawaga Indian village, Montgomery counted only 750 Continentals at the siege. Weighing the possibility of crossing to the Island of Montréal soon, he hoped for more men. On 27 October, he received his first reinforcements in weeks: additional New York troops and the First Connecticut Regiment of 335 men, under General David Wooster.[39]

This regiment spent the summer guarding the New York coast, where they transitioned from Connecticut-provincial to Continental service; and with new orders to head north, only General Wooster and a couple of officers expressed any interest in venturing across Lake Champlain. Many of the Yankee soldiers were anxious about how the transfer to Continental duty would affect them, and they feared being stuck in the province all winter, well past their original enlistments, where they would die of cold or sickness. Eventually 150 were discharged or held at Ticonderoga, sick or "sham sick"; their elderly general skillfully chided and cajoled the rest into committing to a Canadian campaign.[40]

Washington and Schuyler actually feared Brigadier-General Wooster would be a disruptive influence in the Northern Army command; but his troops were needed and would not deploy without him. The old Connecticut general, a seasoned colonial war veteran, had been cantankerous in adapting to Continental service as well. In the summer of 1775, he was particularly miffed to receive a Continental brigadier's rank, a step down from his Connecticut major-general status. At one point, he even returned his brigadier's commission to the Continental Congress.[41]

Schuyler sent Wooster north only after a terse exchange, explicitly confirming that the Yankee brigadier would not contest Montgomery's command. Once the Connecticut regiment arrived in Canada, Montgomery, senior in rank but a quarter century younger than Wooster, deliberately showed the elder officer the utmost respect, offering to take his advice "as a son would that of his father." Within a couple of days, after letting the Connecticut brigadier lead the main transfer of troops to the new north batteries, Montgomery reported that Wooster was highly cooperative, while the Connecticut regimental chaplain observed "great Harmony" between the generals. The younger New

York brigadier had ulterior motives, though; Montgomery was seeking his own replacement, deciding that he had neither the "talents nor temper for such a command," being forced to act "totally out of character to wheedle flatter & Lie" to accommodate the free-spirited Continental soldiers. Montgomery hoped to resign whenever circumstances permitted him to do so honorably.[42]

Meanwhile, in Montréal, committed loyalists were exasperated by Carleton's persistent passivity following the Verchères incident. Continentals further provoked them, marching between Laprairie and Longueuil on a daily basis, shooting muskets, and playing fifes and drums "in mockery of the city." The city's Tory hawks begged for an opportunity to seize Longueuil. The governor vented some pressure by authorizing frequent scouting cruises along the south bank, yet specifically ordered participants not to fire on the rebels, to preclude engagements. The missions also kept the Continentals vigilant and poised to respond to a landing-in-force, and it resulted in additional reinforcements being sent to join Warner in anticipation of a decisive assault.[43]

On 26 October, Carleton escalated his activities, gathering three hundred militiamen and asking if they would join in a descent on Longueuil. They enthusiastically scrambled for bateaux and launched into the river. Approaching the southern banks, loyalists peppered Continentals with bateaux-mounted swivel guns and received return musket fire. After a few such exchanges over a couple of hours, the governor recalled his boats to Montréal, sorely disappointing his supporters, who did not get to set foot on rebel-occupied land. While it was another half-measure, it appeared that Carleton might be preparing a major south-shore operation.[44]

Finally, on 30 October, Carleton declared his intention to cross to Longueuil, relieve Major Preston at Fort St-Jean, and unite with a column on the Richelieu under Colonel Maclean. The governor commanded 600 citizen and habitant militiamen, 80 Indians, and 130 British redcoats in the landing operation. His second-in-command, elected among the *Canadiens*, was Claude Lorimier, the same loyalist who had brought Moses Hazen out of blockaded Fort St-Jean. The force embarked in forty boats, equipped with a few light cannon and swivel guns, as a host of Montrealers gathered to watch the spectacle.[45]

A rebel force, less than half the loyalist strength, waited on the far banks. From the old turreted French "stone château," Fort Longueuil, Colonel Seth Warner commanded roughly three hundred troops, a mix of Green Mountain Boys and Second Regiment Yorkers, with a single artillery piece — recently arrived from Chambly. South-shore habitants, while friendly to the Continentals, abstained from taking an active role in the coming battle.[46]

Around noon, Longueuil's Continental garrison saw the armada headed toward its position; every man was called to arms. Warner moved most of his troops south of town when it appeared that the loyalists intended to land there, keeping only thirty men and the cannon at the fort. The Continentals met the first scout boats with steady fire, driving them back to the middle of the St. Lawrence.[47]

Governor Carleton sent his flotilla back upriver toward Ile-Ste-Hélène, a low island above Longueuil. Through miscommunication, three Indian- and Canadian-manned boats landed at the island. By mid-afternoon, the most spirited men waded through the shallow, rocky shoals separating the island from the south shore. The Continentals laid down a hail of musket fire, pinning the loyalists behind islets and rocks. Meanwhile, the governor ordered another move downriver to attempt a landing near Fort Longueuil, which he now perceived was weakly defended; yet the few Continentals there fended off approaching bateaux long enough for Warner to march and join them, opening a "perpetual firing" between the boats and the shore. When Warner deployed his single cannon, unleashing grapeshot on the exposed attackers, Carleton conceded and withdrew the entire expedition. The mission was a colossal failure.[48]

The Continentals mopped up the Indians and Canadians left between Ile-Ste-Hélène and the riverbank. When darkness fell, Warner's men captured two *Canadiens* there and found three Indians: two dead and one mortally wounded. Perhaps fifty other loyalists had been killed or wounded in the boats during the day's battle; the sole rebel casualty suffered an inconsequential flesh wound. Aided by Carleton's indecisive leadership, Warner's Continentals achieved a significant victory.[49]

In early October, Carleton had also ordered Colonel Allan Maclean to establish a loyalist camp in Sorel, at the mouth of the Richelieu. The colonel marched about one hundred Royal Highland Emigrants from Québec City to that destination, recruiting on the way with limited success. Maclean crossed the St. Lawrence from Trois-Rivières to Nicolet, where he made his fruitless mid-October attempt to force militia mobilization. After marching to Sorel—a port-village of about fifty houses—the force met an armed schooner and two cargo boats carrying sixty British regulars, as well as guns to arm the valley. At first, Maclean seemed successful, issuing weapons to five hundred habitant militiamen in the first week. Then, in the last week of October, Carleton notified the colonel that the Montréal corps was ready to cross to Longueuil. Maclean marshaled his task force and led it up the Richelieu, to link up with the governor's column and relieve Fort St-Jean.[50]

James Livingston and Jeremiah Duggan were already well prepared to meet the advancing loyalist brigade, as partisans had destroyed the low bridges spanning the innumerable streams feeding the lower Richelieu. In St-Marc, roughly midway between Sorel and Chambly, the Chambly patriot cell's summer chairman, Dominique Mondelet, gathered intelligence and provisions. Captain Augustin Loiseau rallied additional habitants, bringing Livingston's lower Richelieu partisan strength to more than five hundred—on a par with Maclean's loyalist *Canadien* militia. Montgomery augmented Livingston with about three hundred Continentals under Massachusetts Colonel James Easton.[51]

As Maclean moved up the Richelieu, he immediately experienced a desertion problem. After receiving the King's muskets and ammunition, habitant militiamen disappeared in alarming numbers. News of Fort Chambly's fall may have had some impact, but it was widely suspected that the patriots sent men to join Maclean just long enough to be issued arms, and then "desert" back to the "*Bastonnais* camp." Even more alarming for the colonel, a few Royal Highland Emigrants fled as well.[52]

It took Maclean's force three days to move eighteen miles from Sorel to St-Denis, "disturbed" en route by Richelieu partisans. At that point, Maclean received orders to abandon his mission; Carleton had failed to land at Longueuil. Word in the province was that, upon "Colonel Maclean's party hearing of [Carleton's] repulse, his Canadians all left him and retired to their homes." General Montgomery chose to believe that Maclean's militiamen fled because they had joined the loyalists only "through fear of fire and sword." Maclean's Highlander and redcoat cadre returned to Sorel, embarking on the ships, some heading to Montréal and others to Québec City.[53]

While cleaning up the lower Richelieu, Livingston captured the St-Ours militia-captain, whose name was not recorded, and sent him to Montgomery; the *Canadien* prisoner was guilty of leading his militiamen to join Maclean, despite having sworn to support the patriot partisans. Livingston was infuriated by this "notorious villain," telling Montgomery that "hanging is too good for the rascal." The partisan commander's emotionally charged response implied that this sort of "closet loyalist" behavior was highly unusual in the valley.[54]

Richelieu patriots exacted local vengeance on other individuals who supported Maclean, as well. Captains Duggan, Loiseau, and Jean-Baptiste Allin were the instigators in a handful of documented acts. Minor offenses included forcing loyalists to sell goods at reduced prices, and emptying liquor stores. More drastic impositions included seizing goods without payment and forcing people from their homes. These acts seemed more reckless than previous ones, yet still targeted loyalists, who suffered property loss, not physical harm.[55]

━━━━━

At Fort St-Jean, a midday flag of truce interrupted the exchange of fire on 1 November. Major Preston permitted a blindfolded man to approach the redoubts, bearing a message from General Montgomery. The messenger was Mr. La Coste, one of the two Canadians captured by Warner's troops after the Battle of Longueuil.[56]

Preston read Montgomery's letter, which informed the major of Carleton's failed relief and requested the fort's surrender. General Montgomery warned that if the siege continued, "I will assemble the Canadians, and shall deem myself innocent of the melancholy consequences which may attend it." It is unclear whether the general was implying merely that he would be reinforced by added habitant manpower to storm the fort, or if it were an odd twist of frontier siege conventions that frequently threatened unrestrained Indian ravages if a post failed to yield on demand.[57]

Preston called for a cease-fire, promising to respond formally the next morning. On the second, Preston made a typical defender's last-ditch counteroffer. To begin with, he questioned La Coste's credibility—the man was reputedly "subject to fits of insanity"—but agreed to surrender if no attempt were made to relieve the fort in four days. In reference to Montgomery's "Canadian threat," Preston added, "In whatever way the fate of this garrison may be determined, I flatter myself it will never depend on the assembling of Canadians, who must have rendered themselves equally contemptible to both parties."[58]

The Continental general was impatient—enlistments were running out and winter fast approaching—so he provided an ultimatum. This was the garrison's last chance to negotiate a conditional surrender. Jean-Baptiste Despins, the other loyalist prisoner of war from Longueuil, was permitted to speak with a garrison parley, confirming La Coste's account. Seeing that his time was up, with no relief in sight, his fort increasingly shattered, and only a week's reduced rations left, Preston agreed to surrender with honors and with his troops' baggage secured. He sought to have *Canadien* volunteers sent home, but Montgomery insisted they be treated as part of the garrison. The two officers agreed to terms that evening.[59]

At 8 A.M. on 3 November, Preston formally surrendered Fort St-Jean along with almost seven hundred soldiers, volunteers, militiamen, sailors, and carpenters (and fifty women), concluding the "most tedious seige of 45 days." The loyalist garrison had lost twenty killed and twenty-three wounded in the course of the campaign. There is not a single-source record of patriot losses, but they were comparable. Upon entering the fort, Montgomery also recovered six Northern Army deserters, who were subsequently sentenced to death.[60] The general rushed to send out official letters reporting the good news, but he also was not one to rest on his accomplishments, planning to "proceed immediately to Montreal." That very day, carts rolled up and down the Laprairie road carrying Northern Army equipment and baggage to the banks of the St. Lawrence.[61]

Montgomery also requested new troops from General Schuyler; his men's enlistments were rapidly expiring. Schuyler had already raised this and numerous other issues with Congress. In a mid-September rapid-fire string of queries, the major-general again begged for details on the future shape of the Northern Army in Canada, its men and provisions, as well as plans "to defend that Province against any attacks that may be made on it in the ensuing year." Schuyler urged the immediate deployment of three thousand men to winter in Quebec; "so large a body of troops" would help the Canadians commit to "act with vigour and spirit, next year," when the Ministry would certainly attempt to recover the province. He also asked a most critical question: who was going to determine the "mode of government" for Canada, to prevent "anarchy and confusion." Regarding the Continental command in Canada, Schuyler advised that the best candidate was "the gentleman who now commands the Army there, if he will remain"; yet Montgomery still longed to resign and return to New York.[62]

In sum, the Northern Army's Canadian campaign seemed to have paid off. The Chambly patriots were liberated, the southern gateway to Quebec Province was open, and Montréal might fall in a matter of days. More important, during Montgomery's deliberate advance, very few "common" Canadians seriously opposed Northern Army operations. Although the royal governor drew a significant number of habitants to arms in Montréal, he failed to bring them to battle in any numbers; meanwhile, James Livingston's *Canadien* patriots, numbering in the hundreds, were firmly united with the patriot cause and closely integrated with Continental operations. Other less zealous Canadians, hesitant to commit to either party, seemed satisfied to supply the *Bastonnais* as long as they were paid in hard cash. Summarizing the Richelieu Valley campaign, Colonel Allan Maclean offered his opinion on the source of the government defeat: "it's a certain fact that 2000 of those fellows [Continentals] never could have done us any mischief had they not been joined by the Canadians"; while Governor Carleton abjectly mused, "The entrenched Camps that might have been formed near Chambly & St. John's, were effectually prevented by the corruption, & I may add, by the stupid baseness of the Canadian Peasantry."[63]

Chapter 10

ANOTHER PATH TO THE
HEART OF QUEBEC

*Canada's Capital, Hannibal's Heir,
and the Kennebec Expedition*

Matters grew daily worse & worse; the insolence of the habitants was insufferable. | *Loyalist account from Québec City, in the "Journal of the Most Remarkable Events Which Happened in Canada"*

The inhabitants have been very kind to us since we have been among them. | *Rhode Island soldier Caleb Haskell, Chaudière Valley, 8 November 1775*

Meanwhile, far from the rebel Northern Army, Quebec and Three Rivers Districts demonstrated their own share of resistance and rebellion, with habitants opposing both government orders and Church authority. The first downstream resistance sprang up just as the rebel army made its second landing near Fort St-Jean; yet its origins were entirely local. On 11 September, seigneur and retired Major Henry Caldwell led a small party across the St. Lawrence to the south-shore ferry point of Pointe-Lévy (see Map 5), intending to raise a militia corps to help drive the rebels from St-Jean. Pointe-Lévy sat in one of several seigneuries that the forty-year-old Caldwell acquired after the Conquest. Coincidentally, his most prominent companion on the mission was fellow seigneur Gabriel-Elzéar Taschereau, whose nearby Nouvelle-Beauce seigneury had resisted Carleton's first mobilization efforts in May.[1]

The seigneurs reached the south shore and initially believed they were going to mobilize a thousand men. By the next day, their hopes were dashed. A cadre of eight rebellious *Canadiens* rallied locals against the call-up and requested support from downstream parishes. A large portion of the Pointe-Lévy militia, perhaps a hundred men, formed a "Seditious Assembly," in

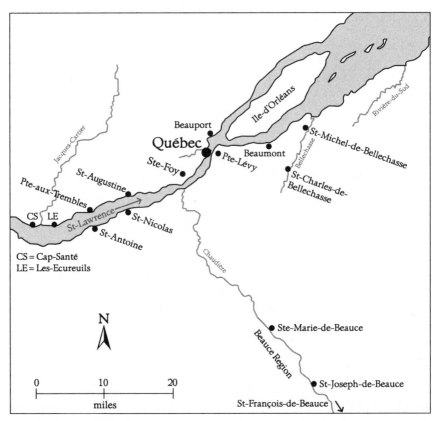

MAP 5: Upper Quebec District.

which they sought "to strengthen each other's resolve not to take up arms for the government." Within twenty-four hours, four hundred habitants from nine different parishes gathered from as far as thirty miles away. Many were unarmed; the "assembly" was as much a political demonstration as it was a show of force. The habitants "abused" Caldwell, Taschereau, and their cohorts and drove them off; the seigneurs returned to the capital "without a man."[2]

The south-shore habitants realized that the government forces might return to suppress the little rebellion, so men from fourteen parishes stood guard "to resist the government's punishment that they feared they might receive," not just at Pointe-Lévy, but also in nearby parishes such as Beaumont, St-Michel, and Montmagny. Within a fortnight, the last militiaman stood down as the government's impotence became obvious.[3]

Nearby Ile-d'Orléans had its own "Seditious" response to militia mobilization. That long island, about five miles downstream from Quebec City, splits a twenty-mile stretch of the St. Lawrence. Its riverbank grain fields were easily discerned from the capital, and five island parishes formed "a most beautiful prospect, a clear open country, with villages, and churches innumerable . . . all whitewashed on the outside." In October, Lieutenant-Governor Cramahé sent a committee, consisting of councilor Judge Adam Mabane, wealthy Scots merchant-seigneur William Grant, and Court Clerk Nicolas-Gaspard Boisseau, to command the island militia levies. Mabane's arrogance immediately rankled patriot-inclined habitants; soon a mob of 250 islanders, armed with sticks, threatened to beat the officers if they did not depart immediately. The loyalist party sensibly fled.[4]

In addition to militia-levy resistance, there was an ideological struggle under way in the Quebec District as well. Parish agitators beat the drum for the patriot cause: men such as Chateau-Richer innkeeper Pierre Gravel, who "used his house to hold meetings to foster the spirit of rebellion," and women such as Augustin Chabot's wife, on Ile-d'Orléans, who "perverted" "almost all the people" in St-Pierre parish "by spreading her seditious remarks as she went door to door" politicizing the normally docile countryside. Many parishes had counterparts to Gravel and Chabot.[5]

Churches became a scene of conflict as well. Some of it was subtle, such as in Trois-Rivières, where a few parishioners admitted they had asked God "that the 'Bostonians' should win" when Vicar-General St-Ongé led prayers for "victory." In several parishes, though, outspoken individuals raucously challenged the Church's overt and unconditional support of controversial government policies.[6]

The single most egregious act of defiance was an outburst in St-Michel-de-Bellechasse during the late September St. Michael's Day Mass. A guest priest's sermon on "the obedience owed to temporal powers" was shouted down by an unidentified parishioner who exclaimed that "there had been too much preaching for the English." The parish's infuriated *curé* immediately reported the event to the bishop, who was equally irate. Briand demanded to know the insolent habitant's identity. If the individual could not be identified, St-Michel and the neighboring parishes would be cast under a collective proscription until the affair was resolved; the Church moved beyond general threats and prepared to impose specific interdicts in an attempt to reform rebellious souls. Under his episcopal authority, Briand would forbid intractable parishioners access to the sacraments until they reformed their ways; for committed Catholics, this was a tremendous deterrence, as it would remove them from the principal practices of their faith.[7]

Less than a month later, Briand provided a similar response to an incident in St-Thomas-de-Montmagny, where the parishioners blatantly opposed their priest's call to support the militia quota. The bishop specifically spelled out the details of their proscription: no marriage without an oath of obedience, no baptism or communion "without retraction and public restitution for the scandal," no burial of defiant Catholics on sacred ground, and even entrance to the church was forbidden. As an extra measure, the church would be locked, except for Mass, denying rebellious parishioners an opportunity to subvert the faith by holding unsanctioned services without their priest.[8]

Viewing the situation across Quebec, Bishop Briand claimed that resistance to Church authority was so widespread that almost the entire diocese deserved to be placed "under the interdict." A patriot Quebecker snidely observed that it was not even "in the power of their clergy with all their threats and interdictions . . . to make the Canadians take up arms." Bishop Briand seemed to agree, concluding in early November, "Troops are needed; they would provide better persuasion than the Word of God."[9]

In Québec City, similar to Montréal, citizens did not refuse militia assemblies en masse; instead, individuals passively resisted and simply chose not to show up when called. By mid-September, when militia companies began regular evening guard duty, loyalists became particularly suspicious of the "French." Only a quarter of the New Subjects were reporting for duty in their turn.[10]

Emboldened by General Montgomery's successes, Old Subject patriots also became increasingly active. The "anarchi[c]al method of calling town meetings" was adopted in the capital, and patriots implied it was time to ensure "good treatment from the friends of Liberty" who would inevitably take the town. Lieutenant-Governor Cramahé was exasperated, scolding patriot Zachary Macaulay that it was their "damned Committees that had thrown the province into its present state and prevented the Canadians from taking arms." On 17 September, loyalist morale suffered another major blow, as word spread that Governor Carleton had ordered Lady Carleton and their children back to England, a clear sign that things were not going well.[11]

The tide changed the following day; Colonel Allan Maclean arrived and almost single-handedly restored Tory confidence. The commander of the Royal Highland Emigrants took charge of the city's defensive needs, wasting no time assembling the "British" militia and implementing regular garrison procedures. He also directed an engineer and carpenters to commence improvements on the city's dilapidated fortifications.[12] Cramahé, who had been relatively timid, seemed inspired by Maclean's energy and dedication. On 21 September, the lieutenant-governor issued a proclamation requiring visitors to report to authorities or be treated as spies. A week later, he officially detained all ships in the harbor; their sailors might augment the city's defensive manpower. To boost morale after Ethan Allen's Longue-Pointe defeat, the administration ordered four hundred broadside copies of an "Account of the Battle of Montreal," detailing the rebel debacle in French and English. After a shaky phase, Québec City found some renewed commitment to the loyalist cause.[13]

The capital's next ideological struggle focused on "French" citizens. Anonymous authors sought to foster loyalist support in the *Canadien* community, publishing two French-only appeals in the *Quebec Gazette*. In the first, printed on 5 October, "Civis Canadensis"[14] sought to "lift the veil" from his neighbors' eyes, so they would not have to beg *"Mea Culpa"* for their current conduct. The piece relied heavily on religious authority, indicating that it may have been written by a clergyman, and alluded to fears raised by "Le Canadien Patriote" back in July; with the rebels in Canada, their religion and property were in grave danger.[15]

The anonymous author "*Canadiens*" provided a similar letter the next week, encouraging fellow subjects to implore the King's mercy immediately; there was still time to "reject the evil counsel" of the rebels and remedy errors. This address was not just printed in the newspaper, but hundreds of French broadsides were produced for "friends of government" to distribute around the province. In the last October issue of the *Gazette,* another "French" writer opined, "Alas! If the rural inhabitants . . . had not let themselves be corrupted by rebels and dangerous minds" and had instead followed the example of the seigneurs and "educated Canadians . . . the rebels would never have tried to disturb our tranquility by making incursions in this province." Despite this focused effort to encourage common *Québécois* support, that community showed little change in its sentiments.[16]

In another early October development, Québec City lost its most ardent defender; Governor Carleton recalled Colonel Maclean from the capital to lead the Richelieu Valley operation described in the previous chapter. Almost immediately, a group of militia officers went to the lieutenant-governor to complain about fellow citizens, "Americans," who were not participating with the militia. They asked Cramahé to force the resisters "either to take arms or be sent out of the place." Eternally cautious, he stalled rather than taking action, promising an answer in a few days. In a short while, however, the lieutenant-governor would receive startling new information that would demand action.[17]

Cramahé and his Québec City supporters were soon to be challenged by a second column of Continental invaders, approaching under the command of Benedict Arnold. Unlike shooting-star rival Ethan Allen, whose dazzling volunteer-officer career burned out at Longue-Pointe, Arnold found an independent command that would give him an enduring influence over the Canadian campaign. After departing from Ticonderoga in the summer, Arnold traveled to Philadelphia and Cambridge, where General Washington and dynamic Connecticut delegate Silas Deane became convinced of the young colonel's tremendous "abilities & activity." By 8 September, Washington found the perfect mission to employ Arnold's energy, skills, and recent experience: leading the Kennebec Expedition that the commander-in-chief had discussed with Schuyler at the end of August. With confirmation that the Northern Army's invasion was under way, Washington gave Arnold command of a detachment from the main Continental Army outside Boston.[18]

Arnold would guide his corps up the Kennebec River, through the Maine region, portage over a chain of lakes on the highlands, and follow the Chaudière River down to Québec City (see Map 2). While raiding parties had occasionally used this path, and a handful of Yankee scouts, messengers, and spies had covertly taken it to enter Quebec over the summer, it had never been used by a large military force.[19]

Washington and Arnold prepared this mission without the involvement of civilian leadership; Congress was still in recess as the plan was fleshed out. The commander-in-chief designed the operation "to take possession of Quebec [City] if possible, but at all Events to create a diversion in favour of General Schuyler." Washington was guardedly optimistic. Intelligence indicated that the Canadian capital was essentially ungarrisoned, and amicable citizens might freely open the gates for Arnold's Continentals.[20]

General Washington armed Arnold with an address, encapsulating the Quebec campaign's core revolutionary liberation ideology, which he could use to explain his mission to the Canadians. In this manifesto, Washington announced that, "by the Advice of many Friends of Liberty" in Quebec, Congress had sent troops into the province "not to plunder, but to protect you; to animate, and bring forth into Action those Sentiments of Freedom you have disclosed, and which the Tools of Despotism would extinguish." The Continental Northern Army would respect property, and traditional religious differences were irrelevant in the patriot struggle—there was no reason for Canadians to "flee as before an Enemy." Instead, they should join the other colonies in an "indissoluble Union" and freely range themselves "under the Standard of general Liberty." English and French broadside copies were printed and sent to Arnold and Schuyler.[21]

Before Arnold departed from Cambridge, Washington provided exquisitely detailed instructions on a huge range of topics; such an operation was a tremendous responsibility for a young colonel. The fundamental theme was that both Canadians and Indians had earned the right to be respected as "Friends and Brethren." Arnold was explicitly warned to maintain strict discipline, ensuring that the troops did not "Plunder or insult" Canadian allies. They were to pay "full Value for all Provisions," and Arnold was accordingly given £1,000 in specie. The corps was also to "avoid all Disrespect or Contempt of the Religion of the Country." If Arnold found the Canadians opposed to his mission, he was ordered to terminate it, to avoid "irritating them against" the United Colonies. Finally, with his prickly Ticonderoga record, Arnold was reminded that he was not a "separate or independent command"; he was expected to follow Schuyler's directions upon "union" and to "avoid all contention about rank."[22]

Arnold led a small, but capable, force of roughly one thousand men, consisting of two provisional battalions of New England volunteers and three Continental rifle companies, hardy frontier sharpshooters from Pennsylvania and Virginia. This corps left Cambridge on 13 September. After a short coastal sail, detachments gathered at Fort Western (Augusta, Maine) on the Kennebec a week later, making final preparations for their wilderness trek. It was only at this point that Washington informed the recently reconvened Congress about the expedition. Despite the general's delay in sharing his plans with Philadelphia, the operation was hardly a secret, as any meaningful activity in the camp at Cambridge quickly became local knowledge. When the troops departed, British General Gage knew not only the mission's destination, but also its size. Newspapers, both Tory and Whig, freely printed details. Patriots had high expectations; a Philadelphia paper optimistically ventured that "in a few weeks we shall hear of his [Arnold's] possessing Quebec," and that every indication promised "that e'er long that great province will accede to the American league."[23]

Colonel Arnold waited at Fort Western for a few days, as essential bateaux were completed; most turned out to be rushed, slipshod jobs, made of green wood, which would not survive the challenging voyage. The advance guard departed on 25 September; shortly thereafter, Arnold received copies of Washington's letter to the Canadians. It seemed the entire mission was ready to venture into Quebec, but as Silas Deane feared, the United Colonies may have waited too long—winter was just around the corner.[24]

Benedict Arnold and his thousand-man force had embarked on an epic journey, clearly worthy of the many books documenting its drama.[25] The "extraordinary March" was thought to "equal Han[n]ibal[']s over the Alps." The men wrangled with the elements, fought to find their path, and through sheer willpower and brute force, drove their way up to the "Height of Land" separating Quebec from New England. Arnold's men faced one challenge after another: bateaux were smashed, men died, supplies were lost, and the weather turned.[26]

Upon reaching the Dead River, after one hundred miles of upstream travel, Arnold dispatched a flurry of messages on 13 October. This included his first attempt to contact patriot friends in Québec City, a letter addressed to John Dyer Mercier, who was a second-echelon patriot and an acquaintance from Arnold's earlier Canadian business trips. This letter heralded the expedition—its strength (well-inflated) and purpose—and asked for intelligence, specifically what the Continentals might expect from "Canadians and merchants in the city." Arnold sent the letters by a pair of friendly Indians and a French-speaking Continental soldier.[27]

Under disputed circumstances,[28] government authorities intercepted the letter to Mercier, and on 28 October, Cramahé was handed this undeniable proof of treason in the capital. He sent the town-sergeant to detain Mercier and imprisoned the patriot in the guardroom. Unaware of the incriminating evidence, the Old Subject community was distressed by this seemingly arbitrary breach of fundamental English rights. The city's "English" gentlemen urgently assembled a committee to meet with the lieutenant-governor and "know the cause of so remarkable a step." Cramahé told them "he was not at liberty to acquaint them with his reasons"; yet the next day he shared his justification with a select group of militia officers, indirectly calming some fears. The Mercier arrest was a major turning point in Québec City. Not only had the government finally acted against a seditious citizen, but they were now aware of Arnold's expedition, including its aim and general strength.[29]

=====

Arnold received a tremendous setback on 25 October; his trailing division commander, Lieutenant-Colonel Roger Enos, decided to turn around on the Kennebec with roughly a quarter of the expedition's force and many supplies, having determined that his men could not go on. Two days later, Arnold reached Lake Megantic on the Quebec side of the mountains. His scouts brought word that Canadians in the frontier hamlet of Sartigan appeared "very friendly" and would "very gladly receive" the expedition. The trek-worn Continentals desperately needed immediate local support, having consumed or lost all of their provisions; retreat was no longer an option.[30]

When they stumbled into Sartigan, Arnold's starving troops appeared "more like ghosts than men." While the Chaudière valley residents could easily have crushed the "weak and naked rebels," they instead received the Continentals with warm hospitality. Arnold immediately requested provisions for his men, paying in hard cash. The colonel augmented his force, as well. After educating local Indians on the "nature of the quarrel between the King and his children," he offered to enlist "as many of them as were fit to go to war" for eight dollars per month, with a two-dollar advance; thirty-two immediately joined.[31]

For the next week, the Kennebec Expedition ventured down the Chaudière River toward the St. Lawrence. Friendly Canadians distributed copies of General Washington's manifesto throughout the valley, preparing their neighbors for the *Bastonnais'* arrival. In the two largest Beauce-region settlements, St-Joseph and Ste-Marie (see Map 5), militia officers eagerly received the address and publicly read it to their parishioners. By the time Arnold reached the southern end of the well-settled Chaudière *côte*, St-François parish locals rang their church bell and informed the colonel that they considered him "sent from heaven to restore them liberty." *Beaucerons* graciously accepted and supported the Continental troops, supplying provisions, giving them lodging, and transporting incapacitated soldiers downriver — but almost always for money. Notably, while they were supportive, none of the habitants armed themselves to join the Continentals. The Chaudière valley would not provide active partisan counterparts to James Livingston's many Richelieu companies.[32]

Arnold's men started concentrating in the village of Ste-Marie-de-Beauce, where Militia-Captain Étienne Parent and his outspoken patriot wife welcomed the Continentals, perhaps sharing tales of their role in Jabez Matthews's May escape.[33] Rebel journal keepers also fondly recorded a dinner at the home of *Curé* Jean-Marie Verreau—naturally no friend to the rebel cause; whether from fear or hospitality, the priest had laid out a fine spread of roast turkey and wine for several guests.[34]

Another newfound patriot friend had already sent Arnold an anxious message from the banks of the St. Lawrence. Ignace Couture, one of the September Pointe-Lévy "Seditious Assembly" ringleaders, sought out a *Bastonnais* advance party with which to share intelligence and encourage cooperation. He informed them that a loyalist detachment had already visited the south shore, seizing or destroying all boats and canoes, and provided a horse for the Continentals to speedily deliver that message back to their colonel in Ste-Marie. Still fearing a punitive visit from government forces, Couture asked Arnold to hasten to Pointe-Lévy. The Continental advance guard subsequently pressed on to reach the St. Lawrence on the night of 7 November, joined shortly thereafter by Arnold. The rest of the expedition followed a day or two behind, carrying canoes purchased on the Chaudière based on Couture's information.[35]

When Arnold reached Pointe-Lévy, he received an important visitor, Québec City merchant John Halsted. The active New Jersey–born patriot had been in a self-imposed exile on Ile-d'Orléans, but hastened across the river to help the Continentals. He immediately pointed out loyalist Major Caldwell's Point-Lévy mill, where they could supplement their provisions with the seigneur's flour. Late that night, Arnold received an even more significant set of messengers; two Indians brought a letter from General Montgomery—the two Continental corps were finally communicating along the St. Lawrence. Based on Montgomery's reported success, Arnold believed the army might soon unite near the capital.[36]

Arnold established his headquarters in Caldwell's mill, where he could gaze upon the forbidding cliffs and walls of Québec City across the cold St. Lawrence; his objective was finally in sight. The colonel had two choices: he could attempt to seize the capital with his meager force, or he could continue upriver to join Montgomery near Montréal. Lingering in Pointe-Lévy was not an option. Winter was rapidly approaching; habitants were preparing for the coming onslaught of cold, cutting firewood and adding paper insulation

A General View of Québec from Point Levy, by Pierre-Charles Canot (1761). Note Lower Town at the base of the hill on the far side of the river and Upper Town above. Library and Archives Canada, Acc. No. 1970-188-6, W. H. Coverdale Collection of Canadiana.

to their stone houses. Local militiamen on guard duty were bundled up in their gray hooded wool *capots,* sealed shut with colorful woven sashes, their legs warmed by thick stockings and moccasins. The Continentals had none of these seasonal necessities. They required shelter and winter clothing very soon.

Arnold went with his natural inclination toward bold yet rational action: they would try the city. While waiting almost a week for his men to assemble on the St. Lawrence, Arnold hired Canadians to make scaling ladders and other equipment needed to assault the city walls. On 9 November, the Continentals had their first encounter with the enemy when a Royal Navy boat landed near the mill. The *Bastonnais* surprised and drove off the party, capturing one midshipman, who provided some useful intelligence.[37]

By Sunday, 12 November, Arnold's men were almost ready to cross the river as the Pointe-Lévy locals invited them to "a fine Ball." The Continentals enjoyed *Canadien* fiddling and dancing, and each soldier received an extra dram of rum and piece of bread. The feast may have been linked to St-Martin's Day—also the traditional day for paying seigneurial dues. In tumultuous 1775, few seigneurs appeared at their manors to receive rents, an excellent excuse for many habitants to avoid payment—all the more reason to celebrate; at the time, loyalist Hugh Finlay even imagined brazen habitants declaring "our seigneur is no more." On the feast night, as Arnold finalized plans for the river crossing and capital assault, he received more letters from General Montgomery, reporting the Richelieu campaign's great success.[38]

On the night of 13 November, the Kennebec Expedition men quietly pushed their canoes off from the south shore, bound for Wolfe's Cove, the very point where British forces landed in 1759. Despite the presence of nearby warships, multiple echelons crossed unhindered; but due to the shortage of canoes, scaling ladders and about 150 men were left at Pointe-Lévy at dawn. From the cove, the Continentals ascended the steep slope and gathered on the Plains of Abraham, southwest of the capital. Arnold established his headquarters in a nearby manor, coincidentally belonging to Major Caldwell, Pointe-Lévy's seigneur. Arnold reassessed his situation; having received new information that the garrison numbered more than a thousand, lacking a quarter of his own force, and without basic assault equipment, he decided it was no longer prudent to execute his original plan to storm the capital that morning. Instead, Arnold had his men establish a perimeter to blockade Québec City.[39]

Later that day, Arnold thought he might bait the garrison out or spark an insurrection behind the walls. He gathered his men within three hundred yards of the ramparts, where they gave three huzzahs. "The parapet was lined by hundreds of gaping citizens and soldiers" who shouted three cheers of defiance and responded with cannon blasts in the rebels' direction. The Continentals beat a retreat and found they had not suffered a single casualty; yet they failed to achieve their purposes.[40]

Arnold's next approach was a psychological attack; he would demand the city's surrender—there was a possibility that friendly elements in the city would offer to capitulate, or that the lieutenant-governor might flinch and actually surrender. Arnold composed a formal message, but in the end, it did not matter what the letter said. Before dusk on 14 November, Continental envoys approached the walls under a white flag, and the garrison responded with an aimed cannon blast, forcing the rebels to scramble for cover. Arnold's envoys tried again the next day and received a similar response.[41]

Forced to await Montgomery's anticipated arrival, the rebel army spent the next couple of days scouting their new locale and getting their units in order. The troops took up crowded, yet comfortable, quarters in warm houses and enjoyed "provisions of every kind in abundance." Arnold again distributed copies of Washington's address to explain the army's purpose, and *Canadiens* visited the camp to express satisfaction with the Continentals' arrival. The habitants also established a "pretty good market," with plenty of "eatables" and other soldiers' necessities. A few suspicious individuals floated around. After overcoming initial qualms about offending the locals, Arnold arrested a pair, who subsequently claimed to be city militia officers on an intelligence mission. Continental pickets captured livestock and other provisions destined for the city; along with notorious Tories' property, including Major Caldwell's, these seemed to be the only goods requisitioned by Arnold's corps — everything else was purchased.[42]

In the early weeks of November, even before the Continentals appeared on the north shore, the situation had been fairly gloomy for "friends of government" in Québec City. It was evident that the habitants were not going to take up arms to defend the province. Then, within a week, citizens heard not only of Arnold's entrance into the province, but also that "His Majesty's mail was robbed by the rebels near Berthier[-en-haut]," almost halfway between Montréal and Trois-Rivières; the capital was being pressed from two directions. The only relief was the arrival of ships carrying more than one hundred Royal Highland Emigrant recruits from Newfoundland, and a Royal Navy frigate, which augmented the city's defensive manpower with fifty marines. Lieutenant-Governor Cramahé tried to help where he could, but one attempt to improve security backfired. He required all canoes entering or leaving town to obtain an official pass, with the result that most habitants simply did not visit to deliver goods, limiting the flow of provisions just as a siege loomed on the horizon. On 11 November, one last ship was authorized to leave the province, taking Chief Justice William Hey to deliver administration views to London and carrying prisoner Ethan Allen to face justice in England.[43]

That same evening, Québec City loyalists were dramatically encouraged by the surprise return of Colonel Allan Maclean, fresh from his failed Sorel expedition, but still adamant that the capital would not fall to the rebels. The colonel was informed of alarming rumors that citizens had been holding private meetings, arguing that the "best course of action for them was to deliver the city to the armies of Congress." To address this situation, Maclean invited the Old Subjects to a meeting. Believing that these merchants' primary objection was the seemingly preferential government treatment "constantly given to the [French-]Canadians," the colonel probably emphasized that the current situation was an opportunity to earn government respect and future consideration through loyal action. In any case, his "spirited exertions" restored order in the Old Subject community, and patriots began moderating their activities.[44]

Maclean then turned to addressing the city's military needs. He reestablished his headquarters and the city command center at Prentice's Tavern, and "prudently set about the organization of all the means of defence." For three days before Arnold's arrival, the colonel was constantly vigilant, inspecting and correcting defenses night and day.[45]

When Lieutenant-Governor Cramahé held a council of war on 16 November, with the city blockaded, Maclean's steely determination fostered a unanimous council resolution to "defend the Town to the last Extremity." Among the measures taken to show their commitment, they ordered Royal Navy sailors ashore to form a defensive battalion, and parties were directed to destroy houses immediately outside the walls, "which may afford Shelter to ye Enemy," especially in the southwest St-Jean suburb. With Maclean's military leadership, it seemed Québec City was ready to endure an isolated winter of a blockade and perhaps even direct assaults.[46]

The day after Cramahé's council of war, a Royal Highland Emigrant deserted to the rebel camp on the Plains of Abraham. He brought intelligence that prompted Arnold to immediately reconsider his plans: Maclean, buoyed by a good sense of rebel strength, planned to sally out and attack the Continentals. The navy would help block the rebel retreat as well, landing artillery on the route to Montréal.[47]

Arnold's officers assessed their units' readiness before meeting in a council of war. They found that weapons were "deficient in numbers"; they had no bayonets and averaged just five rounds of ammunition per man. The rolls showed 680 Continentals in camp, many of them sick. In addition, rumors from the city held that the "French" militia was unwilling to surrender in the face of such a meager force—it would be "an eternal scandal"—but they would consider doing so if confronted by a larger army. The council weighed the facts, and with its concurrence, Arnold decided it was "proper to raise the siege, and proceed up the river St. Lawrence, 8 leagues to Point Aux Tremble."[48]

While his men packed for the march, Arnold penned another letter to Montgomery, informing the general of the changing situation. Then, the Continentals took one last opportunity to pick loyalist Major Caldwell's house and barns clean before they departed. On 19 November, Arnold's corps departed for Pointe-aux-Trembles, "attended by the regrets of a host of well-wishers among the peasantry."[49]

Once the rebels moved upriver, Colonel Maclean sent detachments out from the capital, which returned to report that Arnold's men had left a favorable impression among the habitants. The locals said the rebels were "a good sort of men who take nothing by force," and who "pay liberally for every thing they purchase." Yet reaching Pointe-aux-Trembles, Arnold indicated that such munificence had taxed his war chest, writing that he would "soon have occasion for [more] hard money."[50]

The rebels' retreat gave the city an opportunity to draw provisions from the countryside, but there was "an enormous price" for this reopened communication: "The country people brought in several Copys of the [Washington's] Manifesto." The city did not need any more fuel for internal dissent, as they fully anticipated Arnold's swift return, augmented by Montgomery's successful Richelieu campaign veterans.[51]

Chapter 11

TO WINTER IN CANADA

"Free" Montréal and Fortress Québec

The inhabitants are very friendly and give all the assistance they dare
to do at present. | *Colonel Benedict Arnold to General Richard Montgomery,
Pointe-aux-Trembles, 20 November 1775*

The Enemy without, however, are not to be dreaded as much as their
numerous Friends in the Town. | *Lieutenant-Governor Hector Cramahé to
Secretary of State Dartmouth, Québec City, 19 November 1775*

Montgomery's Northern Army rapidly departed from the St-Jean area within
days of the fort's surrender, and the general joined his men at Laprairie on 6
November. The haggard Continentals quickly erected a camp, but the frosty
November air made it "very uncomfortable living in tents." Spying over the
St. Lawrence, they could discern their next objective, Montréal, with its in-
viting accommodations.[1]

As the main army arrived on the St. Lawrence, detachments spread out
to expand the patriot presence in the district. Colonel Warner's men moved
from Longueuil to Boucherville, a half dozen miles northeast. At the mouth
of the Richelieu, Colonel Easton's Continentals established themselves at
Point Sorel, having cleared the valley of loyalists. Always a trailblazer, John
Brown led a party over to the north shore and roved from Lachenaie down
to the defiant parish of Berthier. It was this detachment that intercepted His
Majesty's mail there on 6 November. The noose was rapidly tightening on
the King's forces.[2]

Militarily, Montréal offered Governor Carleton little hope for defense. The
city's fortifications were "an apology for a wall," and would be "little more
than an Egg Shell" to even light cannon fire. The only reliable defenders were
eighty British regular troops in the city, plus a detachment at Lachine; the

habitant militia and Indian auxiliary force had dwindled to insignificance. Assessing the city militia, the governor believed that "the greatest part of the lower people will not act," and there were plenty of suspected "Traytors within." On 6 November, a merchant committee approached the governor to divine his intentions; he confessed that he would leave in a couple days, at which point "they might take care of themselves." Yet Carleton held on as long as possible, demonstrating his determination while hoping for a fortuitous change of circumstances—he would be disappointed.[3]

Montréal merchants reacted to Carleton's statements by sending a letter to Montgomery, inquiring about Continental plans. On the seventh, the general responded with a letter "to the Inhabitants of Montreal," endorsed to Pierre du Calvet, calling on patriot citizens to encourage fellow inhabitants or "bourgeoisie" to dissuade Carleton from a "futile Resistance," preventing the unnecessary suffering that would result from a bombardment. The letter's tone implied that Montgomery would soon enter the town, one way or another. The general added a postscript addressing rumors that Continentals intended "to give up the town to plunder"; proudly referring to the Northern Army's record, he asked the Montrealers, "Have you heard any one complain of such an act on our part since our Entrance into your Province?" The citizens, however, did not immediately respond, as Carleton and his troops lingered in town.[4]

On 11 November, after a few cold, cloudy days at Laprairie, Montgomery ordered about two hundred Continentals to cross the St. Lawrence. The previous night's snow melted, leaving muddy sludge on the riverbanks as soldiers loaded bateaux and pushed off for Ile-St-Paul (Ile-des-Soeurs). That island, about two miles long, was separated from the main Island of Montréal by a narrow channel three hundred yards wide. Once on Ile-St-Paul, the troops consolidated their position and pitched tents. That evening, two patriot Montrealers, George Measam and James Price's business partner William Haywood, crept over Montréal's walls, rambled two miles to the island, and conferred with General Montgomery, sharing the city's latest developments.[5]

It was clearly time for Governor Carleton to leave Montréal. Seeing the rebel's south-shore buildup, he had already directed his men to load the King's stores, as well as any known merchants' gunpowder, on eight transports "night and day." Any military stores that could not be removed were to be dumped into the river. With the air of "the saddest funeral," Carleton bade farewell to several prominent Montréal loyalists and boarded the last ship. The little flotilla, escorted by a Royal Navy brig and two armed schooners, embarked

An East View of Montreal, in Canada, by Pierre-Charles Canot (1762). Library and Archives Canada, Acc. No. 1970-188-1928, W. H. Coverdale Collection of Canadiana.

for Québec City before dusk. By evacuating, the governor hoped to preserve strength for the capital's defense. He also precluded his own immediate capture and negated the possibility that the invaders might demand surrender of the upcountry posts in conjunction with Montréal; no one remained behind with such authority. The city gates remained closed as devout loyalists still stood guard, but most other militiamen returned home.[6]

Meanwhile, Continentals crossed the narrow channel from Ile-St-Paul and slowly advanced into the Recollet suburb, outside the city's southwest wall, where Montrealers sent envoys to parley. The general reassured them that he "came as a friend," but expected to march his cold, fatigued men through the gates very soon. In town that evening, prominent citizens assembled to discuss their options. After inconclusive debates, they sent another dozen delegates to consult with the general, whence that cross-section of "French" and "English" gentlemen drafted nine proposed articles of capitulation. The terms primarily showed the Montrealers' concerns with a smooth transition of authority, securing property, and trade rights. With so many political issues at stake, this was a moment when Brigadier-General Montgomery truly needed

Congressional civilian advisors. Rather than accept or deny terms outright, Montgomery chose a third option.[7]

After spending a full day in negotiations, the general decided that Montréal could "claim no title to a capitulation" in its unarmed and ungoverned state. Instead, he offered reassurances that he would act in their interest, framed on the citizens' proposed articles. Montgomery readily promised to "ensure peaceable enjoyment of property" and freedom of religion, and to swiftly establish courts "conformable to the British Constitution." One citizen was excluded from all terms though, St-Luc de La Corne; in light of the seigneur's treacherous overtures, the general threatened to treat him separately.[8]

Economically, the merchants asked for freedom to conduct upcountry trade and sought exemption from Continental Association restrictions, but the general could promise only to "promote commerce" whenever it did not endanger "the troops and the publick good," while confessing his impotence to "engage for freedom of trade to the Mother Country."[9]

On military terms, Montgomery offered no guarantees regarding Canadian prisoners of war, but would encourage his superiors to release them on "Motives of humanity." Similarly, he did not expect to billet troops in citizens' homes—but might, "when necessity requires"—and explicitly stated that he was the sole judge of such need. Finally, the general reassured the citizens that he would not compel them to "take up arms" or "contribute, in any manner" toward fighting the Crown.[10]

Surprisingly, there was no recorded conversation about local government, other than Montgomery's expressed desire to see "a virtuous Provincial Convention assembled." Anticipating his imminent departure from the city, the general added that his responses were "binding on any future commanding officer." Montgomery concluded the terms by dictating that his army would enter the city at 9 A.M. on the 13th, and his officers would be given "the keys of all public stores." All things considered, Montgomery's response was a careful balancing act—the best compromise he could offer without explicit Congressional guidance, pressed by the need to expeditiously enter Montréal.[11]

Within the next few days, about forty patriot residents of the Recollet, St-Laurent, and Québec suburbs (see Map 6) sent their own message to Montgomery, a warm greeting, using glowing, ideological phrases that contrasted starkly with the city's stiff, businesslike negotiations. Many of these suburbanites, living in the spread of wooden homes outside the three city gates, were committed opponents of Carleton and the Quebec Act—men such as James Livingston's father John, and Jacques Roussain, who had plotted with Ethan Allen. French-born Canadian Valentin Jautard authored this letter. Jautard was a post-Conquest arrival who had been a Montréal lawyer for seven years. Imbued with Enlightenment ideals, he relished the Continental spirit of liberty.[12]

The suburbanites' response was exactly what Congress had hoped for when penning its Canadian addresses and sending the liberating Northern Army. The patriot suburb dwellers celebrated that their "chains are broken" and enjoyed their return "to a happy freedom." They wanted to assure Congress that their "hearts always desired union," and they embraced the Continentals as their own. Instead of being treated "under terms" like their Montrealer counterparts, they sought a "pact of association and fraternal union."[13]

On the morning of 13 November, Montgomery led his troops through Montréal's Recollet Gate. Some citizens were shocked to see the campaign-worn Continentals; a priest noted his humiliation, "seeing everything under the control of people dressed in such a way, I assure you that a beggar in Europe would be better dressed than they were." A column of troops marched up the westernmost of Montréal's two primary streets, destined for the citadel barracks. The Continentals had to be impressed as they passed scores of imposing whitewashed, tin-roofed stone houses, accented by green fireproof shutters and doors, and the sizeable Notre-Dame Church with its prominent bell tower. The unpaved streets, however, were "half leg deep" in November mud.[14]

On the north end of town, the Continentals arrived at the citadel. The square, wooden structure offered soldiers' bunks aplenty, but was considered "a place of no strength." After posting two cannon in front to demonstrate their authority, troops labored to restore the barracks. The quarters were so damaged by Carleton's departing troops that the Continentals spent their first Montréal night in a nearby storehouse. The barracks were occupied the next day, and quickly reached capacity as additional troops poured into town. Other soldiers moved into family homes, sparking loyalist complaints that despite Montgomery's promises, they were already being "made to lodge the greatest part of the force."[15]

Meanwhile, the Continentals enjoyed Montréal's markets and shops. After months of deprivation, they found a wealth of goods in the "Rich city."

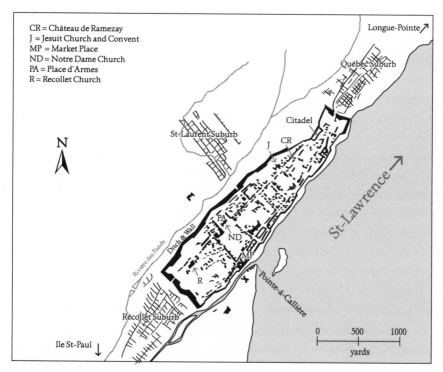

CR = Château de Ramezay
J = Jesuit Church and Convent
MP = Market Place
ND = Notre Dame Church
PA = Place d'Armes
R = Recollet Church

Longue-Pointe↗

Québec Suburb

Citadel

St-Laurent Suburb

CR

J

N

St-Lawrence→

Rivière des Fonds

Ditch & Wall

PA

ND

MP

R

Pointe-à-Callière

Récollet Suburb

Ile St-Paul ↓

0   500   1000
yards

MAP 6: Montréal City Environs.

Near the lower market, soldiers might even imagine they were home; with more than forty English traders nearby, one heard "almost as much English spoken" on Rue St-Paul, "as in the streets of Albany." The "liberators" found that Montréal offered "very comfortable Winter Quarters," although most ached to head home.[16]

General Montgomery's next priority, a matter that caused him "great uneasiness," was to determine how many soldiers he would have to garrison "liberated" regions and conduct follow-on operations over the winter. All soldiers' enlistments expired within the next fifty days, and the troops were tremendously hesitant to advance any deeper into Canada. They grew "exceedingly Turbulent & indeed Mutinous" in their desire to get home.[17]

On 15 November, General Montgomery issued a proclamation, offering his troops generous terms if they would reengage until 15 April 1776 — a date he saw as a compromise, permitting rural troops to return for spring farm work, while giving the colonies time to generate replacement regiments. He publicly hoped none of the men would "leave him at this critical juncture, but such whose affairs or health absolutely require their return home," but surely he knew better. To encourage reenlistments, and as a measure of efficiency, he issued new uniforms, from captured government stores, only to soldiers who extended their service commitment.[18]

Soldiers' responses varied. From the Connecticut regiments, Easton's Massachusetts Regiment, and Bedel's New Hampshire Rangers, fewer than three hundred Yankees agreed to extend in Canada. Yorkers reenlisted in slightly larger numbers, giving Montgomery about seven hundred Continentals in and around Montréal. Most other troops wasted no time racing for home; having completed their obligations, they needed to beat the season and avoid being trapped north of Lake Champlain while they waited for the lake to freeze. Both Schuyler and Montgomery denigrated these men for abandoning the cause at a critical hour, but in the context of colonial armies, it made perfect sense to the soldiers. As Connecticut Governor Trumbull observed, "The pulse of a New-England man beats high for liberty. His engagement in the service he thinks purely voluntary; therefore, in his estimation, when the time of inlistment is out, he thinks himself not holden without further engagement." New York Lieutenant-Colonel Ritzema, for one, was glad to be free of the "lame . . . the lazy and the . . . home sick." He was pleased to send them back "to their Mommies and Daddies and Wives and pumkin Pies" and to avoid wasting effort and matériel on reluctant or malingering soldiers.[19]

Carleton's ships did not get far after leaving Montréal. They were delayed when a ship temporarily ran aground, and then passed only thirty miles downriver before the wind "changed and violently blew from the northeast," forcing them to anchor. In four days, the flotilla sailed just forty-five miles.[20]

Meanwhile, Colonel James Easton's men sat waiting for Carleton's arrival at Sorel, having built a six-gun battery on the St. Lawrence, augmented by two gondolas[21] (gun boats) brought down the Richelieu from St-Jean. With the adverse winds and aided by a fence of canalizing downriver islands, even these relatively meager defenses posed a severe threat to the royal flotilla. On 15 November, some of Carleton's vessels crept into range and the battery opened fire, prompting the ships to withdraw upriver, out of range. Easton sent General Montgomery an urgent request for reinforcements to help block the governor's retreat.[22]

Montgomery immediately called Warner's Green Mountain Boys and Be-del's New Hampshire Rangers to rush to Easton's aid. To help motivate the men, the general took a step "beyond the letter of the law," offering to give "All public stores, except ammunition and provisions" to troops who captured Carleton's ships. Bedel's Rangers and a Canadian partisan detachment under Augustin Loiseau gathered at Sorel, but Montgomery complained that the "Rascally Green Mountain Boys" left him in the lurch, declining action as they prepared to return home.[23]

Still facing the adverse winds, drawing fire whenever the ships ventured too close to the shore, fearing the "strong batteries" rumored at Sorel, and seeing "gunboats among the islands on the opposite bank," Carleton called a council of war aboard his ship on 16 November. The captains felt the governor "had to try every means possible to get to Quebec . . . where his presence was of the utmost importance." Among the proposed courses of action, Captain Bouchette volunteered to swiftly and stealthily transport Carleton past the enemy guns in a rowboat. This option prevailed; the governor and the captain departed later that night, leaving the flotilla under General Prescott's charge.[24]

Unaware of the governor's departure, Easton sent Major Brown to open negotiations with the ships. Brown skillfully exaggerated patriot strength and demanded the ships' surrender.[25] By 19 November, General Prescott had decided his situation was futile. He ordered all gunpowder and shot dumped into the river before telling Brown he was ready to surrender. After nego-tiating advantageous terms, the Continentals secured the general and one hundred British soldiers as prisoners and seized more than a thousand barrels of provisions. They also liberated two government prisoners from the ships: Thomas Walker and Moses Hazen. Immediately thereafter, Easton, who had "shewn so much zeal & activity," departed to recruit his regiment anew, as only eighty of his men had reenlisted, remaining in Canada under Brown.[26]

Governor Carleton, meanwhile, escaped with his aide-de-camp de La-naudière and Chevalier Niverville; Captain Bouchette guided them past the Sorel battery in the late hours of 16 November, oars covered in cloth to muffle their noise. Accelerating in the relative safety of Lac-St-Pierre, they reached Trois-Rivières on the seventeenth, where the governor heard of Arnold's activity at Québec City and Pointe-aux-Trembles. Leaving Trois-Rivières before a rumored rebel arrival, Carleton and Lanaudière reembarked and soon encountered the friendly armed ship *Fell*, which carried them to the capi-tal on 19 November — the same day Prescott surrendered his ships at Sorel.

Carleton had made a wise choice; a royal governor's capture would have had immeasurable value for the patriot cause.[27]

In his escape, when Governor Carleton made his short 17 November stop at Trois-Rivières, he was unaware that its citizens were already considering surrender to the rebel army. That initiative had been prompted by Colonel Maclean's visit nine days earlier, in retreat from his Richelieu Valley debacle; his men seized all the King's stores and merchants' gunpowder from the city before continuing to cruise for the capital. With government forces in flight and "no more hope or resources" to resist rebel invaders, twenty-one prominent Trifluviens (citizens of Trois-Rivières) drafted a capitulation, even though nobody had yet seen a hint of the Northern Army's approach.[28]

In a message worded more like a plea than a surrender, the citizens simply asked to "be treated as favourably as those who fell into your hands in the course of your various conquests." Much like the Montrealers, they seemed most worried that soldiers might "insult or disturb their property . . . private interests . . . personal security." The Trifluvien embassy to Montgomery stagnated the next morning, however, when one of their delegates requested advance payment for the delivery mission; nobody paid him, and with the demand unresolved, the message sat undelivered for a week.[29]

Then, with Carleton's subsequent short visit and rumors of the rebel army's impending arrival, "English" citizens decided to reinitiate the effort. They turned to city notary Jean-Baptiste Badeaux, who agreed to join William Morris in delivering the terms to Montréal. Reaching that city on 20 November, Morris and Badeaux were taken directly to Montgomery. Warmly welcoming the envoys, the general told them he was embarrassed they had traveled so far, as they had no need to fear his troops. The Trifluvien duo politely replied that it was not the Continentals they dreaded, but rebel Canadians. Montgomery reassured them that he would issue orders ensuring the security of Trois-Rivières, and he wrote a kind letter to its citizens, as well.[30]

Montgomery's letter shared his mortification that people would fear for their property at his troops' hands. Continentals were liberators who "came to protect, and not to destroy," and he hoped they would "never be tarnished by any allegations of cruelty." The general concluded with the thought that, God willing, the province would soon have "a free and happy government." Canada's third city received the assurances it sought, and as Badeaux and Morris departed for home, Montgomery gained confidence that Trois-Rivières would not hinder his advance toward Québec City.[31]

Montgomery's meeting with the Trois-Rivières delegates was one of thousands of tasks he handled as the United Colonies' senior representative in Canada. The general was already "exceedingly sorry" Congress had not "favoured" him with a committee to guide Quebec's civilian affairs. Prioritizing military missions over political activities, the brigadier promised Schuyler he would lose "no time in calling a convention" for Canadian Congressional delegates, but only after his "intended expedition" was finished. He had "made the Inhabitants acquainted with the views of Congress" relative to the province, but liberated Canadians were not clamoring for political representation, so they could wait.[32]

While Montgomery hoped the habitants, bourgeois, and even seigneurs would become politically "enlightened," he was frustrated with the priests who had done "all the Mischief in their power," and were now denying absolution to patriots in many parishes. Still, he proudly reported he had "shewn all the respect in my power to Religion & winked at this behaviour in the Priests for fear of giving Malice a handle." He was also exploring an avenue for potential Church cooperation, a tacit quid pro quo with the Jesuits, as he met with the Montréal superior, Father Pierre-René Floquet.[33]

The Jesuit Order was officially suppressed by Pope Clement XIV in 1773, but Canadian authorities agreed to tolerate their continuation. Still Floquet "complained of some little indignities shewn their order," especially the government's use of their house as the "Common Prison." Montgomery "promised redress" and indicated that the Order might be able once again to enjoy its broad holdings in Quebec if the province should "accede to the General Union." The general did not ask for any specific favors, but he hoped "this hint may be of service."[34]

In more mundane matters, Montgomery appointed patriot Montrealers to several offices: George Measam was made postmaster; Levy Solomons was appointed "Purveyor to the American Hospitals in Canada"; *Canadien* Jean-François Hamtramck was promoted from partisan to Continental commissary. The general also appointed patriot militia colonels for both the Quebec and Montreal Districts: Regnier de Roussi, a recent Boston transplant, and active patriot François Cazeau, respectively. The latter was appointed secretly, so he could "live among the enemy," one of his principal contributions being to provide intelligence on Montréal loyalists. Theoretically, all these men relieved Montgomery of some administrative duties, permitting him to focus on his two biggest Northern Army challenges, money and manpower.[35]

Financially, Montgomery pestered General Schuyler for more hard cash. The brigadier had established a productive partnership with Montréal patriot merchant James Price, whom he considered "active and intelligent, so warm a friend to the measures adopted by Congress." The invaluable Price loaned the army £5000 (York)[36] for temporary relief, but Montgomery warned Schuyler that it would not be "sufficient to answer all expenses."[37]

Militarily, after the Northern Army's weak reenlistment response, Montgomery turned to his only other immediate source of troops: the Canadians. On 19 November, he authorized James Livingston to recruit a Continental Canadian regiment; Congress had encouraged Schuyler to raise such a unit "at the Expence of the Continent," if any Canadians were inclined to "take up Arms." Montgomery boldly reported, "I can have as many Canadians as I know how to maintain"; yet in reality, recruiting was not that easy for newly commissioned Colonel Livingston. The Canadian leader had gathered volunteers whenever needed during the Richelieu Valley campaign, where habitants had the freedom to leave camp and check on their families and farms. Now, however, Livingston was asking them to engage for a full year, likely for deployment far from home, a very different undertaking. Trusted partisan lieutenants such as Loiseau and Allin promptly scoured the district for volunteers.[38]

Before leaving Montréal, Montgomery had one more military issue to address: Canadian loyalist prisoners of war. His inclination was toward leniency: he permitted the city's loyalist militia officers and half-pay retired officers to remain; at least three minor Fort St-Jean prisoners also were allowed to return to the city; and he was considering similar petitions from Hertel-de-Rouville, captured at Fort St-Jean, and Rigauville, captured at Verchères. The most contentious, though, were the Canadians captured aboard Prescott's ships; Montgomery had let them come ashore on parole while he pondered the best course of action.[39]

Such tolerance irritated a zealous Yorker officer faction, led by radical Captain John Lamb. On 23 November, these officers presented Montgomery with a remonstrance, protesting the dangerous "indulgence" shown to "some of the officers of the King's troops" and requesting those Tories' removal from Canada. The general was apoplectic over such presumptuous behavior, and in a fit of anger, informed the officers he was resigning.[40]

The Yorkers rushed to comfort Montgomery, pleading that their move was not driven by "a want of confidence" in him, but purely for "public Safety," and reassured him that all their Canadian friends shared similar sentiments. They also maintained that their remonstrance was intended to help the general justify loyalist removal, not to force a decision upon him. With a little added persuasion from General Wooster, Montgomery considered their apology sufficient to "resume the command with some propriety."[41]

Many prisoners of war were procedurally sent to the United Colonies, although Montgomery told Schuyler that he had no issue with the "Canadian Soldiery" returning home. The brigadier pondered the rectitude of disarming prominent loyalists who remained in Montréal, but showed an inexplicable degree of mercy to infamous Tory troublemakers; he permitted active "friends of government" St-Luc La Corne and Hertel-de-Rouville to remain in Canada on parole. John Fraser, taken aboard Prescott's ships, was also informed that he could remain in the province, but because of the "very great uneasiness" expressed by Montgomery's patriot friends, Fraser needed to quietly "remove to some village on the other side of [the] St. Lawrence River." On the loyalist prisoner issue, Montgomery's liberal predispositions were warped by radical patriot demands, resulting in an apparently arbitrary set of decisions toward Canadian Tories.[42]

Almost 150 miles downriver, Arnold's men reached Pointe-aux-Trembles (Neuville) on 19 November, after a twenty-mile march from the Plains of Abraham. Habitant families hosted the 676 weary Continentals with "kindness and hospitality," inviting them to enjoy "as much comfort as tight houses, warm fires," and their "scantiness of clothing would permit." Arnold also purchased provisions aplenty from the extremely cooperative *Canadiens*. With the troops' shelter and food needs met, Colonel Arnold sent Montgomery express requests for "cloathing, shoes & Money."[43]

Despite the fact that "few or none" of the Pointe-aux-Trembles habitants spoke English, they aided Arnold's corps considerably, gathering food and providing transportation. Some petitioned to be enlisted, but Arnold no longer had money to pay such an auxiliary corps — he would have to rely on volunteers. Fortunately, he already had a tremendous friend in the parish.[44]

Maurice Desdevens-de-Glandon, another French-born Canadian, had been a provincial surveyor since 1768 and was very familiar with the land and people. The thirty-three-year-old apparently fed Montgomery with intelligence early in the invasion. The general eventually asked Desdevens to assist Arnold outside the capital, where he probably inspired the colonel's decision to withdraw specifically to Pointe-aux-Trembles. As an unofficial patriot militia-captain, Desdevens also encouraged habitants to take up arms in the cause of liberty, gather intelligence, and guide Arnold's men to loyalist seigneur property worth requisitioning.[45]

On 28 November, Arnold also called on his "old friends" at Pointe-Lévy, asking those south-shore *Canadiens* to "prevent any kind of provisions or forage to be brought to the garrison" in Québec City. They cooperated; all winter, not a single canoe crossed with food from there. On the twenty-eighth, Arnold also allied his troops with upstream Canadians to address a more immediate threat. Militia-Captain Joseph-Etienne Pagé requested Continental assistance to challenge a few Royal Navy ships patrolling near Cap-Santé, ten miles southwest of Pointe-aux-Trembles, and the colonel promptly dispatched a seventy-man detachment to join him. Arnold was particularly worried that these ships might intercept Montgomery's corps on the St. Lawrence, so he also sent a slew of messages to constantly update the general on the enemy vessels' status, even employing Canadian patriot John Halsted as a courier. In the end, there was no fight on the river; the threat waned as the ships passed downstream on 30 November. Anticipating Montgomery any day and itching to return to Québec City, Arnold also sent Captain Daniel Morgan with another seventy-man detachment to surveil the capital environs and offer reassurances to habitants living near the Plains of Abraham, who feared the garrison might sortie to burn and plunder their houses.[46]

═══════

At his Montréal headquarters, Montgomery still hoped to be replaced as Continental commander in Canada, even offering his own recommendation, Major-General Charles Lee. He also reiterated his wish for a "respectable Committee of Congress," pleading that he did not have "weight enough to carry on business" himself. For now, however, Quebec's Continental leadership consisted of Montgomery and General David Wooster. As the commander headed to the capital, he gave Wooster command of the rear areas. To help the touchy Yankee brigadier, Montgomery left trusted New York

Lieutenant-Colonel Rudolphus Ritzema to assist "in the Duty of the Garrison" at Wooster's request.[47]

Before General Montgomery moved downriver to assist Arnold, he set about "new modelling" the army. The reenlistees came from a hodgepodge of different units, so they were consolidated on provincial lines: reduced-strength New York and Connecticut "regiments" and a small mixed unit of Easton's Massachusetts men and Bedel's New Hampshire Rangers, under Major Brown. The men were also issued the promised replacement clothing, including red British uniform coats found in Montréal. Montgomery took advantage of other captured assets to hasten to the capital, loading men, provisions, ammunition, and equipment aboard Prescott's recently captured ships. On the morning of 25 November, they sailed for Pointe-aux-Trembles. The general brought along an important partner, James Price, who would be an unofficial civilian advisor and might provide additional financial support when necessary. Initially, the Continental maneuver corps consisted of fewer than two hundred New York troops, including the artillery company. The flotilla picked up the Sorel battery guns en route; Brown's detachment and more Yorkers followed a few days later, also by boat.[48]

The new Canadian Continental troops also joined the move downriver. Captain Jeremiah Duggan led an advance-guard company by land to Ste-Anne-de-la-Pérade, northeast of Trois-Rivières. In that parish, they received an ammunition supply landed from Montgomery's ships, and they escorted it thirty miles by road to avoid any lingering Royal Navy threat and ensure prompt, safe delivery to Arnold at Pointe-aux-Trembles. Duggan and his Canadians delivered that precious load on the evening of 30 November.[49]

The rest of the Canadian Regiment traveled by land, a few days behind. Colonel Livingston led a total of just two hundred newly enlisted Canadian Continentals; his recruiting had been cut short after only eight days, when Montgomery ordered the unit's march to the capital. Leading them into Trois-Rivières en route, Livingston faced a new test of his authority almost immediately. An overzealous Rivière-du-Loup patriot, François Guillot *dit* Larose, had detained seigneur Councilor Conrad Gugy and brought him to the district capital. Larose made various accusations against Gugy: that he had forced the militia to march against the *Bastonnais* under threat of flogging and that he had called the Continentals "a band of beggars," Duggan a "rogue," and Livingston "a bankrupt." Gugy pleaded innocent on all counts.

Serving as an ad hoc judge, Livingston admonished the patriot accuser, ordering Larose to calm down; his overeager behavior was hurting the cause. The colonel cleared Gugy of the false accusations and armed him with a written notice to post at his parish church, publicizing the verdicts on the accuser and accused. Loyalist notary Jean-Baptiste Badeaux recorded the incident; he must have been astonished that the rebel Old Subject grain merchant issued such wise justice.[50]

On the morning of 1 December, the two Continental corps finally united as the eleven rebel ships arrived off Pointe-aux-Trembles, completing a "remarkably quick passage." Arnold's men received their general at the riverbank, and Montgomery gave them an "energetic and elegant speech" before they started unloading the ships. The first order of business for Arnold's men was to receive clothing; each man was issued "an excellent blanket coat," as well as "a new red regimental coat."[51]

That same day, Montgomery recognized Maurice Desdevens's invaluable contributions right away, commissioning him a militia-captain in Congress's pay. Wasting no time, he then asked Captain Desdevens to assemble local manpower to unload heavy cargo from the ships and to provide all the sleighs he could furnish. Within eighteen hours, the ships were unloaded and the Continentals had enough *calèches* (sleighs) to support the entire army's deployment.[52]

Without the generous assistance provided on the Chaudière, at Pointe-Lévy, and in Pointe-aux-Trembles, Arnold's expedition would have shattered. Instead, as a Canadian priest wrote of Arnold's expedition, "they appeared without supplies, having neither ammunition nor food, and in very small numbers, at the beginning of the most inclement season of the year: but were pleasantly surprised when, in the middle of this situation, they found everything in their favor . . . they could get the Canadians to act counter to their faith . . . their oaths." Quebec District habitants may not have taken up arms to support the Continentals in 1775, but they still played an absolutely vital role in promoting war against Carleton's government.[53]

———

In the capital in mid-November, Colonel Maclean thought he had become the province's senior officer, believing Carleton had been captured. The colonel and garrison were pleasantly surprised to see the governor's miraculous 19 November arrival. After receiving a formal welcoming salute, Carleton ascended to Upper Town and immersed himself in improving the government's last bastion against rebellion.[54]

While Carleton had been in Montréal, Lieutenant-Governor Cramahé had done little to suppress patriot agitation. Loyalists still feared that "the town was in great danger of being given up, through the cabals of the disaffected, whom Cramahé permitted to remain in town." Even Carleton agreed; upon his return he noted, "we have so many Enemies within . . . I think our Fate extremely doubtful." On 22 November, the governor tackled this situation, issuing a proclamation that required every militia-eligible man who refused to take up arms "to quit the Town in four Days . . . together with their wives and children." If they did not depart from Quebec District by 1 December, they could be "treated as Rebels or Spies." These "enemies of the state" also had to leave behind any provisions, but would be compensated. Loyalists "were now rid of their fears from the treachery of the Anti-Royalists," who had been more feared than the "avowed rebels without the walls."[55]

After settling personal business as best they could, patriot exiles shuffled out the city gates, leaving "all their property behind, except some wearing apparel and a little household furniture." The precise number of patriot refugees is unknown, but they included several "principal inhabitants," British Party leaders John McCord, Zachary Macaulay, and Jonathan Welles among them. Even an individual such as lawyer Edward Antill, who had recently signed Montréal's "articles of the loyal association," elected to flee from this "new tyranny." Arnold's sentries at Pointe-aux-Trembles met the first exiles on 26 November, several of whom offered their services to the Continental effort; the most prominent posting was Antill's, as the army's chief engineer.[56]

With the internal threat neutralized, Carleton and Maclean made final preparations for a siege: inspecting defenses, examining everyone passing through the gates, and even issuing new green provincial uniforms to the militia, tailored from material found in the city. A census and inventory of stores proved they had sufficient provisions to feed the city's sixteen hundred armed men and thirty-two hundred women and children for eight months, although firewood would be scarce. Meanwhile, the 30 November *Quebec Gazette* announced it was "impossible to continue the publication," a superfluous extravagance in a city facing imminent siege. Under the fearless and decisive leadership of Carleton and Maclean, the capital's defenders were prepared to meet all challenges and hold Québec City until a British relief fleet might arrive, no sooner than May.[57]

Chapter 12

TIME TO CONSIDER POLITICS

The Continental Congress, the Northern Army,
and a Committee for Canada

If We should be successful in that Province, a momentous, political Question
arises. What is to be done with it? | *John Adams to Joseph Warren, Philadelphia,*
8 October 1775

I am entirely of your Opinion that We shall be undone unless the most
spirited Measures are pursued. | *Rhode Island Delegate Samuel Ward to Henry*
Ward, 8 January 1776

Even before the fall of Fort Chambly, New Hampshire delegates believed:
"We are likely soon to be in possession of St. John's [St-Jean] and Canada,"
and John Adams noted the "very promising Intelligence concerning the operations of the Northern Army." It was easy to forget that many measures
were needed to ensure military and political success, and especially to defend
Quebec once liberated. General Schuyler did all he could to remind Congress
that the army needed strategic guidance, reinforcements, money, supplies, and
support with Canadian politics. Congress, however, was distracted by more
immediate, persistent, and louder demands: the siege of Boston, governance in
the absence of Royal authorities, defiant New York loyalists, a continent-wide
gunpowder shortage, finances — the list was almost endless; and Canada
seemed to be progressing so well.[1]

On 9 October, when Congress read General Schuyler's letters of 19 and 29
September, it spurred an initial round of discussions about long-term plans
for Canada. In the first letter (described in Chapter Eight), reporting early
struggles around Fort St-Jean, the general asked important strategic questions about Canadian politics and the Northern Army's future. The second

emphasized Montgomery's request for a committee to help establish a free Canadian government.

John Adams, perhaps after previewing Schuyler's letters, was already pondering such issues. He saw that a new Quebec government was necessary, but asked what form it should take: "Shall the Canadians choose an House of Representatives, a Council and a Governor?" Adams made it clear that "It will not do to govern them by Martial Law, and make our General Governor," replacing one form of oppression with another. But, there was always a lurking, fundamental question — "Is there Knowledge and Understanding enough among them [the Canadians], to elect an assembly, which will be capable of ruling them and then to be governed by it?"[2]

Congress considered Schuyler's letters for a few days, before President John Hancock responded on 11 October. In Hancock's words, the United Colonies' primary objective was to induce the Canadians "to accede to an Union with these Colonies, and that they form from the several Parishes a Provincial Convention and send Delegates to this Congress." They recommended a Georgia-style approach: "in the present unsettled State of that Country, a regular Election can hardly be expected, we must acquiesce in the Choice of such Parishes and Districts as are disposed to join us." This model had been proven successful over the summer, when a proper Georgian provincial delegation joined the St. John's Parish representatives, officially adding the thirteenth colony to the Continental confederation. While Congress agreed upon "the Necessity of attending to the Situation of Canada," the body trusted that Schuyler's "Care and Prudence" would render any Congressional delegation "unnecessary, at least for the present."[3]

Also, while Congress could have tackled the issue of Northern Army replacement units directly, they deferred to Schuyler. After requesting the commander's assessment of troop needs, Hancock also asked him to suggest "the best Method of procuring men," a decision that clearly belonged in Philadelphia or colonial capitals. By passing these issues to Schuyler's hands, Congress delayed resolution, effectively ensuring a significant gap in Northern Army troop strength over the winter; and this was being done before Fort Chambly had even fallen.[4]

General Schuyler was distinctly displeased with Congress's response, which he received around 20 October. The Northern Army commander immediately and frankly replied that Congress was "not in Sentiment" with him on the subject of a committee. Schuyler explained that a delegation was an absolute necessity. In an ideal army, "in which discipline and subordination are established, and prevail," a general might handle such political tasks, but the Northern Army was clearly not in that situation. Both he and Montgomery were overwhelmed with martial demands, and they simply could not spend adequate time on Canadian politics.[5]

A couple of weeks later, Schuyler addressed the Northern Army troop strength question. He felt that three thousand men would be sufficient for the winter: one thousand each in Québec City and Montréal, and five hundred in both Trois-Rivières and the Richelieu. Once spring came, however, more troops would be vital to face the much-anticipated Ministerial relief force, and Schuyler warned that it "may not be prudent to place too much dependance" on Canadian supporters. For the next season at least, the United Colonies would have to bear the burden of defending Quebec.[6]

While Congress and the Northern Army took months to address the Canadian expedition's critical issues, the United Colonies' newspapers kept their people informed about the situation in Quebec. Letters from military participants were reprinted regularly for mass consumption, with no censorship, so colonial readers had a fairly accurate view of campaign progress, allowing for several weeks' delay. Plenty of erroneous reports were mixed in—with no basis in reality—of fantastic Northern Army victories and catastrophic defeats. In late 1775, however, the American progress was really being driven by key events outside Canada.[7]

Patriots throughout North America received a series of bitter rebuffs from Great Britain in the fall of 1775. On 18 October, the Royal Navy shocked colonists by burning Falmouth (Portland, Maine). Less than two weeks later, Congressional delegates received copies of a monumental Royal proclamation in which King George III declared that the "many of our subjects in divers[e] parts of our Colonies," who had been "misled by dangerous and ill designing men," were in a clear state of rebellion—effectively declaring every Congressman and Continental soldier a rebel, as well as anyone who did not actively resist them. Patriots who still clung to hopes for reconciliation received another slap in the face on 9 November. A letter from London agents reported that the King had refused to receive Congress's 8 July petition and had said that "no answer would be given." If the King preferred to prosecute savage war rather than read a petition, what hope did the colonies have for a future role in the empire? Patriot military victory and political success in

Canada seemed one of very few measures that might shock the Ministry and Crown into rational compromise with the colonies.[8]

During this same time frame, an apparent sideshow in the Continental Army camp at Cambridge directly reflected changing revolutionary attitudes. The fifth of November marked Guy Fawkes' Day, otherwise known as Pope's Day, traditionally observed in New England with the "ridiculous and childish Custom of burning the Effigy of the pope." Now, Washington strictly forbade the Continental Army from such exhibitions. In his orders, the general expressed astonishment that officers and soldiers would be "so void of common sense, as not to see the impropriety of such a step at this Juncture," when Catholic brethren were actively taking up the cause in Canada. Washington astutely educated his men on the strategic significance of apparently minor or frivolous actions, and ensured that his army did not provide loyalists with further evidence of United Colonial hypocrisy in their efforts to bring Quebec into the confederation.[9]

—————

General Schuyler's sharp 21 October response to Congressional dithering finally triggered action to create a Committee to the Northern Army. On 2 November, the Philadelphia assembly established a committee of three, to "repair northward, to confer with Gen[era]l Schuyler." The delegates were all New Englanders—John Langdon, Robert Treat Paine, and Eliphalet Dyer, from New Hampshire, Massachusetts, and Connecticut, respectively.[10]

This committee followed on the heels of a similar effort, a Committee to the Camp at Cambridge, which spent most of October consulting with General Washington on the Continental Army's future. In that conference, the commander-in-chief deliberately excluded Northern Department issues from discussions, paving the way for the Langdon-Paine-Dyer committee. The Cambridge Committee presented its report on 3 November; over the next few days, Congress responded with a slew of resolutions, standardizing and shaping a "new army" under Washington.[11]

All that Congressional activity, however, delayed the completion of the Northern Army Committee's instructions. In the meantime, Connecticut's Eliphalet Dyer "excused himself from going northward," due to an "indisposition." New York delegate Robert R. Livingston Jr. was selected to replace him—General Montgomery's brother-in-law. None of these three committee members had specific Northern Department qualifications, but all had excellent patriot *bona fides*.[12]

Not yet thirty, Robert R. Livingston was the young political star of his influential family. Ironically, the Hudson Valley Livingstons probably had more in common with Quebec's seigneurs than with Canadian rebels; as manorial lords, they had even seen their tenants recently resist mobilization for the patriot cause, an event rooted in long-standing struggles over land-holding terms. The committee's eldest member, Robert Treat Paine, was a preeminent Massachusetts lawyer, a prosecutor in the Boston Massacre trials. Paine was a good detail man, heavily involved in committees, but had not been a major innovator.[13]

John Langdon was a New Hampshire merchant who had risen to prominence in that colony's patriot ranks. His most famous moment came in mid-December 1774, when he led two hundred men to seize provincial powder from Portsmouth's island "Castle," Fort William and Mary. He was an effective leader in the committee room and the field of action. Langdon also recently spurred New Hampshire's push to create a new revolutionary form of government — the province had been left "Destitute of Legislation" by the "Sudden & Abrupt Departure" of their royal leadership; Congress approved this move on 3 November. Langdon's assignment to the Northern Army Committee, just as his pet project was set into motion, understandably caused him some consternation.[14]

While Montgomery was optimistic about these delegates, two fellow ex-British officers were more guarded. General Charles Lee felt Paine was too provincial to handle the French-Canadiens, lacking the proper "*mannieres*." Adjutant General Horatio Gates hoped there were "Brains and Language sufficient in those upon that Delegation, to influence the Canadians to support all our Measures," and wished Benjamin Franklin had been selected as a member; yet Paine, Langdon, and Livingston were the only representatives sent north by Congress.[15]

Unlike the military-focused Committee to Cambridge, the Northern Army Committee's 8 November instructions included political elements; the trio was instructed to consult with General Schuyler on the "best and most efficacious method . . . of engaging the inhabitants of the colony of Canada to accede to the Association of the United Colonies" and for protecting the Canadians. Their general guidance on Quebec was a reiteration of John Hancock's 11 October advice to General Schuyler: persuade the Canadians to join the union, reassure them of their rights, and raise the Canadian Continental regiment. Congress also proclaimed an intention to "procure as much hard money as will be necessary . . . to be used in Canada," and approved Schuyler's plan for Canadian loyalist prisoners—loose confinement in the United Colonies. Other military guidance included direction regarding fortifications, provisions, reenlistments, recruiting, and pay.[16]

Two days later, John Hancock advised Schuyler of the committee's mission, enclosing a copy of their instructions, so the general could prepare to confer with the delegation. With orders in hand, the committee members left Philadelphia on 12 November. They did not arrive in Albany until 21 November and reached Fort George on the twenty-sixth; they had spent time inspecting the Hudson Valley fortifications en route, as part of their official duties. In Hackensack and Albany, they passed British prisoners from both Fort Chambly and Fort St-Jean, confirming the Northern Army's recent success. Delayed for two days at Fort George, due to "extream severe weather," they reached Ticonderoga on the twenty-eighth. Upon arrival, they happened upon General Prescott and a number of officers captured on the St. Lawrence. Their serial encounters with Ministerial enemies, so recently vanquished from Canada, must have reinforced the committee's confidence in a northern victory.[17]

The delegation did not take long to conduct business after their arrival at Ticonderoga. While the Cambridge Committee consulted Washington for a month, the Northern Army Committee spent just three days with Schuyler. Paine, Langdon, and Livingston contributed little of substance, finding that the generals had "anticipated" their instructions. Without further insight into their conversations, it seems they were glorified couriers and cheerleaders. After only one day of consultation, Robert R. Livingston wrote to Montgomery, "I believe we shall leave you to manage what you have so prosperously begun, I sh[oul]d almost say finished." The delegates took another day to coordinate with General Schuyler, and as their last act before returning to Philadelphia, composed a long letter to Montgomery.[18]

In that letter, the committee's only meaningful guidance concerned the establishment of a Canadian patriot government. The delegates repeated Congress's broad instructions and asked Montgomery, in their own words, to "Cherish the first dawnings of liberty among a people, who have early testified their sense of its Value." Langdon, Paine, and Livingston gave the general one solid task: to use his "utmost endeavours to procure a free meeting of the people in their several Parishes," as the first step in generating a provincial government and selecting delegates for Philadelphia. Of course, this had been a basic point in Congressional plans since October 1774.[19]

The delegates also reiterated that, if needed, Congress was prepared to accept partial representation from "Such Towns, Parishes and districts, as may think it proper to send deputies." Paine, Livingston, and Langdon offered an additional morsel of their own; if the Canadians found they needed political advice, Congress would be pleased to send another committee "to meet and Confer with them . . . at Albany, Montreal, or any other place," at a time when "the Communication is more open." The committee was oblivious to the Canadians' overall apathy toward political union and did not realize that Montgomery was too preoccupied with a demanding military campaign to nurture Quebec's taste for liberty. The province absolutely needed hands-on assistance, not long-distance advice.[20]

If Langdon, Paine, and Livingston were truly exerting their "utmost endeavours" for any or all of these objectives, it would seem that they would have left Ticonderoga for Montréal, rather than returning to Philadelphia. Even the committee members confided that they had a perceived duty to enter Canada. In early November, Langdon wrote of his appointment to "a Committee to go to Canada." After their return, Paine also admitted he "had some expectation" of proceeding farther when they set out on the mission. Instead, they turned south from Ticonderoga on 1 December. The scope of their mission really called for a much more dynamic, aggressive, and energetic approach.[21]

According to the committee members, their decision to avoid Canada hinged on a number of arguments, and Schuyler was allegedly in agreement. The first and most obvious point was "the Advanced season of the year." It was "too late to pass Safely by Water & too early to pass on the Ice," and the trip could not be made "without the greatest difficulty and hazard." While the trip would undoubtedly have been challenging, it was far from impossible, especially for a small group. In this same season, Schuyler was advising that troops could be sent to Canada with little difficulty, even before Lake Champlain's ice set. The delegates also maintained that the previous actions taken by Schuyler and Montgomery had "render[e]d a Journey into Canada in some measure unnecessary at present"; yet the generals had actually done little to directly foster Canadian government and the union, beyond distributing manifestos and offering suggestions, as they were so busy.[22]

In the committee's 30 November letter to Montgomery and late-December report to Congress, they also argued that Montgomery would be too busy to assist *them,* "that their Journey there, would be of little use to the publick." At the very point when Montgomery most needed someone to assume responsibility for civil affairs in liberated Canada, precisely because he was so heavily engaged in military business, the committee used that as a justification for cutting their voyage short, lacking the initiative to lead political activity. Instead, it left vital governance issues to be handled in Montréal by the cantankerous Brigadier-General Wooster.[23]

Perhaps the best insight into the committee's core rationale for stopping short of Quebec comes from Robert R. Livingston's letter to his close friend John Jay, in which he confided that his "strongest objection" was that the committee was "by no means adapted to the manners of the people with whom they were to deal." He was confident they "would not greatly raise the reputation of the congress, nor answer any good purpose among the polished people." It turned out that the assessments of Generals Gates and Lee had been correct. Perhaps this was also why General Schuyler so readily concurred with the committee's excuses for not moving on to Canada; maybe he likewise anticipated they would have little effect, or perhaps might even hurt the cause in Montréal.[24]

═══════

While the Committee to the Northern Army was halfheartedly conducting its mission, the general spirit in Congress was tremendously optimistic. News of victories at Chambly and St-Jean, followed by Montréal's "quiet submission," led many to believe that Québec City would undoubtedly fall quickly. Richard Henry Lee reflected a common view when he reported, "Success, equal to the justice of the cause, has followed this undertaking," and that "No doubt is entertained here, but that this Congress will be shortly joined by Delegates from Canada, which will then complete the union of 14 provinces." President John Hancock believed victory in Quebec would prove to be a "most mortifying Contravention to the ministerial System of enslaving" that province. Meanwhile, Generals Washington and Schuyler struggled to remind Congress that success was not guaranteed and understood there would "certainly be a strong army to retake Canada in the spring." On 4 December, the commander-in-chief subtly nudged Congress, noting that "the Reduction of Quebec is an Object of Such great importance that I doubt not the Congress will give every assistance in their power for the Accomplishing it this Winter."[25]

Without waiting for the Northern Army Committee's report, Congress officially lauded Schuyler and Montgomery. Hancock also offered personal encouragement to Schuyler, who had frequently expressed his intention to resign. The president of Congress thanked the Northern Army's third general, Wooster, as well for his "very important Assistance" in "spreading the Banners of Freedom over the greatest Part of Canada." On 9 December, Congress recognized Montgomery's efforts, promoting him to major-general—a rank commensurate with command of all Continental forces in Quebec—although he would still be subordinate to Schuyler as part of the Northern Army.[26]

It was not until 23 December that John Langdon presented the Northern Army report to Congress, as the only committee member in attendance. All three members had delayed together at Albany to participate in an Indian conference, until Livingston rushed home on the tenth, after hearing of his father's death. At mid-month, Langdon rode for Philadelphia on horseback, while Paine opted for a slower return by sulky. He would not reach Philadelphia until five days after Langdon presented the committee report, despite his friends' appeals for haste to promptly present "the state of our affairs in Canada" in Congress.[27]

Langdon's report reflected the delegates' priorities; it was heavily focused on military matters, with only a small fraction of the report addressing Quebec's political affairs. Amidst the wealth of army concerns, the report quibbled with Montgomery's uniform issue at Montréal, suggesting that perhaps it was proper to charge troops for the clothes the general had given them. Regarding troop strength in Canada, the committee concurred with Schuyler's recommendations almost verbatim: three thousand men for the winter, with more in the spring to prepare defensive works and defend the province. In just two sentences on the Canadian Regiment, they found Congress's direction "had been Complied with before the Arrival of your Committee, and the Command given to Colonel James Livingston."[28]

Their report on Canadian politics was only a paragraph long, effectively focused on their committee's activities—their reasons for not going to Quebec and the advice they had given Montgomery—rather than on an analysis of the province's status in relation to the United Colonies. The committee explained how they "concluded by a letter to General Montgomery to inform the Canadians of the Sent[i]ments of Congress" and left the commander responsible for finding "a proper Opportunity to Communicate them," and they described their offer to send a second committee to the north, "when the ice should render the Journey more practicable, and when it may probably be attended with Salutary effects."[29]

Congress waited until after the New Year to act on the report, in contrast to their immediate response after receiving the Cambridge Committee report in early November. The Northern Army situation was different, though, in that most administrative matters had already been taken care of, except for the two most strategic issues: finding thousands of replacement troops and helping to establish a provincial government in Quebec.

—————

After ushering in 1776, Congress slowly returned to consider Quebec's needs. On 2 January, the body took a few moments to write British commander General Howe to ensure that Ethan Allen and the other Continental prisoners from Longue-Pointe would not be punished for treason and that the conditions of their confinement would be improved. The United Colonies declared that they would treat their British prisoners of war the same way as the Americans were being treated in Ministerial hands, including a threat to place General Prescott in chains, as Ethan Allen had been in Canada.[30]

Four days later, the "Committee on General Schuyler's Letters" provided an update from the Northern Army. In a 31 December letter, the Northern Army commander, begging "a thousand pardons of Congress" for his "importunity" on the matter, repeated his wish "that a considerable force should be immediately sent into Canada." He contended that "unless such a measure be adopted, we shall severely repent of it, perhaps when too late to afford a remedy."[31]

Finally, on 8 January, Congress sealed their plan for Northern Army reinforcements, almost three months after the receipt of Schuyler's first inquiry on the matter. In a full-day session dedicated to Canada, the United Colonies determined to post nine battalions (regiments) in the Province of Quebec—theoretically sixty-five hundred Continentals—to conquer Québec City, secure the province, and counter a Ministerial relief force. Three battalions would come from Canada—Livingston's Canadians and two formed from the remnants of Montgomery's and Arnold's corps. The other six units would be drawn from New Hampshire, Connecticut, New York, New Jersey, and two from Pennsylvania, to be "kept up and maintained" through 1776.[32] The Jersey battalion, and one of Pennsylvania's, were immediately ordered to join Schuyler; the others would need time to form.[33]

A proposal to promote Benedict Arnold to brigadier-general followed, unanimously approved on 10 January. Turning to recognize patriot Canadians, John Hancock officially praised James Livingston for having "signally exerted himself in the cause of America." Likewise, Congress expressed its "grateful Sense" for James Price's support to the "American Cause" and promised immediate repayment of the money he had advanced to the Northern Army.[34]

─────

As 1775 drew to a close, celebrated New York City patriot Alexander Mc-Dougall presented an astute set of questions to delegate John Jay—the sort of strategic inquiries that ought to have been asked before ever launching the invasion, but which were equally poignant at this point. Nominal commander of the First New York Regiment, because of his political skill and influence, Colonel McDougall had been vigorously entreated to stay in the province when his unit deployed to Canada. Sufficiently removed from the daily hubbub of Philadelphia, Cambridge, or Canada and well informed by two of his officers in Montréal, Lieutenant-Colonel Ritzema and "old Friend" Captain William Goforth, McDougall discerned strategic issues that were lost in the torrent of daily demands saturating the Congressional delegates' and Continental generals' attention.[35]

McDougall postulated that as "the Army was sent to Canada to enable the inhabitants to speak out, if they Chose it, and join the Virtuous Confederacy," Montgomery's recent victories had achieved the campaign's military objective. But, he pondered, what would happen if the Canadians did not take advantage of their situation and failed to develop a patriot government to join the United Colonies before the spring thaw? Could a large army "compel" the habitants to join the confederation, or would Quebec merely become an indefensible position? McDougall suggested that these questions "should be well and early considered," so that success in Canada did not "weaken, instead of strengthening the Confederacy."[36]

McDougall also foresaw the looming Ministerial juggernaut that would hit Quebec in the spring. With British naval superiority, in a province dominated by a single navigable line of communication, would Continental forces not "be exposed to have their communication cut off with Montreal, by the Enemy's landing Troops and intrenching between those places?" A plan, with troops to execute it, was an immediate necessity; the colonel suggested that at least six thousand men should be sent quite soon.[37]

A question McDougall left unasked was what measures, beyond military activity, might convince the Canadians to join the confederacy and thus achieve the campaign's principal objective: Canadian unity in the Continental Congress. The critical intermediate step was the formation of local government in the liberated districts of Quebec; yet as the calendar turned to 1776, the only notable Canadian patriot leaders were engrossed in military activity: Livingston and his officers, Maurice Desdevens, and even James Price. Somebody needed to be building a government—hardly a thought for Quebec's revolutionaries to this point—and even with the enticement of the Georgian "parish" model for partial congressional representation, there was not the slightest move to send Canadian delegates.

Beyond grand addresses, the United Colonies had made no earnest effort to mentor the habitants, bourgeois, and prominent *Canadiens* in proven political mechanics that might foster a patriot government and achieve the principal Continental goal in Canada. Without functioning committees of correspondence or safety, Canada was years behind the confederated colonies in developing an effective patriot political organization and clearly needed help to catch up. The critical moment came when Montréal fell; as the Canadians failed to show sufficient initiative in governing themselves, they needed a boost—exactly what a timely Congressional delegation might provide. The Northern Army Committee was almost perfectly timed, but its decision to return from Ticonderoga precluded any opportunity for nurturing early Canadian government leadership. The void of Canadian civilian government at the end of 1775 bade ill for Quebec's union with the confederated colonies.

Congress also ignored military considerations for far too long. It was no secret that most enlistments expired in late 1775. Even if Schuyler and Montgomery had stayed at Ile-aux-Noix and never advanced to the mainland, they would have needed replacements before the end of the year—an effort that should have been initiated the moment Congress heard the invasion had been launched. By waiting until early January to identify units for the 1776 campaign, the Philadelphia assembly put the Northern Army months behind. The dearth of congressional decisions in the fall would reverberate on the St. Lawrence in December and May. The United Colonies simply failed to posture themselves to exploit their initial military gains in Canada.

Chapter 13

CONTEST OF WILLS AT QUÉBEC

The Fortress Capital—Key to Victory?

I fear the Canadians will not relish a union with the Colonies, till they see the whole Country in our hands. | *General Richard Montgomery to General Philip Schuyler, headquarters outside Quebec, 18 December 1775*

Let not one small disaster among so many noble deeds, discourage the Sons of Liberty. | Pennsylvania Packet, *19 February 1776*

Isolated behind Québec City's ramparts, loyalists were disgusted by the unwillingness of the habitants to bring provisions into the capital following Arnold's 19 November departure. Whether from "ingratitude, or fear of the resentment of the rebels," the locals were "neither bringing provisions nor allowing them to be brought by others." Citizens, especially Old Subjects, maligned their rural neighbors as "traitorous, faithless, ungrateful villains." It was an "absurdity" that "a party of fifty rebels hinders a body of from 4 to 5,000 Canadians from doing as they please."[1] Capital loyalists were correct; the habitants were making a clear statement. Arnold's men had been eagerly attended when settled around the Plains of Abraham; Carleton's garrison received virtually nothing. It obviously was not about money; the governor's coin was just as valuable as the rebels'. Thirty miles downriver in the southshore community of Pointe-à-la-Caille, the habitants took a more drastic step. When loyalists loaded a vessel in that parish with livestock and provisions for Québec City, locals "forcibly detain'd" the boat. A party of ardent patriots from St-François-du-Sud, ten miles away, helped block the shipment and subsequently redirected it to the rebels—the only thing reaching the capital from Pointe-à-la-Caille was demoralizing news of the incident.[2]

For the first few days of December, a long string of brilliantly decorated

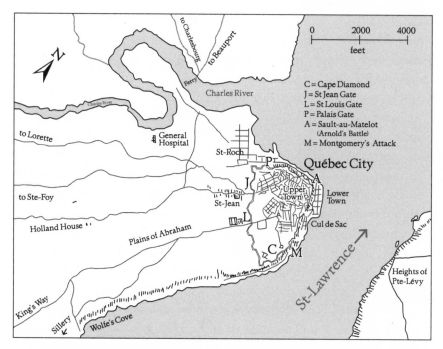

MAP 7: Québec City Environs.

habitant sleighs, heavily laden with soldiers and baggage, jingled toward the snow-blanketed Plains of Abraham. With Arnold's rifle companies in the lead, the Continentals deployed in a sweeping arc surrounding the capital, ranging from Charlesbourg in the north to Ste-Foy (see Map 7). They found cozy accommodations and hospitable hosts in numerous "low and pretty country houses" a few miles from the capital fortifications. General Montgomery established his headquarters at Holland House, the estate home of provincial surveyor-general Major Samuel Holland and the leased residence of legislative councilor and "Le Canadien Patriote" author Hugh Finlay, conveniently situated on the Ste-Foy road at the southwest end of the Plains; Caldwell's house, which had been Arnold's headquarters, was no longer habitable. By 6 December, the army was adequately arranged "to prevent any further supplies arriving" for Québec City.[3]

Amidst the snowy fields, light woods, and whitewashed habitant homes interspersed along Continental lines, there was one anomaly: a substantial compound less than a mile from the capital's St-Jean gate, the General-Hospital (*Hôpital-Général*). Near the Charles River, the hospital's large, main stone structure had been called "the finest building in all Canada," surrounded by gardens, outbuildings, and even a windmill. A religious home for the city's indigent elderly and infirm, run by thirty nuns, this facility would be the stage for an intriguing interplay between its loyalist staff and Continentals.[4]

In November, Arnold's corps had explored the General-Hospital's military possibilities; so when the army returned, hundreds of troops sought quarters in the substantial edifice. Nuns feared the rebels would draw artillery, but Continentals were rightly convinced that Carleton had forbidden all fire toward the charitable institution—a benefit to both soldiers and sisters. Equally disturbed by the overwhelming mass of guests, Father Superior Charles-Régis Bergères-de-Rigauville[5] visited Holland House to politely protest the imposition. Montgomery, Arnold, and the father returned, finding the building so full of troops that they could barely enter the door. The general surveyed the situation and issued new orders, relocating most Continentals; only Captain Henry Dearborn's New Hampshire company remained. Just ten days later, they were moved as well, to make room for Doctor Isaac Senter's principal army hospital.[6]

―――――

General Montgomery, while focused on establishing the blockade, had not completely ignored Canadian politics. On 4 December, his translator produced a French version of John Hancock's 11 October letter to Schuyler, describing Congress's recommendations for a Canadian provincial convention, and once again, Captain Desdevens helped disseminate copies. Montgomery also met with fervent Canadian patriot Christophe Pélissier, visiting from St-Maurice Forges near Trois-Rivières. The French-born Pélissier had lived in Quebec for more than twenty years and ran the iron forges—the province's only significant industrial operation. He had an Enlightenment-inspired libertarian zest, as well as "prompt abilities" and an "Enterprising Genius." At the general's request, Pélissier tried to promote a Canadian convention in Montréal and Trois-Rivières circles, "to the end that Deputies might be chosen to join the Continental Congress," but quickly decided it was impracticable. Countless urban loyalists were "continually intimidating the people with supposed consequences" of joining the United Colonies, promoting "odious and contemptible ideas of the American Confederation." Pélissier convinced Montgomery that a convention "ought not be attempted till after the reduction of Quebeck," when Canadians would be convinced of their interest in joining the union.[7]

The Canadian militia was also notably absent from the Continental blockade lines, by Montgomery's choice, not from lack of volunteers. Despite Colonel Livingston's view that local Canadians should be included, Montgomery declined to invite large parties of armed habitants in camp; however, he was happy to use their labor, carriage, and provisions. The core factor in the general's choice was probably discipline; capitulating Montréal and Trois-Rivières citizens had expressed serious apprehensions about habitants running amok in their cities. Montgomery may have decided that the volunteers' marginal military contributions were outweighed by the detrimental impact they might have on his immediate objective: the capital's surrender.[8]

Livingston's Canadian Regiment, more trusted, led the combined Continental corps's first raid. On the night of 5 December, Captain Jeremiah Duggan led a party to the suburb of St-Roch, dominated by the capital's northwest fortifications, which loomed atop a steep hill, directly over the *ville*. The Canadian Continentals came to disarm St-Roch, apparently at the suburbanites' invitation. Duggan's men met no resistance, seized weapons, required locals to "give their Paroles not to carry arms," and then withdrew before dawn. Many St-Roch residents subsequently packed up their possessions and fled for refuge from the anticipated siege.[9]

The next day, Duggan's men and one of Arnold's rifle companies moved to Beauport, one parish downriver from Québec City, to "watch the motions of the enemy." While there, they opportunistically seized a ship full of provisions, livestock, and government money. The Continentals also paid a visit to the nearby seigneurial manor of Antoine Juchereau-Duchesnay, a loyalist gentleman volunteer captured at Fort St-Jean. Duggan haughtily declared himself "master of the house," demanded food, killed pigs, and seized the seigneur's choicest wares, "striking in their quality and value," which he locked in the granary for future recovery.[10]

After Duggan's St-Roch raid, Montgomery established forward posts in that suburb and St-Jean, which lay before the southwest city gate of that name, well within cannon shot, but clearly visible to defenders on the parapets. Many Continentals still hoped a demonstration of intent might prompt the city's fall from within. Carleton's 22 November proclamation made such a popularly driven capitulation doubtful; no patriot agitators were left to foster unrest. Still, Montgomery endeavored to spark a spontaneous surrender if he might, developing a pair of messages to sow dissent among the defenders.

The first was a letter to "Friends & fellow Subjects," both in English and French, inviting them to promote his "peaceable Admission" to the city. The general warned of dire consequences if he were forced to dislodge the Ministerial troops: "The City in Flames at this severe Season . . . The Confusion, Carnage & Plunder." He also assured them, despite aspersions about Continental "Inhumanity," that people and property would be respected. His army came solely with the intention of "eradicating Tyranny & giving Liberty and Security" to the "oppressed Province."[11]

The second message was a surrender request, presented "in very extraordinary language," as Carleton later described it. Montgomery bragged of his army's success and insulted the "wretched" garrison and defenses, while threatening to hold the governor accountable for persisting in "an unwarrantable defence" and for "destroying stores of any sort, public or private." Composing the letters was easy—delivery was the challenge.[12]

Not bothering to send another flag of truce, Montgomery tried smuggling his messages into town with an old woman on 7 December. Gate guards apprehended the "perfidious female" after entry, and Carleton ceremoniously burned the unread letters. Unwilling to abandon their "psychological operation," the Continentals attached additional copies to arrows, which Sartigan Indian auxiliaries fired over the walls. Although loyalist accounts maintained that the arrows "were immediately picked up and carried to the Governor," Continentals were confident that copies were circulated about town.[13]

The capital defenses were not impermeable. A few Continental deserters were admitted through the Palais Gate. Two loyalist agents crept out of the city and were captured along the St. Lawrence with "300 dollars in specie," trying to purchase provisions. As deserters and spies crossed the lines, the Continentals were also visited by a virulent menace—smallpox. The camp was vulnerable: most of the army had been neither inoculated nor exposed to the disease, especially the troops from New England, where inoculation was tightly controlled. Officers forbade the practice of inoculation to avoid losing troops for weeks as they fought the disease, and to preclude inadvertent exposure to others within their units. Tight quarters in habitant homes also encouraged the infection's easy spread.[14]

The first documented report, dated 6 December, noted, "The small pox is all around us, and there is great danger of its spreading in the army." There was a known outbreak in the capital; some habitants probably had spread the contagion as Continentals billeted with them. To mitigate the impact, Montgomery promptly established a smallpox hospital in Sillery on the St. Lawrence shore, far from the main camp; yet by 21 December, Private Caleb Haskell recorded "The small pox spreads fast in our army."[15]

There were accusations that Carleton deliberately introduced smallpox to aid his defense. Québec City exile Hector McNeill made the most direct, contemporary charge: that Carleton inoculated "the poor people at government expence for the purpose of giving it to our army." Yet the outbreak probably sparked from casual *Canadien*-Continental interaction, kindled in campaign-weakened constitutions and further fanned by self-inoculating soldiers.[16]

Another scourge, not medical but moral, began to manifest itself in Arnold's corps as well. On 2 December, three of his New England companies threatened to return home. Connecticut Captain Oliver Hanchett, in particular, started a pattern of insubordination. The captain refused orders on two occasions: to transport heavy cargo from Pointe-aux-Trembles to Sillery, and to man a hazardous post in St-Jean. Arnold tried to overlook Hanchett's insubordination, ordering other companies to perform these duties, but a combination of campaign fatigue and personality conflict with their commander was eroding his men's incredible discipline and epic endurance.[17]

After fruitless attempts to coax the city into surrender, Montgomery began establishing artillery batteries, a prospect posing two major hurdles. First, the Continentals lacked siege guns and were outgunned by any measure. The second challenge was seasonal: frozen ground made it impossible to erect normal battery fortifications. Habitants had already helped assemble plenty of fascines and gabions[18] to frame earthworks, but there was no dirt fill to complete them.

Employing "Yankee ingenuity," on 9 December, Montgomery ordered construction of an "ice battery" on the outskirts of the St-Jean suburb. Snow-covered gabions and fascines were dampened to freeze into solid ice. During five days of construction and gun hauling, British cannon harassed the rebels, killing one and wounding several. The Continental battery finally opened fire at dawn on 15 December, but the gunners found their medium-weight guns could inflict little "material damage except throwing down a few chimneys." Effective loyalist counterbattery fire cracked at the ice works, persuading Yorker artillerymen that the position was "too feeble for the purpose it was erected"; by Christmas Eve, they had abandoned their shattered "heap of nonsense." In his private correspondence, Montgomery confessed that the battery's real mission was "deception."[19]

Another Continental battery had begun operating in St-Roch on 8 December. Using mortars sheltered near the base of the capital's steep hill, besiegers lofted high-angle shot into the city. Continentals hoped the mortars might terrorize the population into submission or put the garrison "into some confusion." With memories of the heavy 1759 bombardment, "proprietors of houses dreaded the effect of the enemys shells," but after a few impacts from rebel bombettes, citizens reportedly "walked the streets laughing at their former fears." Riflemen from Arnold's corps achieved greater effect. Using concealed posts high in St-Roch houses and the old Intendant's Palace, they sniped at sentries on the capital parapets, killing and wounding several. Of course, traditionalist defenders disdained such "savage" and "contemptuous" warfare; "Lie in wait to shoot a sentry! a deed worthy of Yanky men of war." Yet sharpshooters, however deadly, would never reduce a fortress to surrender by themselves.[20]

Montgomery concurrently expanded the blockade, ordering a small detachment to Ile-d'Orléans, the same downstream island that vehemently had opposed loyalist mobilization in October. On 8 December, Pennsylvania Rifle Lieutenant William Cross, a "handsome little Irishman, always neatly dressed," led twenty of Captain Matthew Smith's troops to the island, "to keep all provisions from going to town." Upon arrival, the lieutenant called a habitant assembly, confirming every islander's support for the Continental effort.[21]

During his command tenure, Cross excelled in gathering provisions. Finding "some Ships on the Island whose Owners were Inimicable to the Continent," he seized their cargos. The lieutenant subsequently directed habitants to "assemble a number of slays," and delivered the confiscated goods to the siege lines. The lieutenant also found a stable of horses off-loaded from a ship, which coincidentally had belonged to Benedict Arnold from one of his pre-Ticonderoga business endeavors. At least three patriot steeds were sent to Holland House, while others served on the island.[22]

Cross, however, exploited his remote command. Within a couple of weeks, patriot islanders visited Holland House protesting the lieutenant's behavior: "Cross had extorted from them their wines and other liquors, and all kinds of provisions," without compensation. Allegedly he was keeping an "open house," splitting the spoils with his men, and abusing his authority. Another soldier observed it was all the more shocking because "the people of the isle were our friends." On 29 December, based on habitant complaints, Arnold terminated the lieutenant's "luxurious and merry reign over that charming spot." His successor's orders reflect the nature of Cross's indiscretions; in addition to enforcing the blockade, the new commander was counseled to "be assiduous in gaining the esteem of the inhabitants, who are now complaining that they have been treated in a rigorous manner" and to keep his men "under strict discipline, and not suffer them to have too much liquor." Lieutenant Cross's haughty marauding, following Arnold's New England officers' recalcitrance earlier in the month, began to taint the great reputation of the Kennebec Expedition's officers.[23]

On the mainland, other riflemen were looting too, but theirs was focused against loyalists, not friends. In mid-December, a "scoundrel Canadian" informant led another rifle company detachment on unauthorized expeditions to ransack property, allegedly belonging to the lieutenant-governor, "or some other inhabitant of Quebec." On consecutive nights, they raided two estates, seizing livestock, food stores, and luxury items such as "costly feather beds" and silverware sets. They did not leave until the ill-gotten goods spilled out of their sleighs. The recorder of these incidents, Pennsylvania rifleman John Joseph Henry, proudly reported, "With this disreputable exploit, marauding ceased"; given time to reflect on their behavior, the pillagers became contrite. Henry still emphasized that their only targets were "known tories," also boasting: "The clergy, the nobles, and the peasantry, were respected and protected, especially the latter, with whom, to use a trite expression, we fraternized."[24]

While the rebels were blockading, sniping, bombarding, and marauding, loyalists established a defensive routine. Adapting to regular garrison duty, militia, regulars, Emigrants, and sailors manned posts around the fortress. Carleton and Maclean tweaked the militia organization, consolidating "French" militia companies and creating an "invalids" company to employ less-hardy citizens for noncombat duties.

Having written off the suburbs, the garrison still had two starkly different areas to defend: Upper and Lower Towns. Upper Town was naturally fortified by steep ground on its north, norteast, and south sides; the remaining sides were protected by stone walls—not perfect, but still formidable. The extensive ramparts were interrupted by three gates: the northwest Palais Gate, above St-Roch, and two opening to the southwest, St-Jean and St-Louis Gates. Internally, Upper Town was highly defensible; reminiscent of a medieval European city, the streets were "generally irregular and uneven," and the "shabby awkward" stone buildings were effectively miniature forts.[25]

Mercantile port Lower Town was quite different. Isolated at the city's northeast tip, it was a narrow strip of tall trade houses, aligned on a couple of long streets conforming to the waterfront, with numerous crossroads leading to the docks. Lower Town's only connections to Upper Town were a road and paths winding up the steep-pitched rocky hillside. The garrison built a barrier midway up, where the roadway was actually cut into the rock, and added barricades at both ends of Lower Town. The walls high above St-Roch and the St. Lawrence dominated the northern and eastern approaches as well.

Montgomery, however, was not yet ready to storm the capital. On 15 December, shortly after the "ice battery" commenced fire, the general made a final attempt to encourage surrender. Arnold and Montgomery's aide-de-camp, Colonel John McPherson, marched cautiously toward the walls under a flag of truce. Their reception was predictable, if less violent than previous episodes. The two colonels were informed that the governor would have "no manner of communication with rebels," so they trudged back to Holland House, their mission unfulfilled.[26]

After his last embassy was rebuffed, Montgomery wrote a telling letter to brother-in-law Robert R. Livingston, addressing the news that the Congressional committee would not arrive in 1775. The general was "mortified" that Livingston and fellow delegates found it unnecessary to go to Quebec. In Montgomery's eyes, the oft-requested committee would have served two critical purposes: curbing "licentious" Continental troops by improving discipline and morale, and promoting Canadian public interest by "influencing the people to a choice of representatives." The embassy also would have precluded the "disagreeable necessity" of Montgomery determining policy on his own, "running the hazard of mistaking the intentions of Congress."[27]

Shortly before drafting this letter, Montgomery had committed to assaulting Québec City, recognizing the futility of his "endeavors" to bring Carleton or the citizens to an "accommodation." He felt compelled to take action by twin pressures. Militarily, almost all of Arnold's New England men would depart on New Year's Day—their enlistments expired—removing about half of the Kennebec Expedition's troops. Politically, Montgomery feared the Canadians would not join the union until all of Quebec Province was clearly in Continental control; thus, conquest of the capital was critical to achieving the campaign's ultimate aim. If not for the combination of factors, the general would have continued the blockade in hopes of starving out the garrison.[28]

After the failed 15 December parley, Montgomery called a council of war. His field officers agreed to storm the capital, although James Livingston again suggested that a large number of habitant volunteers might give the army sufficient mass to convince the defenders to surrender—a notion the general declined. When "the first strong northwester" brought a storm, the Continentals would make a night attack. A third of the troops would make a feint on the Lower Town, while the main body attacked the relatively isolated southeastern Cape Diamond bastion by "Escalade," scaling the walls with ladders. The general still fretted about manpower, observing that he had "not much above 800 men fit for duty," and then adding the quip, "exclusive of a few Raggamuffin Canadians," presumably a reference to volunteers rather than Livingston's Continentals, whose numbers seem to be part of the aforementioned total. Yet Montgomery was willing to try the "experiment," exclaiming "*Audaces fortuna juvat*" (Fortune favors the brave). Having learned to consult his "democratic" soldiers, the general conferred with them on 23 December and was reassured that they supported the plan.[29]

Meanwhile, the capital garrison was on edge. Frequent snowstorms fostered a rash of false alarms; it was easy to imagine shadowy figures in the distance, shuffling behind undulating curtains of falling flakes. The first call came on the dark morn of 16 December; the entire garrison ran to battle posts, only to find no enemy approaching. The cycle was repeated on the eighteenth and twice on the twentieth. Sentries, standing guard in pairs due to bitterly cold weather, were definitely skittish, but regained their composure after the 20 December incidents.[30]

The garrison began receiving encouraging news from outside, by foot and canoe. The rebel army was reportedly in a bad state; Canadians were abandoning them, while Yankees and Yorkers tired of the expedition. The letters also brought cause for worry. One warned there was a "machination of some of the Captains of the militia"—Québec City garrison officers were allegedly keeping "secret correspondence" with the rebels. Of course, Old Subject commentators hastily concluded that the traitors were "those of the French part of the population."[31]

The most important intelligence, however, came on 22 December. Major Caldwell's clerk Joshua Wolf, under rebel arrest for a month, escaped and crept into Lower Town. He told of a rebel plan to storm the city on the night of the twenty-third, alleging that General Montgomery had boasted he "wou'd dine in Quebec or in Hell on Christmas." A Continental deserter corroborated Wolf's military information and provided further details of Montgomery's assault plan. Carleton put the garrison on full alert that evening, issuing extra ammunition.[32]

On the blizzard-veiled Plains of Abraham, Montgomery was actually preparing his Continentals to attack. Around 2 A.M. on Christmas Eve, at least some of the troops formed, but were ordered back to regular duty after dawn. Montgomery hesitated to launch the attack after learning of Wolf's escape, correctly assuming the element of surprise had been lost. At least the general had regained confidence in his men; poised on the edge of the precipice, they seemed willing to leap when ordered. Later in the day, "General Montgomery returnd his most hearty thanks to his men because they turned out the night before with such full spirits to go through with what he had desired them."[33]

Montgomery used the subsequent downtime to write one more letter to General Schuyler, mostly addressing finances. Montgomery was "amazed no money is yet arrived"; by the end of the month, the war chest held less than £500. A short-term effort to introduce paper money in Montréal had failed; very few businessmen accepted the bills, and the notes were widely rejected by those burnt by France paper money in the French and Indian War, and by Old Subjects too. As a result, the few cooperative Montrealers required Continentals to exchange bills at highly depreciated values, prompting termination of the experiment. The general also took the opportunity to further praise patriot financier James Price: "a faithful friend to the cause indeed." Montgomery even credited the Montréal merchant with being "the first mover" of all the Canadian measures "which have been attended with so many and great advantages to the United Colonies." Price's dedicated endeavors had built to this point—a climactic conquest of the capital and complete liberation of Quebec. Price coincidentally left for Montréal on the twenty-third, on an unspecified mission.[34]

‗‗‗‗‗‗‗

By the end of December, Continental discipline was tenuous. As John Pierce, Arnold's surveyor and engineer noted, some men continued to "Plunder the French Inhabitants," causing "great uneasiness." One more documented incident had occurred on the eve of the cancelled assault. Under Arnold's orders, a semi-legitimate escort mission to St-Roch sought to secure a patriot merchant's wares, but was disrupted by the careless "noise and bustle" of a Continental Canadian party marauding nearby. The ruckus drew a volley of garrison artillery directed at Livingston's band, driving both parties from the suburb.[35]

The next day, things suddenly turned black for Montgomery. The general discovered, to his "great mortification, that three companies of Colonel Arnold's detachment" were "very averse" to storming the city. The discontented New England units, "within a few days of being free from their engagements," may simply have been expressing self-interest, but Montgomery suspected something more. On 26 December he wrote, "There is strong reason to believe their difference of sentiments from the rest of the troops arises from the influence of their officers"—three New England captains, Goodrich, Hubbard, and the problematic Hanchett, all tired of Arnold's leadership. The mutinous captains offered to follow orders only if they could serve in a "separate command" away from Arnold, and even recommended an acceptable field officer, presumably Major John Brown.[36]

Montgomery, "much embarassed" by the affair, stood by his deputy commander and refused to accommodate the captains' cabal. The general took two measures to quell dissent. First, he had an *éclaircissement*—a heart-to-heart talk—with the "field officer," persuading him to disassociate himself from the troublemaking officers. Resolving the issue with the companies in question, Montgomery bypassed the officers and appealed directly to the men. On 27 December he met the soldiers and gave a speech that hit its mark. The troops agreed to participate in the upcoming assault.[37]

Having restored order in his force, Montgomery was still pressed for time;

he knew he had to act before the enlistments expired. The general ordered all preparations for an assault that night. Troops gathered with the "greatest cheerfulness and Alacrity," but were once again stood down before dawn. The overt rationale was unpromising weather. Presumably, Montgomery also had a nagging assumption that deserters had conveyed even more details of the assault plans to Québec City and the defenders would be fully prepared to meet his assault; a few of his men had disappeared both before and immediately after the Christmas Eve marshaling of forces.[38]

In fact, Governor Carleton had expeditiously improved the Upper Town defenses with his latest intelligence. He ordered extra cannon placed on the flank of each bastion, loaded with grapeshot and canister shells, which were particularly well suited for mowing down storming parties. A blockhouse was also completed at Cape Diamond, the primary rebel objective in the compromised original plan, providing additional forward defenses with improved fields of fire.[39]

To address the apparent fact that his scheme of attack was known by the enemy, Montgomery devised a new plan. The primary difference would be the main objective, now Lower Town—a change that Arnold and Antill advocated, and which James Price had encouraged before his departure for Montréal. These trade-minded individuals were convinced that the capital's remaining merchants would force the city to capitulate if their riverfront stores were jeopardized in rebel hands. This time, Montgomery shared his plan only with field officers, otherwise keeping the details from the rest of the men. Two of three columns would attack Lower Town, one from each end: Arnold would attack through St-Roch with his Kennebec corps, Sartigan Indians, and a sled-borne cannon; Montgomery and his Yorkers—Richelieu Valley veterans and recent reinforcements—would approach the town from the opposite direction, along the icy St. Lawrence banks under the Cape Diamond bastion. Colonel James Livingston would lead the third force, a diversion by the Canadian Continentals and Brown's men, feigning attacks on Cape Diamond and St-Jean Gate. It was audacious, tactically unsound, and fraught with risk. Montgomery divided his numerically inferior force into detachments incapable of mutual support, and with no reserve, while attacking an enemy with "internal lines," capable of moving forces from one threat to another. Even if the Continentals took Lower Town, operational success was totally contingent on Upper Town choosing to surrender. Yet, given the tools at hand and time constraints, with his better initial plan compromised, it was all Montgomery had to offer.[40]

Montgomery kept his men poised for an assault each night, awaiting favorably snowy weather. On 29 December, the general ordered additional preparatory measures to ensure surprise, sending two missions to detain individuals suspected of feeding intelligence to the garrison. Arnold's men arrested one man in a short fight at Drummond's stillhouse, near the Charles River; Captain Duggan's Canadians arrested another, probably in St-Roch, where the garrison reported seeing "arm'd rebels crossing the Streets," some clad in the red coats acquired at Montréal.[41]

On 30 December, General Montgomery also took measures farther afield, sending orders to patriot Militia-Captain Pierre Langlois at Les-Ecureuils, a neighboring parish of Pointe-aux-Trembles. Montgomery obviously doubted some of his men's commitment, ordering Langlois to "stop all the soldiers of the Continental Army who have no passes." The orders also broadly authorized Langlois "to act in all things for the best service of the Honorable the Continental Congress."[42]

When snow and rain showers began on the night of 30 December, Montgomery issued alert orders to assemble the forces. Around 4 A.M. on New Year's Eve, all troops were formed up: Arnold's at the General-Hospital, Montgomery's down at Wolfe's Cove, and Livingston's on the edge of St-Jean. Despite the snow showers, Emigrants Captain Malcolm Fraser claimed to discern "very uncommon" lights in the distance around 5 A.M. and called the guards to arms. Loyalist defenders sprang to action.[43]

General Montgomery's Yorkers advanced "in a narrow file, upon a path rendered extremely rugged by large blocks of ice thrown by the currents of the tide and the river," a steep riverbank on one side and the sheer rock wall of Cape Diamond hanging over the other. After carpenters cut down a first set of undefended pickets blocking their path, Montgomery and his senior officers led the troops from the front, tearing through a second layer of barricades to penetrate into the east edge of Lower Town. Loyalist defenders opened fire from a blockhouse — the first cannon blast killed the general and aide-de-camp McPherson. About a dozen men lay beside them, dead and wounded. "This fatal stroke" threw the troops into confusion. New York Colonel Donald Campbell now found himself in charge. Campbell had significant field experience to rely on, having served as a junior Highlander officer in the French and Indian War, including participation in General James Abercromby's futile frontal assault on French works at Fort Carillon (Ticonderoga) in 1758, and the following year's more successful campaign up Lake Champlain.

Quickly weighing the situation, perhaps under the shadow of his past combat ordeals, the colonel elected to withdraw—the entire eastern attack was shattered in minutes.[44]

Arnold's wing got a late start, missing the rocket signal launching the assault; but the troops rushed toward their objectives after hearing the din of fire from Livingston's diversionary attack. Once again, the commander was one of the first casualties. Passing the first barriers at Lower Town's north end, a shot from the high fortress walls hit Arnold in the leg; he tried to persevere, but blood loss forced him back to the General-Hospital.[45]

Unlike Montgomery's wing, Lieutenant-Colonel Christopher Greene and his captains took the initiative and pressed on after their leader fell. Continentals captured several loyalist positions in "a most dreadful conflict and carnage" of house-to-house fighting. Unaware that the other arm of the assault had failed, they fought with the same determination that drove them through the Appalachian wilderness into Canada. Carleton outflanked them, however; having repelled Montgomery's column, the governor concentrated his forces on the sole remaining battle. While Arnold's men were engaged in the pitched Lower Town battle, the governor sortied a hundred-man detachment through the Palais Gate just after the light of day, attacking the Continentals from the rear and cutting off escape. The fight continued for a short while, but after a few dramatic episodes, the surrounded, forlorn rebels were compelled to surrender as the sun broke the horizon.[46]

The only northern Lower Town attackers who escaped capture were either wounded early in the fight, like Arnold, or dared to flee across the treacherous ice in St-Charles Bay—the Sartigan Indians and a few Canadian volunteers. From about 500 men in Arnold's wing, 372 men were captured, 35 were killed, and 33 were wounded. The successful defenders marched the prisoners up to confinement in the Recollet College; as Customs-Collector Thomas Ainslie noted, "the Flower of the rebel army fell into our hands."[47]

On the Plains of Abraham, where Livingston and Brown's men were creating their diversion, defenders observed "a heavy and hot fire from a Body of men posted behind a rising ground within eighty yards of the guardhouse on Cape Diamond"; these were Brown's men, who subsequently did not move from that protected position. Concurrently, Livingston's Canadian Continentals "appeared in the suburbs of St. John," but never reached the St-Jean Gate barricades, which they intended to set ablaze. Colonel Campbell attributed the incomplete Canadian feint to "an early alarm in the town" that brought a withering fusillade, "kept up from the whole extent of the city walls incessantly"; yet since he was with Montgomery, assaulting Lower Town at the beginning of the attack, his assessment is presumably based on others' reports.[48]

While minor in the overall scheme of the attack, Livingston's men were singled out for harsh criticism, gaining a negative reputation that only grew worse farther from the scene. The sole firsthand report came from Doctor Senter at the General-Hospital. By his record, the Canadian regiment "made the best of their way off soon after the heavy fire began." He hinted that many Canadians fled beyond the limits of the camp; but Colonel Campbell's account referred to "Colonel James Livingston, with some of his regiment," being deployed between the General-Hospital and the city even as Arnold's attack was still in question, and did not immediately mention a significant Canadian flight. Three months later, Campbell recollected that men deserted by "10, 20 & 30," but that was in reference to both Arnold's and Livingston's men fleeing later in the day. The Canadians, however, made an easy scapegoat; it did not help anyone in the United Colonies to point fingers at the Yorkers' fragile attack, although that is exactly where Arnold's imprisoned troops laid the blame.[49]

While the battle was still in question, Arnold astutely sent messages to help stabilize the situation, regardless of its outcome. He sent an express dispatch from the General-Hospital to inform Wooster of Montgomery's death. With remarkable presence of mind, the painfully wounded Arnold also sent orders to nearby militia-captains, requesting immediate assistance; more men were surely needed now. Shortly thereafter, Colonel Campbell, assuming that Arnold was incapacitated, sent his own express to Wooster, detailing the defeat and making recommendations for Montréal's security. Canadian engineer Edward Antill carried this message; "well acquainted on the road," he could ensure its prompt delivery.[50]

In the immediate aftermath of the attack, Antill's version of events was the one that reached the United Colonies. By his account, the Canadians failed miserably in combat, a detail neither Arnold nor Campbell highlighted. Weeks later, in Albany, Antill's account easily fit General Schuyler's preconceptions: "the Canadians, as I have heretofore observed, are not to be depended upon; only one hundred and sixty were at Quebeck with Colonel Livingston, and those behaved ill." With Schuyler's stamp, this view became an accepted fact among most Continental leaders.[51]

The General-Hospital's history provides one last notable vignette from that chaotic New Year's Eve morning. A wounded Canadian Continental was brought in, "near death," and Father Superior de Rigauville was asked to administer last rites. Generously applying an in extremis exception to Bishop Briand's interdict against rebel Canadians-in-arms, the priest "made this young man publicly confess that he recognized that he was quite guilty, and that he was sincerely penitent." In the presence of other *Canadiens* and Continentals, de Rigauville admonished the dying soldier before giving him absolution. While Father de Rigauville went to the limits of his authority to mitigate the bishop's proscription and comfort the young soldier on his death-bed, Continental officers viewed the father superior's actions as abusive — an insult to their Canadian compatriots. Tensions grew, fueling additional confrontations in the following weeks.[52]

The failed assault presented an entirely new environment for both sides. Carleton was impressed with his militia, who had "behaved gallantly"; notably, loyalist *Canadien* losses reflected their dedication and critical role in the Lower Town fight. Of the garrison's five killed and thirteen wounded, the "French" had one killed and six wounded, two mortally. The victory dispelled most doubts about the capital's survival and offered great encouragement for the King's cause in Canada. That same day, Bishop Briand rushed to celebrate the event, proclaiming a *Te Deum* — a special hymn of praise or thanks — to celebrate the rebel defeat.[53]

Meanwhile, Governor Carleton showed "Every possible mark of distinction" to Montgomery's corpse and treated his prisoners of war well. On New Year's Day, he permitted a captured Continental major to visit Holland House, arranging for the officer prisoners' baggage — just as Montgomery had done for loyalists at St-Jean. After escorting the Continental major out of the Palais Gate, Carleton's aide-de-camp Charles de Lanaudière spied a rabble of Canadians "at the end of St Roc[h]," allegedly waiting to loot the city, presuming the rebels had been victorious. Quickly relieved of their misconceptions, they dispersed after dark. Such activity lends credence to the citizens' fears of marauding habitants; this persistent theme hints that there was substantive underlying resentment between habitants and Canadian city dwellers, maybe even with some ties to the previous summer's unrest.[54]

As word of the disaster spread from Québec City to Montréal, and on to the United Colonies, most patriots were stunned by the defeat, fearing it would negate all the recent northern gains; but a surprising number took the military loss in stride and expected a quick recovery. General Montgomery's death, however, was universally mourned and lamented. In Philadelphia, Congress ordered an oration and monument to "express the veneration of the United Colonies for their late general, Richard Montgomery," the new patriot martyr.[55]

Chapter 14

THE QUESTION OF LOYALISTS

General Wooster and "Liberated" Montréal, 1775

Would it not be prudent to seize on those Tories who have been, are, and that we know will be active against us? | *General George Washington to Rhode Island Governor Nicholas Cooke, 15 November 1775*

General Wooster is taking the most prudent and spirited measures to put it in the best order possible. | *A Continental Officer writing from Montréal, 2 December 1775*

While Québec City had a vital role in the United Colonies' military effort, Montréal was the natural focus for political activity. The city had been home to Canada's most outspoken patriots and was now freed from Ministerial rule. After Montgomery's late November departure to join Arnold outside the Canadian capital, the Northern Army's least inspirational leader, General David Wooster, was left alone in Montréal to face a slew of emerging political and military challenges.

General David Wooster was the eldest Continental Army general, sixty-five years old. The tall man "with a high sense of public duty" had served in all his generation's wars, participating in the 1745 Louisbourg siege and serving as a French and Indian War provincial brigade commander, including duty in the 1760 Lake Champlain campaign and resultant occupation of Montréal. He was even rewarded with a lucrative regular captain's commission, from which he retired to half-pay. One of New Haven's influential leaders, he founded the province's first Masonic lodge in 1750. In his hometown's history, Wooster is most famously credited as the selectman sent to deter Captain Arnold from seizing ammunition from the city powder house immediately after Lexington and Concord, as the upstart rushed to lead volunteers to Boston—an incident in which Arnold persevered and was given access re-

*David Wooster Esq'r.—
Commander in Chief
of the Provincial Army
Against Quebec* (detail).
Library of Congress
Prints and Photographs
Division.

luctantly to the military stores. While Wooster's military credentials were as good as any other colonial-born Continental general's, it also seemed he might be past his prime.[1]

After Arnold marched off for Boston, Wooster committed himself to the patriot cause by resigning his British commission; Connecticut also appointed him major-general and commander of its First Regiment. During his subsequent service around New York City, Wooster dealt with the complicated political and command technicalities of his regiment's service in a neighboring province, along with the added complication of growing Continental authority. Wooster did not have many friends among Continental leadership, and his behavior continued to raise questions about his competence and value to the cause—resulting in a polarizing historical legacy.[2] His chief contemporary detractor was Connecticut delegate Silas Deane, who considered Wooster an "old woman" who was "totally unequal to the service" in a Continental brigadiership.[3]

Among his traits, Wooster was very lenient with his men, and also their strongest advocate, with a reputation as "the soldier's protector and friend." His conduct in the fall of 1775 serves as a fine example. Resisting incorporation under Continental authority, his soldiers refused to sign the Continental Articles of War, and his officers deliberately held back muster rolls, insisting that they had enlisted in Connecticut provincial service. Wooster elected to passively ignore General Schuyler's orders on the matter, appeasing his Yankee boys. He also subverted the Continental supply system, contracting through provincial sources to obtain better provisions for his men, inspiring "jealousies . . . among the other troops." In addition, Wooster sparked a sharp spat with Schuyler by holding court-martials under Connecticut, rather than Continental, rules. The Northern Army commander was shocked to find a subordinate administering high military justice without his consent. General Washington was also unhappy with Wooster's liberal granting of paid furloughs to men not going to Canada, rather than discharging them. In Philadelphia, sources reported that "the majority of the members [of Congress] are by no means pleased with the conduct of the Connecticut troops," at least in part because of their general. Wooster brought this troublesome reputation with him to Montréal, undoubtedly contributing to Montgomery's decision to leave one of his best regimental commanders behind as a deputy, Lieutenant-Colonel Ritzema.[4]

Dutch-born Rudolphus Ritzema had just proven his martial skill in the Fort St-Jean siege. Although he was raised in New York, he attended divinity school in the Netherlands where, distracted by military opportunities in the Seven Years' War, he enlisted in the Prussian army, and "Being a large, tall, rawboned fellow, he was put into the grenadiers." When his regiment disbanded after the war, he returned to America, practicing law. As Alexander McDougall's deputy in the First New York Regiment, he took the unit into the field when the colonel stayed in New York City. Some of Ritzema's radical peers bristled at his strict methods, but Montgomery praised his remarkable talents: "Out of the sweepings of New York Streets he has made something more like Regular troops, than I have seen in the continental service." Teaming with Wooster, Ritzema's traditional European military skills could counterbalance the Connecticut general's Yankee leniency.[5]

Receiving the Montréal command, Wooster established his headquarters in Thomas Walker's house—the city's "best built, and perhaps the best furnished"—and surrounded himself with a suite of staff officers and secretaries. His French civilian secretary was Valentin Jautard, the fervent patriot who had composed the inspirational "suburbs" letter in mid-November. Wooster regularly hosted civilian and military guests, seldom dining with less than twenty gentlemen, serving "the best provisions the country afforded." Some would consider this extravagant, but the Northern Army commander, Schuyler, believed that such "excess" was important for Continental prestige. Despite his sizeable entourage, Wooster had a paltry military force to provide military rule in the Montreal and Three Rivers Districts. Ritzema wrote, "Our garrison does not exceed four hundred effective men — a small number to awe such a country as this." The command consisted of the consolidated reenlistees from three Connecticut regiments and three companies of New York troops, one stationed at Fort St-Jean.[6]

Wooster found he had surprisingly few Montréal patriots to rely on in governing the city. The most active were busy supporting the Northern Army. James Price was serving outside Québec City with Montgomery; George Measam was employed as postmaster and undertook new duties as "Commissary of Provisions." Other patriots, easily the majority, supported the cause by making loans and donations to the military operation, and generally "exerted their Influence" to encourage *Canadien* support, but otherwise were preoccupied with trade. This group included men such as William Haywood, John Blake, Joseph Bindon, William McCarty, and David Salisbury Franks. They made considerable personal financial sacrifices, but none stepped up as a political leader.[7]

François Cazeau was an anomaly, with his secret militia-colonel's commission. He temporarily resumed his past role as patriot distributor for three hundred copies of Washington's manifesto, when they reached Montréal. Cazeau also claimed that he gave many habitants "entire absolution from the debts they owed him," as inducement to join the cause. There is no evidence proving that other patriots offered similar enticements to heavily indebted Canadians, but it would not be surprising. In loyalist Simon Sanguinet's view, many supporters aligned themselves with the patriots in hopes of easing their "bad business," presumably debt-ridden.[8]

Of all the patriots, it was Thomas Walker who functioned as Wooster's chief advisor. The brash radical, only recently "delivered . . . from the cruel hand of tyranny and oppression," had been irritable and antagonistic before his close confinement on General Prescott's ships; now he was vindictive and bitter. When Prescott and his officers came ashore as prisoners, Walker mocked them on the Montréal riverfront, making "several insolent personal gestures." His advice naturally tended to foster division and internal conflict when Wooster needed to promote political cooperation and activity. After a few months, both Washington and Schuyler expressed fears that the general paid too much attention to Walker, whose "private resentment will hurt our cause."[9]

Initially, Walker was still popular in his country home, L'Assomption. When he returned to his country estate around the end of November, habitants prepared a maypole and built a huge bonfire to honor him—a fantastic reception for the parish's famous patriot leader. Walker, however, was incapable of nurturing goodwill for long. Returning to L'Assomption a few days later, he called the habitants to take up arms in the Continental cause. When no one joined, he was insulted and left, bearing a grudge against his seemingly fickle neighbors.[10]

Wooster's Continentals demonstrated particularly good discipline over the winter months, thanks to officers such as Ritzema, who "exerted themselves publicly to prevent tyranny and oppression." A British officer reported, "the rebel army conducted themselves much more to the satisfaction of the inhabitants of Montreal, than could reasonably have been expected from men under such unprincipled leaders," the "unprincipled leaders" apparently being those in Philadelphia. The troops' behavior was not flawless, though. On the night of 15 December, King George III's Upper Town Square bust suffered another indignity; his "head was severed from his body" and dumped in a well on the Place d'Armes.[11]

Wooster was preoccupied with other matters. He met with the Caughnawagas at the end of December, "urging them to keep their neutrality," and the Indians agreed "to everything he wanted." The general also made a token effort to mobilize district militia, using the same fifteen-men-per-parish quota that Carleton had attempted—essentially no one responded. Meanwhile, several Island of Montréal parishes, including Pointe-Claire, Ste-Geneviève, and Sault-au-Récollet, complained to Wooster about their militia-captains, who treated them unfairly and "oppressed" them. The general did not immediately intervene, but these habitant protests certainly factored into the decisions he would make early in 1776.[12]

As regional commander, one of General Wooster's primary concerns was Montreal District loyalist opposition. Like Montgomery, Wooster's natural inclination was to be lenient. Even though Montgomery had ordered retired Major John Campbell out of Montréal, Wooster let him stay. The Connecticut brigadier also told Claude Lorimier, an old acquaintance from the 1760 Montréal occupation, that he "had nothing to fear," even though the Canadian had actively served as a division commander in the failed Longueuil landing operation. Authorities in the United Colonies echoed the generals' conscientiousness about detaining civilians; a Continental colonel in Albany even wanted to know "the Crimes" of Fort St-Jean *Canadien* volunteer prisoners before he would allow them to be taken to detention in Connecticut.[13]

Patriot Montrealers, however, were displeased with such scrupulous philosophies. Many considered themselves injured by loyalist rivals and felt those Tories now deserved punishment. Wooster warned Schuyler, "Our friends in this country are very sorry to see so many prisoners returning," specifically referring to the loyalists from Prescott's fleet, whom Montgomery permitted to stay in Canada on parole.[14]

Rumors persisted that loyalist plots were afoot. Probing a far-fetched scheme, the Continental Fort St-Jean garrison was ordered to search for "7000 stand of arms" allegedly buried before the surrender, intended to arm loyalist Canadians and Indians "to assist the ministerial troops" in a future counterrebellion. Then, only days after Montgomery left town, Wooster received an anonymous letter from Boucherville (see Map 8) prompting immediate, direct action: St-Luc de La Corne was reportedly leading a handful of loyalists "complotting Measures for the Destruction" of Montréal's Continentals. Late on the night of 1 December, Colonel Ritzema and 150 New York troops crossed the icy St. Lawrence with orders to investigate loyalists identified in the informant's letter. The Continentals were to examine suspects' personal papers, arresting them if there was any incriminating evidence, and to seize any arms and ammunition.[15]

Their first stop was Longueuil, visiting seigneur Joseph-Fleury Deschambault and Judge John Fraser, his son-in-law. The soldiers escorted the gentlemen to a nearby tavern, where they interrogated them as troops searched their houses. Ritzema reported that they found "nothing having any evil Tendency," and he released Deschambault and Fraser to their homes. Based on Ritzema's contemporary letters, there is good reason to believe he would have acted if there had been even the slightest evidence of a plot.[16]

Then the Continentals moved ten miles downriver to Boucherville, calling on La Corne and his son-in-law, Indian Superintendent Major John Camp-

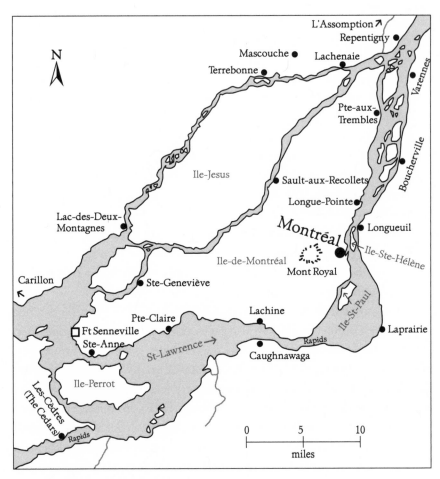

N

L'Assomption ↗
Repentigny ●
Mascouche ● Lachenaie
Terrebonne ●
Pte-aux-Trembles ●
Ile-Jesus
Sault-aux-Recollets ●
Longue-Pointe ●
Lac-des-Deux-Montagnes ●
Montréal
Longueuil ●
Ile-Ste-Hélène
Ile-de-Montréal
Mont Royal
Carillon
↙
Ste-Geneviève ●
Lachine
Pte-Claire ●
Ft Senneville □
Ste-Anne ●
St-Lawrence →
Rapids
Laprairie ●
Caughnawaga ●
Ile-St-Paul
Boucherville
Varennes
Ile-Perrot
Les-Cédars (The Cedars)
Rapids ●

0   5   10
miles

MAP 8: Island of Montréal Environs.

bell, once again finding "Nothing that had an inimical Tendency." Still, as a precaution, Ritzema detained the perpetually shady La Corne, intending to send him to the United Colonies. Campbell was sent to Montréal for Wooster's examination. One of the Continental officers participating in the raids did not believe the tips were "supported by sufficient evidence," but also felt Wooster had no choice but to act as he did, especially since La Corne "was known to be a very dangerous person in Canada."[17]

Over the next few days, confusing and oft-changing guidance emanated from Wooster's headquarters. First, Ritzema was sent to Longueuil, notifying Major Fraser to prepare for a gentleman's confinement in Fort Chambly. Then the general reconsidered La Corne's exile, authorizing his return to Boucherville when the old *Canadien* villain claimed he was "exceedingly ill," unfit for travel up Lake Champlain.[18]

Despite the general's merciful, if unpredictable, tendencies, prominent Tories frustrated Wooster time and again. Major Edward William Gray, the Montréal Crown Sheriff, unabashedly dismissed rebel prospects in public; by one report, the "whole tenour of his discourse in the coffee-house . . . was against the honourable Continental Congress and their measures." The general also complained that Major Campbell, after his release in the Ritzema raid, "behaved himself in a very extraordinary manner," similarly haranguing against the patriot cause.[19]

Luc de la Corne, dit Chaptes de La Corne ou La Corne Saint-Luc. Archives of the City of Montreal, BM1, No. P1049.

Judge Fraser gave Wooster even more difficulty in a highly convoluted series of interactions. After the judge had been warned to prepare for Fort Chambly incarceration, Wooster generously informed Fraser he was "at liberty to return to the town." When the loyalist subsequently visited Montréal, he courteously called on Wooster, and all seemed well; yet while visiting the general again two days later, they had a heated exchange. In the time between meetings, patriot friends informed Wooster that over the summer, the judge had been involved in holding "depositions, bonds, &c.," which Governor Carleton had demanded from prominent patriot Montrealers. Vindictively, the general demanded a similar bond from Fraser. Patriot Pierre du Calvet, who had a long-standing feud with the judge, undoubtedly contributed to Wooster's change of heart. Fraser promised to deliver a bond, but then reconsidered his offer within days, writing that he would not meet the obligation. Then, as if to add fuel to Wooster's predictable ire, Fraser announced that he held official papers, but that he would not, "on any account deliver them, nor any paper of any transaction prior to the capitulation of Montreal." Wooster fumed, "Your breach of promise and insolent letter . . . justly merit a set of iron ornaments"; but instead of following the Ministry's "inhuman and infamous example" of fettering Walker and Allen, Wooster once again ordered Fraser to Fort Chambly, to "remain in close abode till further orders."[20]

Much as Montgomery had been unable to please radical New York officers with his treatment of loyalist prisoners at the end of November, Wooster's policies sparked concern among some Montréal patriots. On 22 December, an anonymous group called "The Faithful Union with Liberty" wrote an appeal to General Montgomery. The letter observed that Crown officeholders captured on Prescott's ships were going "in and out of almost every house in the city," leading discussions "most disadvantageous to the cause of Liberty." In the "Union's" view, the only appropriate response was to exile all of these "Insolent" loyalists; Tories were abusing Montgomery's "Humanity & Generosity" to the detriment of the cause. Notably, the "Union" wrote their letter in French; presumably, Cazeau, Jautard, or du Calvet authored it. This may have been tactical; the appeal might carry more weight if it appeared to come from *Canadiens*. The general never had an opportunity to respond, however. The document did make its way to Albany, though, where it may have influenced General Schuyler early in 1776.[21]

On 2 January, General Wooster launched another loyalist suppression mission; a Yorker detachment under Captain William Goforth visited suspicious "Country Gentlemen." Most probably, this was the same mission described by the loyalist Sanguinet, in which Thomas Walker, James Price, and a Continental party came to L'Assomption to seize weapons.[22] Sanguinet maintained the detachment's target was the entire parish, as a punishment for their failure to take up arms under Walker. The generous characters of Price and Goforth, and the practical limitations of such a small party conducting a parishwide search on a short winter's day, would suggest the mission really was aimed against a few select individuals. In any case, the *Bastonnais* seized weapons from "only three or four" L'Assomption residents.[23]

Perhaps the most flagrant claim laid against the Continental regime in Montréal alleged that "General Wooster had shut up the Mass Houses (in Montreal) on Christmas Eve; which with other Matters has turned the Canadians." This oft-cited accusation implicitly indicts Wooster for bigotry, tyranny, and indifference to the *Canadien* populace. The limited documentary evidence, however, puts the entire event in extreme doubt. The sole primary source record came from London in late January 1776. Major Andrew Skene, detained for months after the Ticonderoga operation, found his way to a Royal Navy ship off New York and then to England, around the New Year. Skene could not have had firsthand knowledge of Wooster's Montréal activities; his distance from Canadian reality is proven later in the same letter, where he wrote, "it is imagined Wooster & Easton . . . are taken, or fled from Montreal." Lending considerable doubt to the possibility that Wooster made such a Christmas order, Montréal loyalists such as Sanguinet carefully recorded every potentially inflammatory Continental act, yet made absolutely no mention of this "event." Thus, Wooster's most infamous charge, the Montréal "Christmas Mass-Houses" order, seems in all likelihood to be the product of a fruitful imagination or the mutated product of a long chain of underground Tory correspondence.[24]

The entire allegation still reflects the precarious situation Wooster faced in Montréal. The general's indulgent character complicated many situations; his inconsistent decisions, characterized by the La Corne and Fraser episodes, exaggerated the "arbitrary" nature of his loyalist treatment; yet he was in a "damned if you do, damned if you don't" situation. If he let the archloyalists run free, the district's security was endangered; if he detained them, he gave his enemies ammunition to "prove" that patriots were hypocritical "defenders of British rights." The general's core problem, however, was that he had no civil authority to guide and support such decisions—he was in over his head, unaided by Continental authorities, local government, or a civilian judicial system.

General David Wooster was not the only colonial leader challenged by loyalist issues in late 1775 and early 1776. There were several concurrent anti-Tory measures and operations undertaken in the other rebellious colonies, which provide an important context in examining the Continental measures in Canada—a factor that has generally been ignored in the harsh criticism of Wooster's Montréal activities. While suppression of the political opposition had previously been handled on local committees' own initiative—disarming obstinate foes and requiring oaths from known "friends of government"—on 6 October 1775, the Continental Congress issued a broad resolve that patriot bodies (Assemblies, committees, and so forth) should arrest and secure anybody "whose going at large may, in their opinion, endanger the safety of the colony, or the liberties of America." Before the end of the year, the Continental Army actively entered this fight against loyalist opposition, particularly in Rhode Island and New York.[25]

Rhode Island Governor Nicholas Cooke initiated the first Continental military involvement. On 19 December, as Wooster was ordering Fraser's detention in Fort Chambly, Cooke asked General Washington for a general and troops to help suppress Tories who were covertly assisting British foraging parties on the province's outer islands. Washington did not send any Continental units, but did send Major-General Charles Lee.[26]

Lee had the strongest military credentials of any of the Continental generals. Born in England, Lee received a gentleman's education in Switzerland, where "he obtained a thorough knowledge of the French language," before launching a distinguished British Army career. In his extensive French and Indian War service, he was wounded at Ticonderoga and served in Amherst's 1760 campaign, leading to Montréal's capitulation. After the peace, Lee dabbled in British Whig politics before accepting a short term of service as a "mercenary" general on the continent. Returning to England, he became so disgusted with perceived government corruption that he departed for America in 1773, settling in Virginia. He heartily embraced the patriot movement and visited the first Continental Congress. The next summer Lee was rewarded with the Continental Army's second major-generalship.[27]

In December 1775, Lee left Cambridge to meet Rhode Island's call for assistance, conducting a five-day mission in the province. Keenly discerning the Revolution's political nature and eager to act, he "took the liberty, without any authority, but the conviction of the necessity, to administer a very strong oath to some of the leading tories," arresting three defiant Newport loyalists. Even though he infringed on provincial government prerogatives, Rhode Island patriots thanked him. Washington praised the operation as well, declaring, "I am of oppinion, that if the same plan was pursued through every Province, it wou'd have a very good effect."[28]

———

Lee's next mission was in New York, a divided province that had been painfully slow in addressing its Tory opposition, especially on Long Island and Staten Island. Monitoring New York's political developments and seeking to follow up on his recent Rhode Island success, on 5 January 1776 General Lee suggested that Washington permit him to gather a force of Connecticut volunteers and enter New York to improve fortifications and "purge" leading Tories. The commander-in-chief approved. While Lee gathered volunteers, the Continental Congress took the Long Island situation into its own hands, sending New Jersey Colonel Nathaniel Heard to disarm notorious islander loyalists—a mission completed by 18 January.[29]

Four days later, Lee boldly announced that he was ready to enter New York, disarm the "manifestly disaffected," demand bonds for Tory good behavior, and administer "the strongest oath that can be devised." This radically intrusive approach shocked both the New York Committee of Safety and delegates in Philadelphia. Lee was urgently asked to keep his men at the border until political representatives consulted with him, and the general cooperated. The New York Committee and a hastily dispatched Continental Congress committee conferred with Lee and asserted the supremacy of civil authority. The general declared his pleasure with this development, as it would ensure he did not draw "the enmity of the whole Province" for his zeal in the common cause.[30]

Lee cooperated in meetings with the committees in New York, but ordered key loyalists to be disarmed and prevented communication with Royal Navy ships. When the provincial congress failed to adopt his recommendation for the arrest of arch-Tory suspects who refused a loyalty oath, he implemented the policy on his own initiative. The New York government again protested, reminding the general that "the right of apprehending, trying, and punishing citizens" belonged to civilian, not military authorities. Lee replied that his own conscience, in the face of imminent military threats, "dictated the necessity of the measure." The Continental Congress weighed in, as well, subsequently resolving, "That no oath by way of test be imposed upon, exacted, or required of any of the inhabitants of these colonies, by any military officers." The civil-military crisis was defused conveniently by the unrepentant Lee's timely 7 March departure; he had orders to attend to a new Southern Department command in Virginia. While many conservative Yorkers were infuriated by the audacious major-general's actions in their province, he left the Tories in a weakened state, a minimal threat for the near future.[31]

———

Almost simultaneously, General Schuyler conducted another anti-Tory mission in Tryon County, New York, northwest of Albany. Spurred by intelligence that Sir John Johnson and his loyalist Highlander supporters possessed Crown arms, ammunition, and Indian blankets—dangerous commodities in the opposition's hands—a Continental Congress committee directed Schuyler to secure all such items at the Johnson Hall estate. The committee also gave the general discretion to detain anyone he deemed "too dangerous to go at large" and to disarm loyalist "Scotch Roman Catholic Soldiers."[32]

In mid-January, General Schuyler cooperated with the local patriot committees and militia to move on Johnson's Tory stronghold, where he respectfully negotiated terms directly with Sir John. The loyalist leader consented to surrendering his own and his Highlanders' weapons; Johnson would be on liberal parole, and Schuyler would choose a dozen prisoners as surety for loyalist behavior. As a result, Schuyler gathered arms from more than six hundred Tryon County Tories, neutralizing a significant internal threat in New York and earning Washington's approval. Governor Trumbull congratulated Schuyler as well, observing that, "Suppressing such enemies to American liberty is of very great importance."[33]

Lee and Schuyler applied two very different approaches in the United Colonies' nascent antiloyalist effort. Schuyler's early success was initiated by Congressional guidance and was achieved through close cooperation with local political committees. Lee boldly acted on broad military orders and had to be reined in by local and Continental government leadership. In both cases, in conjunction with civil authorities, the generals applied "oppressive" measures to neutralize threats from ideological foes.

In Montréal, at essentially the same time, Wooster would apply similarly "tyrannical" methods, but lacked the benefit of civilian political guidance, positive or negative. As Montgomery had noted, Congress was "too far distant" to provide meaningful guidance on internal Canadian security issues, and had failed to provide a committee on the scene, or even broad operational guidelines. Despite Washington's fear that Wooster was "not of such Activity as to press thro' Difficulties" of overall command in Canada, necessity soon forced the major-general to take dramatic action against Quebec loyalists. Although his measures were not dissimilar to Schuyler's and Lee's, Wooster alone faced intense contemporary and historical scrutiny and blame for his acts and their alleged consequences.[34]

Chapter 15

A CRITICAL MONTH

Wooster's Montréal, January 1776

This affair puts a very different face upon our interests in this country; however, we must make the best of it. | *General David Wooster to General Philip Schuyler, 5 January 1776*

There are still in this province certain ill-disposed persons who wish to damage the common cause which we uphold. | *General David Wooster to Canadian Militia Officers, Montréal, 6 January 1776*

On 3 January 1776, frozen, road-worn Canadian Edward Antill arrived in Montréal, delivering the first word of Montgomery's Québec City defeat. The catastrophe threw tremendous weight on General David Wooster's shoulders; his responsibilities grew severalfold as the command of all Continental troops in Canada devolved to him. He had not only to manage Montréal's turbulent politics, but also to direct the shattered corps 150 miles downriver. Within the next forty-eight hours, the general received additional advice, thorough reports, and urgent requests from both senior colonels on the capital siege lines. Arnold, now commanding the Quebec District force, begged "for God sake, order as many men Down as you can possibly spare Consistent with the safety of Montreal"; Campbell specifically called for two hundred men. They both expressed that Wooster's presence was needed in their camp too; Arnold expected to be incapacitated for two months with his wounded leg.[1]

Both Arnold and Campbell shared another concern with Wooster: Montréal's security. The city was critical to lines of communication and supply, but was also the ground where they hoped to nurture Canadian patriot government. Colonel Campbell wrote, "I Leave it to you to Judge the propriety of Disarming the Tories of Montreal." Arnold observed that "the lenity shown to our prisoners heretofore in Montreal and places adjacent" was now "highly imprudent and dangerous," and known loyalist leaders "should be immediately sent over the Lake without respect of persons." He provided new intelligence supporting his recommendation, including a copy of a letter Carleton disseminated to militia-captains, "to prevail on them to raise their Parishes" against the Continentals; there was good reason to suspect a "French" Montréal plot was already under way.[2]

Meanwhile, Wooster sent news of Montgomery's misfortune on to General Schuyler, requesting immediate assistance. For this mission, James Price suggested Edward Antill, who had arrived from the capital forty-eight hours earlier. He would "be of infinite service" in making Congress "thoroughly acquainted with the minds of the Canadians in general, as well as what steps will be necessary for securing this Province and uniting it to the other Colonies." Moses Hazen joined Antill on the trip, having made a firm commitment to the patriot cause after his "unjust" fall imprisonment by Governor Carleton. The pair departed on 5 January.[3]

That same day, Wooster held a council of war. Most significant, his officers agreed to a man that Wooster should remain in Montréal. Physically, the "Severe Season of the Year" and the general's "advanced age" made travel impractical; militarily, Montréal's security was more important than the capital siege; and politically, the officers felt the general had "now form'd Considerable Connections with the Inhabitants"—his presence was important "to Conciliate their Affections." Only two individuals went to Arnold's immediate relief: New York Colonel James Clinton and the indispensable James Price, who hoped to help raise Canadian volunteers.[4]

Writing to the New York Committee of Safety at this same time, Colonel Rudolphus Ritzema summarized the Canadian situation. Until reinforcements arrived, he believed, "The most that can be expected from us, is to maintain our ground here, and keep a watchful eye towards the Canadians." Patriot Old Subjects had already been "stripped of their money and goods" supporting the Northern Army, and the colonel claimed there were no "French friends, to assist us." Yet all was not hopeless: "the peasantry are, in general, at present for us." But Ritzema suspected, for most Canadians, it was "from no other motive than that we are the strongest side"; only "Some few" were committed "from principle." His plea was simple: "Let us have men and money, otherwise, by Heavens, Canada is lost." Ritzema also requested "a General to command us," as Montgomery's loss was immediately felt.[5]

To stabilize the military situation, Wooster directed the Fort St-Jean garrison "to stop the deserters who fled from all directions"—a number of Continentals had deserted, or left at the expiration of their enlistments, from both the Québec City corps and Montréal—and the general sent back, "Every Rascal" caught. Wooster also ordered the troops to be retained beyond their enlistments, justifying the measure by military necessity. With no authority, but based solely on the "present exigency," he wrote Seth Warner asking for more than five hundred Green Mountain Boys to serve under Continental pay. Wooster begged for haste; rather than waiting for an entire regiment, "let them be sent by Tens-Twenty-Thirtys-Fortys-or Fiftys as they can be Collected." Even such small parties would have "good effect on the minds of the Canadians, to see Succours coming on." Less than two weeks after the general's desperate appeal, Warner reported recruiting efforts were "very encouraging," having sent "one hundred and upwards" to Canada, with "a number more . . . ready to march soon."[6]

By 14 January, Wooster determined the immediate risk in Montréal had subsided enough to send Arnold 120 men under New York Major Peter Gansevoort, "all that could with prudence be spared." A week later, he added another seventy Yorkers. The total numbers might seem trifling, but this removed almost half of Wooster's city garrison strength.[7]

The old general's most immediate concern was neutralizing the loyalist threat in Montréal. Tory notary Simon Sanguinet reported that "immediately" after receiving word of the New Year's Eve disaster, Wooster sent a sizeable party of Continentals to disarm about a dozen "Friends of the Crown," including Sheriff Edward William Gray, District Militia-Major St-Georges Dupré, and Sanguinet himself. By that loyalist's account, soldiers also searched for evidence to justify exiling the "good royalists," but found nothing.[8]

On 6 January, General Wooster established the foundation for a new, less permissive Continental regime, issuing a proclamation that defined acceptable standards of Canadian behavior. Loyalists, of course, saw this as further evidence of the arbitrary, hypocritical rebel "liberation," an oppressive tool "preventing the public from speaking about their business, and to keep them silent." Wooster similarly was criticized by contemporaries in the United Colonies and generations of historians; yet in the context of the times, he was providing "legal" justification for counter-Tory actions, paralleling measures already adopted in Philadelphia, Rhode Island, Connecticut, and New York. Yet without a credible Canadian civilian authority, he had no choice but to implement it by military fiat.[9]

According to Wooster's proclamation, anyone found "opposing or in any way injuring the interest of Congress and the progress of Arms," would be "declared enemies of public liberty, traitors to their country." As such, they would be "punished with severity, made prisoners and even banished from the province if their case requires it." Criminal loyalist opposition could take the form of "speeches and injurious remarks," harboring deserters, or "obstinate refusal and disobedience" to Continental officers.[10]

To ensure that Canadians could not plead ignorance, Wooster used traditional channels to disseminate the proclamation. Militia-captains were called to "publish" it at church doors. The general also asked those officers to remind habitants of the United Colonies' intent in the province: "to drive out the Ministerial troops as well as to protect the inhabitants from the general enslavement," which London intended for all the colonies. Addressing popular rumors that the Northern Army was abandoning Canada, he added, "Congress has since determined to reinforce the said army with another body of troops, even more considerable than the first," which would arrive as soon as the lake route was passable.[11]

Wooster was convinced that loyalist foes were numerous. The seigneurs and clergy continued to demonstrate their commitment to the Crown. But many seigneurs were already prisoners or were holed up in Quebec City; those still roaming Montréal were kept under close watch. By default, the Church's opposition role grew. The general noted how, "The Clergy almost universally refuse absolution to those who are our friends & preach to the people that it is not now too late to take Arms against us."[12]

From the St-Maurice Forges, near Trois-Rivières, patriot Christophe Pélissier wrote to Congress, concurring with Wooster's observations. Montgomery's defeat had made the loyalists "more audacious than ever." They were insinuating that habitants, "being guilty of rebellion," would have to join the large Ministerial force arriving in the spring "to obtain their pardon, without which their houses will be pillaged and burnt, and themselves punished with death." The loyalists sought to render Congress, "together with liberty itself, contemptible in the eyes of the Canadians."[13]

Pélissier offered a three-part plan to secure Canadians for the patriot cause. First, Continental authorities should secure all Tories who held Crown offices, as well as "other Royalists." Second, Pélissier insisted that no effort should be made to tax Canadians; loyalists were spreading rumors that the United Colonies conquered the province simply to impose taxes to "pay all the expense of this war." The third recommendation aligned with every previous expression of Congressional intent: despite the Church's opposition, Pélissier advocated leaving habitants "in possession of their bishops, their priests, and the free exercise of religion."[14]

Arnold, meanwhile, preempted Wooster's policies, having already arrested a notorious loyalist. On 4 January, the colonel sent Captain François Bellette upriver for detention in Montréal or the colonies. Bellette, "the villain who destroyed the powder" on the ships off Sorel before surrender and had subsequently been set at liberty by Montgomery, was behaving "Exceeding ill" around the Continental camp. It appears that the loyalist ship captain was then detained in Montréal, with no record of him being sent to the United Colonies.[15]

Armed with his 6 January proclamation, General Wooster prepared to crack down on obstinate Tories. On the fourteenth, he warned General Schuyler that some loyalist prisoners, recently returned from New York, were "very busy in reporting Stories" prejudicial to the patriot cause—especially Meshech Seers, a Montréal volunteer captured near St-Jean in September, who was subsequently released under lenient Continental policies around the New Year, along with many *Canadien* prisoners from the fall campaign. Due to the loyalists' troublesome behavior and Montréal patriots' warnings, the Connecticut brigadier saw the "great necessity" of returning troublemakers and "ringleaders of the Tories in this Country" to Schuyler. Two days later, Wooster appointed a new Montréal "brigade-major," an army officer responsible for the day-to-day management of garrison duties, billeting, discipline, and civil-military affairs. Isaac Melchior received this posting—a Kennebec Expedition volunteer officer, he had been sent to the city bearing Arnold's messages immediately after the Battle of Québec City.[16]

On 16 January, the first day in his new post, Melchior was sent to detain Sheriff Gray and the obnoxious Justice René-Ovide Hertel-de-Rouville, a Fort St-Jean prisoner paroled by Montgomery. There is no record of the evidence against these two, but if Wooster had to pick leading representatives of both "English" and "French" Tory communities, these were excellent choices. Thomas Walker also had a long-standing grudge against de-Rouville, and may have bent Wooster's ear on the subject. As Melchior detained the duo, Montrealers gathered to protest the arrests, telling Wooster that such action was counter to Montgomery's terms for the city. Although the written terms had no direct connection with the current situation, Wooster relented. Freeing the loyalists, the general promised, or threatened, to make a list of sixty-four

Tories who might be sent as prisoners to the colonies. His intent is unclear; were the listed loyalists simply suspects, or as some interpreted, were they hostages for the city's good behavior? That same January day, Brigade-Major Melchior also was ordered to disarm the three Montréal suburbs. Wooster presumably had intelligence supporting this action, perhaps from Cazeau; or as Sanguinet portrayed it, the Continental general just may have made an arbitrary decision. In any case, the suburbanites, so zealously patriotic upon the Northern Army's arrival, were now suspected Tories. Only two days later, Wooster reattempted de Rouville's arrest; and again citizens, presumably including a large percentage of Tories, intervened. The exasperated general told the protestors that he "considered everyone present to be enemies and rogues, and that in a while, things would go differently."[17]

While publicly threatening Crown officeholders and their friends, Wooster still treaded carefully around the Church, even though a growing number of habitants complained that their priests were refusing absolution to patriot supporters. The general made one half-measure; during one of James Price's short Montréal stays, probably between 20 January and 7 February, Price and two Continental officers visited Vicar-General Montgolfier. The Canadian patriot merchant informed Montgolfier that he and several priests were being ordered to the colonies. The still-cautious Wooster revoked the order within days, though; perhaps he reconsidered the act or merely intended it as a threat—Sanguinet credited James Price's wife for intervening with the general on the clergymen's behalf. Still, the vicar-general was reminded that priests were being monitored and Continental restraint had limits.[18]

After all these false starts, several loyalists finally were arrested on 20 January and sent in a convoy to New York. Guided by Canadian patriot Jean-Baptiste de Gas, the train included forty sleds of loyalists, their servants, and the ample baggage permitted for gentlemen prisoners. Wooster described most as paroled prisoners of war; but a few were individuals who had "by their base ungenerous conduct, shewn themselves to be our bitterest Enemies," a group known to include La Corne's son-in-law Major Campbell, Meshech Seers, Judge Fraser—held in Fort Chambly for the last month, and the oft-targeted de Rouville. Wooster justified their exile in letters to Schuyler, detailing Campbell's and Seers's offenses, and attaching affidavits "concerning Mr. De Rouville's conduct."[19]

Schuyler, meanwhile, offered guidance for handling the loyalist problem—sent on 26 January, immediately on the heels of his own Tryon County disarmament mission. However, it would not be received in Montréal until early February. The major-general recommended that Wooster introduce a tribunal forum in Canada. The accused should be called before the general, "confronted with their accusers," and given an opportunity to "exculpate themselves." If deemed guilty, Wooster was to send them to Albany "in close confinement, together with the affidavit ascertaining their guilt." This would have been a notable contribution to the patriot cause in Montréal: even a military tribunal was better than arbitrary exile at the general's "whim"; while not exactly "constitutional," at least the accused had an opportunity to face charges and present a defense. Yet in the same letter, Schuyler provided apparently contradictory guidance, telling Wooster to "send to this place all prisoners"—unless specifically granted parole by capitulation terms—"together with such persons as may be dangerous to our cause, if suffered to remain in Canada." Wooster seemed to focus on the latter direction; there is no record of Wooster conducting any such tribunals.[20]

At his core, Wooster felt, "There is but little confidence to be placed in the Canadians." In calling Warner for reinforcements, the general had commented, "You know as well as any other man, the temper and disposition of the Canadians; that they are not to be depended upon." He also compared the *Canadiens* to Indians, "fond of choosing the strongest party." Despite these misgivings, the old Connecticut general exerted his best efforts to engage the Canadians in the fight for liberty.[21]

With Montréal's first train of loyalist prisoners on its way, Wooster turned his attention to the countryside. Prompted by an appeal from "sundry captains of militia," the general ordered all militia officers to surrender royal commission papers, which he would replace with Continental equivalents. Wooster saw a wealth of "happy Consequences" in this measure. Much like a test oath, those who refused to surrender their commissions would prove themselves dangerous to the cause of liberty, justifying their arrests. Rather than simply replacing the governor's commissions, Wooster also gave habitants the opportunity to elect their own officers, a process that fostered "democratic" activity in the parishes. In his bigoted view, the general also calculated that "those who take Commissions under the Congress will be afraid to desert our Cause, and no principle opperates so strongly upon the Minds of the Canadians as fear."[22]

By 21 January, Wooster boasted that many commissions were turned in, parishes were pleased to elect officers, and there were "but few instances that they have not chosen a zealous friend to our cause." Loyalists such as Sanguinet viewed Wooster's policies in a different light. The Tory notary considered them as a "means to sow dissension between the Canadians, in order to set one against another," distracting them from the Continentals' weak position.[23]

While the general reported great success in the parishes, Montréal militia officers, especially senior field officers, passively resisted his order, refusing to provide their commissions. Then on 25 January, Tory citizens posted an "anonymous seditious paper" on Montréal church doors. The "very artfully written" letter pointed out the horrid state of Continental arms in Quebec and asked *Canadiens* "what Benefit they cou'd Expect to Reap from so mobby a Banditry." The invaders were "without money without Arms without Discipline without Clothes and without Credit." The author called Canadians to join in "Driving this handfull of Rebels from amongst us." There was no uprising; but Christophe Pélissier visited Montréal around that time and found more "Royalists" than he imagined, and feared that if they were left "unbridled," they might "change the good disposition of the country people." Pélissier warned Congress that expeditious reinforcements were critical; "quartered in the country," they might stem the loyalist tide.[24]

Coincidentally, on the same day the Tory letter was posted, the first fresh troops arrived from the United Colonies—western Massachusetts men. After seeing Wooster's letter to Seth Warner requesting hasty reinforcements, Berkshire County authorities rushed troops forward as volunteers without waiting for colonial authorization. With Schuyler's coordination, another partially formed Massachusetts regiment was expedited north under Major Jeremiah Cady as well. Detachments from these units, and the Green Mountain Boys, entered Canada in a small but steady flow. Wooster noted that their arrival added "fresh Spirits to our men." Another patriot observer described their "very good effect"; Canadians were convinced that "Bostonians are coming thick as the trees in the woods," and Tories were "quite crest-fallen."[25]

Wooster was emboldened, concurrently informing Schuyler of his plan for a Montréal Committee of Safety and Correspondence. The brigadier hoped that a local committee would relieve him of a "very great Burthen" by resolving "a thousand trifling Disputes," and thought "perhaps other places in the Country will be inclined to follow the Example, and by Degrees they may be led to chuse a provincial Congress and of course Delegates for the Continental Congress." Hopeful, but not deluded, Wooster confessed there was "at least a plausibility in the Scheme"; yet with no further record of a Montréal committee, the whole initiative was apparently stillborn.[26]

As troops flowed in, the Northern Army still remained "in great want of cash." The army only continued to "rub along" with the assistance of Canadian supporters; but local friends had already been "drained . . . of the most of their cash." Arnold and Wooster agreed that "Mr. Price is our only resource"; by now, the merchant and his partner Haywood had advanced more than £20,000. Although the generals floated various schemes to give Continental bills "currency" in Canada, hard cash remained absolutely vital—as Wooster said, it was "next to impossible to do anything without it." In early January, some Montréal-based troops even had refused to perform duties until paid, making "the whole Garrison full of Clamor." On 27 January, General Wooster finally received supplemental specie; he was "very happy to receive the Cash," but immediately requested more, the most recent shipment being consumed in paying off debts.[27]

With reinforcements and a little cash in hand, Wooster was still hesitant to leave Montréal himself, but was comfortable sending his deputy, Colonel Ritzema, across the lakes to consult with General Schuyler. The colonel was to discuss "the best Means . . . for a speedy Reduction of Quebec" and placing New York troops in Canada "on a permanent Footing" after their ad hoc November reenlistments. Ritzema reached Albany on 5 February and spent a day consulting with Schuyler, after which the general dispatched him to Philadelphia, so that "Congress may have an Opportunity of examining him as to our affairs in Canada." After his conversation with Ritzema, Schuyler noted, "The civil police [policy] of that Country I am very certain claims immediate Attention," and reminded Congress that civilian administration "ought not to be left to any Military Commander who must necessarily have his Hands full of other Business," a statement that applied to all the Northern Army generals. Without explicitly stating it, Schuyler reminded President Hancock of the persistent need for a Congressional committee in Canada.[28]

═══════

In Philadelphia, Edward Antill arrived to play the same role he had in Montréal and Albany, bearing first news of defeat at the Battle of Québec City. On 17 January, the Canadian delivered letters to Congress from Schuyler, Wooster,

Arnold, and Campbell. The following day, Antill was called to provide two hours' testimony to the Continental assembly—"a very clear Account of every Circumstance" in the province. In his view, Canadians were "between Hawk and Buzzard," facing dangers from both sides, yet would "generally join our Side if we send a strong Force there immediately."[29]

One day later, the same Northern Army letters reached Washington in Cambridge. Schuyler had written, "I tremble for our people in Canada; and nothing, my dear sir, seems left, to prevent the most fatal consequences, but an immediate reinforcement, that is nowhere to be had, but from you," a theme captured in Wooster's and Arnold's dispatches as well. Washington called a council of war, and although General Gates noted that "many here think Worcester [sic] put the worst complexion upon his Intelligence that he might be succoured the more expeditiously," they resolved to send three regiments north. Informing Congress of their decision, Washington also repeated the sentiments of Wooster and Schuyler, noting that "Canadians and Indians" are "too well disposed to take part with the strongest." The Northern Army needed to show its strength soon.[30]

Back in Philadelphia, the shock of Montgomery's demise sparked an unprecedented flurry of activity in Congress; after months of procrastinating and taking half-measures on Canada, it took just two days for the body to issue a plethora of resolutions for troops, money, powder, generals, and more. On 19 January, they resolved, "That the American army in Canada be reinforced with all possible despatch, as well for the security and relief of our friends there, as for better securing the rights and liberties not only of that colony, but the other United Colonies." The Congress ordered Washington to detach a Cambridge batallion "to march with the greatest expedition possible to Canada"; and it ordered two of the regiments already slated for Canada, one each from New Jersey and Pennsylvania, to send forward any ready companies—expediting reinforcements, but at a risk to unit integrity and discipline. Congress also recommended that "the ruling Powers in every Colony" gather "all the gold and silver coin they can," specifically for Quebec. The colonies responded energetically, but it took months to produce meaningful results.[31]

Based on Edward Antill's recommendation, Congress also ordered the formation of another Canadian army unit. The new Second Canadian Regiment was given a curious French organization with four battalions of 250 men each—a third bigger than the standard Continental unit. The new Canadian arrangement also reduced the number of soldiers under each officer, potentially improving discipline, while increasing the quantity of prestigious officer positions.[32]

Antill offered a nomination for command of the unit: his travel companion from Canada, retired British ranger officer Moses Hazen, whose patriotism Schuyler endorsed. On 22 January, Congress appointed that veteran Canadian to command, with Antill as his lieutenant-colonel. The arrangement, however, slighted Jeremiah Duggan, Livingston's battle-proven deputy in the Richelieu Valley and Québec City operations. In contrast, Hazen had not led troops in the current struggle, and Antill had been a staff officer for only about a month; yet they were on the scene in Philadelphia to earn appointments, and Hazen's reputation from the last war was substantial.[33]

The next day, a question arose about Hazen's qualifications—whether he was under parole not to serve against the King. With a multitude of paroled Tories across the confederation, the United Colonies had good reason to avoid setting a precedent for breaking such terms. Antill was nominally commander for a few days, until Hazen persuaded Congress that he had no obligations and was reappointed to command the Second Canadian Regiment.[34]

While resolving these issues, Congress officially recognized the Continental Army's bilingual nature. With hundreds of French-Canadian soldiers serving the United Colonies, a 23 January resolution ordered the Articles of War translated into French. This gave both Livingston and Hazen a tool "for the better regulating of the continental troops"—standards of discipline and punishment in their troops' native tongue.[35]

Unfortunately for Wooster, Congress still prevaricated on sending proper political support, producing another resolution announcing that it was not "expedient at present to send a committee" to Canada. The Continental Congress did not send any detailed political instructions to guide affairs in Montréal in the meantime, either. While the United Colonies proved willing to implement military and financial measures for Quebec, they habitually failed to address the most critical civil government needs.[36]

Hesitant to send a delegation to Quebec, Congress resorted to its conventional means for promoting Canadian acquiescence to the union. On 23 January, William Livingston, Thomas Lynch, and James Wilson were appointed as a committee to "prepare a letter to the Canadians." There were no Dickinsons, Lees, Samuel Adamses, or Jays for this job; dynamic intellects were tackling bigger issues as the colonies grew further apart from the Crown. At that very time, one political pamphlet was enjoying particular popularity, guiding patriot hearts toward American independence: Thomas Paine's *Common Sense*—coincidentally, the archradical author offered his profits to buy mittens for troops headed to Quebec.[37]

The third Congressional address to Canada focused heavily on encouragement. In light of the recent "vicissitudes and disappointments," Congress reiterated its enduring commitment to Quebec, promising, "We will never abandon you to the unrelenting fury of your and our enemies." The letter offered details about the sizeable Continental force recently ordered to Canada, while inviting Canadians to "seize with zeal and eagerness the favourable moment to co-operate in the success of so glorious an enterprize." The address's closing point repeated the call for homegrown patriot government in Quebec, advising and exhorting Canadians "to establish associations in your different parishes" replicating those "which have proved so salutary to the United Colonies," to form a provincial assembly, and from that body, "to appoint delegates to represent them in this Congress." A full union between Quebec and the thirteen colonies was still the ultimate objective; yet it remained solely the Canadians' responsibility to make it happen. The letter was promptly approved and translated; Fleury Mesplet again printed French copies. Hazen and Antill, preparing to return to Quebec, were handed stacks of addresses for delivery to Montréal.[38]

Coincident with these other developments, the United Colonies demonstrated their theoretical unwillingness to abandon Quebec, even for the benefit of the other thirteen colonies. When developing plans for a peace delegation to England, among a dozen specific guidelines, Congress directed negotiators to insist upon "Pardon & indemn[it]y to Inhabitants of Canada." This, of course, was not publicized at the time, but indicates Congressional regard for Canadian patriots.[39]

During January 1776, in Montréal and Philadelphia, the United Colonies implemented serious measures to recover from Montgomery's catastrophic Québec City defeat. Wooster's response was characterized by his 6 January proclamation for Tory suppression and his demand that militia officers exchange their commissions. When compared with General Lee's success in

Rhode Island and New York, Wooster's measures seem prudent; yet his indecisive implementation exaggerated "arbitrary" aspects and exposed him to criticism from both loyalist Canadians and fellow patriots.

Congress's immediate reactions showed resolve, but specific political support for Canada remained the most glaring shortfall. It seems it was easier for Congress to demand action from others—the army and the colonies—than it was to call on its own members to make the personal sacrifice to remove themselves from Philadelphia for several months and make the arduous trip to Quebec. As a result, the military remained the sole manifestation of Continental authority in Canada.

Ultimately though, the United Colonies had limited ability to steer events in the north; the Canadians had the most critical role. Seigneurs and clergy were indisputably attached to the Crown, and the rebels' hold on the province was too tenuous to temper their zeal; but habitants and bourgeois could have a decisive voice if they threw their weight behind the patriot cause. The Ministry, of course, had its own cards to play. Behind Québec City's walls, Carleton defied the rebels; his loyalist friends fostered resistance elsewhere in the province; and the spring arrival of British Army reinforcements would, of course, tremendously influence the military situation. The Continental Congress and Northern Army had a limited window, from January through May 1776, to fortify their military and political positions and secure what General Washington described as "the only link wanting in the grand chain of Continental Union." If the United Colonies failed in either realm, Canada's fate was sealed.[40]

Chapter 16

EVOLVING OCCUPATION

Montréal and the Struggle for the Canadian Spirit

There are so many Civil and Political Affairs that require the greatest Care and most Delicate Management. | *General David Wooster to the Continental Congress, Montréal, 11 February 1776*

A crueler dictatorship had never been seen. | *Simon Sanguinet "To the Inhabitants of Canada," March 1776*

With renewed confidence at the end of January 1776, General David Wooster decided it was time to confront the Montréal militia officers decisively on exchanging their royal commissions for Continental equivalents. The general believed that "the whole posse of Tories"—men such as outspoken Tory Edward William Gray—"used their utmost endeavours to dissuade the French officers from complying" with his orders. Recognizing that Continental authority would "appear contemptible in the eyes of the Tories and Canadians" if he did not enforce his demands, Wooster issued a final warning that resisters could expect confinement at Fort Chambly.[1]

On 2 February, James Price and William Haywood called a Montréal citizens' meeting "to sound their opinions on different subjects." After the city's "respectable citizens" had gathered in the Recollet Church,[2] Price immediately stole the floor, "ineloquently" arguing for the militia officers to surrender their commissions. Tired of the extended patriot monologue, coffeehouse owner Loubet interjected, suggesting a breakaway meeting in which other citizens might actually express their opinions. According to loyalist Claude Lorimier, Price promptly ordered Continental soldiers to take Loubet away, resulting in a general scramble for the doors. As citizens massed near the exit, Lorimier harangued against rebel injustice, declaring he would never surrender his commission. Without the solid foundation of a Montréal patriot committee organization to build upon, this chaotic episode utterly failed to introduce a rebel "meeting culture" to the city—"an essential ingredient of revolution." Instead of establishing a collective social force that might promote individual commitment to the patriot cause, the Continentals' friends undoubtedly left their citizen peers disgusted with the arbitrary and tyrannical proceedings they witnessed at the Recollet Church.[3]

No Montrealers seemed to have been arrested that day, but on the next, Wooster ordered Lorimier to headquarters. In the ensuing interview, the loyalist did not deny or recant his previous day's statements, in which he had referred to "lousy" Americans. In response, the general informed Lorimier that he could see plenty of "well-disciplined" and uninfested troops, as he would be sent to New York within the week.[4]

When senior Montréal militia officers still failed to deliver their commissions that day, Wooster ordered the principals sent to Chambly, "pursuant to General Schuyler's orders and my own sentiments." Edward Gray, long a marked man, was accompanied by militia officers Colonel Dufy-Desauniers, Lieutenant-Colonel Neveu-Sevestre, and Major St-Georges Dupré, all of whom were allegedly sowing "improper conversation" and "refused to give parole" not to act against the Continentals. On 6 February, these gentlemen were escorted from the city. Twelve days later, another train of prisoners was sent farther, to the United Colonies. They were "British officers and their families, who had been permitted, for their accommodation, to remain at Montreal," but who had subsequently proven themselves dangerous to good order in the city. Critics, both loyalists and conservative patriots, marked the 6 February militia officer arrests as a decisive point in Montréal's "arbitrary" rule; yet in light of the contemporary anti-Tory activities of Lee and Schuyler, Wooster's decisions seem prudent in this phase of the growing continental revolution, although his vacillating implementation of loyalist suppression measures warrants some criticism.[5]

General Wooster faced another critically important issue in Montréal in early 1776. As fur traders began to assemble spring shipments, they wondered if Continental authorities would permit their annual trade. If denied, the city's principal business would be destroyed for the year. The issue was not new; merchants had raised it after John Brown's spring 1775 visit and during Montréal's November capitulation. Albany fur traders faced a similar challenge, yet New York had the benefit of patriot government bodies to weigh in and prudently balance economics with security. In Montréal, the decision rested on a single heavily burdened Continental general, with no particular expertise on the subject.[6]

In late January, Wooster called a meeting of citizen "Indian traders." When he asked whether they "expected passports in the spring to carry their goods, &c., into the Indian country as usual," they replied affirmatively. The merchants certainly must have referred Wooster to Montgomery's November promises to "promote commerce" and "grant passports for the upper countries when required." Wooster hesitated; for "the safety of the troops and the publick good," he would not "grant passports without the direction of Congress." It was too easy for trade goods to be diverted to British Army posts or serve as gifts encouraging Indians to ally with Ministerial forces.[7]

Addressing this situation, Wooster suggested that the merchants "choose a committee to wait upon Congress for their direction." On 5 February, just three days after Price's chaotic town meeting, the fur traders assembled in the same Recollet Church. They initially discussed sending a twelve-man delegation to Philadelphia, an idea linked to Price and Haywood. Loyalists, however, feared such a party would be transformed into a de facto provincial delegation to Congress. As an alternative, they chose to send a single messenger with a petition focused solely on fur-trade licensing. The bearer would be Benjamin Frobisher, a signer of the 1774 British Party petitions for an assembly and against the Quebec Act, but who was also heavily tied to British metropolitan business interests.[8]

───

In order to handle all these political and strategic issues, Schuyler relentlessly pressed Congress for help in Montréal. On 10 February, he wrote, "I dare confidently venture to prophecy, that unless a respectable Committee of Congress be with all expedition sent to Canada, our affairs will not only greatly suffer, but that, in all probability we shall lose the affections of the Canadians." Before that letter reached Philadelphia though, Congress heard firsthand accounts from two individuals fresh from Montréal, aligning with the general's views. In a mid-February meeting with Congress, Colonel Ritzema elucidated the possibility of additional Canadian units, offered advice on reorganizing Continental troops already in the province, emphasized Wooster's desire for replacement generals, and harped on the need for cash. He also offered opinions on Canadian Continental leaders, particularly extolling Jeremiah Duggan. After his testimony, Ritzema headed for New York, where he would be called to form a new regiment, leaving Canadian concerns behind.[9]

Shortly after Ritzema's visit, a "French" Canadian arrived in Philadelphia, Prudent Lajeunesse. He was a Longueuil resident and Richelieu valley campaign partisan captain, most recently serving in Montréal. On 20 January, Wooster had provided him with an envoy's passport, to "give Congress true Information" about the "Sentiments and way of Thinking of his Countrymen." Upon arrival, the *Canadien* conferred with the important Committee of Secret Correspondence, including such powerful members as Benjamin Franklin, John Dickinson, and John Jay. That committee provided its Lajeunesse Report on 14 February.[10]

The *Canadien* described the ongoing struggle for habitant loyalties, pitting seigneurs and clergy against Continentals and their patriot Canadian friends. By his report, Congress's letters "made little Impression, the common People being generally unable to read." Therefore, Lajeunesse noted, "it would be of great Service if some Persons from the Congress were sent to Canada" to explain, face-to-face, the nature of the current conflict. He opined that "unless some such Measure is taken," Continental affairs would "meet with continual Difficulty and Obstruction."[11]

After months of generals' requests for a Congressional committee, Lajeunesse's testimony was the straw that broke the camel's back. On 14 February, the very day that the Committee of Secret Correspondence provided its report, Congress decided to send a committee to Canada. The new committee would consist of two members of Congress, augmented by specially qualified civilians. A long series of delays, however, kept the delegation in Philadelphia, during which time additional visitors arrived from Canada.[12]

When Montréal merchant representative Benjamin Frobisher departed from his home city on 11 February, General Wooster sent James Price, Thomas Walker, and John Bonfield with him. The general asked those patriot leaders, well "acquainted with this province and with the tempers and dispositions of the Canadians," to share their views with Congress, including "what can be said for and against" the merchants' petition. En route, they picked up a letter from Schuyler, supporting Wooster's decision against opening the fur trade. On 4 March, Frobisher presented "the memorial from sundry merchants of Montreal, respecting Indian trade" in Philadelphia. Congress referred the petition to committee, soon transferring it to the new Committee to Canada, which preferred to see conditions in Quebec before rendering a verdict on the matter. Despite the Montréal merchants' best efforts to follow Wooster's prompting, Congress failed to give an efficient reply.[13]

Formally, Price and Walker did not receive a much better reception. A proposal that Congress "examine" the gentlemen was "opposed as unnecessary and dropt." With the Committee to Canada already established, any further action by the whole of Congress would only confuse matters. However, James Price was appointed deputy-commissary general for Canada, a move strongly endorsed by General Schuyler. Unlike all the other Philadelphia visitors, Price and Walker also sparked unusual rumors and misperceptions. On the one hand, in Rhode Island they were reported to be "Delegates from Montreal to the Congress." On the other hand, Canadian loyalist circles imagined the duo had been arrested in Philadelphia because Congress blamed the two "instigators" for misleading the United Colonies into invading Quebec.[14]

Back in Montréal, Moses Hazen returned in early February, bearing copies of Congress's third letter to the Canadians. François Cazeau again circulated the message, reporting that it was "productive of much good." The Tory Sanguinet, however, claimed it was a failure; he was absolutely correct in observing that the Canadians still "did not want to establish an assembly—and desired even less to send deputies to Congress."[15]

═════

As patriot officers and envoys traveled across the lakes to communicate between Canada and the United Colonies, New York's Royal Governor William Tryon established his own parallel correspondence. While returning from his New York detention, *Canadien* loyalist prisoner of war Joseph-Marie Lamotte secreted a packet of letters, for delivery to Vicar-General Etienne Montgolfier in Montréal. Lamotte and several peers had been generously released by Continental authorities. By 31 January, the vicar-general received Tryon's congratulations for the Canadian government's victory on New Year's Eve, and intelligence from the lower colonies, including a "true copy of the letter that General Wooster sent to Congress." This was the Connecticut general's letter to Seth Warner, which showed "contempt" for the Canadians and would play a more important role in a few weeks, once Montgolfier's agents forwarded the letters to Québec City.[16]

In late February, Montgolfier sent Lamotte, and associate Joseph Papineau, as couriers to the capital. Carrying walking sticks hollowed out to conceal letters, the pair proceeded along the St. Lawrence's south bank, "walking by day in the woods and by night on the highways," and receiving shelter from friendly priests on a painstakingly cautious eleven-day voyage. Passing over to Ile-d'Orléans, they sheltered in the St-Pierre presbytery before crossing to the capital, in the cover of a blinding snowstorm on the night of 8 March.[17]

As Tryon and Montgolfier furthered the loyalist cause with their cooperative correspondence, Schuyler and Wooster were sidetracked in an inopportune dispute over their own letters, the latter euphemistically observing that they "were not upon the most friendly terms." In a triangle of correspondence between the two generals and Congress, Schuyler had been offended by Wooster's mid-January complaints regarding the prisoners' return to Canada. For almost a month, the major-general protested that Wooster had damaged his reputation and honor, and shown contempt for his authority. Wooster stood his ground, but expressed "great unhappiness" that they could not agree and made it clear that he wished to "let the matter rest." Schuyler finally let the issue pass in late February. Meanwhile, Congress investigated the spat, carefully avoiding blame for either general; both generals were critical to the cause at this moment. John Adams, however, took the opportunity to provide a counterpoint to the growing number of Wooster detractors, noting that the Connecticut general had "done that in Canada" which Schuyler could not have done: "He . . . kept up an Army there through the Winter."[18]

Thereafter, the generals' correspondence returned to more important themes — particularly finances. Wooster added new emphasis to the army's need for hard cash, noting that "we must either starve, quit the country, or disgrace our army and the American cause, by laying the country under contribution; there is no other alternative." Given the scope of Continental debt in the parishes, he predicted that by mid-March the United Colonies would be unable to procure habitant transportation. Meanwhile, Schuyler helped sustain the army by sending $5,300 in cash, drawn on his personal credit.

Continental commissaries also reached Canada in March; they did not bring money, but might limit costly "waste of provisions."[19]

Ever since Congress had heard of Montgomery's death, it had been understood that a replacement general was needed in Canada. Even though there was almost universal consensus on the perfect candidate for the job, there was no solution for almost a month. Montgomery, Arnold, and Ritzema, as well as several Congressional delegates, all reached the same conclusion offered by Horatio Gates: "I know no man but Lee capable of commanding in Canada."[20]

General Charles Lee, however, was productively engaged in suppressing the New York Tories, probably a key reason that Congress did not immediately send him north. By the second week of February, though, Washington, Robert Morris, and Benjamin Franklin all corresponded with Lee on the possibility of a Canadian command. The major-general admitted he found the idea flattering: a "most tempting field of honour." He reassured General Washington, "Wherever I can be of most service, there I should like to be." Lee's interest in Canada stretched back to the first Continental Congress, and he frequently offered peers his views on creative considerations for the province—from Northern Army officer qualifications, to recruiting Canadian regiments for deployment outside that province; most recently, he had consulted with Lieutenant-Colonel Ritzema to gather the latest Quebec intelligence.[21]

The long-anticipated appointment finally came on 17 February. Prominent delegates such as Benjamin Franklin and Robert Morris quickly penned letters congratulating Lee. John Adams praised the major-general's "Address, his Fluency in French, his Activity, his great Experience and Skill," observing, "If We fail now, I shall be easy because I know of nothing more or better that We can do."[22]

Even though Lee was busy handling New York's issues, he energetically prepared for the Canadian command, promptly requesting French and English secretaries and asking to be accompanied by an additional brigadier-general.[23] Yet just as Lee informed Congress that he was ready to head north, on 28 February, President John Hancock changed the general's orders. Lee was to hold fast in New York. Congress had begun redistricting Continental military commands, and as John Adams had earlier informed Lee, he was in high demand: "We want you at N[ew] York—We want you at Cambridge[.] We want you in Virginia." South Carolinian Edward Rutledge specifically asked Hancock to ensure that Lee did not get too far away; with district commanders to be selected on 1 March, Rutledge eyed the much-vaunted Lee for the new Southern Department.[24]

That day, Hancock informed General Lee that he was, in fact, reassigned to the Southern Department. Even Lee was shocked: "As I am the only General Officer, on the Continent, who can speak and think in French, I confess I think it would have been more prudent to have sent me to Canada"; yet he was a good soldier and would "obey with alacrity, and hope[fully], with success." Washington concurred, writing that Lee would have "done more essential service to the common cause in Canada."[25]

With all the other district commands filled, Congress took five more days to identify a new commander for Quebec, as John Thomas was finally ordered to "immediately repair" to Canada from Cambridge, and was simultaneously promoted to major-general. Thomas was a respected leader from Washington's main Continental camp. Like Montgomery, Wooster, and Lee, he also had served in the decisive 1760 campaign up the Champlain-Richelieu corridor, commanding a Massachusetts regiment. Fifteen years later, as the Revolution opened, he was a provincial general, and in the summer of 1775, became one of the original Continental brigadiers. Now, upon his new promotion and appointment as district commander, John Hancock and John Adams encouraged him, but the dour Adams could not help but note, "The Department to which you are destined has been in Great Confusion." Meanwhile, Congress reassured General Schuyler that the Colonies would still "rely greatly" on his support for Quebec as well—consistent supplies were critical to "not only the success, but the existence of the Army in Canada."[26]

———

As Congress dawdled about appointing a new commander and took time sending its new Committee to Canada, General Wooster continued to direct efforts on his own. With so many leading Tories confined in Chambly or the colonies, one infamous loyalist still remained at liberty—the "noted Indian Partizan" St-Luc de La Corne. The "old villain" had remained in Boucherville for two months on the general's authority, until Moses Hazen returned from Philadelphia to vouch for La Corne's return to Montréal. Some of La Corne's friends, however, counseled that it was unwise for him to linger in the city;

he might seem too close to the *Bastonnais,* especially after his subversive fall correspondence with Montgomery. Through an arrangement facilitated by Hazen, La Corne was sent as a prisoner to the United Colonies. He departed on 20 February, escorted by Brigade-Major Isaac Melchior. Unaware that Wooster was taking such measures, General Washington coincidentally had his secretary write to Montréal, advising that it would be "pleasing to his Excellency" and "of very great service to the American cause" for La Corne to be "sent out of the Province."[27]

With Melchior's departure, Wooster called junior New York Lieutenant George Nicholson to fill the vacant brigade-major position. In contrast to his predecessor's commendable performance, Nicholson quickly earned a reputation for abusing authority. He reportedly did "nothing but pillage, & commit outrages on the Inhabitants" of Montréal. When Nicholson confined a man in a "flagrant act of violence," citizens finally issued a formal complaint to Wooster. Rather than removing the troublesome brigade-major from the city, on 7 March, the general transferred him to a new position at headquarters—a promotion to aide-de-camp, shocking Montrealers of all stripes. Yet despite Nicholson's indiscretions, general relations between citizens and soldiers remained surprisingly friendly.[28]

Meanwhile, a handful of lesser loyalists were sent out of Canada in March. Half-pay British officer Simon Evans and Monsieur Beaubassin were exiled for "inveterate" opposition to Continental authority. Several others were sent up from the Québec City lines: Mr. Woolsy and Mr. Winter both violated their paroles and were caught trying to enter the capital; Joseph Launière and François Robitaille were arrested as spies from the capital.[29]

One notable loyalist would not be exiled, however. Even though General Wooster had told Claude Lorimier that he would be sent to New York in the first week of February, the loyalist Indian expert was permitted to linger in the city for more than a month. On 6 March, Lorimier slipped from Montréal in "a secret manner," headed up-country. He had two coconspirators with him, Richard Walker and Stanley Goddard, and the three "rank tories" were last seen at the Indian village of St-Régis before disappearing from patriot sight. Their departure did not bode well for Montréal's exposed western approaches. After the escape, Wooster wrote to General Schuyler, informing him there was "reason to apprehend some mischief contriving against us in the upper Counties."[30]

This was not a completely new development. Wooster had already shared concerns that the Montréal Tories were communicating with the King's troops in the up-country, planning to gather Indian allies and "make a descent upon this Town when our Troops are gone to Quebec," but Lorimier's departure amplified the threat. The general repeated appeals for reinforcements, encouraging their arrival before the lakes thawed and restricted communications for weeks. Wooster also suggested that Schuyler launch an expedition to Oswego, to interdict any British parties coming from the Great Lakes.[31]

General Wooster kept a steady eye on the reinforcements arriving from the south. He knew the decisive battle would take place as soon as the St. Lawrence was navigable and prodded Congress: "our every thing depends upon our having a force upon the spot superior to them." On 18 February, the first official Continental reinforcements reached Montréal, but in the haste to send units forward, these companies from Colonel John Philip De Haas's First Pennsylvania Battalion arrived "very incompleat." Men rushed north "hanging upon the Sleighs like Bees about a Hive," but by 6 March, Schuyler already had reported that the southernmost lakes were thawing, effectively halting the troop flow to Canada. Only a week later, Wooster found that "there has not yet arrived from the Colonies fifteen hundred men," less than a quarter of what was intended for the spring.[32]

These new troops, however, quickly proved counterproductive in promoting good Canadian relations. Even while still in New York, General Schuyler complained of the lead Pennsylvania and New Jersey regiments: "I am ashamed of the Conduct of our Troops—Tories and Whigs are indiscriminately the Object of plunder whenever a fair Oppertunity offers." Congress reacted with a 17 February resolution calling Continental officers to "use their utmost diligence" to prevent plunder, and punishing offenders "according to the strictest discipline," but little changed.[33]

In contrast to Montgomery's remarkably restrained troops in the fall campaign, the newcomers arrived ill disciplined and arrogant; their conduct was "absolutely shocking" and habitants were "ill used." A civilian Continental teamster even reported that these troops abused Canadians' religion: "The inhabitants were fired at as they went to mass. The priests themselves were robbed and outrages of every description were committed." As Schuyler later commented, the troops' ignorance and disdain gave the "Canadians about Sorrel . . . too much Reason" to complain of "ill Treatment."[34]

Northern Army finances only exacerbated the situation. When soldiers did not simply steal what they wanted, they paid in certificates or promised payment, sometimes demanding a lower price than market value. Habitants found that when they tried to cash in certificates, the quartermaster-general regularly "rejected them for informality." Friendly Richelieu Valley Canadians found "their Labour & Property lost and the Congress & United Colonies Bankrupts." Official policies also grated on the *Canadiens*. West of Montréal, Wooster issued orders "forbidding anyone to drive any stranger . . . without permission from an American general officer." In the city itself, loyalists were "forced to leave their houses to make room" for the new reinforcements. Continental authorities also called on rural habitants to perform compulsory *corvée* labor, primarily providing transportation. While *corvée* duty was a traditional means of employing *Canadiens* for government work, it was never popular.[35]

The situation seemed ripe for a loyalist uprising. In early March, Montréal notary Simon Sanguinet composed and posted an anonymous letter to the "Inhabitants of Canada." The loyalist scolded his brethren for passivity in the face of the *Bastonnais'* "tyrannical power"—now was the time to act "to avoid the solemn punishment" that they deserved for their disloyal conduct to the government. The letter noted how the Canadians were ransacked and insulted by the rebels, yet continued to endure the abuse. Were they not bothered when given "despotic commands" or called for unpaid *corvées?* Sanguinet hoped to rouse them from their slumber; yet once again, there was no response. Montrealers remained immersed in their self-interested, politically apathetic lethargy.[36]

With the river ice ready to break, fur-trade merchants prepared their spring shipments even though Congress had not responded to their petition. None of the merchants wanted to lose the trade, but some had even more incentive to ignore Continental restrictions: a few Old Subject merchants had just relocated from New York to avoid the Continental Association's trade limitations, and most "French" traders had struggled for the last decade to establish their position in the British Imperial trading system. Neither group was likely to sacrifice their business just because the current Continental régime was bureaucratically incompetent.

General Wooster's informants warned that some merchants intended to "send off their goods in the spring, with or without passports," and he responded with an order "prohibiting the carrying any coarse goods out of the city, except such as were wanted by the country people." A few merchants defied the order, covertly shipping goods from Montréal; and in one notable case, Wooster had sufficient intelligence to intercept the "smugglers." On 20 March, about thirty miles west of Montréal, a Continental party stopped seven of twenty-nine sleighs in a Bernard & Wadden Company caravan. The "coarse goods" were confiscated, and Commissary of Public Stores George Measam distributed them to Continental consumers.[37]

While such merchants tried to skirt Continental authority, their ardent patriot counterparts continued to drain their own accounts in support of "the cause," granting liberal credit to the army and circulating Continental bills. A long list of businessmen claimed they supported the Northern Army at a hefty loss: Joseph Bindon, John Blake, John Dyer Mercier, François Cazeau, Pierre du Calvet, David Salisbury Franks, Jacob Vanderheyden, and Benjamin Thompson. Hospital Purveyor Levy Solomons incurred even more personal debt in the execution of his office, as the army could not even pay for the "Preservation of the Sick." All Wooster could offer them was his praise and a vain promise to repay their loans. While they were neither risking their lives in the field nor leading political action, Montréal's patriot merchants proved their willingness to sacrifice their fortunes in the fight for liberty.[38]

=====

After his return to Montréal from Philadelphia, Colonel Moses Hazen swiftly began recruiting his new regiment—a symbol of Canadian patriot support in 1776, intended to be almost 10 percent of the Continental force in Quebec. Hazen's first announcement went out on 10 February, authorizing recruiters to enlist men "to defend their just rights and privileges." The term was one year, at 40 *livres* (₶) per month, equal to standard Continental private pay, with a 40₶ recruiting bonus.[39]

Hazen tried to emphasize the selection of good officers; Wooster helped by delegating appointment authority to the regiment's colonels. Hazen gave all the field officer positions to Old Subjects, perhaps to ease communication with other Continental units, but relied heavily on *Canadien* company commanders, including Laurent Olivier, Philip Liebert, and Brindamour. Jean-François Hamtramck, Pierre du Calvet, and Pierre Boileau were among the junior officers appointed. One of the chief qualifications for company commanders was personal wealth; Hazen lacked hard money, so officers were forced to pay their soldiers' recruiting bonuses and a few months' pay from personal accounts. Predictably, loyalists disparaged the Canadian Continental officers, but even Hazen admitted that his first officers were not well qualified—being forced to make do with the few candidates available.[40]

Hazen tied officer appointments to recruiting success, giving proper commissions only to those in adequately manned companies. In the end, only half of the twenty authorized companies would be fielded, the lack of hard cash being the biggest obstacle. After one month, the colonel reported that "my money is now exhausted and am not like to get any men until it arrives from below." By mid-March, in the Montreal District, Hazen had recruited only about one quarter of his desired end strength, and again the quality was questionable. Loyalists characterized the Canadian Continentals as "scoundrels . . . the largest number of whom were French soldiers who had stayed in Canada after the Conquest," although theoretically such men should have been disciplined, experienced warriors. Still, Hazen doubted his own men's reliability, predicting they would desert or switch sides if "the Canadians in general join against us."[41]

Lieutenant-Colonel Antill was sent to the Quebec District to find more men, where Hazen encouraged him to poach recruits from Jeremiah Duggan, who was reportedly having success there. The colonel prodded Antill to "Lay aside the delicate Gentleman" and send out aggressive recruiting officers. By 1 April, however, Hazen suspended recruiting, noting, "The want of money obliges me to stop . . . not a man more will now engage." The best estimate of the Second Canadian Regiment's progress maintained that "Four Hundred and Seventy-seven Men were, in a very short Time, inlisted, armed, accoutred, and clothed, chiefly at the Expence of the Officers of the Regiment, and carried into actual Service." It was far below expectations, but given the monetary hurdles and unstable situation, was not a complete failure.[42]

Once his companies were raised and deployed, Hazen lost operational control over most of them. The first four companies were scattered around the province—two to support Arnold at Québec City and one at Fort Chambly—leaving one with the colonel in Montréal. Additional companies subsequently were deployed to Fort St-Jean, and west to Les-Cèdres (The Cedars). The Second Canadian Regiment stayed "In this dismembered Situation" for the duration of the campaign. Moses Hazen, however, remained anchored in Montréal for a while.[43]

By mid-March, General Wooster had stabilized Montréal for more than two months and finally reported that "the service of the United Colonies make it necessary that I repair immediately to the Camp before Quebec." Wooster identified Moses Hazen as his Montreal District successor, notifying the Canadian colonel of his new responsibilities on 23 March. The general trusted Hazen to pursue his "best Judgement and Skill, in the Discharge of the Trust," simply asking him to keep his superiors informed of "any extraordinary occurences that may happen." There were a few specific guidelines, though. First and foremost, Hazen was to "keep up Strict Discipline," and if necessary, to "defend the Town to the last extremity." He was also to enforce Wooster's ban on fur-trade shipments. Once Lake Champlain opened, Hazen was directed to send loyalist prisoners from Chambly down to Albany; and he was also granted authority to send away "any other Persons that may be Esteemed dangerous and inimical to the Cause of the United Colonies."[44]

Several patriot Montrealers still doubted Hazen's commitment to their cause. As William Haywood, James Price's business partner reported, "Colo[nel] Hazen [was] generally suspected of being unfriendly." Instead of arresting Tories, other patriots observed that the colonel always "exerted his interest to get our enemies released." Some even labeled Hazen an enemy, "Dangerous to an Extreme."[45]

Wooster packed up his baggage, bade adieu to friends, and departed from Montréal on 27 March. Hazen established a new headquarters, settling into one of the city's most elegant buildings, the Château de Ramezay. The long, palatial stone home, perched on the city's high ground, was built in 1705 for the governor of New France. The Château had since served as headquarters for the French colonial *Compagnie des Indes* and most recently as a residence for visiting officials. Hazen co-opted this traditional symbol of authority in Montréal, while distancing himself from Thomas Walker's influence.[46]

As he entered his new command, Hazen offered to keep General Schuyler regularly informed "of every material Circumstance," and suggested he might add his "own Ideas of the whole Country and affairs in General." Such communication was not necessarily appropriate by protocol—Wooster was still Hazen's immediate superior, yet the demands of long-distance communications provided a convenient excuse for skipping an echelon of command—and Schuyler did nothing to discourage Hazen's correspondence.[47]

Just days after Wooster left town, Moses Hazen's first such letter to Schuyler provided an invaluable assessment of the deteriorating state of Quebec—a damning indictment of Continental maladministration in Canada. The pessimistic colonel noted a perceptible shift in Canadian loyalties; in contrast to the warm welcome Richelieu Valley habitants provided in the fall, Hazen warned, "we are no more to look upon them as friends"; instead, they were "waiting an Opportunity to Join our Enemies." He reported that among the "better sort of people . . . both French & English seven eighths are Tories, who would wish to see our Throats cut and perhaps would readily assist in doing it."[48]

Hazen identified a number of policies and affairs contributing to the drift in support. The Clergy had "been Neglected, perhaps in some Instances Ill used." Habitants had been disenchanted by forced requisitions and payment in paper money or useless hand receipts. They also lacked confidence in the United Colonies, because they had never seen "Sufficient force in the Country to protect them." The Northern Army was a hollow shell, weak in numbers, decimated by smallpox, with troops yearning to depart the moment their enlistments were complete. Canadian regiments were inadequately manned and could not hope to reach full strength until hard money arrived.

General Schuyler certainly knew things were tenuous in Quebec, but even with all Wooster's situation reports and pleas for additional support, and Arnold's stark assessments from outside the capital, the situation had never been painted so black. The ever-gloomy Hazen portrayed a "whole Country left without any other kind of law, than that of the Arbitrary & Despotic power of the Sword in the hands of the several Commanding Officers, too frequently abused." The most poignant line in the letter maintained "We have brot about ourselves by Mismanagement what Gov[erno]r Carleton himself could never Effect," driving the Canadians to support the loyalists.[49]

Only one day before Hazen composed his letter, Montréal patriot George Measam shared a similarly bleak view of the situation, addressed to New York's Alexander McDougall. In the Montrealer's perspective, the province had been "most shamefully neglected," having "neither money nor Credit, nor a third part the number of troops we ought to have." While Canadians were "friendly inclined," Measam maintained that Quebec had to be treated as a "Conquered Province," even if it were a "Voluntary Conquest," as the Continentals could not depend on the Canadians. Unlike Hazen, the merchant pointed a finger at Congress, noting: "Matters have not been politically managed with regard to this Province, a starved war is the most expensive, and dangerous; we now have many enemies among us which might have been friends to the cause, had a Committee of sensible men been sent up from the Congress with some money, to regulate the police [policy] of the Country."[50]

Yet, as would be evidenced in coming months, Wooster made a convenient scapegoat. By mid-March—within weeks of Congressional reports from Frobisher, Walker, and Price—sharply critical judgments spread from Philadelphia, that "Old Wooster was throwing every Thing into Confusion." The sexagenarian general was past his prime, more reactive than dynamic, and may not have been charismatic; but blaming David Wooster for incompetently driving Canadians into the loyalist camp is patently unfair. The general even had a few contemporary civilian patriot supporters in Canada, notably Québec City exile Hector McNeill, who reported he had "never seen any thing in General Wooster but the greatest care." Brigadier-General John Sullivan—who would command the final phases of the Canadian operation—told a post-campaign Congressional committee, "The Common reports were in favour of General Wooster," and as best Sullivan could determine, Wooster had conducted himself "well."[51]

Seminal Canadian Campaign historian, Justin H. Smith, however, described Wooster as "the one insurmountable obstacle that prevented the Americans from winning Canada," subsequently a widely accepted historiographical view. While contemporary loyalists generally indicted Wooster for decisions that mirrored, or anticipated, the very same things that garnered General Charles Lee praise in New York, modern historians have tended to focus on three specific incidents to condemn Wooster: the failure to grant fur-trade licenses, the closing of the Mass houses on Christmas Eve, and clergy arrests. However, Wooster had a proven role only in the first of these; in that case Schuyler firmly supported the brigadier's position, and Congress was given an explicit opportunity to overrule it. The second issue, the alleged closing of Montréal churches, is essentially unsubstantiated—based on hearsay rather than any surviving hard evidence. The final accusation, of arrested priests, is based on a composite of several events, some anecdotal, others that happened later in the campaign, which were initiated by Canadians, not Continentals. The reality is that, while he may have threatened it, no record is extant of Wooster arresting or exiling any Church representatives for pro-loyalist preaching, or for denying sacraments to patriot Canadians.[52] The sole, documented early 1776 arrest of priests occurred in Three Rivers District, when patriot Canadian James Price encountered and detained three Recollet priests who had sortied from Québec City; suspected of being Governor Carleton's messengers, they were escorted upriver and held in Montréal, for obvious security reasons.[53]

While far from perfect, Wooster's Montréal command has been unjustly maligned; his decisions inevitably have been portrayed in the worst possible light, without consideration of contemporary events, his superior's concurrence, or Congress's response (or lack thereof) to his frequent pleas and warnings. General David Wooster was bound by limited resources, military and financial, much more than his personal deficiencies. As commemorative Wooster orator Henry Deming observed, "With two thousand men he was called upon to achieve all the impossibilities demanded by the nation." Given the United Colonies' political goals in Canada, Montréal patriots and Congress shared much greater blame for the failure to establish civilian leadership, guidance, or control for the province in the winter of 1776.[54]

Chapter 17

A SPIRIT OF COOPERATION
AND UNDERSTANDING

William Goforth, Jean-Baptiste Badeaux, and Trois-Rivières

This district laying between the army of Quebec and Montreal I conceive to be the quietest part of Canada at present. | *Captain William Goforth to John Jay, Three-Rivers in Canada, 8 April 1776*

The United Colonies' adventure in Canada was heavily focused on Montréal and Québec City. While the province's third city, Trois-Rivières, had a relatively minor role in the overall campaign, it offers a particularly interesting case study in Continental-*Canadien* relations. During one New York captain's two-month tour of duty in that city, he fostered remarkably strong relations with its citizens, while effectively minimizing loyalist conflict and dissent.

=====

Trois-Rivières sits on the north bank of the St. Lawrence, midway between the capital and Montréal. The city was so named because the St-Maurice River, about a half mile north, splits into three channels as it meets the St. Lawrence, creating the appearance of "three rivers." Even if the little city was not massive or opulent, contemporary visitors considered it a "pleasant place," with about one thousand "Trifluviens," as city residents are called. With "well cultivated" wheat fields on the city's south and west sides, citizens were "more devoted . . . to agriculture than to trade," the only other significant local business coming from the forges six miles up the St-Maurice. The city's "small and indifferent" homes were almost exclusively made of wood, unlike the stone edifices predominant in Montréal and Québec City; a few regional seigneurs kept "exceedingly nice houses furnished very respectably." The only substantial structures were the parish church, the "government house" barracks, and the Recollet and Ursuline Convents.[1]

Trois-Rivières had been guardedly loyal in the fall campaign. Sixty-seven citizen militiamen marched toward Montréal in October, until intercepted by the patriots at Berthier-en-haut. Then, the short November visits-in-flight by Maclean and Carleton were immediately followed by the Morris-Badeaux embassy to Montréal, through which the Trifluviens offered their long-distance capitulation to Montgomery on the twentieth.[2] About one week after Colonel James Livingston's Canadians were the first Continentals to march through the city, another Canadian Continental company visited in early December, also en route to the capital. During their short stay, Captain Augustin Loiseau had his men disarm Trois-Rivières' most prominent loyalists—including Militia-Colonel Louis-Joseph Godefroy-de-Tonnancour, his deputy Louis Cressé, and active loyalist seigneur Joseph Boucher-de-Niverville, who had just returned to the city from accompanying Governor Carleton on his harrowing Laurentian escape. The Continentals seized an odd assortment of weapons—swords, handguns, and a few muskets—more novel and sentimental than dangerous; yet that evening, local patriots informed Loiseau that Tonnancour had additional powder and weapons hidden on his property. The captain demonstrated prudence; instead of pursuing the questionable tip, Loiseau led his company out of town the next morning to join Montgomery.[3]

District patriots had already started to exert their influence in the countryside. In Ste-Anne-de-la-Pérade, thirty miles downstream from Trois-Rivières, partisan habitants persistently harassed Louis Gouin, a loyalist who had shown "great zeal" for the government's October militia call-up. A party of fellow patriots from south bank St-Pierre-les-Becquets, opposite la-Pérade, even crossed the St. Lawrence to help vex Gouin. When the les-Becquets *curé* subsequently denied them sacraments, the patriot partisans petitioned General Montgomery to punish their priest. No troops were sent, but the *curé* received a written reprimand from the general's aide. Meanwhile, the parish continued as the district's hub for patriot activity.[4]

The two most prominent regional patriots, though, happened to be at the St-Maurice Forges: transplanted Frenchmen Christophe Pélissier and Pierre de Sales-Laterrière. Both viewed the Continental invasion as an opportunity to bring Enlightenment principles of liberty to their Canadian home. While Pélissier was busy visiting with the Continental generals and encouraging patriot activity in Montréal, Laterrière kept the forge fires burning.[5]

Militia-Colonel Tonnancour,[6] seigneur of several nearby parishes, was

View of Trois-Rivières [Three Rivers], by James Peachey (ca. 1784). This view is from the south, around Pointe-du-Lac. Library and Archives Canada, Acc. No. 1983-33-1609, Collection James Peachey.

the district's senior loyalist and one of Governor Carleton's most trusted allies; but the sixty-three-year-old remained relatively inactive during the fall. There were insinuations that Tonnancour kept a closer eye on his business than his politics; the patriot Laterrière even claimed that Tonnancour sent a shipment of rum to the rebel camp outside Québec City, hedging bets on the campaign's outcome.[7]

After its November capitulation, Trois-Rivières remained ungarrisoned for more than two months. Someone posted Wooster's 6 January proclamation on the church doors, yet there was no one to enforce it. The only solace for local patriots was word that a large number of *Bastonnais* were on their way.[8]

With the first wave of west Massachusetts and Green Mountain Boy reinforcements reaching Montréal in the last week of January, General Wooster finally dispatched a company of New Yorkers to "Curb the Tories" in Trois-Rivières. Captain William Goforth received orders to govern the city and "furnish Horse Carriages . . . for the passing Army and see them supplied with provisions" on their march to the capital. On 8 February, Goforth led almost one hundred soldiers into Trois-Rivières, establishing Continental authority in the city. Constant Freeman, a patriot refugee from the capital, welcomed them to town and offered his services as an interpreter — an important contribution since none of the Yorkers spoke French. The troops moved into the centrally located barracks and began improving that "out of repair" facility. Goforth's men stayed on the ample stone building's ground floor and prepared the upper level to accommodate transiting soldiers. Rather than billeting with local families in typical officer fashion, Goforth and Lieutenant Stephen McDougall quartered themselves in the barracks as well, keeping a close eye on their men and the provisions stored between their rooms.[9]

Captain William Goforth had been an active, if less famous, New York City patriot leader. A Philadelphian by birth, he moved to New York as an adult and prospered as a cordwainer — a shoemaker. Goforth was well educated for an artisan, even owning the *Encyclopaedia Britannica,* when most "mechanic" peers possessed only a Bible and maybe an almanac. By 1769, he began to support Alexander McDougall's patriot politics. Six years later, the forty-four-year-old Goforth translated business acumen and patriot commitment into a growing political role. After the first Continental Congress, he served on the city's new "Committee of Sixty," which expanded citizen tradesmen's political involvement. As a committee man, he helped secure the city's privately held cannons and also inspected ships "suspected of having goods on board not admissible."[10]

When the First New York Regiment was formed in June 1775, Colonel McDougall chose his old friend as a captain. Early in his service, Goforth represented his fellow officers in delivering a petition to the provincial congress, seeking resolution of pay and commission issues before the regiment marched north. Goforth's company remained in the city for a few weeks after the regiment's lead elements deployed, joining the Fort St-Jean campaign at the end of September. There, the men saw "something of the nature of Carrying on a Seige" before the fort surrendered. Once the main army moved to Montréal, Goforth remained with Colonel Ritzema, garrisoning the city as Montgomery left to join Arnold.[11]

One of Captain Goforth's chief characteristics was his empathetic concern — for his family, his soldiers, and the *Canadiens.* With all the tensions in New York City, the captain was "much distress'd" for his wife Catherine and five children, expecting the Royal Navy might bombard the city; so he asked McDougall to watch over them. By March, the colonel helped move the family to the countryside, earning the captain's deepest appreciation and providing great comfort.[12]

Goforth, meanwhile, kept an eye on the regiment's young officers in Canada, especially the colonel's two sons, tending to their interests and providing fatherly advice as their "Dada Goforth"; McDougall's youngest son Stephen even served as his lieutenant. A late November incident also demonstrated Goforth's deep concern for his soldiers. Almost immediately after Montgomery gave uniforms to reenlisting Continentals, rumors circulated that cost of the clothing would be deducted from the soldiers' meager pay. Piqued by the very idea of such a shortsighted, ungrateful imposition, Goforth wrote a fiery letter to McDougall. He warned that Continental leaders appeared to be "Mistaken" in their understanding of the soldiers' limits. In a tone bordering on insubordination, the captain informed his commander, "we intend to make you pay them." In the end, the issue passed, yet Goforth's ire over the potential abuse of his military "sons" was indicative of the deep emotion underlying his leadership.[13]

In his new Trois-Rivières command, Captain Goforth was not one for sitting quietly behind a desk, reporting, "I generally find myself very Busy all day." By his third day in the city, Goforth sought out a more professional interpreter—better service than the volunteer Constant Freeman could offer—asking notary Jean-Baptiste Badeaux to provide an official translation of General Wooster's recent militia commission orders. Badeaux somewhat grudgingly agreed to cooperate with the new town "leader."[14]

Jean-Baptiste Badeaux had served nine years in his office, becoming so fluent in English that he had been mistaken for a *Bastonnais* during his capitulation-delivery trip to Montréal. The thirty-four-year-old Trifluvien had other community roles, acting as attorney for the city's Ursuline Convent and serving as the master cantor of the parish choir. But Goforth perceived an opportunity to use Badeaux's booming voice for more mundane tasks—as an invaluable tool for communicating with "others," not just "French," but Old Subject Tories as well. Any support the notary gave the captain would also co-opt traditional local government authority, lending credibility to Continental actions.[15]

That Sunday, Goforth had the Badeaux-translated orders published at the church doors, and additional copies were sent to all district parishes. On Monday, five "principle Inhabitants came to pay their Respects" to Captain Goforth, handing over their royal commissions. Five more visited the next day, apologizing for their delay; all the city militia officers had complied with Wooster's order, with the notable exception of "the Chief Colonel." Goforth sent Lieutenant McDougall to visit Colonel Tonnancour's home, only a few hundred feet from the barracks, to deliver a written inquiry about his commission. The seigneur-leader pleaded that he did not comprehend the English letter and called Badeaux to interpret. Once Tonnancour understood Goforth's demand, he protested to McDougall that he was under no obligation to surrender his commission, since it was a personal possession and Montgomery had promised to "defend all citizens' property"; so the lieutenant, militia-colonel, and notary called on Goforth for resolution.[16]

Captain Goforth was not looking to harshly impose authority; he did not want to be like British officers, whom he had seen "Violent in abuseing the Canadians because they were not true to [British] Tyranny." When Tonnancour and McDougall appeared at his office, the captain calmly explained that based on Wooster's orders, he had no alternative. Tonnancour would have to appeal to the general himself, and Goforth gave him two days to depart for Montréal or hand over the commission—a firm, but not overly oppressive solution.[17]

When the next couple of days brought "terrible weather . . . with snow and a great chill," Tonnancour opted to relinquish his commission rather than venture upriver. The three-day episode served as a promising overture for Continental-Trifluvien relationships. Goforth came away as a winner, establishing authority without publicly insulting his foes. The captain recognized that, as "a man of the Greatest property in these parts," Tonnancour was "by a Common Consequence of the greatest influence"; and having peacefully resolved the situation with the district's most prominent loyalist, Goforth expected that "all will go smooth and Easy in other Parishes."[18]

Captain Goforth wasted no time following up on his early success. The following Sunday, 18 February, he called all Trifluviens to the barracks for a militia election. Citizens chose officers for both of Trois-Rivières' militia companies, but feared Goforth would be displeased when they voted to keep the incumbent "city" company commander, Militia-Captain Jean-Baptiste Fafard *dit* Laframboise.[19] The Continental captain reassured them that he supported their free decisions.[20]

Goforth spent the next few weeks encouraging similar elections in the district's sixteen rural parishes (see Map 9), sending more than thirty names to General Wooster for commissions. In most parishes, especially on the north shore, incumbent captains were elected to continue in service. In Bécancour and Ste-Anne-de-la-Pérade, habitants ousted former militia officers; and the small, defiant parish of Gentilly elected its first militia-captain in more than a decade, having refused officers under Carleton in 1775. Several officers zeal-

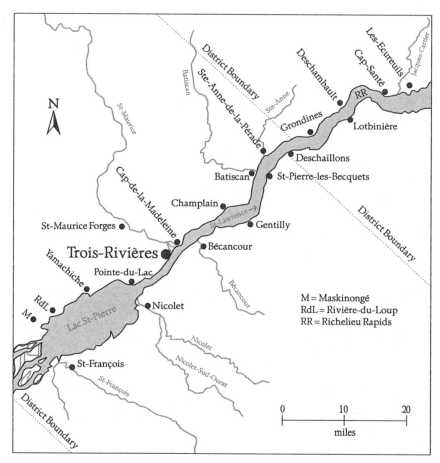

MAP 9: Three Rivers District.

ously accepted their new Continental authority, but a few were notably "shy of Receiving the post," expressing fear that they would be abandoned by the United Colonies if Congress achieved its goals with Britain, or if Ministerial troops drove the Continentals from Quebec.[21]

Goforth was not just proud of the election results, but also noted, "In some Parishes there have been three or four candidates for the Captaincy; and I receive information that bribery and corruption is already beginning to creep into their elections." For the "popular" New York City leader, now captain, it must have been a warm reminder of home. While Goforth was not directly involved in most of the parish elections, he noted, "At some, the disputes run so high that I am obliged to interfere." The captain gave his all to ensure that the militia was "well settled" before Ministerial troops reached

Canada in the spring. At the end of March, he reported that his constitution was broken by fatigue, claiming he was "Scarcely able to put that Cheerfull Countenance on matters which good policy Requires." Yet as he dealt with the *Canadiens* day in and day out, he sustained pleasant local relations — a powerful attribute in civil affairs.[22]

In one of the contentious elections requiring Goforth's intervention, the fervently patriotic habitants of St-Pierre-les-Becquets were extremely disturbed that fellow parishioners voted to retain their old militia-captain. So when they called for assistance, the captain set out on leap day for south bank les-Becquets, at the far eastern end of the district, bringing Badeaux as interpreter. Traveling down the King's Way, Captain Goforth heard that the parish of Champlain was preparing a funeral for their late priest, and decided to stop and pay his respects. His kind act, however, brought him into another local controversy, as habitants bickered over where the funeral should be held, inviting the captain to resolve their dispute. Evaluating the arguments, Goforth decided the funeral "would be held in the parsonage, according to tradition." Once again, he chose a prudent course, demonstrating his authority without appearing to impose "arbitrary" innovation.[23]

After paying their respects to the departed *curé*, Goforth's party pressed on to St-Pierre-les-Becquets. Three days prior, the habitant assembly had voted to keep Militia-Captain Pierre Viola, whom local patriots accused of having "an English heart." The previous summer, Viola had accepted Carleton's commission when fellow parishioners refused. But he had also cooperated with Continental authority: posting Wooster's orders, surrendering his commission, and holding the recent elections. In Badeaux's words, Captain Goforth's verdict was "a very judicious answer." The Continental captain told them that the incumbent could "be just as good a subject for Congress, as he was faithful to General Carleton," but called for a new election to end all dispute. Viola was on the verge of being reelected when he decided to withdraw his name, so a new captain and lieutenant were chosen. William Goforth had again demonstrated his political dexterity, managing relations and disputes with the "foreign" population, ably aided by the invaluable Badeaux.[24]

Badeaux's 1776 journal provides tremendous insight into William Goforth's character, but the notary could not discern the captain's deeper sentiments. A

22 February letter, from the captain to Benjamin Franklin, gives great insight, however. The bold captain offered his unsolicited views to the most famous American, in the hope that Franklin could apply his political genius to solve the Canadian conundrum. Like many observers, Goforth conveyed that the Canadians generally were disposed to the cause of liberty, but they hesitated to commit for fear of suffering Ministerial wrath; an influx of ten thousand troops, however, would "Relieve the People from their fears." Even though the Northern Department had been neglected, Goforth still believed that the Continentals might take the capital and that the Canadians would "have members in Congress and a Civil Government Established."[25]

Goforth observed that many fellow Continentals were "quite out of humour" with habitants who had changed sides during the struggle, but offered his own educated perspective, noting that no one would think their behavior odd "who is in the least acquainted with the history of the Cevil wars in England." Unlike many peers, he viewed the Canadians as rational actors in the rebellion, rather than mere sheep. But he also considered the Canadians "in General very poor . . . very Unlearnt," prompting some less enlightened views. The Baptist captain suggested that Protestant clergymen, schoolmasters, and doctors be brought in to educate the Canadians — not only to ensure they were "qualified for places of Profit and Honour" in the province, but also "to open their Eyes and raise their Appetite for freedom," while conveniently introducing them to Protestantism; he dubbed it "Proselytizing without Persecution." He was clearly aware that the United Colonies could not be perceived to be imposing religious change.[26]

Meanwhile, district patriots were challenging Church authority on their own, emboldened by the Continentals' presence. During Trois-Rivières' 21 February Shrove Tuesday Mass, a citizen openly "ridiculed some expressions" that Vicar-General St-Ongé used in his sermon. In nearby Cap-de-la-Madeleine, a habitant publicly implied that the bishop and vicar-general had been "paid to preach submission to the King." And in Champlain, when the militia-ensign was advised to take a long-standing parish rectory conflict to the vicar-general or bishop, he boldly and defiantly announced that he refused to acknowledge either's authority; he would take his complaints to someone he respected and recognized, Captain Goforth in Trois-Rivières — a radical declaration indeed.[27]

Still, the Church held fast to its loyalist position. During the Easter festival, starting 7 April, Vicar-General St-Ongé specifically prayed for God's blessing on the King's arms, even with Continentals garrisoning his city. Two weeks later, he announced a novena, a nine-day prayer vigil, for God's "Blessing on this province and for the preservation of our religion," clearly promoting royal rule. Badeaux, however, noted that some Trifluvien patriots continued to mock the vicar-general's prayers.[28]

In addition to administering the Three Rivers District, Captain Goforth's other major responsibility was assisting the Continentals' movement to the Québec City siege. The trickle of reinforcements progressively grew to a 1 March surge of 158 men, which included the lead echelon of the First Pennsylvania Battalion, expedited by Congress after Montgomery's defeat. Normally these troops traveled in small parties, averaging about twenty-five men; yet over February and March, they cumulatively totaled thirteen hundred soldiers, and brought a host of discipline issues with them.

The first notable incident occurred on St. Patrick's Day in March 1776. With more than two hundred troops from the Second New Jersey Regiment gathered in town, a host of Irish soldiers celebrated the holiday in raucous form. They marched through town, "swords and bayonets in hand," accompanied by fifes and drums and flying a makeshift banner—a white silk handkerchief fluttering on a fir trunk with two bayonets attached as a cross. Marching through the north end of town, the rambunctious crowd "serenaded" the Ursuline nuns. Returning down Rue Notre Dame, they stopped at the Tonnancour residence, shouting, "God damn this house and everyone in it," until satisfied they had adequately irritated the Tory family. From there, the mob proceeded to a more hospitable reception at Militia-Captain Laframboise's home; he gave each soldier two shots of rum, and the officers were invited inside to share "half a dozen bottles of liquor." The celebration eventually died out after the soldiers visited a few more "friendly" houses.[29]

Other troops stirred up more trouble in the following days, wandering through the city, claiming they were starved, and begging for food. Merciful Trifluviens showed pity, but their generosity waned; they could not be responsible for feeding all the miserable *Bastonnais*. In one event, a dozen troops barged into Tonnancour's home, trying to steal meat from a fireplace spit, leading the seigneur to shoo them out. Through Badeaux, Goforth offered his apologies after the fact and requested that Tonnancour call him immediately in any similar recurrence, promising to "put it in good order."[30]

Discipline issues only worsened through March and April, especially in outlying parishes, where Goforth's influence on the troops was particularly limited. Dealing with the fallout from the widespread Continental misbehavior, Goforth grimly reported that "the minds of the Canadians are much soured, some of them think they have been insulted by Vagabond part of our Soldiery in which there is too much truth." The captain provided Colonel Hazen with a list of the "flagrant abuses" committed by "Private Soldiers on their March to Quebec," as Pennsylvania and New Jersey detachments crossed his district. A priest's house was "entered with great Violence," and the *curé* had his watch "plundered from him." In several incidents, women and children were "terrifyed and forced with the point of the Bayonet to furnish homes for Private Soldiers"; frightened *Canadiens* eagerly surrendered horses and carts to soldiers, just to be rid of the marauders. And in the most violent case, Goforth reported that Continentals ran up a twenty-shilling debt with a habitant, and when asked for payment, they "Run him through the neck with a Bayonet." Goforth was powerless to find the offenders on his own. Whenever he informed transiting Continental officers about troops' depredations, he said they did "every thing in their power to detect the perpetrators and make Reparation," yet rarely had any success. Goforth went so far as to authorize district militia-captains to "Raise their men" and bring such wildly undisciplined *Bastonnais* to him in the city.[31]

Goforth wrote to his influential commander and friend, Alexander McDougall, identifying the root problems behind this intolerable criminal licentiousness. The small parties of ten, twenty, and thirty rushing toward Québec City were being led by sergeants and junior officers—generally "fine promising young Gentlemen," who were simply being asked to do too much with their limited experience and authority. Thus, Goforth recommended marching troops as a full company, joined by all unit officers, and hoped "Strict orders of this kind" would be given.[32]

Inadequately supervised troops were only part of the problem. Even officers managed to insult friendly Canadians, as evidenced in a Trois-Rivières episode. When the ever-generous Militia-Captain Laframboise hosted "a big dinner where there were several *Bastonnais,*" one of the Continental guests, a minister, offered an English blessing as they sat down for the meal. The host did not understand the foreign prayer, but upon later inquiry, was informed that the tactless guest had asked God to "damn all the Canadians and the Royalists" and to pour the fire of His anger on the province. Fortunately, Laframboise laughed off the insult, but this sort of crass behavior certainly eroded local goodwill for the Continentals.[33]

With more troops passing through the province, habitants also faced increasing demands to provide transportation. Payment was problematic; *Canadiens* treated Continental bills "with the utmost Contempt" and preferred certificates describing the services performed, believing such receipts might actually be exchanged for cash at some point. On other occasions, Continental officers summoned sleighs or carts and drivers through the *corvée* system, and habitants bristled at performing such unpaid duty. In all cases, district Tories took the opportunity to remind their neighbors of the increasingly unpleasant cost of doing business with the *Bastonnais*.[34]

When Wooster reached Trois-Rivières on 29 March, travelling downriver to lead the Québec City siege, Goforth took the opportunity to dine with him. The general noticed that Goforth "stood well with the people," and tried to persuade him to stay on as city commander even after his men's enlistments expired in mid-April. Wooster sweetened the deal, offering extra pay as a commissary, but the captain preferred his "Liberty to Return" home and declined all offers. Thereafter, the general rewarded patriot Constant Freeman with the role of "Issuing Commissary" for the city. Wooster also used his short stay to confer with Christophe Pélissier. The Canadian patriot warned that pro-patriot sentiment was in decline, and no progress had been made toward Canadian local government. Parting on good terms the next day, Pélissier loaned "his covered cariole and two horses with his coachman" to carry the aging commander to his new headquarters in relative comfort.[35]

Shortly after Wooster left Trois-Rivières, Jean-Baptiste Badeaux called Goforth on a different sort of business. Representing the Ursuline Convent, Badeaux inquired about Continental debt owed to the sisters. The black-habited nuns ran a fourteen-bed hospital and had willingly comforted sick Continentals. The army had incurred more than £30 of debt with the convent, but the captain had no hard money to settle the account. When Badeaux pressed for payment, Goforth asked that the sisters "remain patient and they will be paid." The notary teased that he would tell the ladies to feed the soldiers "patience," and the captain could see how fat they got on such a diet. Goforth could only laugh and offer that "there would soon be some cash," and he signed to verify the account ledger. The Continental officer shifted the discussion to a related topic, asking Badeaux why local merchants still refused to accept Continental bills. The notary responded that since the United Colonies "were not masters of the country . . . the capital still belonged to the King," and only the province's sovereign could change its currency. Paper bills would never be accepted until all Quebec was conquered.[36]

Despite Trois-Rivières' relative isolation, Goforth managed to keep abreast of affairs in the province. A pair of New York Continental peers regularly fed him information from the capital siege lines, and passing troops brought the latest news from Montréal and the United Colonies. Goforth concurrently did his part to share information with friends back home, including April correspondence to John Jay and Alexander McDougall, offering his perspectives two months after his Franklin letter.[37]

Goforth noted a subtle, but broad shift in Canadian sentiments, expressing fears that "the Congress is sinking fast in their Esteem." Habitant disenchantment had grown, as a result of "Neglect of payment for their Labour and forcing paper money upon them" and because of the Continentals' insults. Goforth still believed the *Canadiens* were "humane and Breathing after freedom," but were also willing to "make their Peace with [the Ministerial] Administration . . . to save their property and to prevent their families from being Debauched and Butchered."[38]

Goforth offered several nonmilitary recommendations to address this situation. He reported that "a printing office is much wanting"; properly run, it would "be of great use to the cause of Liberty." With his recent experience as district arbiter, the captain also noted, "The establishing regular Courts of Justice is much wanted and ardently called for by many of the best people." More strategically, he observed that "something ought to be done to divert the trade of the merchants in Canada." Canadian traders were hesitant to "sacrifice their trade," and in Goforth's opinion, "one great reason why we have so many Tories is because the dread to shut their Stores" to comply with the Continental Association.[39]

Militarily, Goforth reported the weak state of the Québec City siege camp: the large number of sick, "the officers of the different Provinces . . . continually stigmatizing each other," and the motley reinforcements. The captain also observed that "one Single twenty-Gun Ship" could wreak havoc up and down the river unless proper defenses were built to stop the Royal Navy. In fact, Militia-Captain Laframboise and other Canadian gentlemen had shown him a perfect spot to contest river navigation, on a confined stretch of the St. Lawrence just downriver from the city. Goforth was also aware of an even more defensible choke point at the Richelieu Rapids (not to be confused with the Richelieu River), farther downstream near Deschambault. Even though Montgomery had identified the latter area's importance before his demise, and Goforth's "hearty friends" now encouraged some sort of riverside fortifications, there was "not a Single Battery being Erected for the defence of any [of] the Towns or Vilages"; the Continentals simply lacked the money, manpower, and weapons for such an endeavor.[40]

<hr />

Only a few weeks after General Wooster left Trois-Rivières on his downriver voyage, Brigadier-General Arnold came the other way, hastening toward a new command at Montréal, in relief of Colonel Hazen. On the night Arnold arrived in town, he hosted prominent Trifluvien Joseph-Claude Courval for dinner. When it was time for the guest to return home, he stepped out to find that the thawing St. Lawrence had risen and he was unable to get home on dry land. Arnold ordered some soldiers to take Courval on their shoulders, and they "carried him over the water" to his abode, setting him down safe and dry on his own doorstep. Arnold also visited Christophe Pélissier in St-Maurice, delivering a commission to him as the new district militia-colonel, in place of the Tory Tonnancour. Pélissier had no martial experience to justify such a posting; although Goforth noted that the forge master had recently become "well versed with Theory and in some measure with some of the practical parts of War," the Canadian patriot's primary qualification was clearly his revolutionary commitment.[41]

A few short days later, on 15 April, the garrison company's enlistments expired. Goforth had employed all his skills just to keep his "Solid Boys" on duty to the end, garrisoning the city through a critical period in which they believed Wooster might make another assault on the capital. They were dismissed on the morning of the sixteenth, and jubilantly departed upriver for the long journey back to New York, technically ending Captain William Goforth's obligations in Trois-Rivières.[42]

The city's "principle French Inhabitants" were alarmed to hear that the captain might depart. They shared their concern with the reliable Goforth and "pressed" him to stay, noting the "Connection" and "good Understanding" he shared with the citizens. Sympathizing, and not wishing to abandon his Trifluvien friends, Goforth remained in the city for another week with a few volunteers, until General Wooster summoned him to headquarters. Captain William Goforth's Trois-Rivières tour of duty concluded without ceremony; he even had to snag his own replacement under the general's authority, transferring the city command to a passing Massachusetts captain leading a detachment of twenty-four men. Only Lieutenant McDougall joined the captain as he headed down the King's Way on a new mission.[43]

Continental troops continued to transit through Trois-Rivières after Goforth's departure, but the lack of a committed garrison commander had an almost immediate impact. Apathetic soldiers accidentally started a barracks chimney fire and made no effort to fight the blaze; the troops simply grabbed their packs and resumed their march toward Québec City. Tonnancour and a few nearby Trifluviens intervened to extinguish the fire, preventing a destructive conflagration.[44]

Up at St-Maurice, Pélissier persevered in his Continental support, providing "iron, stores, and every other material" in his power. Like Montréal's patriot merchants, Pélissier also made immediate financial sacrifices by accepting Continental bills. In a more direct military contribution, he had the forges cast shells and shot for Continental guns, which he hoped to deliver by mid-May — after four months' preparation time.[45]

Returning to Goforth's tenure in Trois-Rivières, Jean-Baptiste Badeaux's journal and other contemporary records show the captain was an extremely capable military governor. Despite ideological differences, the Yorker captain clearly had earned the loyalist notary's respect. Unlike Simon Sanguinet's comparable record of events in Montréal — a catalog of Continental officers' failures in Canada — Badeaux's journal reads like a glowing performance appraisal for Goforth.

The captain identified and co-opted an able assistant in Badeaux, read local sentiment, reined in zealous patriots, and controlled his troops, without arresting or exiling any district loyalists. As he departed from his Trois-Rivières post, Goforth believed the district was "the quietest and best Disposed part of Canada," but humbly offered that it was due to the "happy influence of French Gentlemen in and about this Town"—no doubt thinking of "neutrals" such as Militia-Captain Laframboise and loyalists such as Badeaux, as much as his patriot friends Pélissier and Laterrière. Goforth's amiable local relations were reflected in his observation that he had lived "Considerable happy among the people in this District"; yet one of Goforth's Continental peers also noted that the captain was "more respected and feared than any man" in the region. While the New York officer may not have brought every Trifluvien to the patriot cause, Goforth certainly did not squander Canadian goodwill like some of his cohorts in Montréal. It is interesting to postulate what may have happened in that critical western city, and subsequently the rest of the province, if General Wooster had selected Goforth as brigade-major, instead of the troublesome George Nicholson.[46]

Goforth's next duty was entirely different. On 24 April, General Wooster gave him command of the armed schooner *Maria*[47] to ensure that Royal Navy ships did not venture upriver from the Québec City basin. Lieutenant McDougall served as his first mate. This naval career was destined to be short-lived, and the captain found himself back in New York City by the end of May. He was promoted to major in a new regiment under Colonel Lewis Dubois and Lieutenant-Colonel Jacobus Bruyn, but this prompted him to retire from army service; Goforth considered both men "junior" to him, and with a particular sensitivity about promotion by seniority, he could not tolerate the perceived slight. Goforth left New York as the British occupied the city that summer and moved to Pennsylvania for the duration of the war. His enduring patriot credentials were recognized upon his return, when the Sons of Liberty successfully promoted his election for two terms as a New York State assemblyman. Seeking new opportunities to overcome wartime financial losses, he moved to the Ohio territory, where he rose to prominence as a judge, Northwest Territory legislator, president pro tem at the 1802 Ohio Constitutional Convention, and a Jeffersonian-Republican presidential elector in 1804.[48]

Chapter 18

PATRIOT ZEALOTS

Benedict Arnold, Canadian Patriots, and the Québec City Blockade

They have stirred the people, enlisted them for the service of Congress, and ridiculed and threatened royalists. | *Baby-Taschereau-Williams Commission, on Germain Dionne and Clément Gosselin, Ste-Anne-de-la-Pocatière, 13 July 1776*

The Habitants below Point Levy are ready to take arms to drive the Bostonois out of the Country, they have no cash, they begin to hang their heads. | *Journal of Captain Thomas Ainslie, 15 March 1776*

Downriver, outside Québec City, Benedict Arnold faced a tremendously taxing situation after the New Year's Eve defeat. Seriously wounded and bedridden, Colonel Arnold had to restore order among his remaining troops, maintain a blockade around the capital, aggressively press General Wooster and Congress for support, and promote sustained Canadian participation in the patriot cause. Yet for a man of Arnold's indomitable will, these demanding and diverse responsibilities were manageable. As the colonel assessed his newly inherited command from a General-Hospital bed, he counted fewer than eight hundred men, and almost half of this force was Canadian — Livingston's Continental Regiment, still "of about 200," and "some Scattered Canadian Forces, amounting to 200 more." Not only were the troops spread thin, but the duty was hard as the bitterest northern chill pervaded the countryside and snow reached a depth of five feet. Arnold slightly modified his lines, removing the forward-most batteries and relocating their guns to defend the powder magazine, much farther from the walls. Conscious of Canadian patriot morale, the colonel opted not to move the magazine from the edge of the Plains of Abraham, "lest it should make unfavourable impressions on the Canadians, and induce them to withdraw their assistance." Arnold "thought it most prudent to put the best face on matters, and betray no marks of fear."[1]

.

Habitant support to Arnold's Continentals was critical in these first few days of 1776, and reports of their contributions varied considerably. Colonel Livingston maintained that most Canadians declined calls to join; after their mid-December overtures were rebuffed, "they did not think proper to come after the Retreat." Carleton's garrison saw things differently, recording on 2 January, "Many of the ungrateful Canadians have joined the enemy," supported by a patriot account that "A number" of habitants "Immediately marched to Quebec" upon hearing of the New Year's repulse. The Continentals' local friends in nearby Beauport, Charlesbourg, and Ste-Foy called neighbors to assemble, but there is no quantification of their results. Weighing the diverse reports, Arnold's estimate of two hundred habitant auxiliaries seems to have been reasonably accurate for that first week of January.[2]

In any case, Arnold found that the number of friendly "country people" in camp exceeded the number of weapons available. On 4 January, the colonel requested every musket that could be sent from Montréal, to equip Canadian auxiliaries. Arnold was taking Congress's guidance to heart, working "to conciliate the affections of the Canadians, and cherish every dawning of liberty which appears among them," and by the eleventh was confident to report, "The disposition of the Canadians is very favourable to your wishes."[3]

On New Year's Day, Colonel Arnold also had turned to his stalwart Canadian allies upriver, calling reliable Militia-Captains Maurice Desdevens and Pierre Langlois to raise as many habitants as possible and march to join him. Two days later, the militia duo also was ordered to "visit all houses" and seize any weapons they found "belonging to the Congress." By mid-month, Arnold again asked these captains to halt Continental deserters and return them, a repeat of Montgomery's late December orders. Desdevens sent back at least two dozen fleeing Yorkers, and one of Arnold's New Englanders reported that twelve compatriots similarly had been "Stopt by the French Guard" and returned to camp.[4]

On 12 January, Arnold took a more deliberate step to bring the Canadians under arms. Having already called Desdevens and Langlois to start recruiting companies, the Colonel decided to form them into another Continental regiment of three hundred Canadians. The new unit would be led by the Canadian Colonel Livingston's right-hand man, Jeremiah Duggan, "a man universally known in Canada and greatly esteemed."[5]

Colonel Arnold could only beg Congress's forgiveness for acting "without authority" in creating a new Canadian unit, but expressed "the exigency of our affairs will justify the step I have taken." By his order, Duggan's regiment would receive "the same pay, and be under the same regulations, as the Continental forces," with terms of enlistment to end on 31 May, or upon Québec City's surrender. With firearms still an issue, Arnold expanded the militia-captains' authority to confiscate *all* habitant weapons, not just the Continental arms, offering receipts and reassurances that either the weapons would be returned or the owners would be properly compensated. Desdevens undertook his responsibilities "with as much zeal as affection," appointing four sergeants, actively drumming up enlistments in his home parish, and gathering fifty muskets. There is no record that Langlois raised any troops, and in nearby Cap-Santé, Militia-Captain Joseph-Etienne Pagé "tried to enlist people to bear arms . . . but to no avail." Closer to the main camp, Beauport's Captain Pierre Parant and Ile-d'Orléans's Captain Jean-Baptiste Leclair only raised about fifteen men between the two of them. Meanwhile, Arnold recognized the need for a French version of the Articles of War—"for the better disciplining of the Canadians"—almost three weeks before Congress issued a similar resolution; Northern Army interpreter, Swiss-Yorker Jean-Pierre Têtard produced the Québec camp's translation.[6]

Colonels Arnold and Livingston took an additional step to encourage Canadian enlistments. Believing Bishop Briand's proscriptions against rebellious Canadians were having a detrimental impact on recruiting, they found a Catholic priest willing to serve as chaplain for Livingston's Regiment, in defiance of Church authority. The individual, "Reverend" Louis Lotbinière, had a troubled past, being removed from his St-Laurent (Ile-d'Orléans) parish in late 1772 and placed under an interdict for insubordination. Continental officers saw promise in the Lotbinière solution, but were unaware that according to Catholic practice, the ex-priest was not permitted to provide sacraments—his religious services had only notional meaning to those ignorant or contemptuous of the Church's rulings on his status. In return for Lotbinière's service, Arnold promised him a Continental chaplain's pay and rations. Loyalists reported that the rebels also promised "to appoint him Bishop, when they take Quebec," but there is no evidence supporting that claim.[7]

———————

Shortly after repelling the rebel assault, Governor Carleton mirrored Arnold's call for Canadian support. He sent at least one appeal to Militia-Captain

Magné in the Montreal District parish of Varennes, which had been so earnestly committed to Carleton's government in the fall. The governor called Magné to mobilize the entire parish, march toward the capital, and "raise all the other Parishes Coming down," anticipating a cascade of loyalist support. The King's commissary in Montréal, Jacob Jordan, would support the effort. In reality, Carleton's militia enterprise was nipped in the bud. Incredibly, the governor entrusted the message's delivery to an Acadian prisoner, captured earlier in rebel service; once outside the city, the courier handed the Magné order to the Continentals, prompting Arnold's early warnings to Wooster about potential uprisings and justifying the general's strict treatment of prominent Montréal loyalists.[8]

Carleton made another equally miserable attempt to augment his Québec City garrison on 8 January. Having captured more than 370 Continentals on New Year's Eve, the governor offered a deal: if they volunteered to enlist in Colonel Maclean's Royal Highland Emigrants, he would "free" them for that service. About ninety accepted, "all from Britain or Ireland," and technically free of Continental obligations at the end of 1775. They proclaimed that they "wish'd to attone for their past error," swearing loyalty to His Majesty. Initially, it seemed a wise decision by the governor, as the recruits faithfully manned their posts; but two weeks later, they began disappearing over the walls. In a three-week period starting from 21 January, fifteen Emigrants deserted, almost all ex-Continentals, but occasionally accompanied by some of Maclean's earlier recruits. Not only did Carleton lose manpower, but the rebels also gained valuable intelligence. On 16 February, the governor ordered all remaining "new recruits" reimprisoned, "to frustrate their traitorous designs."[9]

In his army's precarious state, Benedict Arnold easily could have justified terminating the blockade and withdrawing upriver; yet this was not in his character. He was convinced he could maintain the blockade and, with adequate reinforcements, even take the town. Arnold's wound limited his leadership impact. James Price noted that the colonel gave "good orders," but did not ensure they were obeyed; that "Guards neglect their duty utterly"; and that negligent junior officers failed to issue orders, occasionally leaving the "same men on guard 48 hours."[10]

Amazingly, troops with "so little subordination" maintained a respectable blockade. The snow helped; as garrison journal keepers noted, "The first storys of many houses are under snow, the windows of the second serve as doors by which to pass into the streets." Man-size drifts channeled anyone exiting from the capital gates directly into Continental checkpoints, where most were returned to town. All this was accomplished with fewer than five hundred effective troops, spread over a five-mile arc around the city, on Ile-d'Orléans and at Pointe-Lévy. The first 120-man relief from Montréal did not arrive until 26 January.[11]

Arnold also continued to harass the capital defenders: his men sniped at sentries, fired random signal rockets, and burned houses in St-Roch to deny the garrison firewood. On 22 January, the colonel also ordered a bold raid on the river's edge, near Lower Town. A small group of Continental Canadian soldiers with proven "zeal, bravery and fidelity," including Livingston's trusted Captains Augustin Loiseau and Jean-Baptiste Allin, went to burn two moored vessels. Stealthily passing within musket range of city ramparts, they reached their targets and set the ships ablaze before making their escape.[12]

Outside the walls, at the General-Hospital, smoldering tensions also flashed between Continentals and their less-than-enthusiastic hosts. A colonel, presumably Livingston, wrote to Father Superior de Rigauville complaining about the treatment given to the dying Canadian soldier on New Year's Eve — in which the priest forced the rebel *Canadien* to disavow his rebellious activities before receiving absolution. The colonel threatened to remove the father from the hospital, and he also accused the nuns of compromising Montgomery's attack by "ringing bells" and "showing lights at night" to warn the garrison before the failed assault. This new charge prompted a rebuttal from the father superior, who thought the Continentals were being unreasonable: "No Earthly power can influence the function of our ministry" in the sacraments, and dismissed the accusations against the nuns as nonsense. After this flare-up, relations at the General-Hospital returned to an uncomfortable détente. The hospital history only documents one other notable incident, in which an officer complained to the mother superior about the care given to Continental patients. Unsatisfied with the nun's brusque response, the officer protested to Father de Rigauville, becoming so enraged that he raised his sword during his tirade. A Continental doctor, presumably Isaac Senter, reported the event to headquarters — prompting Arnold to order the offending officer's immediate departure from hospital grounds; the Continental command wanted to prevent irreparable harm to the invaluable, but tense, relationship with the guardedly helpful staff.[13]

Meanwhile in the capital garrison, all sorts of rumors flourished about the rebels. It was comforting for loyalists to believe that their opponents really were banditti, intent on terrorizing the population, so numerous reports of plundering and injury to Canadians were particularly popular. When an especially shocking tale about the robbery and murder of civilians reached the capital, however, a Tory journal keeper had to comment, "This story is most probably fabricated in Town."[14]

⸻

Remarkably, Quebec District habitants offered persistent support for Arnold's army after the failed assault. Historian John Hare found that nearly one in five habitants were considered "bad subjects" by a mid-1776 government commission that evaluated fifty-four parishes' rebel support.[15] Perhaps more significant, more than one-third of Carleton's 1775 militia officers and sergeants were accused of supporting the Continentals to some degree. Hare also highlighted seven "bad parishes" (see Map 10), where more than 30 percent of militia-age men were "bad subjects"—a level of rebel support probably comparable to many regions in the Thirteen Colonies.[16] Six of these communities sat in a seventy-five-mile south-bank strip, from Pointe-Lévy, opposite Québec City, to Rivière-Ouelle in the northeast. As a sample characterization of these "bad parishes," the governor's commission found that Pointe-Lévy was "generally seditious and opposed to the King's orders; in summary, zealous and very fond of the rebels."

Well before Wooster ordered militia elections in January, Benedict Arnold had been appointing friendly militia officers, a system Montgomery supported. Maurice Desdevens was the most notable of at least seven officers named in parishes near Continental camps, including the Pointe-aux-Trembles area, the capital neighborhood, and on Ile-d'Orléans. Some militia-captains actively curried these appointments from Arnold, including north-shore L'Ange-Gardien's Nicolas Lecomte, Charlesbourg's Jacques Allard, and Jean Acelin from Ile-d'Orléans. In their duties, most of these patriot militia-captains adequately balanced Continental needs and respect for fellow habitants; but both Lecomte and Acelin were accused of "having acted harshly" toward their neighbors. In other areas without patriot-appointed militia-captains, another

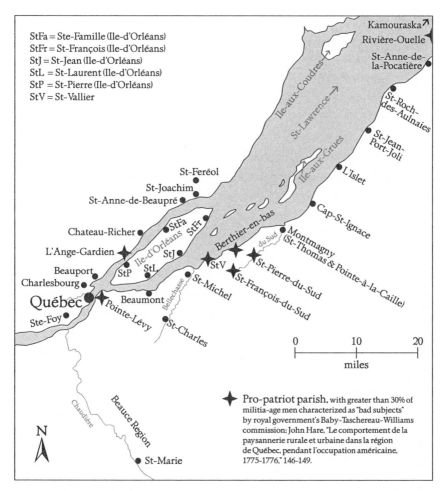

Kamouraska
Rivière-Ouelle
St-Anne-de-la-Pocatière
St-Roch-des-Aulnaies
St-Jean-Port-Joli
L'Islet
St-Lawrence
Ile-aux-Coudres
Ile-aux-Grues
St-Feréol
St-Joachim
St-Anne-de-Beaupré
Cap-St-Ignace
Chateau-Richer
StFa StFr
Berthier-en-bas
Montmagny (St-Thomas & Pointe-à-la-Caille)
L'Ange-Gardien
Ile-d'Orléans StJ
StV
du Sud
Beauport
StP StL
St-Pierre-du-Sud
Charlesbourg
Bellechasse St-Michel
St-François-du-Sud
Québec
Beaumont
Ste-Foy
Pointe-Lévy
St-Charles

0   10   20
miles

Pro-patriot parish, with greater than 30% of
militia-age men characterized as "bad subjects"
by royal government's Baby-Taschereau-Williams
commission: John Hare, "Le comportement de la
paysannerie rurale et urbaine dans la région
de Québec, pendant l'occupation américaine,
1775-1776," 146-149.

N

Chaudière
Beauce Region
St-Marie

MAP 10: Lower Quebec District.

nine parishes provided generous and efficient support through the winter, arranged unhesitatingly by either the Carleton-appointed militia officers or unofficial community leaders.[17]

Unlike his counterparts in Montreal and Three Rivers Districts, Benedict Arnold did not press for the implementation of Wooster's militia commission order. The colonel chose not to risk alienating militia officers who were already providing satisfactory support, by demanding they surrender a piece of paper. Only two Quebec District parishes actually held elections during Arnold's tour as commander, apparently unprompted by Continental authorities. In January, patriot hotbed Pointe-Lévy voted to retain one militia-captain and replace another. Deschambault, a large parish on the extreme western end of the district, selected a completely new slate of officers in February, probably inspired to hold elections by Captain Goforth's activity in nearby Three Rivers District.[18]

<hr />

The struggle for rural support assumed an increasingly revolutionary form in early 1776, as a number of patriot advocates motivated, educated, and propagandized fellow habitants. Less-active supporters simply posted or read Continental orders and letters; the more fanatical actively spread fact and rumor across the countryside to stir partisan support. These proselytizers and agitators rarely were militia-captains, but often held other positions of authority: notaries, surveyors, road menders, and junior militia officers; a few operated businesses: an innkeeper, a baker, and a cobbler. Yet others were just motivated habitants, the most famous being a St-Joachim resident called Lesperance, known for his outspoken "preaching" against the government in north-shore communities downstream from the capital.[19]

These activists employed diverse tactics. Michel Montigny, militia-ensign for St-Pierre (Ile-d'Orléans), "encouraged the habitants to sedition" and "prevented them" from following their curé's advice. In Ste-Anne-de-la-Pocatière, local patriot partisans told their priest to "take a walk," so that they could freely discuss Continental messages with fellow parishioners. A St-Thomas-de-Montmagny notary even drafted petitions, "which he had several habitants sign, inviting the rebels to come." Parishes close to Québec City regularly dispatched representatives to consult with Arnold and his colonels, returning to share the latest news with fellow habitants.[20]

While Arnold and his senior officers appreciated partisan political support, the Continentals' most immediate local benefit came in the form of provisions. Since the long, tenuous supply line from New York clearly lacked sufficient capacity, the army depended on the parishes for flour and meat staples, which were gathered at magazines in Pointe-Lévy and on the edge of the Plains of Abraham. To help manage this effort, Montgomery had appointed Canadian John Halsted as commissary officer. In turn, Halsted and his agents relied on militia officers and patriot parish leaders to gather and deliver goods to the Continental depots.[21]

Continental commissary agents frequently paid for provisions and transportation using debt certificates in Halsted's name, but they occasionally requisitioned goods or relied on compulsory *corvée* transportation. In general, the habitants grudgingly complied with these demands, arranged through militia-captains, although there were a few cases of passive resistance. While the provision system and *corvée* calls certainly strained Continental-habitant relations, they also gave local patriots an opportunity to exercise leadership.[22]

Some Quebec District patriots went even further and organized pillaging expeditions in support of the cause. In February 1776, habitants led Continentals to gather flour requisitions from the St-Roch-des-Aulnaies seigneurial mill and the St-Vallier manor — belonging to loyalist seigneur and prisoner of war Antoine Juchereau-Duchesnay and Carleton's aide-de-camp Charles de Lanaudière, respectively. Chaudière valley patriots took even greater vengeance on seigneur Gabriel-Elzéar Taschereau's property. Even though the Beauce region was remarkably placid after Arnold's November passage, vindictive habitants not only seized money and wheat from their seigneur's mill, but also conducted an auction of "all the household goods, farm tools, and assets" found at his Ste-Marie-de-Beauce estate. The event was widely attended by local habitants, who snatched up their seigneur's goods. Another event in out-of-the-way St-Nicolas parish fit this same pattern of Tory property confiscations. In all these cases, Continental officers may have endorsed the marauding, but habitants identified the targets and chiefly executed the missions.[23]

Canadian patriots also supported the Continentals with armed detachments. North-shore parishes below the capital manned a blockade post at "the Sault" near Beauport, opposite Ile-d'Orléans. Some of these guards were forced to serve, but a "great number seem to have done so most willingly and the rest without much resistance." The Ile-d'Orléans parishes kept another post at the island's south tip — again, some habitants eagerly served and others were forced; a few actually refused duty. Completing an arc of Canadian posts on river approaches to Québec City, Pointe-Lévy habitants guarded the southern end of the ice bridge to the capital. The loyalist garrison noted that "The Canadians keep up an unremitted Patrole to cut off all communication with the Town," closing approaches the Continentals could not have adequately manned on their own.[24]

In their own communities, patriot partisans played another critical role in the revolutionary struggle — suppressing Tory opponents. Often, these activists just harassed and intimidated loyalist opposition through public denunciations and threats. A few patriot enforcers actually took physical action, including Langlois and Lecomte, who disarmed problematic loyalists, and Desdevens, who led a punitive pillaging expedition. In cases on Ile-d'Orléans and south-shore St-Vallier, zealous patriot regulators arrested Tory troublemakers and delivered them to the Continentals, in accordance with Wooster's 6 January proclamation. The culprits were held for ten days, a "sentence" useful for intimidation, with the implied threat of worse punishment if they persisted in unacceptable behavior. In Pointe-aux-Trembles, Desdevens even imprisoned "several" local enemies aboard the *Gaspée*, left grounded after Montgomery's troops arrived in November.[25]

Although rare, patriot *Canadiens* even acted against the parishes' premier loyalist advocates: their *curés*. Loyalist Simon Sanguinet maintained that "many" priests were "sought out with guards and led to the Bastonnois camp," while Continental Captain Gershom Mott offered a more moderate report, that "priests in two or three parishes" had been brought to headquarters "on Acc[oun]t of their Diabolical Conduct & were released on Solemn promises of Amendment." Of the five cases documented in any detail, patriots from St-Pierre (Ile-d'Orléans), Charlesbourg, and St-Thomas-de-Montmagny only lodged "complaints" and "allegations" against their priests. In the extreme northeast, habitants in the "bad parish" of Rivière-Ouelle led their priest out of town, but let him return before traveling too far. Only north-shore patriot Lesperance actually delivered *curés* into Continental hands, two defiant priests from Ste-Anne-de-Beaupré and St-Joachim — presumably the individuals to whom Mott referred. Even in this case, less radical parishioners trekked twenty-five miles to the Continental camp and obtained their priests' prompt release. Arnold's officers were undoubtedly happy to have an excuse to free the clergymen, minimizing fallout from Lesperance's unsolicited action against "protected" Church representatives.[26]

In the late winter and spring of 1776, a dedicated Canadian patriot trio made an indelible mark amidst Quebec's lower south-shore parishes. Clément Gosselin and his father-in-law Germain Dionne, both from Ste-Anne-de-la-Pocatière, along with Pierre Ayotte of Kamouraska, formed a dynamic partnership that "assisted the enemies of government in any way," enforcing Continental will along a hundred-mile swath. Ayotte had been a longtime "Merchant of furs, &c." operating in the up-country, until he caught the spirit of liberty in 1775 and returned to his remote north Laurentian home parish. Twenty miles upriver, Clément Gosselin was an unusually prosperous La-Pocatière habitant, sufficiently wealthy to advance "money, provisions, and ammunition" for the patriot war effort. Even though he was not yet thirty, he was referred to as "*sieur*," an indication of community status. His father-in-law, forty-four-year-old Germain Dionne was another invaluable patriot activist. One of his parish's most prominent residents, Dionne was first bailiff and a "rich" businessman.[27]

The younger two, Ayotte and Gosselin, were volunteers in Montgomery's camp before the general's death, but rocketed to regional notoriety when Colonel Duggan appointed them captains in his new Canadian regiment. In late January, they began to roam the lower south-shore parishes on various Continental missions. Almost immediately, Ayotte established the nucleus of a company—perhaps a dozen men—who were soon posted to support the Pointe-Lévy Continentals as their captain sought more enlistees. Ranging the snow-blanketed countryside, Ayotte and Gosselin were not simply recruiters, but also served as agitators and enforcers, "preaching rebellion everywhere." Back in La-Pocatière, Germain Dionne gave critical logistical support; he "provided the necessaries, supplies, shoes, etc." for their Continental recruits. The parish *curé*, Pierre-Antoine Porlier, commented that "Aiot [*sic*], Gosselin and Germain Dionne did what they wanted" in the south-bank parishes. Visiting different communities, they served as the principal Continental authority, acting as judges, sheriffs, commissaries, and substitute militia-captains, as needed.[28]

Despite this relative influence and their leading role as Continental recruiters, Gosselin and Ayotte only enlisted about 130 *Canadiens* in 1776. Half came from parishes within thirty miles of Gosselin and Dionne's La-Pocatière home. The recruits were primarily young unpropertied habitants, looking to help their families with their 40ł monthly pay while still being able to return to their farms in late spring. Gosselin and Ayotte found the same thing that Hazen had observed in Montréal: the lack of hard money was the biggest detractor to recruiting success. In mid-March, Ayotte wrote to Arnold emphasizing the urgent need for cash; a couple of weeks later, he added, "Bricks without straw we cannot make." Unsurprisingly, Québec City loyalists described these Canadian Continental recruits as "about 100 of the most idle profligate wretches in the Country" and "the outcasts of Canada." While it was true that Ayotte and Gosselin did not enlist prominent *Canadiens,* their new soldiers were typical habitants' sons, poor but not particularly dissolute.[29]

Despite their limited recruiting success, Gosselin, Ayotte, and Dionne provided the sort of local patriot leadership that was wanting in most of the province; but once again, it was channeled into military activity rather than government. These three clearly had an exceptional commitment to their political views, a sort of zeal lacking among "common" loyalist *Canadien* rivals. Their only comparable peer, Maurice Desdevens, continued to prove his worth in Pointe-aux-Trembles and was rewarded with appointments as notary and surveyor by "the Honorable Congress." It is notable that these were civilian duties, another potential seedbed for local patriot governance, but Desdevens remained preoccupied with martial duties.[30]

In mid-February, Ayotte and Gosselin's commander, Colonel Jeremiah Duggan, departed the Continental camp, heading upriver to consult with the Northern Army's generals. In Montréal, Wooster regretfully informed the colonel that Congress had given the Second Canadian Regiment's command to Moses Hazen. Duggan promptly headed south to meet with Congress and seek an appropriate command. When the Canadian officer passed through New York, Major-General Schuyler gave him an endorsement emphasizing Duggan's "influence with the Canadians" and his invaluable assistance during the Fort St-Jean siege.[31]

In Philadelphia, a Congressional committee conferred with Duggan. His service clearly warranted a prestigious Canadian posting; so on 28 March, Congress presented him with $1000 "for his past Services" and created a new command for him. Commissioned as a Continental lieutenant-colonel, he would lead three 100-man companies of "Rangers in Canada." But he would have to start from scratch; Gosselin's and Ayotte's companies, along with Hamtramck's Chambly-region company, all originally recruited for service with Duggan, were incorporated into Hazen's Second Regiment.[32]

At Québec City, the Continental blockade continued while patriot Canadians worked the rural parishes. Military operations on both sides of the lines were quite different. Governor Carleton's garrison remained confident in their defensive routine, enjoying the shelter of the fortified capital while awaiting relief in the spring. The Continentals, meanwhile, suffered from increasingly

A Continental Three-Dollar Bill, Issued 10 May 1775 (*Exitus in dubio est* = The outcome is in doubt). Reproduced from the original held by the Department of Special Collections of the Hesburgh Libraries, University of Notre Dame.

poor morale, harsh weather, and long and frequent duty. Only Arnold's energy, supported by a "few Officers of Spirit," managed to keep the effort together.[33]

The Continental camp was also being decimated by smallpox. By the end of February, one hundred of Arnold's eight hundred men were quarantined in the riverside smallpox hospital. A Continental officer reported that over the winter, more than one hundred succumbed to the disease. In response to the ravages of smallpox, Arnold took a radical step, which must have sparked habitant resentment—ordering residents around his camp to leave their homes and move "into the country." His soldiers might spread the disease amongst themselves, but this order theoretically eliminated Canadians from the cycle of contagion.[34]

The financial situation was equally desperate; Colonel Livingston reported that there had been "several Mutinies . . . owing in a great Measure to our want of Money to pay the Troops," who found Continental bills useless in the local economy. On 4 March, Arnold took an even more unpopular step with the Canadians. He issued a proclamation "giving our paper money a currency; promising to exchange it in four months for hard cash, at the same time declaring those enemies who should refuse it." In subsequent weeks, the Continentals paid out about $15,000 in bills: "Many received it willingly, but the greater part of the people were averse to taking it." Always seeking the positive, Arnold hoped that at least "those who have received it will be interested in keeping the credit of it good." A more pragmatic Continental officer noted, "Chagrin & discontent universally appeared in the faces of those who received" the bills, "and with it is gone the affections of the people in General." Tory agitators took the opportunity to remind *Canadiens* that they had been warned repeatedly about such consequences from associating with the rebels.[35]

With his general military situation seemingly under control, Governor Carleton still worked very hard to win the battle for the minds of the citizens and soldiers. While he turned back two flags of truce, on 11 February and 14 March, loyalist informants and deserters still were given entry to the city. Their news varied; some of it was fairly accurate, but often it was just wild rumors. A popular theme was that the rebels were "talking of going away," but that the perfidious Canadians, "alarmed" at the prospect of restored Ministerial authority, kept the invaders from retreating and exclaimed, "as you have brought us into a scrape of this description, you must bring us out of it again, and take Quebec."[36]

On 5 March, the blockaders and garrison began a slightly humorous exchange of long-distance "communications," as the Continentals raised a pair of red flags outside the city, one near the General-Hospital and the other "at the guard house at the West end of St Roc[h]." Some loyalists were concerned that these were signals to rebel prisoners in the city, possibly indicating an imminent attack; others believed the banners commemorated the 5 March 1770 Boston Massacre — unfortunately, none of the Continentals seem to have recorded the flags' true purpose. The banners sparked further curiosity as they reappeared intermittently for several days. By coincidence, the garrison raised its own elevated "signal" on the seventh. On the highest part of Cape Diamond, the defenders "set up a mast of 30 feet with a sentry box atop," insulated with hay, as an observation point to spy upon the enemy camp and to peer farther downriver for the spring relief fleet. From Pointe-Lévy, Continentals were not able to identify the new object on the Québec City skyline. Noticing Yorker rebels squinting at the mast and trying to discern its purpose, a few south-shore "Canadian Royalists" told them that the strange construction was "a wooden horse with a bundle of hay" and that Carleton had declared "he would not give up the Town until the horse has ate his hay," adding that "the General is a man of his word."[37]

On 8 March, the most significant of all the loyalist messengers arrived at the capital—Lamotte and Papineau, sent by Vicar-General Montgolfier with news from New York Governor Tryon. Their reports, both official and informal, cheered the "King's faithful subjects . . . coop'd up" in the Canadian capital, but questionable tales of "mutiny among the rebels at Montreal" and other far-fetched reports led a loyalist journal keeper to note skeptically that their many "encouraging accounts" had perhaps been "made on purpose." A few days later, more suspiciously good news arrived, that "the Indians in the upper Countries have proposed among themselves to come down to the relief of this place."[38]

The next phase of the Quebec blockade really began on 14 March, sparked by events that General Wooster unwittingly initiated in Montréal back on 6 January. Among the messages Lamotte and Papineau delivered was a copy of General Wooster's "indiscrete" letter to Seth Warner, which included disparaging comments about "the Tempers, Dispositions and Character of the Canadians." This had been surreptitiously obtained by New York Governor Tryon and forwarded by Vicar-General Montgolfier. Within a week of receiving this valuable information, Carleton ordered a special two-week resurrection of the *Quebec Gazette* so that he could employ this written ammunition against his rebel foes. The newspaper printed Wooster's letter as its lead article on the fourteenth, exposing the general's anti-Canadian biases and implying duplicity in all Continental authority. The paper also provided printed extracts from two of Benedict Arnold's letters, written on 6 and 14 January; although they were not insulting to the Canadians, they painted the Continental military situation in a desperately unfavorable light. In the next week's issue, the *Gazette* included a copy of General Montgomery's surrender letter delivered by arrow back in mid-December; obviously, the governor had refrained from burning at least one copy. This was the letter in which Montgomery pointed out "the absurdity of resistance," while deriding the garrison as "a few of the worst Troops who ever stiled themselves Soldiers."

Normally, these antirebel exposés might seem insignificant; the capital city was still blockaded after all, but another circumstance gave added relevance to the *Quebec Gazette* special editions.[39]

By coincidence, south-shore Tory Hugh Fraser had dispatched two Canadians—St-Vallier notary Joseph Riverin and miller Jean-Baptiste Chasseur—to sneak into the capital by canoe from Beaumont, only eight miles downstream from Pointe-Lévy. After landing in the capital, the pair delivered loyalist letters to the governor and described the situation in the Quebec District countryside. By their account, there was growing unrest in the lower south-shore parishes; aggravated habitants were weary of the occupiers and ready to drive them out. Broke, demoralized, and unable to raise Canadian recruits, the rebel foe was reeling and might crumble with a well-timed blow. Governor Carleton sent Riverin and Chasseur on a return trip two nights later, carrying "letters, [G]azettes and instructions to some of our friends below." Those messages would ignite a new loyalist fire in the south-shore communities below Quebec; Wooster's damning letter printed in the *Quebec Gazette* would help serve as kindling, resulting in a small but intense flare-up on the tiny St. Lawrence tributary known as Rivière-du-Sud.[40]

Chapter 19

SPRING OF UNREST

A Canadian Battle in the Quebec District

The Canadians taking up Arms so early against us, is of the most
Important consequence. | *Colonel Moses Hazen to General Philip Schuyler,
Montréal, 1 April 1776*

Even as Captains Clément Gosselin and Pierre Ayotte roved the south-
shore parishes recruiting Canadian Continentals, loyalist resistance began to
congeal in the very same region (see Map 10). Ste-Anne-de-la-Pocatière's
priest Pierre-Antoine Porlier served as a secret Tory rallying point. In the late
winter of 1776, the parish's elderly Militia-Captain Augustin Roy *dit* Lauzier
consulted with the *curé* about launching an uprising; loyalists had been chaf-
ing under the rebels, especially the Canadian Continental officers—Porlier
counseled patience. More surprisingly, shortly thereafter, a patriot commissary
agent, Jean-Baptiste Féré, shared a late-winter political confession with the
priest. Although Féré had played an important role in promoting the United
Colonies' invasion, serving as a key 1775 Lake Champlain messenger, he had
since reconsidered his allegiance. The unrelieved Continental weakness following Montgomery's defeat opened the commissary's eyes to the reality
of the situation: the rebels were destined to fail. Now, Féré hoped to lead
an insurrection to drive the rebels from Pointe-Lévy, restoring government
authority and redeeming himself. Porlier, however, advised Féré to bide his
time as well—the right time for action would come soon.[1]

Suddenly, on 20 March the situation changed. Loyalist couriers Joseph
Riverin and Jean-Baptiste Chasseur arrived in La-Pocatière, having completed
a long, bone-chilling downriver trip from Québec City. The two brought
news and instructions to mobilize the south shore. The previous day, they
had stopped on a narrow Laurentian island, twenty-five miles upstream from
Porlier's parish, to deliver the governor's orders for Ile-aux-Grues seigneur

Louis-Liénard de Beaujeu-de-Villemonde to lead the operation. This sixty-year-old noble son of New France was one of the few prominent loyalist leaders remaining in the district, sheltered by his insular existence.[2]

In a thirty-seven-year military career, ranging from the Mississippi to Acadia, de Beaujeu earned the *Croix de St-Louis* for dedicated French service. After the Conquest, he warmed slowly to British rule, initially remaining on the remote Mississippi. In 1769, he moved to his wife's Ile-aux-Grues seigneury, settling into the life of a country lord. Despite de Beaujeu's age and unproven loyalties, Carleton had Riverin deliver a new commission to him with orders to immediately raise regional militia for the King's service, and provided an amnesty for all volunteers, as well as the 14 March *Quebec Gazette* with Wooster's inflammatory letter. As the two messengers left the island for La-Pocatière, de Beaujeu took several hours to prepare for the coming redemptive fight, hoping to drive the rebels from the Quebec District.[3]

La-Pocatière loyalists were excited by the news that Riverin and Chasseur delivered. After a short hesitation to weigh the consequences of their commitment, the habitants decided to save their parishes "from the stain of rebellion" and rallied to their loyalist militia-captain. Lauzier raised a Union Jack near his home, and local Tories buzzed with energy, rushing to spread the word to other parishes. The next day, de Beaujeu landed on the south shore as Canadians gathered from Kamouraska, Rivière-Ouelle, La-Pocatière, and St-Roch-des-Aulnaies. While these lower parishes provided critical initial support, success depended on an equally positive reception in the southern upstream parishes; so a seminary priest, Charles-François Bailly-de-Messein was sent to gather intelligence there, before the main party marched on the Continentals at Pointe-Lévy.[4]

Abbot Bailly was a Montréal-born, Paris-educated director of Québec City's *Petit-Séminaire,* sent to the south shore early in 1776 to encourage the habitants' loyalty; he found kindred spirits in Porlier and Lauzier. Now, de Beaujeu gave him a small party of men to visit the Rivière-du-Sud, a Laurentian tributary, on the pretext of buying seed, but really to evaluate regional loyalist support. In the little ten-mile valley that joins the St. Lawrence in Montmagny, the party was shocked to find very few habitants willing to take up arms for the government. Yet Abbot Bailly still called de Beaujeu to march south immediately; rebel habitant opposition was already brewing, and the loyalists needed to strike preemptively. Meanwhile, the priest and his party would wait at Pointe-à-la-Caille, in Montmagny Parish.[5]

On the morning of 23 March, de Beaujeu led 106 loyalists south from La-Pocatière. Spreading word of the amnesty ahead of their advance, they hoped hundreds of supporters would rally to the government and assist their upriver march to Pointe-Lévy. Instead, the band faced obstacles. Deep snow had started to melt, turning the roads into a muddy morass, while large drifts still precluded off-road travel. In St-Jean-Port-Joli, less than twenty miles into the march, boisterous habitant opponents hindered the loyalists' march; L'Islet, the next parish upriver, presented similar challenges. Regional loyalties were split, though; twenty-four Tory volunteers joined de Beaujeu from those same parishes. In the next community, Cap-St-Ignace, the militia-captain and another dozen loyalists rallied; from that parish on, patriot habitants verbally discouraged the loyalists, but did not obstruct their progress. After two days, the slowly growing force traveled forty miles, reaching Montmagny, at the mouth of the Rivière-du-Sud, about halfway to their ultimate target. As de Beaujeu linked up with Abbot Bailly, another dozen locals joined the loyalist corps; about 150 progovernment partisans settled into the Pointe-à-la-Caille community, under the gloomy sky of an intolerably cold 24 March night.[6]

—————

Somehow, Continental Captain Pierre Ayotte obtained a tip that there was a Canadian traitor on the south shore—probably a reference to commissary agent Féré—and warned General Arnold. There were clearly some moles in the nascent loyalist uprising. One was likely Cap-St-Ignace lawyer Jean-Baptiste Lebrun-de-Duplessis, marching with de Beaujeu, who had "displayed at times the conduct of a zealous subject, and, at others, that of an extreme rebel." He had a known relationship with Féré, teaming with the commissary to confiscate seigneurs' wheat earlier in the year. When the loyalist corps reached Pointe-à-la-Caille, someone—perhaps Lebrun—sent a young Cap-St-Ignace habitant to alert local patriot leaders "that a group of royalists was forming under Mr. Beaujeu's command."[7]

On 24 March, Captain Clément Gosselin and two patriot companions spied de Beaujeu's vanguard at Pointe-à-la-Caille; the captain was probably on a tip-based "scouting trip." The trio rushed to Pointe-Lévy to warn the Continental camp "that there was a royalist force readying against them." General Arnold promptly received slightly inaccurate word that "a party of sixty men had landed there from Quebeck, and that two hundred and fifty

Canadians had joined them." A second part of the report held that the loyalists "had seized a convoy of provisions coming to the camp, with two Commissaries"; Féré may have connived to "surrender" himself and his provisions to de Beaujeu's force as part of his Tory conversion.[8]

Later that day, as the loyalists assembled at Pointe-à-la-Caille, Arnold ordered Major Lewis Dubois to lead eighty Yorker Continentals across to Pointe-Lévy and seize the loyalist "Standerd (which the[y] have Erected) and bring it to head Quarters." The vigilant and sharp-minded Arnold also anticipated a broader potential uprising, ordering three Continental companies to secure Ile-d'Orléans and posting armed vessels off Pointe-Lévy to protect cross-river communications.[9]

As Dubois's heavily outnumbered detachment left camp, a fretting Continental officer lamented, "God and he only, can determine our Fate." South-shore habitants, however, still had a principal role in shaping the Continentals' destiny. Almost one hundred friendly, armed *Canadiens* met Dubois at Pointe-Lévy—the Canadian Continentals under Gosselin and Ayotte, and more than a dozen Pointe-Lévy militia volunteers. Twenty-five miles downstream, zealous patriot bailiff Joseph Morancy independently secured Continental-*Canadien* surprise by arresting Tory Donald MacKinnon in Berthier-en-bas; the loyalist had seen Gosselin's scouting party returning from Montmagny to Pointe-Lévy and would otherwise have warned de Beaujeu that the Continentals were aware of his position. Meanwhile, patriot habitants gathered in numerous south-shore parishes—some called by Gosselin and Ayotte, others on their own initiative. Within twenty-four hours, more than fifty-five Canadians were gathered to oppose their fellow habitants' southward march.[10]

Quebec District's lower south-shore parishes braced for their own small-scale civil war. Habitants from eight communities north of Montmagny rallied under the Union Jack, opposed by patriot militia gathered south of Pointe-à-la-Caille. With no deep-rooted cause for this geographic division, the split seems to have developed circumstantially, simply because de Beaujeu ignited the uprising in La-Pocatière, while the Continentals were focused at Pointe-Lévy. There were patriots aplenty in the northern parishes, and numerous loyalists in the southern communities; they simply lacked opportunities to rally to the flags of their choice. In fact, most of Gosselin and Ayotte's Canadian Continentals were from lower parishes, having cast their allegiances well before the present situation developed. Only "middle-ground" habitants in the Rivière-du-Sud parishes were given the chance to join the side of their choosing; a dozen supported de Beaujeu, while more than seventy marched with the patriots.[11]

Sitting at Pointe-à-la-Caille, Captain de Beaujeu made a fateful decision on the evening of 24 March, sending a detachment "to gather arms and men" from the Rivière-du-Sud parishes. Popular L'Islet Tory Jean-Baptiste Couillard-Després led an "advance guard" with Abbot Bailly and about thirty other loyalists, to the home of St-Pierre-du-Sud's Militia-Captain Michel Blais. A successful second-generation Canadian habitant, Blais had accumulated local property to become coseigneur of two Rivière-du-Sud holdings. In the 1760s, he was a militia-captain, then a bailiff after the militia was abolished. Governor Carleton restored the sixty-year-old Blais to his captaincy in 1775, supported by his militia-lieutenant son.[12]

Captain Blais and his "large house" were appropriate rallying points. His home was a symbol of strength, the only stone house in the parish, and with its relative opulence showed that the river's most successful habitant stood behind his king. In the freezing morning of 25 March, Couillard led his loyalist detachment to Blais's house; the party, now numbering more than forty, hoisted "the King's standard" and awaited the arrival of more Rivière-du-Sud Tories.[13]

Their progovernment insurrection, however, was again betrayed from within. Militia-Sergeant Augustin Blanchet, sent by Captain Blais to gather parish militia, instead visited local patriot Jean Dessince to "warn the rebels of this development." The two found Major Dubois with his strong Continental-partisan corps of 135 men and pointed them toward Blais's home. Ayotte quickly rallied forty more St-Pierre patriots, while Gosselin gathered thirty-five militiamen from neighboring St-François, who were perhaps less willing—the Continental captain allegedly threatened to pillage and burn their homes if they did not cooperate. On the frighteningly cold late March day, the habitants suddenly found themselves pitted against their peers and neighbors. Simon Sanguinet even maintained "that fathers were seen fighting against their children, and children against their fathers"—there were, in fact, Gendrons, Thibaults, and even Blaises participating on either side.[14]

The *capot*-shrouded, *tuque*-capped habitants and dirty, winter-uniformed

Continentals cautiously approached Blais's home; the low surrounding hills hid their approach from the west. Spying the Union Jack fluttering in the wind, the advance guard cautiously crested the hill and saw enemy habitants milling about the house. The loyalist defenders were caught "unawares" in a less-than-ideal fighting position. The stone house provided cover, but the Tories were trapped at the bottom of a half-bowl valley, with the rebels holding the high ground. Dubois also had a three-to-one numerical advantage.[15]

Both sides exchanged fire, but the disadvantaged loyalists surrendered quickly. As smoke cleared from the St-Pierre skirmish, the victors scrambled to pull down the King's standard, and Major Dubois found only one patriot "slightly wounded," shot through the shoulder. On the opposing side, three loyalist habitants lay dead on the frosty mud, and ten others were wounded, including Couillard and Abbot Bailly, "dangerously wounded" with "two balls thro' his body." By some accounts, zealous patriot habitants wanted to massacre their prisoners, but Dubois's Continentals intervened to shield the Tories. Most captured loyalists were taken quickly across the St. Lawrence to the main Continental camp, but Abbot Bailly was left behind. In the parish rectory, the local surgeon and the parish *curé* tended to Bailly's critical abdominal wound. Berthier Bailiff Joseph Morancy, however, was infuriated to hear of the abbot's "lenient" treatment and arrested the surgeon and Bailly, treating both "very harshly." Morancy's vindictive treatment shows the degree of enmity that reigned between some Canadians in early 1776.[16]

In Pointe-à-la-Caille, de Beaujeu received word of the shattering St-Pierre defeat later that day. With more than one hundred men at hand, and a Lauzier-led rear guard arriving soon, de Beaujeu still might have met Dubois in a near-equal battle. The old military leader, however, felt he had lost the most critical factor: his ragtag militia corps' morale. "[W]earied with repeated misfortunes, and finding themselves hardly capable of coping with their foes," the little army "dispersed and returned home" as de Beaujeu fled to his island sanctuary. The panicked Féré flew to La-Pocatière crying, "All is lost . . . save me, save us!" *Curé* Porlier advised him to keep fleeing north, out of Continental reach. Exposed to the harsh light of reinvigorated Continental and patriot *Canadien* energies, the loyalist uprising melted away much quicker than it had snowballed on its roll toward Pointe-Lévy.[17]

When Arnold heard about the battle, he sent Yorker Lieutenant-Colonel John Nicholson[18] to command the entire south-shore operation "in pursuit of the enemy," with an additional seventy Continentals. Nicholson and Dubois employed local partisans to visit known loyalists, gathering all copies of the governor's letter that had "induced them to take up arms" and all de-Beaujeu–issued commissions. Four suspected Tories were also arrested from the downstream parishes. Elsewhere in the district, patriot Canadians suppressed other signs of loyalist activity. On the north shore, the radical Lesperance disarmed ten suspects apparently "readying themselves to join" de Beaujeu. Much closer to the battle site, patriot habitants ferreted out messenger Jean-Baptiste Chasseur in a St-Michel-de-Bellechasse mill and turned him over to Continental officers. In St-Nicolas, southwest of Pointe-Lévy, patriot leaders twice hunted down reported parties of Canadian "strangers," delivering their quarry to Arnold's camp.[19]

Up north in Ste-Anne-de-la-Pocatière, parishioners harassed *Curé* Porlier for leading their husbands and sons into such folly. Surprisingly, despite their stark ideological differences, archpatriot Germain Dionne comforted the forlorn priest, telling him that the Canadian Continentals would "treat him reasonably" and adding that "Aiot [*sic*] is good, he will save you." As fifty partisans and Continentals subsequently descended on the parish, Ayotte proved Dionne correct, convincing fellow Continental officers that "they would undermine their position if they pushed things to extremes, especially if they seized the priests." Instead, La-Pocatière merchant William Ross seemed to bear the brunt of retribution, since he was an Old Subject who had willingly been one of de Beaujeu's lieutenants. He was "assaulted repeatedly by the rebels," and over the following weeks, Continentals seized a "large amount of provisions" from him, loaded them on Ross's own schooner, and shipped them to the army upstream.[20]

At the other end of the Quebec District, General Arnold dispatched eighteen St-Pierre insurgent prisoners to Montréal. As they passed Trois-Rivières on 3 April, Jean-Baptiste Badeaux observed that "there is nothing more detestable and more repugnant to nature than to see these poor people conducted by their compatriots, who are completely unaffected; on the contrary, the poor boors guide them along with unparalleled joy." The Trifluvien notary obviously was not familiar with the ugly face of civil war. Eventually, seven captives[21] were led to the lower colonies, and the others were sent home on parole.[22]

The capital garrison did not seem overly concerned when it heard of the

St-Pierre encounter's outcome. The "victory" had a more substantial impact among leading Continental officers and especially in the United Colonies. One officer observed, "This insurrection is occasioned by the seeming neglect shown to this province," and Colonel Hazen felt the event was of the "utmost Importance and the most dangerous Consequence," requiring the "immediate attention of Congress." Almost a month after the fact, on 23 April, Congress heard of the battle from a Hazen letter. In a flurry of activity almost on a par with that after Montgomery's defeat, delegates scrambled to address the likely sources of Canadian unrest. President of Congress John Hancock provided a keen assessment of the news: "I cannot help suspect that the Defection of the Canadians is more the Result of Policy than Inclination . . . finding the Force of the United Colonies in Canada fall much Short of Expectation, they naturally throw themselves into the Scale which they believe begins to preponderate."[23]

The Battle of St-Pierre was an indicator of how rapidly the Canadian situation was souring. Congress focused more on remedies than causes, passing a series of resolutions "calculated both to increase our military Force in that Country, and to allay the Fears & Apprehensions of the People." Richard Henry Lee noted that their hope now rested on the "Committee, better discipline, and the large body of troops going thither" to sufficiently restore the Canadian environment to patriot advantage. What was ignored, however, in both battle reports and Congress's reactions, was the remarkable patriot habitant contributions — in both intelligence and manpower — that won the Battle of St-Pierre and ensured the insurrection's quick suppression.[24]

Toward the end of March, things began to look slightly more promising for the Continentals outside Québec City. The leading edge of the new Pennsylvania and New Jersey troops finally trickled into camp, noticeably strengthening the rebel camp. General Arnold's wounds improved so that he could ride about on horseback and reconnoiter on foot. And in just a week or two, the countryside would rapidly cast off its white blanket, "the fields and Forrests" would "put on a Green garment," and siege works finally could be constructed.[25]

Despite the lack of "An able Engineer," Arnold ordered the construction of two new artillery batteries: one on Pointe-Lévy's heights — "in the same Place where Wolf had his Gun Battery last war" — and the other near the failed St-Jean "ice battery." The general hoped that cannon might still force a surrender, but noted that "in case they fail, we have ladders, &c. for a storm." One of his soldiers concurred, writing on 28 March, "We have great hopes of taking the town soon, the troops arriving so fast, and two batteries being almost ready to play upon the town."[26]

A company from Hazen's Second Canadian Regiment also had been ordered to join the siege. The colonel sent Captain Brindamour's unit, even though Lieutenant-Colonel Antill had issues with the captain, and the company was not even half complete—indicative of the regiment's desperate recruiting situation. Brindamour's men gave their colonel little reason for optimism in their mid-April march. Nine men deserted en route, so only a dozen reached Arnold's camp, when a full-strength company should have had fifty. Hazen blamed the chronic pay problem, observing that it was "impossible to march" Canadian troops until they were paid in hard cash. The colonel was frustrated and embarrassed, noting how Wooster had ordered him to deploy "the handful of men I have," but emphasized his men's disproportionate strategic significance, warning, "It will not do to break faith with the Canadians."[27]

Governor Carleton had his own "French" garrison incident on 17 March, when six *Canadien* militiamen, "one after the other refus'd to stand Sentry" on the edge of Lower Town, where General Montgomery had died. Some claimed they were "afraid of riflemen, and others declared their dread of ghosts of the persons lately slain there." The former fear was reasonable—rebel fire had killed four New Subject militiamen that month. The scared, disobedient *Canadiens* were imprisoned overnight and then publicly reprimanded "on the parade." They apparently overcame their fears of both spirits and sharpshooters, thereafter resuming sentry duty when and where assigned.[28]

In addition to the snipers, there were a number of small skirmishes outside the city walls, especially in St-Roch suburb where Continental pickets encountered garrison parties seeking firewood. At the end of March, though, Carleton was handed an opportunity to do something more. By chance, loyalist guards discovered a rebel prisoner-of-war plot, not only to escape, but also to facilitate a *coup-de-main* on the city—and they had already communicated the plan to Arnold. The prisoners would break out on "the first dark stormy night" and signal the Continentals by setting buildings ablaze, at which point the escapees would open St-Jean Gate for their cohorts. Instead, Carleton secured the prisoner-of-war conspirators and decided to replicate the sights and sounds of the prison break, hoping to lure Arnold's Continentals into a trap. At two o'clock in the morning, on 1 April, the entire garrison was posted; fires were set, guns were shot, "church bells were set ringing, and the drums beating," and a garrison party "kept hallooing, Liberty, Liberty for ever!" The Continentals, however, failed to take the bait.[29]

While unable to draw the main rebel army to the walls, deserters from the Continental reinforcements willingly crossed over to the enemy by ones and twos, seemingly as soon as they reached the Plains of Abraham. Almost daily, these defectors informed the garrison of rebel camp developments. An occasional Canadian loyalist slipped past the Continental blockade as well, delivering more trustworthy news. On the morning of 5 April, "Monsieur Loiseaux an honest Canadian came in at Sau[l]t au Matelot." All of his news had a good loyalist slant and some was remarkably accurate—the rebels were "sickly" and "many of them are under inoculation"—while other items were exaggerated or warped. Relaying additional news about the St-Pierre engagement, Loiseaux erroneously reported that "all the priests and inhabitants . . . of consequence" from lower parishes were being kept by the Continentals "as hostages for the frustration of any more such attempts." A variety of similar claims from other sources drew particular Tory attention, as they apparently fit a projected pattern they expected from their rebel counterparts.[30]

On 9 April, another informant arrived from the rebel camp, "a decent looking" man named Chaucer. While suspected of being a spy, he talked a lot. One item drew special attention: he said the rebels were preparing to attack by the fifteenth, before many Continental enlistments expired. This potential replay of Montgomery's attack gave the garrison good cause to remain highly vigilant for the next week.[31]

On 1 April, General David Wooster arrived at Holland House to take command of the Continental operation. Assessing troop returns, he found a strength on paper of 2,505 men, including 329 Canadian Continentals; yet fully one-third of the army was sick, mostly with smallpox. The next day, Wooster surveyed enemy positions with Arnold and Antill, and the new Pointe-Lévy battery fired its first shots. With the St-Jean battery and an additional gun position being constructed north of the Charles River, the Continental lines were finally beginning to look and sound more like a siege, albeit a weak one.[32]

After evaluating his force and the enemy, General Wooster addressed logistics. The army was still short of provisions, it had no cash to pay for them, and even paper money was becoming scarce. Accordingly, on 2 April, the general ordered Commissary John Halsted "to take all the wheat necessary for the usage of the army," providing only a "receipt to pay . . . at the current price." While at first glance this might seem a severe imposition, it really was an improvement over Arnold's 4 March order that required Canadians to accept the despised Continental bills; the people much preferred receipts.[33]

Wooster's most pressing concern, however, was enlistments. The army was in danger of losing 60 percent of its capital-blockade manpower on 15 April: Warner's Green Mountain Boys, the Massachusetts volunteers and Cady's Detachment, Livingston's Canadians, and all the New York and Connecticut men reengaged back in November. To help lubricate new enlistments, Wooster ordered the paymaster to settle old accounts and offered a bounty for soldiers willing to sign on for a full year; all this was met with little enthusiasm.[34]

Shortly after Wooster's arrival, Arnold fell from his horse and reinjured his leg, causing him to be confined to quarters for several days and keeping the younger general from taking "an Active part" in operations. He suffered a second, emotional wound as he languished in recovery: "Wooster did not think proper to consult" with Arnold "in any of his matters." Neglected, the young brigadier became convinced he would be more useful in Montréal and asked Wooster's permission to depart, which was "very readily granted." As he left camp, Arnold's perspectives darkened. Where he had once had "great hopes" for the Continental siege, now embittered by his relationship with Wooster and plagued by troublesome wounds, he became "very Dubious" of the army's success.[35]

═══════

To be fair to Arnold, the longest-serving Continentals had become increasingly restive and insubordinate as their obligations neared an end. Soldiers and officers fought amongst themselves — particularly between different colonies. None of the troops seemed inclined to reenlist, particularly those who had not seen their families for most of a year already; and without hard cash for pay, Colonel Hazen believed "very few, if any" of Livingston's Canadians would reengage. It seemed that the army, built so slowly, was destined to be half dismantled at mid-month.[36]

On the other side of the capital ramparts, the garrison anticipated another

Continental assault, even though the weather was not conducive to a massed attack. A loyalist defender observed, "If the rebels should attempt to approach the walls in the present state of the snow especially when loaded with ladders, they'll be mowed down by our grape and canister shot." As dusk settled on the evening of 14 April, Tories noted, "Every thing in motion among the enemy." The garrison stood ready on the crisp, clear night; "fire balls were lighted" to illuminate approaches, and guards were issued signal rockets for alarms; yet the hours passed quietly. Wooster did not feel compelled to attack as Montgomery had; instead, he opted to wait for new men.[37]

General Wooster hoped that many soldiers could "be prevail'd Upon to Stay a few days longer, untill the Expected Recruits arrive . . . at a time when by staying they may render perhaps almost Infinite Service to their Country"; yet he was certainly aware that most soldiers would not willingly extend. Prompted by concerns about the lack of discipline of homebound troops, on the fourteenth the general required all soldiers leaving camp to have an officer to "lead & Command them while in this Country." The next day, as enlistments expired, Wooster reminded "those Soldiers who have utterly refus'd to Continue" that he considered them "subject to the law Martial while in this Country." The general then introduced administrative delays, forcing units to wait two or three extra days to formally muster out, promising pay settlement and proper provisions on the return march as incentives to await proper dismissal. Then, on the eighteenth, Wooster added further restrictions: "no man or Body of Men, Under penalty of suffering the Severity of Military Punishment," was to "leave the Camp till the boats come down" to transport them upriver, ensuring that departing troops had no opportunity to maraud the Canadian countryside on a homeward march.[38]

Remarkably, the previously steady stream of Continental desertions tapered off. The trapped troops complained and stirred, but there was only one major protest. "[A]bout 40 of the Yorkers Paraded themselves" by Holland House, "to git Liberty to go home" on 17 April. Wooster warned that they would receive no provisions if they left camp on their own, after which the soldiers threatened to "plunder the inhabitants" and fired off guns near the powder magazine, posing the threat of an explosion. Wooster called New York Colonel James Clinton to suppress the little riot—with Canadian Continentals reportedly "most forward" in restoring control, as fifteen mutineers were "carried to the gard house and put in irons." Finally, on 29 April, the troops were officially released to board ships. Wooster had effectively coaxed and cheated two weeks' extra service from these men—quite a feat, given the circumstances—providing time for hundreds of new reinforcements to reach the camp.[39]

The fresh Continental forces joined the siege with considerable vigor. Night pickets ventured "so close to the walls" that they could "hear the sentries converse with one another." On 22 April, a new battery opened near the General-Hospital. While the Pointe-Lévy battery played "sweetly upon the lower town" and scored hits on ships at anchor, the other guns "plumpt" shells "into the thicket" of Upper Town; although by a loyalist's report, the rebel artillery could "make no manner of impression on the Town . . . As yet they have killed a boy, wounded a sailor, and broke the leg of a turkey." The Continentals simply lacked the proper artillery for bombarding a fortified city to meaningful effect.[40]

When the lower St. Lawrence's ice broke up and the river became navigable, a battle loomed for control of the river. Carleton was fitting up HMS *Lizard,* HMS *Hunter,* and a few provincial ships to sail from icebound berths at Québec City, preparing to challenge the rebels and show the flag until spring reinforcements arrived with decisive naval superiority. In opposition, the Continentals had the captured Royal Navy sloop *Gaspée,* the provincial armed schooner *Maria,* and a gondola available upriver at Pointe-aux-Trembles, and by the end of April, the other captured transport ships were used to carry discharged soldiers to Sorel or Montréal. Wooster appointed Canadian Hector McNeill as his naval captain, responsible for preparing this flotilla to challenge the Royal Navy ships, intercept loyalist supplies, and perhaps, directly contribute to taking the capital.[41]

Early in April, Wooster approved another naval plan: to "burn the English Frigates and Transports" moored at Lower Town, with a fireship. They would use Arnold's merchant brigantine *Peggy* for the mission; the ship had been recovered by Continental detachments in December, off Île-d'Orléans, where it was moored after Canadian government authorities seized it during the previous summer's unrest. "Hay and Hogsheads" were left aboard as flammable material, and a team of Continental soldiers added other fuel and explosives in preparation for the ship's final cruise. The plan lost its element of surprise, however, when a deserter warned the garrison by 9 April. As a result, Carleton and Royal Navy Captain Thomas Mackenzie had "Boats row guard every night," and they put "guns on all the wharfs, and strong guards and picquets in different parts of the Lower Town." Their preparations were tested on the night of 27 April; at ten o'clock, a Cape Diamond sentry "call'd out A FIRESHIP! A FIRESHIP!" Alarms rang and the garrison was posted in minutes. With more careful examination, the fire "proved to be a house or a heap of rubbish in a blaze on the beach, on the Point Levy side," and the men stood down.[42]

Meanwhile, Wooster and McNeill struggled to find semicompetent ship captains for their little navy. For example, in April the *Maria* was commanded by New York Captain Barent Teneyck for a few days, until he was replaced by William Goforth, fresh from Trois-Rivières duty. Wooster ordered the brig *Gaspée* to be piloted by anyone available, but the ship was simply left standing offshore at Jacques-Cartier, manned by a party of soldiers. Down at Québec City, *Canadien* loyalist Militia-Captain Henri Laforce initiated spring river operations as he "hauled out" a provincial schooner from the capital basin on 21 April, drawing fire from Pointe-Lévy. Five days later, he ventured farther into the river and "chased some canoes." On 2 May, Captain Goforth led a Continental naval patrol to search "every Creek, River and Harbour, as far as Sorrell; and to seize and secure" any boats that might be carrying supplies to the capital defenders — he did not find anything. The naval "contest" remained an uneventful series of minor patrols, awaiting escalation by the fireship or Royal Navy reinforcements.[43]

———

As the main camps engaged in stalemates on the Plains of Abraham and the St. Lawrence, Captain Clément Gosselin took center stage in the previously contested lower south-shore parishes. Beginning in St-Pierre-du-Sud, Gosselin led elections to replace loyalist Militia-Captain Michal Blais and his son; the new officers included Jean Dessince, who had helped guide the Continentals to the battle. Then Gosselin sped to Ste-Anne-de-la-Pocatière, the heart of the suppressed loyalist uprising. The Continental captain, his father-in-law Germain Dionne. and notary Joseph Dionne interrogated parish habitants about the circumstances leading to the insurrection and the escapes of messenger Riverin and turncoat Commissary Féré. Once the "tribunal" was complete, Gosselin dealt with the other parishes that had shown support for the King, while Ayotte hunted Féré, who now had "a price on his head."[44]

Gosselin's pacification solutions varied, based on each community's demonstrated loyalties during the uprising. In "loyalist" Cap-St-Ignace, he imposed new militia officers appointed under Congressional authority. In "neutral" L'Islet and St-Roch-des-Aulanies, militia-captains were forced to exchange their old commissions for Continental equivalents. The "patriot" parishes of St-Jean-Port-Joli, St-Vallier, and Berthier-en-bas all held elections; several men who had provided critical intelligence, or participated in the St-Pierre affair, were given these new militia offices. The most interesting developments were in St-François, just up the Rivière-du-Sud from the battle site. That parish, which later claimed it had been coerced into joining the 25 March St-Pierre engagement alongside the Continentals, "drafted a petition requesting permission to appoint officers." The patriot element had clearly taken charge in St-François, and Gosselin returned to preside over their ensuing elections.[45]

Also in April, Gosselin undertook another military mission supporting General Wooster; establishing a south-shore chain of signal fires from Rimouski, 150 miles downstream from the capital, all the way to St-Michel-de-Bellechasse, where a signal fire would be visible from the principal Continental camps. The system was designed to provide headquarters with almost immediate warning when the much-anticipated Ministerial relief fleet finally reached the settled St. Lawrence valley. Many local militia-captains supported the enterprise, and a few were zealous. Rivière-Ouelle's Bazil Dubé not only led construction of his parish's signal stacks, but also went so far as to inspect the entire network, traveling all the way down to Rimouski. Dubé was a rising patriot zealot—almost on a par with Ayotte, Gosselin, and Dionne—encouraging fellow habitants, actively supporting Continental recruiting efforts, and oppressing loyalist neighbors in his travels.[46]

These key Canadian patriots proved critical in restoring and expanding Continental authority after de Beaujeu's uprising. Gosselin, Ayotte, Dionne, and Dubé began to make a meaningful mark in the lower south-shore parishes, yet their progress would soon be interrupted by military developments at the capital. Regardless of their temporary gains, eventually they would have had to deal with the principal problems vexing patriots throughout the province: the United Colonies' miserable finances, poor Continental troop discipline, and an unimpressive patriot military presence.

A LATE-CHANGING CAST

New Continental Leadership for Canada

I must confess I have very great Confidence, in the Abilities and
Integrity, the Political Principles and good Disposition of this Committee. |
John Adams to James Warren, Philadelphia, 18 February 1776

A General Thomas, (lately an Apothecary), was on his way with 1200 men
to join the Rebels in Canada, where they may arrive the beginning of May. |
Journal of the Siege and Blockade of Quebec . . . , *23 April 1776*

The composition of Congress's Committee to Canada, officially named on
15 February, contrasted with November's Committee to the Northern Army,
which had consisted of New Englanders and one New Yorker. The new committee members were all middle colonists: Pennsylvania's Benjamin Franklin
and Maryland's Samuel Chase, both members of Congress; and Marylander
Charles Carroll of Carrollton, a welcome observer in Philadelphia, but not
an official delegate. When Congress named these three commissioners, they
also requested that Charles Carroll "prevail on Mr. John Caroll to accompany
the committee to Canada, to assist them in such matters as they shall think
useful"; John Carroll, Charles's cousin, happened to be a Jesuit priest.[1]
 There were at least two other Congress members who expressed a desire to
be part of the Committee to Canada, who would have been interesting addi-
tions. John Adams told his wife Abigail, "I wish I understood French as well
as you. I would have gone to Canada, if I had"; but it is hard to imagine his
fellow delegates unleashing the brash radical upon the Canadians at such a
sensitive juncture. Robert R. Livingston Jr., who had been on the November
Committee to the Northern Army, similarly confided to New York delegate
John Jay, "If a Committee should be sent to superintend the operations of the
Canada expedition I'd like to be one of the number." Livingston, however, faced

two critical challenges. First, he was in poor health and severely depressed after his grandfather, father, and brother-in-law General Richard Montgomery all died in a six-month span. Politically, Livingston had also opposed the Canadian campaign on principle, and believed "it is most evident the Canadians are not to be relied on"—challenging views to overcome for committee success. However, Adams and Livingston were not seriously considered; by February, there was a general consensus to appoint Franklin, Chase, and Carroll.[2]

Benjamin Franklin, the "First American," scientist-philosopher, and longtime political agent, was eminently suited for the Canadian mission. Shortly after the nominations, John Adams listed the doctor's impressive qualifications: "His masterly Acquaintance with the French Language, his extensive Correspondence in France, his great Experience in Life, his Wisdom, Prudence, Caution, his engaging Address, united to his unshaken Firmness in the present American System of Politicks and War." Two years later, in France, Adams would find that he had oversold Franklin's ability with the foreign tongue, where experience proved that the doctor "spoke it poorly" and "stumbled badly in conversation," but the raconteur made up for those limitations with his brilliant charm. His most significant downside was his age, having turned seventy just a month before his Canada committee appointment.[3]

Franklin also had a wealth of Canadian connections. As a chief advocate for the British acquisition of New France in the French and Indian War peace settlement, he authored his famous "Canada Pamphlet." In the post-Conquest era, Franklin visited the province as the North American postmaster, establishing the New York-to-Montréal mail route. He had also been present for Parliament's 1774 Quebec Bill debates, before returning to Philadelphia completely disenchanted with the Ministry and joining the second Continental Congress. Drafting the United Colonies' Articles of Confederation, the doctor included a clause ensuring that Canada was "entitled to all the Advantages of our Union." The septuagenarian was willing to serve where called, but was not overly enthusiastic to hear of his new committee appointment.[4]

Franklin's delegate counterpart, thirty-five-year-old Samuel Chase, offered complementary skills. He was a leading Annapolis Son of Liberty who had fervently supported the cause since the Stamp Act Crisis. He honed his political talents in Maryland's colonial assembly and patriot committees, producing appointments to both Continental Congresses. Chase was an effective orator, writer, and organizer; his biggest limitation was his overwhelming zeal. Based on early Philadelphia experiences, John Adams noted how the Maryland archpatriot had been "violent and boisterous" in Congress, while Tory rivals labeled him "A turbulent man." Yet by the time Chase had been identified for duty in Quebec, Adams comfortably could observe that the younger delegate was "deeply impress'd with a sense of the Importance of securing Canada, very active, eloquent, spirited, and capable." When viewed as a team, the energetic young Marylander provided a good balance for Franklin's relative frailty and smooth diplomatic approach.[5]

In Congress, Chase showed a recurring interest in Canada, soliciting "every Intelligence" on the province after the first Congress. It was Chase who wrote General Schuyler to clarify Congressional guidance during the August 1775 recess, emphasizing the criticality of the Canadians' "Approbation" for any invasion. The Marylander stressed the "infinite importance" of Quebec and even offered his own January 1776 plan for a "Committee go to Canada as soon as the Lakes are frozen hard enough," which would "call a Convention, explain the Views and designs of Congress, and persuade them to send Delegates." Chase politely and ironically added, "My Inclination to serve my Country would induce Me to offer my Services, if I did not esteem Myself unable to discharge the Trust."[6]

As a leading advocate for colonial independence, on a par with John Adams, Chase was unlikely to let concerns about reconciliation temper his decisions in Canada. A bigger challenge was his militant stand for strict compliance with the Continental Association's commercial restrictions. Earlier, when Georgians sought a trade exemption in Congress, Chase ranted, "Did they come here to ruin America?" and argued that their proposals would "bring Destruction upon all N[orth] America." The serious economic concerns of the Montréal merchants were unlikely to alter his core principles on trade issues.[7]

Samuel Chase's role on the Committee to Canada generally has been lost in the shadows of legendary cohort Ben Franklin and their novel Catholic companions, the Carrolls. In reality, Chase was the committee's de facto leader. The Marylander made the most significant contributions in forming the mission in Philadelphia, and in generating action in Canada.

There was good reason to weight the committee so heavily toward the Maryland representation of Chase and the Carroll cousins; their colony was founded as a Catholic haven in the British Empire and had a substantial practicing population. Yet by the time of the Revolution, Catholicism was scarcely tolerated; the Church was severely restricted, and the province's approximately sixteen thousand Catholics were banned from government office. Biases were slowly eroding though, and Charles Carroll of Carrollton was the revolutionary vanguard who led Maryland's slow advance toward religious freedom.[8]

Charles Carroll of Carrollton (differentiating him from his father, Charles Carroll of Annapolis) came from an exceptionally wealthy landed family. He spent his teen years studying in Flanders and France, and concluded his legal education in London. Of course, Carroll was a "compleat Master of French Language" when he returned, and he brought his own copies of Montesquieu and Voltaire, as well. He did not rise to political prominence until 1773, when he authored a brilliant riposte under the *nom de plume* "First Citizen," opposing the governor's declared right to establish officials' fees by proclamation. After discovering "First Citizen's" identity, patriots eagerly recruited Carroll for the Annapolis Committee of Correspondence, where he served with Samuel Chase. Although still technically unelectable in Maryland on religious grounds, Carroll employed his patriot genius in extralegal conventions and county committees, particularly valuable while his closest "friends of liberty," Chase and William Paca, were busy in Philadelphia.[9]

Charles Carroll was so intrigued by the Continental Congress that he periodically visited nearby Philadelphia to observe and confer with the delegates. In January 1776, it was Samuel Chase who first recommended Carroll for Canada, noting "His attachment and zeal to the Cause, his abilities his Acquaintance with the Language, Manner & Customs of France and his Religion, with the circumstances of a very great Estate." Carroll's 15 February committee appointment might be seen as a small reward in a world that legally denied him public office based on his faith, yet it was a step forward. Charles Carroll, at the age of thirty-eight, proved that a Catholic could be trusted to represent the United Colonies; religion had become less important than patriot credentials, offering hope for all North American Catholics.[10]

Meanwhile, Carroll's cousin, Father John Carroll, seemed to provide a promising solution to Canadian religious challenges. John Adams and several other delegates, ignorant of Catholic practice, believed that the Jesuit could provide the sacraments to "Friends in Canada," as the "Anathemas of the Church" were "very terrible." General Charles Lee, after consulting with Price and Walker, hinted at another purpose; a liberty-loving Catholic priest from Maryland would provide physical "proof" of the United Colonies' religious tolerance, even if it was still largely notional. As a teen, John Carroll left Maryland to study in Europe with his cousin Charley. Having taken a religious track, in 1771 he became a Jesuit father at the age of thirty-six. Just two years later, that order's suppression prompted his return to America, where he quietly tended to Maryland Catholics. Realistically, John Carroll's only real qualification for the Quebec mission was his fluent French; a fish out of water on the commission, he was quite unprepared to be a patriot political advocate.[11]

Father Carroll happened to capture his thoughts on committee duty shortly after his appointment, viewing himself as "a very unfit person to be employed in negotiations," for which he had "neither experience or systematical knowledge." He also had issues with Quebec's revolutionary role; the Father believed Canadians did not have "the same motives for taking up arms against England," as they had "not tried the success of petitions & remonstrances" like their southern neighbors — perhaps he was ignorant of Canada's British Party efforts in the last decade. Most important, Carroll hesitated to join the committee because he had "observed that when the ministers of Religion leave their duties of their profession to take a busy part in political matters, they generally fall into contempt; & sometimes even bring discredit to the cause." He did not wish to ruin his own reputation, nor do disservice to the United Colonies, but ultimately chose not to disappoint Congress's expectations. Historian Thomas O'Brien Hanley suggested that Father Carroll's decisive motivating factor might have been to gain religious freedom for Catholic compatriots at home; bringing a larger number of coreligionists into the cause might encourage the restoration of true religious toleration in Maryland.[12]

A week after Congress named the Carrolls, Chase, and Franklin to the Committee to Canada, it also authorized an adjunct member. On 26 February, French-born printer Fleury Mesplet was approved to go to Montréal at Congress's expense to "set up his press and carry on the printing business" there. Like prominent Canadian patriots Pélissier and Cazeau, the master printer had matured in the French Enlightenment and brought its spirit of liberty and reason with him to Philadelphia in 1774. Mesplet first came to Congress's notice in October of that year, when they commissioned him to print French copies of the first "Address to the Inhabitants of the Province of Quebec." Early in 1775, Mesplet had ventured to Canada on his own, to evaluate the possibility of establishing provincial competition for William Brown's Québec City print shop, but he returned to Philadelphia and continued serving Congress's French print needs instead.[13]

It was Samuel Chase, again, who recognized that the committee needed a skilled French printer. He knew Mesplet was perfect, "on account of his Language and known attachment to the interests of the United-States [*sic*]." Before Congress officially supported the printer's relocation to Canada, President John Hancock and veteran printer Franklin interviewed him for a "Verification of his Abilities," after which Mesplet swiftly packed his professional equipment and family possessions and hired a typesetter, two journeymen, and a servant to join his new Canadian enterprise. The entire team and kit were assembled and prepared to depart in less than three weeks; Mesplet would actually leave Philadelphia before Chase, Franklin, and the Carrolls.[14]

The committee's departure was delayed more than a month; they needed guidance and commissions from Congress, and those items proved contentious. On 17 February, a committee was appointed to frame the United Colonies' intentions for their envoys, but it did not even present a first draft for six days. Not anticipating any meaningful delays, on 7 March President Hancock believed that Franklin, Chase, and the Carrolls might set out within a week; yet the second draft did not appear for another two days and sparked "3 or 4 hours" debate. John Jay and other conservatives opposed recommendations that the Canadians "form a Constitution and Government for themselves without Limitation [of] Time," viewing it as license for "an Independency"—too drastic a step at this point. Thus, the instructions bounced back and forth from the committee to Congress for almost two more weeks.[15]

Meanwhile, the Canada commissioners stood by, expecting to leave with just a few days' notice for a mission of unknown length. Charles Carroll hoped they might depart soon, settle "matters in that country to the satisfaction of Congress, & with tolerable dispatch" return by mid-May. On 16 March, Mesplet, his wife, and four workers left Philadelphia. Two days later, with the instructions still in draft form, Carroll chafed at the delays, writing, "I begin to hope my journey to Canada will not take place."[16]

On 20 March, Congress finally approved painstakingly long instructions for the "Canadian Mission." The committee was "to repair to Canada, and make known to the people of that country, the wishes and intentions of the Congress with respect to them." A good portion of the document summarized the United Colonies' Canadian objectives, emphasizing their "inclination, that the people of Canada may set up such a form of government, as will be most likely, in their judgment, to produce their happiness." The most critical challenge, the strategic stumbling block for so many months, was to "urge the necessity" for the Canadians to immediately take "some decisive step, to put themselves under the protection of the United Colonies." Franklin, Chase, and Carroll were charged with educating their Canadian counterparts on patriot government principles and to "press them to have a complete representation of the people assembled in convention, with all possible expedition, to deliberate concerning the establishment of a form of government, and a union with the United Colonies." If the Canadians offered objections, Congress wanted details and the terms on which they might yet join the Union — perhaps foreseeing insurmountable issues with the Continental Association's trade restrictions.[17]

In more specific responsibilities, the committee was charged "to settle all disputes between the Canadians and the continental troops," making necessary regulations and reforming abuses. The commissioners were also given authority over some military affairs; they could "sit and vote as members of councils of war, in directing fortifications and defences to be made, or to be demolished, by land or water," preapproved for up to $100,000 of defensive works; they were also "empowered to suspend any military officer from the exercise of his commission." Addressing the Montréal merchants' February petition, the committee was authorized "to promote and encourage the trade of Canada with the Indian Nations, and to grant passports for carrying it on as far as it may consist with the safety of the troops, and the public good." Canadian external trade would be "on an equal footing with . . . the trade of the United Colonies," little comfort for a province so dependent upon transatlantic fur and wheat trades focused toward London. More immediately, the commissioners were implored to "use every wise and prudent measure to introduce and give credit and circulation to the continental money in Canada."[18]

These instructions were supported by individual commissions for Franklin, Chase, and Charles Carroll, establishing any two of them as a committee "for and on behalf of us, and all the People of the United Colonies," their authority remaining in force until specifically revoked. By the commissions, they

Château de Ramezay, by Henry Richard S. Bunnett (1886). The Château was only slightly modified in the century after 1776. Copyright © McCord Museum No. M309.

were authorized to call on "all officers, soldiers, and others" who might help their Canadian negotiations. Charles Carroll trembled "at the thoughts of this very important & almost unbounded trust," yet was "determined not to fail thro' inattention, or for want of application." He also reassured his father that he and his fellow delegates were "determined not to abuse" their "great powers." Chase and the Carrolls were ready to leave almost immediately, but Franklin needed more time. The four committee members finally departed Philadelphia on 26 March.[19]

———

Back in Montréal, Moses Hazen commanded from his new Château de Ramezay headquarters and sent weekly situation reports direct to General Schuyler. His 1 April letter had caused a stir in both Albany and Philadelphia, and his next two letters continued with the same foreboding motif—the province was in a "Convulsive state" for a multitude of reasons. One key factor that Hazen emphasized on 8 April was the priests' refusal of "the Ceremonies of the Church to the poor Ignorant people" unless they declared themselves in favor of the King. In his role as a recruiting regimental commander, Hazen saw the Church policy's impact on his current troops, and he began to believe it was affecting his ability to draw additional recruits.[20]

In late February, in an attempt to mitigate these issues, General Wooster employed Duggan in a rebuffed attempt to recruit a city priest as chaplain for the Canadian Continentals. Then, when Colonel Hazen assumed district command, he renewed conversations with the city's neglected Jesuits — revisiting Montgomery's implied invitation for the Order's collaboration. Hazen removed the "common prison" from the Jesuits' Montréal home, and Floquet particularly "enjoyed this beneficence, because it had not been requested." The colonel further cultivated the relationship, inviting the Jesuit father to dinner at the beginning of Holy Week.[21]

Immediately thereafter, Canadian Continentals began approaching the Jesuit superior for absolution. He conditionally agreed, as long as the soldiers assured Floquet "that they would not join in the siege of Quebec, and that they would peacefully serve in Montreal," in which case he would administer to the men as if they were his congregation. Floquet convinced himself that he was acting in the spirit of Bishop Briand's mandates, but Montréal Vicar-General Etienne Montgolfier saw things differently. He rebuked the Jesuit for defying the bishop after having received very specific warnings. Meanwhile, Hazen began referring to Floquet as his chaplain, noting how the Jesuit had given the troops "absolution when the priest in the Country Refused"; the colonel eventually requested Floquet's formal assignment to the regiment.[22]

As spring emerged in upper Canada, Colonel Hazen faced a critical operational military concern; rumors of a combined Indian and upcountry British Army attack on Montréal grew in earnest. Around mid-month, Hazen received reports that fugitive loyalist Claude Lorimier was spotted thirty miles southwest of the city in Les-Cèdres parish, "inlisting men and stirring up the Indians to cut our throats." The "Rascal" Tory was assuring Canadians and Indians "that eight hundred Indians with the garrisons of Detroit, Niagara, &c. would be at the Cedars [Les-Cèdres]" in twenty days. This intelligence prompted Hazen's most significant decision as district commander; he ordered Colonel Timothy Bedel, veteran of the fall Richelieu Valley Campaign, to establish a post at "The Cedars" with his recently arrived and newly recruited regiment of New Hampshire frontiersmen. Les-Cèdres overlooked a set of St-Lawrence rapids, controlling upcountry approaches to Montréal.[23]

Only a few days later, on 18 April, Benedict Arnold limped up to the Château to assume Montréal District's command from Hazen; leadership of the large, critical region really belonged in the hands of a general. Arnold immediately reissued Bedel's orders to "prevent any Goods being sent to the Upper Country, & to guard against a Surprise from the Enemy, or their Indians" at Les-Cèdres, and he also dispatched a sixty-man detachment up the Ottawa, to watch similar rapids at Carillon. Thereafter, fewer than five hundred Continentals remained in Montréal, about half of whom were homeward bound.[24]

Arnold praised Hazen as "a sensable Judicious Officer" who had kept city affairs quiet and prudently addressed the western threat. Now, the general aimed to employ the colonel's talents on a new mission: "to command at St. John's, Chambly, &c." During their short command transition, Arnold read Hazen's 1 April letter—the one that drew so much attention in Congress—and confided to Schuyler, "I am sorry to say, I think most of his Remarks but too true." Arnold maintained, "If we are not immediately supported with Eight or Ten Thousand Men, a good train of Artillery well Served, & a Military Chest well furnished, the Ministerial Troops[,] If they attempt It, will regain this Country."[25]

While General Arnold knew he needed reinforcements in Montréal, he also understood how desperately Wooster needed additional manpower outside Québec City. Because troops and resources were spread so thin, both generals spent the winter reacting to loyalists—counterattacking de Beaujeu and responding defensively to the upcountry threat—rather than seizing the operational initiative. Unfortunately, the mid-March lake thaw coincided with the point when Continental regiments were finally prepared to head into Canada, having finally overcome their own recruiting and equipping challenges. When the waterways cleared almost a month later, General Schuyler expedited troops to the north; yet Moses Hazen calculated that the leading wave could not reach Québec City until 5 May. The new troops would have little opportunity to help take the capital or even prepare defenses against the enemy's anticipated relief army.[26]

Meanwhile, the reinforcements' miserable discipline plagued the Northern Army. Congress was shocked at hearing of their troops' countless depredations, sparking President Hancock's observation: "It is only by cultivating a friendly Intercourse with them, and restraining by exemplary Punishment the Irregularities of the Soldiery, that their [Canadians'] Affections can be ever regained"; yet tremendous damage had been done and continued to be inflicted upon Quebec's habitants. Grappling with the Continentals' despicable behavior, Hancock rationalized it to some degree, arguing that men with a "Love of Liberty & Aversion to military Restraint" posed a fundamental discipline challenge, exacerbated by the degree to which the United Colonies had been forced to take up arms, unprepared, for "Self Preservation." Canada just happened to be the scene where these underlying issues most glaringly manifested themselves.[27]

Some of these spring soldiers behaved more like drunken tavern thugs: abusing civilians, deliberately destroying private property, fighting between units, and defying officers. By mid-May, General Schuyler despaired, "the Licentiousn[ess] [of] some of the Troops that are gone on, has been such, That few of the Inhabitants have Escaped A[buse] Either in their Persons or Property." The general lamented that many carpenters, wagoners, and bateaumen had already quit due to the "criminal Conduct in the Soldiery," directly affecting the insubordinate troops' own welfare, as supplies could not efficiently be forwarded to Canada. Schuyler persistently issued "the most pointed Orders," but every effort failed to stop "those scandalous Excesses." Mitigating the Continentals' depredations, the general ordered units to "march in as close Order as possible," and "that none of the Men be suffered to straggle and enter the Houses or Inclosures of the Inhabitants." If "any outrage should be committed on any Inhabitant or person employed in the public Service," offenders should "be immediately confined and reported to him." In extreme cases, soldiers were sentenced to thirty-nine lashes, or even death, but such punishment had little impact on the army's rampant misconduct.[28]

General Montgomery's long-awaited replacement finally reached Canada in late April with the first wave of post-thaw reinforcements. The tardiness of General Thomas's 6 March appointment guaranteed that he would face the toughest travel conditions while hastening to his new command. This more energetic Yankee major-general, however, was prepared to press ahead as quickly as possible; on 17 April, he and his staff "broke their way through the ice," reaching Montréal on the twenty-sixth.[29]

The fifty-one-year-old Massachusetts general had entered military service as a surgeon in the French and Indian War, but subsequently joined the officer ranks and rose to command a provincial regiment. Early in the revolution, he again answered his province's call, raising a regiment and accepting an appointment as Massachusetts's lieutenant-general, following Lexington and Concord. In the summer of 1775, the Philadelphia Congress appointed him as a brigadier. Like Wooster, Thomas felt slighted by his lesser Continental rank and low seniority (sixth of eight); initially hesitant to serve, he was persuaded to continue after being elevated administratively to first in seniority. With that episode behind him, he thrived as a trusted deputy under General Washington, who reported that Thomas was "much esteemed," an "able good Officer," and "a good man." Thomas's service in the Cambridge camp culminated in his 4 March 1776 mission to seize Dorchester Heights—a move that soon compelled the British to abandon Boston. Almost immediately thereafter, he received his promotion and appointment to Canadian command. Charles Carroll happened to offer his personal observations on the general a month later: "his first appearance does not impress you with any high ideas of his abilities," but the Marylander also offered that Thomas had "a command of temper exceedingly necessary in an officer who is to command in Canada." Regardless of his character, Thomas's key functional deficiency for Canadian command was one common to all Continental generals, excluding Charles Lee: Thomas did not speak French.[30]

As Thomas passed Albany, he consulted with General Schuyler and gained valuable insight, but also adopted Schuyler's biases, subsequently writing: "For Canada, we cannot expect to be able to call in any assistance from the inhabitants, as with the other colonies, in any emergency." If he had known the details surrounding the encounter at St-Pierre, he might have tempered that judgment. Thomas also joined his predecessors in fervently calling for more men and money, even before he reached his new Canadian command.[31]

On 28 April, in Montréal, General Thomas was joined by a new brigadier-general. Where General Lee had requested one or two of the Continental Army's most reliable brigadier-generals to join him when destined for Canada, Thomas, in contrast, received an unproven, newly commissioned foreign volunteer. Prussian Baron Frederick William de Woedtke had just been appointed a Continental brigadier by special election on 16 March. The baron, in his mid-thirties, had served in Frederick the Great's army, rising to the rank of major before leaving the service after "Tyrannical treatment" from the King of Prussia. Venturing to France, de Woedtke met some "friends of liberty" who encouraged him to join the American cause. In Philadelphia, he was advertised as "late a Major Gen[eral] of Cavalry in the Prussian Service and Aid du Camp to that King," celebrated for his "love of Liberty & Military knowledge." Congress was impressed with the baron's inflated qualifications, which outweighed his uncourtly carriage and "most awkward appearance." Since de Woedtke was reportedly "well acquainted with the French language," he seemed a natural choice to send north — although his fluency was as questionable as his résumé. His English may have been even worse, perhaps making the new brigadier more a liability than a benefit. As de Woedtke joined Thomas at the end of April, their late Canadian arrival put them in the same situation as the recently arrived reinforcements, with little opportunity to act before the Ministerial relief fleet came to Quebec. They had days, maybe a couple weeks at most; and the new generals had not even left Montréal. The military staff was in Canada, but the most important leadership component of the United Colonies' Canadian effort had still not arrived — the much-requested and much-delayed committee from Congress.[32]

While General Thomas and the Committee to Canada were venturing toward Montréal, General Washington had a moment to ponder developments in the northern province. Like many patriot leaders, Washington was stunned by Colonel Hazen's early April letters, particularly the reports of the St-Pierre affair, which seemed to indicate a frightening new level of loyalist opposition. In letters to President John Hancock and General Schuyler, the commander-in-chief reiterated Quebec's importance in the United Colonies' overall strategy and the Canadians' role in that plan: "The Security of that Country is of the utmost importance to us, this cannot be done so effectually by conquest as by taking stronghold of the affections and confidence of the Inhabitants." Fearing that the Canadians had been "insulted & Injured" by Continental troops, he added, "Nothing could have a Greater Tendency to ruin our Cause in that Country. For Human Nature is such, that It will adhere to the Side from whence the best Treatment is received." From his headquarters in New York, Washington could only hope that "most of the difficulties" identified by Hazen would be "obviated by the appearance of the respectable Committee of Congress in Canada"; and the new waves of troop reinforcements would be ready to counter the anticipated Ministerial spring reinforcements.[33]

Chapter 21

MAY TIDES

New Arrivals and Massive Change for the Province

Your Commissioners themselves are in a critical and most irksome
Situation, pestered hourly with Demands great and small that they cannot
answer. | *Commissioners to Canada to John Hancock, President of Congress,
Montréal, 8 May 1776*

In the most irregular, helter skelter manner we raised the siege, leaving every
thing. | *Journal of Doctor Isaac Senter*

Following their 26 March departure from Philadelphia, Benjamin Franklin,
Samuel Chase, Charles Carroll, and John Carroll adopted a deliberate pace
toward Canada. Sailing up the Hudson, they surveyed progress on the Hudson River fortifications, reaching Albany on 8 April. Major-General Schuyler
hosted them at his Saratoga estate for almost a week while they were "detained by the present state of the lakes." During that time, the major-general
shared the latest "Advices from Canada." This news increased committee
skepticism for the mission's prospects. Franklin expressed their concerns to
John Hancock, fearing that "we shall be able to effect but little there." The
much younger, and more optimistic, Charles Carroll observed, "Our affairs
in Canada do not wear that flattering aspect as in other places," but hoped "a
proper force & good management may turn the tide once more in our favour"
and politically that they might yet "engage the Canadians if not in the union,
at least to observe the strictest neutrality."[1]

Preparing to depart Saratoga, Franklin expressed worries that the journey
would be too much for his aged body, sitting down to "write to a few friends,
by way of farewell"; the trip proved to be uncomfortable, but bearable. The
committee left Schuyler's company on 16 April only to find that the lakes were
still not yet open. After a few days' delay at Lake George, the ice broke and

they ventured down the Champlain corridor, reaching St-Jean on 27 April. Franklin, Chase, and the Carrolls spent their first Canadian night at Moses Hazen's home on the Richelieu east shore, finding the house a "perfect wreck" with "scarcely a whole pane of glass in the house"—a result of the Continentals' punitive marauding in the fall, back when Hazen was still considered a loyalist. As the committee members awaited transportation to Montréal, they could see a new season springing to life in Canada as nearby habitants were sowing wheat on the freshly thawed ground. The Congressional envoys could only hope to plant equally productive political seeds of their own, but Chase confided to John Adams that he was "afraid all our Efforts to take Quebec will prove fruitless." However, he was still willing to persevere in aiding their northern friends, claiming, "I now esteem Myself a Canadian."[2]

On the evening of 29 April, seven months after General Montgomery's first request and seventy-four days after being chartered by Congress, the Committee to Canada finally reached Montréal. General Arnold and "a great body of officers, gentry, &c." eagerly greeted the delegation. Troops rendered "military honors" and Continental gunners fired a salute from the citadel, as the large party proceeded up to General Arnold's quarters. The committee members and "a number of the friends to liberty spent the evening with decent mirth," which included people "crowding in to pay their compliments" and "an elegant supper"—an unprecedented celebration in the six-month Continental occupation. When the evening was complete, Chase, the Carrolls, and Franklin were guided to Thomas Walker's well-furnished abode, which the owner had offered for their use when they left Philadelphia.[3]

The commissioners had little opportunity to recover from their taxing trip, spending the following day "receiving visits, and dining in a large company." Father Carroll was left alone to face the unrelenting social onslaught, as the three other delegates broke away for a council of war with General Arnold, General de Woedtke, Colonel Hazen, and Pennsylvania Colonel John Philip De Haas in a separate room. General John Thomas was notably absent, already more than one hundred miles downriver in his rush to the Québec City camp. While the committee was authorized to participate in councils of war, their instructions did not specifically authorize them to act independently of the commanding general. Certainly Brigadier-General Arnold encouraged this hasty meeting in the major-general's absence; with easy access to the committee, he had an opportunity to expedite measures he felt were long overdue.[4]

In council, Colonel Hazen and Arnold urged the necessity of immediately preparing fortifications and vessels to defend the St. Lawrence—a second line of defense upriver from the capital. These long-advised measures had not been undertaken "for a very good Reason, No Money or Men of Skill to do it." Now the council agreed to improve and arm both the old fieldworks that blocked the King's Way at the Jacques-Cartier River, near Cap-Santé, and shore fortifications overlooking the key Richelieu Rapids chokepoint, on the St. Lawrence near Deschambault (see Map 9)—between Trois-Rivières and Pointe-aux-Trembles. In the increasingly likely event that the Continentals were forced to withdraw to these works, they could still "keep possession of 7/8ths of Canada." The council, under the committee's authority, sent General Thomas orders to implement this plan.[5]

The council of war also decided to augment the land defenses with an additional "Number of floating Batteries, Row Galleys, &c. to guard the River." The committee ordered the construction of "six gondolas, of a proper size to carry heavy cannon" at Chambly, augmenting General Arnold's previous request for another armed vessel from Crown-Point. Unbeknownst to the council, General Wooster had similar ideas and had sent Chief-Engineer Antill with soldiers, carpenters, and blacksmiths to fortify Deschambault six days earlier. Steadfast Militia-Captain Maurice Desdevens contributed by surveying Jacques-Cartier and Deschambault, but was stricken with pleurisy after being doused and exhausted while surveying a St. Lawrence island for the defenses; in his subsequently weakened state, he remained inactive for the duration of the campaign.[6]

On 1 May, the day after the council of war, the committee composed its first report to Congress, including short updates on military provisions, troop strength, and the Indian trade. The real focus, however, was the financial situation and its horrendous impact on Continental objectives in Canada. Offering an anecdote from their previous travels, they noted that even "the most trifling service" was unobtainable "without an assurance of instant pay in silver or gold"; their advance-agent from St-Jean had been unable to arrange ferry travel to Montréal with paper money, and was delayed in crossing the river to announce the committee's impending arrival until a passing friend obtained coin for him. The committee only secured its own transportation through Canadian patriot William McCarty, who hired *carioles* on personal credit.

The commissioners reported it was impossible to "expect the continuance of our interest with the people here, who begin to consider the Congress as bankrupt and their cause as desperate." Accordingly, the committee requested an immediate supplement of £20,000 in hard money and grimly added, "till the arrival of money, it seems improper to propose the federal union of this Province with the others."[7]

As the commissioners prepared to face myriad issues, they employed a Canadian secretary, Jonathan Welles—he was an early patriot cohort to Walker and Price, and one of the principal Québec City agitators exiled by Carleton's 22 November proclamation; he would be the only consistent local voice in their meetings. The committee issued its first major political decision on 1 May, opening the fur trade. This was the rare case when the envoys could act just in time, as most trade goods were actually sent upcountry later that month. Before granting passports, though, they required bond to ensure that the merchants did "nothing in the upper Country prejudicial to the Continental interests."[8]

In accordance with the commissioners' instructions to "make a strict and impartial enquiry into the cause of the imprisonment" of several loyalists, on 4 May the committee addressed the case of loyalist Judge John Fraser. One of the late January Montréal exiles, he was currently detained in New York. The committee undoubtedly was given evidence in the loyalist's defense while en route to Canada, while conferring with Schuyler, and perhaps even from Fraser himself. Without consulting General Wooster, the commissioners ordered Fraser's release, granting permission for his return to Montréal on parole. A few days later, they authorized militia officers Dufy-Desauniers and St-Georges Dupré, as well as the defiant Montréal Sheriff Edward William Gray, to be freed from their Fort Chambly imprisonment, again without external consultation.[9]

When he heard of these decisions, General Wooster considered the committee's actions "the greatest insult and indignity" and "inconsistent with good policy." In his view, "it naturally rendered general orders contemptible in the eyes of the officers and soldiers of our own Army, as well as of our enemies." According to Wooster, the troublesome Gray returned to Montréal and "put on his sword and cockade and strutted about like a victorious conqueror," while the other released prisoners went into the country "recruiting for the King's Army among the Canadians."[10]

Thomas Walker, although not in Canada at the time, was similarly disturbed and reported "the utter Confusion & despair of the true friends of Liberty" resulting from the committee's decisions. Allegedly, when citizens approached the commissioners to protest the decisions, the patriots were "haughtily" dismissed, and the committee argued "That it was doing the most substantial wrong to exile a man five hundred miles from his own home only because he is disaffected to the Cause." Canadian officers reportedly "pull'd out their Commissions in this Town & trampled them under their feet swearing they wouldn't accept another Comm[ission] under such men who destroyed by a *Coup de plume* [emphasis in the original] what they had risked their lives for." One of them even "damn'd Mr Chace" to his face. A body of diplomats such as Franklin, Chase, and Carroll ought to have recognized the need to consult Wooster or Thomas before issuing their edicts; although it is highly likely that Hazen, notoriously lenient toward Tories, and perhaps even Arnold, unfamiliar with the specific cases in question, may have recommended their selected course of action. "Arbitrary" policy changes were a poor way to shore up and encourage patriot support before the province's imminent military showdown.[11]

While handling fur-trade and loyalist issues in that first week of May, the committee also resolved a minor Continental command issue — this time in favor of a Canadian patriot. Both Colonel Hazen and Connecticut Lieutenant-Colonel Nathaniel Buell separately had been given command of the St-Jean and Chambly region, the former from Arnold and the latter from Schuyler. On 30 April, Arnold recognized the conflict but stood by his appointment, deeming that with Hazen's knowledge of the local terrain, habitants, and the French language, "a more usefull Man could not be employed" there. Buell came to Montréal on 1 May, and after a "warm" five-day spat with Arnold on the issue, the committee was forced to intervene, concurring with the general.[12]

In miscellaneous logistics tasks, the delegates subsequently consulted Hazen about creating Richelieu Valley supply magazines and appointed Canadian William McCarty as deputy quartermaster at St-Jean. On 8 May, they hosted a council of Indian deputies in Montréal, even though such matters were not officially under their purview. In this case, the Indians only delivered "confirmation of their former promises" to remain neutral.[13]

The predominant, recurring focus of the commissioner's activities, though, continued to be money. By 6 May, they harped on the "necessity of a speedy supply of hard money," stressing the difficulty of keeping troops under "proper disciplin without paying them regularly." Supplies, otherwise obtainable in Canada, were out of reach without "recourse to violences . . . which indispose and irritate the minds of the people." They repeated their harsh, but realistic recommendation: "If hard money cannot be procured and forwarded with dispatch to Canada, it would be adviseable, in our opinion, to withdraw our army & fortify the passes on the lakes." Two days later, their next report focused on the universal lack of credit. Not only were the commissioners unable to borrow money publicly or privately, but they also learned that patriot Canadians had anticipated that the committee would bring a considerable amount of money to pay off debts. They observed that the resultant "Disappointment has discouraged every Body, and established an Opinion that none [no money] is to be had, or that the Congress has not Credit enough in their own Colonies to procure it." Again, a minimum of £20,000 was absolutely vital to reestablish Continental credit in Canada and make the United Colonies "respected instead of being hated by the people." Back in Philadelphia, President John Hancock had already warned the New England colonies, "In order to give Success to the Expedition into Canada, Nothing is so much wanted at this Juncture, as a Supply of Specie," seeking their immediate financial assistance; but in May 1776 there simply was no ready cash in Continental hands, not in Philadelphia or Montréal.[14]

By 8 May, so soon after ordering the release of prominent Tory prisoners, Franklin, Chase, and Carroll finally began to understand the loyalist threat in their midst, seeing firsthand how their enemies exploited every patriot weakness to stir up both citizens and habitants. On a daily basis, the commissioners learned of "Intimations of Plots hatching and Insurrections intended for Expelling Us, on the first News of the Arrival of a British Army"; yet the sole committee optimist, Charles Carroll, still wanted to believe the situation was salvageable; with "a just & conciliating conduct" the United Colonies might "reestablish our affairs in this Colony and fix the affections of this People to the Colonies."[15]

While Franklin, Chase, and Charles Carroll were heavily engaged with committee business, the other two members of the Congressional delegation were struggling to contribute. No flood of Catholics sought out Father John Carroll—certainly not the clergy. Upon arriving in Montréal, Carroll provided Jesuit Father Floquet with a letter of introduction from Philadelphia's Father Ferdinand Farmer, but still met with a reserved reception. Floquet did not invite Carroll to stay at the Jesuit home, and hosted him only once for dinner. Somewhat surprisingly though, Vicar-General Montgolfier actually granted Father Carroll permission to say Mass in the city—undoubtedly a courtesy to a missionary in good standing, despite the Marylander's current choice of companions. All evidence, however, indicates that Father Carroll accomplished extremely little in Canada.[16]

In addition, some of the anticipated benefits of Father Carroll's embassy were offset by another Catholic priest visiting Montréal from the lower colonies—Tory priest John McKenna. The Irish "priest chaplain" of New York's Mohawk Valley Highlanders fled to Canada as a refugee in October 1775. By his mere presence, McKenna was a counterpoint to Carroll's message; the same "freedom loving" people who sent the Jesuit from Maryland had also driven the Irish priest out of New York. Coincidentally, McKenna was well protected from patriot retribution during the Continental occupation, being friends with Moses Hazen and dining regularly with Wooster.[17]

Printer Fleury Mesplet faced even greater challenges than the others. With a ten-day head start on the main delegation, Mesplet and his little company reached Fort George by 8 April, where they waited for the printing press and equipment's arrival on five heavy wagons, and for their subsequent transfer to bateaux for the rest of the journey. Cruising up Lake George as soon as it opened on the eighteenth, they caught fair winds to pass St-Jean by the twenty-second. Frustratingly, while transiting the river rapids above Chambly, the cargo bateaux "shipped so great a quantity of water that they were almost lost." When Mesplet reached Montréal on 6 May and inventoried his equipment, he "found a quantity of goods spoiled"; yet most important, the press arrived intact. Through his dedicated efforts, Mesplet delivered the United Colonies a new tool in the war for Canadian loyalties.[18]

Mesplet's first hurdle in Montréal was to find an appropriate print shop building. Until the master printer found "a house suitable to fullfil the Intentions of the Respectable Congress," the printer and his team were "put up" in a tavern, with all the printing equipment. Finally, after Mesplet found available shop space, the press was readied for operation on 18 May. Despite charming oral history that the press was set up in the cellars of the Château de Ramezay, by Mesplet's own account, the first Montréal print work was done in his shop near the market square, several blocks away. By that time, though, there was little opportunity for the press to influence Canadian sentiments. The concept of a "Printer to Congress at Montreal" was yet another example of a good idea implemented too late to be effective.[19]

=====

Along with all the other obstacles, Continental leadership was horribly disjointed and unsynchronized in the critical first week of May. The committee's political activities were being directed 150 miles from General Thomas's military headquarters. General Arnold's Montréal posting further complicated the issue: he encouraged the diplomat commissioners to issue military orders independent of the commanding general, and Thomas was unable to tap the brigadier's vast Canadian field experience. Meanwhile, Wooster, who had made almost all of the province's key political decisions, was at Holland House, unavailable to consult with the committee; the most experienced Continental voices were at the wrong ends of the province.

The Northern Army's two veteran generals, Arnold and Wooster, received vastly different treatment in May. With no Canadian command remaining after Thomas's arrival, and little encouragement to linger, Wooster prepared to head home to Connecticut. General Arnold, however, impressed the Congressional commissioners: Charles Carroll observed that "General Arnold is the Man," John Carroll held the general in the "highest esteem," and Samuel Chase observed that Arnold was "brave, active & well acquainted in that Country." Similarly impressed with Arnold's reputation, Thomas asked the young brigadier to join him outside the capital, if his wounds permitted, to serve as an experienced, dynamic right-hand man.[20]

On 2 May, General Thomas finally finished his long journey from Cambridge to the Plains of Abraham. The general was shocked to see the poor state of his army: "a Few more than two thousand Men, & Twelve Hundred of which are unfit for Duty, with the Small Pox, &c." Amazingly, six hundred were volunteers, extended past their enlistments to keep up the numbers until reinforcements arrived—another testament to Wooster's underappreciated leadership—and the meager force was still stretched exceedingly thin around the siege lines, Ile-d'Orléans, and the south-shore parishes.[21]

A day later, General Thomas was given the opportunity to witness a long-planned Continental attack. The fireship *Peggy* was finally poised to launch. On a brisk evening, about an hour after sunset, the garrison spied a ship approaching from downriver, headed for Lower Town. Initially, the defenders "apprehend'd She was from Europe and the cry passed thro' the town as such." Carleton ordered the guns to hold fire as picket boats hailed the mysterious ship; when no answer came, the garrison was called to arms and batteries commenced fire on the ship. The brigantine "instantly broke out in a prodigeous Smoak, followed by a great flame, on which all her rigging and sails catched fire," but the captain miscalculated winds and tides. She ran to shore about two hundred yards downstream from her target and "burned to the Water's edge," with tremendous explosions of "shells grenades, petards, pots a feu, &c." While Governor Carleton theorized that the rebels "intended a general assault had they succeeded in setting Fire to the Ships and lower Town," the Continentals were actually unprepared and undermanned to exploit any success after sparking chaos in the capital port. It was a flashy but meaningless effort.[22]

Although unavailable to him at the moment, General Thomas had a host of reinforcements headed his way. In addition to the units ordered by Congress in January 1776, many of which were en route on the King's Way, the general knew that another brigade also was on its way from Cambridge, under General William Thompson. Congress had directed it to Canada on 25 March, the troops becoming available after the recent British evacuation from Boston. Another brigade under General John Sullivan subsequently had been ordered north from Washington's New York camp on 25 April, after Congress received news of the March Quebec District uprising and read Hazen's despondent 1 April letter. The two new brigades totaled more than six thousand men, but were stretched in a three-hundred-mile chain from the Hudson Valley to the St. Lawrence. These reinforcements, intended to inspire respect for the cause and demonstrate commitment to the Canadian populace, seemed more likely to show the pitiful depths to which the United Colonies had already fallen, especially for those remembering French and British regulars of the last war. Jean-Baptiste Badeaux commented on the "poor . . . nude and sickly" Yankees passing through Trois-Rivières; and he felt the diverse, motley soldiers of Colonel Charles Burrall's Connecticut Regiment represented the dregs of society. Equipment-wise, one of Sullivan's men commented that his unit had "fowling-pieces of different sizes and bores and few of them had bayonets"—unimpressive, but typical of Continental units at the time.[23]

After taking a few days to assess his situation, General Thomas called a council of war at Holland House on the afternoon of 5 May, attended by General Wooster and several colonels. The weak force was so widely dispersed "that not more than 300 men could be rallied to the relief of any" one detachment — sizeable Ministerial reinforcements could sweep right through them. The logistics situation was no better, as Thomas noted, "the French Inhabitants much disaffected, so that supplies of any kind were obtained with great difficulty from them."[24]

With these factors clearly evident, General Thomas made the only logical choice, unanimously supported by the council. After "mature deliberation," and armed with the Congressional commissioners' guidance to fortify Jacques-Cartier and Deschambault, the general resolved to send the several hundred sick troops upriver "as quick as possible" and to call in the various detachments "in the Night of the next Day," which would be the evening of 6 May. The army, "as soon as it could conveniently be done," would regroup at "some important posts where there would be a prospect of resisting with success."[25]

Later that evening, ominous news reached the camp. Three signal fires were reported on the distant south shore, near St-Michel parish; more details arrived by express messenger — five British ships were traveling up the St. Lawrence. The Ministerial relief force was arriving at absolutely the worst possible moment for General Thomas's army; some elements were already preparing to withdraw, while others were unaware of the council of war's decision to retreat. It was a recipe for complete chaos.[26]

During these tumultuous events, General Wooster, with his aides and baggage, departed from Holland House. By Wooster's own account, Thomas sent him to rally the soon-to-be-retreating forces at Jacques-Cartier, although it seems the Connecticut general was prepared to leave the camp before the council of war, since his Yankee troops all had completed their service and Thomas had replaced him in command. Behind Québec City's wall, the defenders heard about the imminent Continental withdrawal before they were even aware of their relief force's approach. In the predawn hours of 6 May, a woman approached the Palais Gate, reporting that the rebels "were in extreme confusion loading all the carts they could find with baggage[,] arms &c.," and "that Mr Wooster was gone off."[27]

═══

The relief fleet's May arrival capped a five-month British effort to send a force to recover Quebec Province. Secretary of State George Germain spearheaded plans that sent Major-General John Burgoyne with eight British regiments, a full complement of siege artillery, and at least three thousand German auxiliary troops. Ships, carrying the advance elements of this massive army, approached Ile-d'Orléans on Sunday, 5 May. Passing a parish church, probably St-François, the sailors and soldiers saw "a great Number of Inhabitants coming out of Church," who "Crowded to the beach" upon seeing the ships. The lead vessel hoisted its colors and fired a gun signal — the ship's captain fully expecting that habitants would flock to come on board; instead, when they recognized the squadron's identity "they all dispersed," so that the soldiers and sailors "could hardly see a Creature on shore." With this cold reception, the British force pressed on to the capital.[28]

In the early dawn of 6 May, the citizens and defenders of Québec City scrambled in "inconceivable joy . . . people half drest ran down to the Grand battery to feast their eyes with the sight of a ship of war displaying the Union flag." Carleton called the garrison to arms and assembled them on the parade, announcing that after months of isolation, "the Volunteers of the British and Canadian Militia shoud join the troops and sailors to attack the rebels." At about noon, roughly 850 men, including 200 newly arrived soldiers and marines, marched from the city gates with a tremendously confident air, ready to drive the miserable rebels back to their homes. "The little Army extended itself quite across the plains, making a fine appearance," yet found no meaningful opposition. The rebels were in the midst of their retreat, and after the slightest show of force, "the Plains were soon cleared of those Plunderers." The main British corps returned to the city at around four in the afternoon, as Colonel Maclean led detachments to "examine the houses w[h]ere the rebels had been Quarter'd . . . to bring in all the Sick and Wounded" and gather abandoned Continental arms. The two Royal Navy escort ships sailed upriver to destroy any rebel vessels they found. While Carleton expedited the rebels' flight, he made no effort to cut off their retreat.[29]

In the rebel camp, anarchy had reigned as soon as the Continentals recognized their situation that morning. Although Thomas issued retreat orders to "as many of the troops . . . as time would permit," it was really "every man for himself." Colonel Porter's Massachusetts Regiment covered the main body's withdrawal, exchanging a few out-of-range shots with Carleton's advance party; yet with the cautious enemy approach, the Continental rear guard slipped away before the British Army plodded to the tree line, at the edge of the Plains.[30]

Looking around the rebel camp, Carleton's men found overwhelming evidence of the Continentals' great confusion and violent panic. Many rebels left with just the clothes on their backs, in many cases even dropping their muskets in flight. The British Army "found the roads strewed with arms, cartridges, clothes, bread, pork, &c."; artillery pieces were feebly spiked with "only a Nail put into the Vent which was easyly drawn from thence." In Holland-House, British soldiers found "the Commanding officers Dinner which he had left at the fire" and "orderly books and papers."[31]

The Continental flight was hasty and disorderly. Colonel Porter's men retreated about fifteen miles before halting that night. The bulk of the army was even farther upstream. Yet some Continental detachments—at Beauport, Ile-d'Orléans, and the south shore—lagged behind or never received retreat orders. On the night of 5 May, after the council of war and word of the enemy ships' approach, south-shore commander Colonel Nicholson "precipitately saved himself in his batteau instead of bringing off his men as he was commanded," leaving 270 Continentals to "shift for themselves" at their outposts. This was such an egregiously negligent act, even in the face of mass chaos, that Congress eventually called for Nicholson's investigation, by name.[32]

With the rising sun illuminating the Ministerial relief fleet on the sixth, the abandoned Continentals at Pointe-Lévy and on Ile-d'Orléans saw that it was clearly time to retreat, with or without orders. After a failed effort to cross the river and rejoin the main army, they fled along the south bank, with two Royal Navy warships periodically harassing them with fire. Continentals posted northeast of the capital, in places such as Beauport and even St-Roch suburb, had "no Alternative but to form a circle thro' the Woods" to avoid the enemy deployed on the Plains and reach the King's Way to join the retreat.[33]

Pierre Ayotte and some Canadian Continentals never had any warning that Ministerial relief forces were present. Approaching Pointe-Lévy on regular business, Ayotte was "taken by surprise" by Carleton's troops soon after the main rebel retreat. The dynamic Continental captain, so critical to Canadian patriot support in the district, had been forgotten by his command and became one of the few healthy Continentals captured near Québec City. He was promptly led to imprisonment in the capital.[34]

The war for Quebec Province entered a drastically different stage on 6 May.

Somewhat symbolically, Captain Ayotte's capture signaled the end of the ideologically focused campaign for the province. Many Canadians continued to oppose the Royal government, sometimes in surprisingly large numbers, but Continental leaders no longer focused on drawing the Canadians into the union; the principal and overriding objective was now the United Colonies' immediate defense — stopping the enemy before he penetrated into New York. The Continentals conclusively had lost the strategic initiative. One of the loyalists noted: "Thus was the Country round Quebec freed from very troublesome neighbours, a misguided people, led by designing men, real enemys to the libertys of their Country, tho' they had taken upon them the specious title of the Assertor of American Rights."[35]

Chapter 22

THE SAD NECESSITY

OF ABANDONING CANADA

*Military Collapse and the End
of the Canadian Continental Experience*

Our Affairs have taken a Strange turn Since our Arrival. The Canadians
are Flocking by Hundreds to take a part with us. | *General John Sullivan to
General George Washington, Sorel, 5 June 1776*

The junction of the Canadians with the Colonies, an object which brought
us into this Country is now at an End, let us quit them & Secure our
own Country before it is too late. | *General Benedict Arnold to General John
Sullivan, Chambly, 13 June 1776*

"The poor inhabitants" were confused by the Continental collapse on 6 May.
Seeing "the roads full of people, shamefully flying," it seemed the rebel force
was abandoning Canada. Rather than commit to either side at this point,
General Thomas reported habitants did "not afford us the least assistance, but
kept themselves concealed." Supplies were difficult to obtain, and at numerous
north-shore tributaries, the army found "No conveniences for ferrying our
troops . . . except a canoe or two, and these were rare."[1]

Retreating Continental troops began to regain order at Deschambault
on 7 May, having already fled past the rudimentary landward-focused
Jacques-Cartier works. As officers collected the "poor fugitives," General
Thomas arrived to call a council of war. Assessing their lack of provisions,
insufficient artillery, and overall miserable condition, the commander decided
to withdraw further—to south-shore Sorel, eighty miles upriver. Shortly after
the council, Thomas received word that Arnold was expediting reinforcements
from Montréal, prompting the major-general to keep eight hundred men at

Deschambault and Jacques-Cartier, who could "proceed up or down" the river as circumstances dictated, while the rest of the army retreated. Over the next few days, General de Woedtke reassembled the bulk of the Northern Army around Sorel's old fortifications where, unsurprisingly, the troops still showed a "want of confidence."[2]

Now that General Thomas had demonstrated intent to hold at Deschambault, he was joined by a handful of fervent *Canadien* supporters. Some furnished provisions, while others dug up old French cannon, hidden since the last war, and transported them to the Continental entrenchments. Having overcome their initial shock, these habitants exerted themselves to help keep government forces at bay.[3]

Giving Thomas time, Governor Carleton pursued a cautious course from Québec City, too timid by most loyalist accounts. Consolidating his power, he awaited more reinforcements before advancing his army, but unleashed his ships to harass retreating rebels and "take or destroy" rebel vessels. The Continentals' *Maria*—under Captain Goforth—and *Gaspée* were surprised near Pointe-aux-Trembles; their crews abandoned the ships on the shore, clumsily holing and setting them afire.[4]

One of Carleton's first post-relief acts was to send agents to neighboring parishes, encouraging the habitants to bring goods to the city. Locals came, offering token items for sale, more a peace offering than a business exchange. The governor also implemented an extremely generous policy toward the rebels. On 10 May, he instructed militia officers to gather "his Majesty's deluded subjects of the neighbouring Provinces labouring under wounds & divers disorders . . . dispers'd in the adjacent woods & parishes," promising the rebels that "as soon as their health is restor'd, they shall have free liberty to return to their respective Provinces." In contrast, Bishop Briand remained steadfast in his strict pronouncements against those Canadians who had committed "rebellious crimes and disobedience," insisting they be denied the sacraments until the time "When the King will have issued a pardon, amnesty, remission."[5]

In Montréal, the Committee to Canada digested the news of the army's collapse, recognizing that "retreat was inevitable," but expected that the army would hold at Deschambault or Sorel. Politically, though, they saw their mission at an end. On 10 May they informed Congress, "We are afraid it will not be in our power to render our Country any farther services in this Colony." Chase and the Carrolls initially stayed in the city, worried that an immediate departure might "discourage our troops & friends in the country." The ailing

Doctor Franklin, however, left for Philadelphia on the eleventh in the company of Martha Walker. That odd pair hardly had exited the Island of Montréal when Father Carroll reconsidered his position; having clearly become irrelevant, he would rush to catch Franklin at St-Jean. On the twelfth, fearing a British ship might run up the river and block them in Montréal, Charles Carroll and Samuel Chase relocated to south-shore Laprairie. As Franklin and Father Carroll headed south, several active Canadian patriots adopted a similar course. Within the next couple of weeks, Hector McNeill, William Holton, and John Halsted all made their way to St-Jean and on to the United Colonies.[6]

Having exited the Montréal political scene, Chase and Charles Carroll focused on military matters from the south bank. The somewhat panicked two-man rump committee advised Arnold, "If the Inhabitants of Montreal should break their Capitulation, & molest the Garrison or any of our Friends," he should "instantly seize the principal Citizens and keep them as Hostages." Addressing the nagging issue of provisions, they authorized Arnold and Thomas to confiscate supplies if necessary, offering that "force regulated by a proper Authority" would "prevent the horrors arising from the Licentiousness of a Starving & of course uncontroullable Soldiery." The committee offered a slew of other military recommendations during this time, and all the generals save Arnold interpreted them as orders. In the process, Chase and Carroll muddied an already confusing command situation; the conscientious Major-General Thomas reacted as much to the committee's operational inputs, generated one hundred miles from the front, as he did to his own on-the-scene judgment.[7]

———

Adding to the confusion, another Continental general entered Canada on 13 May — Brigadier William Thompson, at the head of his four-regiment brigade. The fifty-year-old, Irish-born Pennsylvanian, apparently sensing that real authority rested with the committee and Arnold, led his vanguard straight to Montréal rather than joining Major-General Thomas. After conferring with Chase and Carroll, the brigadier left the city on 14 May, ordered to take almost sixteen hundred men to Deschambault. The rump committee informed General Thomas of this latest decision, reminded him of "the great Importance of Jacques Cartier & De Chambault," and added their wish that he and Thompson would "exert the utmost of their Skill and Abilities to defend those passes to the last Extreamity."[8]

General Thomas, however, was already acting on the commissioners' long-distance guidance from three days earlier, when they assured him he was the "best Judge" for military decisions. Accordingly, he had withdrawn his forward-most troops to Trois-Rivières; the army was ill equipped to improve the fortifications at Deschambault and Jacques-Cartier, and was drawing inadequate provisions at those posts. As his troops moved upriver, Thomas visited Sorel to evaluate the main army's situation and hold a council of war.[9]

In the ensuing chaos after their Québec City collapse, Continentals continued to act as an "Army out of Temper & without Controul" along the King's Way, especially around Trois-Rivières, and local Canadian patriots also saw an opportunity to exact vengeance on their neighbors. Jean-Baptiste Badeaux lamented that loyalists were "between death and life" as "fanatical" habitants rose up, intent on pillaging, arresting, or perhaps even murdering leaders such as Militia-Colonel Tonnancour and Legislative Councilor Gugy. In two parishes near L'Assomption — St-Sulpice and Repentigny — emboldened partisans "ignominiously" drove their outspokenly loyalist priests to the rebel camp at Sorel, hoping the *curés* would be taken to the United Colonies as prisoners. L'Assomption's Abbot Pierre Huet-de-la-Valinière and Colonel Moses Hazen both intervened to secure the detained priests' release.[10]

As General Thomas gathered officers at Sorel on 17 May for another council of war, Charles Carroll and Samuel Chase showed their overall exasperation. Chase vented his frustrations in a spectacular letter to Richard Henry Lee, observing that although ten battalions had been sent to Canada, they arrived with horrendously inadequate provisions. The exasperated Marylander concluded, "Congress are not a fit Body to act as a Council of War. They are too large, too slow and their Resolutions can never be kept secret." Meanwhile, Charles Carroll focused his ire on General Wooster, "the ruin of our affairs in this country." Carroll undoubtedly had been prejudiced against the general during his visits with Schuyler en route to Canada and had heard the many complaints of Wooster's Montréal foes — eagerly proffered by both loyalists and patriots; plus, he and the other committee members fundamentally opposed Wooster's "illiberal" approach to Canada's Tory problems. The Marylander further lamented that Wooster had permitted his lackeys to abuse their authority in Montréal the whole winter. The commissioners were spent, reporting "as the possession of this country must finally be decided by the Sword; we think our stay here no longer of service to the public"; but they would "wait with Impatience" for further guidance.[11]

Even without pressure from Carleton, the Northern Army continued to implode. The endemic lack of provisions, smallpox, and chaotic command sapped Continental strength, even as more troops arrived. After meeting with subordinates again on 20 May, General Thomas decided to withdraw all remaining troops from the north shore and concentrate everything at Sorel. Generals Thomas, Arnold, de Woedtke, Thompson, and even the still-lingering Wooster all settled into the confines of the lower Richelieu Valley.[12]

After only a couple of days at Sorel, General Arnold was recalled to Montréal, to handle a developing upcountry enemy attack. On 15 May, Colonel Bedel, commander of the western posts, received intelligence during a meeting in the Caughnawaga village indicating that a loyalist force was finally approaching the Les-Cèdres post, known as Fort Cedars. He rushed to deliver the news to Montréal, triggering immediate action by commissioners Chase and Carroll, in coordination with the acting city garrison commander, Massachusetts Colonel John Paterson. They called for Arnold's immediate return and dispatched Major Henry Sherburne with an additional 150 men to augment the three-hundred-man Fort Cedars garrison. Bedel initially joined this reinforcement, but became so weakened by an emerging case of smallpox that he remained bedridden in Lachine while Sherburne pressed on.[13]

Back on 12 May, the long-prepared upcountry Ministerial force had begun its 120-mile march from Fort Oswegatchie toward Montréal. Captain George Forster commanded the expedition, consisting of forty British soldiers, eleven Canadian volunteers, and more than two hundred Indians. Hearing of Québec City's relief, the party increased its pace toward Les-Cèdres (see Map 8) on the seventeenth.[14]

On the morning of 19 May, Forster's men approached and engaged Fort Cedars. Local seigneur Jean-Baptiste Testard-de-Montigny joined them with another thirty loyalist Canadians and was promptly sent to intercept Sherburne and his Continental reinforcements. Meanwhile, the leadership at Fort Cedars cracked, even though their losses had been negligible in intermittent firefights. Threatening an Indian massacre if the Continentals did not immediately yield, Forster persuaded acting commander Major Isaac Butterfield to swiftly surrender. The following day, Major Sherburne was ambushed after a cautious crossing from the Island of Montréal. After "bravely" fighting an "obstinate engagement" for about an hour, Sherburne was informed of But-terfield's surrender, began to run short of ammunition, and found his retreat blocked; he was convinced to surrender as well. Forster netted 487 Continental prisoners, including ten Canadian Continentals under Lieutenant Jean-François Hamtramck. In less than two days' fighting at the Battle of The Cedars, the British captain's weaker, but more audacious party had eliminated the Continentals' western Laurentian defenses.[15]

Forster rushed to exploit his advantage, reuniting with Montigny and crossing to the Island of Montréal. The combined loyalist force grew to almost five hundred men as more Canadian volunteers joined. On the morning of 24 May, they advanced from Pointe-Claire, eighteen miles from their ultimate objective, the city of Montréal. A few "reputable" Montrealers stopped them short of Lachine village, warning that Arnold was "entrenched" there with "six hundred men with six pieces of cannon" and might have fifteen hundred troops before nightfall. In a loyalist council of war, the party decided to withdraw back to Pointe-Claire. By the time Forster reached that parish, about eighty loyalists and many Indians had slipped away, at which point the rest decided to retreat from the Island of Montréal. In reality, Arnold had assembled only about 350 Continentals at Lachine; however, they were well posted in the strong village of stone warehouses and sturdy wood fences.[16]

Hearing of Forster's retreat, Arnold pressed for aggressive pursuit in a late night council of war. Ignoring dissenting officers, the next day he led five hundred men upriver to attack the loyalist corps at Ile-Perrot, having been augmented by two hundred Caughnawagas and additional troops from Montréal, including two of Hazen's companies. Forster realized he was in a desperate situation; rather than face a battle, which might result in cata-strophic defeat and a potential Indian massacre of the rebel prisoners, the British captain deemed it "expedient" to negotiate a cartel—an accord to transfer the prisoners back into Continental hands—in exchange for his own party's unhindered withdrawal. To ensure the best terms, he slyly reached an agreement with captive Majors Butterfield and Sherburne.[17]

After exchanging fire in the face of an impending attack by Arnold on the evening of 26 May, Forster sent a flag of truce to inform the Continental general of the cartel. Arnold summarily rejected it over an article stating that exchanged Continental prisoners would not "on any pretext whatsoever . . . take up arms against the Government of Great Britain," which was more re-strictive than standard parole terms that lasted only until the released prisoners were administratively "exchanged." Forster agreed to remove it, realizing that he still had a good deal without that article, and the commanders initiated a four-day cease-fire to implement the cartel. Captain Forster's operation had been brilliant. The attack on the Continental rear was particularly well timed and skillfully executed, and might well have shattered the rebel army in Canada if Montréal had been seized. It was only the few Montrealers who fed Forster bad intelligence on his approach to Lachine who stemmed the loyalist tide—although Arnold's energetic defense may have done so if given the chance. Once he lost the initiative, Forster adeptly used the cartel to secure his men's safe retreat.[18]

One significant secondary effect of The Cedars engagements involved the Canadian Continentals. While the cartel did not specifically address the ten prisoners of war from Hazen's regiment, Forster, prompted by Claude Lorimier, treated them separately, "to be considered even in a worse light than deserters from his majesty's armies." All the Canadian prisoners, except Lieutenant Hamtramck, were put in irons to "terrify" other habitants away from the rebel cause; none of the "American" Continentals, including Butterfield and Sherburne, attempted to intervene. Although these Canadian soldiers were eventually released, Colonel Hazen was justifiably irate on principle. How could other Continental officers leave his men as a potential "Sacrifice to the Vengeance of a cruel Enemy?" The colonel reacted by giving his men leave to return home, for their own safety and their families' welfare.[19]

Meanwhile, a vindictive Arnold unleashed Continental troops on loyalist properties in western Island of Montréal parishes. The Continentals burned Montigny's estate near Ste-Anne, including the inactive stone Fort Senneville, ravaged Lorimier's mother's property, and plundered homes in Ste-Geneviève, home to several men who had joined Forster's party; in an unprecedented move, soldiers even marauded the churches in that parish and Pointe-Claire. Only resistance from Hazen and Pennsylvania Colonel De Haas kept Arnold from vengefully razing the Lac-des-Deux-Montagnes Indian villages. As a whole, this pattern was a significant divergence from Arnold's lenient treatment of the south-shore Quebec District parishes after the March insurrection; but the St-Pierre affair had been a decisive patriot victory, and much had changed in Canada over the past two months.[20]

Like so many of his troops on this campaign, Major-General John Thomas entered his own battle against smallpox on 20 May. He temporarily resigned his command to General Thompson, the nearest general. Commissioner Carroll noted that Thompson put the Sorel camp discipline "on a better footing," yet there was still "much confusion, extreme disorder and negligence." Habitants were still being abused and harassed, prompting Thompson to threaten offending troops and to once again encourage officers to prevent unfortunate incidents. At Chambly, General de Woedtke took the extra measure of inviting injured habitants to bring complaints directly to him.[21]

Meanwhile, Samuel Chase and Charles Carroll returned to Montréal for one last round of business. On 26 May, they ordered James Price and William McCarty to visit merchants, requesting delivery of "What the soldiers are in immediate want of." In exchange, the Continentals pledged "the faith of the United Colonies for payment." If businessmen refused, Chase and Carroll added, "our necessity requires, that force should be used to compel a Delivery." Thereafter, the commissioners decided it was time to leave the province, planning one more council of war before departing.[22]

General Thomas was slowly losing his bout with the smallpox. Reports of his demise began to spread on the twenty-ninth, although he actually passed away at Chambly on 1 June. Even though Thompson was notionally in charge, Chase and Carroll observed that "there is not that good understanding & free communication of sentiments between the General Officers." Canadian Deputy Quartermaster William McCarty wrote of the Canadians' anxiety about uncoordinated Continental "Maneouvers, our Marching One day to St. Johns & the next back again &c. Orders Contradicting Orders." Yet when Thomas, on his deathbed, called for General Wooster to take the army's reins, the commissioners intervened. Having irresoluble issues with the old Connecticut general's leadership, Chase and Carroll deemed him "unfit, totally unfit, to Command . . . & conduct the war," and they informed Wooster that "his stay in this Colony is unnecessary & even prejudicial to our Affairs."[23]

Despite the commissioners' pronouncements, as the army's senior general in the field, Wooster still presided over the 30 May Chambly council of war; Chase and Carroll, Generals Arnold, Thompson, and de Woedtke, and thirteen colonels — including James Livingston and Moses Hazen — all participated. They resolved "that, if practicable," it was in the United Colonies' interests "to keep Canada," but since it was not "practicable or prudent" to hold Deschambault, they would keep Sorel as their forward post. Arnold was also directed to lead five hundred troops from Montréal, to attack Forster as soon as the cartel's suspension of hostilities expired. Charles Carroll noted that officers unofficially discussed preparations "to make an orderly retreat out of Canada." The generals also concurred that Arnold was the acting commander in Canada, until the senior Brigadier-General John Sullivan arrived in the next few days. When the council adjourned, the commissioners said their farewells and headed for St-Jean, sailing off on 1 June with "no Expectation of keeping any footing" in Canada, barring a tremendous change of circumstances.[24]

Seeing that Congress's best politicians had given up hope, leading patriots James Price, William Haywood, and committee secretary Jonathan Welles all emulated their exit. With Thomas Walker still traveling through New York, the leading Old Subject Canadian patriots had all conceded the Canadian revolution as lost and abandoned the province; they could only hope to find new homes in the United Colonies and recover their business there. "French" Canadian Christophe Pélissier headed south, too; but François Cazeau remained in Montréal, ready to take his chances if Carleton returned. The soldiers Antill, Livingston, Hazen, and Duggan persevered as long as the Northern Army was in Quebec, as did a few of their soldiers; but most Canadian Continental rank and file left camp—with or without authorization—to rejoin their families as Ministerial reconquest seemed inevitable.

General Carleton still was in no rush to chase the rebels from the province, though; he seemed to give the misguided colonists ample opportunity to see the error of their ways, and return home without unnecessary battles. On 27 and 28 May, the main Ministerial army sailed up to the capital in thirty-nine troop ships—giving Carleton overwhelming numerical superiority in Canada, through regular forces alone. The governor did not call for militia mobilization, but placed parishes on call—a notional commitment that would keep the unreliable habitants out of compromising military situations and preclude rural protests. The ensuing support from the parishes was determined primarily by militia-captains' initiative. The only notable direct local support came from an unspecified number of "stout, zealous, Voluntier Canadian Boatmen" who helped the King's ships slowly navigate up the St. Lawrence.[25]

Meanwhile in the west, General Arnold reached Lachine in the first week of June to find that Forster had fled upriver, out of reach. Returning to Montréal, the general found new guidance from General Schuyler, further complicating the already confusing command picture. The major-general directed a pair of measures to improve the Continental position in case of an exodus from the province. First, he called for "bringing away from Montreal all the goods" possible, either by "pledging the faith of the Colonies for the payment" or confiscation, if necessary. The other call was more radical; Arnold was to "seize and send into the Colonies, all such persons as have been notoriously disaffected to them," specifically "all the prisoners that are in Canada either upon their parole or otherwise," countermanding the commissioners' divisive early May decisions.[26]

Arnold focused on the provisions aspect of the orders, reporting that most Tories had already "absconded." With good commercial intelligence, the general dexterously dispatched Continentals to gather useful matériel from Lachine fur-trade warehouses and Montréal merchants' stores, and promptly shipped the goods to Chambly. Most Canadians declined to accept written promises of payment, fearing they might be a liability to have on hand when the government recovered the city.[27]

Arnold's efficiency ended as soon as the goods left Montréal, though. At Chambly, Hazen "refused to take custody of the confiscated stores," and Arnold's escort detachment left them "heaped in piles" on the shore of Chambly basin. Poorly inventoried goods were "stolen or plundered"; and once moved to St-Jean, many parcels were "broken open, plundered and mixed together in the greatest confusion, and great part missing." Arnold blamed Hazen, but a growing number of rivals and opponents pointed fingers at the general, implying that he intended the goods to be used for his own profit.[28]

On 1 June, the very day that commissioners Chase and Carroll sailed south from St-Jean, a fleet of "about two Hundred Vessels," looking "something like the Grecian Fleet going to the Seage of Troy," came the other way bearing Brigadier-General John Sullivan and regiments from Pennsylvania, New Hampshire, and New Jersey. The thirty-six-year-old Sullivan was young and inexperienced, but energetic—one of New Hampshire's most active patriots. A successful lawyer before the crisis, he rapidly progressed from provincial major to the Provincial Assembly, and then to Philadelphia for both Continental Congresses. He was appointed a Continental brigadier-general in the first June 1775 list and served with the main army under Washington until receiving orders for Canada.[29]

Landing at St-Jean, Sullivan was quite surprised to find that command of the entire army had devolved to him. He spent his first day divining "the true state of affairs" in Canada. He soon concluded that "no one thing is right; everything is in the utmost confusion, and almost everyone frightened at they know not what." Sullivan made a lightning tour of Chambly and Montréal before speeding to the main army camp at Sorel.[30]

There was one very significant and highly unexpected development result-ing from Sullivan's arrival—a dramatic shift in local *Canadien* sentiments. As soon as he landed at St-Jean, a local militia-captain greeted him with an offer to bring out three parishes of men, some six hundred habitants, ask-ing only for provisions and arms. Local patriot leaders confessed that their earlier "Disaffection" from Continental support had been because the army's "Exertions were so feeble that they doubted much" of its long-term prospects and its "Ability to protect them." Now, with a massive influx of Continental reinforcements, Sullivan reported that the Richelieu River banks were "Lined with men Women & Children Leaping & Clapping their hands for Joy" at his arrival. After a few days in country, the general conferred with militia officers who offered not only to raise hundreds of habitants, but also to provide flour for the Northern Army. Volunteers came from as far away as Three Rivers District's north shore Yamachiche parish, and Sullivan issued Continental commissions to several regional patriot leaders.[31]

Yamachiche's Larose was one of the new captains, authorized by Sullivan to raise an "Independent Company." The zealous patriot was ordered to "act in concert with the American Troops, in opposition to the Ministerial Army in Canada." Colonel Jeremiah Duggan also returned to the scene. Within days, he had "Raised & armed upward of 200 men" for his Canadian Ranger companies. Yet he was almost immediately distracted by a spat with Moses Hazen—apparently a popular Continental activity at the time—and sub-sequently refused further service until a court of inquiry resolved an "un-just aspersion" made by Hazen. Duggan temporarily gave Chambly Captain Théodore Chartier command over his recruits, while the colonel publicly bragged of his own accomplishments and disparaged Hazen's value and com-mitment—Canadian Continental leadership was a disaster.[32]

Local partisans stepped up, though, transporting wheat and flour to the Continentals and asking for "nothing in return but Certificates." By 6 June,

Sullivan proclaimed he had "no Doubt of the General Attachment of the Canadians," noting that "perhaps as many according to their Numbers are Really in our favour as in Some other Colonies upon the Continent." Sullivan also received new support from Congress — £1,662 of specie and resolves proclaiming the "absolute necessity of keeping possession" of Canada, which Sullivan said "gave new Life to our Canadian friends."[33]

The local patriot leaders' resurgence brought a growing number of habitant complaints against their "obnoxiously" loyalist priests, whom they wished "to be Secured." Even the friendly Caughnawaga Indians reported that *Canadien* commitment was being moderated "through the influence of their Priests." Sullivan refrained from acting however, writing to Washington that he would "Touch this String with great Tenderness at pres[en]t," knowing the average habitant's dedication to the Church.[34]

The new face of Canadian support and the Northern Army emboldened General Sullivan. By 6 June he believed he could "in a few days Reduce the Army to order & with the Assistance of a Kind providence put a new face to our Affairs." Before Sullivan arrived, Thompson had already dispatched Pennsylvania Colonel Arthur St. Clair with a six-hundred-man detachment to Nicolet, more than thirty miles down the south shore, intending to strike an isolated loyalist force under Colonel Maclean, reported near Trois-Rivières.[35]

———

Carleton's lead British columns had just ventured into Trois-Rivières by 4 June, and General Sullivan's agents, including a "Friendly Canadian who Lived at Three Rivers," informed him that the Ministerial force only numbered three hundred. On 6 June, Sullivan gave Thompson new orders; he was to take two regiments from Sorel, join Colonel St. Clair at Nicolet, cross the St. Lawrence, and attack the isolated enemy detachment. With almost eighteen hundred Continentals, the generals believed Thompson would easily overwhelm Maclean. Yet Sullivan's spies did not understand the nature of Carleton's advance: the bulk of the Ministerial troops were aboard ships, shadowing the march of the advance guard. By 8 June, about two thousand British regulars were at Trois-Rivières, on the river and in the city; Thompson was unwittingly preparing to attack a numerically superior enemy.[36]

Reaching Nicolet, Thompson ordered a river crossing on the night of 7 June. Continental river craft sailed across the funnel end of the St. Lawrence's Lac-St-Pierre, but disembarked roughly nine miles from their intended landing point—differing accounts attribute this to poor navigation or a desire to keep a safe distance from Royal Navy ships. On the north shore, the army did not want to risk being spotted on the exposed riverside King's Way, but patriot guides, including Larose, were unfamiliar with the back roads. Thompson called a nearby Pointe-du-Lac habitant, Antoine Gauthier, to guide the corps. According to popular accounts, however, the Canadian quietly told his wife to warn local loyalists of the surprise rebel landing; their news spread to Trois-Rivières just before dawn. To give the King's forces more time, Gauthier led the Continentals on "several windings" through swampy forests, making Thompson's men wade "three hours through the mud, about mid-deep in general." Long beams of morning light shone through the trees before Thompson's vanguard cleared the woods—with three miles of farm fields still lying between them and their objective. The city alarm sounded before Thompson's troops could assemble on the plain. The Battle of Three Rivers opened as seigneur Joseph Boucher-de-Niverville rushed a party of Trifluvien militia forward to thwart the rebel advance. British soldiers followed, forming on high ground north of the city as artillery and additional troops rapidly poured out from the ships offshore.[37]

Most Continentals never made it out of the woods. British artillery arrived at a critical moment to ensure that their thin red line did not give way to the rebel vanguard; and in the middle of the hot fight, Thompson's army unexpectedly turned to flee—the Continentals saw Royal Navy ships moving upstream, threatening to cut them off from their bateaux at Pointe-du-Lac. The Battle of Three Rivers was instantly transformed into a rout. Perhaps because of this collapse and the ensuing chaotic retreat, Thompson's attack occasionally has been portrayed as pure folly; yet some participants considered it a credible threat to the Ministerial corps. Carleton deemed it "a very bold enterprize, indeed," and a British officer participant even compared it with one of Frederick the Great's bold operations. In his view, without the combination of timely artillery support and delays in the rebel march, Thompson's men "must have Carried their point."[38]

Yet events conspired against Thompson, and hundreds of Continentals were taken prisoner, including the general. Canadians—ardent loyalists and those eager to prove renewed commitment to the King—chased, ambushed, and pestered disorganized rebel parties through the woods. When it became obvious that enemy ships were approaching, the Continental rearguard—some

250 men with the bateaux—took flight with a few hundred retreating troops. A larger number of stragglers emerged from the swamps two days later, meeting Continental pickets near Berthier-en-haut, and were ferried across the river to rejoin the main army at Sorel. In the end, habitants brought in more than two hundred rebel prisoners of war, but other casualties were moderate—the King's forces lost fewer than twenty men, the Continentals around fifty. After dealing the rebels such a serious blow in battle, Carleton formed his army into three brigades and prepared to sail up the St. Lawrence in earnest; yet adverse winds slowed the advance, giving the Continentals a few days to reconsider their plans.[39]

With word of the Battle of Three Rivers defeat, General Sullivan and his deputies recognized that retreat from Canada was inevitable. The enemy clearly had superior numbers, no further reinforcements were expected, and almost one-third of Thompson's corps was lost. The only boost came from another wave of Canadian volunteers, reporting to camps at Sorel, Chambly, and St-Jean. Sullivan had issued a proclamation calling for their support, and up to two thousand were expected to join; yet that came to naught when an 11 June council of war decided to abandon Sorel and retreat to Chambly.[40]

The army hardly had arrived there when Sullivan called another council of war on the thirteenth; Arnold, Hazen, and Antill were all busy elsewhere, but offered written opinions, all gloomy. Arnold recommended a complete withdrawal, emphasizing that there was "more honour in making a Safe retreat, than hazarding a Battle against such Superiority." Once again, the officers-in-council, with General de Woedtke dissenting, felt "a prudent retreat" was necessary; the next morning the army was ordered to St-Jean.[41]

Arnold had been back in Montréal for only two days when, in the late afternoon of 15 June, his aide-de-camp, Captain James Wilkinson, returned from an aborted courier mission to report that the British fleet was off the Island of Montréal's northern tip, well above Sorel. Reacting to the immediate risk of being cut off from the rest of the Northern Army, Arnold promptly evacuated the garrison. Under a pelting rain, three hundred Continentals, many sick with smallpox, frantically embarked in heavily laden bateaux and crossed to Longueuil before sunset. After landing, Arnold ruthlessly threatened south-shore parish priests to gather sufficient carriages for his force. Then the Continentals burned their bateaux and followed the Laprairie Road to St-Jean, arriving on 16 June, ahead of Sullivan and the main army.[42]

Arnold's hasty departure surprised Montréal Tories. Militia-Colonel Dufy-Desauniers emerged from hiding to lead a loyalist citizens' guard for two days, until they were relieved by a party of five hundred regulars, Indians, and Canadians who entered the city from the west. Montréal, the unofficial Continental Canadian capital for more than six months, was restored to British government control without a fight.[43]

Meanwhile, the main Continental corps struggled up the Richelieu, leaving behind twenty cannon and heavy stores before passing the Ste-Thérèse Rapids. The troops torched Fort Chambly as they left, and the rear guard pulled up bridges in their retreat. The entire army finally assembled at St-Jean on the morning of 18 June. In another council of war, Sullivan's officers unanimously agreed "that to attempt holding St Johns would be to Expose the whole Army to [I]nevitable Ruins." Men and equipment expeditiously sailed up to Ile-aux-Noix. Before the last Continentals departed, they set fire to Fort St-Jean and Hazen's manor. Arnold, like a tragic hero in a Greek epic, remained to the very end, flirting around Burgoyne's advance guard until the last boat was ready. He pushed the bateau off himself, so he could be the "the last man who embarked from the shores of the enemy." His May 1775 Fort St-Jean raid had served as the overture for the calamitous Canadian campaign, and now Arnold stood alone as the curtain fell on this sad concluding act.[44]

Governor Carleton's strategy had come to fruition: the rebels were leaving Canada with nary a fight. The pursuing army never caught more than a few stragglers. Landing at Sorel on 14 June, the King's troops trailed the rebel retreat by several miles, closing to reach St-Jean an hour or two after Arnold's departure. Royal Navy Captain Charles Douglas observed that the rebels had been "quite expelled" from Canada, "after a resistance on every occasion hithert[o] as flimsy & absurd as were their Motives for taking up Arms against their Sovereign." Carleton made a "triumphal entry" into Montréal on 20 June, while General Burgoyne consolidated his corps to launch an offensive into New York. The British force, however, would have to build a completely new fleet before it could press up the lakes; the rebels had prudently removed or destroyed all watercraft on the north end of Lake Champlain.[45]

The remnants of thirteen Continental regiments settled onto cramped, swampy Ile-aux-Noix. On the first day, the island was hellish, covered "with the people sick with the small-pox." A regimental surgeon recorded that, while tending to the ill and incapacitated soldiers dumped on the riverbanks, he could not walk without tripping over them because they were so tightly packed. Fortunately, the first loads of departing bateaux carried most of those plagued soldiers up the lake, along with some heavy cannon, critical for defending Crown-Point and Ticonderoga.[46]

Sullivan held onto Ile-aux-Noix for several more days, as the remaining troops were sent up Lake Champlain in waves. The last troops reached Crown-Point on 1 July, on the eve of the United Colonies' decision to declare independence from Great Britain. In the north, both sides were left to pick up the pieces: Governor Carleton had to restore authority in Quebec without fueling further rebellion, and the Continental Congress had to figure out what had gone wrong with its great northern expedition and determine how best to defend itself in the spectacularly different world of July 1776.[47]

Chapter 23

THE CAUSES OF THE
MISCARRIAGES IN CANADA

Carleton and Congress Investigate the Failures

To cure them, It must be first known what are the Causes; & the State physicians must be fully convinced of them before they can apply a Remedy. | *Elbridge Gerry to James Warren, Philadelphia, 15 June 1776*

His Majesty commands me to acquaint you that there still remains another part of your duty to be undertaken which will require all your abilities and the strictest application: the restoring peace and the establishing good order and legal government in Canada. | *Secretary of State Lord George Germain to Governor Guy Carleton, Whitehall, 22 August 1776*

In Philadelphia, delegates reacted to the news of Québec City's relief and the Continental flight with a similar surge of activity to that which had followed Montgomery's defeat and the Battle of St-Pierre. The very day word arrived—16 May—a new committee was formed to address the letters that bore the unfortunate news. It quickly grew to include leaders such as John Adams, Richard Henry Lee, and Robert R. Livingston. Adams had already formed his opinion on the campaign's catastrophic turns—there had been too many words and not enough action—"Where shall We lay the blame? America duped and bubbled with the Phantom of Commissioners, has been fast asleep and left that important Post undefended, unsupported." A 22 May "Letters Committee" report generated several Congressional resolutions, related more to intentions than action, identifying the "two great objects" of the Canadian campaign as "the protection and assistance of our Canadian friends, and the securing so much of that country as may prevent any communication between our enemies and the Indians," showing the emerging emphasis on strategic defense.[1]

Another committee, again including Adams and Richard Henry Lee, was appointed to "confer" with General Washington "upon the most speedy and effectual means for supporting the American cause of Canada." On 24 May, the committee prompted Congress to issue resolves reassuring the "Commanding Officer in Canada" that he had the United Colonies' fullest support and that troops would be "hastened" to Canada, "as soon as provisions can be forwarded for their support." On 29 May, after mulling over reports that ten thousand Ministerial troops were expected in Canada, the committee suggested that a like number of northern patriot militiamen be sent to "reinforce the Army in Canada, and to keep up the communication with that Province." Schuyler disliked the plan, fearing the militia would weaken the army rather than strengthen it. His letters emphasized the militiamen's susceptibility to smallpox, and he must have harbored deep concerns about discipline as well. Yet Congress pressed ahead, calling on the New England colonies "in the most pressing Language, urging them to send forward their Militia." By the time the men were mobilized, though, the Northern Army was long out of Canada.[2]

Congress had similar experience with efforts to deliver hard cash to Canada. The United Colonies were just beginning to see results from the urgent April appeals for specie; it was not until 16 June that President Hancock sent off a wagon with "about twenty two Thousand Dollars in Silver" and "a Quantity of Continental Money" for Schuyler and Sullivan. Of course, Congress was unaware that it was far too late to help Quebec, as the army was already withdrawing to St-Jean.[3]

Early Committee to Canada returnees Benjamin Franklin and John Carroll did not deliver an official account of their northern duty, but offered casual reports to friends on their way home. During their trip, the "Doctor" and the Jesuit had their patience tested by their traveling companions—Martha and Thomas Walker; the latter decided to join his wife in transit south, instead of completing his return to Montréal. Franklin observed how both Walkers "have excellent Talents at making themselves Enemies . . . they will never be long without them." Even the docile Father Carroll was shocked by the Walkers' "impertinence"; Martha Walker loudly proclaimed that the commissioners had been "advised with & been governed by Tories." With Walker as the

United Colonies' most outspoken friend, perhaps the difficulties in organizing Canadian patriot political activity made more sense.[4]

When Samuel Chase and Charles Carroll returned from Canada, they took a more active official role. Passing Fort George, they ordered several Northern Army officers' pay frozen — some charged "with Mal-practices, and others with Neglect of Duty." In New York City, they stopped to share their Canadian observations with General Washington. Arriving in Philadelphia, the commissioners provided a written report, seemingly lost to history, but without real impact; the delegates were already well aware of the desperate situation in the north, with little more to offer as a remedy.[5]

Yet after a few days consideration, Congress decided to try one more fix for Canada. With General Thomas's demise, a new major-general was needed and Congress began to "cast their Eyes" on Adjutant-General Horatio Gates. Samuel Chase wrote to Gates, encouraging him for the role, advising that "Laurels are still to be reaped in Canada," and adding that it appeared the new commander would be sent "with the powers of a Roman Dictator." On 17 June, Congress ordered Gates "to take the command of the forces in that province."[6]

A week later, Gates received his instructions. Fearing that Congress was granting extraordinary powers — Hancock believed they made Gates "Dictator in Canada" — his authority was limited to 1 October. Realistically, Gates was given no more power than Montgomery, Arnold, Wooster, or Sullivan had assumed by necessity. But the new commander had no sooner received his instructions than Schuyler wrote to inform him of the army's Ile-aux-Noix retreat. By 8 July, it had become glaringly obvious that there really was no Canadian command. Instead, Gates and Schuyler were left to manage an ill-defined command relationship in New York, with no more specific guidance than that Congress did not intend to give Gates a command superior to Schuyler's, "whilst the troops should be on this side of Canada," and that they should "cultivate Harmony" between each other. The major-generals cooperated, with Schuyler retaining the overall Northern Theater command, while Gates led the army in the field at Ticonderoga.[7]

———

As a body, Congress did not look to assign personal blame for the Canadian catastrophe, but many delegates rushed to identify a villain — General Wooster. Having been out of the United Colonies for more than six months, and with

Connecticut's unassuming Roger Sherman being the only delegate who might be called a friend in Congress, the general was an easy target. As the "Letters Committee" examined the Canadian situation, Thomas Jefferson hastily gave Wooster "the credit of this misadventure," and Richard Henry Lee wrote of the general's abominable misconduct. However, John Adams—always quick to defend Yankee leaders—bristled at such unsubstantiated conclusions, noting that "Wooster was calumniated for Incapacity, Want of Application and even for Cowardice with[out] a Colour of Proof of either." With his discerning political eye, Adams observed that the prime accusers were the same delegates who perpetually delayed support for Canada with "their indefatigable Obstruction to every Measure which had been meditated."[8]

On 6 June, after receiving the commissioners' letter from Canada declaring Wooster "totally unfit" for command, Congress directed the general to "immediately repair" to Continental Army headquarters in New York City. By 21 June, the Connecticut general was given a de facto retirement and authorized to return home. Wooster subsequently visited Philadelphia and called for Congress to "look thoroughly" into his conduct, so he could be "acquitted or condemned upon just grounds and sufficient proof"; yet he would have to wait for Congress to address the broader aspects of the Canadian debacle before they investigated his personal performance.[9]

General Schuyler's leadership drew scrutiny as well. By the end of May, Schuyler feared an imminent court-martial for "high-treason." A vocal minority of Albany County foes accused him of deliberately "sending all the provisions in this country to Canada" to fall into enemy hands, while Massachusetts opponents wrote to General Washington with concerns about the major-general's "fidelity to his country." Washington, however, was too familiar with the Northern Army commander's challenges and sacrifices to doubt Schuyler's commitment to the cause.[10]

Meanwhile, battered, pockmarked, and starved Continental regiments festered at Crown-Point, then Ticonderoga. The summer air was heavy with acrimony in an environment "void of every idea of discipline or subordination." Intercolonial conflicts fostered "complete disunity" in the ranks, while officers cast aspersions against peers and made accusations against superiors whose leadership they disliked. The Canada commissioners had ordered investigations into several officers' conduct, as well. Only General Sullivan seemed to avoid blame and recrimination—everyone just felt sorry for him and the situation into which he had been cast in Canada.[11]

In the midst of all the "insulting and quarrelling," more Canadian Continental soldiers began to reach the southern Lake Champlain camps as well. Unlike their American counterparts, these soldiers had tarried in Quebec to gather their families and precious belongings before leaving as refugees. Now they sought asylum in New York. By 21 July, Colonel Edward Antill, similarly displaced, was ordered to lead the Canadian Continentals and their families to Albany, for better accommodations and easier supply of provisions. Another group of Livingston's and Hazen's veterans opted to remain at their Quebec farms rather than fleeing their home province, hoping that Governor Carleton would be lenient in his reconquest.[12]

Even before the Canadian campaign ended, there was an undercurrent in Philadelphia intent on examining the debacle and identifying its sources. John Adams developed eight causes for the "Misfortunes and Miscarriages in Canada"; his pet theme, "Diversity of Sentiments in Congress," topped the list. Along with a handful of administrative issues, he also considered unqualified generals-in-chief, bad intelligence, and lack of specie as major factors. In mid-June, fellow Massachusetts delegate Elbridge Gerry offered his own list of focus points, which included the "Supineness" of Congress, the slow formation of regiments, poor supply distribution, and seemingly incompetent officers, while observing that Congress was preparing "to search the wound & probe it to the bottom."[13]

The first official step toward a comprehensive investigation began on 21 June, when Congress ordered General Washington to lead an examination "into the causes of the miscarriages in Canada." With broad guidance, the commander-in-chief was expected to immediately bring all officers "accused of cowardice, plundering, embezzlement . . . and other misdemeanors" to an appropriate inquiry. Washington delegated this "Work of Difficulty & Delicacy" to Schuyler, who ordered numerous investigations over the summer. The extremely preoccupied generals did not, however, deliver a comprehensive Continental Army report on Canada, or testimony in Philadelphia, which the original Congressional resolution requested.[14]

Congress did not wait long to form its own "Committee to Inquire into the Miscarriages in Canada," which came about on 24 June. This large committee, consisting of one member from each confederated colony, did not have particularly high-powered leadership, Robert Treat Paine being its most prominent participant. After a little more than a month, with members distracted by other important tasks such as declaring independence, the committee produced its primary report on 30 July. It did not blame individuals, nor did it tackle the more contentious and fundamental issues behind the campaign—objectives, strategic planning, or Congressional support. It also ignored the basic question of whether Canadians ever intended to join the confederation; instead it focused on three very practical causes for the misfortunes in Canada.[15]

Why had the Northern Army failed, according to the committee? First, "the short inlistments of the continental troops" made them "disorderly and disobedient" and forced "the commanding officers into measures, which their prudence might have postponed"—a reference to Montgomery's New Year's Eve assault. The second cause was "the want of hard money . . . rendering the supplies of necessaries difficult and precarious . . . and the pay of the troops of little use to them." Finally, "a still greater, and more fatal source of misfortune" was "the prevalence of the small pox in that army." That was it: a politically palatable solution that received ready concurrence; one that would neither aggravate tensions between the newly united states, nor pose obstacles to any future attempt to bring Canada into the Union. Of note, Canadian James Price had offered these three exact causes for the "failure of the expedition" when giving testimony to the committee twenty days earlier. The committee's initial report was accompanied by eleven resolutions related to specific incidents or charges against individuals in Canada, from the plundering of General Prescott's baggage, to responsibility for The Cedars debacle—almost all were directed to the Continental Army for further action.[16]

The same committee was also assigned to examine General Wooster's conduct. The old Yankee cooperated by providing testimony and correspondence justifying his actions against the Montréal Tories. Meanwhile, one of the Canada commissioners in Congress, presumably Chase, made "boundless Efforts" to "blast" Wooster's character, representing him "as a most worthless contemptible Felon," and "fixed a deep Prejudice against him in a majority" of Congress. Despite this, in the committee's last major decision, on 17 August it reported: "Upon the whole of the evidence that was before them . . . nothing censurable or blameworthy appears against Brigadier-General Wooster," and Congress agreed. The general did not return to active Continental service, though. While his honor may have been restored, his services were not wanted outside Connecticut, which appointed him major-general of militia. He died less than a year later, at age sixty-seven, from wounds suffered in his state's defense, at the Battle of Ridgefield.[17]

Still sensitive regarding his own honor, General Schuyler interpreted an implied indictment of his own performance by the "Miscarriages Committee" in its lack of blame for others. On 16 August, he requested that Congress investigate his conduct, while proffering more requests to retire from service. The "Miscarriages Committee" took its time, and without much investigation, offered its verdict on 2 October—informing the general not only that he was exonerated, but also that they were "fully satisfied of his attachment to the cause of freedom" and respected "the many services which he has rendered to his country." Two days later, President Hancock wrote to inform Schuyler that, due to his invaluable service, Congress once again could not consent to his oft-requested retirement from the army.[18]

———

At the same time General Schuyler was asking for a Congressional inquiry into his conduct in August, he found himself acting as the custodian of the patriot Canadian refugees gathered at the south end of Lake Champlain. Perhaps with some sense of guilt over the Canadians' "Misfortunes occasioned by their Attachment to our Cause," the major-general issued provisions to all of them, including their families, and granted civilian refugees "a small Matter of Money." Canadian soldiers were still paid as Continentals, and were employed repairing the Albany-to-Fort George road.[19]

During the summer, Congress addressed some Canadian friends' needs as well. Answering numerous petitions, the assembly granted pay and rewards to individuals such as Livingston's Chaplain Louis Lotbinière and Montréal merchant Pierre du Calvet; Christophe Pélissier was appointed an engineer lieutenant-colonel, and Prudent Lajeunesse, whose testimony had finally launched the Committee to Canada, was made a captain in Livingston's regiment. Congress also authorized General Schuyler to give "such rewards and wages as shall appear to have been merited" to everyone who had "acted as volunteers in Canada, and retreated with the army."[20]

The number of refugees grew as other patriots decided they could not remain under Ministerial rule, settled their affairs in Canada, and relocated—men such as the merchant Zachary Macaulay and Continental Captains Joseph Ménard, Loiseau, and Allin exited in 1776, and Captain Gosselin endured two more years before departing Quebec. Joseph Bindon later composed a list of Canadian refugees in America, which could have been a roster of Quebec Province's principal patriot activists from 1774 to 1776, including the likes of Thomas Walker, James Livingston, François Cazeau, John Halsted, Jonas Clark Minot, and John Blake.[21]

Congress eventually accommodated most Canadian Continentals by authorizing James Livingston and Moses Hazen to keep their regiments. When it became clear there were not enough Canadian or foreign volunteers for the units, both colonels were authorized to recruit men from any state. Several Canadians stayed with their regiments for years, while others floated in and out of service. Many refugee soldiers also chose to join units from their newly adopted home states, especially New York. In 1783, in recognition of their particular sacrifices and service, Congress guaranteed land grants for all the Canadian veterans. A 1787 government roster of refugee soldiers, newly settled around Lake Champlain, listed more than fifty Canadian expatriates, including several of the most dedicated Continental officers: General Moses Hazen, Edward Antill, Clément Gosselin, and Pierre Ayotte.[22]

Some civilian refugees, especially the Old Subjects, quickly adapted to their new homes in the United States, establishing successful businesses and seamlessly blending in with their neighbors. Others were not so fortunate and found themselves in dire straits. A few gave up after several years and returned to Canada; perhaps the most prominent of these was Maurice Desdevens. For decades, Congress was beset by a stream of civilian Canadian refugee petitions, seeking compensation for property and fortunes sacrificed in the cause. Many appeals were lost in the young nation's government bureaucracy, some were denied, and others produced token compensation; a good number resulted in land grants — in some cases after a quarter century's delay. The most pitiful of all the petitions came from Chaplain Louis Lotbinière, written in 1787: "Would to God that I had never known either the general [M]ontgomery or [A]rnold in Canada, I would not now starve with hunger and cold."[23]

Finally, there was one other group of Canadians in the United States during the summer of 1776 — the loyalist prisoners. Congress continued to pay their living expenses and moderate stipends, during a very liberal detention. Finally, on 10 October 1776, Congress resolved that all of the prisoners "not taken in arms" be sent home on parole, "not to take up arms against the United States, nor give intelligence to the enemies of these states." There were two exceptions: St-Luc de La Corne and René-Ovide Hertel-de-Rouville. These arch-Tories were held until the spring of 1777, when they were released in a prisoner-of-war exchange.[24]

—————

By the end of the summer of 1776, the United States were ready to move on from their unfortunate Canadian experience. There was little hope that Quebec would become a fourteenth state, although the Articles of Confederation still left that as an option. Over the next seven years of war, an American gaze turned to Canada a few more times and Benjamin Franklin occasionally tried to gain the province in peace negotiations, but there would never be another promising opportunity as there had been in 1775.[25]

There was a price to be paid for the Canadian defeat. The United Colonies' second motive for the invasion had always been their own defense from Ministerial invasion and Indian raids. In the fall of 1776, Carleton launched his aborted invasion, thwarted in part by Arnold on Lake Champlain; and General Burgoyne penetrated to Saratoga the next year. The British recovery of Canada also helped break Iroquois neutrality, fueling several years of bitter frontier warfare in the north. It was almost too easy, though, for the Continental Congress to brush off and forget the defeat in Quebec itself. The United States did not have to repair the damage done in Canada and were heavily focused on protecting themselves. The British government, however, faced a huge challenge in bringing their recovered province back under control, a job that Governor Carleton handled with considerable tact and skill.

—————

Governor Guy Carleton already had demonstrated his reconciliatory intentions in his 10 May 1776 Proclamation, guaranteeing magnanimous treatment for rebel prisoners in his province. Following the Battle of Three Rivers, he reiterated the policy: that prisoners "should be sent to their homes as soon as possible," so that having seen the error of their ways, not only the freed rebels but their neighbors at home might also see "that the way to the Kings mercy is still open." All American prisoners were released from Quebec by the end of July, marking the end of that indulgent policy.[26]

In his first May 1776 dispatches to London, Carleton heaped praise on the loyalty of the clergy, the seigneurs, and the capital garrison—but avoided discussing the habitants. Perhaps he was sidestepping the sensitive issue, or maybe he wanted to gather more facts, having been trapped in the city for almost six months. Secretary of State Lord George Germain, however, was unsatisfied with this gap in Carleton's reports. Even if the House of Commons had voted not to inquire into "the causes of the defection of the people of the Province of Quebeck," as secretary of state, Germain wanted to understand his colonial subjects' character in order to form appropriate policy. The secretary responded that Carleton's silence on "the present disposition of the Canadians" was "much to be lamented," already suspecting "dependence upon the Peasantry" would be "precarious." Before the relief army sailed to Canada at the beginning of the year, he had reminded General Burgoyne that "Management" of the habitants would "require no small share of Address to remove their Prejudices and to convince them how greatly they have been deceived."[27]

Almost immediately after the capital was relieved, Governor Carleton initiated an ingenious plan on those lines to restore government authority in the rural communities. He established a three-man commission to visit each parish, gather facts, determine where the habitants had cooperated with the rebels, identify commendable loyalists, and remove or restore officials as necessary. The Quebec District commissioners were merchant François Baby, seigneur Gabriel-Elzéar Taschereau, and lawyer Jenkin Williams, all of whom had endured the winter siege with the governor.

The trio launched its mission on 22 May in the region closest to the capital, visiting a parish or two each day. They conducted a preliminary investigation in each community, assembled all the militia-age men, read their commission, appointed new officers, reviewed the parishioners, mildly shamed collaborators, and then had the parish assembly cheer "Vive le Roi" before adjourning. In each parish, they also documented the past year's notable incidents, their loyalist and rebellious participants, and whether disloyal activity was coerced or voluntary. It proved to be a very efficient process; in less than fifty days, the commission had visited all the district parishes, as well as the lower half of Three Rivers District.[28]

Baby, Taschereau, and Williams were inclined toward the strictest standards of loyalty—even militia-captains who had been threatened into collaboration were almost inevitably replaced—but the commissioners also dispensed punishment with the greatest lenity. Their treatment of the patriot militia-captain in St-François (Ile-d'Orléans) was characteristic: they called the culprit in front of the assembled parish militia, scolded him, and "condemned him for having the baseness of accepting this [rebel] commission and . . . had him burn it with his own hand." There were no arrests or floggings, no property seizures or home burnings. Once the commission's visit was complete, the slate was essentially wiped clean—a precursor of modern "peace and reconciliation" commissions.[29]

After the province had been completely liberated, Carleton appointed another commission, similar to the Baby-Taschereau-Williams mission, with responsibility for Montreal District and the upper Three Rivers District. Militia-Major St-Georges-Dupré, Sheriff Edward William Gray, and Court Clerk Pierre Panet took much longer to complete their commission tasks; a visit to Berthier-region parishes took place as late as March 1777. Unfortunately, there is almost no trace of their findings; it is not hard to believe that, given the damning nature of the Quebec District report, results from the substantially more rebellious Montreal District might have been intentionally "lost," to protect both habitants and government officials.[30]

===

In his other post-recovery policies, Carleton demonstrated that he had learned important lessons, both from the 1775 rebellion and the invasion. Most important, he did not attempt to mobilize the Canadian militia in 1776, resorting only to *corvée* labor. This way he could assert government authority in terms tolerable to most habitants. In the spring of 1777, Carleton's legislative council also enacted the province's first post-Conquest militia ordinance, defining the terms of militia service largely on a traditional New French framework.[31]

The governor also showed new sensitivity to other habitant needs in 1776. The King's troops and their German auxiliaries were ordered to pay Canadians solely in "ready money" and "on no occasion to give Receipts," an intentional contrast to the bankrupt rebels. At harvest time, the governor ensured that Richelieu Valley farmers had "room for their crops of Corn after the Harvest"; soldiers billeted in barns were to relocate if habitants needed the space. Lower Richelieu farmers were also "exempted from all military services, *Corvées* or Fatigues" during the harvest. These policies were undoubtedly popular with the *Canadiens* and maximized wheat production for army use.[32]

However, Carleton had learned to be less tolerant of known government opponents. Initially, his officers targeted notorious Canadian Continentals such as Captains Pierre Ayotte and Jean-Baptiste Allin, who were imprisoned for short terms in 1776. Maurice Desdevens's house was plundered retributively by Tories, and he was forced to pay for the many muskets he had confiscated under Arnold's orders.[33]

Bishop Briand and Vicar-General Montgolfier conducted their own Church purge after the rebels' departure. L'Assomption's Father Huet-de-la-Valinière was reassigned to lower Quebec District parishes, for being suspiciously friendly with the rebels; he subsequently returned to France in 1779. Briand also placed Jesuit Father Pierre-René Floquet under an interdict for six months, based on his Montréal involvement with Hazen's Canadian Continentals; and Chambly's *curé* Médard Pétrimoux was replaced because he "no longer had authority over" his previously rebellious parishioners.[34]

Before the end of summer 1776, Secretary of State Lord Germain gave Carleton additional guidance, directing policies specifically to reward loyalists and punish those who had rebelled. In this spirit, when it was time to find winter quarters for the army, Carleton ordered a regiment to be billeted in the refractory Nouvelle-Beauce region and "other of the mutinous parishes" south of the river. The governor went so far as to order General Friedrich Riedesel to move his Brunswick auxiliaries out of faithful subjects' houses; the German soldiers could relocate to the abodes of those who had "so shamefully ignored or neglected" their duty to the King. Proven loyal militiamen were also exempted from *corvée* duty.[35]

Carleton kept a particularly close eye on known patriots, but refrained from arresting civilians. Printer Fleury Mesplet and his employees had been detained by Montréal loyalists within hours of Arnold's evacuation, but were released twenty-six days later to reopen the print shop. Government policies of lenity changed, however, when Frederick Haldimand became governor in the summer of 1778. He soon imprisoned at least nine liberally minded Canadian patriots, including François Cazeau, Pierre du Calvet, and Pierre de-Sales-Laterrière.[36]

In 1778, Mesplet coincidentally began publishing Montréal's first newspaper, the French-language *Gazette du commerce et littéraire de Montréal*. The paper's "revolutionary" Enlightenment views disturbed Vicar-General Montgolfier, who complained to the new governor; Haldimand needed little further prompting, imprisoning Mesplet and his business partner, Wooster's ex-secretary Valentin Jautard, in June 1779. The pair remained incarcerated through the end of the war. A few years after his release, Mesplet began publishing the bilingual *Montréal Gazette* newspaper.[37]

Despite all his policies and measures, by the fall of 1776, Governor Carleton could note that the "Noblesse, Clergy, and greater Part of the Bourgeoisie" remained steadfast supporters of government; but he opined to Secretary of State Germain that loyalty from the "lower class" was still in doubt: "I think there is nothing to fear from them while we are in a state of prosperity, and nothing to hope for when in distress." It was no surprise that initial attempts to mobilize three Canadian companies for the 1777 New York expedition suffered from feeble recruitment and heavy desertion. General Burgoyne resignedly observed, "The assistance of Canadians beyond the limits of the province . . . will be little or nothing." Finally, Carleton strong-armed the parishes to keep the units manned, and the companies, along with a few hundred Canadian bateaumen and laborers, joined Burgoyne's march. Despite the slight progress, the governor felt it would take many years to bring the habitants back to a proper state of deference; in the meantime, it would "require a Military Force to support the Civil Authority."[38]

A much lower-ranking British officer seemed to agree, observing, "The lower class of Canadians" was "exceedingly insolent," but attributed it to "the very great indulgence shewn to them by General Carleton." Despite the many benefits they had been given in the Conquest and the Quebec Act, the habitants did not seem to be "well affected to the English Government." This observer felt that many would readily assist the Americans, if there were not such a powerful military force in the province. [39]

Yet with all the new post-recovery policies, there had been only superficial change, the 1777 Militia Ordnance being the most substantial measure that addressed core Canadian revolutionary issues. Even though loyal merchants petitioned against the Quebec Act government again in 1778, they would not see an assembly until the Constitutional Act of 1791, by which time the complexion of the country was dramatically altered by throngs of loyalist refugees from the United States. The seigneurial landholding system would remain in place for another seventy-eight years, until the 1854 "Act for the Abolition of Feudal Rights and Duties in Lower Canada." The province, victorious in its defense, had not been compelled to make hasty changes—and as would be expected, its governors acted as if there were no fundamental problems, correcting only the most obvious causes of Quebec's 1775 *petit* rebellion.[40]

CONCLUSION

Misinterpretations and Missteps in a War to Spread Democracy

Indeed there was benevolence in the whole plan of his expedition. It was to be executed not so much by force as by persuasion. | *William Smith's "Oration in Memory of General Richard Montgomery," 1776*

We now have many enemies among us which might have been friends to the cause, had a Committee of sensible men been sent up from the Congress with some money, to regulate the policy of the Country. | *George Measam to Alexander McDougall, Montréal, 31 March 1776*

In 1776, Congress analyzed the Canadian debacle only in terms of a traditional military campaign, even though they had intentionally launched a revolutionary war in Quebec—a struggle for the will of a people.[1] The delegates did not investigate political-diplomatic failures and did not question why Quebec Province failed to follow the course of its southern neighbors. The catastrophic outcome of the northern enterprise originated from much more than short enlistments, smallpox, and a want of silver. The United Colonies launched a liberation campaign with scant Canadian support, then executed it with insufficient energy and means to achieve its objectives.

The War of American Independence was in many ways the first modern "revolutionary war"—a conflict in which the population's support is the "center of gravity" for strategic victory. In such struggles, people naturally fall into three categories: government supporters, rebels and their friends, and a majority who do not particularly care to get involved, being sufficiently satisfied with their lot to avoid "unnecessary" tumult and change. This was the case in the Thirteen Colonies, and in Quebec Province as well.[2]

Governor Guy Carleton's administration was backed by a small cadre of outspoken, aggressive Tory seigneurs and officeholders such as William

Edward Gray, John Fraser, Hertel-de-Rouville, Adam Mabane, Henry Cald-well, and Gabriel-Elzéar Taschereau, and Bishop Briand with his vicars and priests. They were supported by a similarly small number of less zealous but loyalist-inclined individuals who supported the King when called, or after carefully weighing their options. This group included the conservative faction of Canada's prewar British Party and prominent French-Canadians such as St-Luc de La Corne and Godefroy-de-Tonnancour, as well as a few parish leaders. This progovernment column was a product of Carleton's long-term strategic plans. When he came to office in the 1760s, Carleton clearly identified the Canadian population as the critical component for provincial security in a potential conflict, imperial or revolutionary. With that vision, he applied governing principles that theoretically were biased toward the colony's vast "French" majority, culminating in the Quebec Act of 1774. Arguably, his plan had a fundamental flaw: he founded his state structure on a thin aristocratic foundation, at the cost of distancing a loud middle-class faction and many habitants. Yet it is fair to say that in Canada's revolutionary episode, the clergy and seigneurs delivered on Carleton's investment, serving as a levee against the flood of popular rebellion, giving the British military time to sweep in and push back the tide before a rebel government could be established.[3]

At the other end of the spectrum, there were two streams of opposition to the government. Small cells of liberty-minded patriot activists found di-rect, common cause with the United Colonies on political and ideological grounds. This numerically inconsequential, but economically powerful element included the radical British Party faction—Thomas Walker, James Price, William Haywood, and Zachary Macaulay—and French-born Canadians such as François Cazeau, Christophe Pélissier, and Maurice Desdevens. A more significant anti-administration element came directly from the habitant majority. Thousands of rural *Canadiens* joined the few hundred British Party radicals when the parishes reacted to the Quebec Act's government innova-tions, manifested in local policy and brought to alarming reality as seigneurs visited the parishes to assert new authority under martial law. The habitants' 1775 rebellions in the Terrebonne region, the Richelieu Valley, Berthier-en-haut, and the Beauce demonstrated their anger and disenchantment with the government. Independently, these two marginal or fleeting currents of opposition—the Continental patriot movement and the provincial resistance to the Quebec Act government—probably were manageable for the admin-istration. The real danger to the Crown came when they converged, became intertwined, and fed each other—especially in the Richelieu Valley, but also in the late fall Pointe-Lévy and Ile-d'Orléans "seditious assemblies."

In the middle were tens of thousands of habitants, artisans, and merchants who simply wanted to continue their lives undisturbed; these people were the contested "terrain" over whom the Ministry and rebels fought. Either side could achieve a meaningful victory if they could persuade a sizeable number of these *Canadiens* to align with their cause. Until that point, when pushed, the mass of people might circumstantially support one side or the other: to oppose "invaders," when local leaders called them to action against haughty seigneurs or "rebel banditti," or to succor forces marching through their communities. Many contemporaries and subsequent historians characterized this ambivalence as a particularly Canadian "neutrality" or "fickleness,"[4] yet the habitants' positions directly paralleled many North American colonists' general conduct in the Revolution; and this conservative, noncommital tendency has become an acknowledged fact of modern "revolutionary" wars. The historical record shows that Canadian support for the "invading" Continental Northern Army in 1775 was comparable to that shown for the patriot cause in many American regions under similar circumstances; and the habitants' loyalist "rebound," following Ministerial reconquest, was more reserved than that demonstrated in other states, such as British-occupied 1776 New Jersey. In December of that year, Washington lamented, "A large part of the Jerseys have given every proof of disaffection [to the patriot cause] that a people can do . . . instead of resistance," they were "offering Submission & taking protections" from Crown authorities—a contrast to the passive reception given to restored royal government in Quebec.[5]

———

The British Party's brazen Quebec Act opposition, and reports of habitant anti-administration rebellions, led the United Colonies to see their Canadian neighbors as a people begging to be liberated—a nation poised to join the rest of British North America, if just given the chance. On the eve of the 1775 invasion, Connecticut Governor Jonathan Trumbull succinctly described the Continental perspective: "Our enemies are the Ministerial Troops in Canada, while the Canadians are our friends, and will join us at a time when they are able and not forced to the contrary by our enemies." Projecting their own sentiments on their neighbors, the rebels assumed that the Canadians, as a "rational people," would embrace the United Colonies' form of British liberty, as expressed in "American" popular government. The few Richelieu Valley Canadians who communicated across Lake Champlain in the decisive summer of 1775 encouraged these views.[6]

This led to a critical Continental error in that—based on sparse intelligence and a proclivity to read "indications of sentiment" as they expected them to be—the United Colonies misinterpreted Quebec's antigovernment position. In reality, only the tiniest Canadian element had any inclination to unite with the Thirteen Colonies; although many more Canadians wanted to change their local government and correct its recent innovations, their opposition was class based, localized, or situational. The only meaningful Canadian encouragement for a Continental intervention came from the nascent Chambly patriot cell. When the United Colonies decided to invade Quebec in the summer of 1775, they did so based on inadequately developed intelligence and erroneous assumptions, stepping into an environment that did not offer broad, provincial support, and in which most classes and parties were still weighing their interests and loyalties in the growing North American struggle.

Yet once the "liberation" began, even though Continentals initiated the Quebec campaign on poorly evaluated pretenses, it appeared that the United Colonies might succeed with only modest initial Canadian support. In less than three months, the Ministerial "house of cards" collapsed, and Carleton's supporters were huddled in the capital, abandoning Montréal and the rest of the province to the rebels.

At the most fundamental level, the United Colonies lost the war for Canada at the point that Generals Montgomery and Schuyler acted on discretionary orders and sailed north on Lake Champlain. This was not because the campaign was inherently doomed in concept, but because the Continental Congress launched a juggernaut that it was unprepared to control, adequately guide, or properly support. As John Adams recognized, in large part this was because Congress was still in its own internal turmoil, without a common understanding of the means the colonies were willing to employ in their overall struggle. The invasion simply should not have been launched without deliberate consideration of how the United Colonies might foster a Canadian patriot movement if it failed to bloom after being relieved from Ministerial oppression, and without a contingency plan for handling irremediable Canadian apathy toward self-government. Congress also should have provided explicit consent in the form of a "go" decision, as well as a set of operational bounds for any northern campaign, based on rational analysis of intelligence at the time of the intended invasion and a calculated assessment of men and supplies available—measures that would have involved the Philadelphia delegates from the start. Instead, Congress's coincidental summer recess ensured a void of civilian government guidance for Schuyler at the critical moment he launched the operation, and made certain that the Continental confederation would be politically, financially, and logistically behind from the start.

Once the invasion commenced, the United Colonies suffered from a deadly combination of faults: overcommitment and complacency. When General Washington decided to send Arnold up the Kennebec, he effectively forced Montgomery to operate on a 150-mile span of the St. Lawrence, a massive chunk of territory that the Northern Army was ill equipped to control and influence under the best circumstances—even if Arnold had seized Québec City. The spring 1776 campaign would have had a completely different complexion if Montgomery had secured the Montreal District and spent the winter consolidating patriot power, while fortifying, arming, and manning Jacques-Cartier and Deschambault, instead of firing his bolt at the capital.

The fall of Fort St-Jean, and then Montréal, led many in the United Colonies to view Canada's complete liberation as a given. Schuyler's and Montgomery's pleas for everything—troops, money, political guidance—fell on deaf ears, as invaluable months passed. Only the New Year's Eve defeat, the Battle of St-Pierre, and the May siege collapse broke Congress's characteristic complacency on northern affairs. In large part this was because the Colonies had so many other pressing issues. As John Adams lamented, "Many Things are to be done here and many more to think upon by day and by night. Cares come from Boston, from Canada, from twelve other Colonies, from innumerable Indian Tribes, from all Parts of Europe and the West Indies." No one represented Quebec's needs in Congress, so Canada and the Northern Army were generally out-prioritized until the next crisis. The United Colonies simply did not pursue the timely measures needed to wage the war they had authorized.[7]

The Continental military effort clearly could have been better controlled: troop strength, provisions, and finances all suffered from horrible neglect and mismanagement. Yet militarily, some degree of Northern Army defeat was almost inevitable in the spring of 1776. With the Ministry's naval supremacy and overwhelming military resources, the United Colonies were hard pressed to challenge Leviathan in the narrow river-dominated province. Even if properly manned, equipped, and supplied, the rebels would have needed considerable skill and luck to hold the line at Deschambault; regardless, military success was only a means to achieve the real strategic objective: Canadian unity with the Continental confederation.

For the campaign to succeed in its ultimate aim, some form of Canadian political commitment to the Continental cause had to exist. Local support was paramount, and if fostered appropriately, might have generated a durable patriot government—one that could survive Ministerial occupation, even if "in exile." A great opportunity existed for Canadian patriots and Continental authorities to nurture the cause of liberty in Quebec Province and politically consolidate their military gains; they needed to persuade Canadians that it was in their interest to unite with the other colonies and collectively challenge the Ministry's unpopular actions.

Most significant, the core of zealous, militant Canadian patriots failed to exploit the advantages the Continental Northern Army had handed them. Both the urban merchant opposition and the rebellious habitants in the Richelieu Valley, Lac-St-Pierre, Beauce, and Pointe-aux-Trembles regions—many of whom adopted the patriot cause—did not make the slightest step toward coordinated political action. They fatally hesitated when it was time to take the next step in the revolutionary struggle. Instead of developing local, district, or provincial governing bodies, Quebec's partisan leadership focused exclusively on military operations, forming Canadian units and supporting the Northern Army. There were no committees of safety, chains of correspondence, or political gatherings to foster a "liberty"-based model of popular government. While the Canadian opposition factions proved ready to overthrow the "oppressive" Crown government, they were completely unprepared to offer an alternative. The small revolutionary elite failed to implement the "first step in the mobilization process—creation of [political] organizations." As historian T. H. Breen has observed, in the other colonies, "The people were not . . . neutral spectators. The committees drew them into the revolutionary process," and "determined the progress of the revolution." Yet Quebec never achieved a functional committee system. Canada's rebel leaders lacked the vision, capacity, or will to launch a new revolutionary government; and Northern Army leaders willingly kept the province's most-committed patriots preoccupied in military pursuits. Without a foundation of organized local political support, over time "liberators" became "invaders" and "occupiers," and Canadian patriot partisans became "collaborators" instead of "revolutionaries."[8]

A particularly critical step that Congress failed to take, one which offered game-changing impact in Canada, was to send an early political committee to invigorate and guide Quebec's patriots, and to assess and communicate the province's true situation to Philadelphia. Generals Montgomery and Schuyler left no doubt that both the patriot Canadians and the Northern Army were suffering tremendously from the lack of political guidance. The timing of the November 1775 Paine-Langdon-Livingston committee was almost perfect, but that team was not prepared to handle the work really needed in Montréal—fostering a revolutionary government system and taking critical political decisions out of military hands. Canadian historian Stanley Ryerson astutely assessed that the United Colonies failed in Canada because "the war was not yet being waged in a revolutionary way," and Continental "hesitations were reflected in the failure to combine a political offensive with a military one." Having launched a "revolutionary" war, Congress did not execute it as one, neglecting to provide the political means needed to reach its ends, until half a year too late.[9]

Perhaps the greatest obstacle that prevented many influential Canadians from joining the Continental confederation came in the economic realm. As historian D. G. Creighton observed, "The Canadian merchants were reluctant to accept even for a moment the embargo which the Americans had adopted as a war-time measure . . . They had no desire to endanger their own commercial system, even for an interval." Thomas Walker and James Price had emphasized this point, months before the invasion, and the Montrealers expressed the same sentiment in their November 1775 terms of capitulation. In Quebec, the Continental Association for nonimport/nonexport had a much greater impact than for its neighbors. Isolated from other colonies and less self-sufficient as a province, a lost fur-trade and wheat-marketing season would be economically devastating. In a North American struggle that was essentially about the control of property, the United Colonies were asking Canadians to make a disproportionate sacrifice for the cause. If the Continental governments truly sought to bring Quebec Province into their confederation, they needed to offer an ingenious alternative to the Association's strict rules; yet Congress ignored the economic issue altogether, until Montréal fur traders pressed the issue in 1776 — producing a long-delayed and localized, temporary solution, only by default. Given the close relationship between the Association's enforcement committees and revolutionary mobilization, the Quebec merchants' inability to consider participation in the Continental trade measure and Congress's unwillingness to compromise were significant obstacles to the development of a patriot Canadian government, as well.[10]

There was one aspect of economic "property security," though, that initially appeared promising for the rebels. Canada's summer 1775 parish rebellions and Continental "liberation" from the Quebec Act government offered habitants an opportunity to keep more of their grain profits, as the newly reentrenched seigneurial dues and Church tithes were undermined by the revolutionary invasion. But by the spring of 1776, this proved to be a mirage. In fact, the Northern Army's paper purchase of habitant goods and services proved to be nothing short of theft — an absolute loss of Canadian property. The new waves of ill-disciplined, marauding Continental reinforcements added even more danger, threatening habitants' lives and limbs, in addition to their property.

Yet what was truly amazing, and that clearly indicates there was fertile ground to grow a patriot Quebec alongside the United Colonies, was the repeated resurgence of Canadian support for the weak, bankrupt Continentals: after the New Year's Eve defeat, in response to de Beaujeu's progovernment insurrection, and even after the rebels' chaotic retreat in the face of the Ministerial relief fleet. The fact that as late as June 1776, Richelieu Valley habitants gathered men and wheat to support the severely drubbed Continentals, and lined up to cheer General Sullivan's arrival, indicates that there was some deeper ideological connection — one that went dormant when the cause seemed helpless, but which bloomed at the moment circumstances offered the slightest hope for a continued, productive relationship with the rebels. Once again, this is analogous to patriot behavior in many parts of the United States throughout the war. In the end, though, the confederated colonies and Canadian patriots failed in Quebec on both military and political lines of operation, ensuring catastrophic defeat for the patriot cause; and because of Quebec's geographic isolation and overwhelming Ministerial military dominance on the St. Lawrence, once lost, there was little hope for the United

States to ever relight the lamp of liberty that shined so promisingly to the north from 1775 to 1776.

━━━━━━

The United Colonies' "intervention" in Canada was no more quixotic than the patriot struggle to control divided New York or government-dependent Georgia, or in fact, the entire concept of the American Revolution. Canada's 1775 parish rebellions paralleled other localized resistance movements that were incorporated under the "Banners of Freedom" as the Revolutionary War grew—the Green Mountain Boys being just one example—and Quebec's factional politics were no different from most colonies. The rebellion that spread from Boston, to unite thirteen colonies, was expected to cover the settled continent and incorporate diverse strains of anti-Ministerial sentiment into a common cause. In Quebec, this was manifested in the miscalculated and horribly executed attempt to "liberate" the Canadians from a government they apparently did not want, which was supposed to allow latent "democratic" inclinations to flourish.

Inadequate intelligence, psychological projection of "American" political values, and military miscalculation led the United Colonies to launch their inept Canadian invasion. Once initiated, even though the principal political goal—bringing Quebec Province into the United Colonies—was clearly spelled out at the beginning and a "democratic" political model was repeatedly offered, appropriate resources were never applied until the situation was unsalvageable. By default, the military became the "tool of necessity" for implementing what was, at its core, a political and diplomatic challenge. The Canadian patriots' impotence and Congress's neglect and mismanagement guaranteed the failure of the Quebec campaign in the face of a determined and powerful British Ministerial foe.

Appendix 1

CANADIAN VOICES

A Note on Sources

One of the chief challenges in examining the 1774–1776 Revolutionary crisis in Quebec is the relative national imbalance of firsthand primary source records. Continental "American" documentation covers a wide range of civilian, military, government, and newspaper sources; while outside of high-level British government correspondence, the available Canadian accounts principally derive from three select categories: journals from Québec City's Old Subject Tories, government-associated New Subjects' journals and memoirs, and the Baby-Taschereau-Williams commission's report. Each of these sources provides valuable insight into specific segments of the Canadian population, but also has notable shortcomings.

Among the most heavily referenced Canadian sources are the several journals generated by Anglo-Tories in Québec City during the blockade. The most popular of these is Thomas Ainslie's journal, last published in 1968.[1] The Literary and Historical Society of Quebec published several other journals from 1876 to 1906.[2] Yet perhaps the most refined Old Subject journal remains unpublished, the "Journal of the Most Remarkable Events . . . ," held in the Library and Archives Canada. These accounts record many details within the capital, showing their authors' proximity to government and military leaders and providing good insight into hard-line "English" Canadian loyalists' views. However, they all suffer from two key weaknesses. First, their notably similar content indicates considerable collaboration or iterative production; they cannot reliably be used as independent sources. For any given day, there are only shades of difference or minor details varying between the several journal keepers' entries. Second, since the authors roamed about in less than one square mile of the gigantic province for almost six months, trapped behind fortress walls, they relied tremendously on secondhand accounts and rumors to flesh out events occurring outside of the capital city—and unsurprisingly, many of these reports were erroneous or exaggerated. In several cases, earlier historians of this campaign have been overly reliant on, and uncritical of, these journals' indirect "observations," treating them as fact, while such accounts often do not withstand scrutiny when weighed against other primary sources.

Another highly referenced documentary collection comes from five French-Canadian journals and memoirs kept by the notaries Sanguinet, Badeaux, Berthelot, and Foucher, and active loyalist Claude Lorimier.[3] These different authors provide significant eyewitness accounts of events in their own surroundings: Sanguinet in Montréal, Berthelot in Québec City, Badeaux in Trois-Rivières, Foucher at St-Jean, and Lorimier reflecting on his adventures. However, being written by *Canadiens* who clearly aligned themselves with the government, they are distinctly partisan accounts, with Badeaux's uniquely balanced journal being the exception.

Clergy views are also fairly well documented, with numerous collected and published letters from Bishop Briand and Vicar-General Montgolfier.[4] Although this author did not have the opportunity to investigate archdiocese holdings or individual parish records and other local resources, some of these may yet offer interesting details for future research.[5]

Somewhat curiously, seigneurs and merchants left little firsthand documentation for this period. The available fragments of seigneurs' correspondence are miniscule and do not offer any great insight. Only a scant few of the radical patriot Quebec merchants left records in their letters or appeals to Congress,[6] and a handful of loyalist *Canadien* bourgeois accounts are captured in Verreau's *Invasion du Canada* and Pierre Foretier's "Notes and Reminesces" from Montréal's occupation.[7]

In examining the bulk of the populace, Quebec's largely illiterate habitants did not leave a meaningful record of their perspectives and experience; so their motivations and local activities have to be gleaned and interpreted from others' accounts. The best sources for the summer 1775 parish rebellions in Montreal District come from Francis Maseres's partisan compilations of anti-administration sources in contemporary publications,[8] which must be weighed accordingly. Likewise, there are many diverse accounts of radical Canadians' activities in this period among the *Papers of the Continental Congress*. The documents offering the most detail, however, tend to have been composed years after the fact, and generally these were written to justify claims for Congressional compensation. They help complete the picture of

Canadian views and events, but must be scrutinized carefully with their original purpose in mind.

The one distinctly essential source for habitant activity in this period, however, is the Baby-Taschereau-Williams report from the Quebec and lower Three Rivers Districts, translated and published in 2005.[9] That document is key to deciphering the details of the Beauce region's defiance, Pointe-Lévy's "Seditious Assembly," and the Ile-d'Orléans uprising, as well as the 1776 St-Pierre episode.

Given these gaps and limitations in the period's Canadian documentary record, Continental American sources are important to flesh out many aspects of those episodes where there was cross-border engagement with Quebec—collaboration or direct conflict. This leaves the habitants' summer of 1775 resistance as the weakest segment of the primary source story and as a clear opportunity for future study.

Appendix 2

THE POLARIZED LEGACY
OF GENERAL DAVID WOOSTER

By almost any measure, David Wooster has been given short shrift in the American historical record. His biographical background and abbreviated Revolutionary War career have been examined in remarkably few works; more significant, the sparse sketches of Wooster's life and military experience come almost exclusively from extreme perspectives: either those lauding his patriotism and zeal for his troops, or those portraying him as a doddering incompetent. The limited amount of treatment falling between those poles tends to be peripheral.

In the pro-Wooster catalog, a number of hagiographic—and often derivative—nineteenth-century biographies are typified by Henry C. Deming's "An Oration Upon the Life and Services of Gen. David Wooster" and Cornelius Moore's *Leaflets of Masonic Biography*.[1] These accounts proudly extol a Connecticut warrior, aristocratic yet popular with many of his troops, who was martyred early in the Revolutionary cause while countering the 1777 Danbury Raid in his home state.

On the other side, two important historians of the Canadian campaign—Justin Smith and Kenneth Roberts—are among Wooster's harshest critics, and their view seems to prevail among most modern historians.[2] Roberts boldly asserted that Wooster "antagonized everyone with whom he came in contact," and that "nobody, from Washington down, had anything good to say about Wooster during his stay in Canada"—both statements being incorrect, at least in their extreme scope. Roberts also impugned the general by claiming he "drank large amounts of flip [a popular Connecticut mixture of rum, pumpkin, beer, and brown sugar] each day, and was 'countrified' in his appearance and conduct."[3] There is only marginal support for these characterizations in sparse historical anecdotes, which referred to the general's preferred beverage and his somewhat shocking willingness to fraternize with "common" men.[4] Smith similarly portrays Wooster as "a bluff, hearty man of the people," opining that the old Yankee "must have been a very effective general in the opinion of a hay-field. All the farmers within reach of his voice would have nodded approval."[5] With the little extant primary source material on Wooster, such views seem to be the historians' projections of their own biases, rather than well-supported assessments of the historical individual.

This work was not intended to rehabilitate Wooster's historical reputation, but in research and writing, the author found that the general's story was far more complex than the near-caricatures offered by earlier historians. Given the scant amount of surviving Wooster correspondence, and the polarized character of secondary accounts, this book's picture of the general has been pieced together from a wide array of documentary sources, carefully weighed in a deliberate effort to accurately record General Wooster's neglected role in the confused early days of the Continental Army and in many of the Canadian campaign's most contentious moments.

NOTES

Source Abbreviations

AA4   Peter Force, ed., *American Archives, Fourth Series.*

AA5   Peter Force, ed., *American Archives, Fifth Series.*

AMP   Alexander MacDougall Papers, 1756–1795, NYHS.

ASP   Walter Lowrie, ed., *American State Papers, Documents Legislative and Executive, of the Congress of the United States, Class IX, Claims.*

BTW   Michael P. Gabriel, ed., *Quebec During the American Invasion: The Journal of François Baby, Gabriel Taschereau and Jenkin Williams.*

CAD   Adam Shortt and Arthur Doughty, eds., *Canadian Archives: Documents Relating to the Constitutional History of Canada, 1759–1791.*

CCA 1904 *Concerning Canadian Archives for the Year 1904.*

CCoC   *Dear Papa, Dear Charley: The Papers of Charles Carroll of Carrollton, 1748–1782*, Vol. 2, Ronald Hoffman, ed.

CO5   Colonial Office Fonds, CO 5. America and West Indies, Original Correspondence, etc., MG11-CO5, Microfilm B-3898. LAC.

CSSAR   Connecticut Society of the Sons of the American Revolution.

CTG   Thomas Gage, *The Correspondence of General Thomas Gage with the Secretaries of State,* Clarence E. Carter, ed.

DAR   K. G. Davies, ed., *Documents of the American Revolution, 1770–1783.*

DCB   *Dictionary of Canadian Biography Online/Dictionnaire biographique du Canada en ligne,* LAC.

EAK   John J. Duffy, ed., *Ethan Allen and His Kin, Correspondence, 1772–1819. A Selected Edition in Two Volumes.*

FHV   Fonds Hospice-Anthelme-Jean-Baptiste Verreau, MG23-GV7, LAC.

HGP   Horatio Gates Papers, NYHS.

HMNF   Historical Section of the General Staff, ed., *A History of the Organization, Development, and Services of the Military and Naval Forces of Canada, From the Peace of Paris in 1763 to the Present Time.*

JCC   Worthington C. Ford, ed., *Journals of the Continental Congress, 1774–1789.*

JMRE   "Journal of the Most Remarkable Events Which Happened in Canada between the Months of July 1775 and June 1776," MG23-B7, LAC.

JMRO   "Journal of the Most Remarkable Occurrences . . . ," in *Historical Documents Relating to the Blockade of Quebec by the American Revolutionists in 1775–1776.*

JOPO   "Journal of the Principal Occurrences," in Fred Wurtele, ed., *Blockade of Quebec in 1775–1776 by the American Revolutionists (Les Bastonnais).*

JPCM   William E. Lincoln, ed., *The Journals of Each Provincial Congress of Massachusetts in 1774 and 1775.*

JSBQ   *Journal of the Siege and Blockade of Quebec by the American Rebels in Autumn 1775 and Winter 1776.*

LAC   Library and Archives Canada.

LOD	Paul H. Smith, ed., *Letters of Delegates to Congress, 1774–1789*.
MACC	James Sullivan, ed., *Minutes of the Albany Committee of Correspondence, 1775–1778*.
MHC	Moses Hazen Collection, MG23-B4, LAC.
NDAR	William Bell Clark, ed., *Naval Documents of the American Revolution*.
NYHS	New-York Historical Society.
NYPL	New York Public Library.
PBF	Benjamin Franklin, *The Papers of Benjamin Franklin*, William Willcox, ed.
PCC	U.S. National Archives, Papers of the Continental Congress.
PGWRWS	George Washington, *The Papers of George Washington: Revolutionary War Series*, Philander Chase, ed.
PMP	Perceval-Maxwell Papers, MG40-R89, LAC.
PSP	Philip Schuyler Papers, NYPL.
PTJ	Thomas Jefferson, *The Papers of Thomas Jefferson*, Julian P. Boyd, ed.
QG	*Quebec Gazette*.
RWP	United States National Archives, M804, Revolutionary War Pension and Bounty-Land Warrant Application Files.
Sanguinet	Simon Sanguinet, "Temoin Oculaire de L'Invasion du Canada par les Bastonnois," in Abbé Verreau, ed., *Invasion du Canada, Collection de Memoires recueillis et annotes*.
SAP	Samuel Adams Papers, NYPL.
SP2	Haldimand Papers, MG-21, Papers relating to State Prisoners and suspected persons (Volume 2), 1775–1784, Microfilm A-765, LAC.

Name Abbreviations

AM	Alexander McDougall
BA	Benedict Arnold
BF	Benjamin Franklin
CCC	Charles Carroll of Carrollton
CL	Charles Lee
Cont Congr	Continental Congress
CT	Connecticut
DW	David Wooster
EA	Ethan Allen
EM	Etienne Montgolfier
EoD	Earl of Dartmouth
GC	Guy Carleton
GW	George Washington
HG	Horatio Gates
(IO)	Ile-d'Orléans
JA	John Adams
JB	John Brown
JH	John Hancock
JL	James Livingston
JOB	Jean-Olivier Briand
JS	John Sullivan
MA	Massachusetts
MH	Moses Hazen
NH	New Hampshire
NY	New York

RM   Richard Montgomery
RRL   Robert R. Livingston, Jr.
RTP   Robert Treat Paine
SA   Samuel Adams
TW   Thomas Walker
WG   William Goforth

Introduction

William Smith, *An Oration in Memory of General Montgomery, and of the Officers and Soldiers, Who Fell with Him, December 31, 1775, before Quebec* (London: J. Almon, 1776), 26.

1. Conceptually different from insurrectionary "wars of liberation" fought within a state (i.e., anticolonial, nationalist, or Communist).

2. Eliot A. Cohen has coincidentally explored this aspect of the campaign in his *Conquered into Liberty: Two Centuries of Battles Along the Great Warpath That Made the American Way of War* (New York: Free Press, 2011).

Chapter 1. The Only Link Wanting

Epigraph: Worthington C. Ford, ed., *Journals of the Continental Congress, 1774–1789* (hereafter cited as *JCC*), (Washington, DC: Government Printing Office, 1904), 1: 111.

1. Thomas Jefferson, "A Summary View of the Rights of British America," 1774, in *Tracts of the American Revolution*, ed. Merrill Jensen (Indianapolis: Bobbs-Merrill, 1967), 263–64.

2. Silas Deane to the Committees, 4 June 1774, in *Correspondence and Journals of Samuel Blachley Webb*, Worthington C. Ford (New York: Wickersham, 1893), 1: 25.

3. *JCC*, 1: 32–37. Key motivations behind Congress's approval of the Suffolk Resolves are examined in T. H. Breen, *American Insurgents, American Patriots: The Revolution of the People* (New York: Hill and Wang, 2010), 129–59.

4. Jack Rakove, *The Beginnings of National Politics: An Interpretive History of the Continental Congress* (New York: Knopf, 1979), 51–52; *JCC*, 1: 79; David W. Conroy, "Development of a Revolutionary Organization, 1765–1775," in *The Blackwell Encyclopedia of the American Revolution*, eds. Jack P. Greene and J. R. Pole (Cambridge, MA: Basil Blackwell, 1991), 228; Breen, *American Insurgents*, 168.

5. *JCC*, 1: 82.

6. House of Lords debates on the Quebec Bill, 18 June 1774, in *American Archives, Fourth Series . . .* ed. Peter Force (hereafter cited as *AA4*), (Washington, DC: 1837), 1: 214.

7. John Penn to Earl of Dartmouth (hereafter cited as EoD), 5 September 1775, in *Documents of the American Revolution, 1770–1783* ed. K. G. Davies (hereafter cited as *DAR*), (Dublin: Irish University, 1975), 8: 186.

8. John Adams, *Diary and Autobiography of John Adams*, ed. L. H. Butterfield (Cambridge, MA: Belknap, 1962), 2: 147.

9. "To the Canadians . . . ," *Essex Journal* (Newburyport, MA), 19 October 1774.

10. Ibid.

11. The Association, 20 October 1774, in *JCC*, 1: 79.

12. "Halifax, October 25," *Nova Scotia Gazette and the Weekly Chronicle* (Halifax, NS), 25 October 1774.

13. *JCC*, 1: 106–112.

14. Ibid.

15. Pierre Monette, *Le Rendez-vous manqué avec la révolution américaine* (Montréal: Chez Tryptique, 2007), 73; "To the Inhabitants of the Province of Quebec," 26 October 1774, in *JCC*, 1: 108.

16. "To the Inhabitants . . . ," 26 October 1774, in *JCC*, 1: 108; Michael Schudson, "Was There Ever a Public Sphere? If So, When? Reflections on the American Case," in *Habermas and the Public Sphere*, ed. Craig Calhoun (Cambridge, MA: MIT Press, 1992), 151.

17. *JCC*, 1: 112.

18. Ibid.

Chapter 2. New Subjects to the King

Epigraph: Public Archives of Canada, *Documents Relating to the Constitutional History of Canada, 1759–1791*, eds. Adam Shortt and Arthur Doughty (hereafter cited as *CAD*), (Ottawa: S. E. Dawson, 1907), 1: 65.

1. Notes of Witnesses' Testimony concerning the Canadian Campaign, James Price, 20 July 1776, in Thomas Jefferson, *The Papers of Thomas Jefferson* (hereafter cited as *PTJ*), ed. Julian P. Boyd (Princeton: Princeton University Press, 1950), 1: 449; Francis Maseres, *Additional Papers Concerning the Province of Quebeck* (London: W. White, 1776), 6.

2. Frances Brooke, *The History of Emily Montague* (London: J. Dodsley, 1769), 1: 13; Richard C. Harris, *The Seigneurial System in Early Canada: A Geographical Study* (Montréal: McGill-Queen's University Press, 1984), 167–68, 182.

3. Philippe Aubert de Gaspé, *Mémoires* (Ottawa: G. E. Desbarats, 1866), 26n; "A Canadian," *A Political and Historical Account of Lower Canada . . .* (London: William Marsh and Alfred Miller, 1830), 112. "Jean-Baptiste" was the most common *Canadien* name and was used to personify French-Canadian characteristics in the same way that John Bull represented Englishmen.

4. "A Canadian," *Historical Account*, 127; William Stone, trans., *Letters of Brunswick and Hessian Officers during the American Revolution* (Albany, NY: Joel Munsell's Sons, 1891), 31; Brooke, *Emily Montague*, 1: 13.

5. Harris, *Seigneurial System*, 38.

6. Brooke, *Emily Montague*, 1: 13; "Francis Maseres to Charles Yorke," 27 May 1768, in Francis Maseres, *The Maseres Letters, 1766–1768*, ed. W. Stewart Wallace (Toronto: Oxford, 1919), 97.

7. Allan Greer, *Peasant, Lord and Merchant: Rural Society in Three Quebec Parishes, 1740–1840* (Toronto: University of Toronto Press, 1985), 28–30.

8. "A Canadian," *Historical Account*, 122.

9. Greer, *Peasant, Lord and Merchant*, 163.

10. Stone, *Letters*, 16.

11. Comité Culturel et Patrimonial de Beauceville, "Missionnaires, desservants et curés," accessed 26 February 2012, http://www.ccpb.ca/missionnaires-desservants-et-cures.

12. William B. Munro, *The Seigneurs of Old Canada: A Chronicle of New World Feudalism* (Toronto: Glasgow, Brook and Co, 1914), 118; Owen Chadwick, *The Popes and European Revolution* (Oxford: Clarendon Press, 1981), 133, 149; Roger Magnuson, *Education in New France* (Montréal: McGill-Queen's University Press, 1992), 86.

13. Gilles Chaussé, "French Canada from the Conquest to 1840," in *A Concise History of Christianity in Canada*, eds. Terrence Murphy and Roberto Perin (Toronto: Oxford University Press, 1996), 57–58, 63.

14. "Bouchard," accessed 15 March 2011, http://freepages.genealogy.rootsweb.ancestry.com/~chatweb/b80.htm#P26032.

15. Stone, *Letters*, 22–23.

16. *Quebec Gazette* (hereafter *QG*), 22 August 1765; Ordnance Establishing Civil Courts, 1764, in *Documents of the Canadian Constitution, 1759–1915*, ed. W.P.M. Kennedy (Toronto: Oxford, 1918), 39–40; Donald Fyson, "Judicial Auxiliaries Across Legal Regimes: From New France to Lower Canada," paper presented to the colloquium *Les auxiliaires de la justice: intermédiaires entre la justice*

et les populations, de la fin du Moyen Âge à l'époque contemporaine, Québec, September 2004, accessed 17 January 2010, http://www.hst.ulaval.ca/profs/Dfyson/Auxiliaries.pdf.

17. Pierre-Georges Roy, *La Famille Godefroy de Tonnancour* (Quebec: Laflamme, 1904), 51–57; "Batiscamp, 3 November 1776," in Stone, *Letters*, 45–46; "Godefroy de Tonnancour, Louis-Joseph," *Dictionary of Canadian Biography Online* (hereafter cited as *DCB*), accessed 30 October 2010, www.biographi.ca.

18. The *Moulin Seigneurial de Pointe-du-Lac*, Pointe du Lac, Quebec, ten miles southwest of Trois-Rivières.

19. Harris, *Seigneurial System*, 64–77.

20. Hilda Neatby, *Quebec: The Revolutionary Age, 1760–1791* (Toronto: McClelland and Stuart, 1966), 104.

21. Maseres, *Additional Papers*, 165; Neatby, *Revolutionary Age*, 60.

22. Greer, *Peasant, Lord, and Merchant*, 159–172; "Jacobs, Samuel," *DCB*.

23. Business agreement between Benedict Arnold and Samuel Jacobs, 4 October 1774, Benedict Arnold Collection, MG23 B27, LAC.

24. David T. Ruddel, *Québec City, 1765–1832: The Evolution of a Colonial Town* (Ottawa: National Museums, 1987), 57; "Allsopp, George," *DCB*.

25. "Guy, Pierre, 1738–1812," *DCB*; Hilda Neatby, "Pierre Guy: A Montreal Merchant of the Eighteenth Century," *Eighteenth Century Studies* 5, no. 2 (Winter, 1971–1972): 224–42.

26. See José Eduardo Igartua, *The Merchants and Negotiants of Montreal, 1750–1775: A Study in Socio-economic History* (Ann Arbor, MI: University Microfilms International, 1980); and Dale Miquelon, "The Baby Family in the Trade of Canada, 1750–1820," Master's thesis, Carleton University, Ottawa, 1966.

27. Yvan Lamonde, *Histoire Sociale des Idées au Québec*, Vol I: *1760–1896* (Montréal: Fides, 2000), 70.

28. William Smith, "The Post Office, 1763–1841," in *Canada and its Provinces: A History of the Canadian People and Their Institutions by One Hundred Associates*, eds. Adam Shortt and Arthur Doughty (Toronto: Glasgow, Brook, 1914), 4: 731; *QG*, 23 May 1765. Ship traffic analysis is derived from *QG* customhouse reports, April–November 1774.

29. Richard D. Brown, *Knowledge Is Power: The Diffusion of Information in Early America, 1700–1865* (New York: Oxford University Press, 1989), 112–16; Magnuson, *Education in New France*, 90–91; GC to EoD, 11 November 1775, *DAR*, 8: 229. The "Journal Kept in Quebec in 1775 by James Jeffry," *Historical Collection of the Essex Institute* 50 (April 1914): 97–150, shows that the coffeehouses and taverns of Québec City and Montréal were communication hubs on a par with those in other North American cities.

30. F-J Audet, "William Brown (1737–1789), premier imprimeur, journaliste et libraire de Québec; sa vie et ses oeuvres," *Transactions of the Royal Society of Canada, Third Series* (1932) 26: 97; "Brown, William," *DCB*.

31. *QG*, 21 June 1764; Pierre du Calvet, *The Case of Peter du Calvet, Esq., Of Montreal in the Province of Quebec* (London, 1834), 60–61.

32. *QG*, 2 January 1772 and 15 April 1773.

Chapter 3. Fuel for Rebellion

Epigraph: *CAD*, 1: 411–12.

1. Major Moncrief, *A Short Account of the Expedition Against Quebec . . .* , ed. E.G.G. Lewis (Quebec: Franciscan Convent, 1901), 50.

2. John Knox, *An Historical Journal of the Campaigns in North America* (London: W. Johnston, 1769), 1: 303–4; "Journal of Malcolm Fraser," in George M. Wrong, *A Canadian Manor and Its Seigneurs: The Story of a Hundred Years, 1761–1861* (Toronto: Macmillan, 1908), 253–55.

3. John Faragher, *A Great and Noble Scheme: The Tragic Story of the Expulsion of the French Acadians from Their Homeland* (New York: W.W. Norton, 2005), 436–37; Pierre-Maurice Hebert, *The Acadians of Quebec* (Orange Park, FL: Quintin, 2002), 265.

4. Guy Fregault, *Canada: The War of the Conquest* (Toronto: Oxford, 1969), 270–72; "General Murray's Report of the State of the Government of Quebec," 5 June 1762, in *CAD*, 1: 49; Roeliff Morton Breckenridge, "The Paper Currencies of New France," *Journal of Political Economy* 1, no. 3 (June 1893): 426–31.

5. *CAD*, 1: 6–7, 21–29.

6. "Dubreil de Pontbriand, Henri-Marie," *DCB*.

7. John S. Moir, *The Church in the British Era: From the British Conquest to Confederation* (Toronto: McGraw-Hill Ryerson, 1972), 39–41; "Montgolfier, Étienne" and "Briand, Jean-Olivier," *DCB*. The most pressing need for a bishop was to ordain new priests.

8. Mason Wade, *The French Canadians, 1760–1945* (Toronto: Macmillan, 1956), 55–56.

9. James Murray to Earl of Halifax, 30 October 1764, in Wade, *French Canadians*, 57.

10. Thomas Gage to Earl of Halifax, 23 February 1765, in *The Correspondence of General Thomas Gage with the Secretaries of State, 1763–1775*, ed. Clarence E. Carter (hereafter cited as *CTG*), (New Haven: Yale University Press, 1931), 1: 51–52.

11. Ibid.

12. Neatby, *Revolutionary Age*, 128–29.

13. "James Murray to the Captains of Militia in the Parishes above Quebec, 22 March 1764," in *A History of the Organization, Development, and Services of the Military and Naval Forces of Canada, From the Peace of Paris in 1763 to the Present Time*, eds. Historical Section of the General Staff (hereafter cited as *HMNF*), (Quebec: King's Printer, 1919), 1: 72–73.

14. Of the sixteen officers, several would play an active role in the 1774–1776 crisis: Major Jean-Baptiste-Marie Bergères-de-Rigauville, Captain Antoine Juchereau-Duchesnay, Lieutenant Joseph-Hippolyte Hertel-de-St-François, and a Lieutenant Dupré, presumably St-Georges Dupré or his brother Jean-Baptiste; *HMNF*, 1: 100.

15. Proclamation for raising Canadian Volunteers . . . , 6 March 1764 in *HMNF*, 1: 61; Frederick Haldimand to Thomas Gage, 25 March 1764, and Frederick Haldimand to Halifax, 18 April 1764, in Michel Brunet, *Les Canadiens Après La Conquête, 1759–1775: De la Révolution canadienne à la Révolution américaine* (Montréal: Fides, 1969), 66–67.

16. Copy of a letter from Quebec, 30 September 1766, in D. G. Creighton, *The Commercial Empire of the St. Lawrence, 1760–1850* (Toronto: Ryerson, 1937), 58–59; Wilfred B. Kerr, "The Stamp Act in Quebec," *English Historical Review* 47 (1932): 648–51.

17. Paul David Nelson, *General Sir Guy Carleton, Lord Dorchester: Soldier-Statesmen of Early British Canada* (Cranbury, NJ: Associated University Presses, 2000), 20–29. See also Paul H. Smith, "Sir Guy Carleton: Soldier-Statesman," in *George Washington's Opponents: British Generals and Admirals in the American Revolution*, ed. George A. Billias (New York: Morrow, 1969); "Carleton, Guy, 1st Baron Dorchester," *DCB;* and Arthur G. Bradley, *Sir Guy Carleton (Lord Dorchester)* (Toronto: University of Toronto Press, 1966).

18. Nelson, *Guy Carleton*, 19, 31

19. Guy Carleton to Lord Shelburne, Quebec, 25 November 1767, in *HMNF,* 1: 110.

20. See Philip Lawson, *The Imperial Challenge: Quebec and Britain in the Age of the American Revolution* (Montréal: McGill-Queen's University Press, 1990) for a comprehensive study of the issues surrounding Quebec's government within the British Empire.

21. Coffeehouses were just another form of public house, serving coffee and other potables (rum, ale, etc.). In many cities, they were the preferred gathering places for the merchant community and generally catered to a higher-class clientele than typical taverns.

22. Petition for a General Assembly, in *CAD*, 1: 291–292; Francis Maseres to Richard Sutton,

14 August 1768, in Maseres, *Maseres Letters*, 113; Guy Carleton (hereafter GC) to Earl of Hillsborough, Quebec, 28 March and 25 April 1770, in *DAR*, 2: 69, 81–82.

23. Petition for the Restoration of French Law and Custom, in *CAD*, 1: 292–93.

24. Account Transmitted to Maseres by "principal English Inhabitants of Quebec, and Petition to the King," 31 December 1773 and 10 January 1774, in *CAD*, 1: 343–44, 348–49. Huguenots were Protestants driven out of France following the 1681 Revocation of the Edict of Nantes, which ended that country's religious toleration.

25. Cramahé's Reply to Petition for Assembly, 11 December 1773, and note to "Memorial to Dartmouth," 15 January 1774, in *CAD*, 1: 346, 1845; Memorial of British in Quebec to EoD, 31 December 1773, in *DAR*, 6: 268.

26. Petition of the Roman Catholic Inhabitants of Quebec, December 1773, in *AA4*, 1: 1849.

27. "His Majesty's Most Gracious Speech to both Houses of Parliament," *QG*, 15 September 1774.

28. *Massachusetts Gazette and Boston Post-Boy*, 29 August 1774; GC to EoD, 11 November 1774, in *DAR*, 8: 230.

29. GC to EoD, 23 September 1774, in *CAD*, 2: 583; Nelson, *Guy Carleton*, 54.

30. Creighton, *Commercial Empire*, 56–57; "Extract of a Letter dated the 9th of October, 1774, from a Gentleman in Montreal, to his Friend in New-York," *Boston Evening-Post*, 21 November 1774.

31. John Jay, quoted in James Duane's "Notes of Debates," 15–17 October 1774, in *Letters of Delegates to Congress, 1774–1789*, ed. Paul H. Smith (hereafter cited as *LOD*), (Washington, DC: Library of Congress, 1976), 1: 199. Jay's points match Lord Camden's points of objection to the Act, raised in the House of Lords debates and printed in colonial newspapers over the summer; "Substance of Lord Camden's Speech . . . May 17, 1775," *Rivington's Gazette* (New York), 13 July 1775.

32. Samuel Sherwood, "The Church's Flight into the Wilderness: An Address on the Times," New York, 17 January 1776, in *Political Sermons of the American Founding Era*, vol. I (1730–1788), ed. Ellis Sandoz (Indianapolis, IN: Liberty Fund, 1998), 502. See Francis Cogliano, *No King, No Popery: Anti-Catholicism in Revolutionary New England* (Westport, CT: Greenwood, 1995), and Charles H. Metzger, *The Quebec Act: A Primary Cause of the American Revolution* (New York: United States Catholic Historical Society, 1936), for broader assessments of colonial anti-Catholic sentiment.

33. "London, August 16," *Connecticut Journal and the New-Haven Post-Boy*, 21 October 1774.

34. *JCC*, 1: 111; "London . . . June 21," *Dunlap's Pennsylvania Packet* (Philadelphia), 29 August 1774; "From the London Evening Post of June 30," *New York Journal*, 29 September 1774.

35. "London . . . June 28," *Dunlap's Pennsylvania Packet* (Philadelphia), 29 August 1774; "Novanglus," 30 January 1775, in Jensen, *Tracts*, 311; "London, August 11" and "August 13," *Connecticut Journal and the New-Haven Post-Boy*, 21 October 1774.

36. Frustrated Ohio Valley investors included George Washington, Benjamin Franklin, Richard Henry Lee, and Patrick Henry, among many other entrepreneurial Virginians and Pennsylvanians. See Clarence W. Alvord, *The Mississippi Valley in British Politics: A Study of the Trade, Land Speculation, and Experiments in Imperialism Culminating in the American Revolution* (Cleveland, OH: Arthur H. Clark, 1917); Thomas P. Abernethy, *Western Lands and the American Revolution* (New York: Russell and Russell, 1959); and Shaw Livermore, *Early American Land Companies: Their Influence on Corporate Development* (Washington, DC: Beard, 2000).

37. NY Assembly, 3 March 1775, in *AA4*, 1: 1300; "Representation and Remonstrance of the General Assembly of the Colony of New-York," *Rivington's Gazette* (New York), 27 April 1775. The customs post provision in the Quebec Revenue Act was amended in May 1775, but word did not reach the colonies until the Revolution was well in motion; Bernhard Knollenberg, *Growth of the American Revolution, 1766–1775* (Indianapolis: Liberty Fund, 2003), 146–49.

38. Benjamin Hallowell to Grey Cooper, 5 September 1774, in *DAR*, 8: 191.

Chapter 4. Authors and Agitators

Epigraphs: "Extract of a Letter dated the 9th of October, 1774, from a Gentleman in Montreal, to his Friend in New-York," *New-York Journal*, 10 November 1774; Samuel Adams Papers (hereafter cited as SAP), New York Public Library (hereafter cited as NYPL).

1. "Oliver Cromwell," *Boston Gazette*, 19 October 1772; Jonas Clarke Minot to Arnold Welles, 6 September 1774, and Boston Committee to J. C. Minot, 10 October 1774, in Massachusetts Historical Society, *Collections of the Massachusetts Historical Society*, Ser. 4 (Boston: Little, Brown, 1858), 4: 70–71. Historian T. H. Breen identified these charitable donations as the "first step" in the political mobilization of many colonists and the development of continental patriot networks; T. H. Breen, *American Insurgents*, 17. Of note, the content of the Boston Committee letter does not match the description of the mysterious "General Congress" letter to Québec City, mentioned in the 25 October *Nova Scotia Gazette*, which reportedly invited Canada's "principal merchants" to join the other colonies' protest measures (see the discussion in Chapter One).

2. GC to EoD, 11 November 1774, in *DAR*, 8: 229–30; Petition to the King, 12 November 1774, in *CAD*, 1: 415. Note that Haywood's name is often spelled "Heywood."

3. "Extract of a Letter dated the 9th of October, 1774, from a Gentleman in Montreal, to his Friend in New-York," *New-York Journal*, 10 November 1774.

4. "Extract of a Letter from Quebec, dated Octo. 24, 1774," *Boston Evening-Post*, 21 November 1774.

5. GC to EoD, 11 November 1774, in *DAR*, 8: 229–30; "Extract of a Letter dated at Quebec, October 30," *Massachusetts Gazette and the Boston Weekly News-Letter*, 24 November 1774.

6. GC to EoD, 11 November 1774, in *DAR*, 8: 229–30; *Journal of the most remarkable events which happened in Canada between the months of July 1775 and June 1776* (hereafter cited as *JMRE*), MG23-B7, p. 11, LAC.

7. Petitions for Repeal of the Quebec Act, 12 November 1774, in *CAD*, 1: 414–18. The list of petitioners included almost every notable future Canadian patriot; the loyalists included a large segment of less politically active traders such as Simon, Alexander, and Malcolm Fraser, Simon McTavish, William Grant, Samuel Jacobs, and Aaron Hart.

8. Simon Sanguinet, "Temoin Oculaire de L'Invasion du Canada par les Bastonnois" (hereafter cited as Sanguinet), in *Invasion du Canada, Collection de Mémoires recueillis et annotés*, ed. Abbé Verreau (Montréal: Eusèbe Senecal, 1873), 4; John Brown to Boston Committee of Correspondence, 29 March 1775, in *AA4* 2: 243; Breen, *American Insurgents*, 101, 18.

9. *JCC*, 1: 122; Monette, *Rendez-vous manqué*, 88.

10. "Extract of a Letter from Montreal, Jan. 17," *Boston Evening Post*, 6 March 1776; Monette, *Rendez-vous manqué*, 98–100.

11. "Le Canadien Patriote," 26 December 1774, in Francis Maseres, *An account of the proceedings of the British, and other Protestant inhabitants, of the province of Quebeck, in North America, In order to obtain an House of Assembly in that Province* (London: B. White, 1775), 269–73.

12. "Cugnet, François-Joseph," *DCB*.

13. "Le Canadien Patriote," 26 December 1774, in Maseres, *Account of the Proceedings*, 269–75.

14. Ibid., 264.

15. Francis Maseres, *The Canadian Freeholder: In Two Dialogues between an Englishman and a Frenchman Settled in Canada* (London: B. White, 1777), 27–28.

16. "An Answer to the anonymous Letter written in December 1774, and signed *Le Canadien Patriote*, dated Indian Lorette," 8 February 1775, in Maseres, *Additional Papers*, 52–57.

17. Ibid.

18. "Extract of a Letter from Montreal, dated January 18, 1775," *Pennsylvania Gazette*, 22 February 1775.

19. "Extract of a Letter from Canada, dated Montreal, 24 March 1775," in *AA4*, 2: 231.

20. *JCC,* 1: 88.

21. Memorial of Thomas Walker (hereafter TW), 22 January 1785, Papers of the Continental Congress, (hereafter cited as PCC), M247 r52 i41 vio p665; Sanguinet, 19, translation from E. B. O'Callaghan Papers (throughout), Courtesy of The New-York Historical Society (hereafter cited as NYHS); "Indemnity for Losses Sustained by Francis Cazeau of Montreal," in *American State Papers: Documents, Legislative and Executive, of the Congress of the United States. Class IX. Claims,* ed. Walter Lowrie (hereafter cited as *ASP*), (Washington, DC: Gales and Seaton, 1834), 516.

22. "Indemnity for Losses Sustained by Francis Cazeau of Montreal," in *ASP*, 516; "Cazeau, François," *DCB*; Corinne Rouleau, "Une Incroyable et Véridique Histoire: L'Affaire Cazeau, 1776–1893," *Bulletin de la Société historique Franco-Américaine* (1946–1947): 5–6.

23. Sanguinet, 20; "Copy of Intelligence received the 5th April, 1775, dated 2 Apr.," and "Paper of Intelligence from Montreal," 10 April 1775, in *HMNF*, 1: 137–39.

24. Committee of Worcester, Massachusetts to Timothy Bigelow, 4 October 1774, in *DAR*, 8: 204–6; William Lincoln, ed., *The Journals of Each Provincial Congress of Massachusetts in 1774 & 1775, and of the Committee of Safety with an Appendix Containing the Proceedings of the County Conventions* (hereafter cited as *JPCM*), (Boston: Dutton and Wentworth, 1838), 41, 59.

25. GC to EoD, 11 November 1774, in *DAR*, 8: 230; Jeffry, "Journal," 101, 110; Edward Gray to Hugh Finlay, 13 February 1775, Edward William Gray Fonds, MG23-GII3, LAC.

26. *JPCM*, 100.

27. The Committee of Correspondence of Boston to the Inhabitants of the Province of Quebec, Boston, 21 February 1775, in Samuel Adams, *The Writings of Samuel Adams,* ed. H. A. Cushing (New York: 1907), 3: 119.

28. James Price and Alexander Hay to the Members of the Committee of Donations for the Town of Boston, 9 February 1775, in Massachusetts Historical Society, *Collections,* 4: 234.

29. John Brown (hereafter JB) to Samuel Adams (hereafter SA), Cambridge, 13 February 1775, SAP, NYPL; "The Committee of Correspondence of Boston to John Brown, Boston," 21 February 1775, in Adams, *Writings,* 3: 119. There were several types of "pounds" in North American circulation, including English pounds sterling and various colonial standards. Documents rarely clarify this, but most Continental references are to a colonial pound, roughly valued somewhere between three-quarters and two-fifths of the English standard. Common specie (hard cash) came in a similarly diverse mix of French, Spanish, and English mints, with its own complicated exchange rates. See Simon L. Adler, "Money and Money Units in the American Colonies," *Rochester Historical Society Proceedings* 8 (1929), 143–73; and Fernand Ouellet, *Economic and Social History of Quebec, 1760–1850: Structures and Conjunctures* (Ottawa: Carleton University Press, 1980), 60.

30. Archibald M. Howe, *Colonel John Brown of Pittsfield, Massachusetts, the Brave Accuser of Benedict Arnold* (Boston: W. B. Clarke, 1908), 5.

31. JB to the Committee of Correspondence in Boston, 29 March 1775, in *AA4,* 2: 243–44.

32. Ibid.; "Extract of Letter to Guy Carleton," 7 April 1775, in *DAR,* 9: 93.

33. JB to the Committee of Correspondence in Boston, 29 March 1775, in *AA4,* 2: 243–44; "Extract of a Letter from Montreal, dated 3d April, 1775," and "Copy of Intelligence received the 5th April, 1775, dated 2 Apr.," in *HMNF,* 2: 135, 137.

34. JB to the Committee of Correspondence in Boston, 29 March 1775, in *AA4,* 2: 243–44; "Extract of a Letter from Montreal," 7 April 1775, in *HMNF,* 2: 138. The Latin *in terrorem* means "by way of threat, terror, or warning."

35. JB to the Committee of Correspondence in Boston, 29 March 1775, in *AA4,* 2: 243–44.

36. Ibid.

37. *AA4,* 2: 305.

38. "Extract of letter to GC," 7 April 1775, in *DAR,* 9: 93. In 1775, Todd was a key advisor in reorienting the Phyn and Ellice Company from New York to Montréal, mitigating the impact

of the Quebec Revenue Act and Continental Association on its business. By 1779, Todd's growing ventures with James McGill, the Frobishers (Joseph and Benjamin), and Simon McTavish would expand to become the famed North West Company; "Todd, Isaac," *DCB;* R. H. Fleming, "Phyn, Ellice and Company of Schenectady," in *Contributions to Canadian Economics* (Toronto: University of Toronto Press, 1932), 28–30.

39. William Hey to the Lord Chancellor, 20 August, 11 and 17 September 1775, in *HMNF,* 2: 70; Sanguinet, 21.

Chapter 5. Preemptive Strikes

Epigraphs: *AA4,* 2: 243–44; William Lindsay, "Narrative of the Invasion of Canada by the American Provincials . . . William Lindsay, Lieutenant in the British Militia, 1775," *Canadian Review* 2 (1826): 340.

1. "Intercepted Letter, dated Montreal, 6th May, 1775, Dear Finlay," *Connecticut Gazette* (New London), 16 June 1775; Martha Walker, "A Diary of the Invasion of Canada, 1775. Being a Narrative of Certain Events Which Transpired in Canada, During the Invasion of that Province by the American Army, in 1775. Written by a Mrs. Walker," in *The Collections of the New Hampshire Antiquarian Society, No. 2,* ed. Silas Ketchum (Contoocook, NH: Antiquarian Society, 1876), 35; Henry Livingston, "The Journal of Major Henry Livingston of Third New York Continental Line August to December 1775," ed. Gaillard Hunt, *The Pennsylvania Magazine of History and Biography* 22 (1898): 29.

2. Sanguinet, 24; *QG,* 11 May 1775.

3. Edward Gray to Andrew P. Skene, 6 May 1775, Edward William Gray Fonds, MG23-GII3, LAC; EoD to Thomas Gage, 27 January 1775, in Peter King, "Documents on the American Revolution," accessed 7 January 2011, http://http-server.carleton.ca/~pking/.

4. *Connecticut Journal and the New-Haven Post Boy,* 12 April 1775.

5. "Journal of Captain Edward Mott," in Connecticut Historical Society, *Papers Relating to the Expedition to Ticonderoga, April and May, 1775* (Hartford: Connecticut Historical Society, 1860), 165–67; Edward Mott to the Massachusetts Congress, 11 May 1775, in *AA4,* 2: 558.

6. Benedict Arnold (hereafter BA) to Committee of Safety, 30 April 1775, and Orders to BA, 3 May 1775, in *AA4,* 2: 450, 485; *JPCM,* 185.

7. Brown/Neilson Shop Records, September 1773, in Patricia L. Fleming and Sandra Alston, *Early Canadian Printing: A Supplement to Marie Tremaine's A Bibliography of Canadian Imprints, 1751–1800* (Toronto: University of Toronto Press, 1999), 446; and Business agreement between Benedict Arnold and Samuel Jacobs, 4 October 1774, Benedict Arnold Collection, MG23 B27, LAC. For recent treatments of Arnold, see James K. Martin, *Benedict Arnold, Revolutionary Hero: An American Warrior Reconsidered* (New York: New York University, 1997); Willard Sterne Randall, *Benedict Arnold: Patriot and Traitor* (New York: William Morrow, 1990); and Barry K. Wilson, *Benedict Arnold: A Traitor in Our Midst* (Montréal: McGill-Queens University Press, 2001).

8. Edward Mott to the Massachusetts Congress, 11 May 1775, in *AA4,* 2: 558; JB to Committee of Correspondence in Boston, 29 March 1775, in James P. Baxter, ed., *Collections of the Maine Historical Society, Second Series,* Vol. 14 (Portland: Maine Historical Society, 1910), 241.

9. Alexander Graydon, *Memoirs of a Life, Chiefly Passed in Pennsylvania Within the Last Sixty Years; with Occasional Remarks Upon the General Occurrences, Character and Spirit of that Eventful Period* (Hartsburgh, PA: John Wyeth, 1811), 223; Edward Mott to the MA Congress, 11 May 1775, in *AA4,* 2: 558; Edward Countryman, "Consolidating Power in Revolutionary America: The Case of New York, 1775–1783," *Journal of Interdisciplinary History* 6, no. 4 (Spring 1976): 656. See also Michael Bellesiles, *Revolutionary Outlaws: Ethan Allen and the Struggle for Independence on the Early American Frontier* (Charlottesville: University of Virginia Press, 1995).

10. Edward Mott to the MA Congress, 11 May 1775, in *AA4,* 2: 558.

11. Ethan Allen (hereafter EA) to Committee of the City of Albany, 11 May 1775, in William Bell Clark, ed., *Naval Documents of the American Revolution* (hereafter cited as *NDAR*), (Washington, DC: Government Printing Office, 1964), 1: 314; Seth Warner and Peleg Sunderland to the Governor, Council and General Assembly of CT, Crown Point, 12 May 75, in Lucius E. Chittenden, *The Capture of Ticonderoga: Annual Address Before the Vermont Historical Society* (Montpelier, VT: Tuttle, 1872), 109.

12. Seth Warner and Peleg Sunderland to the Governor, Council and General Assembly of CT, Crown Point, 12 May 75, in Chittenden, *Capture of Ticonderoga,* 109; EA to the MA Congress, 11 May 1775, John J. Duffy, ed., *Ethan Allen and his Kin, Correspondence, 1772–1819. A Selected Edition in Two Volumes* (hereafter cited as *EAK*), (Hanover, NH: University Press of New England, 1998), 1: 20–21; Walker, "Diary," 36–37. It is not clear who specifically brought Arnold's letter to Canada. Arnold had many contacts from previous Quebec business trips, but according to Mrs. Walker, ultimately the letter was delivered by Moses Hazen, who was completely unaware of its content.

13. The elder Skene founded the settlement after serving in the French and Indian War, and was called "Governor" because he had been recently granted royal lieutenant-gubernatorial responsibilities for the Ticonderoga-Crown Point region. Governor Skene, who had been visiting England, would be detained by Congressional authorities upon his Summer 1775 return to North America; *JCC,* 2: 82; William F. Skene, ed., *Memorials of the Family Skene of Skene; from the Family Papers and Other Illustrative Documents* (Aberdeen: New Spalding Club, 1887), 58–60.

14. EA to Jonathan Trumbull, 12 May 1775, in *EAK,* 1: 22; BA to the MA Committee of Safety, 14 May 1775, *NDAR,* 1: 330.

15. James Hadden, *Hadden's Journal and Orderly Books. A Journal Kept in Canada and Upon Burgoyne's Campaign in 1776 and 1777* (Albany, NY: Joel Munsell's Sons, 1884), 35; Arent Schuyler DePeyster, *Miscellanies, By an Officer,* ed. J. Watts De Peyster (Dumfries, UK: C. Munro, 1813), 26.

16. Bateaux (sing. Bateau) were the primary utility watercraft of Canada and the northern lakes; flat-bottomed vessels, pointed at each end, they could be rowed or equipped with rudimentary sails; although not particularly maneuverable, they were known for their excellent carrying capacity.

17. "Hartford, May 29. Extract of a Letter from Ticonderoga, dated May 23," *Connecticut Courant and Hartford Weekly Intelligencer,* 29 May 1775.

18. Ibid.; BA to the Committee of Safety, 19 May 1775, *JPCM,* 702.

19. "Hartford, May 29. Extract of a Letter from Ticonderoga, dated May 23," *Connecticut Courant and Hartford Weekly Intelligencer,* 29 May 1775.

20. Sanguinet, 28–29.

21. *QG,* 25 May 1775; BA to the Committee of Safety, 23 May 1775, in *JPCM,* 703.

22. EA to James Morrison, et al, in *AA4,* 2: 639; GC to EoD, 7 June 1775, in *DAR,* 9: 157.

23. Sanguinet, 29.

24. Verreau, *Invasion,* 305; Sanguinet, 27–31. The *Canadien* appointees were Thomas Dufy-Desauniers, Joseph-Dominique-Emmanuel Le-Moyne-de-Longueuil, Pierre Panet, St- George Dupré, Pierre-François Mézière, Simon Sanguinet, Pierre Guy, and Jacques-Joseph Lemoine-Despins, Sr., all solid loyalists; Sanguinet, 31.

25. Sanguinet, 32.

26. Ibid.

27. "Moses Hazen," *DCB*; Philippe Demers, *Le Général Hazen, seigneur de Bleury-Sud: essai de monographie régionale* (Montréal: Librairie Beauchemin, 1927).

28. "The following is a copy of a circular letter . . . ," *QG,* 27 April 1775; *JCC,* 2: 15.

29. The Georgian St-John's Parish sat about thirty miles south of Savannah on the Atlantic Coast, in modern Liberty County.

30. Kenneth Colemen, *The American Revolution in Georgia, 1763–1789* (Athens: University of Georgia Press, 1958), 43, 49–50.

31. *JCC*, 2: 56.

32. Ibid., 2: 54

33. Nathaniel Wales, Jr. . . . to the Speaker of the Assembly of Connecticut, 23 May 1775, *AA4*, 2: 685.

34. Silas Deane's Diary, 27 May, in *LOD*, 1: 412; *JCC*, 2: 64, 67–70.

35. Letter to the Inhabitants of Canada, 29 May 1775, *JCC*, 2: 68–70.

36. Ibid.; Sanguinet, 39; Monette, *Rendez-vous manqué*, 62.

37. NY Provincial Congress, 25 May–3 June 1775, in *AA4*, 2: 1252–53, 1270, 1275; Address of the NY Provincial Congress to the Inhabitants of Quebeck, 2 June 1775, in *CAD*, 2: 57; Monette, *Rendez-vous manqué*, 176; French translation of Resolution and Address, in Colonial Office Fonds, CO 5. America and West Indies, Original Correspondence, etc., MG11-Co5, Microfilm B-3898 (hereafter cited as Co5),1107, p. 242, LAC; William Tryon to EoD, 5 January 1776, in *Concerning Canadian Archives for the Year 1904* (hereafter cited as *CCA 1904*), (Ottawa: S. K. Dawson, 1905).

38. BA to TW, 24 May 1775, in *HMNF, 2:* 48; BA to the MA Committee of Safety, 23 May 1775, in *JPCM*, 703–704.

39. BA to TW, 20 May 1775, in BA to TW, 24 May 1775, in *HMNF*, 2:47–48; BA to MA Committee of Safety, 26 May 1775, in NDAR, 1: 539.

40. Sub-committee of the City and County of Albany to the Provincial Congress of NY, 26 May 1775, and CT Assembly to the Albany Committee, 2 May 1775, in *AA4*, 2: 713, 731.

41. *JCC*, 2: 73–75.

42. R. Lamb, *An Original and Authentic Journal of Occurrences During the Late American War, From Its Commencement to the Year 1783* (Dublin: Wilkinson and Courtney, 1809), 78.

Chapter 6. *That Damned Absurd Word "Liberty"*

Epigraphs: *AA4*, 3: 963; Maseres, *Additional Papers*, 70.

1. See the previous chapter for a list of these officers.

2. Sanguinet, 34; GC to EoD, 7 June 1775, in *DAR*, 9: 158.

3. *JMRE*, 7–8; Pierre Guy to François Baby, 19 June 1775, in Verreau, *Invasion*, 306–307.

4. Mandate, Pour la Visite des Paroisses du Diocèse en 1775, 22 May 1775, in Henri Têtu and C. O. Gagnon, *Mandements, Lettres Pastorales et Circulaires des Évêques de Québec*, Vol. 2 (Québec: Imprimerie Générale, 1888), 259–64; Instructions to priests on back of Mandement, in Laval Laurent, *Québec et l'église aux États-Unis sous Mgr. Briand et Mgr. Plessis* (Washington, DC: Catholic University of America, 1945), 40. An interdict is "an ecclesiastical sentence which forbids the right of Christian burial, the use of the sacraments, and the enjoyment of public worship or ecclesiastical functions" until removed; while excommunication has similar practical characteristics, it also removes the excommunicated from the greater Church body. Bishop Briand had the authority to interdict or excommunicate individuals, or to interdict entire parishes within his diocese. John Thein, *Ecclesiastical Dictionary* (New York: Benziger Brothers, 1900), 291–92, 364.

5. *The Bible* (King James Version), Romans 13:1–2; Jean-Olivier Briand (hereafter JOB) to a French Bishop, 10 March 1775, in John S. Moir, *The Church and State in Canada, 1627–1867: Basic Documents* (Toronto: McClelland and Stewart, 1967), 104; *The Bible*, Romans 13:1–7.

6. JOB to St-Ongé, cited in Auguste Gosselin, *L'Église du Canada après la conquête, Deuxième Partie, 1775–1789* (Québec: Laflamme, 1917) 7; Mandate "Au Sujet de l'Invasion des Américains au Canada," in Têtu, *Mandements*, 264–65; "Serment prêché pour expliquer le mandement du 22 mai, 1775," in Gustave Lanctot, *Canada and the American Revolution, 1774–1783* (Cambridge, MA: Harvard University Press, 1967), 53.

7. Many *Canadiens* referred to all their southern neighbors as *Bastonnais* (Bostonians), without regard to their colony of origin.

8. Copy of Intelligence received the 5th April, 1775, dated 2 Apr., in *HMNF,* 1: 137; Michael P. Gabriel, ed., *Quebec During the American Invasion: The Journal of François Baby, Gabriel Taschereau and Jenkin Williams* (hereafter *BTW*) , trans. S. Pascale Vergereau-Dewey (East Lansing: Michigan State University, 2005) 60, 62.

9. *BTW,* 63. *Curé* Verreau's background is provided in Chapter Two.

10. Matthews was accompanied by David Dinsmore of New Gloucester, a man named Moore, and possibly Remington Hobby or John Getchell of Vassalboro. A second three-man team, perhaps including New Gloucester's Benjamin Hammon, had executed a similar mission a week earlier, but was never seen again. That party may have been lost in the wilderness expanse between the Maine settlements and the Chaudière; Thomas Smith, *Extracts from the Journals Kept by the Rev. Thomas Smith, Late Pastor of the First Church of Christ in Falmouth* (Portland, ME: Thomas Todd, 1821), 46; William Williamson, *The History of the State of Maine; From Its First Discovery,* A.D. *1602, to the Separation,* A.D. *1820, Inclusive,* Vol. 2 (Hallowell, ME: Glazier, Masters and Co., 1832), 418.

11. "Extract of a Letter from Hon. Enoch Freeman, to the Massachusetts Congress," 5 May 1775, in *JPCM,* 217; Smith, *Journals,* 46; *BTW,* 60.

12. *BTW,* 60; *JMRE,* 6; Smith, *Extracts,* 46.

13. State of Two Companies of His Majesty's Royal Regiment of Artillery, 7th (or Royal Fusiliers) and 26th Regiment of Foot, Montreal, 5 June 1775, in *CCA 1904,* 369.

14. GC to EoD, 7 June 1775, in *DAR,* 9: 158; "Extract of a Letter, intercepted at Ticonderoga . . . Signed, A. Mabane. Woodfield, (in Canada) April 26," *Connecticut Journal and New-Haven Post-Boy,* 7 June 1775; Extract of a Letter from Thomas Gage to GC, 4 September 1774, in *CAD,* 2: 583–84.

15. GC to EoD, 7 June 1775, in *DAR,* 9: 158.

16. This report may have originated from a late-May bloodless encounter between Green Mountain Boy scouts and loyalist forces near Fort St-Jean, referred to in the 1 June Proclamation of Colonels Allen and Easton, discussed later in this chapter; *JPCM,* 715–17.

17. Ibid.; Governor Carleton, 9 June Proclamation, *QG,* 15 June 1775.

18. Sanguinet, 34; GC to EoD, 26 June 1775, in *DAR,* 9: 208–209.

19. Letter from Quebeck, 25 October 1774, and Extract of a letter from an English merchant in Quebeck, 9 November 1775, in Maseres, *Additional Papers,* 85–86, 103–104; "Hertel de Rouville, René-Ovide," *DCB.*

20. Sanguinet, 37.

21. Hector Cramahé to Earl of Hillsborough, 25 July 1772, in *DAR,* 5: 151; A Narrative of the tumultuous conduct of the freeholders of divers seigniories in the province of Quebeck in the summer of the year 1775, in Maseres, *Additional Papers,* 71; Extracts of Letters Received in England, 9 November 1775, in *AA4,* 3: 1418.

22. "Letter to Maseres, 22 June 1775," cited in Justin H. Smith, *Our Struggle for the Fourteenth Colony: Canada and the American Revolution* (New York: Knickerbocker Press, 1907), 1: 221.

23. Proclamation of Cols. Allen and Easton, 1 June 1775, in *JPCM,* 715–17; Monette, *Rendez-vous manqué,* 183.

24. "*On s'y soit qui mal y pence à celui qui ne suivra le bon chemin*"; Jeremiah 6:16 is the closest biblical parallel.

25. NY Provincial Congress to the Gentlemen Merchants of the Province of Quebeck, 12 June 1775, in *AA4,* 2: 1294; Sanguinet, 38–39; Information from Capt Richard Jenkins, 10 September 1774, Philip Schuyler Papers (hereafter cited as PSP), NYPL; "Capt Jenkins . . . ," *Constitutional Gazette* (New York), 20 August 1775; GC to EoD, 14 August 1775, in *DAR,* 9: 74–75.

26. Etienne Montgolfier (hereafter EM) [to JOB], 12 June 1775, Fonds de l'Église catholique, Archevêché de Montréal, MG17-A5, LAC; Maseres, *Additional Papers,* 134–36.

27. Maseres, *Additional Papers*, 134–36; Sanguinet, 39; Allan Greer, *The Patriots and the People: The Rebellion of 1837 in Rural Lower Canada* (Toronto: University of Toronto Press, 1993), 118–19; *JMRE*, 6–7; Deposition from John Baptiste Féré, 10 August 1775, PSP, NYPL.

28. Sanguinet, 38–39; A Narrative of the tumultuous conduct . . . , in Maseres, *Additional Papers*, 72–74; Jeffry, "Journal," 116–17.

29. This number seems significantly inflated, probably exceeding the valley's entire militia-age male habitant population; even several hundred would still be a significant show of defiance.

30. Deposition by John Duguid, 2 August 1775, and Deposition of John Shatforth, 2 August 1775, PSP, NYPL; A Narrative of the tumultuous conduct . . . , in Maseres, *Additional Papers*, 75–76. The timing is placed "about three weeks" before 3 August 1775, by "Samuel Mott to Jonathan Trumbull, Sr.," 3 August 1775, *AA4*, 3: 18.

31. Narrative of the tumultuous conduct . . . , in Maseres, *Additional Papers*, 75–76; "Cuthbert, James," *DCB*.

32. Documentation of these incidents comes primarily from anti-administration British Party sources; the quotes are clearly filtered by their lens, but the core complaints ring true.

33. Extract of another Letter from Quebeck, 1 October 1775, in *AA4*, 3: 926; Pierre Guy to François Baby, Montreal, 19 June 1775, in Verreau, *Invasion*, 306; Testimony of James Price, 10 July 1776, in *PTJ*, 1: 449.

34. GC to EoD, 14 August 1775, in *DAR*, 9: 73.

35. Sanguinet, 38; Thomas Ainslie, *Canada Preserved: The Journal of Captain Thomas Ainslie*, ed. Sheldon S. Cohen (New York: New York University Press, 1968), 19; Narrative of the tumultuous conduct . . . , in Maseres, *Additional Papers*, 80–81.

36. Sanguinet, 38–40; Ainslie, *Journal*, 19; Narrative of the tumultuous conduct . . . , in Maseres, *Additional Papers*, 80–81; Jeffry, "Journal," 122; Extract of a Letter from Montreal to a Gentleman in England, 10 July 1775, in *AA4*, 2: 1623.

37. *DCB*, "Maclean, Allan," "Nairne, John," and "Fraser (ffraser), Malcolm"; Mary Beacock Fryer, *Allan Maclean, Jacobite General: The Life of an Eighteenth Century Career Soldier* (Toronto: Dundurn Press, 1987), 119; *QG*, 10 August 1775; David Stewart, *Sketches . . . of the Highlanders of Scotland; with Details of the Military Service of the Highland Regiments* (Edinburgh: Archibald Constable, 1822), 2: 183. In 1761, Maclean had raised his own Highlanders regiment in Scotland, the 114th (Maclean's) Highlanders.

38. James Livingston (hereafter JL) to Philip Schuyler (hereafter PS), [n.d.] August 1775, in *AA4*, 3: 469; Thomas Gage to George Germain, 20 September 1775, in *CCA 1904*, 385; "Extract of a letter from an officer at Ticonderoga. . . . dated August 23," *Essex Gazette* [Salem, MA], 7 September 1775; Fryer, *Allan Maclean*, 121–25.

39. GC to EoD, 25 October 1775, and EoD to Guy Johnson, 24 July 1775, in *DAR*, 11: 166, 56. Also see Paul L. Stevens, "His Majesty's 'Savage' Allies: British Policy and the Northern Indians during the Revolutionary War, The Carleton Years, 1774–1778," Doctoral dissertation, State University of New York–Buffalo, 1984).

40. "Extract of a Letter from Montreal, dated the 30th Ult," *QG*, 3 August 1775; Guy Johnson, "Journal of Colonel Guy Johnson from May to November, 1775," ed. E. B. O'Callaghan, in *Documents Relative to the Colonial History of the State of New York* (Albany, NY: Weed, Parsons, 1857), 8: 659; Daniel Claus, *Daniel Claus Memoranda, 1775* (Quebec: Literary and Historical Society of Quebec, 1906), n.p.

41. Johnson, "Journal," 660.

42. Presumably a reference to the St-Jean raids by Arnold and Allen, and the Matthews's mission on the Chaudière, or perhaps the late May patriot scout encounter near St-Jean.

43. "L'Imprimeur est prié d'inférer la paragrafe . . . ," *QG*, 13 July 1775.

44. In this appearance, "Le Canadien Patriote" was bilingual Scottish-Canadian merchant

Hugh Finlay, legislative councilor and deputy postmaster general, not François Cugnet, who wrote in December 1774 under the same name. A *Canadien* named Du Croix helped Finlay with the translation. Jeffry, 124; and "Finlay, Hugh," *DCB*.

45. "Reponse d'un Canadien à un Étranger," *QG*, 27 July 1775; "An English Farmer to the People of Canada," *QG*, 17 August 1775.

46. Sanguinet, 38; Jeffry, "Journal," 117–126. Montréal merchant Udney Hay was one of the patriots detained by Carleton; he was subsequently released and went on to deliver Indian intelligence to the Albany Committee's Dirck Swart (see the following chapter); 20 June 1775, in James Sullivan, ed., *Minutes of the Albany Committee of Correspondence, 1775–1778* (hereafter cited as *MACC*), (Albany, NY: J. B. Lyon, 1923), 1: 91.

47. Neatby, *The Administration of Justice under the Quebec Act* (Minneapolis: University of Minnesota, 1937), 25; William Hey to Lord Chancellor, 28 August 1775, in *CAD*, 2: 668–71.

48. William Hey to Lord Chancellor, 28 August 1775, in *CAD*, 2: 668–71.

49. Ibid.

Chapter 7. To Erect the Glorious Standard

Epigraph: *Constitutional Gazette* (New York), 9 September 1775.

1. Intercepted Canadian mail, read 26 May 1775, in *MACC*, 1: 42.

2. Ibid.; Elisha Phelps to General Assembly of CT, 16 May 1775, in Chittenden, *Capture of Ticonderoga*, 112.

3. EA to Continental Congress (hereafter Cont Congr), 29 May 1775, EA to NY Provincial Congress, 2 June 1775, and EA to the MA Congress, 9 June 1775, in *EAK*, 33–39.

4. EA to Cont Congr, 29 May 1775, EA to NY Provincial Congress, 2 June 1775, and EA to the MA Congress, 9 June 1775, in *EAK*, 33–39.

5. James Easton to the Provincial Congress, 6 June 1775, in *JPCM*, 714–15.

6. BA to the Cont Congr, 13 June 1775, and BA to Jonathan Trumbull, 13 June 1775, in *AA4*, 2: 976–978.

7. Ibid.

8. Richard Buel, Jr., *Dear Liberty: Connecticut's Mobilization for the Revolutionary War* (Middletown, CT: Western University, 1980), 39; Jonathan Trumbull, Sr. to Benedict Arnold, 19 June 1775, in *AA4*, 2: 1026–27.

9. *MACC*, 1: 91, 93, 155–56.

10. Benjamin Franklin (hereafter BF) to Thomas Life, 5 June 1775, in *LOD*, 1: 445.

11. *JCC*, 2: 89.

12. James Wilkinson, *Memoirs of My Own Times*, vol. 1 (Philadelphia: Abraham Small, 1816), 60. See also Don R. Gerlach, *Philip Schuyler and the American Revolution in New York, 1733–1777* (Lincoln: University of Nebraska Press, 1964).

13. Deane was such a zealous advocate for action on the Ticonderoga model, that he was being nick-named "the Affair at Ticonderoga" and earned a reputation as "a Schemer" in Congress; Silas Deane to Elizabeth Deane, 18 June 1775, in *LOD*, 1: 505.

14. Ibid.

15. *JCC*, 2: 103–105.

16. Cont Congr to NY Provincial Congress, 24 June 1775, and Cont Congr to PS, 1 July 1775, PSP, NYPL.

17. Thomas Johnson, Jr. to John Dickinson, n.d. [1 June 1775], in *LOD*, 1: 431; George Washington (hereafter GW) to PS, 25 June 1775, in *AA4*, 2: 1085–86.

18. John Hancock (hereafter JH) to PS, 28 June 1775, in *LOD*, 1: 554; Cont Congr Resolution, 27 June 1775, PSP, NYPL.

19. "To the oppressed inhabitants . . . ," 26 June 1775, in *JCC*, 2: 70.

20. Brook Watson to NY Provincial Congress, 4 July 1775, in *AA4*, 2: 1571.

21. "Declaration on Taking Arms," 6 July 1775, in *JCC*, 2: 152–53; R. H. Lee to Robert Carter, 1 July 1775, in *LOD*, 1: 570.

22. Barbara Graymont, *The Iroquois in the American Revolution* (Syracuse, NY: Syracuse University Press, 1972), 59–60; Reverend Wheelock to the NH Congress, 28 June 1775, in *AA4*, 2: 1542.

23. *JCC*, 2: 175; Silas Deane's Diary, 14 July 1775, in *LOD*, 1: 625; Examination of Garret Roseboom, 14 July 1775, PSP, NYPL; BA to Cont Congr, 11 July 1775, *AA4*, 2: 1647.

24. Edward Mott to Jonathan Trumbull, 6 July 1775, and BA to MA Committee, 24 June 1775, in *AA4*, 2: 1592, 1598–99; MA Committee to BA, 23 June 1775, in *NDAR*, 1: 743.

25. PS to Cont Congr, 27 July 1775, in *AA4*, 2: 1734–35; An Account of the Voyage of Capt. Remember Baker began the 13th day of July . . . , and Capt. Halsey to Philip Schuyler, 30 July 1775, PSP, NYPL.

26. PS to Cont Congr, 21 July 1775, in *AA4*, 2: 1702.

27. Jonathan Trumbull to PS, 17, 24 and 28 July 1775, in *AA4*, 2: 1676–77, 1721, 1747.

28. Charlan Deposition, in *HMNF*, 2: 66–67; and Deposition from John Baptiste Féré, 10 August 1775, PSP, NYPL.

29. Ménard most likely held a 1764 commission or was "elected" captain by fellow parishioners. Although there were contemporary references to other militia-captains in the region's parishes, it does not seem that Carleton issued new commissions on the Richelieu in 1775.

30. Samuel Elmore to PS, 23 July 1775 [1st letter], PSP, NYPL; Charlan Deposition, in *HMNF*, 2: 66–67.

31. Samuel Elmore to PS, 23 July 1775 [2nd letter], and Major Brown's Report from Scout to Canada, 7 August 1775, PSP, NYPL; Memorandum from Lieutenant Colonel Brown to General Schuyler, 27 August 1776, and Petition of JB to the Honorable Cont Congr, 26 June 1776, in Peter Force, ed., *American Archives, Fifth Series* (hereafter cited as *AA5*), (Washington, DC, 1837), 1: 1218, 1220; "Extract of a letter from an Officer at Ticonderoga . . . dated August 23," in *New York Journal*, 7 September 1775; JB to Jonathan Trumbull, 14 August 1775, in *AA4*, 3: 135–36. On their mission to confer with Walker, Ménard and Charlan were detained outside Montréal. An official party of Indians, led by interpreter Louis Perthuis, captured Charlan and delivered him to Montréal authorities, while Ménard escaped; Charlan Deposition, in *HMNF*, 2: 67.

32. Many sources claim that James Livingston was born in Montréal. This is extremely unlikely for his birth year of 1747; apparently the misconception is based on marriage records indicating that he was from Montréal. All of his siblings were born in New York; he was most likely born in Albany.

33. Emma Ten Broek Runk, *The Ten Broeck Genealogy: Being the Records and Annals of Dirck Wesselse Ten Broeck of Albany and His Descendants* (New York: De Vinne Press, 1897), 87–88; Memorial of JL, 7 March 1782, PCC, M247 r50 i41v5 p246.

34. JL to PS, n.d. [August 1775], in *AA4*, 3: 468–69.

35. Samuel Elmore to PS, 28 July 1775, Remember Baker to PS, 31 July 1775, and Samuel Elmore to PS, 1 August 1775, PSP, NYPL.

36. Report of Captain James Stewart of the *Liberty*, 30 July 1775, in *AA4*, 3: 49; Remember Baker to PS, 31 July 1775, Deposition of John Shatforth, 2 August 1775, and Deposition of John Duguid, 2 August 1775, PSP, NYPL.

37. Deposition from John Baptiste Féré, 10 August 1775, PSP, NYPL.

38. PS to NY Congress, 31 July 1775, in *AA4*, 2: 1760; William Gilliland to Cont Congr, 29 May 1775, PCC, M247 r95 i71 v10 p2. Congress had directed Schuyler to appoint the field officers for the Green Mountain Boys, but he considered the issue to be "too delicate" to overrule local election results and issued commissions accordingly; Philip Schuyler to New York Congress, 23 August 1775, in *AA4*, 3: 243.

39. Proceedings of the Provincial Congress, 30 June 1775, in Berthold Fernow, *New York in the Revolution* (New York: Weed, Parsons and Company, 1887), 1: 13; NY Provincial Congress to PS, 8 August 1775, PSP, NYPL; *The New England Chronicle or the Essex Gazette* [Salem], 7 September 1775.

40. For additional background on Samuel Chase, see Chapter Twenty.

41. Francis Lewis to PS, 2 August 1775, and Samuel Chase to PS, 10 August 1775, in *LOD*, 1: 694, 700; NY Provincial Congress to PS, 21 August 1775, and Silas Deane to PS, 20 August 1775, PSP, NYPL.

42. JH to PS, 18 July 1775, in *LOD*, 1: 635; Michael P. Gabriel, *Major General Richard Montgomery: The Making of an American Hero* (Madison, NJ: Fairleigh Dickinson University Press, 2002), 36.

43. Richard Montgomery (hereafter RM) to PS, 10 August and 24 August 1775, and Major Brown's Report, 25 August 1775, PSP, NYPL. See the following chapter for more biographical background on Montgomery.

44. "Extract of a Letter from the same Gentlemen [at Albany], Sept. 5," *New-York Gazette and Weekly Mercury*, 11 September 1775; "Letter from an Officer in the New York Forces, [Extract] The Carrying Place near Ticonderoga, 14 September 1775," *New York Journal*, 28 September 1775.

45. PS to Jonathan Trumbull, 31 August 1775, in *AA4*, 3: 469.

46. Ibid.; PS to GW, 27 August 1775, in *AA4*, 3: 443–44.

47. RM to PS, 29 August 1775, PSP, NYPL.

48. Deposition of soldier Peter Griffin, 25 August 1775, in *AA4*, 3: 670–71; JB to RM, 23 August 1775, in *NDAR*, 1: 1215.

49. JL to PS, 23 or 24 August 1775, RM to PS, 29 August 1775, and RM to PS, 30 August 1775, PSP, NYPL; "Journal of His Majesty's Brig *Gaspee*, Lieut. William Hunter," in *NDAR*, 1: 1259.

50. "Philadelphia, September 20. Intelligence received by the Congress from General Schuyler, Sept. 18, 1775," *New-England Chronicle* (Salem, MA), 28 September 1775; RM to PS, 29 August 1775, PSP, NYPL; Memorial of JL, 7 March 1782, PCC, M247 r50 i41 v5, p246.

Chapter 8. The Canadians Opened the Road

Epigraph: "Letters to Robert Morris, 1775–1782," *Collections of the New-York Historical Society for the Year 1878* (New York: New-York Historical Society, 1879), 399–400.

1. Janet Livingston Montgomery Memoir, in Louise L. Hunt, *Biographical Notes concerning General Richard Montgomery together with Hitherto Unpublished Letters* (Poughkeepsie, NY: News Book and Job, 1876), 4–8. See also the two fine, modern biographies of Montgomery: Michael P. Gabriel, *Major General Richard Montgomery: The Making of an American Hero* (Madison, NJ: Fairleigh Dickinson University Press, 2002), and Hal Shelton, *General Richard Montgomery and the American Revolution* (New York: New York University Press, 1994).

2. John J. Henry, *An Accurate and Interesting Account of the Hardships and Sufferings of that Band of Heroes, Who Traversed the Wilderness in the Campaign Against Quebec in 1775* (Lancaster, PA: William Greer, 1812), 98; Richard Montgomery to Philip Schuyler, 29 and 30 August 1775, PSP, NYPL.

3. William Digby, *The British Invasion from the North: Digby's Journal of the Campaigns of Carleton and Burgoyne from Canada, 1776–1777*, ed. James P. Baxter (Albany, NY: Joel Munsell's Sons, 1887), 134–35, 138.

4. "Narrative of the siege of St Johns Canada," September 17, 1775, in "Appendix B: Papers Relating to the Surrender of St. Johns and Chambly," *Report on the Works of the Public Archives for the Years 1914 and 1915*, ed. Arthur Doughty (Ottawa: L. Taché, 1916), 18; Livingston, "Journal," 29–30; *HMNF*, 2: 7.

5. JL to PS, n.d. [August 1775], and PS to JH, 8 September 1775, in *AA4*, 3: 468–69, 669.

6. Ibid.

7. PS to JH, 8 September 1775, and Letter to a Gentleman in New York from an Officer at Ile-aux-Noix, 16 September 1775, in *AA4*, 3: 669, 723; "Account of the Battle happen'd near the Camp

at St. John's, on the 6th Instant," *QG*, 14 September 1775; Claude Lorimier, *At War with the Americans* (Victoria, BC: Porcépic, 1987), 30; RM to Janet Montgomery, 5 September 1775 [probably 6 September], in Hunt, *Biographical Notes*, 12.

8. Samuel Prindle Narrative, US National Archives, M804, Revolutionary War Pension and Bounty-Land Warrant Application Files (hereafter RWP), S15577, p5; RM to Janet Montgomery, 5 September 1775 [probably 6 September], Hunt, *Biographical Notes*, 12; PS to JH, 8 September 1775, in *AA4*, 3: 669.

9. Council of War at the Camp near St. John's, 7 September 1775, in *AA4*, 3: 672; Rudolphus Ritzema, "Journal of Col. Rudolphus Ritzema, of the First New York Regiment, August 8, 1775 to March 30, 1776," *Magazine of American History* 1 (1877): 99.

10. JL to PS, 8 September 1775, and EA to PS, 8 September 1775, PSP, NYPL; Ethan Allen, *Narrative of Col. Ethan Allen's Captivity, Written by Himself* (Burlington, VT: Chauncey Goodrich, 1846), 20.

11. John Lacey, "Memoirs of Brigadier General John Lacey," *Pennsylvania Magazine of History and Biography* 25 (1901); Ammi R. Robbins, *Journal of the Rev. Ammi R. Robbins, A Chaplain in the American Army in the Northern Campaign of 1776* (Yale, CT: B. L. Hamlen, 1850), 14.

12. JL to PS, 7 September 1775, PSP, NYPL; EA to PS, [1]4 September, 1775, in *EAK*, 50–51; Allen, *Narrative*, 20.

13. EA to PS, 14 September 1775, in *AA4*, 3: 742–43; Petition from John Vincent, January 1785[?], PCC, M247 r56 i42 v8 p84.

14. JL to PS, 7 September 1775, PSP, NYPL; JL to PS, [~26] August 1775, in *AA4*, 3: 468–469.

15. Ibid.; Order from Prescott to Longueuil, 5 and 6 September 1775, in *Documents Inédits sur le Colonel de Longueuil*, ed. Monongahela De Beaujeu (Montréal: Société Numismatique et des Antiquaires de Montréal, 1891), 16; Sanguinet, 43; Widow Benoist to François Baby, 7 September 1775, in Verreau, *Invasion*, 310–11; Richard Prescott to Charles Preston, 11 September 1775, in Doughty, "Papers," 7; GC to EoD, 21 September 1775, in *DAR*, 11: 130.

16. Widow Benoist to François Baby, 9 September 1775, in Verreau, *Invasion*, 311–13; GC to M. de Longueuil, 13 September 1775, in Beaujeu, *Documents Inédits*, 17.

17. Lorimier, *At War*, 28; Walker, "Diary," 39–44; Widow Benoist to François Baby, 9 September 1775, in Verreau, *Invasion*, 312–13; Sanguinet, 49.

18. JL to PS, St-Thérèse, 8 September 1775, PSP, NYPL.

19. Benjamin Trumbull, "A Concise Journal or Minutes of the Principal Movement Towards St. John's of the Siege & Surrender of the Forts There in 1775," *Collections of the Connecticut Historical Society*, vol. 7 (Hartford: Connecticut Historical Society, 1899), 143; PS to Cont Congr, 19 September 1775, in *AA4*, 3: 738; Orders to Colonel Ritzema on his going into Canada, 10 September 1775, PCC, M247 r189 i170 v70 p99.

20. Narrative of the Proceedings of the Army, 10 September 1775, PSP, NYPL; "Extract of a Letter from . . . Isle aux Noix, dated September 16, 1775," *New York Journal*, 5 October 1775.

21. "Extract of a Letter from . . . Isle aux Noix, dated September 16, 1775," *New York Journal*, 5 October 1775.

22. William M. Willett, *A Narrative of the Military Actions of Colonel Marinus Willett, Taken Chiefly from His Own Manuscript* (New York: Carvill, 1831), 36; RM to Janet Montgomery, 12 September 1775, in Hunt, *Biographical Notes*, 11; At a General Court Martial holden at the Isle aux Noix on the 13th Day of September, Richard Varick Papers, NYHS; Ritzema, "Journal," 98.

23. JL to PS, n.d. [15 September?], PSP, NYPL; Hugh Finlay to Anthony Todd, 19 September 1775, in *DAR*, 11: 121.

24. Near modern St-Mathias.

25. JL to PS, n.d. [15 September?], PSP, NYPL; Sanguinet, 44; Richard Prescott to Charles Preston, 15 September 1775, in Doughty, "Papers," 7; Mons. Oriet's Account enclosed in Tryon to Dartmouth, 11 November 1775, Co5, 1106, pp. 693–95, LAC; "Picoté de Bellestre, François-Marie,"

DCB; Item I7, Fonds Hospice-Anthelme-Jean-Baptiste Verreau, MG23-GV7 (hereafter cited as FHV), LAC. Livingston's brothers Richard and Abraham also joined him in the field, subsequently serving as officers in his Canadian Continental regiment; Edwin Brockholst Livingston, *The Livingstons of Livingston Manor* . . . (New York: Knickerbocker Press, 1920), 524.

26. RM to PS, [19?] September 1775, PSP, NYPL; John Vincent Memorial, n.d., Louis Mornais Certification for Jean-Baptiste Allin, April 6, 1779, Augustin Loizeau Petition to John Jay, n.d., PCC, M247 1158 1147 v3 p409–411, and Memorial of Maurice Desdevens, 27 April 1786, PCC, M247 141 135 p252.

27. JL and Jeremiah Duggan to the Captains . . . , 16 September 1775, in *HMNF*, 2: 78; JL to Militia Officers, 18 September 1775, Perceval-Maxwell Papers (hereafter PMP), MG40-R89, LAC.

28. Mons. I. Oriet's Account, C05, 1106, pp. 693–95, LAC; EM to JOB, 20[?] September 1775, in Gosselin, *L'Église*, 43; Sanguinet, 45.

29. Sanguinet, 45; "Extrait mortuaire de Marie Magdeleine Arrivée" (transcription), Carton 9, item II, FHV, MG23-GV7, LAC.

30. Sanguinet, 45; JL to PS, Pointe-Olivier, n.d., PSP, NYPL.

31. RM to PS, 19 September 1775, PSP, NYPL; Moses Hazen (hereafter MH) to JH, 18 February 1776, in *AA4*, 4: 1189.

32. Feu Foucher, "Journal Tenu Pendant Le Siege du Fort Saint-Jean, en 1775," *Le Bulletin des Recherches Historiques* 40 (1934): 138–39, 142; "Quebec News," *QG*, 28 September 1775; "Narrative of the Siege," 18 September 1775, in Doughty, "Papers," 19.

33. "Narrative of the Siege," 18 September 1775, in Doughty, "Papers," 19; RM to PS, 19 September 1775, PSP, NYPL; Timothy Bedel to NH Committee of Safety, 23 September 1775, in *AA4*, 3: 779.

34. PS to Cont Congr, 19 September 1775, and General Montgomery, Return of Men sent northward . . . 28 September 1775, in *AA4*, 3: 738, 955; "Journal of Robert Barwick During the Canadian Campaign," in *NDAR*, 2: 1387–89.

35. Livingston, "Journal," 19–20; Sanguinet, 45–46.

36. EM to JOB, 20 September 1775, in Gosselin, *L'Église*, 43; "Extracts from Records of Indian Transactions . . . of Col. Guy Johnson," in *CCA 1904*, 351.

37. Not the same person as the Captain Joseph Ménard who promoted Chambly-Ticonderoga correspondence in the summer; *dit* (called) is used to indicate a hereditary family nickname, a very common Quebec practice.

38. RM to PS, 19 September 1775, PSP, NYPL; Allen, *Narrative*, 20–21; Jean Menard dit Brindamour Memorial, n.d., PCC, M247 141 135 p163.

39. Allen, *Narrative*, 20–21; EA to RM, 20 September 1775, in *EAK* 51–52; JL to PS, 8 September 1775, and JL to PS, 19 September 1775, PSP, NYPL.

40. GW to PS, 8 September 1775, PSP, NYPL; Foucher, "Journal," 145; Sanguinet, 45–46; Orders to Colonel Ritzema, 10 September 1775, PCC, M247 1189 1170 v70 p99.

41. Maseres, *Additional Papers*, 118–19. Examples of these habitant songs can be found in Bernard Andrès, *La Conquête des Lettres au Québec (1759–1799): Anthologie* (Québec: Presses de l'Université Laval, 2007), 196, 202.

42. Return of Sick Discharged by PS, 25 September 1775, in *AA4*, 3: 797; Foucher, "Journal," 142–43.

43. Foucher, "Journal," 145; Lorimier, *At War*, 32. General Prescott wrote a letter directing Hazen's delivery to Montréal, apparently on the twenty-first, but there is no indication that Preston ever received those instructions at Fort St-Jean; Richard Prescott to Charles Preston, "Thursday" [n.d.], in Doughty, "Papers," 8.

44. Foucher, "Journal," 146; JL to RM, 27 September 1775, in *AA4*, 3: 953.

45. Allen, *Narrative*, 20–21. Montgomery was aware that his free-ranging officers had "a project of making an attempt on Montreal," but knew of no firm plans, noting, "I fear the troops are not fit for it;" RM to PS, 28 September 1775, PSP, NYPL.

46. Allen, *Narrative*, 20–21; Sanguinet, 49; Item I7, FHV, MG23-GV7, LAC.

47. One of the officers was identified as a Canadian-Acadian interpreter, with family in the L'Assomption area; the other seemed to be a leading officer, wearing "a blanket overcoat" with "a feather in his hat," perhaps Seth Warner or another Green Mountain Boy—perhaps even one of Ethan Allen's brothers—yet no one subsequently claimed involvement in this liaison; Copy of Joseph Deschamps Deposition at Montreal, 10 October 1775, *HMNF*, 2: 93.

48. Depositions of J-B Bruyeres and Joseph Deschamps, 4 October and 10 October 1775, and Copy of Germain Le Roux's Deposition, 13 October 1775, in *HMNF*, 2: 86–87, 93–94, 103; Mémoire [attribué à l'abbé Huet de la Valinière], Fonds de la Bibliothèque Sainte-Geneviève, MG7 VI, LAC.

49. Sanguinet, 50; EM to JOB, 23 October 1775, Collection Jean-Olivier Briand, MG23-GIV4, LAC; Allen, *Narrative*, 23.

50. George Measam to PS, 20 November 1775, PSP, NYPL; "Extract of an authentick Letter from Montreal, dated September 28," *QG*, 5 October 1775.

51. Multiple accounts, in *QG*, 5 October and 19 October 1775; "Hartford, November 20. Extract of a letter from an officer of rank, dated Camp before St. John's, Nov. 1, 1775," *Connecticut Gazette*, 1 December 1775; William Tryon to EoD, 11 November 1775, Co5, 1106, p. 692, LAC; EM to JOB, 2 October 1775, Collection Jean-Olivier Briand, MG23-GIV4, LAC.

52. Multiple accounts, in *QG*, 5 October and 19 October 1775; EM to JOB, 2 October 1775, Collection Jean-Olivier Briand, MG23-GIV4, LAC; Allen, *Narrative*, 24.

53. Walker, "Diary," 45; "Extract of a letter from Tionderoga [*sic*], October 5," *Rivington's Gazette* (New York), 26 October 1775; RM to PS, 28 September 1775, PSP, NYPL.

54. EM to JOB, 9 October 1775, in Gosselin, *L'Église*, 45; Brook Watson to William Franklin, 18 October 1775, PCC, M247 r65 i52 VI p275; Brook Watson to William Sheriff, 16 October 1775, in *Pennsylvania Evening Post* (Philadelphia), 24 December 1775; EM to JOB, 2 October 1775, Collection Jean-Olivier Briand, MG23-GIV4, LAC.

55. Cont Congr to PS, 20 September 1775, PSP, NYPL.

56. PS to Cont Congr, 19 September 1775, in *AA4*, 3: 739.

57. RM to PS 24 September 1775, PSP, NYPL; PS to Cont Congr, 29 September 1775, in *AA4*, 3: 839.

58. Extract of a Letter from a Gentleman in Quebeck, to his Father in Ayrshire, Scotland, 30 September 1775, in *AA4*, 3: 845.

59. The one-seventh figure is based on "200 Canadians have join'd Montgomery's Army, commanded by James Livingston" from "Six Parishes on the River Sorrel amounting to 1500 fit to bear Arms," in "Mons. I. Oriet's Account," Co5, 1106, pp. 693–95, LAC; one-fourth is based on 300 under Livingston and 125 additional recruits under Allen after 19 September, allowing for half of Allen's claimed recruits to be Livingston's men and/or bluster; Lt Abraham Palmer of Bedel's Company also reported 500 Canadians "under arms with them" on 6 October; *AA4*, 3: 980.

Chapter 9. The Treachery of the Canadians

Epigraph: *DAR*, II: 189.

1. GC to EoD, 24 October 1775, in *DAR*, II: 165; Memorial of TW, 22 January 1785, PCC, M247 r52 i41 VIO p665.

2. GC Order, 4 October 1775, TW Oath before Samuel Mifflin, 24 April 1776, and Declaration of Bruyere de Belair [Jean-Baptiste Bruyères-de-Belaire], 17 February 1776, in *The Remembrancer, or Impartial Repository of Public Events*, Part 2, ed. John Almon (London: 1776), 244–48; Memorial of TW, 22 January 1785, PCC, M247 r52 i41 VIO p665; Deposition of J-Bte. Bruyeres, 4 October 1775, in *HMNF*, 2: 86–87.

3. TW Oath before Samuel Mifflin, 24 April 1776, in Almon, *Remembrancer*, 244–47; Memorial of TW, 22 January 1785, PCC, M247 r52 i41 VIO p665; Walker, "Diary," 48–49.

4. Trumbull, "Concise Journal," 148–49; RM to Timothy Bedel, 2 October 1775, in W.T.R.

Saffell, *Record of the Revolutionary War: Containing the Military and Financial Correspondence of Distinguished Officers* . . . (Baltimore: Charles C. Saffell, 1894), 22; "Barlow's Diary," 3 October 1775, in New-York Historical Society, *Early American Orderly Books, 1748–1817* (New Haven, CT: Research Publications, 1977).

5. Swivel guns were very light artillery pieces, mounted in pivoting brackets.

6. JL to Timothy Bedel, 5 October 1775, in Saffell, *Record,* 24; "Barlow's Diary," 4 October 1775, in NYHS, *Orderly Books;* "Narrative of the Siege," 4 October 1775, in Doughty, "Papers," 21; RM to PS, 6 October and 9 October 1775, PSP, NYPL. New York Major Herman Zedwitz, commanding the east shore, later reported that about half of the Canadians fled in the face of the attack. This detail is questionable, as no other accounts mention such a flight, and Zedwitz wrote this as part of a self-aggrandizing justification of his overall conduct in Continental service, following his arrest for treasonous acts in the summer of 1776; Defense of Herman Zedwitz, PCC, M247 i78 r104 v24 p675–676.

7. RM to Timothy Bedel, 29 September, 2 and 4 October 1775, in Saffell, *Record,* 22–23; Israel Morey to the NH Committee of Safety, 6 October 1775, in *AA4,* 3: 980.

8. Foucher, "Journal," 152–53.

9. Ibid.; "La Corne, Luc de," *DCB.*

10. Sanguinet, 52–53; RM to JL, 4 October 1775, and John McPherson to JL, 4 October 1775, PCC, M247 r50 i41 v5 p250, 271; RM to Janet Montgomery, 6 October 1775, in Hunt, *Biographical Notes,* 13; RM to PS, 6 October 1775, PSP, NYPL; RM to JB, 6 October 1775, in *AA4,* 3: 1098.

11. Sanguinet, 51–53; RM to PS, 9 October 1775, PSP, NYPL; RM to Janet Montgomery, 9 October 1775, in Hunt, *Biographical Notes,* 14.

12. *QG,* 5 October 1775; EM to JOB, 2 October 1775, Collection Jean-Olivier Briand, MG23-GIV4, LAC; Sanguinet, 54–55; Widow Benoist to François Baby, 3 October 1775, in Verreau, *Invasion,* 317.

13. Jean-Baptiste Badeaux, *Journal des Operations de l'Armée Américaine Lors de L'Invasion du Canada en 1775–76* (Montréal: Eusèbe Senecal, 1871), 3; *BTW,* 32.

14. Sanguinet, 54.

15. "Tarieu de Lanaudière, Charles-Louis," *DCB; BTW,* 35–36; Badeaux, *Journal,* 6–7.

16. Badeaux, *Journal,* 6–7; Guy Carleton to Earl of Dartmouth, 25 October 1775, and Hugh Finlay to Anthony Todd, 1 November 1775, in *DAR,* 11: 166, 171.

17. See Chapter Two for more on Tonnancour's background.

18. Badeaux, *Journal,* 5–6.

19. Ibid., 7–8; Berthelot Journal, in Verreau, *Invasion,* 230.

20. EM to JOB, 9 October 1775, in Gosselin, *L'Église,* 45; Sanguinet, 55–56.

21. *QG,* 19 October 1775; GC to EoD, 25 October 1775, in *DAR,* 11: 166.

22. EM to JOB, 2[0] October 1775, Collection Jean-Olivier Briand, MG23-GIV4, LAC.

23. Rigauville served in the French and Indian War and commanded the Canadian regiment in Pontiac's War.

24. EM to JOB, 2[0] October 1775, Collection Jean-Olivier Briand, MG23-GIV4, LAC; Sanguinet, 63; John Fassett, Jr., "Diary of Lt John Fassett Jr. . . . ," in *The Follet-Dewey Fassett-Safford Ancestry of Captain Martin Dewey Follett,* ed. Harry P. Ward (Columbus, OH: Champlin, 1896), 222; GC to EoD, 20 November 1775, in *DAR,* 11: 186.

25. Sanguinet, 63; EM to JOB, 2[0] October 1775, Collection Jean-Olivier Briand, MG23-GIV4, LAC; RM to PS, 20 October 1775, PSP, NYPL.

26. PS to GW, 6 November 1775, *PGWRWS,* 2: 316.

27. Livingston, "Journal," 21.

28. "Second Book of Minutes of the Court of Inquiry of Damages Occasioned by the Invasion of the Rebels," FHV, MG23-GV7, LAC.

29. RM to Timothy Bedel, 29 September 1775, and RM to Timothy Bedel, 5 October 1775, in Saffell, *Record,* 21–22, 24; PS to JH, 18 October 1775, in *AA4,* 3: 1094.

30. RM to PS, 13 October 1775, PSP, NYPL; Herman Zedwitz to JH, 25 November 1778, PCC, M247 i78 r104 v24 p675–676.

31. RM to PS, 9 October and 31 October 1775, PSP, NYPL; Samuel Mott to Jonathan Trumbull, 6 October 1775, in *AA4,* 3: 974.

32. RM to PS, 13 October and 20 October 1775, PSP, NYPL.

33. Ritzema, "Journal," 106; Memorial of JL, 7 March 1782, and RM to JL, 16 October 1775, PCC, M247 r50 i41 v5 p246, 266; RM to PS, 20 October 1775, PSP, NYPL; Israel Curtiss to Jonathan Chase Cornish, 7 October 1775, Donald F. Clark Collection, NYHS; "Narrative of the Siege," 16 October 1775, in Doughty, "Papers," 23.

34. George Heriot, *Travels through the Canadas* (Philadelphia: M. Carey, 1813), 118.

35. Claus, *Memoranda,* n.p.; Memorial of JL, 7 March 1782; and RM to JL, 19 October 1775, PCC, M247 r50 i41 v5 246, 262.

36. RM to PS, 20 October 1775, PSP, NYPL; Foucher, "Journal," 201.

37. JL to RM, 16 October 1775, in *AA4,* 3: 1195–96; Rhode Island Delegates to Nicholas Cooke, 4 November 1775, in *LOD,* 2: 302.

38. RM to PS, 20 October 1775, PSP, NYPL.

39. RM to PS, 23 October 1775, PSP, NYPL.

40. PS to JH, 18 October and 21 October 1775, PCC, M247 r172 i153 vi p213, 242; PS to JH, 20 October 1775, in *AA4,* 3: 1124; Justus Bellamy Narrative, RWP, S17838.

41. PS to JH, 21 October 1775, PCC, M247 r172 i153 vi p242; GW to PS, 6 October 1775, and Thomas Lynch to PS, 9 November 1775, PSP, NYPL; David Wooster (hereafter DW) to Roger Sherman, 7 July 1775, in Lewis H. Boutell, *The Life of Roger Sherman* (Chicago: A. C. McClurg, 1896), 88; DW to Jonathan Trumbull, Sr., 24 August 1775, in *AA4,* 3: 262.

42. PS to DW, 19 October 1775, and DW to PS, 19 October 1775, in *AA4,* 3: 1107–1108; Justus Bellamy Narrative, RWP, S17838; Extract of a Letter from an Officer in the New York Forces, 3 November 1775, in *AA4,* 3: 1344; Benjamin Trumbull letter, 3 November 1775, in Trumbull, "Concise Journal," 171–72; RM to PS, 31 October 1775, PSP, NYPL. In the stiff 19 October exchange—conducted by letter, even though both were at Ticonderoga—Schuyler also sought confirmation that Wooster considered his regiment under Continental authority. Wooster replied that his men had been enlisted under a "compact" with Connecticut, but were "acting in conjunction with the other colonies in the service, and for the defence of the associated colonies in general." However, he did promise to "use every means" in his "power to give success to the expedition."

43. Sanguinet, 58–60; Fassett, "Diary," 223–24.

44. Sanguinet, 61, 64; Fassett, "Diary," 223–24.

45. Lorimier, *At War,* 38–39.

46. RM to PS, 3 November 1775, PSP, NYPL; "Extract of a Letter from St. John's Camp, North Side of St. John's, Nov. 4, 1775," *New England Chronicle or the Essex Gazette* (Salem, MA), 30 November 1775; Fassett, "Diary," 225.

47. Fassett, "Diary," 225–26.

48. Ibid.; Lorimier, *At War,* 39; Christopher Prince, *The Autobiography of a Yankee Mariner: Christopher Prince and the American Revolution,* ed. Michael J. Crawford (Washington, DC: Brassey's, 2002), 54.

49. Fassett, "Diary," 225–28; Sanguinet, 65.

50. Sanguinet, 59; Berthelot Journal, in Verreau, *Invasion,* 230; Hugh Finlay to Anthony Todd, 1 November 1775, in *DAR,* 11: 171.

51. JB Memorandum of Service to PS, 27 August 1776, in *AA5,* 1: 1219; JL to RM, 26 October 1775, in *AA4,* 3: 1196; Augustin Loizeau Petition to John Jay, n.d., PCC, M247 r158 i147 v3 p409–411.

52. Badeaux, *Journal*, 8; Berthelot Journal, in Verreau, *Invasion*, 230; Hector Cramahé to George Germain, 6 October 1775, Public Record Office, Ser. Q, Canada Correspondence, Canada, Formerly British North America, Original Correspondence, MG11-C042Q, v12, p195–196, LAC.

53. Berthelot Journal, in Verreau, *Invasion*, 230–32; Augustin Loizeau Petition to John Jay, n.d., PCC, M247 r158 i147 v3 p409–411; Extracts of Letters Received in England, Quebeck, 9 November 1775, in *AA4*, 3: 1419; RM to PS, 3 November 1775, PSP, NYPL; GC to EoD, 5 November 1775, in *DAR*, 11: 173.

54. JL to RM, 3 November 1775, in *AA4*, 3: 1341.

55. "Second Book . . . of the Court of Inquiry of Damages," FHV, MG23-GV7, LAC.

56. Foucher, "Journal," 210.

57. RM to Charles Preston [First Letter], 1 November 1775, in *HMNF*, 2: 114.

58. Extract of Another Letter from Fort St Johns, 3 November 1775, and Charles Preston to RM, 1 November 1775, in *AA4*, 3: 1344, 1393. Many British officers and authorities grudgingly respected the Continental rebels' cause, to a degree, but were particularly harsh in judging Canadians for defiance or neutrality in the struggle. See also Colonel Maclean's comments at the end of this chapter.

59. "Narrative of the Siege," 1 November 1775, in Doughty, "Papers," 24.

60. The six Continental deserters' ultimate fate is unclear, based on scant records; only New York soldier Anthony Clarke reported deaths on that otherwise calm day—two of Captain Lamb's artillerymen—but failed to clarify the cause of their demise; Anthony Clarke's Memorandum Book, 1775–1776, p. 3, Minute Books, Account Books and Daybooks, 1745–1815, BV Banyar, Goldsbrow, NYHS, transcribed by Stephen Gilbert, Joe Renkas, and Mary Mulcahy.

61. Articles of Capitulation Proposed by Major Charles Preston for his Majesty's Forts at St. John's, 2 November 1775, in *AA4*, 3: 1394; Livingston, "Journal," 26; Prisoners taken at the different Posts at the North in 1775, n.d., Richard Varick Papers, NYHS; RM to PS, 3 November 1775, PSP, NYPL.

62. PS to JH, 11 September 1775, in *AA4*, 3: 1521; RM to PS, 31 October 1775, PSP, NYPL.

63. Allan Maclean to Viscount Barrington, 20 November 1775, in *DAR*, 11: 189; GC to EoD, 5 November 1775, in *HMNF*, 2: 116.

Chapter 10. *Another Path to the Heart of Quebec*

Epigraphs: *JMRE*, 11; Caleb Haskell, *Caleb Haskell's Diary, May 5, 1775–May 30, 1776* (Newburyport, MA: William H. Huse, 1881), 13.

1. "Caldwell, Henry," *DCB*.

2. Jeffry, "Journal," 135; *BTW*, 55, 58–59, 67, 73–79, 84, 94 (Beaumont, St-Henry, St-Charles, Pointe-Lévy, St-Michel, St-Vallier, Berthier, St-François-du-Sud, St-Pierre-du-Sud, St-Thomas).

3. *BTW*, 75, 111 (St-Michel and Rivière-Ouelle).

4. Lamb, *Authentic Journal*, 69; "Grant, William (1744–1804)," and "Boiseau, Nicolas-Gaspard," *DCB*; *BTW*, 19–23; Le Comte Dupré to François Baby, 21 October 1775, in Verreau, *Invasion*, 319.

5. *BTW*, 15, 23; Hugh Finlay to Anthony Todd, 1 November 1775, in *DAR*, 11: 171.

6. Badeaux, *Journal*, 4–5; *BTW*, 22; Laurent, *Québec et l'église*, 41.

7. JOB to Antoine-Lagroix Huppe, 1 October 1775, in Gosselin, *L'Église*, 29–31; Laurent, *Québec et l'église*, 41–44.

8. Maisonbassé to JOB, 22 October 1775, in Lanctot, *Canada and the American Revolution*, 84; JOB to Maisonbasse, 25 October 1775, in Gosselin, *L'Église*, 37–39.

9. JOB to EM, 25 October and 5 November 1775, in Gosselin, *L'Église*, 35–39, 47–48; Letter from Quebeck, 25 October 1775, in Maseres, *Additional Papers*, 91.

10. Jeffry, "Journal," 134–38; Hugh Finlay to [Anthony Todd], 19 September 1775, in *DAR*, 11: 120.

11. Ainslie, *Journal*, 20–21; Extract of a letter from an English merchant in Quebeck, 9 No-

vember 1775, in Maseres, *Additional Papers,* 101; "Extract of a letter from Quebec, dated Sept. 18," *Constitutional Gazette* (New York), 28 October 1775.

12. In 1770, General Gage bluntly reported, "The Works of Quebec are bad."; Thomas Gage to Hillsborough, 8 September 1770, in *CTG,* 1: 269. The city's defenses not only had been damaged during the French and Indian War, but also deteriorated further in the subsequent decade, as the financially strained London government lacked funds to improve them; in 1776, a British officer observed, "The fortifications are in a ruinous condition which shows the neglect of the late Governors."; Joshua Pell, Jr., "Diary of Joshua Pell, Jr.," *Magazine of American History* 2 (1878): 43. For a technical analysis of the fortifications, see also Andre Charbonneau, A. Y. Desloges, and M. Lafrance, *Quebec the Fortified City: From the 17th to the 19th Century* (Ottawa: Parks Canada, 1982).

13. Robert Lester and Anthony Vialar, *Orderly Book begun by Capt. Anthony Vialar of the British Militia the 17th September 1775, and kept by him till November 16th, when continued by Capt. Robert Lester* (Quebec: Literary and Historical Society of Quebec, 1905); *QG,* 21 September, 5 and 26 October 1775; Hector Cramahé to EoD, 21 September 1775, in *DAR,* 11: 125; Fleming, *Early Canadian Printing,* 448.

14. This *nom de plume* had been used a decade earlier in the *QG,* by an author promoting moderation in the Stamp Act Crisis.

15. "Mea Culpa," *QG,* 5 October 1775; translation in *HMNF,* 2: 88–89; Monette, *Rendez-vous manqué,* 249.

16. Fleming, *Early Canadian Printing,* 448; "Adresse aux Canadiens . . . ," *QG,* 12 October 1775; *QG,* 28 October 1775.

17. Hector Cramahé to George Germain, October 6, 1775, Public Record Office, Ser. Q, Canada Correspondence, Canada, Formerly British North America, Original Correspondence, MG11-C042Q, v12, p195–196, LAC; Jeffry, "Journal," 141.

18. Silas Deane to PS, 20 August 1775, PSP, NYPL; GW to PS, 8 September 1775, PSP, NYPL.

19. The Jabez Matthews scouting party to Quebec was the most recent organized effort to have used the trail, May–June 1775; see the discussion in Chapter Six.

20. GW to Samuel Washington, 30 September 1775, in *PGWRWS,* 2: 72.

21. Ibid.; "Address," c. 14 September 1775, in *PGWRWS,* 1: 461–62.

22. GW to BA, 15 September 1775, in *PGWRWS,* 1: 455–59.

23. GW to JH, 21 September 1775, in *PGWRWS,* 2: 27–28; Thomas Gage to EoD, Boston, 20 September 1775, in *CTG,* 1: 416; "Extract of a letter from Cambridge, September 14 1775," *Story & Humphrey's Pennsylvania Mercury* [Philadelphia], 29 September 1775.

24. BA to GW, 25 September 1775, in *PGWRWS,* 2: 42; Silas Deane to Elizabeth Deane, 2 October 1775, in Silas Deane, *The Deane Papers, 1774–1790,* vol. 1 (New York: New-York Historical Society, 1887), 82; "Journal of Eleazer Oswald on the Quebec Expedition," 25 September 1775, in *NDAR,* 2: 200.

25. Recent works include Thomas Desjardin, *Through a Howling Wilderness: Benedict Arnold's March to Quebec, 1775* (New York: St. Martin's Press, 2006); Arthur S. Lefkowitz, *Benedict Arnold's Army: The 1775 American Invasion of Canada During the Revolutionary War* (New York: Savas Beatie, 2008); and Stephen Darley, *Voices from a Wilderness Expedition: The Journals and Men of Benedict Arnold's Expedition to Quebec in 1775* (Bloomington, IN: AuthorHouse, 2011), which adds to Kenneth Roberts's classic *March to Quebec: Journals of the Members of Arnold's Expedition* (Garden City, NY: Doubleday, 1938).

26. Joseph Hewes to Robert Smith, 8 January 1776, in *LOD,* 4: 58.

27. BA to John Manir [*sic*], 13 October 1775, and BA to Lieutenant Steele, 13 October 1775, in Benedict Arnold, "Letters, September 27–December 5, 1775," *Collections of Maine Historical Society* 1 (1861): 469–70.

28. Different accounts blame the Indians or the soldier, John Hall.

29. Extract of a letter, dated at Quebeck, 9 November 1775, in *HMNF*, 2: 122; Jeffry, "Journal," 143; *JMRE*, 12.

30. BA to GW, 27 October 1775, in *PGWRWS*, 2: 245. Enos was subsequently exonerated of any wrongdoing in a court-martial. However, it did not include testimony from any of Arnold's officers who completed the trek, as they were still in Canada; Court of Inquiry and Court-Martial on Lieutenant-Colonel Enos, 31 May 1776, in *AA4*, 3: 1170–71.

31. Morison Diary, November 4, in Roberts, *March to Quebec*, 531; Lindsay, "Narrative of the Invasion," 2: 352; Matthias Ogden, "Journal of Major Matthias Ogden, 1775, In Arnold's Campaign Against Quebec," *Proceedings of the New Jersey Historical Society, New Series* 13 (1928). It does not appear that Arnold had the specific authority to engage additional men in military service, his only related written guidance simply being to "conciliate the Affections of the Canadians and Indians to the great Interests of America"; GW to BA, 14 September 1775, in *PGWRWS*, 1: 456.

32. Ogden, "Journal."

33. See Chapter Six.

34. 5 November, Ogden "Journal"; Isaac Senter, *The Journal of Isaac Senter, Physician and Surgeon* . . . (Tarrytown, NY: 1915); *BTW*, 61, 63, 68.

35. *BTW*, 60–61, 68; BA to RM, 8 November 1775, in Arnold, "Letters," 480–81.

36. Memorial of John Halsted to Congress, 23 March 1785, PCC, M247 r54 i42 v3 p461; Henry Caldwell to James Murray, 15 June 1776, in Henry Caldwell, *The Invasion of Canada in 1775: Letter Attributed to Major Henry Caldwell* (Quebec: Literary and Historical Society of Quebec, 1887), 3; BA to RM, 8 November 1775, in Arnold, "Letters," 480–81.

37. 9 November, Ogden, "Journal."

38. 12 and 13 November, John Pierce Journal, in Roberts, *March to Quebec*, 674; Hugh Finlay to Anthony Todd, 1 November 1775, in *DAR*, 11: 170.

39. BA to RM, 14 November 1775, and Benedict Arnold to unknown, 27 November 1775, in Arnold, "Letters," 484, 495–96.

40. BA to Captain Hanchet, n.d., in Arnold, "Letters," 485–86; John Henry Diary, 14 November 1775, in Roberts, *March to Quebec*, 354.

41. BA to Hector Cramahé, 14 November 1775, in Roberts, *March to Quebec*, 89; 14 and 15 November, Ogden, "Journal"; *JMRE*, 14.

42. Morison Diary, 14 November 1775, and Henry Diary, 16 November 1775, in Roberts, *March to Quebec*, 533, 356; 15 November, in Nathaniel Shipton and David Swain, eds., *Rhode Islanders Record the Revolution: The Journals of William Humphrey and Zuriel Waterman* (Providence: Rhode Island Publications Society, 1984), 25; *JMRE*, 14–15.

43. *QG*, 9 November and 16 November 1775; Ainslie, *Journal*, 21; *JMRE*, 13.

44. Lindsay, "Narrative of the Invasion," 3: 92; Berthelot journal, in Verreau, *Invasion*, 235; *JMRE*, 8–9; "Maclean Testimonial," 25 May 1776, in *HMNF*, 2: 163.

45. Lindsay, "Narrative of the Invasion," 3: 89; 15 November, in Lester, *Orderly Book*; *JMRE*, 17; Allan Maclean to Viscount Barrington, 20 November 1775, in *DAR*, 11: 190.

46. At a Council of War held at Quebec the 16th of November 1775, *CCA 1904*, 367; Civil and Military Officers of Quebec to Captain John Hamilton, 16 November 1775, *NDAR*, 2: 1039.

47. BA to GW, 20 November 1775, in Arnold, "Letters," 490.

48. 18 November, in Senter, *Journal*, 44; 18 November, John Pierce Journal, in Roberts, *March to Quebec*, 679; BA to GW, 20 November 1775, in Arnold, "Letters," 490; General Return of the Detachment under Command of Benedict Arnold . . . 29 November 1775, in Benedict Arnold Correspondence, BV Arnold, Benedict, NYHS.

49. "Philadelphia, Jan 4. Extract of a letter from an officer under Col. Arnold, dated at Point aux Tremble (in Canada) November 21, 1775," *Providence Gazette*, 3 February 1776; Henry Caldwell to James Murray, 15 June 1776, in Caldwell, *Letter*, 6–8; Henry, *Interesting Account*, 94.

50. *JMRE*, 18–19; BA to GW, 20 November 1775, in Arnold, "Letters," 487–89.
51. *JMRE*, 14–15.

Chapter 11. To Winter in Canada

Epigraphs: Arnold, "Letters," 487–89; *HMNF,* 2: 129.

1. Barlow's Diary, 6 and 7 November, in "The March to Montreal and Quebec, 1775," *American Historical Register* 2, ed. Charles Todd (1895): 648; PS to JH, 11 November 1775, in *AA4*, 3: 1522.

2. JB to RM, 7 November 1775, in *AA4*, 3: 1394.

3. Friedrich Adolf Riedesel, *Memoirs and Letters of Major General Riedesel*, vol. 1, ed. Max von Eelking (Albany, NY: J. Munsell, 1868), 51; William Goforth (hereafter WG) to Alexander McDougall (hereafter AM), 6 April 1776, Alexander McDougall Papers (hereafter cited as AMP), NYHS; GC to EoD, 5 November 1775, in *HMNF,* 2: 116–17; JB to RM, 7 November 1775, in *AA4*, 3: 1395.

4. RM to the Inhabitants of Montréal, 7 November 1775, PMP, LAC; JB to RM, 7 November 1775, in *AA4*, 3: 1394; *HMNF,* 2: 118.

5. 10 November, "Barlow Diary," in Todd, "March to Montreal," 648; Herman Zedwitz to JH, 25 November 1778, PCC, M247 i78 r104 v24 p675–676; Sanguinet, 79–80.

6. Sanguinet, 79–80; Prince, *Autobiography,* 53.

7. Sanguinet, 80–83; "Journal of Robert Barwick During the Canadian Campaign," in *NDAR*, 2: 1394.

8. Articles of Capitulation, in *AA4*, 3: 1597–98.

9. Ibid.

10. Ibid.

11. Ibid.; Sanguinet, 84.

12. "Jautard, Valentin" *DCB*; Monette, *Rendez-vous manqué*, 269–72.

13. Sanguinet, 85–86.

14. Curatteau to [Nantes], 22 October 1776, Fonds des Archives départementales de la Loire-Atlantique, Série E- Papiers de famille, MG6-A5, LAC; Livingston, "Journal," 27–29; Thomas Anburey, *Travels through the Interior Parts of America in a Series of Letters by an Officer* (London: William Lane, 1789), 1: 124–25.

15. Francis Grant, "Journal from New York to Canada, 1767," *New York State Historical Association Proceedings* 30 (1932): 308; "Journal of Robert Barwick," in *NDAR*, 2: 1394; Sanguinet, 70–71; Clarke's Memorandum Book, 4, BV Banyar, Goldsbrow, NYHS.

16. 14 and 17 November, in Fassett, "Diary," 235–37; Livingston, "Journal," 28, "New-York, November 30," *New England Chronicle or the Essex Gazette* (Salem, MA), 30 November 1775.

17. RM to PS, 13 November 1775, PSP, NYPL.

18. RM Proclamation to Troops, 15 November 1775, in *AA4*, 3: 1683.

19. Ritzema, "Journal," 103; RM to PS, 25 November 1775, PSP, NYPL; Rudolphus Ritzema to AM, 19 November 1775, AMP, NYHS; Jonathan Trumbull to GW, 7 December 1775, in *AA4*, 4: 213.

20. Berthelot Journal, in Verreau, *Invasion*, 233; GC to EoD, 20 November 1775, in *DAR*, 11: 185.

21. Gondolas were flat-bottomed vessels, pointed on both ends like bateaux and fifty or sixty feet in length. They were generally rowed, but could be sailed in favorable conditions. These gondolas were the *Hancock* and *Schuyler*, constructed by Schuyler's order on Lake Champlain in the summer of 1775; they had participated in the siege of Fort St-Jean; James L. Nelson, *Benedict Arnold's Navy* (Camden, ME: International Marine/McGraw-Hill, 2006), 86, 228; Douglas R. Cubbison, *The American Northern Theater Army in 1776: The Ruin and Reconstruction of the Continental Force* (Jefferson, NC: MacFarland: 2010), 84.

22. RM to PS, 17 November 1775, in *AA4*, 3: 1633; Prince, *Autobiography,* 55.

23. RM to PS, 20 November 1775, PSP, NYPL; RM to PS, 5 December 1775, PSP, NYPL.

24. Berthelot Journal, in Verreau, *Invasion*, 233–34, Prince, *Autobiography*, 55; TW Oath before Samuel Mifflin, 24 April 1776, in Almon, *Remembrancer*, 246.

25. While the interdiction and coerced surrender of Prescott's flotilla are often attributed solely to Brown's clever bluffs, the highly adverse navigating conditions, legitimate rebel defenses (even if light), and weak fighting power of the flotilla—not to mention the loads of powder, families, government officials, important papers, etc., aboard the ships—indicate that forcing the Sorel batteries may well have been a catastrophic event for the loyalists. The primary nautical account from Prescott's ships lends credence to this perspective; see Prince, *Autobiography*, 55–58.

26. Berthelot Journal, in Verreau, *Invasion*, 233–34, Prince, *Autobiography*, 55; RM to PS, 22 November 1775, PSP, NYPL; JB to PS, 28 November 1775, PSP, NYPL; TW Oath before Samuel Mifflin, 24 April 1776, in Almon, *Remembrancer*, 247.

27. Badeaux, *Journal*, 9.

28. Ibid., 9–10.

29. Ibid.

30. Ibid., 9–13.

31. Ibid.

32. RM to PS, 13 November 1775, PSP, NYPL.

33. Ibid.

34. Ibid.

35. RM to PS, 17 November and 20 November 1775, PSP, NYPL; George Measam to PS, 20 November 1775, PSP, NYPL; Memorial of Levy Solomons, 15 November 1784, PCC, M247 r41 i35 p148; Memorial of Regnier Derousi, 22 February 1777, PCC, M247 r51 i41 v8 p260; William L. Otten, *Colonel J. F. Hamtramck—His Life & Times, Volume One (1756–1783): Captain of the Revolution* (Port Aransas, TX: W. L. Otten, 1997), 21; Indemnity for Losses Sustained by Francis Cazeau, in *ASP*, 517.

36. A New York pound was valued at seven-sixteenths (.4375) of an English pound sterling. See the note in Chapter Four for a discussion on the values of various pounds. The amount of £5000 (York) was still a considerable sum, equivalent to slightly more than Carleton's annual governor's salary; Instructions to Governor Carleton, 1775, in *CAD*, 2: 613.

37. RM to PS, 19 November and 24 November 1775, PSP, NYPL.

38. RM to PS, 19 November 1775, PSP, NYPL; JH to PS, 11 October 1775, in *LOD*, 2: 162.

39. Jean-Baptiste Hertel [de Rouville] to RM, 11 November 1775, PCC, M247 r96 i78 VII p1; Rigauville Parole Request, 23 October 1775, PCC M247 r71 i58 p382.

40. RM to PS, 24 November 1775, PSP, NYPL.

41. Ibid.; James Clinton, John Nicholson, and Lewis Dubois to RM, 23 November 1775, PCC, M247 r179 i161 v2 p441; DW to Roger Sherman, 11 February 1776, in Boutell, *Roger Sherman*, 344.

42. RM to PS, 24 November 1775, PSP, NYPL; RM to John Fraser, 23 November 1775, in *AA4*, 4: 1173.

43. General Return of the Detachment . . . [29 November 1775], Benedict Arnold Correspondence, BV Arnold, Benedict, NYHS; "Extract of a letter from an officer . . . dated at Point aux Tremble (in Canada) November 21, 1775," *Providence Gazette*, 3 February 1776; Henry, *Interesting Account*, 95; 21 November 1775, "The Journal of Captain John Topham," *Magazine of History with Notes and Queries, Extra Numbers* 13, no. 50 (1916): 112.

44. "Extract of a letter from an officer . . . dated at Point aux Tremble (in Canada) November 21, 1775," *Providence Gazette*, 3 February 1776.

45. *BTW*, 27; "Desdevens de Glandon, Maurice," *DCB*; Memorial of Maurice Desdevens, 27 April 1786, PCC, M247 r41 i35 p252.

46. Benedict Arnold Order, 28 November 1775, in J-Edmond Roy, *Histoire de la Seigneurie de Lauzon* (Levis, QC: J-E Roy, 1900), 3: 57; *BTW*, 29, 54; Jeremiah Greenman, *Diary of a Common Soldier in the American Revolution, 1775–1783, An Annotated Edition of the Military Journal of*

Jeremiah Greenman, Robert C. Bray and Paul E. Bushnell, eds. (DeKalb, IL: Northern Illinois University, 1978), 21.

47. RM to PS, 13 November and 24 November 1775, PSP, NYPL; Ritzema, "Journal," 103–104. Jealous New York Major Herman Zedwitz claimed that Ritzema remained behind because he was a coward, suffering from "a Cannon fever"; Herman Zedwitz to JH, 25 November 1778, PCC, M247 i78 r104 v24 p675–676.

48. Rudolphus Ritzema to AM, 19 November 1775, AMP, NYHS; "Journal of Robert Barwick," 29 November 1775, in *NDAR*, 2: 1396.

49. 27–30 November, in Haskell, *Diary*, 31; BA to Jeremiah Duggan, 27 November 1775, in Arnold, "Letters," 497.

50. Badeaux, *Journal*, 13; JL to PS, 22 February 1776, PSP, NYPL.

51. Henry, *Interesting Account*, 141–42; Prince, *Autobiography*, 66.

52. Maurice Desdevens to John Pierce, 9 January 1786, and General Montgomery Order to Maurice Desdevens, 1 December 1775, PCC, M247 r41 i35 p260, 219.

53. Mémoire [attribué à l'abbé Huet de la Valinière] sur l'état du Canada pendant la Révolution américaine, Fonds de la Bibliothèque Sainte-Geneviève, MG7 VI, LAC.

54. Allan Maclean to Viscount Barrington, 20 November 1775, in *DAR*, 11: 190.

55. Henry Caldwell to James Murray, 15 June 1776, in Caldwell, *Letter*, 5; GC to EoD, Quebec, 20 November 1775, in *HMNF*, 2: 134; *QG*, 30 November 1775; *JMRE*, 20; Ainslie, *Journal*, 22–23.

56. Extract of a letter, dated Camp before Quebeck, near the General-Hospital, 6 December 1775, in *AA4*, 4: 204; Henry Caldwell to James Murray, 15 June 1776, in Caldwell, *Letter*, 6–7; "A Journal of Occurrences within the Observation of Return Jonathan Meigs," 26 November 1775, in Roberts, *March to Quebec*, 184.

57. Ainslie, *Journal*, 24; "Advertisements," *QG*, 30 November 1775.

Chapter 12. Time to Consider Politics

Epigraphs: *LOD*, 2: 144; *LOD*, 3: 61.

1. NH Delegates to Matthew Thornton, 7 October 1775, and JA to James Warren, 8 October 1775, in *LOD*, 2: 142, 144.

2. JA to James Warren, 8 October 1775, in *LOD*, 2: 144.

3. JH to PS, 11 October 1775, in *LOD*, 2: 162–63.

4. Ibid.

5. PS to GW, 6 November 1775, in *PGWRWS*, 2: 314; PS to JH, 21 October 1775, in *AA4*, 3: 1130–31.

6. PS to JH, 11 November 1775, in *AA4*, 3: 1521.

7. Good examples of newspapers that printed accounts from Canada in the Fall of 1775 include: *Rivington's Gazette* (New York), *New York Journal*, *Essex Gazette* (Salem, MA), *Pennsylvania Evening Post* (Philadelphia), and *Connecticut Courant* (Hartford).

8. Proclamation "For suppressing Rebellion and Sedition . . . 23 August 1775," *QG*, 8 August 1776; *JCC*, 3: 343; Thomas Lynch to GW, 13 November 1775, in *PGWRWS*, 2: 366.

9. General Orders, 5 November 1775, in *PGWRWS*, 2: 300.

10. *JCC*, 3: 317.

11. Ibid., 3: 318, 321–25.

12. Ibid., 3: 339.

13. Although numerous biographical articles about Livingston and Paine are included in state and national collections and in collections of the signers of the Declaration of Independence, only a few monographs exist on these individuals; see George Dangerfield, *Chancellor Robert R. Livingston of New York, 1746–1813* (New York: Harcourt Brace, 1960); and Sarah Cushing Paine, *Paine Ancestry: The Family of Robert Treat Paine, Signer of the Declaration of Independence* (Bos-

ton: Paine Family, 1912). For more on New York tenant uprisings, see Sung Bok Kim, *Landlord and Tenant in Colonial New York: Manorial Society, 1664–1775* (Chapel Hill: University of North Carolina, 1978), Sung Bok Kim, "Impact of Class Relations and Warfare in the American Revolution: The New York Experience," *The Journal of American History* 69, no. 2 (September 1982): 326–46, and Mark Irving, *Agrarian Conflicts in Colonial New-York, 1711–1775* (New York: Columbia University Press, 1940).

14. Congress at Exeter, 5 January 1776, in Nathaniel Bouton, ed., *Provincial Papers, Documents and Records Relating to the Province of New-Hampshire, from 1764 to 1776* (Concord, NH: Edward Jenks, 1874), 8: 2; *JCC,* 3: 319. For additional biographical details, see also Lawrence Mayo, *John Langdon of New Hampshire* (Port Washington, NY: Kennikat Press, 1970), and Charles R. Corning, *John Langdon* (Concord, NH: Rumford, 1903).

15. Charles Lee (hereafter CL) to Richard Henry Lee, 12 December 1775, in Charles Lee, "The Lee Papers, Vol. I, 1754–1776," in *Collections of the New-York Historical Society for the Year 1871* (New York: New-York Historical Society, 1872), 228; Horatio Gates (hereafter HG) to BF, 5 December 1775, in Benjamin Franklin, *The Papers of Benjamin Franklin* (hereafter cited as *PBF*), ed. William Willcox (New Haven, CT: Yale University Press, 1982), 22: 284–85.

16. Instructions to R. R. Livingston, Robert Treat Paine (hereafter RTP), and John Langdon, Esquires, in *JCC,* 3: 339–41; Richard Henry Lee to GW, 6 December 1775, in *LOD,* 2: 449.

17. Cont Congr to PS, 10 November 1775, PSP, NYPL; Robert R. Livingston (hereafter RRL) to John Jay, 27 November 1775, in John Jay, *John Jay: The Making of a Revolutionary—Unpublished Papers, 1745–1780,* ed. Richard B. Morris (New York: Harper and Row, 1975), 182–83; "Diary of Robert Treat Paine," in Paine, *Ancestry,* 36–37.

18. PS to GW, 27 November 1775, in *PGWRWS,* 2: 453; RRL to RM, 29 November 1775, Livingston Family Papers, NYPL.

19. RRL, RTP, and John Langdon to RM, 30 November 1775, in *LOD,* 2: 414.

20. Ibid.

21. Instructions to RRL, RTP, and John Langdon, in *JCC,* 3: 339–41; John Langdon to Ammi Ruhamah Cutter, 6 November 1775, and RTP to Joseph Palmer, 1 January 1776, in *LOD,* 2: 310, 3: 10–11.

22. RRL, RTP, and John Langdon to RM, 30 November 1775, RTP to Joseph Palmer, 1 January 1776, in *LOD,* 2: 413, 3: 10; PS to Cont Congr, 8 December 1775, in *AA4,* 4: 220.

23. Committee Report, 23 December 1775, in *JCC,* 3: 451.

24. RRL to John Jay, 6 December 1775, *John Jay Papers,* Columbia University, accessed 14 August 2007, http://www.columbia.edu/cu/lweb/digital/jay/search.html.

25. R. H. Lee to Catherine Macaulay, 29 November 1775, in *LOD,* 2: 405; *New England Chronicle or Essex Gazette* (Salem, MA), 24 November 1775; JH to RM, 30 November 1775, in *LOD,* 2: 415; GW to JH, 4 December 1775, and PS to GW, 8 December 1775, in *PGWRWS,* 2: 485, 518.

26. JH to PS, 30 November 1775, PSP, NYPL; JH to DW, 30 November 1775, in *LOD,* 2: 417; *JCC,* 3: 418, 424.

27. "Diary of Robert Treat Paine," in Paine, *Ancestry,* 37; Thomas Cushing to RTP, 19 December 1775, in Robert Treat Paine, *Papers of Robert Treat Paine,* vol. 3 (1774–1777), ed. Edward Hanson (Boston : Massachusetts Historical Society, 2005), 118.

28. Report of Committee, 23 December 1775, in *JCC,* 2: 446–51.

29. Ibid.

30. *JCC,* 4: 33.

31. PS to JH, 31 December 1775, in *AA4,* 4: 480.

32. The new battalions for Canada were to include: Colonel John Philip De Haas's First Pennsylvania; Colonel William Maxwell's Second New Jersey; Colonel Timothy Bedel's New Hampshire; Colonel Charles Burrall's Connecticut; and Colonel Arthur St. Clair's Second Pennsylvania.

33. *JCC,* 4: 40.

34. Ibid., 47; JH to PS, 10 January 1776, and JH to Jonathan Trumbull, Sr., 12 January 1776, in *LOD,* 3: 79–80, 86.

35. Roger Champagne, "New York's Radicals and the Coming of Independence," *The Journal of American History* 51, no. 1 (June 1964): 33–34.

36. AM to John Jay, 19 December 1775, in Jay, *Unpublished Papers,* 207.

37. Ibid.

Chapter 13. Contest of Wills at Québec

Epigraphs: PSP, NYPL; "Extract of another letter," *Pennsylvania Packet,* 19 February 1776.

1. 2 December entry, in "Journal of the Most Remarkable Occurrences . . . ," (hereafter cited as JMRO), in *Historical Documents Relating to the Blockade of Quebec by the American Revolutionists in 1775–1776* (Quebec: Literary and Historical Society of Quebec, 1905), 95; 2 December entry, in *Journal of the Siege and Blockade of Quebec by the American Rebels in Autumn 1775 and Winter 1776* (hereafter cited as *JSBQ*), (Quebec: Literary and Historical Society of Quebec, 1876), 4; "Journal of the Principal Occurrences . . . ," 18 December entry, in *Blockade of Quebec in 1775–1776 by the American Revolutionists (Les Bastonnais),* ed. Fred Wurtele (Quebec: Literary and Historical Society of Quebec, 1906), 62.

2. *JMRE,* 23–24; *BTW,* 83.

3. Meigs Diary, 3 December, and Henry Diary, 2 December, in Roberts, *March to Quebec,* 185, 364; 4 December, in JMRO, 96; RM to PS, 5 December 1775, PSP, NYPL. Multiple Continental accounts claim that Caldwell's house was burned while they were at Pointe-aux-Trembles, but Caldwell specifically reported that the house "was not burned, yet it was torn to pieces," while all the outbuildings were burned; Caldwell, "Letter," 7; "Journal of William Humphrey," 28 November 1775, in Shipton, *Journals,* 29.

4. Thomas Jefferys, *The Natural and Civil History of the French Dominions in North and South America* (London: T. Jefferys, 1760), 8.

5. Brother of seigneur and legislative councilor Jean-Baptiste-Marie Bergères-de-Rigauville, who was captured by the Continentals at Verchères on 18 October 1775.

6. Helena O'Reilly, *Monseigneur de Saint Vallier et L'Hôpital Général de Québec* (Québec: C. Darveau, 1882), 407–408; 5 and 16 December entries, in Senter, *Journal,* 46, 48.

7. Copied by order of Congress at Pointe aux Trembles, this 4th of December 1775, M. Desdevens, deputy Captain, L'Anglois Papers, Haldimand Papers, MG-21, Papers relating to State Prisoners and suspected persons (Volume 2), 1775–1784, Microfilm A-765 (hereafter cited as SP2), pp. 12–18, LAC; WG to AM, 21 April 1776, AMP, NYHS; Christophe Pélissier to JH, 8 January 1776 and 20 July 1776, in *AA4,* 4: 60 and *AA5,* 1: 466–67.

8. JL to PS, February 22, 1776, PSP, NYPL.

9. 5 December, Ainslie, *Journal,* 26.

10. Simeon Thayer, *The Invasion of Canada in 1775, Including the Journal of Captain Simeon Thayer . . . ,* edited by Edwin M. Stone (Providence, RI: Knowles, Anthony, 1867), 25; Declaration of Vincent Giroux, 4 November 1776, MG23-B37, LAC; *BTW,* 15. Other Continentals broke the lock and made off with the goods before Duggan's return.

11. RM "to My Friends & fellow Subjects," 6 December 1775, PMP, LAC.

12. GC to William Howe, 12 January 1776, in *DAR,* 12: 41; Letter from Mr. Montgomery . . . , *QG,* 21 March 1776.

13. 7 December, "Journal of the Principal Occurrences," in Wurtele, *Blockade of Quebec* (hereafter cited as JOPO), 57–58; Lindsay, "Narrative of the Invasion," 3: 94–95.

14. 6 December, in Senter, *Journal,* 46; Ann M. Becker, "Smallpox in Washington's Army: Strategic Implications of the Disease during the American Revolutionary War," *The Journal of*

Military History 68, no. 2 (April 2004): 394; Elizabeth A. Fenn, *Pox Americana: The Great Smallpox Epidemic of 1775–1782* (New York: Hill and Wang, 2001), 39.

15. 6 and 21 December, in Haskell, *Diary*, 14–15; JMRO, 97.

16. Becker, "Smallpox," 405, 407; "Hector McNeill Testimony," in *NDAR*, 5: 875. Those suffering from smallpox due to inoculation tended to have less-threatening symptoms, but some still died—and they were still highly contagious.

17. 7 December, in Thayer, *Journal*, 25; "John Pierce Journal," in Roberts, *March to Quebec*, 689. Thayer and Pierce suggest that Hanchett's insubordination was based on cowardice and a grudge against Arnold for perceived disrespect and mistreatment on their northern voyage and St. Lawrence crossing; Darley, *Wilderness Expedition*, 194. After the failure to capture Québec City by surprise, Arnold's New England companies quietly may have adopted an attitude similar to that expressed by Yankee counterparts in mid-November Montréal, seeking to head home intact, before their enlistments expired; see Chapter Eleven.

18. *Fascines* are bundled sticks, and *gabions* are wicker baskets, used as a foundation for earthworks.

19. "Extract of a letter from Montreal, dated Dec. 17," *Pennsylvania Packet*, 22 January 1776; 13–15 December, "Journal of Robert Barwick," in *NDAR*, 2: 1397–98; Simeon Fobes Journal, in Roberts, *March to Quebec*, 589; RM to Robert R. Livingston, Sr., 16 December 1775, and RM to RRL, 17 December 1775 (transcripts), George Bancroft Collection, NYPL.

20. Extract of a Letter from a Gentleman in the Continental Service, 16 December 1775, in *AA4*, 4: 290; *JMRE*, 28, 32; Ainslie, *Journal*, 27–31.

21. Certification of Wm Cross, Respecting horses belonging to the cargo of the Brigantine *Peggy*, 5 August 1779, PCC, M247 r147 i136 v4 p274; BA to Michael Simpson, 29 December 1775, and note in Henry, *Interesting Account*, 133.

22. Certification of Wm Cross, Respecting horses belonging to the cargo of the Brigantine *Peggy*, 5 August 1779, Certificate of Charles Lee, 27 April 1780, and Certification of Johnathan Taylor, 6 August 1779, PCC, M247 r147 i136 v4 p270–274.

23. BA to Michael Simpson, 29 December 1775, and notes in Henry, *Interesting Account*, 133, 155.

24. 12 and 13 December, in Henry, *Interesting Account*, 103–104.

25. John Melish, *Military Documents Consisting of: A Description of the Seat of War in the Northern Section of the United States and Canada* . . . (Philadelphia: G. Palmer, 1814), 24–25; Letter to Fowler Walker, 14 September 1766, in Wallace, *Maseres Letters*, 43.

26. 15 December, in JMRO, 99.

27. RM to RRL, 17 December 1775 (transcript), George Bancroft Collection, NYPL.

28. Ibid.; RM to PS, 18 December 1775, PSP, NYPL.

29. RM to PS, 15 December 1775, PSP, NYPL; RM to RRL, 17 December 1775 (transcript), George Bancroft Collection, NYPL; December 23 entries, Dearborn and Meigs Journals, in Roberts, *March to Quebec*, 147, 187. Regarding the "Raggamuffin Canadians," at least one loyalist source mentions that hundreds of local inhabitants were being employed in the Continental camp, and the 1776 Baby-Taschereau-Williams commission report referred to many *Canadiens'* presence outside the capital at this time, even if Montgomery was not inclined to arm and organize them; 20 December 1775, JOPO, 63, and *BTW*, passim.

30. *JMRE*, 31; Journal of H.M. Sloop *Hunter*, Captain Thomas Mackenzie, 18 December and 20 December 1775, in *NDAR* 3: 144, 4: 16.

31. 18 December and 20 December 1775, in JOPO, 62–63.

32. 22–24 December 1775, in *JMRE*, 33–34; Ainslie, *Journal*, 30–31.

33. "Journal of Robert Barwick," 23–24 December 1775, in *NDAR*, 3: 1399; *JMRE*, 35. New York artilleryman Barwick provides the sole account positively mentioning troop assemblies on the night of the twenty-third. In the numerous accounts from Arnold's men, only Private Jacob Greenman from Captain Samuel Ward's New England company mentions preparations for storming the

city, but places it on the night of the twenty-second, Greenman, *Diary*, 23; a few others describe more general measures for an imminent storming on the twenty-third. Montgomery may have issued orders to only some of the troops before reconsidering the attack, or perhaps simmering leadership issues in Arnold's corps kept orders from reaching all of his soldiers, forcing the general's hand in cancelling an attack.

34. RM to PS, 26 December 1775, in *AA4*, 4: 465–66; Notes of Witnesses' Testimony concerning the Canadian Campaign, [July 10. 1776. Mr. Price], in *PTJ*, 1: 449.

35. "John Pierce Journal," 23 December 1775, in Roberts, *March to Quebec*, 698; 24 December, in Henry, *Interesting Account*, 109.

36. RM to PS, 26 December 1775, in *AA4*, 4: 464–65; "John Pierce Journal," in Roberts, *March to Quebec*, 689, 701. See the discussion of Hanchett's insubordination earlier in this chapter. Part of Goodrich's ill will toward Arnold may have originated from the captain's home-region ties to John Brown and James Easton, who had their own long-standing issues with Arnold dating back to Ticonderoga; Hubbard's rationale for joining the cabal is not clear; Darley, *Wilderness Expedition*, 191, 194, 198.

37. RM to PS, 26 December 1775, in *AA4*, 4: 464–65; 27 December, Senter, *Journal*, 49.

38. John Lamb to WG, 28 December 1775, AMP, NYHS; Donald Campbell to RRL, 28 March 1776, Robert R. Livingston Collection, MG23-B40, LAC.

39. "Journal of the Siege from 1st December 1775," in Wurtele, *Blockade of Quebec*, 15–16.

40. Donald Campbell to RRL, 28 March 1776, Robert R. Livingston Collection, MG23-B40, LAC; Matthew L. Davis, *Memoirs of Aaron Burr with Miscellaneous Selections from his Correspondence*, vol. 1 (New York: Harper and Brothers, 1836), 70.

41. Topham, "Journal," 118.

42. L'Anglois Papers, SP2, 12–18, LAC; *BTW*, 28.

43. *JMRE*, 37.

44. Lindsay, "Narrative of the Invasion of Canada," 3: 103; Extract of a Letter from Montreal, 5 January 1776, in *AA4*, 4: 582. Campbell served as a lieutenant in the Forty-Second (Highlanders) Regiment, in the French and Indian War. Postwar, he retired from active service on half-pay and led the Scots settlement on New York land grants, west of the New Hampshire Grants (near modern Greenwich). In 1775, he was originally commissioned a major in McDougall's First New York Regiment, before receiving an assignment as Continental deputy quartermaster general for the Northern Department with a colonel's rank. He served at Montgomery's headquarters from the beginning of the Canadian campaign; Frederick B. Richards, "The Black Watch at Ticonderoga," *Proceedings of the New York State Historical Society* 10 (1911): 404, 419–20; *AA4*, 3: 954; *JCC*, 2: 186. Of note, New York Major Herman Zedwitz (who took Campbell's place in the First New York Regiment) was injured in a fall during the short firefight; he proudly claimed responsibility for ordering the initial retreat "without losing one man," not meeting Campbell until "halfway towards Headquarters"; Herman Zedwitz to JH, 25 November 1778, PCC, M247 i78 r104 v24 p675–676.

45. Donald Campbell to RRL, 28 March 1776, Robert R. Livingston Collection, MG23-B40, LAC.

46. Lindsay, "Narrative of the Invasion of Canada," 3: 101–102; Moses Kimball Journal, in Darley, *Wilderness Expedition*, 167.

47. Henry, *Interesting Account*, 119; Journal of Robert Barwick, in *NDAR*, 2: 1400; Ainslie, *Journal*, 37.

48. *JMRE*, 38; Donald Campbell to DW, 31 December 1775, PSP, NYPL.

49. 31 December, in Senter, *Journal*, 53; Donald Campbell to DW, 31 December 1775, PSP, NYPL.

50. Donald Campbell to DW, 31 December 1775, PSP, NYPL; BA to DW, 31 December 1775, in Roberts, *March to Quebec*, 103. Arnold's early call for local militia assistance, and subsequent actions, indicate that he probably shared James Livingston's views on the value of habitant support to the military operation, counter to General Montgomery's opinion.

51. PS to JH, 13 January 1776, in *AA4*, 4: 666.

52. O'Reilly, *L'Hôpital Général*, 411; William E. Addis and Thomas Arnold, *A Catholic Dictionary: Containing Some Account of the Doctrine, Discipline, Rites, Ceremonies, Councils, and Religious Orders of the Catholic Church* (London: Kegan Paul, Trench, Trubner, 1893), 495–96.

53. *JSBQ*, 10; État de Messieurs . . . qui ont servie pendant le Blocus des Américains de 1775 et 1776, British Military and Naval Records, "C Series," Misc. Records, 1714, RG8-I, Microfilm C-3840, n.p., LAC; Briand Mandement, 31 December 1775, in Têtu, *Mandements*, 226.

54. Extract of a Letter from Montreal, 5 January 1776, in *AA4*, 4: 582; *JMRE*, 44–45.

55. *JCC*, 4: 89–90.

Chapter 14. The Question of Loyalists

Epigraphs: *AA4*, 3: 1563; "Montreal, Dec. 2," *New-York Journal*, 11 January 1776.

1. Connecticut Society of the Sons of the American Revolution (hereafter cited as CSSAR), *Catalogue of the Officers and Members of Gen. David Humphreys Branch Since its Organization* (New Haven, CT: General David Humphreys Branch, 1911), 39–42, 45; Cornelius Moore, *Leaflets of Masonic Biography, or Sketches of Eminent Freemasons* (Cincinnati, OH: Masonic Review Office, 1863), 344; Edward E. Atwater, ed., *History of the City of New Haven to the Present Time* (New York: W.W. Munsell, 1887), 42; David Wooster, "Summary of the Life of General David Wooster," in *Genealogy of the Woosters in America, Descended from Edward Wooster of Connecticut* (San Francisco: M. Weiss, 1885), 88–90.

2. See Appendix Two for more on Wooster's historiography.

3. CSSAR, *Catalogue of the Officers*, 41–42; Silas Deane to Elizabeth Deane, 15 July 1775, in Deane, *Papers*, 1: 73.

4. Moore, *Masonic Biography*, 343; "An Aged Subscriber," "Anecdotes of Gen. Wooster," 56–59; Gunning Bedford to JH, 31 August 1775, PCC, M247 r91 i78 v2 p1; Jonathan Rossie, *The Politics of Command in the American Revolution* (Syracuse, NY: Syracuse University Press, 1975), 54; PS to Cont Congr, 14 October 1775, PS to DW, 19 October 1775, and DW to PS, 19 October 1775, in *AA4*, 4: 1065–66, 1107; GW to PS, 16 January 1776, and Gunning Bedford to PS, 9 November 1775, PSP, NYPL.

5. William Hall, "Colonel Rudolphus Ritzema," *Magazine of American History* 2 (March 1878): 163; RM to PS, 31 October 1775, PSP, NYPL. The officers in McDougall's regiment were a balanced, but potentially incendiary mix of radical Sons of Liberty (Captains Marinus Willett, Gershom Mott, and John Quackenbos) and European-trained veterans (Ritzema, Major Herman Zedwitz, and Captain Frederick Weissenfels), along with a handful of other respected, but less prominent, citizens.

6. Journal of Charles Carroll of Carrollton (hereafter CCC), 29 April 1775, in Kate M. Rowland, *The Life of Charles Carroll of Carrollton, 1737–1832, with his Correspondence and Public Papers* (New York: G. P. Putnam, 1898), 1: 392–93); Memorial of TW, 22 January 1785, PCC, M247 r52 i41 v10 p665; Testimony of Samuel Lockwood, July 1776, in *PTJ*, 1: 446; PS to JH, 10 February 1776, and Rudolphus Ritzema to New York Committee of Safety, 5 January 1776, in *AA4*, 4: 991, 1114.

7. Memorial of John Blake, Joseph Bindon, John Dyer Mercier & Benjamin Thompson, Merchants & Traders formerly Inhabitants of the Province of Quebec, PCC, M247 r49 i41 v2 p134; Petition of George Measam, 25 August 1776, in *AA5*, 1: 1157.

8. Report of Committee Regarding Franc[o]is Cazeau, PCC, M247 r26 i19 v1 p555; Indemnity for Losses Sustained by Franc[o]is Cazeau, 31 January 1817, in *ASP*, 516; Sanguinet, 91.

9. "From the Pennsylvania Journal," *Freeman's Journal or New Hampshire Gazette* (Portsmouth), 1 June 1776; PS to JH, 10 February 1776, GW to PS, 27 February 1776, in *AA4*, 4: 990–91, 1515.

10. Sanguinet, 92.

11. Andrew Parke, *An Authentic Narrative of Facts Relating to the Exchange of Prisoners Taken at the*

Cedars (London: T. Cadell, 1777), 3; "Extract of a letter from Montreal, dated Dec 17," *Pennsylvania Packet* (Philadelphia), 22 January 1776; Numismatic and Antiquarian Society of Montreal, *Descriptive Catalogue of a Loan Exhibition of Canadian Historical Portraits . . .* (Montréal: Gazette, 1887), 70. The bust head was recovered sometime later and is currently held at Montréal's McCord Museum.

12. Sanguinet, 92–93; Order of Wooster to Bourdon, 20 December 1775, cited in Lanctot, *Canada and the American Revolution,* 104–105.

13. DW to PS, 20 January 1776, and Goose Van Schaick to PS, 6 October 1775, PSP, NYPL; Lorimier, *At War,* 43.

14. DW to PS, 20 January 1776, PSP, NYPL.

15. "By a letter from St. John's, dated November 24," *Essex Journal and New Hampshire Packet* (Newbury Port, MA), 22 December 1775; Ritzema, "Journal," 104; "Montreal, Dec. 2," *New-York Journal,* 11 January 1776. Further details about the Boucherville "tip" letter (its author and content) are lost to history.

16. Ritzema, "Journal," 104. Discussing New York's Tories and that province's extremely lenient treatment of them, Ritzema recently had written, "such Miscreants ought not to breathe the same Air with Men resolved to be free"; Rudolphus Ritzema to Alexander McDougall, 19 November 1775, AMP, NYHS.

17. Ritzema, "Journal," 104; "Montreal, Dec. 2," *New-York Journal,* 11 January 1776.

18. "Montreal, Dec. 2," *New-York Journal,* 11 January 1776; DW to Timothy Bedel, 4 December 1775, in Saffell, *Record,* 28.

19. DW to Committee of Congress, 5 July 1776, in *AA5,* 1: 6; DW to PS, 20 January 1776, PSP, NYPL.

20. John Fraser to PS, 4 February 1776, and John Fraser to DW, 14 December 1775, in *AA4,* 4: 991–92; Calvet, *Case of . . . ,* 49–56.

21. "The Faithful Union with Liberty" to RM, 22 December 1775, PSP, NYPL.

22. Based on Price's participation, the L'Assomption raid must have occurred sometime between Christmas and 12 January, the dates when Price was away from the Québec City blockade lines.

23. WG to AM, 1 January 1776, AMP, NYHS; Sanguinet, 92–93.

24. Copy of a note from Major [Andrew] Skene to Fitz Maurice, in May Fair [London], 28 January 1776, Co5, 1107, p. 335, LAC.

25. Breen, *American Insurgents,* 237, 239; *JCC,* 3: 280.

26. In General Assembly, Rhode Island, 5 November 1775, in *AA4,* 4: 1376; Nicholas Cooke to GW, 19 December 1775, and GW to JH, 25 December 1775, in *PGWRWS,* 2: 581, 601.

27. "Lee Memoirs," in Jared Sparks, *Lives of Charles Lee and Joseph Reed* (Boston: Little, Brown, 1846), 6. See also John Richard Alden, *General Charles Lee, Traitor or Patriot?* (Baton Rouge: Louisiana State University Press, 1951).

28. CL to JH, 22 January 1776, in Lee, "Papers," 248; GW to JH, 31 December 1775, PCC, M247 r166 i152 vi p384–385.

29. *Connecticut Courant* (Hartford), 27 November 1775; Willett, *Narrative,* 31; CL to GW, 5 January 1776, and GW Orders to CL, 8 January 1776, in Lee, "Papers," 235–37; *JCC,* 4: 19–20. For further details on New York's internal conflicts, see Joseph Tiedemann and Eugene Fingerhut, eds., *The Other New York: The American Revolution Beyond New York City, 1763–1787* (Albany: State University of New York Press, 2005); Joseph Tiedemann, "A Revolution Foiled, Queens County, New York, 1775–1776," *Journal of American History* 75 (1988): 430–32; and Richard M. Ketchum, *Divided Loyalties: How the American Revolution Came to New York* (New York: Holt, 2002).

30. CL to JH, 22 January 1776, NY Committee of Safety to CL, and CL to GW, 5 February 1776, in Lee, "Papers," 249, 242–44; GW to CL, 23 January 1776, in *PGWRWS,* 3: 170; Eliphalet Dyer to SA, 28 January 1776, SAP, NYPL; NY Delegates to NY Committee of Safety, 27 January 1776, in *AA4,* 4: 1091; *JCC,* 4: 92–94.

31. CL to Isaac Sears, 5 March 1776, and NY Provincial Congress to CL, 6 March 1776, in Lee, "Papers," 346, 349–50; CL to NY Provincial Congress, 4 March 1776, and NY Provincial Congress, 5 March 1776, in *AA4*, 5: 334–35, 341; CL to NY Provincial Congress, 6 March 1776, in *NDAR*, 4: 215; *JCC*, 4: 195, 201–204.

32. Committee of Congress [Thomas Kean, Thomas Lynch, and John Jay] to PS, 1 January 1776, in *LOD*, 3: 3; Tryon County Committee to PS, 11 January 1776, in *AA4*, 4: 667–68. Even this sort of general Congressional direction would have been useful for Wooster in Montréal.

33. Jonathan Trumbull to PS, 31 January 1776, in *AA4*, 4: 899; GW to PS, 27 January 1776, in *PGWRWS*, 3: 201. By mid-May 1776, Schuyler would have to order troops back to Johnson Hall to stem further Tory activity, prompting Johnson and hundreds of Highlander associates to secretly flee to Montréal, "thro' the woods"; PS to Elias Dayton, 14 May 1776, in *AA4*, 6: 447–48; Extract of a Letter from a Merchant at Quebec, to his Brother in London, in Almon, *Remembrancer*, 184.

34. RM to RRL, 17 December 1775 (transcript), George Bancroft Papers, NYPL; GW to PS, 6 October 1775, PSP, NYPL.

Chapter 15. A Critical Month

Epigraphs: *AA4*, 4: 669; SP2, 17, LAC; translation from *HMNF*, 2: 140.

1. BA to DW, 2 January 1776, and Donald Campbell to DW, 31 December 1775, PSP, NYPL.

2. Donald Campbell to DW, 31 December 1775, and BA to DW, 5 January 1776, PSP, NYPL; BA to DW, 4 January 1776, PCC, M247 1189 i170 vi p280.

3. James Price to PS, 5 January 1776, in *AA4*, 4: 668; DW to PS, 5 January 1776, PSP, NYPL; Sanguinet, 94.

4. DW to PS, 5 January 1776, PSP, NYPL; WG to AM, 5 January 1776, AMP, NYHS.

5. Rudolphus Ritzema to New York Committee of Safety, 3 January and 5 January 1776, in *AA4*, 4: 1114.

6. DW to PS, 5 January and 14 January 1776, BA to DW, 2 January 1776, PSP, NYPL; DW to Seth Warner, 6 January 1776, Co5, 1107, p. 313, LAC; Seth Warner to PS, 22 January 1776, in *AA4*, 4: 852.

7. DW to PS, 14 January and 21 January 1776, PSP, NYPL.

8. Sanguinet, 93.

9. By early January, Wooster may have been aware that on 14 December 1775, his own home province resolved, "That if any person, by writing or speaking, or by any overt act, shall libel or defame any of the resolves of the honourable Congress of the United Colonies, or the acts and proceedings of the General Assembly of this Colony," they should be "disarmed . . . and rendered incapable to hold or serve in any office," and if still recalcitrant, "shall be further punished either by fine, imprisonment or disfranchisement"; An Act for restraining and punishing Persons who are inimical to the Liberties of this and the rest of the United Colonies [Connecticut], in *AA4*, 4: 270–71. In the aftermath of the early November 1775 burning of Falmouth, MA (Portland, ME), General Washington had also directed New Hampshire officials to seize Crown officials who had "given pregnant proofs of their unfriendly disposition to the cause we are Ingaged In"; Circular Instructions for the Seizure of Certain Royal Officials, 5[–12] November 1775; in *PGWRWS*, 2: 301.

10. DW to Canadian Militia Officers, 6 January 1776, SP2, 17, LAC; translation from *HMNF*, 2: 139–140.

11. Ibid. Wooster's claim about additional troops was either a conjecture or a bluff; Congress did not authorize reinforcements until 8 January 1776.

12. DW to PS, 5 January 1776, PSP, NYPL.

13. Christophe Pélissier to JH, 8 January 1776, in *AA4*, 4: 602–603.

14. Ibid.

15. BA to DW, January 4, 1776, PSP, NYPL.

16. DW to PS, 14 January 1776, PSP, NYPL; PS to Cont Congr, 29 September 1775, *AA4*, 3: 839; WG to AM, 19 January 1776, AMP, NYHS. By this time, Wooster had received not only Arnold's alarming intelligence reports, but also a copy of the 22 December "Faithful Union of Liberty" letter, which warned Montgomery of Montréal Tory subversion. Samuel Lockwood had been Montgomery's brigade-major, but he left to join the Québec City blockade in early December; Samuel Lockwood testimony concerning the Canadian Campaign, in *PTJ*, 1: 447.

17. Sanguinet, 93–94; RM's Response to the Proposed Articles of Capitulation for Montreal, 12 November 1775, in *AA4*, 3: 1598. At this time, Wooster correctly anticipated that Schuyler would be taking similar disarmament measures in Tryon County, suggesting that any confiscated Mohawk Valley loyalists' weapons might be used to replace "bad arms" in use by his Montréal troops; DW to PS, 23 January 1776, *AA4* 4: 1006–1007.

18. Sanguinet, 95.

19. Case of Jean-Baptiste de Gas," 13 April [February?], 1776, in Lee, "Papers," 298–99; DW to PS, 20 January 1776, PSP, NYPL; PS to JH, 31 January 1776, PCC, 1172 i153 vi p490.

20. PS to JH, 25 January 1776, and PS to DW, 26 January 1776, in *AA4*, 4: 851–852, 1003.

21. DW to PS, 5 January 1776, PSP, NYPL; DW to Seth Warner, 6 January 1776, *AA4*, 4: 588. Some of Wooster's prejudices may have been shaped during his French and Indian War campaigning in the Richelieu Valley and during his 1760 Montréal occupation duty.

22. DW to Committee of Congress, 5 July 1776, in *AA5*, 1: 6; DW to PS, 21 January 1776, PSP, NYPL. A Continental militia commission began by recognizing the general's "complete confidence in your leadership, bravery and fidelity, and in your patriotic zeal for the cause of the United Colonies . . . ; Joseph Prevot militia lieutenant commission (transcription) in Carton 9, item I8, FHV, MG23-GV7, LAC.

23. DW to GW, 21 January 1776, in *AA4*, 4: 796; DW to Committee of Congress, 5 July 1776, in *AA5*, 1: 6; Sanguinet, 96.

24. "Extract of a Letter to a Gentleman in New-York, Dated Montreal, January 27, 1776," *New-York Gazette*, 26 February 1776; George Nicholson Statement Regarding Northern Army, n.d., including text of 25 January letter in translation, PCC, M247 r71 i58 p379–380; Christophe Pelissier to JH, 28 January 1776, in *AA4*, 4: 603.

25. Benjamin Simonds to PS, 16 January 1776, DW to PS, 27 January 1776, PSP, NYPL; John Fellows to PS, 27 January 1776, and PS to John Fellows, 28 January 1776, in *AA4*, 4: 882; "Extract of a Letter to a Gentleman in New-York, Dated Montreal, January 27, 1776," *New-York Gazette*, 26 February 1776.

26. DW to PS, 27 January 1776, PSP, NYPL.

27. DW to PS, 14 January 1776, PSP, NYPL; BA to Cont Congr, 11 January 1776, in *AA4*, 4: 628; BA to GW, 14 January 1776, in Roberts, *March to Quebec*, 114; WG to AM, 5 January 1776, AMP, NYHS; DW to PS, 27 January 1776, PSP, NYPL.

28. DW to PS, 27 January 1776, PSP, NYPL; Ritzema, "Journal," 105; PS to JH, 6 February 1776, in *NDAR*, 3: 1147.

29. Richard Smith, "Diary of Richard Smith in the Cont Congr, 1775–1776. II," *The American Historical Review* 1, no. 3 (April 1896): 493–94.

30. PS to GW, 13 January 1776, GW to JH, 19 January 1776, in *AA4*, 4: 666, 773; HG to CL, 22 January 1776, Horatio Gates Papers (hereafter cited as HGP), NYHS.

31. *JCC*, 4: 70–73; JH to GW, 20 January 1776, in *LOD*, 3: 124; Smith, "Diary II," 494. These expedited Continental reinforcements were Colonel John Philip De Haas's First Pennsylvania Battalion and Colonel William Maxwell's Second New Jersey Battalion. The new battalion would be Colonel Elisha Porter's, formed in the western Massachusetts counties; MA Council, 19 January 1776, *AA4*, 4: 1270.

32. Smith, "Diary II," 494; *JCC* 4: 75.

33. PS to JH, 13 January 1776, in *AA4*, 4: 667; *JCC*, 4: 78.

34. *JCC*, 4: 79–80, 92, 95; Smith, "Diary II," 496–97.

35. *JCC*, 4: 79, 168.

36. Ibid., 4: 73.

37. Ibid., 4: 79; Autobiographical sketch in Thomas Paine to Henry Laurens, 14 January 1776, in Thomas Paine, *The Writings of Thomas Paine*, vol. 4, ed. Moncure Daniel Conway (New York: G. P. Putnam's Sons, 1896), 430.

38. *JCC*, 4: 85–86, including "The letter to the Inhabitants of the Province of Canada," 24 January 1776; Monette, *Rendez-vous manqué*, 309.

39. "Commissioners to Negotiate with Great Britain," in *LOD*, 3: 65, 68.

40. GW to DW, 27 January 1776, in *AA4*, 4: 873–74.

Chapter 16. Evolving Occupation

Epigraphs: PSP, NYPL; Sanguinet, 103–105

1. DW to Committee of Congress, 5 July 1776, in *AA5*, 1: 6; Sanguinet, 96; Unsent letter by Edward Gray, 1 February 1776, Edward William Gray Fonds, MG23-GII3, LAC.

2. The Recollet Church sat on the south end of town, far from the barracks and Wooster's headquarters. Perhaps there was a geographic reason behind its selection as the meeting place, rather than the central Notre-Dame Church.

3. Sanguinet, 96–97; Lorimier, *At War*, 43–44; Breen, *American Insurgents*, 86–87.

4. Lorimier, *At War*, 43–44.

5. DW to Committee of Congress, 5 July 1776, in *AA5*, 1: 6; Sanguinet, 96–97; Testimony Concerning the Canadian Campaign, Samuel Blackden, 6 July 1776, in *PTJ*, 1: 446; Willet, *Narrative*, 39.

6. Joseph Hawley to Elbridge Gerry, 20 February 1776, in *AA4*, 4: 1220.

7. DW to Committee of Congress, 5 July 1776, in *AA5*, 1: 7; RM's Response to Proposed Articles of Capitulation for Montreal, 12 November 1775, in *AA4*, 3: 1598.

8. RM's Response to Proposed Articles of Capitulation for Montreal, 12 November 1775, in *AA4*, 3: 1598; Sanguinet, 97. Frobisher and his brother Joseph were key players in the formation of the North West Company, three years later; "Frobisher, Joseph," *DCB*.

9. PS to Cont Congr, 10 February 1776, in *AA4*, 4: 990–92; Ritzema, "Journal," 106.

10. Petition of Prudent Lajeunesse, 4 November 1778, Passport for Prudent Lajeunesse from DW, 20 January 1776, PCC, M247 r30 i22 p213; *JCC* 4: 129, 148–49.

11. Report of Committee of Correspondence on Gentleman from Canada, 14 February 1776, in *JCC* 4: 148–49.

12. Smith, "Diary II," 502; *JCC*, 4: 151.

13. DW to Roger Sherman, 11 February 1776, in Boutell, *Roger Sherman*, 343; DW to Cont Congr, 11 February 1776, PSP, NYPL; PS to JH, 20 February 1776, PCC, M247 r172 i153 vi p548; *JCC*, 4: 182, 200.

14. Smith, "Diary II," 510; PS to JH, 21 February 1776, in *AA4*, 4: 1469; "By a gentleman arrived in this city from Montreal," *Providence Gazette*, 30 March 1776; Badeaux, *Journal*, 28.

15. Indemnity for Losses Sustained by Francis Cazeau, 31 January 1817, in *ASP*, 516; Sanguinet, 100.

16. William Tryon to EM, 31 January 1776, C05, 1107, p. 325, LAC; PS to Cont Congr, 29 September 1775, *AA4*, 3: 839; Dearborn Journal, 5 March 1776, in Darley, *Wilderness Expedition*, 121. Lamotte (sometimes spelled Lamothe) was captured trying to deliver a message to Fort St-Jean early in its siege—the same time frame in which Montréal troublemaker Meschech Seers was captured; Mons. I. Oriet's Account, William Tryon to Dartmouth, 11 November 1775, in *CCA* 1904, 37. At least one account maintained that Lamotte escaped from Connecticut, rather than being released; Item I8, FHV, MG23-GV7, LAC.

17. Pierre Foretier, "Notes and Reminesces of an Inhabitant of Montreal During the Occupation of that City by the Bostonians from 1775 to 1776," *Canada Public Records Report, 1945* (Ottawa: Edmund Cloutier, 1946): xxiii; Ainslie, *Journal,* 60; Item I8, FHV, MG23-GV7, LAC. .

18. DW to Roger Sherman, 11 February 1776, in Boutell, *Roger Sherman,* 343; PS to Cont Congr, 25 January 1776, and PS to DW, 26 January 1776, in *AA4,* 4: 852, 1003; DW to PS, 11 February 1776, PSP, NYPL; JA to John Thomas, 7 March 1776, in *LOD,* 3: 348.

19. DW to JH, 21 February 1776, and PS to GW, 11 June 1776, in *AA4,* 4: 1470, 6: 819; DW to PS, 5 March 1776, PSP, NYPL.

20. HG to unknown, 30 January 1776, in *NDAR,* 3: 2047.

21. CL to Robert Morris, 9 February 1776, BF to CL, 11 February 1776, CL to GW, 14 February 1776, CL to R. H. Lee, 12 December 1775, in Lee, "Papers," 280, 285, 297, 229; CL to JH, 11 February 1776, in *AA4,* 4: 1001.

22. *JCC* 4: 157; BF to CL, 19 February 1776, and Robert Morris to CL, 17 February 1776, in Lee, "Papers," 303–305, 313; JA to James Warren, 18 February 1776, in *LOD,* 3: 276–77.

23. General Lee requested that Brigadier-General Nathaniel Greene or John Sullivan join him from the camp at Cambridge.

24. JH to CL, 28 February 1776, in *AA4,* 4: 1522; CL to JH, 27 February 1776, in Lee, "Papers," 331; Smith, "Diary II," 506–507; JA to CL, 19 February 1776, in *LOD,* 3: 278.

25. JH to CL, 1 March 1776, CL to GW, 3 March 1776, and GW to CL, 14 March 1776, in *AA4,* 5: 37, 50, 224.

26. *JCC,* 4: 186; JH to John Thomas, 6 March 1776, in *AA4,* 5: 84; JA to John Thomas, 7 March 1776, in *LOD,* 3: 348. For additional background on Thomas, see Charles Coffin, *The Life and Services of Major General John Thomas* (New York: Egbert, Hovey and King, 1844), which remains the sole monograph biography on the general, but it is only thirty-three pages and is quite dated.

27. "By several Gentlemen from Albany," *Connecticut Gazette* (New London), 15 March 1776; Sanguinet, 101; Stephen Moylan to DW, 27 February 1776; *AA4* 4: 1515.

28. CCC to Charles Carroll of Annapolis, 17 May 1776, in Charles Carroll, *Dear Papa, Dear Charley: The Papers of Charles Carroll of Carrollton, 1748–1782,* vol. 2, ed. Ronald Hoffman (hereafter cited as *CCoC*), (Chapel Hill: University of North Carolina, 2001), 910; John Blake Testimony Concerning the Canadian Campaign, 1 July 1776, in *PTJ,* 1: 434; Petition of George Nicholson, n.d., PCC, M247 r55 i42 v5 p447.

29. DW to PS, 13 March 1776, Frederick Weissenfels to Sergeant Westerfield, 16 March 1776, and List of Prisoners taken in Canada to be sent down to Hartford, 25 June 1776, PSP, NYPL.

30. DW to PS, 13 March 1776, PSP, NYPL; George Measam to AM, 31 March 1776, AMP, NYHS.

31. DW to PS, 5 March and 13 March 1776, PSP, NYPL.

32. DW to JH, 13 February 1776, and DW to PS, 13 March 1776, in *AA4,* 4: 1132, 5: 417; PS to CL, 29 February 1776, in Lee, "Papers," 339–40; William Tryon to EoD, 15 April 1776, in *CCA* 1904, 365.

33. PS to JH, 6 February 1776, in *NDAR,* 3: 1147; *JCC,* 4: 158.

34. Samuel DeWitt Bloodgood, *The Sexagenary, or Reminiscences of the American Revolution* (Albany, NY: John Munsell, 1866), 39–40; MH to PS, 1 April 1776, PSP, NYPL; PS to JH, 21 May 1776, in *PGWRWS,* 4: 362–63.

35. Bloodgood, *Reminiscences,* 39–40; MH to PS, 1 April 1776, PSP, NYPL; Lorimier, *At War,* 46; Sanguinet, 98.

36. Sanguinet, 103–105.

37. DW to Committee of Congress, 5 July 1776, in *AA5,* 1: 7; Account of Goods seized from Bernard & Wadden, Montreal, 24 March 1776, and Account of Sundry Indian Goods Received in the Public Stores, 2 May 1776, PCC, M247 r26 i19 v1 p317, 321.

38. Memorial of John Blake, Joseph Bindon, John Dyer Mercier & Benjamin Thompson, Mer-

chants & Traders, PCC, M247 r49 i41 v2 p134; Report of Committee Regarding Franc[o]is Cazeau, PCC, M247 r26 i19 vi p555; Memorial of Pierre du Calvet, 27 February 1786, PCC, M247 r53 i42 v2 p194; Memorial of Levy Solomons, 15 November 1784, PCC, M247 r41 i35 p148; David Salisbury Franks Memoirs, in Jacob Rader Marcus, *Memoirs of American Jews, 1775–1865* (New York: Jewish Publication Society of America, 1955), 47; Jacob Vanderheyden to PS, 25 June 1776, PSP, NYPL.

39. MH Recruiting Announcement, 10 February 1776, Haldimand Papers, MG-21, Miscellaneous Papers, Orders and Returns, 1756–1776, Microfilm H-1432, p. 385, LAC. The rate of Canadian pay was expressed in *livres*, a holdover from New France, represented by the symbol ₶. Some contemporary sources expressed the rate as 40 "francs" or translated it to be 40 "pounds"; yet six *livres* equated to a "Spanish milled dollar"—40₶ equaling a Continental private's pay of $6 2/3. See *BTW*, 126 (note 5); Ouellet, *Economic and Social History*, 60; and *JCC*, 2: 90, 103.

40. The Case with Colonel Hazen's Regiment, 3 September 1778, MHC, LAC; Memorial of MH, 16 September 1788, Petition of Capts. Philip Liebert and Laurent Olivier, 6 February 1784, PCC, M247 r55 i42 v6 p85; John Hamtramck Testimony Concerning the Canadian Campaign, 1–17 July 1776, in *PTJ*, 1: 451; Edward Antill receipt to Pierre Du Calvet, Haldimand Papers, MG-21, Documents concernant Pierre Ducalvet et Boyer Pillon, 1776–1786, Microfilm A-774, LAC.

41. MH to Edward Antill, 3 April and 10 April 1776, Haldimand Papers, MG-21, Miscellaneous Papers, Orders and Returns, 1756–1780, LAC; Case with Colonel Hazen's Regiment, 3 September 1778, MHC, LAC; Sanguinet, 94; MH to PS, 1 April 1776, PSP, NYPL. Even in ardently patriotic Connecticut, Governor Trumbull was making similar complaints about the difficulty of mobilizing troops without cash; Jonathan Trumbull to GW, 2 February 1776; *PGWRWS*, 3: 241.

42. MH to Edward Antill, 10 March 1776, Haldimand Papers, MG-21, Miscellaneous Papers, Orders and Returns, 1756–1780, Microfilm A-616, LAC; MH to PS, 1 April 1776, PSP, NYPL; Case with Colonel Hazen's Regiment, 3 September 1778, Moses Hazen Collection, MG23-B4 (hereafter MHC), LAC.

43. Case with Colonel Hazen's Regiment, 3 September 1778, MHC, LAC.

44. DW to MH, 23 March 1776, PCC, M247 r71 i58 p389.

45. William Haywood Testimony Concerning the Canadian Campaign, July 1776, in *PTJ*, 1: 453; Gershom Mott to SA, 21 February 1776, SAP, NYPL.

46. Esther Singleton, *Historic Buildings of America as Seen and Described by Famous Writers* (New York: Dodd, Mead, 1906), 277–80.

47. MH to PS, 1 April 1776, PSP, NYPL.

48. Ibid.

49. Ibid.

50. George Measam to AM, 31 March 1776, AMP, NYHS.

51. Joseph Reed to GW, 15 March 1776, in *PGWRWS*, 3: 474; Hector McNeill Testimony Concerning the Canadian Campaign, 2 July 1776, in *PTJ*, 1: 436; JS Testimony to Committee to Enquire into the Causes of the Miscarriages in Canada, PCC, M247 r71 i58 p385.

52. See Appendix Two: The Polarized Legacy of General David Wooster. Smith, *Fourteenth Colony*, 2: 586–87. For examples of the widespread modern Wooster condemnations on these grounds, see George F.G. Stanley, *Canada Invaded, 1775–1776* (Toronto: A. M. Hakkert, 1977), 110–12; Lanctot, *Canada and the American Revolution*, 110, 120–21; Gabriel, *BTW*, xxxix; Cubbison, *Northern Theater Army*, 13–14; and Wilson, *Benedict Arnold*, 111.

53. The arrested Recollets left the capital on 11 January and encountered Price around 20 January; "Journal of the Siege," in Wurtele, *Blockade of Quebec*, 20; Badeaux, *Journal*, 183; James Price testimony concerning the Canadian Campaign, in *PTJ*, 1: 449.

54. Deming, "Oration," 40.

Chapter 17. A Spirit of Cooperation and Understanding

Epigraph: WG to John Jay, 8 April 1776, John Jay Papers, Columbia University.

1. Stone, *Letters*, 45; Elisha Porter, "Diary of the Canadian Campaign, January–August 1776," *Magazine of American History* 30 (1893): 191; Knox, *Historical Journal*, 2: 361; Isaac Weld, Jr., *Travels Through the States of North America and the Provinces of Upper and Lower Canada during the Years 1795, 1796 and 1797* (London: John Stockdale, 1799), 2: 12.

2. Detailed in Chapter Eleven.

3. Badeaux, *Journal*, 14.

4. *BTW*, 35–36, 49; John Hare, "Le comportement de la paysannerie rurale et urbaine dans la région de Québec, pendant l'occupation américaine, 1775–1776," *Revue de l'Université d'Ottawa* 47, nos. 1 and 2 (January and April 1977): 148–49.

5. "Sales Laterrière, Pierre de" and "Pélissier, Christophe," *DCB*.

6. See Chapter Two for Tonnancour's biographical details.

7. Pierre de Sales Laterrière. *Memoires de Pierre de Sales Laterrière et de sus traverses* (Québec: L'Événement, 1873), 105–106.

8. Badeaux, *Journal*, 15.

9. WG to AM, 27 January, [14] February, and 24 March 1776, AMP, NYHS; Badeaux, *Journal*, 15; James Freeman, "Record of the Services of Constant Freeman, Captain of the Artillery in the Continental Army," *Magazine of American History* 2 (1878): 350. Lieutenant Ranald McDougall went by his middle name, Stephen.

10. WG Daybook and Ledger, John Armstrong Papers, 1772–1950, Indiana Historical Society; New York Committee, 8 June 1775, in *AA4*, 2: 933; William H. Chatfield, *Two Revolutionary War Patriots: Major William Goforth and Captain John Armstrong: Epic Struggles Against British Suppression and Indian Warfare* (Cincinnati, OH: Pendleton House, 2011), 14.

11. Recruiting Notice of 1st New-York, E. B. O'Callaghan Papers, NYHS; New-York Provincial Congress, 2 August 1775, in *AA4*, 2: 1812; WG to AM, 19 [January] 1776, AMP, NYHS.

12. WG to AM, 24 March and 6 April 1776, AMP, NYHS.

13. WG to AM, 22 November 1775, 19 [January] and 24 March 1776, AMP, NYHS.

14. Badeaux, *Journal*, 15–16; WG to AM, 24 March 1776, AMP, NYHS.

15. "Badeaux, Jean-Baptiste," *DCB*; Badeaux, *Journal*, 15–16.

16. Badeaux, *Journal*, 15–16; WG to AM, [14] February 1776, AMP, NYHS.

17. WG to AM, [14] February 1776, AMP, NYHS; WG to BF, 22 February 1776, in *PBF*, 22: 360; Badeaux, *Journal*, 16–17.

18. Badeaux, *Journal*, 16–17; WG to AM, [14] February 1776, AMP, NYHS.

19. Laframboise, a successful bourgeois trader, had also been the city captain before the militia was disbanded in 1764; Marcel Trudel, *Histoire de la Nouvelle France*, vol. 10, *Le régime militaire et la disparition de la Nouvelle France, 1759–1764* (Montréal: Fides, 1999), 105.

20. WG to AM, [14] February 1776, AMP, NYHS; Badeaux, *Journal*, 16–18.

21. *BTW*, 35–47; WG to AM, [14] February, 24 March, and 6 April 1776, AMP, NYHS.

22. "Extract of a Letter from an Officer in the Continental Army dated Trois Rivieres, March 24, 1776," *Constitutional Gazette* (New York), 4 May 1776; WG to AM, 24 March and 6 April 1776, AMP, NYHS.

23. WG to AM, 24 March 1776, AMP, NYHS; Badeaux, *Journal*, 17–18.

24. Badeaux, *Journal*, 17–18; *BTW*, 49.

25. WG to BF, 22 February 1776, in *PBF*, 22: 358–359. Goforth was unaware that Franklin had been named to Congress's Canadian delegation a week earlier.

26. Ibid.

27. *BTW*, 41, 43; Badeaux, *Journal*, 20.

28. Badeaux, *Journal*, 28, 31.

29. Badeaux, *Journal*, 22; "Extract of a Letter from an Officer in the Continental Army, dated Trois Rivieres, March 24, 1776," *Constitutional Gazette* (New York), 4 May 1776.

30. Badeaux, *Journal*, 22.

31. Extracts of a Letter from Captain Goforth, PSP, NYPL; WG to AM, 24 March 1776, AMP, NYHS.

32. WG to AM, 24 March and 21 April 1776, AMP, NYHS.

33. Badeaux, *Journal*, 24.

34. Badeaux, *Journal*, 22; WG to AM, 21 April 1776, AMP, NYHS.

35. WG to AM, 6 April and 21 April 1776, AMP, NYHS; Badeaux, *Journal*, 20; Freeman, "Record of the Services," 350.

36. Weld, *Travels*, 2: 15–16; Badeaux, *Journal*, 25–26; "Second Book . . . of the Court of Inquiry of Damages," and "Account of Ursulines of Trois-Rivières," FHV, MG23-GV7, LAC; "Etat des soldats malades de l'armé du Continent," signed 12 March 1776, PCC, M247, rg360, i35, r41, p113a.

37. Jonathan Brogden to WG, 26 March 1776, PSP, NYPL; Gershom Mott to WG, 26 March 1776, in *AA4*, 5: 869.

38. WG to AM, 24 March and 21 April 1776, AMP, NYHS.

39. WG to John Jay, 8 April 1776, John Jay Papers, Columbia University.

40. Ibid.; WG to AM, 6 April 1776, AMP, NYHS.

41. Badeaux, *Journal*, 29–30; WG to AM, 21 April 1776, AMP, NYHS. Badeaux only records Arnold's dinner guest as "Courval"; this was most likely Joseph-Claude Courval-Cressé, recorded in some sources as Claude-Joseph, onetime inspector of the St-Maurice forges; Roch Samson, *The Forges du Saint-Maurice: Beginnings of the Iron and Steel Industry in Canada, 1730–1885* (Quebec: University of Laval Presses, 1998), 224, 287.

42. Badeaux, *Journal*, 28–30. Goforth referred to himself as the "Father of the Solid Boys in the Northern Army," in his 22 February 1776 letter to Benjamin Franklin, in *PBF*, 22: 358.

43. Badeaux, *Journal*, 28–30; WG to AM, 21 April 1776, AMP, NYHS; Elisha Porter, "Diary," 191.

44. Badeaux, *Journal*, 34–35.

45. Christophe Pelissier to JH, 20 July 1776, in *AA5*, 1: 466–67; BA to PS, 6 May 1776, PSP, NYPL.

46. WG to AM, 6 April and 21 April 1776, AMP, NYHS; Information from Canada to William Paulding, Esq., Chairman of the Committee of Safety, NY, n.d., in *AA4*, 5: 805.

47. The *Maria* was one of Prescott's ships, captured by the Continentals off Sorel in November; it was also referred to as the *Mary*.

48. Chatfield, *Revolutionary War Patriots*, 30. A 1928 biographical entry miscast Goforth's Trois-Rivières garrison service, placing the captain at the Battle of Three Rivers, 8 June 1776; this was an impossibility, as he was in New York at that time. This error has been perpetuated in many subsequent biographical references to Goforth and is not specifically corrected in Chatfield's recent monograph biography; *Dictionary of American Biography*, vol. 1, 1928, cited in Chatfield, *Revolutionary War Patriots*, 11. In contrast to Goforth's relatively calm military-governor service, both Lewis Dubois and Jacobus Bruyn led the Quebec District men in combat duty, including participation in the March 1776 St-Pierre engagement (see Chapter Nineteen).

Chapter 18. Patriot Zealots

Epigraphs: *BTW*, 106; Ainslie, *Journal*, 64.

1. BA to DW, 2 January 1776, PSP, NYPL; BA to DW, 5 January 1776, PCC, M247 r172 i153 vi p460–461; BA to Cont Congr, 11 January 1776, in *AA4*, 4: 628.

2. JL to PS, 22 February 1776, PSP, NYPL; *JSBQ*, 11; John Penn to Thomas Person, 12 February 1776, in *LOD*, 3: 239; *BTW*, 7, 8, 25.

3. BA to DW, 4 January 1776, PSP, NYPL; BA to Cont Congr, 11 January 1776, in Roberts, *March to Quebec*, 110.

4. Aaron Burr to Pierre Langlois, 3 January 1776, L'Anglois Papers, SP2, 12–18, LAC; Maurice Desdevens petition, 17 January 1785, PCC, M247 r41 i35 p224; "John Pierce Journal," 14 January 1776, in Roberts, *March to Quebec*, 711.

5. BA to Cont Congr, 12 January 1776, in Roberts, *March to Quebec*, 113; Extract of a letter, BA to Maurice Desdevens, 13 January 1776, SP2, 18, LAC; BA to Maurice Desdevens, 4 January 1776, PCC, M247 r41 i35 p220.

6. BA to Cont Congr, 12 January 1776, in Roberts, *March to Quebec*, 113; Extract of a letter, BA to Maurice Desdevens, 13 January 1776, SP2, 12–18, LAC; *BTW*, 8, 24, 27, 29–30; *Orderly Books*, 3rd NY Continental Regiment, 9 January 1776, NYHS; "Memorial of Maurice Desdevens," 27 April 1786, *PCC*, M247 r41 i35 p252.

7. Laurent, *Québec et l'église*, 55; *JCC*, 2: 220, 5: 645; *JMRE*, 92–93.

8. Charles Lanaudière, Jr. to Magné & Militia Captains, 4 January 1776, PSP, NYPL; BA to DW, 5 January 1776, PCC, M247 r172 i153 vi p460–461.

9. *JMRE*, 52, 58; "Journal of the Siege," JOPO, 19–25, 78.

10. Benedict Arnold to Cont Congr, 11 January 1776, in Roberts, *March to Quebec*, 111; James Price Testimony concerning the Canadian Campaign, 10 July 1776, in *PTJ*, 1: 449–50.

11. James Price Testimony concerning the Canadian Campaign, 10 July 1776, in *PTJ*, 1: 449–50; *JMRE*, 58; "John Pierce Journal," in Roberts, *March to Quebec*, 707–10; Badeaux, *Journal*, 15; "Journal of the Siege," in Wurtele, *Blockade of Quebec*, 20; Donald Campbell to RRL, 28 March 1776, Robert R. Livingston Collection, MG23-B40, LAC. Continental engineer John Pierce mentions two "fryars," probably Recollets, being detained in departing the capital on 13 January; it is unclear if they were part of the three Recollet brothers transported by James Price as prisoners from Trois-Rivières to Montréal, mentioned in Chapter Sixteen; Roberts, *March to Quebec*, 710.

12. "Extract of a Letter from St Rocks Suburbs . . . dated January 23, 1776," *New-York Gazette*, 26 February 1776; Augustin Loizeau Petition to John Jay, n.d., and Louis Morneau Certification for Jean-Baptiste Allin, 6 April 1779, PCC, M247 r158 i147 v3 p409–411, 273.

13. O'Reilly, *L'Hôpital Général*, 411–13

14. *JMRE*, 54.

15. Hare, "Comportement de la paysannerie," 147–49; *BTW*, 69.

16. South of the St. Lawrence: Pointe-Lévy, St-Vallier, Berthier-en-bas, St-François-du-Sud, St-Pierre-du-Sud, and Rivière-Ouelle; north shore: L'Ange-Gardien; see Map 10.

17. *BTW*, 6, 8–9, 16, 18–19 (Charlesbourg, Beauport, L'Ange-Gardien, St-François (Ile d'Orléans [hereafter abbreviated (IO)]), St-Jean (IO), St-Famille (IO)).

18. Ibid., 31, 66.

19. *BTW*, 6, 13, 72, 82, 106. Based on parish records, it appears that Lesperance was French-born Jacques Talon *dit* Lesperance, or his brother Jean; Université de Montréal Research Program in Historical Demography online, accessed 20 January 2013, http://www.genealogie.umontreal.ca.

20. *BTW*, 22, 106; Pierre-Antoine Porlier, "Mémoire d'observations sur la conduite des habitants des deux paroisses Sainte-Anne et Saint-Roch . . . ," *Bulletin des recherches historiques* 6, no. 5 (mai 1900): 134.

21. John Halsted, *Expense Book of John Halsted, Commissary Under Benedict Arnold, Before Quebec, 1776* (Montréal: C. A. Marchand, 1913).

22. Isaac Guion Attestation, 14 August 1781, PCC, M247 r49 i41 v2 p150.

23. *BTW*, 54, 61, 64, 78, 96, 102–103, 108; Porlier, "Mémoire," 136; Memorial of Charles de Lanaudière, of the Province of Quebec, in *HMNF*, 2: 142.

24. *BTW*, 8, 11, 14, 15–16, 19–20, 22–23; *JMRE*, 69.

25. *BTW*, 9, 23–24, 27–28, 77.

26. Ibid., 13–14, 23; Sanguinet, 95; Gershom Mott to WG, 26 March 1776, AMP, NYHS.

27. *BTW*, 106, 113; Memorial of Pierre Ayot[te], 5 August 1785, and Petition of Capt Gosselin, 6 February 1784, PCC, M247 r54 i42 v3 p256; Porlier, "Mémoire," 135; "Gosselin, Clément," *DCB*; Ernest Monty, "Major Clément Gossélin," *Mémoires de la Société Généalogique* 3 (January 1948): 18, 34.

28. Deposition of Jean Maville, SP2; *BTW*, 90, 106–107; Porlier, "Mémoire," 135–36.

29. *BTW*; Pierre Ayotte to [BA], 16 March 1776, and Letter to Thomas McKean, 28 March 1776, Haldimand Papers, LAC; *JMRE*, 80–82; JMRO, 129.

30. BA to Maurice Desdevens, 12 March 1776, PCC, M247 r41 i35 p220–221.

31. Note (re: Duggan), 21 February 1776, SAP, NYPL; PS to JH, 7 March 1776, in *AA4*, 5: 104.

32. Smith, "Diary . . . II," 515; *JCC*, 4: 238–239; J-F Hamtramck Petition to the Cont Congr, 11 July 1776, PCC, M247 r96 i78 vII p71–73.

33. BA to PS, 10 February 1776, PSP, NYPL.

34. BA to GW, 27 February 1776, in *AA4*, 4: 1513; Hector McNeill Testimony, 2 July 1776, in *NDAR*, 5: 875; Vernon Ives, ed., "Narrative of Uriah Cross in the Revolutionary War," *New York History* 63, no. 3 (July 1982): 289–90.

35. JL to PS, 22 February 1776, PSP, NYPL; BA to Silas Deane, 30 March 1776, in *AA4*, 5: 549–50; Copy of a Letter to Thomas McKean, 28 March 1776, Haldimand Papers, MG-21, Miscellaneous Papers, Orders and Returns, 1756–1776, Microfilm H-1432, p. 382, LAC.

36. JOPO, 81.

37. *JMRE*, 70, 74, 81–82.

38. JMRO, 124–125; *JSBQ*, 15–16; Ainslie, *Journal*, 63.

39. *QG*, 14 and 21 March 1776. It is unclear how Carleton obtained copies of the Arnold letters.

40. *JSBQ*, 17.

Chapter 19. *Spring of Unrest*

Epigraph: PSP, NYPL.

1. Porlier, "Mémoire," 136

2. Ibid., 137; "Liénard de Beaujeu de Villemonde, Louis," *DCB*.

3. "Liénard de Beaujeu de Villemonde, Louis," *DCB*; Donald Chaput, "Treason or Loyalty? Frontier French in the American Revolution," *Journal of the Illinois State Historical Society* 71, no. 4 (November 1978): 245–46; Louis-Philippe Bonneau, *On s'est battu à St-Pierre* (Saint-François, QC: Société de conservation du patrimoine de Saint-François de la Rivière-du-Sud, 1987), 9, 79.

4. Porlier, "Mémoire," 137.

5. Ibid.; "Bailly de Messein, Charles-François," *DCB*.

6. Porlier, "Mémoire," 138; *BTW*, 90–116.

7. Pierre Ayot[te] to [BA], 16 March 1776, Haldimand Papers, MG-21, Miscellaneous Papers, Orders and Returns, 1756–1776, Microfilm H-1432, p. 389, LAC; *BTW*, 95–96.

8. *BTW*, 70; Anthony Clarke's Memorandum Book, 9, BV Banyar, Goldsbrow, NYHS; Extract of a Letter from BA, 26 March and 28 March 1776, and BA to Silas Deane, 30 March 1776, in *AA4*, 5: 512, 550. Féré had received payment from Commissary John Halsted as late as 17 March; Halsted, *Expense Book*.

9. Jonathan Brogden to WG, 26 March 1776, AMP, NYHS; Extract of a Letter from BA, 26 March and 28 March 1776, in *AA4*, 5: 512.

10. Jonathan Brogden to WG, 26 March 1776, and Gershom Mott to WG, 26 March 1776, AMP, NYHS; *BTW*, 58, 68–80.

11. *BTW*, 81–90.

12. Porlier, "Mémoire," 138; *BTW*, 90–112; "Blay, Michel (Michel-Toussaint)," *DCB*.

13. Bonneau, *St-Pierre*, 95; JOPO, 93; *BTW*, 86, 90.

14. *BTW,* 82–88; Sanguinet, 105–106.

15. Bonneau, *St-Pierre,* 96–97; Ainslie, *Journal,* 73.

16. Ainslie, *Journal,* 73; BA to Silas Deane, 30 March 1776, in *AA4,* 5: 550; Clarke's Memorandum Book, 10, BV Banyar, Goldsbrow, NYHS; Thomas Dorsey to Joseph Howell, 30 March 1776, Joseph Howell Manuscripts, NYHS; *BTW,* 79–81.

17. Porlier, "*Memoire,*" 138–139; JOPO, 88.

18. Recently promoted from a captaincy, originally in Clinton's Third New York Regiment—not to be confused with Wooster's controversial aide-de-camp, George Nicholson.

19. Extract of a Letter from BA, 26 March and 28 March 1776, in *AA4,* 5: 512; *BTW,* 14, 54–57, 71–72; Clarke's Memorandum Book, 10, BV Banyar, Goldsbrow, NYHS; Samuel Chase to JA, 21 April 1776, in *LOD,* 3: 568.

20. Porlier, "Memoire," 139–40; *BTW,* 108.

21. Lauzier and his son; St-Roch-des-Aulnaies' François Peltier and his son; Jean Izabel of St-Pierre; William Cather from La-Pocatière; and "John Shellbear"; from List of Prisoners taken in Canada to be sent down to Hartford, 25 June 1776, PSP, NYPL.

22. Badeaux, *Journal,* 26; Sanguinet, 105–106.

23. "Extract of a letter from Montreal, April 1," *New-York Journal,* 9 May 1776; MH to PS, 8 April 1776, PSP, NYPL; JH to PS, 26 April 1776, in *LOD,* 3: 584.

24. *JCC,* 4: 301–303; R. H. Lee to CL, 22 April 1776, and JH to Commissioners to Canada, 26 April 1776, in *LOD,* 3: 572, 583–84.

25. Extract of a letter from Brigadier-General Arnold, 26 March and 28 March 1776, in *AA4,* 5: 512; "An Economic and Social Survey (1772)," Dartmouth Papers, LAC, cited in H. A. Innis, ed., *Select Documents in Canadian Economic History, 1497–1783* (Toronto: University of Toronto Press, 1929), 574.

26. Extract of a Letter from Brigadier General Benedict Arnold, 26 March and 28 March 1776, and BA to Silas Deane, 30 March 1776, in *AA4,* 5: 512, 549; Clarke's Memorandum Book, 9; "Extract of a letter from Camp before Quebec, dated March 28, 1776," *Connecticut Courant* (Hartford), 20 May 1776.

27. MH to Edward Antill, 26 March and 20 April 1776, Haldimand Papers, MG-21, Miscellaneous Papers, Orders and Returns, 1756–1780, Microfilm A-616, LAC; "Memorial of Jean Menard," PCC, M 247 141 i35 p163.

28. *JMRE,* 82; État de Messieurs . . . Nouveau Rôle . . . Le 16 Décembre 1775, British Military and Naval Records, "C Series," Misc. Records, RG8-I , Microfilm C-3840, n.p., LAC.

29. *JMRE,* 82; JOPO, 89–90.

30. *JMRE,* 92; JOPO, 93.

31. *JMRE,* 94–95.

32. BA to PS, Montreal, 20 April 1776—30 March Return of the Troops, in *AA4,* 5: 1100; JMRO, 136.

33. DW to John Halsted, 2 April 1776; John Halsted Certification for Maurice Desdevens, n.d., PCC, M247 141 i35 p221.

34. Orders, Headquarters before Quebec, 8 April 1776, in Doyen Salsig, *Parole: Quebec; Countersign: Ticonderoga, Second New Jersey Regimental Orderly Book, 1776* (London: Fairleigh Dickinson University Press, 1980), 70.

35. BA to PS, 20 April 1776, PSP, NYPL; *JMRE,* 95.

36. WG to John Jay, 8 April 1776, John Jay Papers, Columbia University; Copy of a Letter to Thomas McKean, 28 March 1776, MG-21, Miscellaneous Papers, Orders and Returns, 1756–1776, Microfilm H-1432, p. 382, LAC; MH to PS, 1 April 1776, PSP, NYPL.

37. *JMRE,* 98; 10–15 April, in "Diary of the Weather kept at Quebec in the year of the siege by the Americans in 1776," *Transactions of the Literary and Historical Society of Quebec* New Series, no. 22 (1898).

38. Orders, Headquarters Camp Before Quebec, 14 April and 15 April 1776, in Salsig, *Parole:*

Quebec, 76–77; Adjutant Russell Dewey Declaration, in Louis M. Dewey, *Life of George Dewey, Rear Admiral, U.S.N.; and Dewey Family History* (Westfield, MA: Dewey Family, 1898), 270.

39. Adjutant Russell Dewey Declaration, in Dewey, *Dewey Family*, 270; *JMRE*, 99; Haskell, *Diary*, 19.

40. Samuel Hodgkinson, "Before Quebec 1776," *Pennsylvania Magazine of History and Biography* 10 (1886): 160; *JMRE*, 101–102.

41. Hector McNeill Testimony, 2 July 1776, in *NDAR*, 5: 876; DW to Hector McNeil, 23 April 1776, in "Some Papers of Aaron Burr," ed. Worthington C. Ford, *Proceedings of the American Antiquarian Society* 29 (1919): 68.

42. Certificate of Charles Lee [not General Lee], 27 April 1780, PCC, M247 r147 i136 v4 p270; 9 April and 27 April, in "Diary of the Weather;" *JMRE*, 106. Arnold donated the vessel after the fact; Certificate of Charles Lee above.

43. *JMRE*, 96; James Lockwood to Hector McNeill, 25 April 1776, in *NDAR*, 4: 1244; Memorial of Richard Platt, PCC, M247 r51 i41 v8 pp190–191.

44. *BTW*, 85, 107–108; Porlier, "Memoire," 140; Bonneau, *St-Pierre*, 100.

45. *BTW*, 76–77, 81, 83, 95, 97, 99, 102.

46. Ibid., 76–78, 110–111.

Chapter 20. *A Late-Changing Cast*

Epigraphs: *LOD*, 3: 275; *JSBQ*, 22.

1. *JCC*, 4: 151.

2. RRL to Thomas Lynch, January 1776, and JA to Abigail Adams, 18 February 1776, in *LOD*, 3: 179, 273–274; RRL to John Jay, 15 February 1776, John Jay Papers, Columbia University.

3. JA to James Warren, 18 February 1776, in *LOD*, 3: 276; Stacy Schiff, *A Great Improvisation: Franklin, France, and the Birth of America* (New York: Henry Holt, 1995), 189, *passim*.

4. Proposed Articles of Confederation, 21 July 1775, in *PBF*, 22: 125.

5. James Haw, F. Beirne, R. R. Beirne, and R. S. Jett, *Stormy Patriot: the Life of Samuel Chase* (Baltimore: Maryland Historical Society: 1980), 25; 15 September, in Adams, *Diary*, 2: 172; Extract of a Letter from a Merchant at Annapolis, in Maryland to his Friend in Philadelphia, 28 January 1775, in *AA4*, 1: 1194; JA to James Warren, 18 February 1776, in *LOD*, 3: 276.

6. Samuel Chase to James Duane, 2 December 1774, Samuel Chase to PS, 10 August 1775, and Samuel Chase to JA, 12 January 1776, in *LOD*, 1: 264, 700, 3: 277.

7. Richard Smith's Diary, 14 October 1775, and JA Notes of Debates, 12 October 1775, in *LOD*, 2: 12, 169.

8. Metzger, *Quebec Act*, 5–6.

9. Thomas O'Brien Hanley, *Revolutionary Statesman: Charles Carroll and the War* (Chicago: Loyola, 1983); Ellen Smith, *Charles Carroll of Carrollton* (Cambridge, MA: Harvard University Press, 1942); JA to Abigail Adams, 18 February 1776, in *LOD*, 3: 274.

10. Samuel Chase to JA, 12 January 1776, in *LOD*, 3: 277.

11. JA to Abigail Adams, 18 February 1776, in *LOD*, 3: 273; CL to JH, 27 February 1776, in *AA4*, 4: 1509; John Carroll Brent, ed., *Biographical Sketch of the Most Rev. John Carroll, First Archbishop of Baltimore* (Baltimore: John Murphy, 1843); Peter Guilday, *The Life and Times of John Carroll, Archbishop of Baltimore (1735–1815)* (New York: Encyclopedia Press, 1922).

12. John Carroll to unknown, [February 1776], in John Carroll, *The John Carroll Papers*, vol. 1 (1755–1791), ed. Thomas O'Brien Hanley (Notre Dame, IN: Notre Dame University Press, 1976), 46; Hanley, *Revolutionary Statesman*, 103.

13. *JCC*, 4: 173; J-P Lagrave, *Voltaire's Man in America: A Political Biography of Fleury Mesplet* ... (Toronto: Davies, 1995), 23, 28, 52; R. W. McLachlan, *Fleury Mesplet, The First Printer at Montreal* (Ottawa: J. Hope and Sons, 1906), 200–201; "Mesplet, Fleury," *DCB*.

14. Observations of Fleury Mesplet, 31 December 1784, and Memorial of Fleury Mesplet of Montreal, 27 March 1784, PCC, M247 r51 i41 v6 p341–342, 362.

15. JH to CL, 19 February 1776, in Lee, "Papers," 311; *JCC*, 4: 158; Smith, "Diary II," 505; JH to PS, 7 March 1776, in *AA4*, 5: 100; Richard Smith Diary, 9 March and 12 March 1776, in *LOD*, 3: 365, 370.

16. CCC to Charles Carroll of Annapolis, 4, 8, 13, and 15 March 1776, in *CCoC*, 862, 865, 869, 872; Observations during the voyage of Mr. Fleury Mesplet, 1 August 1783, PCC, M247 r51 i41 v6 p313.

17. 20 March 1776, Instructions & Commission from Congress to Franklin, Carroll, and Chase for the Canadian Mission, in *JCC*, 4: 215–17.

18. Ibid.

19. Commission of Commissioners to Canada, in *AA4*, 5: 411; CCC to Charles Carroll of Annapolis, 22 and 25 March 1776, in *CCoC*, 883 and 886.

20. MH to Edward Antill, 20 April 1776, Haldimand papers, MG-21, Miscellaneous Papers, Orders and Returns, 1756–1780. Microfilm A-616, LAC; MH to PS, 8 April 1776, PSP, NYPL.

21. Curatteau to [Nantes], 22 October 1776, Fonds des Archives départementales de la Loire-Atlantique, Série E–Papiers de famille, MG6-A5, LAC; René Floquet to JOB, 15 June 1776, in Auguste Carayon, *Bannissement des Jésuites de la Louisiane, Relation et Lettres Inédites* (Paris: L'Écureux, 1865), 107–108.

22. René Floquet to JOB, 15 June 1776, in Carayon, *Bannissement des Jésuites*, 107–108; EM to JOB, 17 June 1776, in Gosselin, *L'Église*, 73; MH to Edward Antill, 20 April 1776, Haldimand Papers, MG-21, Miscellaneous Papers, Orders and Returns, 1756–1780, Microfilm A-616, LAC; MH to the Committee of Congress, 24 May 1776, PMP, LAC.

23. MH to Edward Antill, 20 April 1776, Haldimand Papers, MG-21, Miscellaneous Papers, Orders and Returns, 1756–1780, Microfilm A-616, LAC; Benjamin Stevens, "Diary of Benjamin Stevens," *Daughters of the American Revolution Magazine* 44 (August 1914): 138.

24. BA to PS, 20 April 1776, PSP, NYPL. Hazen and Arnold refer to the additional post as "Carrinyon" or "Carrignon" in their letters. While the historical record of this deployment is scant, a detachment at Carillon, on the Ottawa River's Long Sault Rapids, complemented Bedel's post at Les-Cèdres in guarding Montréal's western approaches. Albert G. E. Smith kindly assisted in identifying the location of this post.

25. BA to PS, 30 April 1776, in *AA4*, 5: 1155.

26. MH to Edward Antill, 20 April 1776, Haldimand Papers, MG-21, Miscellaneous Papers, Orders and Returns, 1756–1780, Microfilm A-616, LAC.

27. JH to MH, 24 April 1776, and JH to PS, 26 April 1776, in *LOD*, 3: 580, 584.

28. PS to GW, 27 April 1776 and 10 May 1776, in *PGWRWS*, 4: 147, 264; PS to Captain Bigelow, 27 April 1776, PS General Orders, 6 May and 9 May 1776, PSP, NYPL.

29. Robbins, *Journal*, 9.

30. GW letter, 10 July 1775, and GW to Joseph Reed, 26 February to 9 March 1776 in *PGWRWS*, 1: 89, 375; CCC to Charles Carroll of Annapolis, 8 April 1776, in *CCoC*, 84.

31. JT to John Hancock, 8 April 1776, in *AA4*, 5: 822.

32. *JCC*, 4: 209–10; Smith, "Diary II," 511–12; William Whipple to Joshua Brackett, 17 March and 6 May 1776, in *LOD*, 3: 396, 634–35; John Carroll to Eleanor Darnell Carroll, 1 May 1776, in Carroll, *Papers*, 1: 47; BF to A. M. Woedtke, 13 April 1781, in *PBF*, 34: 546; Cubbison, *Northern Theater Army*, 137.

33. GW to JH, 19 April 1776, and GW to PS, 19 April 1776, in *PGWRWS*, 4: 87, 90.

Chapter 21. May Tides

Epigraphs: Commissioners to Canada to JH, 8 May 1776, in *LOD*, 3: 641; Senter, *Journal*, 57.

1. BF to Josiah Quincy, 15 April 1776, in *AA4*, 5: 947; BF to JH, 13 April 1776, in *LOD*, 3: 518;

CCC to Charles Carroll of Annapolis, 15 April 1776, and CCC to Molly Carroll, 15 April 1776, in *CCoC,* 896, 898.

2. BF to Josiah Quincy, 15 April 1776, in *AA4,* 5: 947; Journal of CCC, 27 April 1776, in Rowland, *Charles Carroll,* 1: 391; Samuel Chase to JA, 28 April 1776, in *LOD,* 3: 598.

3. John Carroll to Eleanor Darnell Carroll, 1 May 1776, in Carroll, *Papers,* 1: 47; "New York, May 15. Extract of a letter from Montreal, May 1, 1776," *Constitutional Gazette* (New York), 18 May 1776.

4. John Carroll to Eleanor Darnell Carroll, 1 May 1776, in Carroll, *Papers,* 1: 47; At a Council of War, held at Head-Quarters, 30 April 1776, in *AA4,* 5: 1166; BA to PS, 30 April 1776, and Council of War, 1 May [*sic*] 1776, PSP, NYPL.

5. BA to PS, 30 April 1776, and Council of War, 1 May [*sic*] 1776, PSP, NYPL; At a Council of War, 30 April 1776, in *AA4,* 5: 1166–67; MH to PS, 1 April 1776, PSP, NYPL; CCC to Charles Carroll of Annapolis, 30 April 1776, in *CCoC,* 901.

6. MH to PS, 1 May 1776, and BA to PS, 20 April 1776, PSP, NYPL; At a Council of War, 30 April 1776, in *AA4,* 5: 1166–67; Edward Antill to Maurice Desdevens, 30 April 1776, and Edward Antill certification for Maurice Desdevens, 17 June 1781, PCC, M247 r41 135 p222.

7. Commissioners to Canada to JH, 1 May 1776, in *LOD,* 3: 611–13.

8. Samuel Chase to HG, 13 June 1776, HGP, NYHS; Testimony of John Blake to Committee on Canada, 1 July 1776, in *PTJ,* 1: 434; Commissioners to Canada to JH, 6 May 1776, in *LOD,* 3: 613.

9. Instructions & Commission from Congress to Franklin, Carroll and Chase for the Canadian Mission, 20 March 1776, in *JCC,* 4: 218; Commissioners to Canada to PS, 4 May 1776, PSP, NYPL; Commissioners to Canada to JH, 6 May 1776, in *LOD,* 3: 629–30; Samuel Blackden Testimony to Committee on Canada, 6 July 1776, in *PTJ,* 1: 446.

10. DW to Committee on Canada, 5 July 1776, in *AA5,* 1: 6–7.

11. TW to SA, 30 May 1776, SAP, NYPL.

12. BA to PS, 30 April 1776, Nathaniel Buell to PS, 3 May 1776, and Commissioners to Canada to PS, 6 May 1776, PSP, NYPL.

13. Samuel Chase and CCC to MH, 6 May 1776, Samuel Chase Manuscripts, NYHS; Commissioners to Canada to JH, 17 May 1776, in *LOD,* 4: 257.

14. JH to MA, NH, RI, and CT, 30 April 1776, and Commissioners to Canada to JH, 6 May and 8 May 1776, in *LOD,* 3: 605, 629–30, 641.

15. Commissioners to Canada to JH, 8 May 1776, in *LOD,* 3: 641; CCC to Charles Carroll of Annapolis, 5 May 1776, in *CCoC,* 904.

16. René Floquet to JOB, 15 June 1776, in Carayon, *Bannissement des Jesuites,* 109; Lanctot, *Canada and the American Revolution,* 135.

17. EM to JOB, 20 October 1775, in McMaster, "Parish in Arms," 117–18; Testimony of Samuel Blackden to Committee on Canada, 6 July 1776, in *PTJ,* 1: 446.

18. Observations during the voyage of Mr Fleury Mesplet, 1 August 1783; Observations of Fleury Mesplet, 31 December 1784; and Memorandum of Expenses made by Fleury Mesplet, PCC, M247 r51 141 v6 p313, 341–42, 362.

19. Memorandum of Expenses made by Fleury Mesplet, PCC, M247 r51 141 v6 p362; McLachlan, *Fleury Mesplet,* 204–205; Smith, *Fourteenth Colony,* 2: 334.

20. CCC to Charles Carroll of Annapolis, 5 May 1776, in *CCoC,* 904; John Carroll to CCC and Samuel Chase, 28 May 1776, in Carroll, *Papers,* 49; Samuel Chase to HG, 13 June 1776, in *LOD,* 4: 203.

21. Copy of John Thomas to BA, [May 2, 1776], PSP, NYPL.

22. "Journal of the Siege," in Wurtele, *Blockade of Quebec,* 49–50; GC to George Germain, 14 May 1776, in *NDAR,* 5: 86; *JMRE,* 109–100. Wooster reportedly had his men pre-position ladders outside the walls before this incident, but diverse Continental accounts fail to mention any specific coordination for an assault in conjunction with the fireship attack; Extract of a Letter from Que-

bec, 10 May 1776, in Almon, *Remembrancer,* 120. A week earlier, on 25 April, the general apparently marshaled troops for a fireship effort, but dismissed them when rainy weather was deemed unfavorable for the mission; Adjutant Russell Dewey Declaration, in Dewey, *Dewey Family,* 270–71.

23. *JCC,* 4: 236, 302; Badeaux, *Journal,* 34–35; John Greenwood, *The Revolutionary Services of John Greenwood, of Boston and New York, 1775–1783* (New York: Devine Press, 1922), 25. Thompson's Brigade consisted of one New Hampshire battalion under Colonel Enoch Poor and three Massachusetts battalions under Colonels John Paterson, John Greaton, and William Bond, totaling 2,177 men; Return of the Regiments Going on Command to Canada, 17 April 1776, HGP, NYHS. Sullivan's Brigade consisted of two New Hampshire battalions, under Colonels James Reed and John Stark; two Pennsylvania battalions, under Colonels Anthony Wayne and William Irvine; and two New Jersey battalions under Colonels Elias Dayton and William Winds, totaling 3,848 men; Return of the Regiments Going on Command to Canada, 28 April 1776, HGP, NYHS.

24. "New-York, May 23," *The Freeman's Journal* (Portsmouth, NH), 1 June 1776; John Thomas to Committee of Congress, 7 May 1776, PSP, NYPL.

25. John Thomas to Committee of Congress, 7 May 1776, PSP, NYPL; Porter, "Diary," 192.

26. *BTW,* 75; John Thomas to Committee of Congress, 7 May 1776, PSP, NYPL.

27. DW testimony concerning the Canadian Campaign, 4 July 1776, in *PTJ,* 1: 445; *JMRE,* 111.

28. George Germain to Lords of Admiralty, 22 January 1776, George Germain to GC, 17 February 1776, and George Germain to William Howe, 28 March 1776, in *DAR,* 12: 50, 57, 11: 95; John Enys, *The American Journals of John Enys,* Elizabeth Cometti, ed. (Syracuse, NY: Syracuse University Press, 1976), 8.

29. *JMRE,* 112; Enys, *American Journals,* 12; GC to William Tryon, 17 May 1776, C05, 1107, p. 739, LAC.

30. Senter, *Journal,* 57; Porter, "Diary," 192–93.

31. *JMRE,* 112; Enys, *American Journals,* 12.

32. Porter, "Diary," 193; TW to SA, 30 May 1776, SAP, NYPL; *JCC,* 5: 623.

33. Jean Maville Deposition, SP2; Clarke's Memorandum Book, 12–13, BV Banyar, Goldsbrow, NYHS.

34. JL Certificate for Bartholomew von Heer, 8 February 1785, PCC, M247 r56 i42 v8 p71; Memorial of Pierre Ayot[te], 5 August 1785, PCC, M247 r53 i42 vi p66a.

35. *JMRE,* 113–14.

Chapter 22. *The Sad Necessity of Abandoning Canada*

Epigraphs: John Sullivan (hereafter JS) to GW, 5 June 1776, PSP, NYPL; BA to JS, 13 June 1776, in Sullivan, *Letters,* 237.

1. Senter, *Journal,* 56; Extracts of a letter from an officer in the army at Deschambault, 9 May 1776, in *AA4,* 6: 398; John Thomas to GW, 8 May 1776, in *PGWRWS,* 4: 232.

2. Robbins, *Journal,* 17; John Thomas to Committee of Congress, 7 May 1776, PSP, NYPL; Council of War, 7 May 1776, in *AA4,* 6: 454; "New-York, May 23," *The Freeman's Journal or New Hampshire Gazette* (Portsmouth, NH), 1 June 1776.

3. *BTW,* 32–33.

4. Charles Douglas to Philip Stephens, 8 May 1776, in *NDAR,* 4: 1452. Goforth's lieutenant, Stephen McDougall, lingered too long on the *Maria* and was captured in this event. Subsequently, he was included by his proper name (Ranald McDougall) on a 1776 list of officer prisoners held in Quebec, almost all of whom were Arnold's men, captured in the assault. Since that list misqualified the prisoners as having all been " . . . taken on December 31st," there is a long-standing misperception that Lieutenant McDougall participated in Montgomery's assault on Québec City; Roberts, *March to Quebec,* 289.

5. *JMRE*, 113; 10 May Proclamation, in Ainslie, *Journal*, 95; JOB to Louis Sarault, 11 May 1776, in Gosselin, *"L'Église,"* 77.

6. Commissioners to Canada to JH, 10 May 1776, in *LOD*, 3: 646–47; CCC to Charles Carroll of Annapolis, 10 May 1776, in *CCoC*, 907–908; Journal of CCC, 12 May 1776, in Rowland, *Charles Carroll*, 1: 393.

7. Commissioners to Canada to BA, 12 May 1776, in *LOD*, 3: 666; CCC to John Thomas, 12 May 1776, Thomas Addis Emmet Collection, MG23-I1, LAC.

8. William Thompson to PS, 19 May 1776, PSP, NYPL; Commissioners to Canada to John Thomas, 15 May 1776, in *LOD*, 3: 681.

9. CCC to John Thomas, 12 May 1776, Thomas Addis Emmet Collection, MG23-I1, LAC; John Thomas to Committee of Congress, 15 May 1776, PCC, M247 171 i58 p253.

10. Thomas Stone to James Hollyday, 20 May 1776, in *LOD*, 4: 51; Badeaux, *Journal*, 36–39; Mémoire [attribué à l'abbé Huet de la Valinière] sur l'état du Canada pendant la Révolution américaine, Fonds de la Bibliothèque Sainte-Geneviève, MG7 VI, LAC; Testimony of William Haywood to Committee on Canada, 18 July 1776, in *PTJ*, 1: 453.

11. Samuel Chase to Richard Henry Lee, 17 May 1776, and Commissioners to Canada to JH, 17 May 1776, in *LOD*, 4: 21–22, 25; CCC to Charles Carroll of Annapolis, 17 May 1776, in *CCoC*, 909–10.

12. John Thomas to Commissioners in Canada, in *AA4*, 6: 592.

13. Ibid.; "Colonel Bedel's Defence," 9 July 1776, "Rolls and Documents Relating to Soldiers in the Revolutionary War," in *New Hampshire Provincial and State Papers*, vol. 17, ed. Isaac W. Hammond (Manchester, NH: John B. Clarke, 1889), 58–59; *JCC*, 5: 534; Commissioners to Canada to JH, 17 May 1776, in *LOD*, 4: 24. Bedel maintained that he obtained his first positive intelligence of Forster's advance during the meeting at Caughnawaga and that the Indians convinced him to take the news to Montréal himself, rather than immediately returning to Fort Cedars. Other accounts state that Bedel was well aware of the threat before his Caughnawaga visit, but none of them specify that the imminent approach of the loyalist force had actually been confirmed. In the ensuing Congressionally ordered court-martial, Bedel was found guilty of "quitting his post at the Cedars," but not for "declining to return to the same with Major Sherburne's reinforcement." "Bedel's Defence," 59; Stevens, "Diary," 138; Testimony of Joseph Easterbrooks and Daniel Wilkins, 2 June 1776, PCC, M247 136 i29 v p255; *JCC*, 5: 618; General Orders from HG, 1 August 1776, in *AA5*, 1: 801; Cubbison, *Northern Theater Army*, 94–95.

14. Parke, *Authentic Narrative*, 21–23.

15. Ibid., 23–30; Greenwood, *Revolutionary Services*, 26–27; An authentic account . . . by an officer of the detachment it principally concerns, in Almon, *Remembrancer*, 205; *JCC*, 5: 535, 538. Butterfield was later court-martialed and found guilty of "surrendering the post," a euphemism for cowardice. Sherburne, unlike Bedel and Butterfield, was respected for his fight and was not court-martialed; General Orders from HG, 1 August 1776, in *AA5*, 1: 801.

16. Parke, *Authentic Narrative*, 29–31; Lorimier, *At War*, 57–58; James Wilkinson to Nathaniel Greene, 24 May 1776, in Wilkinson, *Memoirs*, 1: 43–44.

17. MH to Committee of Congress, 24 May 1776, PMP, LAC; BA to Congressional Committee, 25 May 1776, in *NDAR*, 5: 243; Wilkinson, *Memoirs*, 46; Parke, *Authentic Narrative*, 31.

18. Parke, *Authentic Narrative*, 36–37. For additional secondary source descriptions of the Battle of the Cedars, see Cubbison, *Northern Theater Army*, 92–99; and Samuel E. Dawson, "Massacre at the Cedars," *Canadian Monthly and National Review* 5 (June 1874): 305–23.

19. Parke, *Authentic Narrative*, 35; *JCC*, 5: 537; Testimony of John Hamtramck to Committee on Canada, 1–17 July 1776, in *PTJ*, 1: 451–52; Lorimier, *At War*, 57; J-F Hamtramck Petition to the Cont Congr, 11 July 1776, PCC, M247 196 i78 vii p71–73; Case with Col. Hazen's Regiment, 3 September 1778, MHC, LAC; Isaac Butterfield Testimony Respect[in]g a Breach of the Convention at the Cedars, June 1776, PCC, M247 136 i29 p245.

20. Memorial of Montigny de Louvigny, 7 April 1784, Thomas Townshend, 1st Viscount Sydney fonds, MG23-A3, LAC; Berthelot Journal, in Verreau, *Invasion*, 282; Lorimier, *At War*, 58; "Second Book . . . of the Court of Inquiry of Damages," FHV, MG23-GV7, LAC; BA to the Commissioners, 2 June 1776, PCC, M247 r36 i29 v p256–257; MH to Committee of Congress at Montreal, 24 May 1776, PMP, LAC; Wilkinson, *Memoirs*, 1: 46.

21. Journal of Charles Carroll, 21–23 May 1776, in Rowland, *Charles Carroll*, 1: 395–96; Porter, "Diary," 195; "Woedtke's Orderly Book," 7 June 1776, cited in Lanctot, *Canada and the American Revolution*, 147.

22. Commissioners to Canada to John Thomas, 26 May 1776, in *LOD*, 4: 77; Samuel Chase and CCC to PS, 28 May 1776, PSP, NYPL.

23. Commissioners to Canada to JH, 27 May 1776, in *LOD*, 4: 82–83; William McCarty to PS, 1 June 1776, PSP, NYPL.

24. Council of War held at Chambly, 30 May 1776, in *AA4*, 6: 628; Journal of CCC, 30 May 1776, in Rowland, *Charles Carroll*, 1: 397; Samuel Chase to PS, 31 May 1776, PSP, NYPL.

25. Charles Douglas to PS, 24 May 1776, in *NDAR*, 5: 225.

26. PS to Commander of the Army in Canada, 4 June 1776, in John Sullivan, *Letters and Papers of Major-General John Sullivan, Continental Army*, vol. 1 (1771–1777), ed. O. G. Hammond (Concord: New Hampshire Historical Society, 1930), 215–16.

27. BA to PS, 10 June 1776, PSP, NYPL; Wilkinson, *Memoirs*, 48.

28. Benjamin Thomson's Acct of Goods Taken at Montreal by B. Arnold, PCC, M247 r71 i58 p397; BA to PS, 13 June 1776, in *AA4*, 6: 1038.

29. John Lacey, "Memoirs," 194; Thomas C. Amory, *Military Services and Public Life of Major General John Sullivan of the American Revolutionary Army* (Boston: Wiggin and Lunt, 1868).

30. JS to JH, 1 June 1776, in Sullivan, *Letters*, 213; JS to GW, 5 June 1776, PSP, NYPL.

31. JS to GW, 5 June 1776, PSP, NYPL; JS to JH, 1 June 1776, and JS to GW, 6 June 1776, in Sullivan, *Letters*, 213, 220.

32. Commission to Francis Guillot of River Daloup [du Loup], 6 June 1776, and Jeremiah Duggan to JS, 5 June 1776, in *AA4*, 6: 923–24.

33. JS to GW, 5 June 1776, PSP, NYPL; JS to GW, 6 June 1776, in Sullivan, *Letters*, 220; *JCC*, 4: 388.

34. JS to GW, 6 June and 8 June 1776, in Sullivan, *Letters*, 219, 231.

35. Ibid.; William Thompson to GW, 2 June 1776, in *PGWRWS*, 4: 429.

36. JS to GW, 6 June 1776, in Sullivan, *Letters*, 219; Instructions for General Thompson from General Sullivan, 6 June 1776, in *AA4*, 6: 923.

37. William Thompson to JS, 7 June 1776, in *NDAR*, 5: 408; William Irvine, "Gen. Irvine's Journal of the Canadian Campaign, 1776," *Historical Magazine* 6 (1862): 115–16; Thomas Hartley to Jasper Yeates, 12 June 1776, in *Pennsylvania-German Society Proceedings* 17 (1908): 95–101 [extract printed in *Pennsylvania Evening Post* (Philadelphia), 11 July 1776]; Berthelot Journal, in Verreau, *Invasion*, 238–39. There has yet to be a monograph dedicated to the Battle of Three Rivers; for recent treatments, see Cubbison, *Northern Theater Army*, 110–19, and Pierre Cécil, "La bataille de Trois-Rivières, 8 juin 1776," *Traces* 38, no. 2 (Mars–Avril 2000): 25–27. Pointe-du-Lac has an Antoine Gauthier Park, commemorating the habitant's contribution to the victory. It is noteworthy that the Trois-Rivières militia formed under a seigneur; yet this was a significantly different situation from the numerous 1775 mobilization debacles—this case involved an "urban" militia, there was an imminent threat, a large British military force was at hand, and the locals had directly suffered from Continental depredations in the last few months.

38. Cubbison, *Northern Theater Army*, 119; GC to George Germain, 20 June 1776, in Almon, *Remembrancer*, 178; Griffith Williams to George Germain, 23 June 1776, in *NDAR*, 5: 694; Enys, *American Journals*, 15. When word of the battle reached Continental prisoners still held in Québec City, the bearer of the news claimed, "if the General had been one hour sooner, he would have

carried the post"; Francis Nichols, "Diary," *Pennsylvania Magazine of History and Biography* 20 (1896): 507.

39. "Extract of a Letter Dated Crown-Point, 3 July 1776," *Pennsylvania Evening Post* (Philadelphia), 18 July 1776; Digby, *Journal*, 108, 113; Harry M. Ward, *General William Maxwell and the New Jersey Continentals* (Westport, CT: Greenwood Press, 1997), 34.

40. JS to GW, 8 June 1776, PSP, NYPL.

41. JS to PS, 19 June 1776, in *AA4*, 6: 1103; BA to JS, 13 June 1776, in Sullivan, *Letters*, 237–38; Edward Antill to JS, 13 June 1776, PSP, NYPL; De Woedtke to BF, 3 July 1776, trans. in Cubbison, *Northern Theater Army*, 138.

42. BA to JS, 16 June 1776, in *AA4*, 6: 930; Greenwood, *Revolutionary Services*, 32, 35; Memorial of Levy Solomons, 15 November 1784, PCC, M247 r41 i35 p148.

43. Sanguinet, 132–33; EM to JOB, 17 June 1776, in Gosselin, *L'Église*, 70.

44. JS to PS, 19 June 1776, PSP, NYPL; Wilkinson, *Memoirs*, 55.

45. Digby, *Journal*, 113–19; Charles Douglas to Philip Stevens, 26 June 1776, in *NDAR*, 5: 749; EM to JOB, 21 June 1776, in Faucher de Saint Maurice, *Notes Pour Servir a L'Histoire du Général Richard Montgomery* (Montréal: Eusèbe Senecal, 1893), 28–30.

46. "Extract of a Letter dated Crown-Point, 3 July 1776," *Pennsylvania Evening Post* (Philadelphia), 18 July 1776; John Trumbull, *Autobiography, Reminesces and Letters of John Trumbull, from 1756 to 1841* (New Haven, CT: B. L. Hamlen, 1841), 299–300; William Chamberlin, "Letter of General William Chamberlin," *Proceedings of the Massachusetts Historical Society, Series 2*, 10 (1896): 498.

47. See Cubbison, *Northern Theater Army*, for a thorough, modern examination of the events in this chapter and the subsequent campaign to defend Lake Champlain, Crown Point, and Fort Ticonderoga.

Chapter 23. The Causes of the Miscarriages in Canada

Epigraphs: Elbridge Gerry to James Warren, 15 June 1776, in *LOD*, 4: 221; *DAR*, 12: 187.

1. *JCC*, 4: 359, 362–63; JA to James Warren, 18 May 1776, in *LOD*, 4: 32–33.

2. *JCC*, 4: 376–99, 410; PS to GW, 11 June 1776, in *AA4*, 6: 820; JH to GW, 26 June 1776, in *LOD*, 4: 326–27.

3. JH to GW, 16 June 1776, in *PGWRWS*, 4: 526.

4. TW to SA, 30 May 1776, SAP, NYPL; BF to Commissioners to Canada, 27 May 1776, in *LOD*, 4: 86; John Carroll to CCC and Samuel Chase, 28 May 1776, in Carroll, *Papers*, 49.

5. PS to John Trumbull, Jr., 7 June 1776, PSP, NYPL; GW to JH, 9 June 1776, in *PGWRWS*, 4: 470–71.

6. Samuel Chase to HG, 13 June 1776, HGP, NYHS; *JCC*, 5: 448.

7. Orders and Instructions for HG . . . from GW, 24 June 1776, HGP, NYHS; JH to HG, 18 June 1776, and JH to HG, 8 July 1776, in *LOD*, 4: 262, 408; Cubbison, *Northern Theater Army*, 140.

8. Thomas Jefferson to Thomas Nelson, 16 May 1776, in *PTJ*, 1: 293; JA to James Warren, 18 May 1776, and Richard H. Lee to CL, 18 May 1776, in *LOD*, 4: 33, 37; Adams, *Diary*, 3: 409.

9. *JCC*, 4: 421; Commissioners to Canada to JH, 27 May 1776, and DW to JH, 26 June 1776, in *AA4*, 4: 82, 6: 1081.

10. PS to Commissioners in Canada, 28 May 1776, and Berkshire County Committee to GW, 7 June 1776, in *AA4*, 6: 610, 745.

11. Jonathan Trumbull, Jr. to Jonathan Trumbull, Sr., 12 July 1776, in Trumbull, *Autobiography*, 302–303; Baron de Woedtke to BF, 3 July 1776, in Cubbison, *Northern Theater Army*, 138.

12. Jonathan Trumbull, Sr. to William Williams, 26 July 1776, in *AA5*, 1: 607; Orders, Headquarters Ticonderoga, 21 July 1776, in Salsig, *Parole: Quebec*, 178.

13. JA to Samuel Cooper, 9 June 1776, and Elbridge Gerry to James Warren, 15 June 1776, in *LOD*, 4: 177, 221.

14. *JCC*, 5: 472; JH to GW, 21 June 1776, in *LOD*, 4: 285; GW to PS, 15 July 1776, in *PGWRWS*, 5: 331.

15. *JCC*, 5: 474.

16. Ibid., 5: 617–20; James Price testimony to Committee on Canada, 10 July 1776, in *PTJ*, 1: 449.

17. William Williams to Jonathan Trumbull, Sr., 10 August 1776, in *LOD*, 4: 650; Ford, *JCC*, 5: 665; *AA5* 3: 458; CSSAR, *Catalogue of the Officers*, 44. The disdain Chase and Carroll showed for Wooster undoubtedly had its roots in legitimate differences regarding the handling of Canadian affairs, perhaps originating in Philadelphia consultations with Lajeunesse, Walker, and Price. Such views would have been aggravated by Wooster's Montréal opponents, offering unrebutted perspectives after the delegation arrived in the city. The general's sharp, insolent words over the committee's hasty countermanding of his policies, without consultation, must have further intensified already negative feelings.

18. PS to JH, 16 August 1776, in *AA5*, 1: 983; *JCC*, 5: 841; JH to PS, 4 October 1776, in *LOD*, 5: 303–304.

19. PS, "Memorandum from the Northern Army," Albany, 6 November 1776, PCC, M247 r30 i21 p93.

20. *JCC*, 5: 615, 645–647; The Following Persons Refugees from Canada now in the United States, [n.d.], PCC, M247 r49 i41 v2 p140; At a Board of War, 21 August 1776, in *AA5*, 1: 1094.

21. *QG*, 5 September 1776; Notes from verbal examination of Loiseau and Allin, [summer] 1776, in *AA5*, 1: 799; List from Bindon, PCC, M247 r49 i41 v2 p140–141.

22. *JCC*, 6: 900, 940, 24: 269; Liste des officiers Canadiens, soldats et Refugies, 11 August 1787, PCC, M247 r53 i42 v2 p230.

23. "Desdevens de Glandons, Maurice," *DCB*; Petition of Louis Lotbiniere, 3 February 1787, PCC, M247 r54 i42 v4 p418.

24. *JCC*, 6: 865; Koert Dubois Burnham and David Kendall Martin, *La Corne St. Luc: His Flame* (Chazy, NY: Northern New York American-Canadian Genealogical Society, 1991), 94.

25. BF to James Hutton, 1 February 1778, BF to Vergennes, 25 February 1779, and BF to JA, 20 April 1782, in *PBF* 25: 562, 28: 603, and 37: 177.

26. General Orders, Three Rivers, 18 June 1776, Haldimand Papers, MG-21, General Orders, Microfilm A-617, p. 3, LAC; Digby, *Journal*, 132.

27. George Germain to GC, 21 June 1776, in *DAR*, 12: 154; House of Commons, 20 February 1776, in *AA4*, 6: 265; George Germain to John Burgoyne, 28 March 1776, in *CCA* 1904, 363.

28. *BTW, passim*.

29. Ibid., 17; Bonneau, *St-Pierre*, 111.

30. Lanctot, *Canada and the American Revolution*, 152; GC to Friedrich Riedesel, 23 March 1777, Haldimand Papers, MG-21, General Orders, Microfilm A-617, p. 388, LAC. The 1777 Dupré-Gray-Panet Commission's visit to the Berthier region actually focused on parish activities after the Continental expulsion from the province; transcripts of reports, FHV, Boite 9, No. 25.

31. Digby, *Journal*, 119; *HMNF*, 2: 38; Ernest Chambers, *The Canadian Militia: A History of the Origin and Development of the Force* (Montréal: L. M. Fresco, 1907), 30.

32. General Orders, 5 June 1776 and 16 August 1776, and GC to Brigadier Powell, 24 August 1776, Haldimand Papers, MG-21, General Orders, Microfilm A-617, pp. 4, 28, 35, LAC.

33. Memorial of Pierre Ayot[te], 5 August 1785, John Welles Certification for Jean-Baptiste Allin, 16 October 1778, and Memorial of Maurice Desdevens, 27 April 1786, PCC, M247 r41 i35 p252.

34. EM to JOB, 12 August 1776, in Martin Griffin, *Catholics and the American Revolution* (Ridley Park, PA: M. Griffin, 1902), 78; "Floquet, Pierre-René," and "Huet de la Valinière, Pierre," *DCB*; Gosselin, *L'Église*, 89–90; EM to JOB, 17 June 1776, in Gosselin, 72–73.

35. George Germain to GC, 22 August 1776, in *DAR*, 12: 187; General Orders, 28 October 1776 and 20 November 1776, and GC to Friedrich Riedesel, 20 December 1776, Haldimand Papers, MG-21, General Orders, Microfilm A-617, pp. 58, 65, 313, LAC.

36. Frederick Haldimand to George Germain, 25 October 1780, in *CAD*, 2: 721; Indemnity for Losses Sustained by Francis Cazeau, 31 January 1817, in *ASP*, 516; List from Joseph Bindon—The Following Gentlemen Suffering in Gaol in Quebec & Montreal, PCC, M247 r49 i41 v2 p140–141; Laterrière, *Mémoires*, 104; Papers belonging to L'Anglois of the Ecureuils, taken the 5th of Septr. 1779, SP2, 12–18.

37. Memorial of Fleury Mesplet, 27 March 1787, PCC, M247 r51 i41 v6 p362; "Mesplet, Fleury," *DCB*. Mesplet's primary legacy, the *Montréal Gazette*, still remains in print as of this book's publication. There is also a small Fleury Mesplet Park at the northeast end of Old Town Montréal.

38. GC to Lord George Germain, 9 May 1777, in *CAD*, 2: 460; John Burgoyne to George Germain, 22 June 1777, in *HMNF*, 2: 224; John Burgoyne, *A State of the Expedition from Canada, as Laid Before the House of Commons . . .* (London: J. Almon, 1780), 7; Sanguinet, 144–45; GC to George Germain, 28 September 1776, in *DAR* 12: 234.

39. Anburey, *Travels*, 1: 67, 183.

40. Petition of Merchants for Repeal of the Quebec Act, in *CAD*, 2: 694.

Conclusion

Epigraphs: Smith, *Oration*, 26; George Measam to Alexander McDougall, 31 March 1776, AMP, NYHS.

1. David Galula, *Counterinsurgency Warfare: Theory and Practice* (Cambridge, MA: Harvard University Press, 1964), 4.

2. Robert M. Calhoon, "Loyalism and Neutrality," in *Encyclopedia of the American Revolution*, 247; Galula, *Counterinsurgency Warfare*, 52–55.

3. See Arthur L. Burt, *Guy Carleton, Lord Dorchester, 1724–1808, Revised Version* (Ottawa: Canadian Historical Association, 1968), 5–7, for a critical view of Carleton's politics.

4. Almost all Old Subject loyalist journals, and many letters, single out the *Canadiens* for their passivity or neutrality; as an example, see *JMRE*, 23–24. Several Continentals emphasized Canadian political apathy and unreliability, as well; the most famous being David Wooster to Seth Warner, 6 January 1776, in *AA4*, 4: 588. Canadian historians have tended to dwell on habitant neutrality, without contemporary comparison to popular attitudes in other North American colonies; characteristic examples include Gustave Lanctot, *Les Canadiens et leurs voisins du sud* (Montréal: Bernard Valiquette, 1941) and Fernand Ouellet, *Histoire économique et sociale du Québec, 1760–1850* (Montréal: Fides, 1966), both excerpted and translated in G. A. Rawlyk, *Revolution Rejected, 1775–1776* (Scarborough, ON: Prentice Hall, 1968), 108–12, 119–27; and G. A. Rawlyk, "The American Revolution and Canada," *Encyclopedia of the American Revolution*, 501. Gustave Lanctot highlights the limited nature of Canadian participation in the Continental Army, identifying that only five hundred men served under Congress, from an estimated population of ninety thousand—about 0.5 percent of the total population; Lanctot, *Canada and the American Revolution*, 116. While this number seems remarkably small, the author's best quantified estimate of the Thirteen Colonies' 1776 "Continental" service would be roughly 1.1 percent, from a population that had been progressively mobilized over the course of two years. The 1.1 percent calculation is based on peak reports of twenty-four thousand men serving in 1776 "Continental" duty (excluding units on limited state or militia service), from an estimated "free" population of 2.1 million. These numbers are open to ample debate on two accounts, though: first, that historical strength reports are inconsistent, and second, that the distinction between "Continental" and local service is open to broad interpretation. Depending upon one's definitions, extreme ranges of men in Continental service could be

as low as .6 percent and as high as 2.3 percent of the population. Charles H. Lesser, ed., *Sinews of Independence: Monthly Strength Reports of the Continental Army* (Chicago: University of Chicago Press, 1976), 18–21, 24–27, 32–41; Merrill Jensen, *The Founding of a Nation: A History of the American Revolution, 1763–1776* (New York: Oxford University Press, 1968), 8–10.

5. John Shy, "The American Revolution: The Military Conflict Considered as a Revolutionary War," in Stephen Kurtz and James Hutson, eds., *Essays on the American Revolution* (Chapel Hill: University of North Carolina, 1973), 134; Thomas B. Allen, *Tories: Fighting for the King in America's First Civil War* (New York: Harper, 2010), 188–91; Mark V. Kwasny, *Washington's Partisan War: 1775–1783* (Kent, OH: Kent State University Press, 1996), 91; George Washington to Lund Washington, 10–17 December 1776, in *PGWRWS*, 7: 291.

6. Jonathan Trumbull to Philip Schuyler, 18 August 1775, in *AA4*, 3: 160.

7. John Adams to James Warren, 12 May 1776, in *LOD*, 3: 662.

8. Rebecca K. Starr, "Political Mobilization, 1765–1776," in *Encyclopedia of the American Revolution*, 231; Breen, *American Insurgents*, 206, 162.

9. Stanley Ryerson, *The Founding of Canada: Beginnings to 1815* (Toronto: Progress, 1972), 214.

10. Creighton, *Commercial Empire*, 58; David L. Ammerman, "The Tea Crisis and Its Consequences, Through 1775," *Encyclopedia of the American Revolution*, 203–205; Breen, *American Insurgents*, 170.

Appendix 1

1. Thomas Ainslie, *Canada Preserved: The Journal of Captain Thomas Ainslie*, ed. Sheldon S. Cohen (New York: New York University Press, 1968).

2. *Journal of the Siege and Blockade of Quebec by the American Rebels in Autumn 1775 and Winter 1776* (Quebec: Literary and Historical Society of Quebec, 1876); "Journal of the Most Remarkable Occurrences since Arnold Appear'd Before the Town on the 14th November 1775," *Historical Documents Relating to the Blockade of Quebec by the American Revolutionists in 1775–1776* (Quebec: Literary and Historical Society of Quebec, 1905); and Fred Wurtele, ed., *Blockade of Quebec in 1775–1776 by the American Revolutionists (Les Bastonnais)* (Quebec: Literary and Historical Society of Quebec, 1906).

3. Abbé Verreau, ed. *Invasion du Canada, Collection de Memoires recueillis et annotes* (Montreal: Eusebe Senecal, 1873); Feu Foucher, "Journal Tenu Pendant Le Siege du Fort Saint-Jean, en 1775," *Le Bulletin des Recherches Historiques* 40 (1934). So far, the only translation of these documents has been Claude Lorimier, *At War with the Americans: Translation of 'Mes services pendant la guerre américaine,'* trans. and ed. Peter Aichinger (Victoria, BC: Porcépic, 1987).

4. In particular, see Auguste Gosselin, *L'Église du Canada après la conquête, Deuxième Partie, 1775–1789* (Quebec: Laflamme, 1917); John S. Moir, *The Church and State in Canada, 1627–1867: Basic Documents* (Toronto: McClelland and Stewart, 1967); and Collection Jean-Olivier Briand, MG23-GIV4, LAC.

5. An example of such a local gem, already published, is Pierre-Antoine Porlier's "Mémoire d'observations ...," *Bulletin des recherches historiques* 6, no. 5 (mai 1900), which is absolutely essential for understanding the St-Pierre uprising story.

6. Diverse letters and petitions are captured in Force's *American Archives,* Papers of the Continental Congress, and scattershot through other collections. James Jeffry's "Journal Kept in Quebec in 1775 by James Jeffry," *Historical Collection of the Essex Institute* 50 (April 1914): 97–150, helps to connect many of the province's 1775 events, as well.

7. Pierre Foretier, "Notes and Reminesces of an Inhabitant of Montreal During the Occupation of that City ...," *Canada Public Records Report, 1945* (Ottawa: Edmund Cloutier, 1946).

8. Francis Maseres, *An account of the proceedings of the British, and other Protestant inhabitants,*

of the province of Quebeck, in North America, In order to obtain an House of Assembly in that Province (London: B. White, 1775); and *Additional papers concerning the province of Quebeck . . .* (London: W. White, 1776).

9. Michael Gabriel, ed., *Quebec During the American Invasion: The Journal of François Baby, Gabriel Taschereau and Jenkin Williams*, trans. S. Pascale Vergereau-Dewey (East Lansing: Michigan State University, 2005)

Appendix 2

1. *Proceedings at the Completion of the Wooster Monument* (New Haven, CT: Storer and Morehouse, 1854); and Cornelius Moore, *Leaflets of Masonic Biography, or Sketches of Eminent Freemasons* (Cincinnati, OH: Masonic Review Office, 1863); similarly, see Connecticut Society of the Sons of the American Revolution, *Catalogue of the Officers and Members of Gen. David Humphreys Branch Since Its Organization* (New Haven, CT: General David Humphreys Branch, 1911).

2. See the note in the conclusion of Chapter Sixteen for a listing of more recent historians who have joined in this view.

3. Roberts, *March to Quebec*, 103–104. Smith offers similar views in *Fourteenth Colony*, 2: 229–230, but confesses that his harsh portrait is derived from very limited documentary reference points.

4. See 'An Aged Subscriber,' "Anecdotes of Gen. Wooster," *American Historical Magazine* 1, no. 1 (January 1836): 56–59; and Thomas Jones, *History of New York During the Revolutionary War and of the Leading Events in the Other Colonies at that Period*, Vol. 1 (New York: New-York Historical Society, 1879), 180.

5. Smith, *Fourteenth Colony*, 230.

SELECT BIBLIOGRAPHY

Archives

BIBLIOTHÈQUE ET ARCHIVES NATIONALE DE QUÉBEC

Commerce maritime de Benedict Arnold à Québec. Accessed 20 October 2009. http://pistard
.banq.qc.ca

Procès entre Germain Dionne et consorts. Accessed 20 October 2009. http://pistard.banq.qc.ca

Testament, généalogie, biographie et correspondance de Pierre Huet de la Valinière. Accessed 20
October 2009. http://pistard.banq.qc.ca

COLUMBIA UNIVERSITY

John Jay Papers. Accessed 14 August 2007. http://www.columbia.edu/cu/lweb/digital/jay/search
.html

INDIANA HISTORICAL SOCIETY

John Armstrong Papers, 1772–1950 (microfilm)

LIBRARY AND ARCHIVES OF CANADA

MG6-A5. Fonds des Archives départementales de la Loire-Atlantique. Série EPapiers de famille

MG11-C05. CO 5. America and West Indies, Original Correspondence, etc. Microfilm B-3898

MG11-C042Q. Q Series. Canada, Formerly British North America, Original Correspondence

MG7 VI. Fonds de la Bibliothèque Sainte-Geneviève

MG17-A5. Fonds de l'Église catholique. Archevêché de Montréal

MG-21. Haldimand Papers. Microfilm A-616, A-617, A-671, A-765, A-774, H-1432

MG23-A3. Thomas Townshend, 1st Viscount Sydney Fonds

MG23-B4. Moses Hazen Collection

MG23-B7. Journal of the most remarkable events which happened in Canada between the months
of July 1775 and June 1776

MG23-B25. Certificate of Lt. Col. Allan Maclean

MG23-B27. Benedict Arnold Collection

MG23-B35. Collection Amable Berthelot

MG23-B37. Declaration of Vincent Giroux

MG23-B40. Robert R. Livingston Collection

MG23-GII3. Edward William Gray Fonds

MG23-GIV4. Collection Jean-Olivier Briand

MG23-GV7. Fonds Hospice-Anthelme-Jean-Baptiste Verreau

MG23-I1. Thomas Addis Emmet Collection

MG40-R89. Perceval-Maxwell Papers

RG8-I. British Military and Naval Records, "C Series," 1713, 1714. Miscellaneous Records. Microfilm C-3840

NEW-YORK HISTORICAL SOCIETY ARCHIVES

Benedict Arnold Correspondence, 1772–1782, BV Arnold, Benedict
Horatio Gates Papers (microfilm)
John Lacey Transcripts, 1849–1854, BV Lacey, John
Alexander MacDougall Papers, 1756–1795 (microfilm)
Minute Books, Account Books and Daybooks, 1745–1815, BV Banyar, Goldsbrow—(Copy of
    Anthony Clarke Memorandum Book, 1775–1776. Transcribed by Stephen Gilbert, Joe Renkas,
    and Mary Mulcahy)
E. B. O'Callaghan Papers
Richard Varick Papers, 1774–1830

NEW YORK PUBLIC LIBRARY ARCHIVES

Samuel Adams Papers (microfilm)
George Bancroft Collection
Livingston Family Papers
Philip Schuyler Papers (microfilm). Reel 12: 1772–1775; Reel 13: 1 January–15 May 1776; Reel 14:
    16 May–September 1776

UNITED STATES NATIONAL ARCHIVES

M247. The Correspondence, Journals, Committee Reports, and Records of the Continental Con-
    gress (1774–1789)
M804. Revolutionary War Pension and Bounty-Land Warrant Application Files

Published Primary Sources and Collections

Note: Where applicable, bibliographic preference is given to the primary source author, rather
than the editor, for the various collections of papers, letters, and diaries.

Adams, John. *Diary and Autobiography of John Adams.* Edited by L. H. Butterfield. Cambridge,
    MA: Belknap, 1962.
Adams, Samuel. *The Writings of Samuel Adams.* Edited by H. A. Cushing. New York: Putnam, 1907.
Ainslie, Thomas. *Canada Preserved: The Journal of Captain Thomas Ainslie.* Edited by Sheldon S.
    Cohen. New York: New York University, 1968.
Allen, Ethan. *Narrative of Col. Ethan Allen's Captivity, Written by Himself.* Burlington, VT:
    Chauncey Goodrich, 1846.
Almon, John, ed. *The Remembrancer, or Impartial Repository of Public Events.* Part 2. London: J.
    Almon, 1776.
Anburey, Thomas. *Travels Through the Interior Parts of America. In a Series of Letters. By an Officer.*
    Vol. 1. London: William Lane, 1789.
Archives de la Province de Québec. *Recensement des Gouvernements de Montréal et des Trois-Rivières
    pour 1765.* Québec: Imprimerie du Roi, 1937.
Arnold, Benedict. "Letters, September 27–December 5, 1775." *Collections of Maine Historical Society*
    1 (1861): 447–98.
Aubert de Gaspé, Philippe. *Mémoires.* Ottawa: G. E. Desbarats, 1866.
Badeaux, Jean-Baptiste. *Journal des Operations de l'Armee Americaine Lors de L'Invasion du Canada
    en 1775–76.* Montreal: Eusebe Senecal, 1871.
Beaujeu, Monongahela de, ed. *Documents Inedits sur le Colonel de Longueuil, Annotés et Publiés par
    Monongahela de Beaujeu.* Montreal: Société Numismatique et des Antiquaires de Montréal, 1891.
Bloodgood, Samuel DeWitt. *The Sexagenary, or Reminiscences of the American Revolution.* Albany,
    NY: John Munsell, 1866.

Bouton, Nathaniel, ed. *Provincial Papers, Documents and Records Relating to the Province of New-Hampshire, from 1764 to 1776.* Vols. 7 and 8. Nashua, NH: Green C. Moore, 1873–1874.

Brent, John Carroll, ed. *Biographical Sketch of the Most Rev. John Carroll, First Archbishop of Baltimore.* Baltimore: John Murphy, 1843.

Caldwell, Henry. *The Invasion of Canada in 1775: Letter Attributed to Major Henry Caldwell.* Quebec City: Literary and Historical Society of Quebec, 1887.

Calvet, Pierre du. *The Case of Peter du Calvet, Esq., Of Montreal in the Province of Quebeck.* London: P. du Calvet, 1834.

A Canadian [attributed to Pierre de Sales Laterrière]. *A Political and Historical Account of Lower Canada: With Remarks on the Present Situation of the People, as Regards their Manners, Character, Religion, &c., &c.* London: William Marsh and Alfred Miller, 1830.

Carroll, Charles. *Dear Papa, Dear Charley: The Papers of Charles Carroll of Carrollton, 1748–1782.* Vol. 2. Edited by Ronald Hoffman. Chapel Hill: University of North Carolina Press, 2001.

Carroll, John. *The John Carroll Papers.* Vol. I, *1755–1791.* Edited by Thomas O'Brien Hanley. Notre Dame, IN: University of Notre Dame Press, 1976.

Carter, Clarence E., ed. *The Correspondence of General Thomas Gage with the Secretaries of State.* New Haven, CT: Yale University Press, 1931.

Chamberlin, William. "Letter of General William Chamberlin." In *Proceedings of the Massachusetts Historical Society, Series 2.* Vol. 10 (1896): 497–99.

Chipman, Daniel. *Memoir of Colonel Seth Warner, to which is added the Life of Ethan Allen, by Jared Sparks.* Middlebury, VT: L. W. Clark, 1848.

Clark, William Bell, ed. *Naval Documents of the American Revolution.* Washington, DC: Government Printing Office, 1964–1970.

Claus, Daniel. *Daniel Claus Memoranda, 1775.* Quebec City: Literary and Historical Society of Quebec, 1906.

"Colonel Bedel's Defence." Edited by Isaac W. Hammond. In "Rolls and Documents Relating to Soldiers in the Revolutionary War." *New Hampshire Provincial and State Papers.* Vol. 17. Manchester, NH: John B. Clarke, 1889.

Concerning Canadian Archives for the Year 1904. Ottawa: S. K. Dawson, 1905.

Connecticut Historical Society. *Papers Relating to the Expedition to Ticonderoga, April and May, 1775.* Hartford: Connecticut Historical Society, 1860.

Darley, Stephen. *Voices from a Wilderness Expedition: The Journals and Men of Benedict Arnold's Expedition to Quebec in 1775.* Bloomington, IN: AuthorHouse, 2011.

Davies, K. G., ed. *Documents of the American Revolution, 1770–1783.* Dublin: Irish University, 1975.

Deane, Silas. *The Deane Papers, 1774–1790.* Vol. I, *Collections of the New-York Historical Society for the Year 1886.* Edited by Charles Isham. New York: New-York Historical Society, 1887.

Dewey, Louis M. *Life of George Dewey, Rear Admiral, U.S.N.; and Dewey Family History.* Westfield, MA: Dewey, 1898.

"Diary of the Weather kept at Quebec in the year of the siege by the Americans in 1776." *Transactions of the Literary and Historical Society of Quebec,* n.s., Vol. 9, no. 22 (1898): 1–5.

Digby, William. *The British Invasion from the North: Digby's Journal of the Campaigns of Carleton and Burgoyne from Canada, 1776–1777.* Edited by James Phinney Baxter. Albany, NY: Joel Munsell's Sons, 1887.

Doughty, Arthur, ed. "Appendix B: Papers Relating to the Surrender of St. Johns and Chambly." In *Report on the Works of the Public Archives for the Years 1914 and 1915.* Ottawa: L. Taché, 1916.

Douglas, William. "Letters Written During the Revolutionary War by Colonel William Douglas to His Wife Covering the Period July 19, 1775 to December 5, 1776." *The New-York Historical Society Quarterly Bulletin* 12 (1929): 149–54.

Duffy, John J., ed. *Ethan Allen and His Kin, Correspondence, 1772–1819. A Selected Edition in Two Volumes.* Hanover, NH: University Press of New England, 1998.

Enys, John. *The American Journals of John Enys.* Edited by Elizabeth Cometti. Syracuse, NY: Syracuse University Press, 1976.

Fassett, John, Jr. "Diary of Lt John Fassett Jr. during a trip to Canada and return in Captain Weight Hopkins' company of Colonel Warner's regiment, under General Montgomery, from September 1st to December 7th, 1775." In *The Follet-Dewey Fassett-Safford Ancestry of Captain Martin Dewey Follett.* Edited by Harry P. Ward. Columbus, OH: Champlin, 1896.

Faucher de Saint Maurice. *Notes Pour Servir à L'Histoire du Général Richard Montgomery.* Montreal: Eusebe Senecal, 1893.

Force, Peter, ed. *American Archives: Fourth and Fifth Series.* Washington, DC: M. St. Clair Clarke and Peter Force, 1837.

Ford, Worthington C., ed. *Journals of the Continental Congress, 1774–1789.* Washington, DC: Government Printing Office: 1904.

Foretier, Pierre. "Notes and Reminesces of an Inhabitant of Montreal During the Occupation of that City by the Bostonians from 1775 to 1776." *Canada Public Records Report* (1945): xxv–xxvi.

Foucher, Feu. "Journal Tenu Pendant Le Siege du Fort Saint-Jean, en 1775, Par Feu M. Foucher, Ancien Notaire de Montréal." *Le Bulletin des Recherches Historiques* 40 (1934): 135–59, 197–222.

Franklin, Benjamin. *The Papers of Benjamin Franklin.* Edited by William Willcox. New Haven, CT: Yale, 1982.

Freeman, James. "Record of the Services of Constant Freeman, Captain of the Artillery in the Continental Army." *Magazine of American History* 2 (1878): 349–51.

Gabriel, Michael P., ed. *Quebec During the American Invasion: The Journal of François Baby, Gabriel Taschereau and Jenkin Williams.* Translated by S. Pascale Vergereau-Dewey. East Lansing: Michigan State University, 2005.

Grant, Francis. "Journal from New York to Canada, 1767." *New York State Historical Association Proceedings* 30 (1932): 181–96, 305–22.

Graydon, Alexander. *Memoirs of a Life, Chiefly Passed in Pennsylvania Within the Last Sixty Years; with Occasional Remarks Upon the General Occurrences, Character and Spirit of That Eventful Period.* Hartsburgh, PA: John Wyeth, 1811.

Greenman, Jeremiah. *Diary of a Common Soldier in the American Revolution, 1775–1783: An Annotated Edition of the Military Journal of Jeremiah Greenman.* Edited by Robert C. Bray and Paul E. Bushnell. DeKalb, IL: Northern Illinois University Press, 1978.

Greenwood, John. *The Revolutionary Services of John Greenwood, of Boston and New York, 1775–1783.* New York: Devine Press, 1922.

Hadden, James M. *Hadden's Journal and Orderly Books. A Journal Kept in Canada and Upon Burgoyne's Campaign in 1776 and 1777.* Albany, NY: Joel Munsell's Sons, 1884.

Halsted, John. *Expense Book of John Halsted, Commissary Under Benedict Arnold, Before Quebec, 1776.* Montreal: C. A. Marchand, 1913.

Haskell, Caleb. *Caleb Haskell's Diary, May 5, 1775–May 30, 1776.* Edited by Lothrop Withington. Newburyport, MA: William H. Huse, 1881.

Henry, John J. *An Accurate and Interesting Account of the Hardships and Sufferings of That Band of Heroes, Who Traversed the Wilderness in the Campaign Against Quebec in 1775.* Lancaster, PA: William Greer, 1812.

Heriot, George. *Travels Through the Canadas, Containing a Description of the Picturesque Scenery on Some of the Rivers and Lakes; with an Account of the Productions, Commerce, and Inhabitants of Those Provinces.* Philadelphia: M. Carey, 1813.

Historical Section of the General Staff, ed. *A History of the Organization, Development, and Services of the Military and Naval Forces of Canada, From the Peace of Paris in 1763 to the Present Time.* Quebec: King's Printer, 1919.

Hodgkinson, Samuel. "Before Quebec 1776." *Pennsylvania Magazine of History and Biography* 10 (1886): 158–63.

Hunt, Louise L. *Biographical Notes Concerning General Richard Montgomery Together with Hitherto Unpublished Letters.* Poughkeepsie, NY: News Book and Job, 1876.

Innis, H. A., ed. *Select Documents in Canadian Economic History, 1497–1783.* Toronto: University of Toronto, 1933.

Irvine, William. "Gen. Irvine's Journal of the Canadian Campaign, 1776." *Historical Magazine* 6 (1862): 115–17.

Ives, Vernon, ed. "Narrative of Uriah Cross in the Revolutionary War." *New York History* 63, no. 3 (July 1982): 431–69.

Jay, John. *John Jay: The Making of a Revolutionary—Unpublished Papers, 1745–1780.* Edited by Richard B. Morris. New York: Harper & Row, 1975.

Jefferson, Thomas. *The Papers of Thomas Jefferson.* Edited by Julian P. Boyd. Princeton, NJ: Princeton University Press, 1950.

Jefferys, Thomas. *The Natural and Civil History of the French Dominions in North and South America.* London: T. Jefferys, 1760.

Jeffry, James. "Journal Kept in Quebec in 1775 by James Jeffry." *Historical Collection of the Essex Institute* 50 (April 1914): 97–150.

Jensen, Merrill, ed. *Tracts of the American Revolution, 1763–1776.* Indianapolis: Bobbs-Merrill, 1967.

Johnson, Guy. "Journal of Colonel Guy Johnson from May to November, 1775." Edited by E. B. O'Callaghan. In *Documents Relative to the Colonial History of the State of New York.* Vol. 8. Albany, NY: Weed, Parsons, 1857.

"Journal of the Most Remarkable Occurrences since Arnold Appear'd Before the Town on the 14th November 1775." In *Historical Documents Relating to the Blockade of Quebec by the American Revolutionists in 1775–1776.* Quebec: Literary and Historical Society of Quebec, 1905.

"Journal of the Siege and Blockade of Quebec by the American Rebels in Autumn 1775 and Winter 1776." In *Historical Documents of the Literary and Historical Society of Quebec.* 4th Ser. Quebec: Literary and Historical Society of Quebec, 1876.

Kalm, Peter. *Travels into North America; Containing its Natural History, and a Circumstantial Account of its Plantations and Agriculture in General, With the Civil, Ecclesiastical, and Commercial State of the Country, The Manners of the Inhabitants, and Several Curious and Important Remarks on Various Subjects.* Vol. 3. London: 1771.

Kennedy, W.P.M., ed. *Documents of the Canadian Constitution, 1759–1915.* Toronto: Oxford University Press, 1918.

Knox, John. *An Historical Journal of the Campaigns in North America, 1757, 1758, 1759, 1760.* London: W. Johnston, 1769.

Lacey, John. "Memoirs of Brigadier General John Lacey, of Pennsylvania." *Pennsylvania Magazine of History and Biography* 25 (1901): 191–207, 341–54, 498–515.

Lamb, R. *An Original and Authentic Journal of Occurrences During the Late American War, From Its Commencement to the Year 1783.* Dublin: Wilkinson & Courtney, 1809.

Laterrière, Pierre de Sales. *Mémoires de Pierre de Sales Laterrière et de sus traverses.* Quebec: L'Evenement, 1873.

Lee, Charles. "The Lee Papers, Vol. I, 1754–1776." In *Collections of the New-York Historical Society for the Year 1871.* New York: New-York Historical Society, 1872.

Lester, Robert, and Anthony Vialar. *Orderly Book begun by Capt. Anthony Vialar of the British Militia the 17th September 1775, and kept by him till November 16th, when continued by Capt. Robert Lester.* Quebec: Literary and Historical Society of Quebec, 1905.

"Letters to Robert Morris, 1775–1782." In *Collections of the New-York Historical Society for the Year 1878.* New York: New-York Historical Society, 1879.

Lincoln, William, ed. *The Journals of Each Provincial Congress of Massachusetts in 1774 & 1775, and of the Committee of Safety with an Appendix Containing the Proceedings of the County Conventions—Narratives of the Events of the Nineteenth of April, 1775—Papers Relating to Ticonderoga and Crown Point and Other Documents.* Boston: Dutton and Wentworth, 1838.

Lindsay, William. "Narrative of the Invasion of Canada by the American Provincials, under Montgomery and Arnold, with a particular account of the Siege of Quebec, from the 17th September, 1775, the day on which the British Militia was embodied in that place until the 6th May, 1776, when the siege was raised. William Lindsay, Lieutenant in the British Militia, 1775." *Canadian Review* 2 and 3 (1826).

Livingston, Henry. "The Journal of Major Henry Livingston of Third New York Continental Line August to December 1775." Edited by Gaillard Hunt. *The Pennsylvania Magazine of History and Biography* 22 (1898): 9–33.

Livingston, Henry Beekman. "Colonel Henry Beekman Livingston Letter, Camp Before St. Johns, 6 Oct 75." Edited by Maturin L. Delafield. *Magazine of American History* 21 (1889): 256–58.

Lorimier, Claude. *At War with the Americans: Translation of 'Mes services pendant la guerre américaine.'* Translated and edited by Peter Aichinger. Victoria, BC: Porcépic, 1987.

Lowrie, Walter, ed. *American State Papers, Documents Legislative and Executive, of the Congress of the United States. Class IX. Claims.* Washington, DC: Gales and Seaton, 1834.

Maseres, Francis. *An account of the proceedings of the British, and other Protestant inhabitants, of the province of Quebeck, in North America, In order to obtain an House of Assembly in that Province.* London: B. White, 1775.

———. *Additional papers concerning the province of Quebeck: being an appendix to the book entitled, "An account of the proceedings of the British, and other Protestant inhabitants, of the province of Quebeck, in North America, In order to obtain an House of Assembly in that Province."* London: W. White, 1776.

———. *The Canadian Freeholder: In Two Dialogues Between an Englishman and a Frenchman Settled in Canada.* London: B. White, 1777.

———. *The Maseres Letters, 1766–1768.* Edited by W. Stewart Wallace. Toronto: University of Toronto, 1919.

Massachusetts Historical Society. *Collections of the Massachusetts Historical Society.* Series 4. Vol. 4. Boston: Little, Brown, 1858.

Moncrief, Major. *A Short Account of the Expedition Against Quebec Commanded by Major-General Wolfe in the Year 1759, by Major Moncrief, from the Corps Papers of the Royal Engineers.* Edited by E.G.G. Lewis. Quebec: Nuns of the Franciscan Convent, 1901.

New-York Historical Society. *Early American Orderly Books, 1748–1817.* New Haven, CT: Research Publication, 1977.

Ogden, Matthias. "Journal of Major Matthias Ogden, 1775, in Arnold's Campaign Against Quebec." *Proceedings of the New Jersey Historical Society,* n.s., 13 (1928): 17–30.

Oliver, Peter. *Peter Oliver's Origin & Progress of the American Revolution: A Tory View.* Edited by Douglass Adair and John Schutz. San Marino, CA: Huntington Library, 1961.

Paine, Robert Treat. *Papers of Robert Treat Paine.* Vol. 3, *(1774–1777).* Edited by Edward Hanson. Boston: Massachusetts Historical Society, 2005.

Paine, Sarah Cushing. *Paine Ancestry: The Family of Robert Treat Paine, Signer of the Declaration of Independence.* Boston: Paine Family, 1912.

Parke, Andrew. *An Authentic Narrative of Facts Relating to the Exchange of Prisoners Taken at the Cedars.* London: T. Cadell, 1777.

Porlier, Pierre-Antoine. "Mémoire d'observations sur la conduite des habitants des deux paroisses Sainte-Anne et Saint-Roch au sujet de l'invasion des Bostonnais rebelles et l'exécution des ordres de son excellence Mons. de Carleton pour les repousser de la Pointe Levy sous les ordres de M. de Beaujeu." *Bulletin des recherches historiques* 6, no. 5 (mai 1900): 132–40.

Porter, Elisha. "Diary of the Canadian Campaign, January-August 1776." *Magazine of American History* 30 (1893): 187–205.

Prince, Christopher. *The Autobiography of a Yankee Mariner: Christopher Prince and the American Revolution.* Edited by Michael J. Crawford. Washington, DC: Brassey's, 2002.

Riedesel, Friedrich Adolf. *Memoirs and Letters of Major General Riedesel.* Vol. 1. Edited by Max Von Eelking. Albany, NY: J. Munsell, 1868.

Ritzema, Rudolphus. "Journal of Col. Rudolphus Ritzema, of the First New York Regiment, August 8, 1775 to March 30, 1776." *Magazine of American History* 1 (1877): 98–107.

Robbins, Ammi R. *Journal of the Rev. Ammi R. Robbins, A Chaplain in the American Army in the Northern Campaign of 1776.* New Haven, CT: B. L. Hamlen, 1850.

Roberts, Kenneth, ed. *March to Quebec: Journals of the Members of Arnold's Expedition.* Garden City, NY: Doubleday, 1938.

Rowland, Kate M. *The Life of Charles Carroll of Carrollton, 1737–1832, with his Correspondence and Public Papers.* Vol. 1. New York: G.P. Putnam, 1898.

Saffell, W.T.R. *Record of the Revolutionary War: Containing the Military and Financial Correspondence of Distinguished Officers . . .* Baltimore: Charles C. Saffell, 1894.

Salsig, Doyen. *Parole: Quebec; Countersign: Ticonderoga, Second New Jersey Regimental Orderly Book, 1776.* London: Farleigh Dickinson, 1980.

Senter, Isaac. *The Journal of Isaac Senter, Physician and Surgeon . . .* Tarrytown, NY: Historical Society of Pennsylvania, 1915.

Shipton, Nathaniel N., and David Swain, eds. *Rhode Islanders Record the Revolution: The Journals of William Humphrey and Zuriel Waterman.* Providence: Rhode Island Publications Society, 1984.

Shortt, Adam, and Arthur Doughty, eds. *Canadian Archives: Documents Relating to the Constitutional History of Canada, 1759–1791.* Ottawa: S. E. Dawson, 1907–1918.

Smith, Paul H., ed. *Letters of Delegates to Congress, 1774–1789.* Washington, DC: Library of Congress, 1976–2000.

Smith, Richard. "Diary of Richard Smith in the Continental Congress, 1775–1776." *The American Historical Review* 1, nos. 2 and 3 (January and April 1896): pp. 288–310, 493–516.

Smith, Thomas. *Extracts from the Journals Kept by the Rev. Thomas Smith, Late Pastor of the First Church of Christ in Falmouth.* Portland, ME: Thomas Todd, 1821.

Stevens, Benjamin. "Diary of Benjamin Stevens." *Daughters of the American Revolution Magazine* 44 (August 1914): 137–140.

Stone, William, trans. *Letters of Brunswick and Hessian Officers During the American Revolution.* Albany, NY: Joe Munsell's Sons, 1891.

Sullivan, James, ed. *Minutes of the Albany Committee of Correspondence, 1775–1778.* Albany, NY: J. B. Lyon, 1923.

Sullivan, John. *Letters and Papers of Major-General John Sullivan, Continental Army, Volume 1, 1771–1777.* Edited by O. G. Hammond. Concord: New Hampshire Historical Society, 1930.

Têtu, Henri, and C. O. Gagnon. *Mandements, Lettres Pastorales et Circulaires des Évêques de Québec.* Tome 2. Quebec: Imprimerie Générale, 1888.

Thayer, Simeon. *The Invasion of Canada in 1775, Including the Journal of Captain Simeon Thayer, Describing the Perils and Sufferings of the Army Under Colonel Benedict Arnold, in the March Through the Wilderness to Quebec . . .* Edited by Edwin M. Stone. Providence, RI: Knowles, Anthony, 1867.

Todd, Charles, ed. "The March to Montreal and Quebec, 1775." *American Historical Register* 2 (1895): 641–49.

Topham, John, "The Journal of Captain John Topham." *Magazine of History with Notes and Queries, Extra Numbers* 13, no. 50 (1916): 89–132.

Trumbull, Benjamin. "A Concise Journal or Minutes of the Principal Movement Towards St. John's of the Siege & Surrender of the Forts There in 1775." In *Collections of the Connecticut Historical Society.* Vol. 7. Hartford: Connecticut Historical Society, 1899.

Trumbull, John. *Autobiography, Reminesces and Letters of John Trumbull, from 1756 to 1841.* New Haven, CT: B. L. Hamlen, 1841.

Verreau, Abbé, ed. *Invasion du Canada, Collection de Memoires Recueillis et Annotes.* Montreal: Eusebe Senecal, 1873.

Walker, Martha. "The Shurtleff Manuscript, No. 153. A Diary of the Invasion of Canada, 1775. Being a Narrative of Certain Events Which Transpired in Canada, During the Invasion of That Province by the American Army, in 1775. Written by a Mrs. Walker . . ." Edited by Silas Ketchum. *The Collections of the New Hampshire Antiquarian Society No. 2.* Contoocook, NH: Antiquarian Society, 1876.

Washington, George. *The Papers of George Washington: Colonial Series.* Edited by Philander Chase. Charlottesville: University of Virginia, 1995.

————. *The Papers of George Washington: Revolutionary War Series.* Charlottesville: University of Virginia, 1985–1991.

Weld, Isaac, Jr. *Travels Through the States of North America and the Provinces of Upper and Lower Canada During the Years 1795, 1796 and 1797.* London: John Stockdale, 1799.

Wilkinson, James. *Memoirs of My Own Times.* Vol. 1. Philadelphia: Abraham Small, 1816.

Willett, William M. *A Narrative of the Military Actions of Colonel Marinus Willett, Taken Chiefly from His Own Manuscript.* New York: G. & C. & H. Carvill, 1831.

Wurtele, Fred, ed. *Blockade of Quebec in 1775–1776 by the American Revolutionists (Les Bastonnais).* Quebec: Literary and Historical Society of Quebec, 1906.

Secondary Sources

Aldrich, Edgar. "The Affair of the Cedars and the Service of Colonel Timothy Bedel in the War of the Revolution." In *The Proceedings of the New Hampshire Historical Society.* Vol. 3, *June, 1895 to June, 1899.* Concord: New Hampshire Historical Society, 1902.

Audet, F.-J. "William Brown (1737–1789), premier imprimeur, journaliste et libraire de Québec; sa vie et ses oeuvres." *Transactions of the Royal Society of Canada, 3rd Series* 26 (1932): 97–112.

Bailyn, Bernard, and John Hench. *The Press and the American Revolution.* Worcester, MA: American Antiquarian Society, 1980.

Beauregard, Ludger. "Le peuplement du Richelieu." *Revue de géographie de Montréal* (1965): 43–74.

Becker, Ann M. "Smallpox in Washington's Army: Strategic Implications of the Disease During the American Revolutionary War." *The Journal of Military History* 68, no. 2 (April 2004): 381–430.

Beirne, Francis F. "Mission to Canada: 1776." *Maryland Historical Magazine* 60 (1965): 404–20.

Bellemere, J. E. *Histoire de Nicolet, 1669–1924.* Quebec: Athabaska, 1924.

Bellesiles, Michael. *Revolutionary Outlaws: Ethan Allen and the Struggle for Independence on the Early American Frontier.* Charlottesville: University of Virginia, 1995.

Berger, Carl. *Broadsides and Bayonets: The Propaganda War of the American Revolution.* Philadelphia: University of Pennsylvania, 1961.

Berkshire County. *History of Berkshire County, Massachusetts, with Sketches of Its Prominent Men.* Vol. 2. New York: J. B. Beers, 1885.

Bonneau, Louis-Philippe. *On s'est battu à St-Pierre.* Saint-François, Québec: Société de conservation du patrimoine de Saint-François de la Rivière-du-Sud, 1987.

Boutell, Lewis H. *The Life of Roger Sherman.* Chicago: A. C. McClurg, 1896.

Breen, T. H. *American Insurgents, American Patriots: The Revolution of the People.* New York: Hill and Wang, 2010.

Brisebois, Michel. *The Printing of Handbills in Quebec City, 1764–1800: A Listing with Critical Introduction.* Montreal: McGill University, 1995.

Brooke, Frances. *The History of Emily Montague, in Four Volumes.* London: J. Dodsley, 1769.

Brown, Gayle K. "The Impact of the Colonial Anti-Catholic Tradition on the Canadian Campaign, 1775–1776." *Journal of Church and State* 35 (Summer 1993): 559–75.

Brunet, Michel. *Les Canadiens Après La Conquête, 1759–1775: De la Révolution canadienne à la Révolution américaine.* Montreal: Fides, 1969.

———. *French Canada and the Early Decades of British Rule, 1760–1791.* Ottawa: Canadian Historical Association, 1981.

Buel, Richard, Jr. *Dear Liberty: Connecticut's Mobilization for the Revolutionary War.* Middletown, CT: Wesleyan University Press: 1980.

Burnett, Edmund C. *The Continental Congress.* New York: Macmillan, 1941.

Burnham, Koert DuBois, and David Kendall Martin. *La Corne St. Luc: His Flame.* Chazy, NY: Northern New York American-Canadian Genealogical Society, 1991.

Canadian Broadcasting Corporation. *Canada: A People's History.* Vol. 3, *A Question of Loyalties (1775 to 1815).* Produced by Mark Starowicz. Toronto: Morningstar Entertainment, 2000. DVD.

Carayon, Auguste. *Banissement des Jésuites de la Louisiane, Relation et Lettres Inédites.* Paris: L'Écureux, 1865.

Castonguay, Jacques. *Les défis du fort Saint-Jean. L'invasion ratée des Américains en 1775.* Saint-Jean, QC: Les Éditions du Richelieu, 1975.

"Catholics and the American Revolution." *The American Catholic Historical Researches for 1907,* n.s., 3 (April 1907).

Cécil, Pierre. "La bataille de Trois-Rivières, 8 juin 1776." *Traces* 38, no. 2 (mars-avril 2000): 25–27.

Chambers, Ernest. *The Canadian Militia: A History of the Origin and Development of the Force.* Montréal: L. M. Fresco, 1907.

Charland, Thomas-M. "La Mission de John Carroll au Canada en 1776 et l'interdit du P. Floquet." *La societé d'histoire de l'Église catholique* (1933–1934): 45–56.

Chatfield, William H. *Two Revolutionary War Patriots: Major William Goforth and Captain John Armstrong: Epic Struggles Against British Suppression and Indian Warfare.* Cincinnati, OH: Pendleton House, 2011.

Chittenden, Lucius E. *The Capture of Ticonderoga: Annual Address Before the Vermont Historical Society, Delivered at Montpelier, Vt. on Tuesday Evening, October 8, 1872.* Montpelier, VT: Tuttle and Co, 1872.

Clark, S. D. *Movements of Political Protest in Canada, 1640–1840.* Toronto: University of Toronto Press, 1959.

Cogliano, Francis. *No King, No Popery: Anti-Catholicism in Revolutionary New England.* Westport, CT: Greenwood, 1995.

Colemen, Kenneth. *The American Revolution in Georgia, 1763–1789.* Athens: University of Georgia Press, 1958.

Commission des biens culturels du Québec. *Étude de caractérisation de l'arrondissement historique de Trois-Rivières.* Quebec: Commission des biens culturels du Québec, 2005.

Connecticut Society of the Sons of the American Revolution. *Catalogue of the Officers and Members of Gen. David Humphreys Branch Since Its Organization.* New Haven, CT: General David Humphreys Branch, 1911.

Copeland, David. *Colonial Newspapers: Character and Content.* Newark, NJ: University of Delaware, 1997.

Creighton, D. G. *The Commercial Empire of the St. Lawrence, 1760–1850.* Toronto: Ryerson, 1937.

Crowley, Terrence. "Thunder Gusts: Popular Disturbances in Early French Canada." *Canadian Historical Association, Historical Papers* (1979): 11–31.

Cubbison, Douglas R. *The American Northern Theater Army in 1776: The Ruin and Reconstruction of the Continental Force.* Jefferson, NC: MacFarland, 2010.

Davidson, Philip. *Propaganda and the American Revolution: 1763–1783.* Chapel Hill: University of North Carolina Press, 1941.

Demers, Philippe. *Le Général Hazen, seigneur de Bleury-Sud: essai de monographie régionale.* Montreal: Librairie Beauchemin, 1927.

Deming, Henry C. "An Oration Upon the Life and Services of Gen. David Wooster." In *Proceedings at the Completion of the Wooster Monument.* New Haven, CT: Storer and Morehouse, 1854.

Desjardin, Thomas. *Through a Howling Wilderness: Benedict Arnold's March to Quebec, 1775.* New York: St. Martin's Press, 2006.

Dictionary of Canadian Biography Online/Dictionnaire biographique du Canada en ligne. Library and Archives Canada. Accessed 30 October 2010. www.biographi.ca.

Everest, Allan S. *Moses Hazen and the Canadian Refugees in the American Revolution.* Syracuse, NY: Syracuse University, 1976.

Fleming, Patricia L., and Sandra Alston. *Early Canadian Printing: A Supplement to Marie Tremaine's A Bibliography of Canadian Imprints, 1751–1800.* Toronto: University of Toronto Press, 1999.

Fregault, Guy. *Canada: The War of the Conquest.* Translated by Margaret M. Cameron. Toronto: Oxford University Press, 1969.

French, Allen. *The First Year of the American Revolution.* New York: Houghton Mifflin, 1934.

Fryer, Mary Beacock. *Allan Maclean, Jacobite General: The Life of an Eighteenth Century Career Soldier.* Toronto: Dundurn Press, 1987.

Gabriel, Michael P. *Major General Richard Montgomery: The Making of an American Hero.* Madison, NJ: Fairleigh Dickinson University Press, 2002.

Gerlach, Don R. *Philip Schuyler and the American Revolution in New York, 1733–1777.* Lincoln: University of Nebraska Press, 1964.

———. "Philip Schuyler and the Road to Glory or a Question of Loyalty and Competence." *The New-York Historical Society Quarterly* 49, no. 4 (October 1965).

Gosselin, Auguste. *L'Église du Canada après la conquête, Deuxième Partie, 1775–1789.* Quebec: Laflamme, 1917.

Greer, Allan. *Peasant, Lord, and Merchant: Rural Society in Three Quebec Parishes, 1740–1840.* Toronto: University of Toronto Press, 1985.

———. *The Patriots and the People: The Rebellion of 1837 in Rural Lower Canada.* Toronto: University of Toronto Press, 1993.

Griffin, Martin. *Catholics and the American Revolution.* Ridley Park, PA: M. Griffin, 1902.

Hall, William. "Colonel Rudolphus Ritzema." *Magazine of American History* 2 (March 1878): 162–67.

Hanley, Thomas O'Brien. *Revolutionary Statesman: Charles Carroll and the War.* Chicago: Loyola University Press, 1983.

Hare, John. "The American Revolution and the Beauce, Quebec: 1775–1783." *Culture* 20 (1959): 131–48.

———. "Le comportement de la paysannerie rurale et urbaine dans la région de Québec, pendant l'occupation américaine, 1775–1776." *Revue de l'Université d'Ottawa* 47, nos. 1–2 (janvier et avril 1977): 146.

Harris, Richard C. *The Seigneurial System in Early Canada: A Geographical Study, with a New Preface.* Montreal: McGill-Queen's University Press, 1984.

Haw, James, F. F. Beirne, R. R. Beirne, and R. S. Jett. *Stormy Patriot: The Life of Samuel Chase.* Baltimore: Maryland Historical Society, 1980.

Igartua, José Eduardo. *The Merchants and Negotiants of Montreal, 1750–1775: A Study in Socio-economic History.* Ann Arbor, MI: University Microfilms International, 1980.

Irving, Mark. *Agrarian Conflicts in Colonial New York, 1711–1775.* New York: Columbia University Press, 1940.

Ketchum, Richard M. *Divided Loyalties: How the American Revolution Came to New York.* New York: Holt, 2002.

Knollenberg, Bernhard. *Growth of the American Revolution, 1766–1775.* Indianapolis: Liberty Fund, 2003.

Lagrave, J-P. *Voltaire's Man in America: A Political Biography of Fleury Mesplet, Printer from Lyon, Agent of Benjamin Franklin, Friend of Liberty, Disciple of the Enlightenment.* Translated by Arnold Bennet. Toronto: Davies, 1995.

Lanctot, Gustave. *Canada and the American Revolution, 1774–1783.* Translated by Margaret Cameron. Cambridge, MA: Harvard University Press, 1967.

Langston, Paul. "'Tyrant and Oppressor!' Colonial Press Reaction to the Quebec Act." *Historical Journal of Massachusetts* 34, no. 1 (2006): 1–17.

Laurent, Laval. *Québec et l'église aux États-Unis sous Mgr. Briand et Mgr. Plessis.* Washington, DC: Catholic University of America Press, 1945.

Lawson, Philip. *The Imperial Challenge: Quebec and Britain in the Age of the American Revolution.* Montreal: McGill-Queen's University Press, 1990.

———. "'Sapped by Corruption:' British Governance of Quebec and the Breakdown of Anglo-American Relations on the Eve of Revolution." *Canadian Review of American Studies* 22, no. 3 (1991): 301–23.

Lefkowitz, Arthur S. *Benedict Arnold's Army: The 1775 American Invasion of Canada During the Revolutionary War.* New York: Savas Beatie, 2008.

Leroy, Perry Eugene. "Sir Guy Carleton as a Military Leader During the American Invasion and Repulse in Canada, 1775–1776." Doctoral thesis, Ohio State University, 1960.

Magnuson, Roger. *Education in New France.* Montreal: McGill-Queen's University Press, 1992.

Main, Jackson Turner. *The Social Structure of Revolutionary America.* Princeton: Princeton University Press, 1965.

Mason, Edward G. "Sketch of Pierre Menard." *Chicago Historical Society Collections* 4 (1890): 142–48.

McLachlan, R.W. *Fleury Mesplet, The First Printer at Montreal.* Ottawa: J. Hope & Sons, 1906.

Metzger, Charles H. *The Quebec Act: A Primary Cause of the American Revolution.* New York: United States Catholic Historical Society, 1936.

———. *Catholics and the American Revolution.* Chicago: Loyola University Press, 1962.

Michel, Louis. "Un marchand rural en Nouvelle-France: François-Augustin Bailly de Messein, 1709–1771." *Revue d'histoire de l'Amérique française* 33 (1979): 215–62.

Miquelon, Dale. "The Baby Family in the Trade of Canada, 1750–1820." Master's thesis, Carleton University Press, 1966.

Monette, Pierre, ed. *Le Rendez-vous manqué avec la revolution americaine.* Montreal: Chez Triptyque, 2007.

Monty, Ernest. "Major Clément Gossélin." *Mémoires de la Société Genéalogique* 3 (January 1948): 18–38.

Nadeau, Charles. "La Stratégie lors de l'Affrontement Anglo-Américain au Canada (1775–1776): Objets politiques et objectifs militaires." Thesis, University of Laval, 2008.

Neatby, Hilda. *The Administration of Justice Under the Quebec Act.* Minneapolis: University of Minnesota, 1937.

———. *Quebec: The Revolutionary Age, 1760–1791.* Toronto: McClelland and Stuart, 1966.

———. "Pierre Guy: A Montreal Merchant of the Eighteenth Century." *Eighteenth Century Studies* 5, no. 2 (Winter 1971–1972): 224–42.

Nelson, Paul David. *General Sir Guy Carleton, Lord Dorchester: Soldier-Statesman of Early British Canada.* Cranbury, NJ: Associated University Presses, 2000.

O'Reilly, Helena. *Monseigneur de Saint Vallier et L'Hôpital Général de Québec.* Quebec: C. Darveau, 1882.

Otten, William L. *Colonel J. F. Hamtramck His Life & Times, Volume One (1756–1783): Captain of the Revolution.* Port Aransas, TX: W. L. Otten, 1997.

Ouellet, Fernand. *Economic and Social History of Quebec, 1760–1850: Structures and Conjunctures.* Ottawa: Carleton University Press, 1980.

———. "The British Army of Occupation in the St. Lawrence Valley, 1760–1774: The Conflict Between Civil and Military Society." In *Armies of Occupation.* Edited by Roy A. Prete and A. Hamish Ion. Waterloo, ON: Wilfrid Laurier, 1984.

Pronovost, Claude. *La Bourgeoisie Marchande en Milieu Rural (1720–1840).* Ste-Foy, QC: Université Laval, 1998.

Proulx, Georges-Etienne. "Les Canadiens ont-ils payé la dîme entre 1760 et 1775?" *Revue d'histoire de l'Amérique française* 11, no. 4 (1958): 533–62.

Query, Jacques. "Montréal Sous L'Occupation Américaine, 1775–1776: Répercussions Socio-Économiques." Master's thesis, University of Montreal, 1977.

Rakove, Jack. *The Beginnings of National Politics: An Interpretative History of the Continental Congress.* New York: Knopf, 1979.

Rawlyk, George. *Revolution Rejected: 1775–1776.* Scarborough, NY: Prentice Hall, 1968.

Riddell, William R. "Benjamin Franklin and Canada." *Pennsylvania Magazine of History and Biography* 48 (1924): 97–110.

———. "Benjamin Franklin's Mission to Canada and the Causes of Its Failure." *Pennsylvania Magazine of History and Biography* 48 (1924): 111–58.

Rossie, Jonathan. *The Politics of Command in the American Revolution.* Syracuse, NY: Syracuse University Press, 1975.

Rouleau, Corinne Rocheleau. "Une Incroyable et Veridique Histoire: L'Affaire Cazeau, 1776–1893." *Bulletin de la Société historique franco-américaine* (1946–1947).

Roy, J-Edmond. *Histoire de la Seigneurie de Lauzon.* Vol. 3. Levis, QC: J-E Roy, 1900.

Roy, Raoul. *Les Canadiens français et les Indépendantistes américains, 1774–1783: Une occasion manquée.* Montreal: Éditions du Franc-Canada, 1979.

Séguin, Maurice. *La "Nation canadienne" et l'agriculture (1760–1850): essai d'histoire économique.* Trois Rivières: Boréal, 1973.

Sévigny, Pierre André. "Le commerce du blé et la navigation dans le bas Richelieu avant 1849." *Revue d'histoire de l'Amérique française* 38 (1984): 5–21.

Shelton, Hal. *General Richard Montgomery and the American Revolution.* New York: New York University Press, 1994.

Shy, John. "The American Revolution: The Military Conflict Considered as a Revolutionary War." In *Essays on the American Revolution.* Edited by Stephen Kurtz and James Hutson. Chapel Hill: University of North Carolina Press, 1973.

Smith, Justin H. "The Prologue of the American Revolution." *Century Magazine* 65 (April 1903): 72–91, 351–69, 529–44, 713–33, 899–916.

———. *Our Struggle for the Fourteenth Colony: Canada and the American Revolution.* New York: Knickerbocker Press, 1907.

Stanley, George F.G. Stanley. *Canada Invaded, 1775–1776.* Toronto: A. M. Hakkert, 1977.

Stevens, Paul L. "His Majesty's "Savage" Allies: British Policy and the Northern Indians During the Revolutionary War, The Carleton Years, 1774–1778." Doctoral dissertation, State University of New York, Buffalo, 1984.

Tiedemann, Joseph, and Eugene Fingerhut, eds. *The Other New York: The American Revolution Beyond New York City, 1763–1787.* Albany: State University of New York Press, 2005.

Trudel, Marcel. *Louis XVI, le congres américain et le Canada (1774–1789).* Québec: Les Éditions du Quartier-Latin, 1949.

———. *Le régime militaire dans le gouvernement de Trois-Rivières 1760–1764.* Trois-Rivières, QC: Bien public, 1952.

———. *The Seigneurial Regime.* Ottawa: Canadian Historical Association, 1976.

———. *La tentation américaine, 1774–1783. La Révolution américaine et le Canada, textes commentés.* Sillery, QC: Septentrion, 2006.

Les Ursulines de Trois Rivières Depuis Leur Établissement Jusqu'à nos Jours. Tome Premier. Trois-Rivières, QC: Pierre Ayotte, 1892.

Wade, Mason. *The French Canadians, 1760–1945.* Toronto: Macmillan, 1956.

Wilson, Barry K. *Benedict Arnold: A Traitor in Our Midst.* Montreal: McGill-Queens University Press, 2001.

Wrong, George. *A Canadian Manor and Its Seigneurs: The Story of a Hundred Years, 1761–1861.* Toronto: Macmillan, 1908.

———. *Canada and the American Revolution: The Disruption of the First British Empire.* New York: Macmillan, 1935.

INDEX

Acadians, 32, 262, 380n47
Adams, John, 171, 290, 332–33, 335
Adams, Samuel, 9, 52–53, 67
addresses, Continental Congress: to People of
  Great Britain, 10, 50–51; to Quebec (first),
  6, 10–12, 14–16, 48, 50–51, 84–85; to Quebec
  (second), 67–68, 77–78, 229; to Quebec
  (third), 223–24, 230; "to St. John's, &c.,"
  10–11
addresses, other: Allen and Easton to "French
  people," 77, 373n16; New York Provincial
  Congress, 68, 77; Schuyler manifesto, 104–5,
  107, 111; Washington to Canadians, 144–47,
  151, 153, 203
Albany Committee, 62, 69, 87, 90
Allen, Ethan, 92, 97; letters, 77, 88; Longue-
  Pointe, 116–18; partisan operations, 105,
  107–8, 110–12, 114; prisoner, 118, 151, 179; St-
  Jean, 63–64; Ticonderoga, 60–62
Allin, Jean-Baptiste, 136, 164, 263, 338, 342
Antill, Edward, 169, 197, 213–14, 221–22, 336;
  Canadian Continental officer, 223–24, 238,
  283, 305, 324
Arnold, Benedict, 180, 190, 200, 329–30;
  Battle of Québec City, 190, 194–96, 213;
  Battle of St-Pierre, 277–78, 280; Canadian
  business, 26, 188; Canadian militia, 260–61,
  264–66; Fort St-Jean, 62–63; Kennebec
  Expedition, 144–53, 165–67; letters, 88–89,
  93–94; Montreal District, 256, 298–99, 304–
  5, 307, 310, 320–23; property confiscations,
  318, 323, 325; Québec City blockade, 217, 259,
  262–63, 271–72, 282, 284–85; Ticonderoga,
  59–62, 68–69
Articles of War, 223, 261
assembly, Quebec general, 12, 37–39
Association, Continental, 9–10, 13, 67, 174, 296,
  370n38; Canadian concerns, 50, 54–56, 157,
  236, 255, 351–52

Ayotte, Pierre, 268–70, 277–79, 281, 289, 314,
  339, 342

Baby-Taschereau-Williams Commission,
  341–42, 355, 357
Badeaux, Jean-Baptiste, 126, 162–63, 247–48,
  250, 254–55, 281, 356
bailiffs, 23, 33, 74
Bailly-de-Messein, Charles, 276–77, 279–80
Baker, Remember, 94, 96, 98–100
Bastonnais, 4, 372n7
Beauce, 73–74, 147, 267, 343
Beaujeu, Louis de, 276–80
Beaumont, 140, 274, 383n2
Beauport, 185, 260, 267, 402n17
Bedel, Timothy, 113–14, 122, 298–99, 320
Bedel's Regiment (New Hampshire), 298,
  389n32
Berthier-en-bas, 278, 289, 383n2, 402n16
Berthier-en-haut, 80–82, 125–26, 151, 154, 329
billeting, 157–58, 236
Bindon, Joseph, 63–65, 203, 237, 339
Blais, Michel, 279–80, 288
Blake, John, 46, 54, 203, 237, 339
Boucherville, 154, 205, 207, 233
Briand, Jean-Olivier, 22, 33, 356; government
  advocacy, 115, 198, 317; interdicts, 115, 141–42,
  343; mandates and letters, 71–73, 78
Brindamour, Jean Ménard *dit*, 114, 237, 283
British Army, 35, 55, 75; Canada relief,
  313–14, 324, 327–30; Montréal garrison,
  63–65, 69, 75, 117–19, 133, 135, 154; Richelieu
  Valley operations, 104, 110, 112; upcountry
  garrisons, 234–35, 298–99, 320–21, 330
British Party, 34–35, 37–39, 64–65;
  factionalization, 50, 56, 81–82; propaganda,
  71–73, 75, 78, 84–86; Quebec Act response,
  40–41, 46–52, 54–56, 67. *See also* petitions
Brown, John: liaison mission, 53–56; Montreal

Continental service, 92, 97, 113, 133–34, 161, 215, 220, 285

Gugy, Conrad, 167–68, 319

habitants, 18–21; in support of Continentals, 185, 191, 198, 264–68, 317, 329

Halsted, John, 148, 166, 266, 285, 318, 339

Hamtramck, Jean-François, 110, 163, 237, 270, 321

Hanchett, Oliver, 189, 193

Hay, Udney, 90, 375n46

Haywood, William, 46, 155, 221, 226, 228, 324

Hazen, Moses, 108, 214, 230, 233–34, 339; correspondence, 239–40, 282, 297, 299, 302, 311; Fort St-Jean command, 299, 304–5, 307, 319, 323–26; messenger, 63, 65, 371n12; Montreal District commander, 239, 297–99; questionable allegiances, 106, 112–15, 161, 239, 309; regimental commander, 223–24, 237–38

Hey, William, 56, 81, 85–86, 152

Hoyt, Winthrop, 54–55, 88, 98, 101

Ile-aux-Noix, 101, 104, 106–7, 109–11, 119, 330–31

Ile-d'Orléans, 140–41, 188, 263, 267, 313–14

Indians: Continental diplomacy, 54, 107–8, 111, 204, 307; Crown policy, 83–84; Loyalist auxiliaries (Richelieu Valley), 84, 99, 104, 106, 110, 133; Loyalist auxiliaries (western Quebec), 235, 273, 298, 320–22, 330. See also Caughnawagas; Sartigan Indians

intelligence, 95–97, 100–101; "escaped prisoner report", 68–69, 87; Swart report, 90, 92–93, 375n46

interdict, 115, 141–42, 163, 198, 216, 297

Jacques-Cartier, 288, 305, 312, 316–19

Jautard, Valentin, 158, 202–3, 343

Jay, John, 67, 176, 180, 229, 255, 295

Jesuits, 163, 298, 309

Kahnawakes. See Caughnawagas

Kennebec Expedition, 99–100, 144–53, 165–66, 168, 184, 191; Battle of Québec City, 194–96; discipline issues, 187–89, 193

Lachenaie, 79, 154

Lachine, 54, 75, 321–22, 324–25

La Corne, St-Luc de, 67, 84, 88; Continental treatment, 124–25, 157, 165, 205–7, 233–34, 339

Laframboise, Jean-Baptiste Fafard dit, 248, 252–54

Lajeunesse, Prudent, 229, 338

Lamb's Artillery (New York), 97–98, 113, 167, 188, 383n60

Lamotte, Joseph-Marie, 230–31, 273

Lanaudière, Charles-Louis Tarieu-de, 125–26, 161, 198, 267

Langdon, John, 173–76, 178

L'Ange-Gardien, 264, 402nn16–17

Langlois, Pierre, 195, 260–61, 268

La-Pocatière. See Ste-Anne-de-la-Pocatière

Laprairie, 54, 63, 113, 116, 124, 132, 154–55; Road, 63–65, 109, 112–13, 137, 330

Larose, François Guillot dit, 167–68, 326, 328

L'Assomption, 109, 116–18, 122, 204, 208

Laterrière, Pierre de Sales, 244, 258, 343

Lauzier, Augustin Roy dit, 275–76, 404n21

Lecomte, Nicolas, 264, 268

Lee, Charles, 13, 166, 174, 210–11, 232–33, 332–33

Lee, Richard Henry, 9–11, 177

Les-Cèdres, 238, 298–99. See also Cedars, Battle of the

Lesperance, 266, 268, 281

Liberty, 62, 94, 100–101

L'Islet, 277, 279, 289

literacy, 27–28, 49

Livingston, James, 95, 339; partisan leader, 107–12, 122–24, 129–31, 135–36; Québec City operations, 185, 191, 194–97, 263; regimental commander, 164, 167–68, 178–80, 323–24

Livingston, Robert R., Jr., 102, 173–78, 290–91, 332

Loiseau, Augustin, 110, 116, 118, 135–36, 161, 164, 244, 263, 338

Longue-Pointe, Battle of, 116–19, 143

Longueuil, 79, 95, 116, 119, 127–28, 132, 154, 205, 329; Battle of, 133–35

Longueuil, Joseph Lemoyne-de, 108, 371n24

Lorimier, Claude, 115, 133, 205, 226–27, 234–35, 298, 322, 356

Lotbinière, Louis, 261, 338–39

loyalists: arrests, 217–18, 227, 233–34, 238, 281, 306, 325, 339; Continental depradations (Montreal District), 114, 128, 136, 188–89, 267–68, 281; Continental depradations (Quebec District), 151, 166, 185; disarmed,